FOOD

Under the direction of Jean-Louis Flandrin
and Massimo Montanari

ENGLISH EDITION BY ALBERT SONNENFELD

Translated by Clarissa Botsford, Arthur Goldhammer,

Charles Lambert, Frances M. López-Morillas,

and Sylvia Stevens

FOOD

A CULINARY HISTORY *from*
ANTIQUITY *to the* PRESENT

COLUMBIA UNIVERSITY PRESS   NEW YORK

COLUMBIA UNIVERSITY PRESS

Publishers Since 1893

NEW YORK   CHICHESTER, WEST SUSSEX

Histoire de l'alimentation Copyright © 1996 Gius. Laterza & Figli, Rome, Bari/Librairie Arthème Fayard
Copyright © 1999 Columbia University Press
Paperback edition, 2013
All rights reserved

Library of Congress Cataloging-in-Publication Data
[Histoire de l'alimentation. English]
Food: a culinary history from antiquity to the present /
edited by Jean-Louis Flandrin and Massimo Montanari;
translated by Albert Sonnenfeld
p.   cm. — (European perspectives)
Includes bibliographical references and index.
ISBN 978-0-231-11154-6 (cloth : alk. paper)
ISBN 978-0-231-11155-3 (pbk. : alk. paper)
1. Food—History.   2. Food habits—History.   I. Flandrin, Jean
Louis.   II. Montanari, Massimo, 1949– .   III. Sonnenfeld, Albert.
IV. Title.   V. Series.
TX353.H525   1999
641.3'09—dc21   99-34859

*Columbia University Press wishes to express its appreciation of
assistance given by the government of France through Le Ministère de la
Culture in the preparation of this translation.*

*Casebound editions of Columbia University Press books
are printed on permanent and durable acid-free paper.*

*Printed in the United States of America
Designed by Linda Secondari
Illustrations by Martha Lewis
Cover image © RMN - Grand Palais / Art Resource, NY*

European Perspectives

A SERIES IN SOCIAL THOUGHT
AND CULTURAL CRITICISM

Lawrence D. Kritzman, Editor

European Perspectives presents outstanding books by
leading European thinkers. With both classic and
contemporary works, the series aims to shape the major
intellectual controversies of our day and to facilitate
the tasks of historical understanding.

For a complete list of books in the series, see page 593

CONTENTS

PREFACE

Albert Sonnenfeld

Culinary history has moved to the front burner, joining proliferating recipe collections, cookbooks, and celebrity chef albums as hot items for our age of pluralistic cultural studies. Publication of this English-language edition of *Food: A Culinary History from Antiquity to the Present* could not have come at a more opportune time. "Food is such a powerful dimension of our consciousness as living things," the distinguished anthropologist Sidney Mintz said, "to omit it from the study of human behavior would be egregious."

The American Center for Wine, Food and the Arts, located in Napa, California, and financed by the Mondavi Winery, has broken ground for a 2001 opening. The annual scholarly Oxford University Food Conferences, organized by historian Theodore Zeldin, have long since established the legitimacy of the field in Anglo-American intellectual circles. Alan Davidson's *Petits propos culinaires,* the American Institute of Wine and Food's *Journal of Gastronomy,* and the Cornell-based review *Food and Foodways* provide ongoing scholarly outlets. *The Oxford Book of Food* is soon to appear, and Barbara Haber, director of the culinary collection of the Schlesinger Library at Radcliffe College, not complacent with her own spectacular holdings, is compiling a Web-site directory of relevant materials in other American libraries and private collections. Various "foodie" professional organizations now routinely appoint such learned "visiting scholars" as Dr. B. H. Fussell to educate their membership in historical perspectives.

Culinary history is slowly but surely entering the curriculum as a respectable academic field. Three hundred anthropologists in the United States list food studies as their specialty; courses in food and culture are increasingly widespread at the University of California-Berkeley, Emory University, and the Johns Hopkins University. There are degree-granting programs burgeoning at Boston University, Cornell University, and New York University, even reaching into the ever expanding cooking schools (careers in food services are at the top of job opportunities). With the popularity of historically based "theme restaurants" (one thinks of the historical research in the works of Apicius preceding the opening, say, of Joe Baum's Forum of the Twelve Caesars), and the fashion of recherché fusion cuisine in London and the Zagat-driven cities of America, serious would-be chefs are turning to history to seek out the origins and secrets of the exotic savors of the past. An American chef could now, in theory, open an Etruscan restaurant—thanks to historical research: the authenticity may not be in his blood, but it might well be in his files. Contemporary restaurant criticism, long looked to primarily for excessively personalized hyperventilation leading to a planetarium of quantified stellar ratings, is responding to Chef Mark Miller's stricture: "Most lack intellectual weight, because few critics have the knowledge or experience to put restaurants into a larger historical and social context. The best art, music, and theater critics provide insight that restaurant critics rarely do." But the writings of Mimi Sheraton, Raymond Sokolow, and Jeffrey Steingarten show how historically valid restaurant criticism can become. Even the daily press has moved beyond seasonal recipes and nostalgic reminiscences, enlisting the services of such erudite American food historians as Charles Perry, who might very well hold forth to devotees of the *Los Angeles Times* food section on the philology of yogurt as it relates to the lactic cultures of the Asian steppes!

Food is perhaps the most distinctive expression of an ethnic group, a culture, or, in modern times, a nation. "If you tell me what you eat, I'll tell you who you are" has become a virtual cliché in an age of mass international tourism. Armies travel on their stomachs, to be sure, as Napoleon ruefully learned in his Russian campaign, but the need for food, for condiments to flavor or preserve it, for access to crops and to markets has always driven history, politics, and economics. And now, though we have not yet attained Grimod de la Reyniere's ideal of an endowed professorship of gastronomy in every school, the present volume consecrates the range and depth of culinary history. The historians contributing to this remarkable collection have surveyed feeding strategies from prehistoric times to the era of the Big Mac, from medieval table manners to today's finger food, and in so doing have created cultural history from a new and essential perspective.

"France is a country where they talk about eating. Every country talks about eating but in that country they talk about talking about eating," Gertrude Stein wrote in *Everybody's Autobiography*. The statesman Prince Talleyrand suggested that after one sampled wine with eye, ear, and nose, the next step was not to drink it but "to speak of it." It should therefore come as no surprise that the roots of modern culinary history lie deep in the *terroir* of France. French historians had always been addicted to the vast synthesis, the artfully constructed prose narrative of the past, exemplified by Michelet for politics or, in gastronomy, Brillat-Savarin. Inevitably the focus was philosophical, theoretical, wide, and event-oriented, as befit the numerous French disciples of Hegel and Marx. Long excluded were the supposedly boring and quotidian facts of life lived by the faceless manswarm; these lay buried in forgotten documents gathering dust in obscure provincial archives, in church and state registries. In the 1960s the historians grouped around the Cahiers des Annales found a fertile and until then fallow field in "alimentation," documentation of the whole range of practical and theoretical considerations of a particular society with regard to planting, harvesting, marketing, and consuming food and drink. What the Annales' most illustrious scribe, Fernand Braudel, termed "the structures of everyday life" led from purely quantitative sociological methods (statistics of the consumption of meat over time or in particular locales) to larger questions of cultural approaches and contexts (witness Jean-Louis Flandrin's series of historical gourmet columns in the journal *L'Histoire*).

What had been proposed tentatively in 1970, by J.-J. Hémardinquer in "Pour une histoire de l'alimentation," was to be carried forward by Jean-Louis Flandrin, a historian of collective mentalities often dealing with the early modern family, who, from his perch at the University of Paris VIII-Vincennes, became the leading proponent and exponent of serious, scholarly culinary history for a nation in whose collective consciousness food has been characterized as "perhaps the distinctive ingredient of French identity." As much as his own publications, it was Flandrin's role as one of the founders of the review *Food and Foodways*, as Director of Studies at the Institute for Advanced Study in Social Sciences (EHESS), and as mentor of a generation of culinary historians that gave him the network to collect the essays for the original Franco-Italian edition of this book. He was joined in this formidable task by the medieval historian Massimo Montanari, professor at the University of Bologna and author of works on peasant and urban eating habits and culture in the Middle Ages.

Readability and utility have been the guiding principles of this English-language edition of a monumental historical compendium. To the ever growing public of world travelers, restaurant patrons, cookbook collectors, fascinated by the origins and cultural dimensions of food, this volume offers a veritable feast of diversity. As editor, I suggest that a superb historical overview, from the caveman and antiquity to the democratic dream fulfilled today as a nightmare of universal fast food, can be gleaned by reading in sequence the richly elegant introductions by Flandrin and Montanari to each of the seven sections. Thereafter, the table of contents should be viewed as a menu for pleasurable grazing. The reader can contrive a full gamut of continuities and availabilities: food as medicine would take one from the dietary rules of the ancient Hebrews (Chapter 4) to the link of diet and medicine in the ancient world (Chapter 12), for example, leading to today's taste and health. If now we are cautioned against abuse or even use of alcohol, tea, tobacco, and strong spices, these were once part of a medically virtuous pharmacopoeia. If we know that in the Great Chain of Being, earthbound products—potatoes, onions, leeks—were, as Samuel Beckett well knew, poor people's fodder and that those closer to the heavens acquired the poultry wings of nobility, we can study the relationship of food to class structures from prehistoric banquets through the diets of peasants, warriors, and priests (Chapter 15) to those of society in late medieval and Renaissance Italy (Chapter 24). The focus, to be sure, is on Mediterranean culinary traditions leading from the classical world to the feasts and diets of Christianity, Islam, Judaism, and on to our own secular restaurants and banqueting halls.

In the original collection, many of these essays, inspired by the Annales historians' methodology, contained elaborate documentation: graphs, lists, and statistical charts that made for less than fluent reading. I have eliminated such impedimenta as the page-long count of per-acre yield for artichokes in the Finistere in sixteenth-century Brittany. Overlap and repetition, inevitable in a collection of autonomous essays, gathered rather than culled, have been subjected here to the editorial scissors, and some essays were deemed not worthy of the first cut. The result is, for most English-language readers, a more harmonious and readable volume and less of an omnium gatherum. At the same time, the needs of culinary historians, restaurateurs, and food critics could not be neglected. The invaluable bibliographies have been preserved to encourage researchers and readers alike, and all deletions have been made with a fierce eye to integrity of thought and documentation as well as to continuity and readability.

My challenge has been to be both an editor worthy of the original, noble scholarly efforts of Flandrin and Montanari and an abridger mindful of the almost forty contributing authors. I am, however, primarily responsive to the general reader's need for accessibility and readability. To edit is to absorb a book totally and to rearrange and recalibrate as necessary. Abridging is a form of aesthetic surgery: the patient may cry out in pain under the excising knife, yet the streamlined result makes it worthwhile—responsible, attractive, and pleasurable as well as informative.

FOOD

INTRODUCTION TO THE ORIGINAL EDITION

Jean-Louis Flandrin and Massimo Montanari

Certain ideas about the history of food are part of the general culture. We all know, or think we know, that pasta originated in China, that it was brought back to Venice by Marco Polo, and that it spread from there first throughout Italy and later to the rest of Europe. Or that Charles VIII, returning to France from an expedition to Naples in 1494, brought the melon back with him. Or that Catherine de' Medici, who was crazy about artichoke hearts, made them fashionable in France. Or that the basic techniques of French haute cuisine were developed by Italian cooks working in France. Or that flaky pastry dough was invented by Claude Gellée, better known as Claude Lorrain (1600–1682), who was an assistant pastry maker before going on to make his mark as a painter. Or that *pâté de foie gras* was invented in Strasbourg in 1788 by Marshall de Contades, governor of Alsace. Or was it his cook, Jean-Pierre Clausse, who made a fortune on his discovery? Histories of this sort invariably manage to come up with a specific inventor and date for every famous dish.

If there is a model for this type of history, it is probably the "Catalog of the Inventors of Things That Are Eaten and Drunk" (1548) by Ortensio Lando.[1] This bizarre work, a triumph of fancy and fabrication, is, despite its impressive show of erudition, a catalog of improbable gastronomic and enological inventions. It is an extravagant application to the realm of food of what Marc Bloch called the "myth of origin."

Yet histories that confidently repeat widely held opinions often neglect contradictory evidence. For example, the sources show that pasta did not come to Italy from China by way of Venice but spread northward from the Mezzogiorno, where noodles were eaten long before Marco Polo traveled to the Orient. Furthermore, the fact that Italian pasta is now well known throughout Europe tends to make us forget similar foods that originated in other countries, such as the Polish *kluski*, or that came overland from the east, such as the Tartaric-Lithuanian *kolduni*. Other evidence similarly flies in the face of time-honored tradition: melons were grown in the gardens of Avignon as long ago as the end of the fourteenth century; French cuisine bore less resemblance to Italian cooking in the age of Louis XIV than it did in the Middle Ages; Lancelot de Casteau, who cooked for the prince-bishop of Liège, gave a recipe for flaky pastry in his *Ouverture de cuisine* (1604), a recipe that he probably took from Spanish bakers who may have learned it from the Arabs; and as long ago as 1739 one could read, in *Les Dons de Comus,* about *petits pâtés de foye gras,* as well as a *pâtés de Périgord* that may have been a *foie gras* of duck and a *pâtés de Toulouse* that shared with it the honor of being the most expensive of eighteenth-century dishes; *Le Cuisinier gascon*, moreover, mentioned *petits pâtés de foyes gras aux truffes* in 1740.

To be sure, some of the putative inventors of our most famous dishes may deserve some of the credit that has been bestowed on them. Illustrious personages sometimes did encourage the adoption of certain foods, cooking techniques, or novel flavors. But there are other ways to study the history of what we eat, less sketchy, more fruitful approaches that are not only better suited to our purposes but also more closely aligned with current historical practice, now that history has broadened its horizon beyond the deeds of great men. This is particularly true in regard to the history of everyday life, of which the history of national dietary customs is a part.

The routines of daily life have a structure, and within that structure even the most insignificant events have a necessary place and a precise significance. These structures are relatively static compared with other historical phenomena, which in the jargon of historians are known as events (of short duration) and conjunctural cycles (of medium duration). Structures are not really static, however; they do evolve, but slowly, over a much longer duration than events or cycles. This tripartite division of historical time (events, cycles, and structures) is an idea first proposed by Fernand Braudel. It serves to warn us against the error of assuming that the structures of everyday life have no history, that people's daily routines have always been pretty much what they are today. In fact, daily rituals do change, and so does everything connected with them. Historians can therefore study the history of everyday life. To take just one example, the Greeks and Romans used to lie on couches at banquets. This custom persisted for centuries. But at some point in the early Middle Ages, people in the West began to sit upright at formal dinners. This change in posture was closely related to other changes that occurred at roughly the same time: the upright position freed the left hand for cutting large pieces of roasted meat using knives that became part of the standard dining equipment at this juncture. It is probably no accident, moreover, that it was the same people who used both hands to cut and eat roasted meat and who sat at high tables in high chairs who also invented the fork. Nor was it an accident that the fork did not become a regular table utensil until after the Black Plague, between the fourteenth and the eighteenth century, when the use of plates, drinking glasses, and individual place settings tended to increase the space between diners.

Why are the same foods prepared differently in different countries? Not for whimsical reasons but because of specific technological, economic, and social differences. Take grains, for example. In traditional African societies, where communal activities are common, grains are nevertheless hulled and ground individually by women, who devote much of their time to these chores. And since these societies lack not only grain mills but also ovens, they generally eat their cereals in the form of porridge or mush. By contrast, in medieval Europe landlord-owned mills and ovens saved women a great deal of time but allowed the landlord to dominate his subjects more effectively and made bread the primary staple. Bread is also an important staple in the Muslim world, where some ovens and mills are owned by individual families while others are operated by artisans who sell their services to the public. The bread eaten in this part of the world is very different from European bread, however: loaves are smaller, flatter, and more quickly consumed. Nowhere in the Muslim world do we find large, round loaves suitable for lengthy conservation of the kind that have existed in rural Europe from the Middle Ages to the present.

And why do we eat grains at all? Not because someone at some point had the idea of growing cereal plants that might be good to eat. Grains were consumed for thousands of years before agriculture began. Moreover, the development of agriculture is a complex phenomenon in which religion played a significant part. It was neither an accident nor the invention of some genius. Besides, it is well known that introducing a new plant or animal species into a region does not ensure that the people living there will automatically eat it. While it is true that European aristocrats began eating turkeys as soon as the birds could be bred on the continent, it took centuries for the potato and the tomato to gain acceptance, even though these vegetables now play a far more important role in European cooking than the turkey does. To put the point in the technical jargon of historians, Europe's alimentary structures (in which every item of food has a definite place and function) were for a long time not receptive to American products even though those products had been acclimatized to the Old World. But then, in the eighteenth century, these alimentary structures were disrupted by demographic growth, so the new foodstuffs became part of the European diet.

Finally, consider a more recent example—the triumph of the so-called *nouvelle cuisine* in the 1970s and 1980s. This was not just a vogue launched by the food writers Gault and Millau. The changes in diet advocated by these journalists turn out to have manifested themselves before the two men wrote about them, in many cases long before. For example, short cooking times were linked to the discovery of the importance of vitamins by nutritionists. Similarly, the growing presence of vegetables on restaurant menus, the turn away from flour-based sauces, and the reduction in the quantities of butter and sugar used in both cooking and baking are all phenomena linked to advances in dietetics.

In truth, we are still quite ignorant about both the reasons for these fundamental changes and their precise timing because historians have mainly been interested in other matters. Until well after World War II, they concentrated on the famines of the past and showed how these could be correlated with economic cycles, price movements, agricultural production, and demographics. Owing to the nature of the early modern economy and the state of European agricultural technology at the time, bad harvests tended to recur regularly, leading to food shortages, higher food prices, famines, and staggeringly high mortality.[2] Historians asked why this happened: did people die of hunger as such, of diseases brought on by dubious substitutes for bread, or of epidemics such as the plague, against which malnourished bodies were defenseless?

In the 1960s and 1970s, many historians went even farther, looking into the kinds of physical deficiencies and dietary imbalances that existed even when food was not in short supply. Following the lead of modern nutritionists, they compared the diets of different social groups, of men and women, and of different age cohorts. They figured out how many calories each group consumed on average and what proportion of the diet consisted of starches, proteins, and fats. Finally, they looked into the presence of vitamins and minerals that modern science considers vital to a balanced diet.

Unfortunately, the calculations involved in this kind of work were open to a variety of criticisms. For one thing, the archival sources were often incomplete or imprecise or both. For another, conversions to our modern system of weights and measures were not always easy. Most serious of all, it was pointed out that certain fundamental assumptions were unlikely to be true, since there was no reason to believe that the foods of the past were comparable to the foods of today in nutritional qualities or that people's dietary requirements were similar then and now.

The research in question focused mainly on fourteenth- to eighteenth-century Europe. Reliable results appear to have been obtained concerning the diets of sailors, soldiers in transit via ship, students at boarding schools, and hospital patients. In these institutional settings diets appear to have provided an adequate number of calories and to have been reasonably well balanced.[3] In the absence of adequate sources, however, it proved impossible to gauge what peasants ate, except where they were employed on large estates as hired hands or conscript laborers and fed by the lord of the manor. In western Europe, however, the independent peasantry long constituted the vast majority of the population. There is reason to believe, moreover, that peasants were at times very badly nourished, forced to survive on diets that provided too few calories and virtually no fats or proteins, and this may have been true not just in ancient times but in the relatively recent past.

As for the diet of the wealthy, less is known than one might imagine. Even the wealthiest people seldom bought everything they ate at markets, so the household account books of aristocratic and bourgeois families are unlikely to tell us everything we want to know. Fruits and vegetables were sometimes homegrown, as were grapes for wine. Wheat for bread might be grown on the family estate or come in the form of seigneurial dues, which might also include game. Furthermore, account books rarely distinguished between what was purchased for the masters and what went to servants of various ranks. Yet diet was in those days an essential mark of class difference, so it is meaningless to compute statistical averages in the absence of clear sociological data.

Furthermore, cooks frequently stole from the pantry and sold what they could on the black market. Their masters never ate everything that was served at the dinner table; yet we know very little about what became of the leftovers. Some were served up again at subsequent meals, while others went to the servants, the poor, or the dogs. Hence we are no more capable of using kitchen accounts to gauge the extent to which the wealthy overindulged or suffered from dietary imbalances than we are of measuring the dietary deficiencies of the poor.

Although historical studies of caloric intake and consumption of starches, proteins, and fats are therefore to be treated with caution, other work done in the 1960s and 1970s yielded more reliable and useful results. For example, scholars were able to compile a historical atlas showing where different crops were cultivated.[4] Others looked into the relative density of butchers in various rural areas and calculated per capita meat consumption in medieval and modern cities.[5] Such studies extended the earlier work of two German historians, Schmoller and Abel. Still other historians studied the peasant diet by examining notarial records.[6] Finally, the study of military records has shown that the size of conscripts has increased noticeably since the end of the eighteenth century owing to improvements in diet.[7] While historians were doing quantitative research on nutrition, ethnographers and anthropologists were working on dietary choices, the symbolic significance of different foods, dietary and religious taboos, culinary practices, table manners, and, more broadly, the relation between myth, culture, and social structure.[8]

Among historians, these approaches at first attracted the attention only of a group of Hellenists, who explored the relation between diet and myth, religious sacrifice, and politics in ancient Greece.[9] It was not until the late 1970s that specialists in medieval and early modern history also moved to a culturalist approach of a somewhat different sort. They studied the dietary choices of different countries and social classes as an assertion of social identity.[10] To that end, they compared the culinary techniques and the likes and dislikes of different groups over time, and they examined the influence of religion and dietetics on the selection and preparation of foodstuffs.[11]

As perspectives proliferated and scholars with various interests began to compare their findings, a new history of food began to emerge, a history quite different from the "*petite histoire* of the picturesque and the tragic" that the pioneers of the Annales school of historians attacked in the early 1960s. The new history was no longer *petite*. On the contrary, its ambition was to touch on all aspects of human action and thought. Nor was it, first impressions to the contrary notwithstanding, an "alternative" to traditional history. Humbly but firmly, historians of food insisted on the centrality of their subject, on the strategic role of food as both activity and value in various societies and hence on the possibility of using the history of food to examine a whole range of crucial variables in a manageable way. Clear evidence for the validity of this approach can be seen in the many colloquia and seminars of the 1970s and, especially, the 1980s that brought together scholars of diverse interests from a variety of disciplines around the subject of food. The history of food has demonstrated its ability to unify many different approaches. The old distinction between mind and body, intellect and substance, seemingly vanished in the face of the need to understand the complexity of human behavior with respect to food.

Turning its back on yesterday's myth-begotten histories of food and gastronomy, this book is a compendium of the results of these last thirty years of research. Since many gastronomic myths came into being only because people were ignorant of the periods prior to the time of this or that supposed innovation, we have chosen to begin this history at the dawn of mankind and to follow it right through to the present. And we have asked writers on more recent periods to take account of the results obtained for earlier eras.

The organization of the work is chronological. Part One deals with the prehistoric period and the first great civilizations of the Middle East. Part Two deals with the Greeks and Romans of antiquity. Part Three deals with the crucial epoch of the barbarian invasions and the early Middle Ages (from 400 to 1000) Part Four is concerned with three cultures that had a major impact on medieval Europe: the Hebraic, the Islamic, and the Greek Orthodox. Part Five takes up the middle and latter part of the Middle Ages (from 1000 to 1400). Part Six deals with the early modern era (from 1400 to 1800). Finally, Part Seven is concerned with the nineteenth and twentieth centuries.

Rather than adopt the narrative style of the old myth-filled histories of food, we have chosen a thematic approach. For most of the periods examined, we have included studies of, among other things, economic and demographic factors (that is, the relation between the production of food and its consumption), differences between urban and rural areas, culinary arts, dietetics, meals and table manners, and symbolic aspects of eating.

We have also made an effort to avoid the narrow national outlook that shaped most of the gastronomic myths. To that end, we have called upon historians from many different countries who have contributed in one way or another to recent progress in the history of food, and we have asked them to look beyond their own countries and treat their subjects insofar as possible from a European perspective. Given the current state of knowledge, this is not an easy task.

By and large, we have confined our attention to Europe. However, in order to clarify the nature and inception of the European diet, we do occasionally glance at non-European societies: the reader will find chapters on Mesopotamia, Egypt, and Hebrew society in early antiquity as well as the Byzantine, Arabic, and Jewish societies that were the partners and adversaries of Europeans in the Middle Ages. In addition, the age of discovery and the subsequent opening of markets beyond Europe and the formation of colonial empires on other continents subjected European cuisine to influences from the four corners of the globe.

NOTES

1. Published as an appendix to *Commentary on the Most Notable and Marvelous Things in Italy and Other Places*.
2. A good recent bibliography can be found in M. Lachiver, *Les Années de misère: La famine au temps du Grand Roi* (Paris: Fayard, 1991).
3. The main results are summarized in J.-J. Hémardinquer, *Pour une histoire de l'alimenation* in *Cahier des Annales,* no. 28 (Paris: Armand Colin, 1970), and *Histoire de la consommation* in *Annales: Économies, sociétés, civilisations,* March–June 1975, pp. 402–632.
4. J. Bertin, J.-J. Hémardinquer, M. Keul, and W. G. I. Randles, *Atlas des cultures vivrières*

(Paris: Mouton, 1971). See also Fernand Braudel's interesting thoughts on the relationship between the dominant food crop, the density of population, and social and political structures in *Civilisation matérielle et capitalisme*, vol. 1 (Paris: Armand Colin, 1967), pp. 78–133.

5. On butchers and meat rations, see chap. 2 of the pioneering study by L. Stouff, *Ravitaillement et alimentation en Provence aux XIVe et XVe siècles* (Paris: Mouton, 1970), and Stouff, *La Table provençale: Boire et manger en Provence à la fin du Moyen Age* (Avignon: Barthélemy, 1966).

6. R.-J. Bernard, "L'alimentation paysanne en Gévaudan au XVIIIe siècle," *Annales: économies, sociétés, civilisations,* November–December 1969, pp. 1449–67; and, more recently, J.-M. Boehler, *Une société rurale en milieu rhénan: La paysannerie de la plaine d'Alsace (1648–1789)*, 2d ed. (Strasbourg: Presses Universitaires de Strasbourg, 1995), 2:1679–1730.

7. J.-P. Aron, P. Dumont, and E. Le Roy Ladurie, *Anthropologie du conscrit français* (Paris: Mouton, 1982).

8. The tone was set by Claude Lévi-Strauss, *Mythologiques,* 3 vols. (Paris: Plon, 1964–68). For France, see Y. Verdier, *Façons de faire, façons de dire: La laveuse, la couturière, la cuisinière* (Paris: Gallimard, 1979).

9. Marcel Détienne and Jean-Pierre Vernant, *La Cuisine du sacrifice en pays grec* (Paris: Gallimard, 1979).

10. See M. Montanari, *L'alimentazione contadina nell'alto Medioevo* (Naples: Liguori, 1979); Montanari, *Alimentazione e cultura nel Medioevo* (Rome: Laterza, 1988); Montanari, *La fame e l'abbondanza: Storia dell'alimentazione in Europa* (Rome: Laterza, 1993) [*The Culture of Food,* trans. Carl Ipsen, The Making of Europe (Oxford: Blackwell, 1994)]; and A. Grieco, "Classes sociales, nourriture et imaginaire alimentaire en Italie (XIVe–XVe siècle)" (thesis, École des Hautes Études en Sciences Sociales, Paris, 1987).

11. J.-L. Flandrin, "La diversité des goûts et des pratiques alimentaires en Europe du XVIe au XVIIIe siècle," *Revue d'histoire moderne et contemporaine,* January–March 1983, pp. 66–83; "Le Goût et la nécessité: Sur l'usage des graisses dans les cuisines d'Europe occidentale (XIVe–XVIIIe siècles)," *Annales: Économies, sociétés, civilisations,* March–April 1983, pp. 369–401; *Chronique de Platine: Pour une gastronomie historique* (Paris: Odile Jacob, 1992). B. Laurioux, "Manger l'impur: Animaux et interdits alimentaires durant le haut Moyen Age," in *Histoire et Animal: Actes du colloque "Animal et Histoire,"* Toulouse, May 14–16, 1987, 1:73–88; and "Le lièvre lubrique et la bête sanglante: Réflexions sur quelques interdits alimentaires du haut Moyen Age," *Anthropozoologica,* special issue. J.-L. Flandrin, "La viande: Evolution des goûts et des attitudes," *Entretiens de Bichat,* September 27, 1989, Centre d'Information des Viandes; and "Alimentation et christianisme," *Dossier: Religions et alimentation. Nervure, Journal de Psychiatrie* 8, no. 6 (September 1995): 38–42; J.-L. Flandrin, "Médecine et habitudes alimentaires anciennes," in *Pratiques et Discours alimentaires à la Renaissance,* ed. J.-C. Margolin and R. Sauzet, proceedings of the colloqium of Tours, 1979 (Paris: Maisonneuve et Larose, 1982), pp. 85–95.

P. Jansen-Sieben and F. Daelemans, *Voeding en Geneeskunde: Alimentation et médecine,* proceedings of the Brussels colloquium of October 12, 1990 (Brussels: Archives and Libraries of Belgium, 1993), pp. 177–92. M. Weiss Adamson, *Medieval Dietetics: Food and Drink in Regimen Sanitatis Literature from 800 to 1400* (Frankfurt-am-Main: Peter Lang, 1995).

PART ONE

PREHISTORY *and* EARLY CIVILIZATIONS

INTRODUCTION

THE HUMANIZATION *of* EATING BEHAVIORS

Jean-Louis Flandrin

When and how did the eating behavior of human beings diverge from that of other animal species? Did humans distinguish themselves by the type or variety of foods they ate? By the fact that they prepared their food before eating it? By the ceremonial forms with which they surrounded the act of eating? Or by the conviviality of dining and its characteristic social forms?

Foods

Ancient Egyptian tombs from the fourth millennium B.C.E. show that the diet of the social elite already exhibited considerable variety. By the time of the Nineteenth Dynasty, the pharaoh and his substantial retinue were consuming an even greater diversity of pastries, meats, fish, dairy products, fruits, vegetables, and drinks. But what were ordinary people eating? On this point the sources are far less clear.

It is hard to say exactly when humans began to eat specific foods. Human beings were always omnivores: to one degree or another, they always ate both animals and vegetables. Even before the appearance of hominids, there were already omnivorous primates, so the omnivorous character of the human diet has no historical beginning.

For millions of years most of prehistoric man's calories came to him in the form of a mixture of fruits, leaves, and grains. That the preponderance of man's diet consisted of vegetable matter is suggested by the relatively small range of primitive bands and by certain characteristic wear patterns found in the teeth of humanoid remains. Yet anthropologists who have studied prehistoric man have written more about what he hunted and fished than about what plants he ate. This is partly because traces of vegetal foodstuffs are not as likely to be preserved in the soil. It is also because the chemical and isotopic techniques required to determine the proportions of animal and vegetable products in the prehistoric diet were developed only recently. These new techniques may also shed light on the types of plants eaten.

In recent decades there has been much debate about whether the first hominids—*Australopithecus, Homo habilis,* and later, about 1.5 million years ago, *Homo erectus*—were hunters or carrion eaters. Here it will be argued that man was an active hunter from the beginning, even if he also sometimes robbed other predators of their prey.

In the early Paleolithic period, especially in Europe, hunting and meat-eating took on increased importance. Opportunistic hunting, often of large animals such as bear, rhinoceros, and elephant, was the most common form in the middle Paleolithic period (200,000 to 40,000 B.C.E.). The later Paleolithic (40,000 to 10,000 B.C.E.) saw the development of more specialized forms of hunting involving herds of reindeer, horses, bison, aurochs, and mammoths, depending on the region and local resources.

In the Mesolithic period, as the European climate grew warmer, men were forced to hunt smaller animals such as deer, boar, fur-bearing carnivores, hares, birds, and even snails. Increasing amounts of time were devoted to fishing and gathering. Finally, with the agricultural revolution of the Neolithic period and the advent of the first civilizations, still less time was devoted to hunting, and greater emphasis was placed on rearing and slaughtering livestock of species that are still with us to this day: cows, sheep, goats, and pigs.

The transition to agriculture and husbandry occurred earliest in the Middle and Near East. These activities soon spread to other parts of the Mediterranean. Farther north, hunting and gathering continued to predominate into the Christian era, thus favoring a more balanced, less nutritionally deficient diet.

What types of plants did prehistoric man eat? Roots and tubers? Tender stalks? Leaves? Dry or juicy fruits? Cereals? More precise information would be welcome.

Broadly speaking, consumption of cereals began only after the rise of agriculture, and even then only in the great "civilized" societies—that is, those with cities, such as were found in Mesopotamia, Egypt, Syria, and Iran. In these places we hear of the consumption either of cereals in general or of specific species: first barley, then spelt and wheat and various foods and drinks prepared from these grains, including both leavened and unleavened bread, flatcakes, flatbreads, various kinds of biscuits, and beer.

But how are we to explain the inception of cereal agriculture if people had not already developed a taste for grains and a habit of consuming them? In fact, grains were cultivated in the wild, as has been demonstrated in the case of the Natufian culture, which flourished in the Near East between 12,000 and 10,000 B.C.E., and of Greece throughout the Mesolithic period. Cereals were probably consumed even earlier, since the wear patterns on the teeth of the first hominids, some two to three million years ago, show that they were grain eaters.

In the Mesolithic period humans in temperate zones shifted to a more diversified diet. Let us not be too hasty, however, to interpret this as a sign of progress. Indeed, some scholars see it as a response to the disappearance of the big game animals that abounded in Europe during the Ice Age. Thereafter, in order to round out their diet, men probably had to spend more time hunting small animals, such as the jerboa that was served at Mesopotamian banquets, or gathering wild plants, such as a lentil so small that it took a hundred thousand to make up a pound. By this standard, Esau appears to have been a true sybarite!

Another ambiguous transformation came about in the Neolithic era, but this time the response was quite different from that which had greeted the vanishing of the Paleolithic paradise. Agriculture and husbandry were, among other things, a kind of insurance against climatic changes. Sometimes, however, even this insurance was not adequate, as the biblical story of the seven famished cows in Egypt suggests. The problem was compounded by the fact that, while agriculture and husbandry allowed higher population densities than did hunting and gathering, they also appear to have encouraged natalist ideologies, which favored high birth rates and thus rapid population growth. This tended to increase infant mortality rates and made periodic famines more deadly than ever. In addition, farming, even in the rich, well-irrigated alluvial soil of Egypt and Mesopotamia, required harder labor than the great hunts of the late Paleolithic era. Finally, compared with the hunter-gatherers of Mesolithic Europe, the farmers and husbandmen of the Middle East ate a less varied diet whose nutritional deficiencies reduced their life expectancy.

Not only did nature supply different foods in different parts of the world, but people in every region picked and chose among the foods that nature offered. These choices reflected their different cultures. To this day, for example, Europeans eat no insects, yet people in Africa, South America, and Asia do. Within Europe, the French surprise and scandalize their neighbors by eating frogs and snails, while turtle soup has become an English specialty and haggis (made of the minced heart, lungs, and liver of sheep) a Scottish curiosity. Such differences are plainly cultural, since snails, frogs, turtles, and sheep are found throughout Europe. By the same token, animals prized by most Europeans are of course proscribed on religious grounds elsewhere: pork, eel, sturgeon, caviar, shellfish, and crustaceans are considered impure by Jews and Muslims, and Hindus are forbidden to eat the flesh of any animal. It would be interesting, therefore, to find out when human beings began to choose among the foods provided by nature and what rules guided their choice.

Although this aspect of food history is important and has justifiably attracted the attention of prehistorians, we here examine only one culture in detail: that of the ancient Hebrews. Despite the rigor of the analysis, we must warn against a possible misinterpretation of the results. The analysis is rigorous because it is based on the internal logic of Hebraic thought; the same method could equally well be applied to dietary restrictions in other cultures. The whole system of religious taboos is examined, whereas older "hygienic" theories of dietary restrictions overlooked many aspects. The methodology is therefore widely applicable. Yet it is misleading to treat the ancient Hebrews as a case apart and to examine their dietary practices only in terms of taboos. Even if the Hebrews attached greater importance to dietary restrictions than did other groups, and even if their choices in this respect defined their identity to an unusual degree, they were not as atypical as certain chapters in Part One and later might lead one to believe. Dietary choices are universal, but not all are justified on religious or hygienic grounds. Some are unconscious, and some are justified in other ways. Why, for instance, did the French reject the rutabaga after consuming so much of it during World War II, and why did the English give up flavoring their omelettes with tansy as they did in the Middle Ages?

Cooking

The earliest known recipes date from Mesopotamia in the second millennium B.C.E. It would be rash, however, to conclude that the Mesopotamians invented cooking. They simply had reasons to write down their recipes and were the first, along with the Egyptians, to possess the means to do so: without writing, recipes cannot survive. Yet the absence of written recipes does not rule out an interest in gastronomic matters or the existence of sophisticated culinary techniques. For example, the ancient Egyptians apparently felt no need to write down their recipes, yet we find instructive traces of their cooking methods in tombs dating from as early as the fourth millennium. Still, they did not invent cooking, either.

Some five hundred millennia ago, it appears, man achieved mastery of fire and began to diverge from the hominids, which remained wedded to an animal existence. Students of prehistoric man generally agree that fire was first used for cooking. Other uses appeared only much later. It would seem but a short step from this apparent fact to the statement that cooking made man some 500,000 years ago. Before we take that step, however, let us pause for a moment to consider the evidence for the transition from the raw to the cooked. What is cooking? How does an art of such importance come to be? Why did it develop?

Cooked meat is a natural byproduct of forest fires. In the wake of such fires, carnivores are thus able to sample the taste of cooked flesh. It is sometimes said that all flesh eaters prefer cooked meat to raw and would eat roasted meat every day if only they knew how to make a fire. The suggestion is that as soon as man came into possession of fire, his diet changed.

Let us not be too hasty to embrace this simplistic theory. "Good" and "bad" are not objective qualities; they vary from individual to individual and culture to culture. If any general rule holds, it is that what is known and familiar is generally preferred to what is unknown and unfamiliar. For a Japanese, the best way to serve fresh fish is raw. And at the beginning of the twentieth century, an Eskimo would have preferred raw and quite gamy seal meat to any of the boiled, roasted, or sauced versions that a French chef might have served up. Not all cultures share the age-old European aversion to raw meat and predilection for cooked. Hence one needs to be cautious about explaining the invention of cooking by invoking taste.

Furthermore, the fact that carnivores eat cooked meat after forest fires does not prove that they prefer it to raw meat. Meat on the hoof has to be caught before it can be eaten. Nor does the consumption of accidentally cooked meat prove that the carnivorous animals that do so are prepared to invest the time and energy required to achieve mastery of fire and learn how to cook.

Man domesticated fire some 500,000 years before the birth of Christ. This much seems well established. But it was not the overnight achievement of some ancient Prometheus. Long before man mastered fire, he may well have used it for cooking, as charred bones found at very ancient campsites suggest.

What is cooking? In the chapters that follow, we will learn of plants that are poisonous in their natural state but edible after preparation of some sort—for example, scalding in the case of certain types of mushroom, such as the gyromitra, or turban-tops. Some plants such as manioc require drying, marination, or extensive washing to eliminate bitter or toxic juices. And various types of preservation prevent foodstuffs from becoming toxic. Meat has been dried and smoked since the late Paleolithic period. Later preservation techniques include salting and the use of controlled fermentation to produce storable products such as beer, wine, cider, vinegar, cheeses, sauerkraut, pickles, *nuoc mam* (Vietnamese fish sauce), *garum* (used by the ancient Greeks), soy sauce, *morri* (an ancient Andalusian preparation), and so forth. Such preparations, which were originally intended not so much to enhance the taste of food as to preserve it or make it edible, may be included under the rubric "cooking."

As we shall see, the initial purpose of heating, seasoning, marinating, grinding, slicing, filtering, and other cooking techniques was to make foods digestible and safe as much as, if not more than, to improve their taste. Taste, moreover, depended on culinary customs associated with specific cultural beliefs. The complexity of culinary techniques varied from culture to culture, but even the simplest is worthy of our attention.

Can we therefore say that cooking commenced when the first foods were roasted more than 500,000 years ago? Is that when the "humanization" of animal feeding behavior began? Perhaps, but let us not be too hasty to draw this conclusion. Certain techniques may have originated much earlier, even before the emergence of hominids.

Such, at any rate, is the conclusion suggested by one study of a small population of macaque monkeys on Koshima Island. Japanese primatologists one day observed a young female monkey soaking a sweet potato in a stream before eating it. At first this seemed unimportant. But the female in question developed a habit of soaking her potatoes, and other young macaques imitated her. As the young monkeys matured, they taught this behavior to their offspring. Meanwhile, the behavior itself evolved. Instead of dipping their potatoes in fresh water, as they had done initially, the monkeys came to prefer seawater. Indeed, the whole colony moved closer to the shore in order to facilitate this practice, and this colony of primates soon adopted new foods that they also took to soaking in seawater. Whatever the reason for their behavior, the monkeys were clearly engaged in a kind of culinary practice. Many such techniques may have been developed before the first men began to cook.

Conviviality

What differentiates human alimentary behavior from that of the animals? Culinary techniques, dietary restrictions, and religious rituals associated with eating are certainly part of the answer, but human dining is also believed to be a convivial social function.

Countless texts attest to the existence of banquet rituals as early as the beginning of the third millennium in Sumer and no later than the second millennium in other parts of Mesopotamia and in Syria. Although these texts mainly concern banquets involving gods and princes, they also describe the feasts of various less exalted individuals. Social eating and drinking already served to strengthen friendships and bolster ties between a lord and his vassals, dependents, servants, and even servants of servants. Farther down on the social ladder, merchants sealed bargains by sharing a drink.

In the same period the practice emerged of serving a round of daily meals in the temples of the gods: the "large morning meal," the "small morning meal," the "large evening meal," and the "small evening meal." Men did not eat on as strict a schedule as the gods, nor did they eat as often: there was a small morning meal and a large evening meal. Banquets were also held in the evening.

At Mesopotamian banquets certain foods, condiments, and beverages appear to have been indispensable, and one finds most of the same ingredients at the festive meals of other peoples later on. These included fresh meat, perhaps of a sheep, lamb, deer, or fowl. And then there was that amazing jerboa that served ten thousand people at the palace of Assurbanipal in Kalhu. Or it might be an ordinary goat, as in the fable of the poor man of Nippur. In any case, fresh meat seems to have been an essential ingredient of any Mesopotamian banquet, as it would be of banquets in other times and places.

Also essential were fermented beverages such as barley beer, ale, and liquor made from fermented dates, wine, and the like. Such drinks were perhaps even more typical of festive and convivial occasions. Salt was also shared as a symbol of friendship. Oil is mentioned as a part of every banquet: it was used not to flavor dishes but to anoint the guests' hair. For this purpose it was often perfumed, hence even more precious. Oil thus served a cosmetic function, analogous to that of the water with which diners washed their hands before and after eating.

Other foods whose festive character is less apparent were also consumed: fish, eggs, fruits, vegetables, pastries embellished with fruits or sweetened with honey, flatcakes, and barley bread. At some banquets grains were eaten, either in the kernel or ground into flour but unbaked; these were extolled as extraordinary sources of nourishment. To us this seems odd: in ancient Mesopotamia the agricultural revolution was not yet ancient enough for cereals to have lost their sacred status and become a staple of commoners.

There were also banquets in Egypt as long ago as the Old Kingdom. Here we read of changes in the dinner table, seating, utensils, and the posture of guests at table. In Egypt, as in Mesopotamia, a precise dining ritual and strict etiquette were prescribed, at least for gods and kings.

Did the social function of the banquet originate in the third millennium with the advent of agriculture and husbandry and the concomitant rise of great empires in the East? Probably not. We do not know whether agriculture and husbandry predated alcoholic beverages such as beer, wine, and fruit-based liquors, which played such an important role in festive dining. Mongol horse breeders even drank a liquor made from fermented mare's milk. Nevertheless, archaeologists have shown that beer existed in Iran in the sixth century B.C.E. Feasting may well have been possible even without intoxicating liquors. Finally, it seems likely, though it has yet to be proven, that hallucinogenic plants were used to foster conviviality well before the invention of fermented beverages. Some interpreters of late Paleolithic painting hold that certain images depict visions induced by such plants.

In any case, in the late Paleolithic, groups of families began working together to drive large animals into traps. This form of social organization required a division of the spoils among the several families that participated in the hunt. Very likely there was a division of labor as well. At certain times—after a hunt, for instance—the families probably gathered for a large festive meal at which they consumed part of the fresh kill. Going even farther back in time, to around 500,000 B.C.E. when man first began to cook with fire on a daily basis, the use of a common fire probably encouraged common dining, hence the social function of dining and the development of conviviality.

Does this suggest that meals were not taken in common until food began to be cooked? There is reason to doubt this. Although one should be wary of anthropomorphic interpretations of animal behavior, it is hard to avoid feeling that animals often take pleasure in eating together. Their cooperation in the kill is not incompatible with a hierarchical division of the spoils, a system of priorities, even a kind of etiquette appropriate to an animal society. Nothing similar is observed in the behavior of herbivores. Even before man appeared on the scene, did feasting originate with the division of freshly killed meat?

CHAPTER I

FEEDING STRATEGIES *in* PREHISTORIC TIMES

Catherine Perlès

Even if apes were more omnivorous than is generally believed, man would remain unique among primates for the diversity of his diet. Among the factors contributing to the distinctiveness of human alimentary behavior are the variety and complexity of the underlying economy and the highly socialized, not to say ritualized, nature of human feeding.

The study of prehistoric man's alimentary behavior and its gradual transformation should therefore be an important topic. Despite this importance, however, the current state of research leaves students of prehistory in a paradoxical situation: while we are capable of discussing the fabrication of, say, stone tools in minute detail, the best we can do when it comes to the history of eating is to propose a sketchy and still largely hypothetical portrait.

Chemistry and Prehistory

Some day, perhaps, chemical analysis of fossilized bones will make a full history of the prehistoric diet possible. Bony tissue contains dietary "markers" such as trace elements and carbon isotope ratios.[1] At the present time, however, these advanced methods are mostly still in the experimental stage. There are formidable technical problems to overcome, because many factors can alter the chemical composition of bones after burial. Despite these difficulties, promising results have already been obtained, particularly in regard to fairly recent prehistoric populations. For example, studies of certain North American tribes have demonstrated a regular seasonal alternation between food drawn from the land and food drawn from the water. By contrast, in studies of Danish tribes of the Mesolithic era, no such complementary seasonal cycles have been found to differentiate coastal from inland sites. Apparently the two types of sites were occupied by different groups: fishermen in the one case, hunters in the other. Elsewhere, among agricultural populations, investigators have pointed to the existence of dietary differences between individuals of different social status.

Because of the many technical issues yet to be resolved, these results must be regarded as preliminary. Hence chemical analysis of bones, although an exciting avenue of future investigation, is still a long way from providing us with a complete picture of the prehistoric diet. If we want to trace the history of human eating back to the beginning, we must for the time being rely on traditional archaeological methods, with all their well-known shortcomings.

Those methods are particularly problematic when it comes to the study of diet, since plant matter, like all organic substances, decays in the soil. It is virtually certain, however, that primitive man derived most of his calories from plants, except in extreme latitudes, where the environment was quite special.[2] Indeed, although man, like other primates, is omnivorous, the symbolic importance attached to meat does not reflect its actual nutritional importance. Much of this essay is concerned with meat consumption, but this has to do more with the survival of vestiges of that activity than with its actual importance in the prehistoric diet. But this emphasis also stems, in my view, from the fact that prehistorians themselves wittingly or unwittingly ascribe too much importance to meat-eating in their various theories of "hominization."

The First Hominids: Fierce Hunters or Carcass Snatchers?

To this day, meat, especially meat obtained by hunting wild animals, enjoys a symbolic importance out of all proportion to its place in the human diet. This no doubt accounts for the decisive role traditionally ascribed to hunting in theories of hominization from antiquity to the present.[3] And it probably also explains the hyperbole in recent efforts to refute such theories by showing that the first hominids were scavengers.

In deposits left by the first hominids (*Australopithecus* and *Homo habilis*) in East Africa some 1.5 to 2.5 million years ago, we find substantial numbers of animal bone fragments together with primitive stone implements. The richest sites, located beside lakes and rivers, contain the remains of animals ranging in size from turtles to elephants along with hundreds of chips left from the cutting of stone tools. On the basis of such evidence, these hominids were long considered to be the first primate hunters. By definition they were also permanent bipeds. But bipeds are not particularly well adapted for hunting, particularly when the absence of any long-range projectile weapon made it impossible to hunt from ambush. It was therefore assumed that the males of these species must have cooperated in the hunt.[4] Since the remains of the prey were gathered together at certain sites, these were held to be "campsites" and adduced as evidence for mutual assistance and complementarity between males and females.[5]

Some four to five million years ago, the story goes, diminished rainfall in East Africa reduced the extent of jungle and expanded the savanna, depriving man's ancestors of many plant resources and forcing them to adapt by eating more meat, which required them to band together in organized hunts. This organized hunting led in turn to improvements in communication skills and intellectual faculties and to a gendered division of labor. In other words, the type of social and family organization regarded as typically human allegedly originated with hunting.[6] It was therefore ostensibly because *Australopithecus* became a hunter that he developed human characteristics.

What kind of hypothesis is this? Is it a historical fact or what some ironically call a "scenario," nothing more than a reflection of our own preconceptions? In fact, this reconstruction of the prehistoric past is based on reasoning by analogy.

An American prehistorian, L. Binford, was the first to ask what proof there was that the animal bones and stone implements were left by the same individuals.[7] Perhaps the animal remains were left by wild carnivores and the tools by hominids. After more than a decade of debate, most scholars, particularly in the United States, accept Binford's hypothesis that hyenas gathered most of the carcasses and the hominids arrived to pick over the remains only after the predators were sated. Others, however, hold that the first hominids were sufficiently well organized to snatch freshly killed prey, with considerable meat still left on the bones, and carry it off to sites where stone tools were cached.[8]

In my view, although research in recent years has yielded solid results, the interpretation of those results suffers from methodological errors and is just as prone to ideological bias as the previous interpretation.[9] A broader view precludes seeing our earliest ancestors as miserable scavengers incapable of killing on their own the animals they ate.

Toward a Rehabilitation of the Early Hominids

In order to avoid circular reasoning, one must distinguish two questions. First, who brought the carcasses to the sites where they were deposited? And, second, how were those carcasses obtained?

The fact that animal remains are found together with stone tools and chips is one whose importance should not be underestimated. It is difficult to explain the abundance of both tools and chips if the sites in question were merely the lairs of hyenas picked over by hominids in search of leftover meat and marrow. Carnivores, moreover, do not normally amass bones out in the open. When they tear a carcass apart, they systematically disperse its parts. If they have young to feed, they take portions of the dead animal back to their dens. Thus dispersion is followed by selective accumulation.

When bones are amassed out in the open, therefore, there has to be some reason to explain why the same site was repeatedly reused. At first glance, nothing in the setting (by the side of a lake or river) accounts for this reuse, which is unusual for animal predators but typical of later human hunters. Potts' hypothesis that the presence of tools accounts for the reuse of these sites explains both their character and location. If Potts is correct, most of the carcasses must have been brought to these places by the hominids themselves rather than by hyenas.

Second, analysis of what portions of carcasses are present on the site unambiguously demonstrates that no secondary scavenging was involved. One systematically finds the richest meat-bearing portions (leg, shoulder, etc.). The hominids therefore must have had access to freshly killed animals and not to what was left over after other carnivores had eaten their fill. Indeed, this "rehabilitation" of the early hominids has met with unexpected corroboration in the form of recent findings concerning the behavior of chimpanzees in the wild. Some are skillful hunters: in certain seasons male chimps will hunt smaller monkeys and other prey and eat up to 200 grams of meat per day.[10]

Consequently, it seems difficult to deny that the first hominids were predators in the broad sense. Still, animal protein was probably just a complement to a diet based mainly on plants. There are two kinds of evidence for this assertion: the wear patterns found on the teeth of early hominids, which indicate a plant-based diet, and the range of territory in which they operated. From this we conclude that *Homo habilis* was an opportunistic omnivore.

The Development of Diversified Hunting

There is no evidence that this alimentary strategy was significantly modified in Africa over the next several hundred thousand years. When *Homo erectus* replaced

Homo habilis some 1.5 million years ago, the density of animal remains that we find at surviving sites actually tended to decrease. The bones are also more fractured, which suggests a more intensive consumption of marrow.

By contrast, when *Homo erectus* began to establish himself in more temperate regions, the greater seasonal contrasts and corresponding decrease in plant resources must have led to a greater, though by no means exclusive, nutritional role for meat. In Europe throughout the Paleolithic period we find archaeological evidence for a diversified meat diet, which very early came to depend on an ability to kill large animals.

The variety of animals consumed and the distribution of their ages suggests that hunters went after isolated animals rather than attacking entire herds en masse. Small groups of hunters made regular (though not necessarily daily) forays in search of whatever game they could find. But diversified hunting does not mean random hunting. All hunters observe potential prey even when they are not hunting. On every expedition decisions had to be made: for example, whether to follow the tracks of the first small game encountered or hold out for meatier prey or for something easier to capture. Obviously such choices depended on the day and the season, on experience with previous hunts, on the availability of stored meat, and on the group's knowledge of the abundance of game in the area and of plant resources at that time of year.[11]

Gathering plants was in fact an integral part of hominid alimentary strategies. Because few traces of vegetal foodstuffs have survived, it is difficult to evaluate their consumption either qualitatively or quantitatively. It is nevertheless fair to assume that plants were important both nutritionally and economically, particularly after the domestication of fire opened up a whole new range of resources, namely, plants that, while toxic in their raw state, could be consumed after cooking.[12]

It was some 500,000 years ago that regular domestic use of fire began to have a profound effect on the hominid diet and doubtless on social behavior related to eating as well. Many carnivores have a taste for cooked meat (a natural by-product of forest fires). Yet only man had the ability to eat cooked meat regularly and thus to move from feeding to cooking and ultimately to a whole range of culinary techniques. It is striking to observe that the earliest traces of cooking are contemporary with the earliest vestiges of campfires.[13] Charred bones have been found apart from the remains of the fire itself, indicating that the bones once held grilled meat and were not simply parts of animal carcasses used as fuel. Although grilling was sporadic more than 500,000 years ago, it became common once fire was truly domesticated.

The social impact of cooking was no doubt more immediately apparent than were its nutritional implications. It encouraged *commensalism,* or eating with others, and led to greater division of labor within the group, all of whose members participated in a regular round of activities associated with eating. The result was a more complex group organization.

Specialized Hunting in the Late Paleolithic Period

Toward the end of the middle Paleolithic era we detect the first signs of organized hunting, as individual animals began to be separated from herds by the concerted efforts of groups of hunters. Systems of subsistence based on the exploitation of a selected species of animal became commonplace. Among the species hunted in this fashion in one region or another were reindeer, horses, bison, aurochs, and even mammoths. This new type of hunting called for a socioeconomic structure and range of techniques quite different from those associated with opportunistic hunting. Its economic objectives were also different.

Opportunistic hunting had involved individuals or small groups and required little preparation other than daily maintenance of weapons. Many kinds of weapons and tools were needed to kill and prepare the diverse prey. By contrast, driving herd animals into pits took large numbers of people (often including women and children), usually drawn from groups of families residing separately for much of the year. These periodic assemblies for the hunt suggest that there must have been some means of spreading information and some form of social integration or expanded social structure extending beyond the domestic or residential unit. Hunting herd animals (often migratory) in this way required extensive preparation: pits had to be dug, and large numbers of specialized weapons had to be assembled, along with tools for slaughtering, butchering, and treating hides. In compensation for all this preliminary effort, the hunt could be expected to yield considerable quantities of meat, lard, marrow, hide, sinew, and hair. These reserves of food and materiel might be sufficient for several weeks or months. Hence this type of hunting was more demanding socially and technically as well as more risky (if no animals were captured) but more rewarding if successful. Broadly speaking, it was in areas that practiced this form of hunting that Paleolithic art also developed: sanctuaries, movable objects, and embellishments and ornaments of various kinds. This art, incorporated into communal rituals, no doubt encouraged integration and collaboration. But the art itself was in turn encouraged by the stockpiling of food reserves, which allowed groups to stay put for extended periods.

Collaborative hunting also implied a need to preserve meat after slaughter. The cold, dry climate of the late Paleolithic made this task easier. Meat was dried, smoked, or frozen in pits dug in the earth (in this preglacial climate the subsoil was permanently frozen). Such pits, covered with mammoth tusks, have been found in central and eastern Europe. Elsewhere, whole carcasses, weighted down with stones, were deposited in lakes that froze over in winter, thus preserving the meat.

Stored meats and other foods could be eaten either dry or boiled. Water was boiled either by tossing heated rocks into vessels of wood, bark, or hide, vestiges of which have been found near campfires, or by heating it directly over the fire in animal bellies or skins. Large pieces of meat were also grilled on spits. Traces of spits made of bone have survived. Smaller pieces could be grilled directly on the stones used to line hearths in this period.[14]

The late Paleolithic—a time when primitive man fished for salmon, captured birds, hunted animals in large groups, and developed the ability to depict his prey in art—in many respects marks the apogee of the hunter-gatherer way of life.

Diversity of Diet in the European Mesolithic

As the glaciers began to recede some 8,000 years before the birth of Christ, a moist, temperate climate returned to the middle latitudes of Europe. Tundra, steppes, and prairies gradually gave way to forest. The larger meat-bearing animals were supplanted by smaller prey more difficult to hunt in the dense forest. But other resources became more abundant: not only plants but also fish, mollusks, and birds. The Mesolithic diet was much more diverse than that of the late Paleolithic. Dozens of species from a variety of biotopes could be exploited from a single site. Nevertheless, we must be careful not to confuse diversity with abundance.

If deer, boar, and roe deer had been truly abundant, would Mesolithic man have added rabbit, birds, and snails to his diet? If a few plant species had supplied all of his energy needs, would he have scoured the area around his campsite for fruits, vegetables, and nuts? The very mobility of certain Mesolithic groups, which settled briefly in an area to exploit its resources before moving on, suggests conditions well short of abundance.

Farther north, in game-rich forests close to the sea or to rivers and lakes filled with fish and attractive to migratory birds, we do find traces of more permanent dwelling sites. Here abundant seasonal resources sustained life and made it possible to accumulate reserves. Hence although the Mesolithic tribes living along the Mediterranean were quick to learn agricultural and husbandry techniques imported by immigrants from the Near East, their northern cousins clung for a much longer time to their ancestral ways, even as they began to trade with the sedentary peoples to the south, exchanging fish, game, and gathered plants for ceramics, the meat of domestic animals, and polished stone tools.

Agriculture and Husbandry: Liberation or New Problems?

Although wild cereals had been harvested earlier, it is not until the Neolithic period that we see, first in the Near and Middle East and later in Europe, the beginnings of the economic "revolution" that became the basis for the traditional European diet. This revolution consisted in the cultivation of cereal crops (especially wheat and rye) and the raising of livestock, especially sheep, goats, cows, and pigs. It was at this time that wheat was first used to make both leavened and unleavened bread. The number of millstones that have been found and the care taken with them inside the dwelling indicate just how important a staple grain was from the outset.

There is a tendency, however, to overestimate the benefits of the ensuing dietary transformation. Because all the major western civilizations were founded on foods domesticated in this period, we are apt to view it through rose-colored lenses. In the temperate and northern parts of Europe, cereals and meat from domestic animals were still supplemented by resources from the wild, with the result that people in those parts of the world enjoyed an ample, balanced diet. By contrast, in Mediterranean Europe and the Near and Middle East, little use was made of wild plants or animals. In the early stages of the transition to the Neolithic, in fact, those potential sources of food appear to have been deliberately abandoned, perhaps for ideological reasons: turning his back on the wild, man concentrated on the domestic. The bulk of his diet consisted of cereals, legumes, beef, and mutton. Overreliance on cereals probably had negative effects on health. Dietary deficiencies were probably not the only cause of poor health, however. The growing density of sedentary populations created a propitious environment for epidemics.

Many scholars believe that a second dietary revolution followed close on the heels of the first: this involved the use of earthenware pottery, which allegedly made it possible to cook food in boiling water. Porridge made from various grains became popular as a result. Undue nutritional and dietetic importance has been ascribed to this innovation, however. For one thing, pottery was by no means indispensable for boiling food. As we saw earlier, this method of cooking was already practiced in the Paleolithic era. For another, it now appears certain that in several parts of the world the first ceramics were seldom used for cooking (this is true of Greece and Pakistan, for example). Pottery was used as cookware by these same peoples, but for several centuries they continued to prefer such traditional cooking methods as grilling, baking on heated slabs, or braising in a pit filled with heated stones. Meanwhile, innovations were made in the use of fire: raised hearths were constructed in dwellings and the first closed ovens (similar to traditional bread ovens) were built. Thus "pottage" (in the etymological sense, meaning food cooked in an earthenware pot) did not catch on quickly everywhere. It may have taken hold sooner in colder areas, where it was nutritionally important to preserve fat in the diet, but this remains to be proven. Ceramic containers were in any case used for preparing and storing fermented drinks, which were probably drunk on festive and ritual occasions.

Symbolism and the Origin of Cooking

Various technical and economic developments of the Paleolithic period made for a variety of new methods of preparing and preserving food. Many foods were available to satisfy man's dietetic requirements, and it is likely that cultural preferences, or tastes transmitted from generation to generation, made their appearance at this early stage. Thanks to more numerous and better-preserved artifacts from the Neolithic period, we can be certain that cultural preferences existed by then. Accordingly, it is significant that in Europe hunting regained importance toward the end of the Neolithic. The prey was symbolically significant—the deer—and the renewed interest in hunting coincides with the first evidence of social inequalities and the emergence of elites. The fact that the deer was not domesticated was a true social and cultural choice, and the transfer of wild deer outside of their native habitat confirms the ideological importance attached to the "wild."[15]

Eating, which was at first a response to individual needs, thus gradually became a key element of group structure, a mark of identity, and a symbolic means of expressing thought. Evidence exists of complex culinary creations in the great empires of the Middle East.[16] These impressive states no doubt provided work for a new type of specialist: the cook. By contrast, there is little evidence of culinary sophistication or elaborate cookery in hunter-gatherer societies: preparations were simple, and the use of direct cooking (either by grilling meat or heating it on coals) made it difficult to mix ingredients to achieve new flavors. Menus were quite monotonous.

By contrast, we do find a number of hunter-gatherer societies that were quite adept at combining various substances for the purposes of healing and working magic. These preparations possessed certain features of true culinary art: they were complex combinations of ingredients for other than strictly nutritional purposes. I am therefore tempted to view these practices as forerunners of the more sophisticated culinary techniques that seek to achieve new flavors by means other than mere cooking. The consumption of fermented beverages probably also originated in rituals of one kind or another.

1. For example, the strontium/calcium ratio normally decreases with increasing meat consumption, while the ratio of carbon-13 to carbon-12 can indicate what types of plants were eaten. See, for example, E. Wing and A. Brown, *Paleonutrition: Method and Theory in Prehistoric Foodways* (New York: Academic Press, 1979).

2. This accounts for the interest in measuring the strontium/calcium and carbon-12/carbon-13 ratios in order to determine the proportion of animal and vegetable matter in the diet.

3. W. Stoczkowski, *Anthropologie naïve, anthropologie savante: De l'origine de l'homme, de l'imaginaire et des idées reçues* (Paris: Centre National de Recherche Scientifique, 1994) p. 215.

4. R. Ardrey, *The Hunting Hypothesis* (New York: Atheneum, 1976).

5. G. L. Isaac, "The Food-Sharing Behaviour of Proto-Human Hominids," *Scientific American* 238 (1978): 90–108.

6. G. Mendel, *La Chasse structurale* (Paris: Payot, 1977).

7. L. Binford, *Bones, Ancient Men, and Modern Myths* (London: Academic Press, 1981).

8. R. Potts, *Early Hominid Activities at Olduvai,* Foundations of Human Behavior (New York: Aldine de Gruyter, 1988).

9. For instance: (1) conflation of two distinct questions, namely, who assembled the carcasses and how were they obtained?; (2) the use, by Binford and others, of so-called residual analysis, where only remains different from what carnivores normally leave in their own lairs (the "residue") are attributed to the activity of hominids; from this choice it follows that the hominid cannot be seen as a hunter, because everything characteristic of the behavior of hunters (selection of prey, choice of the portions of the carcass containing the most meat or easiest to dismember, etc.) is automatically attributed to the carnivores; (3) contrary to the views expressed by R. J. Blumenschine in "Carcass Consumption Sequences and the Archaeological Distinction of Scavenging and Hunting," *Journal of Human Evolution* 15 (1986): 639–59, and in *Early Hominid Scavenging Opportunities,* International Series 283 (Oxford: British Archaeological Reports, 1986), interpretations based in part on analysis of carcasses found at excavation sites do not distinguish between hunters and scavengers but between rapid access to the carcass (whether by hunting or theft of fresh kill) and delayed access (secondary scavenging). Rapid access leads to consumption of the best meat, while the poorer leftovers go to the latecomers. But for an exception to the ideological bias that often characterizes the method, see Potts, *Early Hominid Activities.*

10. C. Boesch and E. Boesch, "Hunting Behavior of Wild Chimpanzees in the Tai National Parks," *American Journal of Physical Anthropology* 78 (1989): 547–73; G. Telecki, *The Predatory Behavior of Wild Chimpanzees* (Lewisburg, Penn.: Bucknell University Press, 1973).

11. S. J. Mithen, *Thoughtful Foragers: A Study in Prehistoric Decision Making* (Cambridge: Cambridge University Press, 1990).

12. A. B. Stahl, "Hominid Dietary Selection before Fire," *Current Anthropology* 25 (1984):

151–68; Stahl, "Plant-Food Processing: Implications for Dietary Quality," in *Foraging and Farming: The Evolution of Plant Exploitation,* ed. D. R. Harris and G. C. Hillman (London: Unwin-Hyman, 1989), pp. 171–93.

13. C. Perlès, *Préhistoire du feu* (Paris: Masson, 1977).

14. Ibid.

15. Although deer are easy to domesticate, untamed deer straight from the wild were transported by boat to islands where previously there had been no deer. See J.-D. Vigne, "Domestication ou appropriation pour la chasse: Histoire d'un choix socioculturel depuis le Néolithique," in *Exploitation des animaux sauvages à travers le temps,* XIIIe Rencontres Internationales d'Archéologie et d'Histoire d'Antibes, IVe Colloque International de l'Homme et l'Animal, October 15–17, 1992 (Juan-les-Pins, France: Editions Association pour la Promotion et la Diffusion des Connaissances Archeologiques, 1993), pp. 201–20.

16. J. Bottéro, "Le plus vieux festin du monde," *L'Histoire* 85 (1986): 58–65; Bottéro, "La plus vieille cuisine du monde," *L'Histoire* 187 (1995): 80–85.

CHAPTER 2

THE SOCIAL FUNCTION *of* BANQUETS *in the* EARLIEST CIVILIZATIONS

Francis Joannes

For the Mesopotamians, the society of the gods resembled human society in many ways. We find the clearest demonstration of this parallel in descriptions of banquets attended by the gods. Important decisions were taken at assemblies of the principal deities, assemblies often marked by banquets. One of the primary symbols of the gods' solidarity, these banquets illustrate the human conception of the pleasures of divine life.

When a god from one city visited another, a welcoming dinner was sometimes held. For example, when the goddess Inanna was invited to Eridu, the home of the god Enki, she was welcomed by the city's "vizir," who invited her to sample fresh water, cream, and beer. Later, after sharing many cups of wine with Enki, Inanna took advantage of the god's drunkenness to spirit away certain symbols of his power, which she took with her to her own city, Uruk. Divine banquets were also held to celebrate important victories and other great enterprises. The god Marduk, for example, invited the other gods to dine with him after he tamed the sea and founded Babylon.

Private Banquets

THE PLEASURE OF SHARED MEALS Any formal agreement by a group of individuals, especially individuals of the same family, was apt to be sealed by a shared meal. The dinner symbolized the accord, and the sharing of food and drink was the material counterpart of the written contract. Partaking of the same food and drink bound the participants, and in documents from the beginning of the second millennium we find this formula: "Bread was eaten, beer was drunk, and bodies were anointed with oil."[1] This practice was commonly associated with contracts for the sale of land, over which families frequently enjoyed certain rights. Following the same custom as the gods, the eldest son of the family had the honor of offering guests water to rinse their hands and then of serving them food and drink.

Banquets also sealed contracts to farm a piece of land or hire a boat. Above all they marked weddings. For all these occasions precise rules governed the exchange and sharing of food. To conclude a marriage in Assyria in the late second millennium, it was enough to anoint the head of a marriageable woman and organize a wedding banquet in her honor.

When people—from the highest court officials to the humblest of farmers—drank from the same cup, a kind of fraternity was established.[2] Sharing salt also symbolized a bond between individuals. In the neo-Assyrian period, the phrase *amelu sa tabtiya* (man of my salt) denoted a friend, a person with whom one shared this highly symbolic condiment. A refusal to share one's food was sometimes interpreted as a mark of hostility. Failure to treat a guest politely was a notorious mark of disrespect. The sharing of food mattered more than the ingredients of the meal, since these were of the most basic sort.

THE PLEASURES OF THE INN For less formal occasions people liked to go to places where they could eat and, above all, drink with others. I will use the term "inn" to refer to places of this sort, which could be found in every Mesopotamian town at least as far back as the second millennium. Here visitors found food to eat and were often joined by local residents. The guests were mainly men, but inns were frequently run by women. The most famous such innkeeper is Siduri, who appears in the epic of Gilgamesh. Her inn marks the limit of the civilized world: beyond it, Gilgamesh enters unknown, almost mythic, territory. As an innkeeper, Siduri has a profound knowledge of human nature, and her discussions with Gilgamesh reveal a down-to-earth philosophy of daily life based on a certain number of fundamental principles.

The Royal Banquet

Most of our figurative as well as textual sources concerning banquets and other aspects of early civilization pertain to the royal government. Hence we know a fair amount about why Mesopotamian kings gave banquets and what they were like.

Generally speaking, the sovereign invited guests to his dinner table to help him celebrate some important event: the inauguration of a palace or temple, a military victory, the arrival of a foreign delegation. Such occasions were simply glorified versions of various customary practices. The king was obliged to feed and otherwise compensate people who worked for him, whether in building prestigious monuments or winning battles. He had to welcome the representatives of other kings in a manner befitting his powerful status. And his relationship with the gods, one of the underpinnings of royal ideology, had to be maintained with regular feasts in their honor. The sumptuousness of these royal banquets varied, but they were always a key element in defining the relationship between the king and his people (or, at any rate, some of his people).

In the palaces of Mari and Babylon,[3] kings regularly received illustrious personages—traditional chieftains, royal vassals, foreign ambassadors—at royal banquets that were held in the palace courtyards at night and perhaps also in the great hall adjacent to the innermost courtyard. A strict etiquette governed these occasions: the king was served first, and if he wished to honor one of his guests, he might offer him his own dish. Guests generally sat in groups designated in advance and determined by their status, profession, and country of origin. They were "personal guests" of the sovereign, on whom all eyes were focused, to the detriment of any dinner-table conversation among the guests.

After the guests were seated by rank, servants passed among them with water for washing the hands. Each guest was then given a vial of oil perfumed with cedar, ginger, and myrtle with which to anoint himself at the beginning and end of the meal. Then grilled and stewed meats would be served together with flatbreads and vegetables. Dessert usually consisted of fruits and pastries sweetened with honey. The pastries were often molded, and numerous molds have been found in palace kitchens. Menus sometimes included rarer items: freshwater fish, ostrich eggs, mushrooms (or perhaps truffles), and pistachios. Beverages included wine, beer (brewed from barley or dates), and more unusual drinks such as *dizimtuhhum* and *kiziptuhhum,* flavored with "fragrant reeds," probably styrax, *kikkirenum,* and henbane.

Dinner was accompanied by music, song, and entertainment in the form of clowns, actors, jugglers, and wrestlers. Did female dancers and singers appear at official banquets, or were they reserved exclusively for the king's enjoyment?[4] We do not know how many members of the royal family attended banquets or whether women were invited. Generally the king offered his guests gifts, usually formal attire or objects made of precious metals.

Dinner was served by the palace staff. The cupbearers played a very important role. The grand cupbearer, who was responsible for the complex ritual surrounding the pouring of wine and beer, also served the king and was among the sovereign's most trusted servants. In compensation for their services, servants and entertainers were entitled to eat what was left over or even to partake of the dinner. According to some household accounts, they ate the same food as the official guests.

By the neo-Assyrian period, in the first half of the first millennium, royal banquets had developed into quite sumptuous affairs. The king ate reclining on a couch, while the queen, who was the only guest placed near him, sat on a chair at his feet. The royal couple were surrounded by the usual fly-swatters, musicians, and servants, but they were isolated, and the queen's presence marked the occasion as exceptional.

The neo-Assyrian period witnessed the construction of a number of royal palaces, which were inaugurated with great feasts to which the king invited his subjects. The largest of these banquets was that staged by Assurnasirpal II (883–859) to mark the completion of his palace at Kalhu: 69,574 guests were invited to a feast that lasted ten days.[5] Dozens of items were served in enormous quantities: 1,000 plump oxen, 14,000 sheep, 1,000 lambs, several hundred deer of various kinds, 20,000 pigeons as well as other birds, 10,000 fish, 10,000 jerboa, 10,000 eggs, plus thousands of jugs of beer and skins full of wine. Vast quantities of bread, baskets of fruit and vegetables, and various condiments are also carefully detailed. All the resources of the empire were drawn on, including olives from western Syria. Such royal feasts were a tradition of the Near East: several are mentioned in the Bible, including Balthazar's feast in Babylon, which preceded the collapse of the neo-Babylonian empire (539 B.C.E.), and the feast of Ahasuerus/Xerxes in the Book of Esther.

As the latter example shows, the presence of the queen and other women at these banquets was a relatively rare occurrence. Records of the wine served at the palace of Kalhu show that the "queen's household" maintained wine stores distinct from the king's. This was also true at Mari. Hence the queen's household must have held banquets of its own. At Nineveh there was a regular circuit of food distribution.[6] The highest-ranking personages in the Assyrian empire (the king, queen, royal princes, head eunuch, general-in-chief, and principal provincial governors) donated food for the gods' daily meal,[7] and the administrators of estates belonging to these high nobles also contributed. These items were then redistributed to members of the central administration or served at court banquets.

Another source of supply was the "gifts" brought by people seeking an audience with the king in order to win favor with the monarch and court officials. Lists of recipients of such gifts in kind were compiled in connection with the king's New Year's feast as well as for a gathering to which King Esarhaddon invited

Assyrians in 672 B.C.E. in order to have them swear allegiance to Assurbanipal, his choice as heir apparent. The food served on this occasion was exactly the same as the food served to the gods: beef, mutton, chicken, rabbit, jerboa, fish, bread, fruit, and alcoholic beverages.[8] The guests were grouped by profession according to a strict hierarchy. One banquet included the king's immediate family, top military leaders, members of the royal guard, "scholars," high officials of the royal household, and members of the extended royal family. Of course, the gods also numbered among the king's honored guests. In the first millennium the dishes served to the gods were subsequently eaten by the king. This custom was a royal prerogative.

Religious Banquets

Serving food to the gods was a characteristic feature of Mesopotamian religious life. Every temple employed people for this express purpose: brewers, bakers, butchers, dairymen, and so on. Their job was to prepare dishes to be served to the statues of the gods. For this they were compensated, sometimes with a portion of the food they prepared. When the gods' food was redistributed, they were entitled to certain parts.

Every major temple contained not only an effigy of the principal deity to which the sanctuary was dedicated but also a "divine court": a husband or wife of the god or goddess, a "vizir," and officials of the divine administration. The model was, of course, the royal court of Babylonia or Assyria. Each statue received a portion in keeping with its rank in the hierarchy. For some ceremonies the statues were removed from their chapels and brought together for a feast in honor of the principal god, a feast modeled on the royal banquet. On these occasions priests acted as servants: they set tables, passed bowls for washing the fingers, supplied fragrant oil to anoint the guests, served food and drink, played music, and sang hymns in honor of the assembled deities.

To sum up, the Mesopotamian banquet had two essential characteristics: it was a gathering whose purpose was to celebrate the solidarity of a group, and it involved an elaborate ceremonial. Regardless of whether the guests were gods, members of the royal court, or private individuals, they were generally grouped by rank and seated either in chairs or on the ground. Food and drink circulated, and polite exchanges accompanied this process. When alcohol was consumed, guests were urged to maintain a certain decorum.[9] Banquets were opportunities for their organizers to display wealth and pomp. This ostentatious display, regulated by a strict etiquette, culminated in the neo-Assyrian banquets described by various textual and iconographic sources.

NOTES

1. See J.-M. Durand, "Sumérien et Akkadien en pays amorrite," pt. 1: "Un document juridique archaïque de Mari," *Mari: Annales de recherches interdisciplinaires* (Paris: Editions Recherche sur les Civilisations, 1982), 1:79–89.

2. D. Charpin, "A Contribution to the Geography and History of the Kingdom of Kahat," in *Tall Al-Hamidiya,* vol. 2, ed. M. Wäfler (Göttingen: Vandenhoeck and Ruprecht, 1990), pp. 80–81.

3. Mari, situated on the Euphrates in Syria near the border with Iraq, is the site of a remarkably well-preserved palace from the beginning of the second millennium, a palace where official archives were found in the form of cuneiform tablets. From these two tablets we have been able to learn about the reigns of two kings, Yasmah-Addu (1796?–1776 B.C.E.) and Zimri-Lim (1775–1761 B.C.E.). The palace of Mari was captured, pillaged, and burned by Hammurabi in 1760. Since Hammurabi's palace in Babylon has not been located, the palace at Mari is our fundamental source of information about royal life in this period.

4. One document mentions the award of a sheep to a royal musician, the woman Batahra, suggesting that she might have taken part in an official banquet. See *Archives royales de Mari,* vol. 23 (Paris, 1984), p. 44.

5. Of this number, 47,074 "guests from all the districts of the empire" may in fact have been laborers conscripted for the purpose of building the palace.

6. F. M. Fales and S. Parpola, eds. *Imperial Administrative Records,* pt. 1: *Palace and Temple Administration,* State Archives of Assyria 7 (Helsinki: Helsinki University Press, 1992).

7. A fairly complete list of the main donors for the god Assur in the city of the same name has been established by G. Van Driel, *The Cult of Assur,* Studia Semitica Neerlandica 13 (Assen: Van Gorcum, 1969), pp. 210 ff.; included are the queen, the heir apparent, the majordomo of the prince's household, the general in chief, the grand cupbearer, and the governor of the province of Assur.

8. Bread and fruit were measured by "tables." One text mentions 160 of these, another 74.

9. One way of alluding to lack of decorum was to mention "dining with servants." We find this expression in texts from Mari as well as in letters from Assyrian merchants in Cappadocia: "Since you arrived at my father's house, you have been eating and drinking with the servants." Quoted in C. Michel, "A table avec les marchands paléo-assyriens," *Actes de la rencontre assyriologique internationale de Heidelberg,* July 1992, esp. secs. 1 and 4.

CHAPTER 3

FOOD CULTURE *in* ANCIENT EGYPT

Edda Bresciani

Enough food for everyone was a guarantee of social order for an "ethical" state
such as that controlled by the pharaoh. The maxim "He whose belly is empty is
the one who complains," which we find in the Maxims of Ptahhotpe, a sage who
lived toward the middle of the third millennium, should be understood in this
sense. In accordance with the beliefs that developed in the earliest epochs of
Egyptian history concerning life after death, prayers for the dead requested that
they be given bread and beer, birds and beef. Moreover, tombs were supplied with
victuals, and the dead were always portrayed sitting before a richly laden table
with written lists (the so-called panchart) containing thousands of varieties of
each foodstuff.

The discovery at Saqqara, at the funeral well of the tomb of a Second Dynasty
woman (c. 3700 B.C.E.), of a number of plates bearing assorted foods has provided
a valuable source of information on eating preferences and food preparation during that early period. The meal for the dead included, among other things, a kind
of cereal-based porridge, small barley rolls, cheese, a cooked and decapitated fish,
and two cooked kidneys, probably from sheep. Since we do not possess the equivalent of Apicius' *De re coquinaria* for ancient Egypt, funeral meals of this type are a
primary source of information.

A great deal of information can be derived from the menu of a dinner prepared for a Nineteenth Dynasty pharaoh and his extensive retinue during an offi-

cial visit (the text is part of Papyrus Anastasi IV). This was clearly more than just a meal for the happy few, since the baskets were counted by the hundreds and the food items by the thousands. Nevertheless, the document reveals the preferences, exotic tastes, and range of foodstuffs available during the Ramesside period. The menu includes 10,000 biscuits (*ibescet*), 1,200 Asiatic loaves, 100 baskets of dried meat, 300 cuts of meat (*deghit*), 250 handfuls of beef offal, 10 plucked geese, 40 cooked ducks, 70 sheep, 12 kinds of fish, fat quails, summer pigeons, 60 measures of milk, 90 measures of cream, 30 jars of carob seeds with carob pulp, 100 heads of lettuce, 50 bunches of ordinary grapes and 1,000 bunches of oasis grapes, 300 strings of figs, 50 jars of honeycomb, 50 jars of cucumbers, and 50 small baskets of leek bulbs, equivalent to 120 handfuls. There are also oils: local oils (sesame oil, sweet ben-nut oil) and imported oils (Cyprus oil, oil from the country of the Hittites, *nekefeter* oil from Babylon, oils from Amor, Syria, and Naharina) for charioteers. The list comes to an end with beverages: Syrian beer, Palestinian wine, and *paur* for the servants.

Cereals and Bread

Although there is still no agreement regarding the first cereals to be cultivated in ancient Egypt, barley, along with wheat and spelt, have been found in prehistoric delta settlements dating back to around 4000 B.C.E. The plains that were periodically flooded by the Nile produced cereals in abundance for both domestic use and exportation. Wheat and barley, used for making bread and beer, were staples, while spelt bread was eaten primarily by the poor. Egyptian households adopted very basic techniques for making flour: the grain was first crushed in a stone mortar and then ground between a stone and an angled stone slab; the roughly ground flour was then sieved. To obtain finer flour, the grain was lightly toasted or dried in the sun before being ground (millstones were not used in Egypt until Greco-Roman times). As a result of this technique, bread always contained stone dust, the probable cause of the worn-down teeth that have been found in most Egyptian mummies.

Bread was made by adding water and a pinch of salt to the flour, then kneading the dough by hand or, in large quantities, with the feet in a large container. The flat loaves were then cooked on a stone slab placed directly on the fire or on a shelf in an open oven. Alternatively, the loaves were simply stuck to the oven's inner walls.

Sourdough was used to produce leavened bread. From approximately 1500 B.C.E. on, however, it is possible that bakers also used genuine yeast, such as saccaromycetes, extracted in liquid form during the brewing of beer, work that was typically associated with bread-baking.

The loaves could be round, semicircular, oval, triangular, or conical; loaves intended for temple offerings were baked inside conical clay molds and were sometimes covered with cumin seeds. Wheat cakes in human or animal form were prepared for magical and liturgical rituals. For everyday purposes, however, the names, shapes, and ingredients of cereal products changed as a result of time, tastes, and fashions.

Beer

Beer-brewing methods in ancient Egypt are reasonably well known, thanks to the wall paintings of private tombs and models of breweries. The beer that was produced was strong and identical to *buza*, still brewed in the same way in Sudan and parts of Egypt. In certain working-class areas in Cairo, for example, small loaves of barley or wheat, undercooked in order to preserve the fermenting enzymes contained in the grains, are put into a mixture of water and crushed wheat and left in the heat. The dense liquid is then filtered and left to settle in terracotta jars.

Egyptian texts speak of sweet beer, red beer—the most common—and black beer, which must have been the most alcoholic. All we know of "Syrian beer," presumably imported or brewed using non-Egyptian methods, is that its name is mentioned in some texts.

The Vegetable Garden, the Orchard, and the Vineyard

All Egyptian vegetable gardens produced onions, leeks, and garlic. Egyptian lettuce grew to a considerable size and, because of its shape, was considered a suitable offering for Min, the god of agriculture and fertility. Melons (including watermelons) and cucumbers grew along the fertile banks of the Nile. Legumes—lupines, chickpeas, broad beans, and lentils—were always part of an ancient Egyptian's daily diet, although peas were introduced only during the New Kingdom.

Egyptians also ate the sweet bulb of the lotus, which they boiled or roasted. If we are to believe Theophrastus (*Hist. pl.* IV.8.11), they used it to produce the delicious dish known as *korsion*. The papyrus rhizome, rich with oils and sugars, was good both raw and cooked (*Hist. pl.* IV.2; Herodotus, II.92; Diodorus, I.80), as was the fruit of the mandrake, yellow with green sepals and tasting of pear. The skin of the mandrake fruit contains a high concentration of narcotic toxins, which also produce hallucinations. This may explain its fame as an aphrodisiac as well as the symbolic and erotic significance attributed to it by ancient Egyptians.

Fruit, both wild and cultivated, played a large part in the Egyptian diet. Egyptians ate the fruit of the sycamore, the splendid tree dedicated to the cult of the goddess Hathor, figs (cultivated even prior to the Old Kingdom), and persea fruit (*Mimusops laurifolia*), which was yellow and had an apple flavor and was eaten fresh or dried and ground into flour. They also enjoyed "desert dates" (the fruit of the sweet-fruit tree), cherry-flavored jujubes, dates, and a type of palm coconut (*dum*). Carob pods, with their high sugar content, were used in Egyptian medicine as a vermifuge and digestive. Contacts with neighboring countries, especially in Asia, which became increasingly close from the Eighteenth Dynasty on, introduced new trees to the Egyptian orchard. These included the apple, pomegranate, and olive. Citrus fruits, however, did not exist in Egypt until after the Greco-Roman period.

Grapevines, which already grew in Egypt in the predynastic period, were found throughout the delta, in the Fayum and the western oases (Khargah, Dakhlah, Bahriyah, Farafra). Grown on trellises and arbors, they produced white and black grapes, most of which were used for wine. After the harvest, the grapes were trodden in large vats and the must was then poured into terracotta amphorae, rendered less porous by an internal coat of resin, and sealed with clay. Each amphora bore a "label" indicating the vineyard and the vintage. Egyptians also made date wine, fig wine, which was highly alcoholic, and pomegranate wine (possibly the drink known as *sciadeh*). Wine was also imported from Syria.

Meat and Dairy Products

Animal protein in the Egyptian diet was provided by dairy products, meat, and fish. The milk obtained from breeding and meat animals (cows, sheep, and goats) was made into butter and cheese, remains of which have been found in cylindrical jars in the First Dynasty tombs of Abydos. It is not at all clear whether Egyptians were aware that alum could be used to curdle milk.

The blood of cattle whose throats had been slit for sacrificial purposes was collected to make a kind of blood sausage. Offal was highly prized, especially the spleen and liver, and beef fat was used as a condiment. Fillets and loin chops were roasted or grilled, while less prestigious cuts were boiled. Meat could also be dry-cured.

There is no doubt that pork played a large part in the ancient Egyptian diet or that pigs were raised in large numbers in the villages. The taboo regarding pork had no effect on everyday eating habits, but was probably restricted to ritual offerings since, in Egyptian mythology, pigs were identified with Seth, the god who killed his brother Osiris.

Both wild and reared fowl—geese, ducks, quails, pigeons, and pelicans—were frequently served at Egyptian tables at every social level. Chickens, however, were not introduced until the late Roman period. Geese and pigeons were roasted. Geese, plucked and ready to be cooked, could also be preserved in fat (and possibly in salt) in large containers, as could ducks. Eggs also played a part in the Egyptian diet.

Fish

Teeming with fish, the Nile was generous to rich and poor alike. In tomb decorations from the Old Kingdom on, fishing scenes were often depicted. They reveal the great variety of fish that were caught: mullet, tilapia, catfish, carp, *barbi,* and eels. Fish was not restricted to the poor; it was also eaten at court, and the lakes and ponds of villas were supplied with fish for noblemen to catch with lines. Dried saltfish was part of a soldier's rations. Roe from the mullet, a periodic visitor to the canals of the Nile, was also extracted during the drying process of the fish, to be pressed into large flat cakes and preserved.

It has been noted that fish does not figure on the lists of funerary offerings (pancharts) and only rarely appears among the food left on offering tables. This is probably owing to a kind of taboo connected to its odor.

Honey, Condiments, and Spices

Honey was collected primarily in the delta, whose vast stretches of fertile land offered an ideal environment for bees and bee-keeping. Honey came in two varieties—dark and light—and was preserved in jars with wax-sealed tops.

It is not known for certain whether vinegar was known and used. Kitchen salt, however, came in at least two forms: the so-called northern salt and red salt.

There is no doubt that certain aromatic plants were used in cooking, while the use of others can be assumed from their presence in ancient medicinal recipes: juniper, aniseed, coriander (appreciated by Apicius, III.4.3; X.1.7–8), cumin (Pliny, HN XIX.47.161, mentions Theban cumin and distinguishes it from the Ethiopian variety), fennel, curry-flavored fenugreek (found at the predynastic site of Ma'adi), and poppy seeds. Pepper, on the other hand, was imported from India from the first two centuries A.D. on.

Goose, pork, and beef fat were used for frying and as a condiment. More commonly, oils of various kinds were used: *bak* oil (made from ben-nuts), sesame oil, linseed oil, and castor oil. Olive oil was harder to find. Lists of food deliveries (Papyrus Turin B) mention imported oils: 300 measures of Keftiu oil (from Syria and the Aegean coast) as well as oil from the land of Shasu (Syria-Palestine).

The Dining Room and the Kitchen; Kitchen Slaves

Egyptian ate at least three meals a day: breakfast, lunch, and dinner. They did not use cutlery but ate with their hands. The way in which they sat at table changed over time, at least for the upper classes. During the Old Kingdom, they reclined on rush mats or cushions in front of low tables set for two, on which bread, roasted meat, and fruit were placed, while glasses were placed close by on the floor. As time passed, the upper classes preferred to sit on chairs at normal tables, where they were served. At the end of the meal their servants poured water over their hands. Banquets were enlivened by displays of dancing and music. Wine and beer jars were decorated with garlands, while the guests wore crowns of flowers and offered one another lotus buds to smell.

Simple, mostly cylindrical terracotta ovens could be found in the inner courtyard of all Egyptian houses, even the most modest. Food was cooked in back courtyards on low fires under rush mats or sometimes, as in certain dwellings in El Amarna, on roof terraces. In larger houses, it was possible to find a whole room devoted to cooking, as in the house known as "the house of the three ovens" from the period of Thutmose IV, discovered in Gurna by a University of Pisa expedition. This room had a *canun,* a cooking range with three fires and a surface for pans, as well as a place to put the water jar (a hole carved out of the rock floor with a drainage channel). Clay jars with openings near the base, used to store legumes, cereals, spices, and condiments, stood on the floor.

Cooking methods for meat, fowl, and fish have already been mentioned; they included roasting, spit roasting, grilling, and boiling in pots. Sweet dough for cakes was sometimes fried, as clearly shown in a picture of frying with the explicit caption "Put in the fat and cook the cake." Peasants, who toiled all day in the fields, would roast geese on the spot and drink water from leather flasks left hanging in the shade of trees to keep cool.

Cooking activities required pots and pans to put on the fire. These were made not only of earthenware but also of copper and, later, bronze. The same metals were used to make knives, although stone knives continued be adopted for some purposes. Spoons and ladles, sometimes perforated, were made from wood and metal. Sieves, mortars, and pestles were also used.

Tables were laid with plates, bowls, goblets (earthenware, glazed porcelain, or even gold and silver if the diners were kings or courtiers), and trays of wood, metal, or simply woven vegetable fibers. Small metal strainers were used when pouring wine or beer into the goblets. When extracting the wine or beer from the amphorae, siphons were used to avoid moving the lees.

In places like palaces, large villas, and temples, the organization of kitchens, larders, storerooms, and staff was complex and hierarchical. The Leiden Papyrus 348 (10.4–5), for example, contains a list mentioning brewers, bakers, butchers, pastry chefs, confectioners, bakers specializing in *shat* bread, and wine-tasters, as well as someone who held the position of "house manager for beef fat."

BIBLIOGRAPHY

Biasin, G. P. *I sapori della modernità*. Bologna: Il Mulino, 1991. [*The Flavors of Modernity: Food and the Novel*. Princeton, N.J.: Princeton University Press, 1993.]

Bresciani, E. "L'attività archeologica dell'università di Pisa in Egitto." In *Egitto e Vicino Oriente*. Pisa: Giardini, 1983.

———. "Mense imbandite nell'Egitto antico: Tra ideogramma e realtà." In *L'alimentazione nell'antichità*. Parma, 1985.

———. *Serpente che mangia non ha veleno: Ricette e segreti della mensa dei Faraoni*. Lucca, 1994.

Bresciani, E., comp. *Letteratura e poesia nell'antico Egitto*. Turin, 1990.

Brewer, D. J., and R. F. Friedman. *Fish and Fishing in Ancient Egypt*. Cairo: American University in Cairo Press, 1989.

Caminos, R. *Late Egyptian Miscellanies*. Oxford: Oxford University Press, 1954.

Darby, W. J., P. Ghalioungui, and L. Grivetti. *Food: The Gift of Osiris*. 2 vols. New York: Academic Press, 1977.

Emery, W. B. *A Funerary Repast in an Egyptian Tomb of the Archaic Period*. Scholae Adriani de Buck Memoriae Dicatae 1. Leiden: Nederlands Instituut voor het Nabije Oosten, 1962.

Erman, A. *Life in Ancient Egypt*. Translated by H. M. Tirard. New York: Dover Publications, 1971.

Gamert-Wallert, I. *Fische und Fischkulte im alten Ägypten*. Wiesbaden: Otto Harrassowitz, 1970.

Lepsius, R. *Denkmäler aus Aegypten und Aethiopen*. Louvain, 1849–58.

Malaise, M. "Harpocrate au pot." In *Festgabe Ph. Derchain*. Louvain, 1991.

Manniche, L. *An Ancient Egyptian Herbal*. London: Museum Publications Ltd., 1989.

Posener, G. *Le Papyrus Vandier*. Publications de l'Institut Français d'Archéologie Orientale, no. 626. Cairo: Institut Français d'Archéologie Orientale, 1985.

Reymond, E. A. E., ed. *A Medical Book from Krokodilopolis*. Vienna: Verlag Brüder Hollinek, 1976.

Rossellini, I. *Monumenti dell'Egitto e della Nubia*. 3 vols. Geneva: Editions de Belleslettres, 1977.

Ruffer, A. *Food in Egypt*. Cairo: Institut Français d'Archéologie Orientale, 1919.

Schiaparelli, E. *Relazione sui lavori della Missione Archeologica Italiana in Egitto (1903–1920)*. Vol. 2: *La tomba intatta dell'architetto Cha*. Turin: G. Chiantore, 1927.

Verhoeven, U. *Grillen, kochen, bachen in Alltag und im Ritual Altägyptens*. Rites Égyptiens, no. 4. Brussels: Fondation Égyptologique Reine Élisabeth, 1984.

Wilkinson, J. G. *The Ancient Egyptians: Their Life and Customs*. 2 vols. The History of Nations. New York: Harper & Bros., 1854.

Wilson, H. "Egyptian Food and Drink." In *Shire Egyptology* 9:13, 17, fig. 14. 1988.

CHAPTER 4

BIBLICAL REASONS

The Dietary Rules of the Ancient Hebrews

Jean Soler

"A land of milk and honey" is the biblical phrase for the Promised Land, which is thus symbolically defined in terms of food. But what does the symbol signify, since no one has ever seen a place dripping with milk and honey?

The expression is first used in Exodus 3:8. After leaving Egypt, the Hebrews wandered in the desert for forty years before reaching Canaan. Roaming the parched wasteland with their famished livestock, they dreamed of a place where water would be abundant. Flowing streams would mean fodder for the animals, hence milk for man. In cracks in the rocks, underneath trees, and along riverbanks, flowers would bloom everywhere, so bees could make honey. Not milk or honey but water would flow in the Promised Land, and from this water everything else would come, not just in metaphor but in reality. The Promised Land was the anti-desert.

It was also the anti-Egypt. Egypt, from which the Hebrews had started out, was a fertile country, but it received little rain. All farming was at the mercy of the capricious Nile, which flooded mysteriously every year, normally in midsummer. If the river rose late or not high enough, however, famine ensued. In Pharaoh's dream, interpreted by Joseph in Genesis 41, "lean" cows—without fat on their bones and unable to produce milk—stood for famine. By contrast, in Palestine water from the heavens supplied springs and streams. Rain was a blessing from on high, proof that the Almighty had selected this land for His chosen people: "But the land, whither ye go to possess it, is a land of hills and valleys, and drinketh water of the rain of heaven" (Deut. 11:11).

A "land of milk and honey": milk was the basic food of the Hebrews during their years of wandering; as for honey, in a civilization without sugar, honey was what desserts and candies are for us. It symbolized the good life.

When Moses sent twelve men, one from each tribe, to "spy out the land of Canaan," they returned from their mission with pomegranates and figs and, wonder of wonders, a bunch of grapes so big that it took two men to carry it hanging from a staff (Num. 13:23).

Such was the country of which the Israelites (descendants of Jacob, known in Hebrew as Israel) dreamed while wandering in the desert. Was this Heaven? The Garden of Eden regained? Yes and no. The Bible tells us that Moses, the very man who would lead the Israelites to the Promised Land, had already announced rules restricting or prohibiting the consumption of certain of the foods that awaited them there. For example, the juice of the grape, though it "maketh glad the heart of man" (Ps. 104:15), was declared suspect. Priests would not be allowed to drink wine, not just during services but even beforehand (Lev. 10:9–11). Honey could not be offered up to Yahweh as a sacrifice (Lev. 2:11). Even milk was subject to what might seem at first glance a minor rule but which turns out to be of great significance (it was repeated three times and would be considerably elaborated): "Thou shalt not seethe a kid in its mother's milk" (Ex. 23:19, 34:26; Deut. 14:21).

The most important aspect of the laws of Moses, however, was the prohibition on the eating of certain kinds of meat. Foremost among these proscribed animals, it is commonly believed, even by Jews, was the pig. In fact, pigs are mentioned in the Bible only in conjunction with other animals. It took centuries for the pig to emerge as the most taboo of all. This is usually explained by the fact that poorly cooked pork can serve as a vehicle for transmitting a serious parasitic disease, trichinosis. Underlying this assertion is the hypothesis that the real reason for dietary laws is hygienic. But this hypothesis cannot withstand scrutiny. It assumes that the ancient Hebrews possessed certain medical knowledge when in fact they did not (indeed, they had no doctors) and that they were more perspicacious than their neighbors, the Egyptians, Mesopotamians, and Greeks, all of whom raised pigs and even sacrificed them to the gods, to whom only the most prized foods were offered. Furthermore, if the hygienic theory were valid for pork, it would also have to explain why other animals were proscribed—the camel, say, which was eaten in those days (as it still is today) by nomadic Arabs. Yet no one claims that there was any danger in eating camel meat. Finally, the Bible says nothing about medical concerns. Pig meat is proscribed, it says, because "the swine, though he divide the hoof, and be cloven footed, yet he cheweth not the cud" (Lev. 11:7). Another explanation must be sought.

Animals That May Be Eaten

If there is a rational basis for the dietary restrictions of the ancient Hebrews, we may be able to discover it by examining the Bible. The proscription of certain animals is discussed in two chapters, Leviticus 11 and Deuteronomy 14, the second of which is an abridged version of the first. Moses describes the distinctions invoked to prohibit the eating of certain animals as having been revealed to him by Yahweh on Mount Sinai. No explanatory principle is stated. The proscribed species are described as "impure." Various fowl are enumerated without commentary. However, criteria are given for distinguishing "pure" animals that live on land: they must have "divided feet" and "cloven hooves" and "chew their cud." As for the creatures of the sea, they must have "fins" and "scales" in order to be considered pure.

These criteria primarily involve organs of locomotion: the feet of land animals and the fins of fish. Unlike plants, certain animals have the ability to move about on their own. In order to be considered pure, an animal must move. Aquatic creatures that station themselves on the bottom or cling to rocks are therefore proscribed. The Bible gives no examples of these, but Jewish tradition logically prohibits the eating of shellfish. Also branded as impure are land animals without legs: "And every creeping thing that creepeth upon the earth shall be an abomination; it shall not be eaten" (Lev. 11:41).

Thus only animals with organs of locomotion may be eaten. Not all are acceptable, however. Animal species are divided into three groups according to the environment in which they live: land, water, air. Each group has characteristic organs corresponding to a specific mode of locomotion: walking for land animals, swimming for fish, flying for birds. To the Hebrews, land animals were made for walking, hence they were equipped with feet; fish were made for swimming, hence their fins; and birds were made for flying, hence their wings.

The connection between animals and their environment was especially strong because God created different species expressly for each element: "Let the waters bring forth abundantly the moving creature that hath life, and fowl that may fly above the earth in the open firmament of heaven. . . . Let the earth bring forth the living creature after his kind, cattle, and creeping thing, and beast of the earth after his kind" (Gen. 1:20, 24). In other words, each species belongs to one and only one element, from which it issued and in which it must live, moving about with organs appropriate to that element.

Jewish dietary laws turn out to have been associated with religious beliefs that helped to transform a group of related Semitic tribes into a unified people within a few generations of their exodus from Egypt (which is generally said to have occurred in the middle of the thirteenth century B.C.E.). Central to those beliefs was the idea that a particular god—who later became the one true God—entered into a pact with a chosen people. The terms of this pact were to be scrupulously observed by the parties.

When the Israelites began to think of this god as the creator of the universe, probably in about the eighth century B.C.E., it became even more imperative that they respect the order of the world He had created. That order was most fully set forth in the creation myth with which the Bible begins (whose redaction dates from the fifth or sixth century B.C.E.). The creation process began with the world in an undifferentiated state, described in the text as *tohu* and *bohu* ("without form and void"). This is not "nothingness," as is sometimes maintained, since "darkness" and "waters" are already present (Gen. 1:2). The Creation is described as a series of divisions beginning with the separation of light from darkness ("God divided the light from the darkness" [Gen. 1:4]) and proceeding on to the separation of sky from water ("Let there be a firmament in the midst of the waters" [Gen. 1:6]). Then dry land is brought forth from the water. Finally, the animals are created, in three categories, each associated with one of these distinct environments.

Hence the distinctions that man observes in nature are not arbitrary. They manifest the design of the Creator. It is a religious duty to respect them and, what is more, a condition for the continuation of the pact by virtue of which the Israelites enjoy the protection of the Almighty. Sacred and profane are thus conflated. Dietary rules have the same importance as other religious requirements. All social activities are subject to a series of obligations and prohibitions, which the Bible associates with the revelation on Mount Sinai and subsumes under the term Law.

The Mosaic Law, set forth in the first five books of the Bible (known in the Jewish tradition as the Torah, or Law), is based on one fundamental idea: that the abolition of distinctions is wrong. An animal that straddles two categories, blurring the distinction between, say, the animals of the air and the animals of the water, may not be eaten. The animals were created "each according to its kind." Those which belong to different kinds are stamped with the sign of Evil (which enters into the creation myth of Genesis through the serpent).

If man were to eat these mixed creatures, he would become an accomplice of Evil and, incorporating it, would be contaminated by it. He would likewise become an accomplice of Evil if he were to negate the separation of kinds in any way. "Thou shalt not let thy cattle gender with a diverse kind," commands Leviticus 19:19. Furthermore, "Thou shalt not plow with an ox and an ass together" (Deut. 22:10). A field must be planted in either barley or wheat, never in both: "Thou shalt not sow thy field with mingled seed" (Lev. 19:19). A man may wear a garment of wool or a garment of linen but not of both fibers: "Neither shall a garment mingled of linen and woollen come upon thee" (Lev. 19:19, Deut. 22:11).

These prohibitions beg comparison with the absolute condemnation of homosexuality (for which the sentence is "abomination"; Lev. 18:22). A human being is either a man or a woman. Being a man, he may not comport himself as a woman, or vice versa, for to do so would be to behave as a "hybrid" creature. This ban extends to clothing: "The woman shall not wear that which pertaineth unto a man, neither shall a man put on a woman's garment" (Deut. 22:5).

In incest, also punishable by death, two types of distinction are violated. Mother-son incest is prohibited by Leviticus 18:7: "She is thy mother; thou shalt not uncover her nakedness." This might seem to be tautological: a man may not sleep with his mother because she is his mother. In fact, however, it should be interpreted as saying that no woman may be both mother and wife to the same man, for this would make her a hybrid creature. Sexual relations must not interfere with kinship relations. The order of the world is at issue. Medical considerations are no more germane to the incest taboo than to dietary laws.

Now we are in a better position to understand the only one of these taboos that is repeated three times: "Thou shalt not seethe a kid in its mother's milk." This restriction is aimed at avoiding culinary incest: mother and son no more belong together in the same pot than in the same bed. Cooking fire and erotic heat are related: both can blur differences by inducing distinct elements to coalesce. To explain the expanded importance that this dietary rule assumed in postbiblical Judaism, nothing less than the incest taboo will do, the ban on incest being the strongest of all human prohibitions (as anthropologists and psychoanalysts are well aware). Over the centuries, the rule on milk and meat was broadened to prohibit eating not just the meat of a kid cooked in its mother's milk but any kind of meat cooked in any kind of milk. More than that, to prevent the flesh of mother and child from mixing in the pot or, after eating, in the stomach, combining flesh with milk in the same dish or even in the same meal was also forbidden. If meat was served, no dairy product could accompany it, not even cheese.

If an animal is to be eaten, it must respect the place assigned to it in the plan of Creation. Furthermore, man, in feeding himself, must not disturb the order of Creation in any way. More than that, even if an animal belongs to a pure species, it may be proscribed if it is somehow anomalous with respect to the norm for that species: "And whosoever offereth a sacrifice of peace offerings unto the Lord to accomplish his vow, or a freewill offering in cattle or sheep, it shall be perfect to be accepted; there shall be no blemish therein. Blind, or broken, or maimed, or having a wen, or scurvy, or scabbed, ye shall not offer these unto the Lord, nor make an offering by fire of them upon the altar unto the Lord" (Lev. 22:21–22).

The point is not simply that only perfect animals were worthy of the perfect God. The "peace offering" was in fact a compulsory sacrifice if one wished to eat meat (Lev. 17:3–5). Thus only animals without physical flaws could be eaten. "Purity" meant that the animal had to be intact.

Hence to eat a castrated ox or sheep was an abomination. To castrate a bull was as grave a matter as mating a stallion with a jenny ass to obtain a mule. Both actions interfered with the will of the Creator.

Another consequence of this respect for Creation was the idea that the closer a plant-derived food was to its original state, the purer it was. Foods processed in such a way as to change their nature might be eaten but could not be used in sacrifices. This explains why honey, of which the Hebrews dreamed in the desert, could not be used as an offering. Honey was not created by God in the form in which it is consumed. The same goes for bread, whose preparation required the use of yeast to transform the natural grain. Flour and unleavened bread were suitable for burnt offerings but not leavened bread. Moreover, during Passover, a holiday that commemorates the exodus from Egypt, the birth of the Israelite nation, and the beginning of the religious year when the Jewish people are called upon to contemplate the intentions of the Creator, only unleavened bread may be eaten.

Rules specifying prohibited offerings mention leaven and honey together with fermented things (Lev. 2:11). Hence it is no surprise to find that priests are enjoined to shun wine and other "strong drink" (Lev. 10:9). Those called to perform sacrifices must keep themselves especially pure. They must be without physical defect or "blemish" (Lev. 21:17), like the animals they will immolate. Furthermore, they must not place any processed food on the altar and, when officiating, must refrain from consuming any strong drink that might affect their judgment.

Suspect Swine

While the foregoing analyses account for many Jewish dietary laws, they do not shed much light on the best known of these, namely, the restriction on eating pork. The swine (both the domestic pig and the wild hog) is a land animal with the cloven hoof that is, as we have seen, a mark of purity. The Bible recognizes this but adds that it "cheweth not the cud" (Lev. 11:7, Deut. 14:8).

To understand what this is all about, we need to return to the distinction between animal and vegetable in Genesis 1:30: "And to every beast of the earth, and to every fowl of the air, and to every thing that creepeth upon the earth, wherein there is life, I have given every green herb for meat." This should be interpreted to mean: every green herb *and nothing else*. In the plan of Creation, animals, which, like man, were given "breathing souls," were not supposed to kill and devour one another. Carnivores were not part of God's plan. Hence they were the impurest of the impure. Indeed, the lists of proscribed fowl in Leviticus and Deuteronomy begin with birds of prey: "The eagle, and the ossifrage, and the osprey, and the vulture, and the kite after his kind; every raven after his kind" (Lev. 11:13–15). But how were the carnivores among land animals to be recognized so as not to be eaten? By a simple criterion, namely, rumination: familiar animals like cows and sheep were known to eat nothing but grass, and these animals chew their cud. Hence they are herbivores twice over, and thus doubly pure. Swine, on the other hand, do not ruminate, and this naturally makes them suspect; though indeed herbivores, they are also carnivores. But, as we saw earlier, Hebrew society had an aversion to such hybrid creatures, and this only compounded their impurity.

Having hit on this apparently universal criterion—all ruminants are strict herbivores—the Hebrews might have gone no further. Why, then, did they add the extra criterion of the cloven hoof? Probably because they needed a standard that could be applied to wild animals about whose diet little was known.

Rumination is difficult to observe at a distance. We know this because the Bible classifies hares as ruminants when in fact they are rodents. What very likely happened was that the Hebrews cast about for an anatomical criterion that could serve, on the dead animal, as a visible analogue of the physiological criterion, which can be reliably observed only in domesticated species. They deduced a logical relationship between the nature of the foot and diet: because cloven-hoofed animals lack claws for seizing prey, they were believed to be herbivores. But was this criterion sufficient? Almost, but not quite: it failed to exclude swine, which are omnivorous. Hence both criteria—the cloven hoof and the chewing of the cud—were invoked to identify the pure herbivores.

This prudent definition eliminated some animals that eat only plants, like the hare and camel, because they did not conform exactly to the standard established by the hooves of domestic livestock: a divided foot covered by a cleft shell ("Whatsoever parteth the hoof and is clovenfooted" [Lev. 11:3]). Any deviation from this standard was considered a blemish, and the animal was proscribed.

The Blood Taboo

Yet if an animal belongs to a species declared to be pure and exhibits no abnormality, it may be eaten only if no blood is consumed with its flesh. What is the reason for this?

The key, once again, is to be found in the myth of Creation. The Lord decrees not only what the animals should eat but also what man should eat. Man had this advantage over the animals, that while they were required to eat "green herbs," he was permitted to enjoy grains and fruits (Gen. 1:29). Yet man was not supposed to eat living things any more than animals were. Adam and Eve were created vegetarians. In addition, they were forbidden to partake of the fruit of two trees. But they violated this prohibition after the serpent tempted them by saying, "Ye shall be as gods." Then "the Lord God said, Behold, the man is become as one of us, to know good and evil; and now, lest he put forth his hand, and take also of the tree of life, and eat, and live for ever" (Gen. 3:22).

In order to grasp the import of this passage, one needs to know that the Jewish religion, unlike religions that assert the proximity of man to divinity and seek to meld the former with the latter, insists that man is separated from God by an abyss. Indeed, the Ten Commandments state that God cannot be represented. Life is wholly God's possession (He is sometimes called the Living God, and oaths were sworn on "the life of Yahweh"). Men and animals received but a temporary spark (the idea that there might be life after death did not appear in Judaism until a thousand years after Moses; it was a postbiblical conception).

Now we can understand why Adam and Eve were forbidden to eat of the tree of life and why they were forbidden to eat meat. Had they killed beasts in order to eat them, they would have encroached on the preserve of the Living God. Only the deity who gave life could take it away. The commandment "Thou shalt not kill," though intended to prohibit murder, actually stemmed from a more primitive taboo against killing any living creature, man or animal. Not until after the Flood, which marks a new beginning for humankind, almost a second Creation, is man permitted to eat meat (Gen. 9:3). This permission is granted not as a reward but in recognition of the evil instinct that dwells within the human breast (Gen. 8:21).

Even so, eating meat was permissible only if two rules were respected. The first was that the eating of meat had to be accompanied by a ritual sacrifice, for other-wise the killing of the beast would count as murder. If a man bent on eating meat failed to observe the prescribed ritual, he would be killed just as the animal was. The law of retribution, "life for life, eye for eye, tooth for tooth" (Ex. 21:23–24), would apply to him. "He hath shed blood, and that man shall be cut off from among his people" (Lev. 17:4). Second, the blood of the slaughtered animal, which for the Hebrews was the principle of life, was supposed to be poured on the altar as an offering to God. What the Living God gave had to be returned to Him. When God granted Noah permission to eat animals, He added: "But flesh with the life thereof, which is the blood thereof, shall ye not eat" (Gen. 9:4). Thus the fundamental distance between man and God was reaffirmed. The taboo against eating blood is one of the most powerful in Judaism. Even today, for meat to be kosher, it must be drained of every last drop of blood.

Deciphering these Hebraic dietary laws reveals the logic behind them but tells us nothing about the degree to which their elaboration over the course of several centuries was a conscious or unconscious process. There can be no doubt that the people who honored these laws did not know or try to find out why they exist-ed. For them, to obey the law was enough to demonstrate their faith in God.

There are other ways to honor God, however. What was the purpose of all these rules about eating? The Bible is explicit: "I am the Lord your God, which have sep-arated you from other people. Ye shall therefore put difference between clean beasts and unclean, and between unclean fowls and clean; and ye shall not make your souls abominable by beast, or by fowl, or by any manner of living thing that creepeth on the ground, which I have separated from you as unclean" (Lev. 20:24–25).

Given a world order based on a series of "separations," the Hebrew people were enjoined not to mix with other peoples. "Lo, the people shall dwell alone, and shall not be reckoned among the nations" (Num. 23:9). Hence the Israelites were not allowed to share meals with *goyim*. The food they were required to eat isolated them. The prohibition of "impure" foods played the same role as the pro-hibition of "mixed" marriages, that is, marriages between Hebrews and non-Hebrews (Deut. 7:3). Ultimately, it mattered little what kind of diet was pre-scribed, provided it was different from what neighboring tribes ate. That said, it remains true that the criteria selected were not arbitrary: they were based on a conception of the world that gave the Hebrew people their identity.

The diet of the Israelites, then, was not shaped by nutritional, medical, or gas-tronomic considerations. It was, as Leonardo da Vinci said of painting, essentially a "mental thing."

CHAPTER 5

The PHOENICIANS *and the* CARTHAGINIANS

The Early Mediterranean Diet

Antonella Spanò Giammellaro

Phoenician Agriculture and Its Produce

The land of Canaan, the geographical area that became Phoenicia at the beginning of the Iron Age, was originally occupied by the Canaanites, a group of Semitic origin. During the third and second millennia B.C.E., it was divided into small city-states with close political and cultural links to the great powers of Syria, Mesopotamia, and Egypt.

In the twelfth century B.C.E., political equilibrium in the Near East was disturbed by a progressive deterioration in social and economic organization and the migratory flows of large numbers of groups known as the Peoples of the Sea. As a result, the land of Canaan broke up into a number of nation-states, including Phoenicia.

Phoenician civilization was rooted in the vast cultural world of the Near East. The Phoenician people occupied a narrow strip of territory between the sea and the Lebanon and Anti-Lebanon mountain ranges, where the land available for cultivation was limited but fertile.

CEREALS The Bible refers to cereal consumption in Phoenicia and nearby regions. Barley and wheat were traded between Israel and the Phoenician city of Tyre during the reign of Solomon. Egypt was also mentioned by the prophet

Isaiah (Isa. 23:3) as an important supplier of wheat to the city. This would imply that, despite the great fertility of the soil, Phoenician production was insufficient as a result of the scarcity of farmable land and the density of the population.

Cereals were eaten either boiled (a familiar practice in Near Eastern cooking from prehistoric times) or, very often, in the form of bread or flatcakes of various kinds. The widespread use of these products in the regions around Phoenicia and, in particular, in Ugarit is shown by the many terms used to describe cereal-based porridges and breads. The fact that the Carthaginians, the heirs to the Phoenicians in the west, were still eating these Near Eastern traditional foods in Roman times is further proof of their popularity.

PULSES AND VEGETABLES Cereals were integrated by pulses such as peas, lentils, chickpeas, and broad beans. These were either divided into their component parts (pods, seeds, leaves) or dried and ground into flour. Phoenicians also appear to have eaten large quantities of vegetables. Texts from Ugarit mention vegetable gardens and orchards, while the Bible also refers to well-kept vegetable gardens in Palestine. This is hardly surprising since the area, like that of the entire Syrian-Palestinian coast, was ideally suited to the cultivation of fruit trees and vegetables.

OIL Syria and Palestine began to produce oil from both olives and other seeds in the third millennium. Excavations in Ugarit, at the level of the Bronze Age, have revealed the remains of equipment used to extract oil as well as numerous fragments of large jars intended to contain the precious liquid.

According to the Bible, among the foodstuffs sent by Solomon each year to Hiram, king of Tyre, in exchange for materials and craftsmen for the construction of the temple were "twenty thousand kors" (each *kor* being 450 liters) of "beaten oil" (1 Kings 5:11).

FRUIT The cultivation of fruit trees was widespread. Dates, figs, apples, pomegranates, quinces, almonds, limes, and lotus are mentioned in Assyrian and Babylonian texts, the Bible, and, in more recent times, by classical authors.

There is considerable literary and archaeological evidence for the popularity of pomegranates. The fruit, a symbol of fertility owing to the quantity of seeds it contains, appears in the Bible as a typical product of Palestine alongside figs and grapes. There are at least fifty biblical references to figs, indicating their popularity, while the "Phoenician fig" was considered a delicacy in Egypt until Greek times. Given their sweetness, fresh or dried figs were frequently used in poorer diets instead of more expensive foods such as honey, which was reserved for the rich and aristocratic.

Dates must have been one of the most popular fruits at all levels of society, providing valuable sugars and vitamins. There is no need to list the many regions in which palm trees were cultivated from the fourth millennium on, given that they were present throughout the ancient Mediterranean Near East.

GRAPES AND WINE Grapes were eaten both fresh and dried and were also used to make wine. Raisins were an ingredient in cakes, as can be seen from the royal texts of Ugarit. Egyptian annals refer to "wine running like water in the presses" at Ullaza. The fact that winemaking was highly developed during the second millennium B.C.E. is shown by texts from the cities of Ugarit and Alalakh, both sited just to the north of Phoenicia.

Wine belongs to a venerable tradition. It is known that the *marzeah,* a religious organization also found in Carthage and linked to the cult of certain divinities and the dead, made considerable use of wine during its rites. In biblical tradition, the first references to winemaking and the effects that wine can have are in the story of Noah (Gen. 9:20–21). The soil and climate of Syria and Palestine were so well suited to vine cultivation that nearby countries such as Egypt and Assyria imported their wine.

MEAT Meat was obtained from sheep and cattle, smaller animals such as rabbits, chickens, and doves, and game. Hunting could only have been a secondary source of meat, since it is rarely mentioned in the Bible. Furthermore, the tale of Sinuhe the Egyptian refers to game as a great delicacy, reserved for the rich.

Goats and sheep, on the other hand, were kept throughout Phoenicia, whose mountainous areas provided ample grazing land. Their meat, however, was only rarely eaten, either at the royal tables or following ritual sacrifices.

MILK AND HONEY Quite apart from the many literary and allegorical interpretations that have been made of the phrase, the biblical definition of Canaan as a "land flowing with milk and honey" (Exod. 3:8, 17; 13:5) shows, first and foremost, that milk was highly appreciated.

Honey was one of the products that Tyre and the surrounding region imported from Judah and Israel. There is no doubt that it was also used in the making of cakes.

FISH From the earliest times, fish was an essential element in the basic Phoenician diet, and fishing played an important role in the economy as well. Whales, too, were caught, and an Assyrian inscription refers to a *nakhiru* (a small whale or dolphin?) as one of the gifts presented to Assurnasirpal II by the kings of the Phoenician coast.

Salt extraction complemented the fishing industry. The royal texts of Ugarit refer to salting as the only means of preservation, and saltpans are also likely to have existed in Phoenician cities.

TRADE The Phoenicians played a decisive role in the trading of food and wine in the Mediterranean, which in turn was central to their own economy. Numerous documents testify to the vitality of these commercial links. In the second lament for the fall of Tyre, for example, the prophet Ezekiel mentions the exchange of grain, honey, and oil with Judah and Israel, and of wine with Damascus, in order to illustrate the flourishing trading activities of the city. Archaeological evidence exists in the form of amphorae discovered in Tyre and intended for trade with Palestine.

Homer describes how Phoenician sailors exchanged their produce with food-stuffs (*Od.* XV.403–81), while a cuneiform tablet from Nineveh, dating from the sixth century B.C.E., records a delivery of grain and barley made by two Phoenicians and an Assyrian.

The consumption of beer and drinks made from fermenting cereals, although not widespread, is nonetheless proven not only by the sources but also by the discovery of jars with filters in the Phoenician area.

Agriculture in Carthage

Following the rise of Carthage and the Punic empire in the sixth century B.C.E., agriculture in the western colonies of Sardinia, Spain, and Sicily was controlled by provincial centers, endowed with their own land and resources and operating independently of the main cities.

Cereals appear to have constituted their staple diet. Plautus calls the Carthaginian protagonist of his play *Poenulus* (l. 54) a "big soup-eater" (*pultiphagonides*), suggesting that the *puls,* a porridge of boiled mixed cereals, was the main daily meal and guaranteed a simple basic diet.

The *puls punica* was a nutritious dish. Containing cereals, cheese, honey, and eggs, it provided sugars, fats, proteins, and, to a lesser degree, vitamins. Cato (*Agr. Orig.* 85) recorded the following recipe, adding that a new terracotta cooking pot should be used: "Add a pound of flour to water and boil it well. Pour it into a clean tub, adding three pounds of fresh cheese, half a pound of honey, and an egg. Stir well and cook in a new pot."

Hecataeus of Miletus (fr. 351) calls the peoples of northern Africa "grain eaters," suggesting that cereal production must have been the prevalent feature of the region's noncoastal areas, which are known to have been occupied by

Carthage. Cereals were also the main ingredients of a flatcake called *punicum,* which, according to Sextus Pompeius Festus (see *Punicum*), was delicious.

The presence in numerous houses of small terracotta ovens, similar to the *tabunas* and *tannur* that are still used in Near Eastern and North African regions, testifies to the widespread consumption of both leavened and unleavened bread. A number of votive steles in Carthage bear representations of ears of grain, as do series of Punic coins found in Sardinia.

PULSES AND VEGETABLES Classical sources describe the verdant gardens and orchards of Carthage and the nearby region of Cape Bon, listing a variety of products that range from cabbages and artichokes to cardoons and garlic. At Cartagena, in Spain, highly prized cardoons were cultivated, most of which were destined for export and the tables of the rich.

"Here underneath palms of exceptional size there are olives, under the olives figs, under the figs pomegranates, and under those vines; and underneath the vines is sown corn, and later leguminous plants, and then garden vegetables, all in the same year, and all nourished in the shade of something else." This is how Pliny (*HN* XVIII.188) described the area of Tacape, now Gabes. The largest trees, after palms, were therefore olives. Those called *miliarii,* because they produced approximately 327 kilos of oil each year, were famous in Africa (XVII.93). Mago provides a series of precepts on planting olive groves and cultivating olives (Columella, *Rust.* 17.1; *HN* XVII.128), which, according to some scholars, was first practiced in North Africa by the Phoenicians of Carthage.

FRUIT Numerous documents refer to the cultivation of fruit trees. Different species of pear and apple trees are mentioned by Pliny (*HN* XIII.112), who also defined the pomegranate as *malum punicum* as a tribute to the quantity and quality of Carthaginian production, celebrated by many authors. Mago the farmer offers many recipes for their preservation.

Mago the Carthaginian recommends that seawater should be made exceedingly hot and that the pomegranates, tied with flax or rush, should be let down into it for a short time until they are discolored and then taken out and dried for three days in the sun; afterward they should be hung up in a cool place and, when they are required for use, soaked in cold, fresh water for a night and the following day until the time when they are to be used. The same writer also suggests daubing the fruit, when it is fresh, thickly with well-kneaded potter's clay and, when the clay has dried, hanging it up in a cool place; when it is required for use, the fruit should be plunged in water and the clay dissolved. This process keeps the fruit as fresh as if it had only just been picked.

Mago also recommends that sawdust of poplar wood or holm-oak wood should be spread on the bottom of a new earthenware pot and the fruit arranged so that the sawdust can be trodden in between them; when the first layer has been formed, sawdust should be again put down and the fruit similarly arranged until the pot is full; when it is full, the lid should be put on it and carefully sealed with thick clay (Columella, *Rust.* 12.46.5–6).

Two- and three-dimensional images of the pomegranate can be found throughout the Punic world, above all on steles in northern Africa up to the end of the Phoenician period. The fruit continued to be linked to religion and death in the iconography of sculptors and painters in Africa and Sicily, even under Roman rule.

Figs were also eaten in every part of the western world, Carthaginian figs being so well known that they were exported to Greece and Rome. It is indicative that Cato, in order to demonstrate how close the Punic enemy was, showed the Roman Curia a fig that had been picked in Carthage only three days earlier.

Walnuts, hazelnuts, and almonds, the shells of which have been found in several tombs in Carthage and Lilibeum, must have been a significant source of calories. Pistachios and chestnuts were also known, and large quantities of dates were consumed.

GRAPES AND WINE Grapes were eaten fresh or dried. Raisins were used to produce *passum,* a wine that was highly prized in imperial Rome (*HN* XIV.81). Columella describes how it is made, following Mago's instructions:

> Gather the early grapes when they are quite ripe, rejecting the berries which are mouldy or damaged. Fix in the ground forks or stakes four feet apart for supporting reeds and yoke them together with poles, then put reeds on the top of them and spread out the grapes in the sun, covering them at night so that the dew may not fall on them. Then when they have dried, pluck the berries and throw them into a barrel or wine-jar and add the best possible must thereto so that the grapes are submerged. When they have absorbed the must and are saturated with it, on the sixth day put them all together in a bag and squeeze them in a wine-press and remove the raisin wine. Next tread the wineskins, adding very fresh must, made from other grapes that you have dried for three days in the sun; then mix together and put the whole kneaded mass under the press and immediately put this raisin-wine of the second pressing in sealed vessels so that it may not become too rough; then, twenty or thirty days later, when it has finished fermenting, strain it into other vessels and plaster down the lids immediately and cover them with skins.
>
> (Columella, *Rust.* 12.39.1–2)

According to Pliny, however, the quality of Carthaginian wine (*HN* XXXVI.166) was anything but high, owing to the lime that was added to sweeten it.

MEAT Goats, sheep, and cattle provided milk and other dairy products and, perhaps on special occasions, meat. Alongside rams and short, fat-tailed sheep, still found in Tunisia, votive steles of northern Africa show small animals such as rabbits, chickens, and doves, which were certainly the most common source of meat.

Classical sources reveal that Carthaginians did not eat pork, while they appear to have eaten dogs. Eggshells found in tombs show that eggs were eaten, and this is confirmed by the mention of eggs in a recipe for *puls punica*. It is also possible that ostrich eggs were eaten in those areas where the bird was found, especially if one considers that an ostrich egg was equivalent to between twenty-four and twenty-eight hen eggs.

FISH In many cities along the western Punic coast, fishing and its related industries were the main occupation, representing one of the most flourishing sectors of the economy. The main center was Cádiz, famous among classical authors for its fish-salting plants and the production of *garum,* a highly regarded sauce destined for the tables of Roman gourmets. Many recipes for the sauce have been handed down, but it was basically made by leaving fish innards and flesh of different qualities to ferment in salt water for one or more months with aromatic herbs. The liquid that was produced was collected and preserved in specially made amphorae for exportation.

The most common fish to reach the table, apart from the molluscs and crustaceans whose shells have often been found by archaeologists, were sea bream, red mullet, mackerel, sturgeon, moray eel, sole, and tuna. Numerous representations of these species exist. Images of tuna on several series of coins from Cádiz, Sexi, Abdera, and Soluntum are a clear reflection of the fish's economic importance to those cities. Saltpans were established in these fish-salting centers, and many of those still in use in Sardinia, Sicily, Spain, and northern Africa are near Punic sites.

The honey of Carthage was highly prized, and the hives in the area also produced excellent wax.

FOOD PREPARATION AND CONSUMPTION As we have seen, a picture, albeit incomplete, can be drawn of the food that was available in the regions of Syria-Palestine and the western Phoenician world. However, the scarcity of information makes it almost impossible to talk about the daily diet, the way food was prepared and served, and the circumstances in which it was eaten.

Alvar, J., and C. G. Wagner. "La actividad agrícola en la economía fenicia de la Península Iberica." *Gerion* 6 (1988): 169–85.

Aubet, M. E. "Notas sobre la economía de los asentamientos fenicios del Sur de Espana." *Dialoghi di Archeologia* 2 (1987): 51–62.

Bartoloni, P. "La pesca a Cartagine." In *L'Africa romana: Atti dell'XI convegno di studio*, pp. 479–88. Ozieri, 1996.

———. "Monte Sirai 1982: La necropoli (campagna 1982)." *RSF* 11, no. 2 (1983): 210–14.

———. "Tracce di coltura della vite nella Sardegna fenicia." In *Stato, economia, lavoro nel Vicino Oriente antico*, pp. 410–12. Milan, 1988.

Blansdorf, J., and H. Horst. "Codlia—eine semitische Bezeichnung für garum?" *Zeitschrift für Deutschen Morgenländische Gesellschaft* 138 (1988): 24–38.

Blásquez, J. M. *Historia de España antigua.* Vol. 1, *Protohistoria.* Madrid, 1983.

Bondì, S. F. "L'alimentazione nel mondo fenicio-punico. L'aspetto economico-industriale." In *L'alimentazione nell'antichità*, pp. 167–84. Parma, 1985.

Botto, M. "L'attività economica dei fenici in Oriente tra il IX e la prima metà dell'VlIl sec a.C." *EVO* 11 (1988): 117–54.

Broshi, M. "Wine in Ancient Palestine: Introductory Notes." *IMJ* 3 (1984): 21–40.

———. "The Diet of Palestine in the Roman Period: Introductory Notes." *IMJ* 5 (1986): 41–56.

Callot, O. "Les huileries et l'huile au Bronze récent: Quelques exemples syriens et cypriotes." In *La production du vin et de l'huile en Méditerranée*, ed. M.-C. Amouretti and J.-P. Brun, pp. 55–63. Bulletin de Correspondance Hellénique, suppl. 26. Athens: École Française d'Athènes; Paris: Diffusion de Boccard, 1993.

Caubet, A. 1987. "Archéologie et médecine: L'exemple de Cypre." In *Archéologie et médecine: Actes du VIIèmes Rencontres Internationales d'Archéologie et d'Histoire d'Antibes*, pp. 189–201. Juan-les-Pins, October 1986.

Cecchini, S. M. "Problèmes et aspects de l'agriculture carthaginoise." In *Histoire et archéologie de l'Afrique du Nord: Actes du IIIème Colloque International*, pp. 107–17. Congrès National des Sociétés Savantes, Montpellier, April 1–15, 1985. Paris: C.T.H.S., 1987.

Dentzer, J.-M. *Le Motif du banquet couché dans le Proche-Orient et le monde grec du VIIème au IVème siècle avant J.-C.* Bibliothèque des Écoles Françaises d'Athènes et de Rome, fasc. 246e. Paris: Diffusion de Boccard, 1982.

Desse, G. 1987. "Sur un condiment marin." In *Archéologie et médecine: Actes du VIIèmes Rencontres Internationales d'Archéologie et d'Histoire d'Antibes*, pp. 479–87. Juan-les-Pins, October 1987.

Di Salvo, R. "Analisi osteologica dei reperti scheletrici umani in Lilibeo." In *Lilibeo punica*, ed. C. A. Di Stefano, pp. 57–59. Palermo, 1993.

———. "Gli inumati di Manuzza-Selinunte (Trapani) (IV–III sec. a.C.)." *Archivio per l'Antropologia e la Etnologia* 117 (1987): 259–83.

———. "La necropoli punica della Caserma Tukory: Nota antropologica." In *Di terra in terra: Nuove scoperte archeologiche nella provincia di Palermo*, pp. 293–94. Palermo, 1991.

D'Onofrio, S. "Un forno da pane mediterraneo: Il tannur." In *Il pane,* pp. 57–62. Perugia, 1992.

Etienne, R. "A propos du garum sociorum." *Latomus* 29 (1970): 297–313.

Fales, M. A. "La produzione primaria: I cereali." In *L'alba della civiltà,* 2:165–81. Turin, 1976.

Fantar, M. H. *Carthage: Approche d'une civilisation.* Tunis: Alif-Editions de la Méditerranée, 1993.

Fernández Uriel, P. "Algunas consideraciones sobre la miel y la sal en el extremo del Mediterráneo occidental." In *Lixus: Actes du Colloque Larache,* pp. 332–36. November 8–11, 1989. Rome, 1992.

Grottanelli, C., and N. F. Parise, eds. *Sacrificio e società nel mondo antico.* Rome: Laterza, 1988.

Gsell, S. *Histoire ancienne de l'Afrique du Nord.* 8 vols. Paris: Hachette, 1920–28.

Gubel, E. *Phoenician Furniture: A Typology Based on Iron Age Representations with Reference to the Iconographical Context.* Studia Phoenicia 7. Leuven: Peeters, 1987.

Hadjisavvas, S. "Olive Oil and Wine Production in Ancient Cyprus." *RDAC* 2 (1988): 111–19.

Harden, D. B. *I fenici.* Milan, 1973.

Heltzer, M. "Olive Oil and Wine Production in Phoenicia and in the Mediterranean Trade." In *La production du vin et de l'huile en Méditerranée,* ed. M.-C. Amouretti and J.-P. Brun, pp. 49–54. Bulletin de Correspondance Hellénique, suppl. 26. Athens: École Française d'Athènes; Paris: Diffusion de Boccard, 1993.

———. *The Rural Community in Ancient Ugarit.* Wiesbaden: Reichert, 1976.

———. "Vineyards and Wine in Ugarit." *Ugarit Forschungen* 22 (1990): 119–35.

Laronde, A. "La vie agricole en Lybie jusqu'à l'arrivée des Arabes." *Lybian Studies* 20 (1989): 127–34.

Lipinski, E. "Deux marchands de blé phéniciens à Ninive." *RSF* 3, no. 1 (1975): 1–6.

Liverani, M. *Antico Oriente: Storia, società, economia.* Rome: Laterza, 1988.

———. "Ciocca di capelli o focaccia di ginepro?" *RSF* 3, no. 1 (1975): 37–41.

Mallegni, F., G. Fornaciari, and G. Bartoli. "Su di una serie di reperti umani rinvenuti in una tomba a corridoio dei III–II sec. a.C. della necropoli punica di Cartagine." *Atti della Società Toscana di Scienze Naturali* 87 (1980): 389–445.

Manfredi, L. I. "La coltura dei cereali in età punica in Sardegna e Nord-Africa." *QuadCagliari* 10 (1993): 191–218.

———. "Le saline e il sale nel mondo punico." *RSF* 20, no. 1 (1992): 5–6.

———. "Tharros—XVIII–XIX: Il laboratorio Tharros." *RSF* 21, no. 2 (1993): 206–9.

Martin, R. *Recherches sur les agronomes latins et sur leurs conceptions économiques et sociales.* Collection d'Études Anciennes. Paris: Belles Lettres, 1971.

Milano, L. "Alimentazione e regimi alimentari nella Siria preclassica." *Dialoghi di Archeologia* 3 (1981): 85–121.

Moiner, B. "Lecture moderne de Pline l'Ancienne: Communication sur la production et la consommation de sel de mer dans le bassin méditerranéen." In *L'exploitation de la Mer: Actes du Vèmes Rencontres Internationales d'Archéologie et d'Histoire d'Antibes,* pp. 73–105. October 1984. Valbonne, 1985.

Moscati, S. *I Cartaginesi*. Milan: Jaca, 1982.

———. *I fenici e Cartagine*. Società e Costume 8. Turin: Unione Tipografico-Editrice Torinese, 1972.

Passoni dell'Acqua, A. "Le testimonianze papiracee relative alla Siria e Fenicia in età tolemaica (I papiri di Zenone e le ordinanze reali)." *Rivista biblica italiana* 34 (1986): 233–83.

Picard, C. "Les représentations du sacrifice molk sur les ex-voto de Carthage." *Karthago* 17 (1976): 67–138.

Picard, G., and C. Picard. *La vie quotidienne à Carthage au temps d'Hannibal*. Paris: Hachette, 1958. [*Daily Life in Carthage at the Time of Hannibal*. Trans. A. E. Foster. Daily Life Series. New York: Macmillan, 1961.]

Ponsich, M. *Aceite de oliva y salazonas de pescado: Factores geo-económicos de Betica y Tingitana*. Madrid, 1988.

Ponsich, M., and M. Tarradel. *Garum et industries antiques de salaison dans la Méditerranée occidentale*. Paris: Presses Universitaires de France, 1965.

Pritchard, J. B. *Ancient Near Eastern Texts Relating to the Old Testament*. Princeton: Princeton University Press, 1955.

Provera, M. "La coltura della vite nella tradizione biblica e orientale." *Bibbia e Oriente* 132 (1982): 97–106.

Purpura, G. "Pesca e stabilimenti antichi per la lavorazione del pesce in Sicilia: S. Vito (Trapani), Cala Minnola (Levanzo)." *SicArch* 15 (1982): 45–60.

———. "Pesca e stabilimenti antichi per la lavorazione del pesce in Sicilia: L'Isola delle Femmine (Palermo), Punta Molinazo (Punta Rais), Tonnara del Cofano (Trapani), S. Nicola (Favignana)." *SicArch* 18 (1985): 59–86.

Quittner, V. "The Semantic Background of *socii* in Lat. *garum sociorum*." *Journal of Northwest Semitic Languages* 6 (1978): 45–47.

Rathte, A. "Il banchetto presso i fenici." *Atti del II Congresso internazionale di studi fenici e punici*, Rome, November 9–14, 1987, 3:1165–68. Rome, 1991.

Rivera Núñez, D., and C. Obon de Castro. "La dieta cereal prehistórica y su supervivencia en el área mediterránea." *Trabajos de Prehistoria* 46 (1989): 247–54.

Schaeffer, F. A. "Olive Growing and Olive Oil in Ugarit." In *Olive Oil in Antiquity: Israel and Neighbouring Countries from the Neolithic to the Early Arab Period*, ed. David Eitam and Michael Heltzer. History of the Ancient Near East Studies, no. 7. Padua: Sargon, 1996.

———. *Ugaritica*. Vol. 4. Paris: P. Guethner, 1958.

Spanò Giammellaro A. "L'alimentazione fenicia e punica." In *Atti del Convegno Internazionale sulla cultura dell'alimentazione nei Paesi del Mediterraneo*. Trapani, 1991.

Speranza, I. *Scriptorum Romanorum de re rustica reliquiae*. Biblioteca di Helikon: Testi e Studi, no. 8. Messina: Università degli Studi, 1971.

Tambure'lo, I. "Materiali per una storia dell'economia della Sicilia punica." In *Atti del II Congresso internazionale di studi fenici e punici*, 1:323–41. Rome, November 9–14, 1987. Rome: Consiglio Nazionale delle Ricerche, 1991.

Tlatli, S. E. *La Carthage punique, étude urbaine: la ville, ses fonctions, son rayonnement*. Paris: J. Maisonneuve, 1978.

Uberti, M. L. "Qualche nota sull'alimentazione fenicia e punica: I principali costituenti energetici." *Rivista storica dell'Antichità* 17–18 (1987–88): 189–97.

Van Zeist, W., and S. Bottema. "Paleobotanical Studies of Carthage: A Comparison of Microscopic and Macroscopic Plant Remains." *CEDAC Carthage Bulletin* 5 (1983): 18–22.

Wagner, C. G. "Fenicios en Occidente: la colonización agrícola." *RSF* 17, no. 1 (1989): 61–102.

PART TWO

CLASSICAL WORLD

INTRODUCTION

FOOD SYSTEMS *and* MODELS OF CIVILIZATION

Massimo Montanari

Of the many factors that contribute to defining the food culture of the classical world, one in particular stands out: the desire to be seen as belonging to "civilization"—a privileged corner of the world closed to the alien universe of the "barbarians." Diet played an essential role in this attempt to define a model of civilized life, itself deeply rooted in the concept of the city. In order to distance itself from the "diversity" of the uncivilized noncitizen—and therefore from the "savage" lifestyle of the barbarian populations—three aspects of the food model were stressed: conviviality; the kind of food consumed; and the art of cooking and dietary regimens.

Eating Together

The first thing that distinguished civilized man from beasts and barbarians—regarded as similar in the Greco-Roman value system—was conviviality. Eating did not simply satisfy a bodily urge but transformed the act into a social and communicative event. "We do not sit at table only to eat," wrote Plutarch, "but to eat together." It could be argued that barbarians—and even some species of animals—were equally well acquainted with the habit of eating together. But it was the rules governing it (for example, how to mix wine and water) that made a "civilized" banquet different from a simple meal eaten in company. In Greek society the "correct" way of doing things distinguished civilized men, or citizens, from savages who did not know the rules, and from semi-savages who applied them only occasionally. Conviviality was conceived as a cornerstone of civilization. The *convivium,* or banquet, was the very image of life together (*cum vivere*).

Any group—whether a nuclear family or the entire population of a city—that partook of a banquet around a common table, either in fact or in a symbolic representation, was considered unified. Separate tables, on the other hand, signified that the group was not aggregated. This symbolism pertained to both the relationship between men and that between men and the gods. In the mythical past, men and gods sat at the same table and partook of the same food; after the fall, the tables were separated and the food was differentiated.

It is important to stress that sitting at table together was not only a useful tool for social aggregation and unity but also an instrument of separation and exclusion. Belonging or not belonging to the banquet was highly significant, whether the banquet was "oligarchic"—that is, a representation of the political identity of the city governed by the few—or "democratic," to which practically all were invited. The relationship between participation in the banquet and integration in the community remained strong throughout the Middle Ages in the western world. Excommunication, in the literal sense of exclusion from the community, in lay society as well as in the church and in monasteries, often took the form of being sent away from the table.

In addition to expressing identity, the banquet was also the place where social exchange took place, according to the well-known anthropological paradigm of the exchange of gifts. Food thus took on a different significance at every banquet according to the direction in which the offer was made. From high to low, it denoted generous condescension and social predominance; from low to high it implied humility and subservience; between peers, it demonstrated the communality (however temporary) of the meal.

The banquet also represented hierarchy and power relationships within the group. Status was marked by the position at table of each member, by the criteria of food distribution, and by the kind of food that was served. It was considered perfectly normal to serve different foods at the same meal according to the status of the participant. It must be stressed, however, that in the ancient world this differentiation did not possess the same expressive force or level of formality as it did in the Middle Ages, when different positions were upheld by a precise ideology regarding social differences in food. In classical times, cultural identity was considered more important than social identity. A "civilized citizen" was seen in opposition, above all, to an "uncivilized barbarian," and it was within this main contradiction that the internal dynamics of society moved.

Another important opportunity for social cohesion and for establishing a civilized identity was the symposium, the ritual collective wine-drinking that followed a banquet in the Greek world but that was always strictly separated from it. The symposium celebrated the sacred nature of wine that generates inebriation and therefore facilitates contact with the gods. The Greeks, like the Etruscans, did not usually drink wine with their meals, while the Romans came to consider it a mere beverage and thus stripped it of nearly all its sacred functions. Nonetheless, wine remained a marker of civilization. Civilized man not only invented the magical beverage but also developed forms of self-control and etiquette (knowing when to stop drinking, how to mix wine with water in the appropriate proportions for different social occasions), which proved that he was master over wine and not vice versa. Greek writers never tired of repeating that barbarians were unable to hold to these rules. The shared drinking cup (krater) was yet another symbol of cultural and social regulation and of the superiority of knowledge and technique over instinct.

. . . and Man Created His Plants and Animals

In addition to the rules and rituals of conviviality, food itself played a vital role in establishing human identity. It was food, especially meat, that distinguished men from gods. When Odysseus refused to eat the food of the gods offered by Circe, it was to stress that he belonged to humankind, that he was civilized rather than barbarian. Paradoxically, however, the food that most distinguished men from gods did not distinguish them from the uncivilized world of beasts. It was not meat but bread—an absolute example of artifice, a completely "cultural" product throughout all the phases of its preparation—that became the symbol of civilization and of the distinction between men and animals. Wine and oil were also a mark of a civilized society, which was able to create its own plants and animals by farming the land and raising livestock.

Barbarians were depicted and described by civilized citizens as nomad hunter-gatherers in contrast to those who grew their own produce. Farming the land implied staying in one place, as did sitting at a banquet; the sedentary nature of the feast was thought to be entirely alien to nomad communities. Ovid's myth of Anius and his three daughters who transformed everything they touched into grain, wine, and oil presented a utopia in which nature could be transformed by the human hand. Grain and wine made the eater and drinker human—to the extent that in Homer the term "bread eaters" was synonymous with the word for "men."

Those peoples that did not farm, eat bread, or drink wine were therefore savages or barbarians. Meat was their staple, and milk (an ethnographic projection of the infantile state) their main beverage. Classical writers did not hesitate to add the epithet "Greek" to barbarian populations who were discovered to be bread eaters, a famous example being the Greco-Scythians.

The key factor was the capacity to "construct" one's food by domesticating and overcoming nature, a concept that, in the Greco-Roman world, had a rather negative connotation. The term "hunter-gatherer" (savage, natural) stood in ideal opposition to that of "shepherd-farmer" (domestic, artificial). In practice, this distinction often reflected reality, although shepherds were also commonly associated with hunters because of the similarity between the two activities: they both took place in the uncultivated forests, copses, and natural pastures.

Meat—whether livestock or game—had a strong cultural connotation linking it to savagery, which encouraged its identification as the food of barbarians. The Romans, on the other hand, tried hard to domesticate hunting by setting up controlled reserves of semi-tamed animals. In any case, the savage world was considered "alien" and viewed with diffidence and suspicion; this meant that it was either excluded from the domain of productive activity or forcibly assimilated into the "civilized" world.

Leaving ideology aside, the reality of production was rather different. To start with, cultivated land was not the only source of food. Uncultivated land was exploited for grazing, hunting, fishing, and the gathering of natural foodstuffs. There was a very narrow dividing line between wild and cultivated produce. The process of agricultural domestication was far from completed in the late Roman period—perhaps this explains the intense cultural need that existed to distinguish the wild from the tamed.

Furthermore, wine is not always wine, and bread is not always bread. So-called wine was often watered-down vinegar; bread—the symbol of an ideology—was in many cases more of a cereal pap than a loaf as we know it. Barley cakes and spelt porridge were the main elements of the Greek and Roman food culture. Bread came much later, the result of a long, complex, and typically urban history. Flatcakes cooked under the ashes, together with soups and polenta, were staples—especially in the countryside—for many years to come.

Pulses, mainly broad beans, chickpeas, lentils, and vetch, supplemented the diet dominated by cereals (wheat, barley, spelt, and millet). The Greeks also grew garlic, leeks, and onions in their kitchen gardens, while the Romans cultivated cabbages (which Cato, in his agricultural tract, praised highly), as well as turnips, rape, and aromatic herbs. It is interesting to note that as late as the Middle Ages, the emperor of Byzantium was the laughingstock of the meat-eating continental aristocracy owing to his fondness for these humble vegetables.

There is hardly a trace of these foods in the dietary model constructed by Greek and Roman ideology, however. Rigidly grounded in the three "fundamentals"—bread, wine, and oil—the model left little room for lesser foods such as vegetable soups, low-grade cereal mashes, pulses, and so on. There was even less room for the produce of uncultivated land, culturally marginalized by the dominant value system and therefore concealed by the sources—as if revealing a taste for these products would give away barbarian origins.

The exploitation of pastureland, marshes, and forests, which must surely have had some economic advantages, found its way into the sources almost exclusively in a negative light. Hunting, in particular, was presented as a humble occupation dictated by poverty; what is more, it forced the hunter to spend time away from the seat of civilization, the city. In short, the food ideology presented in Greek and Roman literature should be interpreted as an ideal that corresponded to reality only in part. This does not mean, however, that its importance should be denied; ideology and ideals have always played their part in history.

The concept of frugality was linked to the dominant food model. Bread, wine, and oil (along with figs and honey) were a symbol of the simple life, of a dignified poverty characterized by hard work and humble satisfaction. In Greek sources this idea was contrasted—with obvious ideological and political intentions—with the extravagant and decadent luxury of the Persians. In imperial Rome, writers expressed nostalgia for the good old days when customs were uncorrupted and foods were simple, when there was no need to cross oceans and travel to distant continents to satisfy perverse tastes, and when people were happy to live on the lovingly cultivated fruit of their own land.

Let us not be deceived, however. It was not humility that lay behind the ideal of a rustic way of life lauded by so many Greek and Latin writers. It was, rather, civic pride: every civilization attempted to vindicate its own cultural and historical primacy. The adult initiation ceremony of young Athenians described by Plutarch was purely imperialistic: led to the sanctuary of Agraulus to swear loyalty to their country, they were required to describe their land as being "where wheat, vines, and olives grow." The implicit message was that wherever a Greek settled, he would plant wheat, vines, and olives—which is in fact what happened. Interpreted in another light, however, the message was this: wherever wheat, vines, and olives grew, there the Greeks could claim ascendancy and expand their empire.

The ideology of meat consumption was more problematic. In the classical world, meat had connotations of luxury, festivity, and social privilege; it was not considered a primary food source. Consequently, price controls on meat like the ones imposed on cereals did not exist. In some cases, it was even forbidden to sell meat to the public. The exceptional nature of meat consumption was amplified by sacrificial practices, which conferred an intense symbolic value on meat but, at the same time, placed it out of reach as an everyday food.

Sacrifice was both a tool for expiating guilt (the killing) and an important gesture of solidarity (distributing meat to the people), as well as a means of communicating with the gods (the offering). Clearly of vital importance, much has been written in the last decade, and indeed in the pages that follow, on the subject of sacrifice. One question in particular persists: whether meat consumption was always linked to sacrificial practices. In the Greek world, this seems to have been the case; in the Roman world, on the other hand, it looks as though the link gradually grew weaker. It was maintained on an ideological plane, however, justifying the repeated polemics of early Christians against the consumption of meat after sacrificing animals to "false idols." Only game brought back from the hunt was exempt—for obvious reasons—from the logic of sacrifice. However, its marginality in the Greek and Roman value system confirms that eating meat was a relatively exceptional event.

This cultural analysis dovetails well with an economic consideration: according to a cautious estimate, in the Greek world about 80 percent of calories were provided by cereals; Greek citizens—the recipients of most of the sacrificial meat—ate no more than one or two kilograms (1 kg = 2.2 lbs.) of meat in a year. The philosophical vegetarian sects (in particular, the Orphics and the Pythagoreans) were the ultimate expression of a common non-meat-eating culture. Their rejection of sacrifice (as a refusal to spill blood or a belief in metempsychosis) was an expression of a social phenomenon rather than a dietary prescription in that it represented a rejection of the rules of conviviality and, ultimately, of society.

Respect for the animal's life was also, more prosaically, a matter of economics. Sheep were more useful to the Greeks and Romans alive than dead. They used their wool and their milk to make cheese, which became an everyday food. Cattle were very rare and were used for working in the fields; only when they became old were they killed for their meat. Fish, crustaceans, and cheese rather than meat supplemented the cereals and vegetables in the Greek and Roman diet.

Meat played a more important part in the Roman diet owing to a long-standing tradition on the Italian peninsula of raising pigs, as we shall see in the essay on the Etruscans. Although pork was never an essential element of the diet, it was nevertheless a good source of animal protein. The pig was considered a meat larder on legs. The function of its life, as Cicero put it, was like that of salt: to preserve the meat in perfect condition. Pork took on increasing importance in imperial Rome, and, from the third century on, emperors ordered it to be distributed to the populace together with bread in order to maintain public order as well as underscore the privilege accorded to Roman citizens.

Nevertheless, bread remained the staple food in Roman times. Even soldiers—despite the Homeric image of meat-eating warriors, linked perhaps to sacrificial practices rather than to a specific dietary code—were considered bread eaters. Providing enough bread for soldiers' rations was the foremost concern of army suppliers; without bread, it was thought, no soldier could fight effectively (rations oscillated between 0.8 and 1 kilogram per head in combat).

There was, then, a clear tie between real life and the cultural roots of a civilization that identified *civilitas* with a *civitas* surrounded by *ager*. An ideal soldier, on retiring from active service defending his country, established a country residence in the conquered territory. An ideal general, like Cincinnatus, left his fields to fight and returned as soon as the battle was won. In these figures, ideals blended with reality and mutually reinforced the supremacy of bread as the most important food of all.

This was in stark contrast to the predominantly Germanic culture that followed in the Middle Ages. Meat, not bread, became the food symbol of the warrior, who was, in his turn, assimilated with the figure of the hunter (the hunt being a mirror of war) rather than with that of the farmer-landowner.

The Raw and the Cooked

The preeminence of bread in classical culture was also the result of a science of dietetics (itself almost certainly influenced by the symbolic value attributed to that food), which placed bread at the top of the nutritional table. For Greek and Roman doctors, eating bread provided a perfectly balanced blend of those humors—hot, cold, dry, moist—that Hippocrates considered constituent elements of every foodstuff and, indeed, of everything that existed. "Bread," wrote the great Roman medical writer Aulus Cornelius Celsus, "contains more nutritional material than any other food."

More generally, the science of dietetics was at the heart of the culture of food and gastronomy. The art of cooking in the ancient world was strictly linked with health concerns and with dietetics. The primordial discovery that food could be cooked on the fire was the foundation of a complex food culture that influenced western thought until chemistry took over in the preserving industry.

The fact that barbarians did not cook their food, knew nothing about building fires, and ate everything raw (or, at the most, baked in the sun, like the mythological fish eaters who lived on the banks of the Red Sea), was a commonplace in classical literature. There is little point in stressing this, given the teachings of Lévi-Strauss regarding the value of cooked food as a defining element of civilization.

Suffice it to say that the art of cooking was always aimed not only at making food tastier, but also at transforming its "nature" by adapting it to nutritional needs. In this sense, food and health were always inextricably linked, as Greek and Latin treatises on dietetics, from Hippocrates on, claimed.

Cooking techniques, seasonings, and ways of combining food and drink—these were all seen as being opportunities to "correct" nature. They were also a vital factor in designing a dietary regimen suited to individual needs. A "diet" was a rule to be applied to everyday life (once again, rules defined civilized behavior); the regimen changed according to activities undertaken, age, sex, environment, and season. All these factors, it was believed, affected the combinations of the four humors in the body. The aim of the diet was to redress any imbalances that might have taken place and to bring the body back to that perfect equilibrium, without which health and physical efficiency were impossible. In what was essentially an allopathic view of medicine (although occasional examples of contrary views can be found), the ultimate aim of diet was to maintain a balance by means of "temperate" or "balanced" foods. More often, it was to reconstitute an equilibrium that had been compromised by illness or by any other subjective or objective factor. The diet had to apply different combinations of heat, cold, moisture, or dryness at different levels of intensity in an infinite number of possible proportions.

Cuisine and dietetics thus became part of the same semantic universe. Criteria of taste were intertwined with those concerning health. To identify whether food was good or not, the first elements to come into play were the senses. Although the notion of the four humors was applied to the "nature" of the food, it was more a measure of sensory satisfaction. This meant that what was "good" coincided perfectly with what was "good for you." If this was not the case, the prescriptions of the dietician and doctor were able to correct matters.

City and Country

Both the Greek and the Roman civilizations were eminently urban; the countryside was considered an annex of the *polis* or *civitas*. It supplied the city with food, and citizens took great pride in it, becoming landowners themselves at the first opportunity. Despite this ideological integration, however, the distance between life in the city and life in the countryside—even as far as food was concerned—was considerable. Country dwellers were by no means a homogeneous group—there were slaves and freed slaves, landowners and their employees, rich and poor.

The main distinction between this group and inhabitants of the city was the latter's dependence on the market for supplies or, alternatively, on either public food distribution or private almsgiving institutions—formidable instruments of political, social, and financial control of both the plebeians and the elite. These privileges were particularly marked in Athens and Rome. Another difference, under normal conditions, was the greater variety of resources on the market. In times of difficulty, however, country dwellers enjoyed greater food security since they were closer to the productive land.

This opposition between city and country was present—developing in a non-linear and often contradictory fashion—throughout the Middle Ages and into the modern epoch; it will also be discussed frequently throughout this book.

Crisis of a Model

The food model established by the Greeks and Romans—more ideological than dietetic, as we have seen—began to crumble from the third or fourth century onward, attacked, on the one hand, by Christianity and, on the other, by the newly dominant Germanic culture. Both these forces were "alien" and in many respects incompatible with that model. The biggest change came about with the gradual erosion of the primacy of the Mediterranean triad—grain, wine, and oil—and the increasing acceptability and availability of meat.

The diffusion of Christianity challenged the practice and philosophy of sacrifice. It was rejected at a technical level because the offer was considered wrongly directed at the "wrong" gods (though sacrificial practices aimed at the "true" god persisted, as we shall see later, in certain Christian settlements, especially among the Armenians). Above all, however, its legitimacy was undermined because the practice was considered unnecessarily cruel. It was substituted in the Eucharist with a "vegetarian" sacrifice (bread and wine), which, nonetheless, recalled a far crueler sacrifice that took place once only for the good of all men.

The result was not without contradictions: by making bread and wine sacred and by adopting oil as the sacramental substance par excellence, Christianity reinforced the values of the Roman ideological food model and transmitted it with renewed energy to the generations that followed right into the early Middle Ages. At the same time, the deconsecration of meat turned it into an everyday food.

This phenomenon was all the more significant because, in the same period, Germanic expansion brought with it a food ideology based on exploiting the forests and uncultivated land rather than on farming the land. With the demographic explosion that took place from the third century on and the consequent transformation of the countryside, meat became an even more important element in the diet. Farmland, and therefore production, was reduced, and large-scale landowners began to take over from small holders, turning the land over to pasture.

This was one reason why pork, as mentioned earlier, was distributed to the poor in the streets, and why, in late-imperial Rome, as excavations at Settefinestre have shown, meat appeared in slaves' rations, whereas in Cato's time slaves were given only cereals and vegetables. But there was another reason. The assimilation of meat-eating habits that were once "alien" to the classical world was also linked to an interpretation of the empire. This was no longer a "national" concept; it embraced many different territories and its food model thus became more universal. From Asia, spices and exotic fruit were imported; from the north, the Celtic taste for pork.

With the arrival of the Germanic tribes, however, the new "universal" identity of the empire was challenged. The "barbarian" food model, based on meat consumption, established itself with the same force as its propagators used to invade and conquer the Italian peninsula. The clash between the Romans and the Germanic invaders was also a clash between a value system considered by the Romans "civilized" and another considered "barbaric"—again by the Romans, of course. In the imperial biographies collected under the title *Storia Augusta,* nostalgia for the past was expressed in a eulogy of vegetarian frugality: an emperor's fondness for fruit, vegetables, and bread was an unequivocal sign of loyalty to the Roman tradition; a distaste for bread and vegetables and an exaggerated taste for game and other kinds of meat was a sure sign of incipient barbarism.

Romans and barbarians (with Christians in the middle), farming and the exploitation of forests, bread and meat, domesticated and wild—in the midst of these contradictions, caught between contrasting models of production and consumption, a new phase of food culture and history began with the inception of the Middle Ages.

CHAPTER 6

URBAN *and* RURAL DIETS *in* GREECE

Marie-Claire Amouretti

Less is known about the Greek diet than about the Roman. We do, however, have a fairly good idea of what people ate in the cities of classical Greece, where classical civilization was born in the fifth century B.C.E.

The Agrarian Landscape

The Greek *polis* was a small state (ranging in size from roughly 40 to 4,000 square miles) with a city at its center. Although the ideal was perfect autarky, this was never achieved: some food always had to be imported. Normally the land belonged to the citizens of the *polis*, the basic political community, but there were different categories: communal land (*koina*), often used for pasture; p...ic land (*demosia*), sometimes owned not by the whole community but by a smaller entity, such as the Attic *deme*; sacred land (*hiera*), attached to a temple; and, finally, private property (*idia*). When a colony was founded, its land was divided into lots under various juridical schemes. Established cities employed a variety of systems. In Sparta, for example, the land was owned by the city, which awarded lots to its citizens along with helots to cultivate the land. In actuality, however, these estates were hereditary, and the city could even cede ownership of part of its common land to an individual in recognition of some service. Only sacred land did not change hands, in theory at any rate. In fact, we know from holy wars that these lands were sometimes usurped.

The limited size of the city-state, together with the diversity of tenure, encouraged small farms. Some large estates encompassed a number of scattered farms, but even the largest remained small by our standards: Phainippos' 106-acre estate in Attica, mentioned by Demosthenes, was considered exceptional. An estate of 64 acres passed for large.

Temples owned considerable land. From inscriptions of lease agreements, we know that these were subdivided into numerous farms.

Agriculture relied on natural rainfall. Irrigation was limited to the garden, or *kepos,* which was generally quite small. Considerable effort was invested in improvements to increase yield. Xenophon, in his dialogue *Economics,* composed in about 370 B.C.E., puts the following words in the mouth of a wealthy landowner, Ischomachus (who is actually expressing the ideas of the author): "No improvement is more dramatic than when a once unproductive field begins to yield a whole array of crops. Why, Socrates, I tell you that I myself have taken estates and multiplied their value a hundred times."

Such progress did not come without effort. To obtain decent yields of grain, arid land had to be plowed frequently. Because livestock provided little manure, farmers made compost of grass, straw, and branches. Fields left fallow in alternate years were sometimes planted with legumes.

Although even relatively infertile land was used for grain cultivation, Greek agriculture really revolved around the grape and the olive. Leases carefully detailed the number of grapevines and olive trees to be tended. Despite the importance of these two fruits throughout Greece, cultivation was not intensive. Olive trees were often planted on the edges of fields and roads or scattered throughout fields. Some vineyards were more concentrated, as at Thasos and Chios. A third-century inscription from Rhodes tells us what arrangement of vines was believed to produce a superior grape. In flat territory, cereals and legumes were planted between rows of vines; almond and fig trees grew in many fields.

The landscape became extremely varied as regions developed specialties in certain crops. Sparta produced flax and millet, while varieties of peas were grown on the islands. Grapevines were supported in many different ways: on trellises on some windy islands, on beams protected by low walls on the Chersonese Peninsula, on crossed trellises in Crete, on trees elsewhere. The ancient Greek landscape bore little resemblance to what we see today. For example, the island of Delos, now deserted, was farmed in the classical period, and the plain of Amphissa below Delphi was not yet a green sea of olive trees. Archaeologists, moreover, have found that some Greek islands boasted terraced fields.

Our picture of this much-worked landscape would not be complete without some mention of the *eschatiai,* or "fringes" (that is, marginal land), which were more productive than one might think. Wild herbs grew in the forests. Valonia, saffron, and kermes, used in dyes, were collected by the poor on some islands and in Greek colonies in Asia Minor. Marshes and ponds supplied fish, and eels were taken from Lake Copais in Boeotia.

Rural people thus ate a more diverse diet than one might assume. Some peasants produced enough olives, grapes, fruits, and herbs that they could exchange the surplus for essential grains. But the whole food equation was complicated by the number of city dwellers and the diversity of landownership.

Who Produced the Food?

Recent research has shown that the people who tilled the soil of ancient Greece were a diverse group. In addition to slaves, helots attached to the land, and native laborers employed by Greek colonists, there were of course free farmers and small holders.

Athens was unusual in that it evolved considerably in the classical period. At the beginning of the Peloponnesian wars (431 B.C.E.), the majority of Athenians lived in the country. When Attica was invaded, Thucydides tells us, these rural people were obliged to leave their homes and seek refuge in the beleaguered city. By the fourth century, however, most of the Attic population appears to have been concentrated in Athens, which at that time had somewhere between 300,000 and 500,000 residents. Many citizens were still small holders, however, and either farmed their own land or employed up to three slaves. The largest landowners hired a steward, who supervised the slaves on their land while they resided in the city. According to Plutarch, Pericles was one of the first to sell his farm's produce for cash with which to buy necessary commodities in town. More commonly, to judge from the sources, urban landowners had food from their own farms shipped to town for their personal use.

We can learn a great deal about Greek eating from Hippocrates' *Diet.* The text begins with a discussion of barley, a basic staple. This was consumed in the form of *maza,* a sort of cake made by heating the barley to remove chaff and then grinding it into a whole-grain flour known as *alphita.* Next, liquid was added: water, oil, honey, or milk, to taste, along with various condiments. Finally, this mixture was carefully kneaded. The resulting dough could either be eaten immediately or preserved. This technique has survived in a number of Mediterranean countries (the Tunisian *bsisa,* for example). The ancient Greeks consumed most of their cereal in this form. Some scholars argue that wheat bread began to replace barley cakes in the Greek diet. This did not happen in the period that concerns us here, however.

Barley flour and mint went into a drink known as *cyceon*. Not only was this was the sacred beverage of Eleusis, but country folk liked to drink it as a refreshment. In rural areas barleycorn was eaten green as well as hulled, boiled, and dried. In addition, *ptisane,* a decoction of hulled barleycorn, was recommended as a fever medication.

Wheat has been eaten since prehistoric times. It was used in flatbreads, leavened breads, and cakes. Hippocrates discusses several types of ovens, all fairly small in size. Bakers, who first appeared in Greek cities in the late fifth century, were veritable small businessmen who bought and sold wheat and ground their own flour in addition to baking.

Other cereals such as millet were also grown, as were legumes, which complemented grains in the Greek diet. Hippocrates mentions the fava bean, various kinds of chickpeas, lentils, and vetch, as well as seed plants such as flax, sesame, and poppies, which were prized for their nutritional value. This variety of crops compensated in part for the variability of the grain harvest. Several treatises recommended that city dwellers supplement their diet with these basically rural preparations in time of war.

Hippocrates next turns his attention to animals—not just cattle, pigs, and sheep but also dogs. The Greeks consumed the meat of all these species, but only after ritual sacrifice. They also ate game: boar, deer, hare, fox, and even hedgehog. Various fowl rounded out the meat portion of the Greek diet: ring dove, partridge, pigeon, cock, turtledove, and goose. Ducks and other marsh birds were also appreciated.

Both saltwater and freshwater fish and shellfish are also discussed. Cooked in various ways, these were served along with barley cakes as side dishes (*opson*). Sometimes they were preserved in brine. A bouillon of oyster is discussed. We learn that *garum* was first prepared in Corinth and Delos before being taken up in Carthage and Rome.

Cheese was another key food. Together with barley and figs, it formed the basis of the Spartan diet. Sometimes it was mixed with other ingredients, including honey, and formed into cakes. Honey was frequently used as both a preservative and a sweetener, and it is mentioned in countless recipes for pastries as well as an ingredient of various savory dishes.

Greens, garlic, and onions were also important parts of the Greek diet, as we know from Hippocrates and other sources. Hippocrates begins his list of vegetables with leek, colza, watercress, and turnip, along with several vegetables no longer familiar to us, such as purslane and orache. He also mentions spices such as pennyroyal, marjoram, and thyme. Greens were grown in vegetable gardens as well as fields or simply picked wild. Grains, seeds, and greens all went into soups (*rophema*). Crushed legumes were boiled to make *etnos,* whereas *lekithos* was a boiled mixture of milled seeds, although it is hard to know whether these were thick soups or purees. When times were hard, Greeks gathered squill and mallow, according to a technical treatise by Philo of Byzantium from the third century B.C.E.

As for fruit, melons, grapes, figs, pears, apples, quinces, sorb apples, medlars, pomegranates, and almonds were all eaten both fresh and dried.

The principal drink was wine: warm reds came from Thrace, Thasos, and Chios and light whites from Mende. The Greek lexicon of wine does not always translate readily into ours. The ancients appreciated wine for its color, or robe: dark reds (*melas*) were called purple or blood-colored. White wine (*leukos*) was actually somewhat yellow. A vintage might also be described as harsh (*austeroi*), dry (*xeroi*), mellow (*malakoi*), or sweet (*glukeis*). Wines with a good bouquet were called *ozontes.* Some wines were light (*leptoi*), others thick (*pacheis*). Some were said to be hot (*thermos*), others weak (*asthenestreros*). The most prized vintages were those that were dark, strong, fragrant, and old. Greek vintages should not be confused with Roman ones, which were mainly white. Many specialists hold that certain Greek reds had a high alcohol content: Salviat maintains that *thasos* had an alcohol content of 18 degrees, while Villard argues that it was no higher than 16. This was a slow-fermenting wine with a long maturation period. Well-corked, high-quality amphoras guaranteed a good aging process. Much later, in the third century C.E., the widespread replacement of the amphora by the barrel changed the conditions of aging. By the Middle Ages young wine was preferred to old, probably because few wines could withstand being aged in barrels. Hence the judgments of sixteenth-century authors with respect to ancient wines are misleading. Aging conditions had changed greatly since antiquity. Greek reds were not drunk by peasants, who contented themselves with second pressings or dilute vinegar. In this way, even those with small vineyards produced enough of a surplus to bring it to market.

Finally, although tallow is frequently mentioned as a medicine, we know from other sources that most cooking was done with olive oil. It was nothing like Greek cooking now, however. Cauldrons were used for boiling. Michel Bats has concluded from his study of Greek ceramics that little frying was done before the fifth century B.C.E. Before that, boiling and braising were the preferred cooking methods.

Rural and Urban Menus

Before looking at differences between rural and urban menus, let us first examine some of the general characteristics of the classic Greek diet. As we have seen, barley and wheat were both staples, barley consumed as *maza,* wheat as bread. The Romans, aware of Greek tastes, referred to the Greeks as "barley eaters." This cereal diet was supplemented by legumes (*ospria*), especially vetch, lentils, and peas. Grapes not only provided wine but also figured as ingredients in many dishes. Wherever the Greeks established colonies, vines were planted, even where the natives did not drink wine.

Olive trees also spread with colonization. Olive oil was used by bathers and athletes as well as in cooking. Greek colonies imported oil if they could not produce enough locally. Marseilles, for example, long imported oil from Betica.

Finally, honey was also a staple, despite the vaunted austerity of the Greek diet. Indeed, the Greeks liked to say that they ate simply because they were poor but free, whereas the Persians paid for their sumptuous ways with their freedom. Witness Pausanias' remarks after he defeated the Persians at Plataea in 479 B.C.E., as reported by Herodotus:

> When Pausanias saw [Xerxes' belongings], fitted out with gold and silver and embroidered hangings, he told Mardonius' bakers and chefs to prepare the kind of meal they had made for Mardonius. They did so, and then, when he saw gold and silver couches with their fine coverings, the gold and silver tables, and the magnificent feast, he was amazed at all the good things spread out there and, for a joke, he told his own servants to prepare a typical Laconian meal. When the food was ready, Pausanias was amused to see the huge difference between the two meals, and he sent for the Greek commanders. Once they were all there, he pointed to the two meals and said, "Men of Greece, my purpose in asking you all here is to show you just how stupid the Persian king is. Look at the way he lives, and then consider that he invaded our country to rob us of our meagre portions!"
> (*Histories* IX.82, trans. Robin Waterfield [Oxford: Oxford University Press, 1998])

COUNTRY FOOD Dwelling types were as diverse as forms of landownership and farm sizes. Fairly substantial villages comprised a number of dwelling units. Aristophanes rather regretfully evokes this rural life in his comedies. Although his verses are not directly descriptive and often have a double meaning, they are useful for comparative purposes. In *The Acharnians,* for example, the hero delivers this speech in the agora: "I dread the city and pine for my village, which never told me to buy charcoal or vinegar or oil, where the word 'buy' was unknown."

In what respects did peasants eat differently from city folk? The two were often contrasted to comic effect. In *The Clouds,* for example, Aristophanes describes a peasant who marries a woman from the city: "I had such a nice country life, lolling about in the shade, sprawling amid the bees, the sheep, and the olives, and then I went and married the niece of Megacles, son of Megacles, me, a country yokel, married to a city girl, a lady with her nose in the air. . . . At my wedding feast, seated beside her, I could smell the cheap wine, the baskets of cheese, the wool—the plenty."

In *Peace* Trygeus, a vine tender, evokes peaceful times in the following passage:

> We do not love battles but love to sit with some drinking friends and comrades by the crackling fire, with dry wood, cut in the height of summer, burning brightly, roast chick peas and chestnuts and make love to the Thracian girl while my wife is having a bath! . . . Come wife, prepare three potfuls of beans, mix them with some wheat and bring us your choicest figs. You, Syra, call Manes here. He cannot attend to his vines today, neither can he hoe—the ground is soaked through. Let a servant go inside and bring out some bottled thrushes and those two chaffinches. We should also have some yoghourt in the house and four chunks of tasty preserved hare. . . . If you do find them, boy, bring three pieces to me and give one to father. Then go and ask Aeschinades for some myrtle—with berries on it, mind you—and on your way, shout for Charisades to come here and drink with us." (1125–65)

The comic writers, city people, were struck by the survival of old recipes using such ingredients as green wheat, grilled *chidra, kondros,* ground seed, and pennyroyal, along with large quantities of milk and cheese. In the country, moreover, it was common for slaves, and probably for many free men of modest means, to drink marc rather than wine.

One of the most significant, and paradoxical, differences between the country and the city was that peasants used less grain than their urban counterparts. Comic writers poked fun at rural folk for eating soups of fava beans or chickpeas and herbs such as squill and mallow.

CITY FOOD During the fourth and fifth centuries B.C.E., cities took on increasing importance. The ideal was for each city to draw all its food supplies from the surrounding countryside, or *chora*. In reality, even Sparta, despite its vast territory, was sometimes obliged to import grain.

The grain market was relatively regulated. Barley and wheat were imported from as far away as Sicily and the Black Sea. Because milling was difficult and time-consuming, it became increasingly common in Athens to sell grain in processed form: barley flour for *maza* and wheat flour for bread. Elsewhere, milling was an activity that involved the whole family, although the Athenian practice began to be copied elsewhere. Middlemen bought grain in the market-place and sold it to millers, bakers, and others. In the fifth century B.C.E. the baker Thearion was celebrated in Athens for the quality of his bread.

In the fourth century the gap between the diets of rich and poor widened. The agora became an important marketplace whose stalls featured not only Greek specialties, such as leeks from Megara and eels from Boeotia, but foods from the entire Mediterranean region.

The market infrastructure remained simple. At the port of Piraeus, baskets and goatskins filled with food and drink were loaded onto the backs of donkeys for transport to their destination. Bakeries were modest operations, with no more equipment than a mortar and pestle, a hand mill, and a small oven. Kitchen equipment remained light enough to be transported easily.

Despite this simple equipment, a fairly elaborate cuisine developed. In the late fifth century B.C.E., as the expansion of the Athenian empire led to greater diversity in the food supply, professional cooks appeared in Athens. These professionals maintained a vigilant watch on the quality of foodstuffs and condiments. They used many ingredients in their cooking, especially vinegar, of which the Greeks were particularly fond. Although they never developed tastes as sophisticated as those of wealthy Romans, they did appreciate variety and were willing to spend more for costly foreign items.

Several different grades of olive oil were used: extra virgin oil made from green olives, oil from the first pressing of black olives, and ordinary oil. Presses were everywhere—in the cities as well as the countryside. The earliest known rotary press, an ancestor of the *trapetum* of Pompeii, was found in the city of Olyntha. Olives were also used in preserves and purees.

Wine deserves a special place of its own. There were many local varieties, especially whites, like the one described by Galen at a later date:

> A watery wine is appropriate for the treatment of fever. This should be white and highly refined. Such wine appears to have none of the qualities of other wines: it is neither dry, nor harsh, nor sweet, nor acidic, nor fragrant. Thus it is the only wine that avoids the harmful effects of both wine and water. Every nation has a few wines of this type. In Italy, for example, weak Sabine wine is given to fever patients.
>
> . . . I myself have found wines of this type in Cilicia, Phoenicia, Palestine, Skyros, and Crete. . . . They are unknown outside the countries in which they are produced, however, for two reasons: small quantities of such wines are available everywhere, and they cannot survive long sea voyages, so that merchants are unable to export them to other places.
>
> ("Commentary on Hipponates")

The availability of imported wines was one benefit of living in the city. Among these were sweet wines, including vintages from Thasos and the *biblinos* of Maronea, made from very ripe, sun-dried grapes to which cooked grape juice, known as *siraion* (Latin *defrutum*), was sometimes added to increase the alcohol content (a process known as chaptalization).

Such luxuries were not within the reach of the poor, even in Athens, where the cost of living was relatively low. For people of limited means, it was more difficult to survive in the city than in the countryside. Aristophanes' last two plays (written sometime between 390 and 380 B.C.E.) describe an impoverished milieu in which boiled fava was a luxury. Beggars ate "not bread of mallow shoots or *maza* but scrawny turnip leaves" (*Plutos,* 545). Not even the turnip—just the leaves! In times of scarcity, the urban poor were the most disadvantaged. In 329 B.C.E., for example, grain prices soared while workers' wages stagnated, so the poor went without *maza* or bread.

Later, in the Hellenistic period, it became common for a wealthy benefactor to supply wheat for a city at a low price or to distribute grain free to the citizens. The political transformation consummated by the Alexandrian conquests actually began in the middle of the fourth century B.C.E. From the sources we know that Greeks were aware of an evolution in their culinary customs.

The comic poet Antiphanes contrasted the old cuisine with that current in his day: "Do you see what things have come to? Bread, garlic, cheese, *maza*—those are healthy foods, but not these salted fish, these lamb chops sprinkled with spices, these sweet confections, and these corrupting pot roasts. And by Zeus, if they aren't simmering cabbage in olive oil and eating it with pureed peas!" (*Apud Athenaeum,* 370e).

It is not only old and new that are contrasted here but also country and city. The difference between the urban and rural diet was obviously greater in the fourth century than it was in Aristophanes' day, during the Peloponnesian wars.

The classical Greek diet was thus both more complex and less static than was once believed. What the Greeks ate clearly contributed to their sense of identity. Although the peculiarities of the Greek diet sharpened the distinction between Greek and barbarian, a diversity of culinary customs gradually developed within Greece itself. Regional differences increased, as did the contrast between the urban and rural diets and the eating habits of rich and poor.

BIBLIOGRAPHY

Amigues, S., ed. and trans. *Théophraste: Recherche sur les plantes.* 3 vols. Paris: Belles Lettres, 1988–93.

———. "L'agriculture de la Grèce antique: Bilan de recherches de la dernière décennie." *Topoi* 4, no. 1 (1994): 69–93.

Amouretti, M.-C. "De l'ethnologie à l'économie: Le coût de l'outillage agricole dans la Grèce antique." *Mélanges Lévêque* 7 (1993): 1–13.

———. "L'originalité technique du vin grec et les traditions de la Méditerranée orientale." In *Münsterische Beiträge zur antiken Handelsgeschichte,* 1996, pp. 1–25.

———. Oléiculture et viticulture dans la Grèce antique." In *Agriculture in Ancient Greece,* ed. B. Wells, pp. 77–86. Stockholm: Svenska Institutet i Athen, 1992.

———. *Le pain et l'huile dans la Grèce antique, de l'araire au moulin.* Paris: Belles Lettres, 1986.

———. "Le remède d'Épiménide, aliment pour le temple, la guerre ou la disette?" In *Eykpata: Mélanges offerts à C. Vatin,* pp. 61–72. Aix: Publications Universitaires de Provence, 1994.

Amouretti, M.-C., and J.-P. Brun, eds. *La production du vin et de l'huile en Méditerranée: Symposium international, Aix-Toulon 1991.* Bulletin de correspondance hellénique, suppl. 26. Paris: Diffusion de Boccard, 1993.

Aristophanes. *Two Plays: Peace and Lysistrata.* Trans. Doros Alastos. London: Zeno, 1953.

Bats, M. *Vaisselle et alimentation à Olbia de Provence (v. 350–v. 50 av. J.-C.): Modèles culturels et catégories céramiques.* Revue archéologique de Narbonnaise, suppl. 18. Paris: Editions du Centre National de la Recherche Scientifique, 1988.

Brunet, M. "Campagnes de la Grèce antique." *Topoi* 2 (1992): 33–51.

Burdford, A. *Land and Labor in the Greek World.* Baltimore: Johns Hopkins University Press, 1993.

Chtcheglov, A. *Polis et chora: Cité et territoire dans le Pont-Euxin.* Trans. Jacqueline Gaudey. Annales Littéraires de l'Université de Besanáon, no. 476. Paris: Diffusion Les Belles Lettres, 1992.

Foxhall, L. "Household, Gender and Property in Classical Athens." *Classical Quarterly* 39 (1989): 22–44.

Foxhall, L., and H. Forbes. "Sitometria: The Role of Grain and Staple Food in Classical Antiquity." *Chiron* 12 (1982): 41–90.

Gallo, L. "Alimentazione e classi sociali: Una nota su orzo e frumento in Grecia." *Opus* 2 (1983): 449–72.

Garnsey, P. *Famine and Food Supply in the Graeco-Roman World: Responses to Risk and Crisis.* Cambridge: Cambridge University Press, 1988.

Herodotus. *The Histories.* Trans. Robin Waterfield. Oxford: Oxford University Press, 1998.

Isager, S., and J. E. Skydsgaard. *Ancient Greek Agriculture: An Introduction.* London: Routledge, 1992.

Jameson, M. H. "Agricultural Labor in Ancient Greece." In *Agriculture in Ancient Greece: Proceedings of the Seventh International Symposium at the Swedish Institute of Athens, 16–17 May 1990,* ed. B. Wells, pp. 135–46. Stockholm, 1992.

Marangou, A. *Vins et amphores de la Crète antique.* Paris, 1996.

Osborne, R. *Classical Landscape with Figures: The Ancient Greek City and Its Countryside.* London: G. Phillip, 1987; Dobbs Ferry, N.Y.: Sheridan House, 1987.

Salviat, F. "Le vin de Rhodes et les plantations du déme d'Amos." In *La production du vin et de l'huile en Méditerranée: Symposium international, Aix-Toulon 1991,* ed. M.-C. Amouretti and J.-P. Brun, pp. 151–62. Bulletin de correspondance hellénique, suppl. 26. Paris: Diffusion de Boccard, 1993.

———. "Vignes et vins anciens de Maronée à Mendé." *Recherches franco-helléniques* 1 (1990): 457–76.

Savonnidi, N. "Wine Making on the Northern Coast of the Black Sea in Antiquity." In *La production du vin et de l'huile en Méditerranée, Symposium international, Aix-Toulon 1991,* ed. M.-C. Amouretti and J.-P. Brun, pp. 227–36. Bulletin de correspondance hellénique, suppl. 26. Paris: Diffusion de Boccard, 1993.

Schmitt-Pantel, P. *La cité au banquet: Histoire des repas publics dans les cités grecques.* Rome: École Française de Rome, 1992.

Sparkes, B. "The Greek Kitchen." *Journal of Hellenic Studies* 82 (1962): 121–37; and 85 (1965): 162–63.

———. "A Pretty Kettle of Fish." In *Food in Antiquity,* ed. J. Wilkins, D. Harvey, and M. Dobson, pp. 150–61. Exeter, England: University of Exeter Press, 1995.

Sparkes, B., and L. Talcott. *Black and Plain Pottery of the 6th, 5th, and 4th Centuries B.C.* 2 vols. Princeton, N.J.: American School of Classical Studies at Athens, 1970.

CHAPTER 7

GREEK MEALS
A Civic Ritual

Pauline Schmitt-Pantel

For the Greeks, the production and consumption of food involved numerous social rituals. There were rituals surrounding labor in the fields and rituals associated with exchange in the village agora and urban marketplace. But mealtime rituals are by far the best known. The rules of eating, which can be gleaned from many sources, constituted a rich and varied symbolic system. The mealtime ritual was intimately intertwined with the production and preparation of the simplest of Greek dishes, the foundation of the entire Greek diet: the barley cake, or *maza*. It was also related to the blood sacrifice, a ritual that preceded any meal in which the meat of domestic animals was consumed. At the heart of every banquet was the consumption of meat and grain that had been ritually consecrated to the gods. Finally, many texts and images focused on what came after eating, when the guests raised their glasses and drank together, the so-called *symposion*.[1]

The sacrifice and *symposion* highlight certain fundamental Greek values, such as egalitarianism and communal spirit, which were basic to Greek social life, discourse, and culture. Scenes painted on ceramics from the classical period illustrate these same values. In what follows, I will focus on just one aspect of Greek dining, the communal banquet. The banquet marked a special moment in man's relationship to the gods, in the relationship of Greek to non-Greek, and in the relationship of citizen to citizen within the Greek city-state. Bearing these three relationships in mind, I propose to trace the history of what turns out to have been a rich and varied cultural tradition.[2]

Banquets of Mortals

In the beginning gods and men sat down together at the same banquet table. "In those days meals were shared, and humans and immortals sat together," Hesiod notes, while Pausanias recalls that in times of yore in Arcadia "men, being just and pious, were guests and dining companions of the gods." But then Prometheus stole fire from the gods, arousing the ire of Zeus. From that moment on, humans, who had been entitled to the juiciest portions of the sacrificial meat, were obliged to work for their daily bread; they were obliged to take wives if they wished to reproduce; and they became mortal. No longer did humans dine with the gods, and if ever they feasted on the same occasion, they did so separately. Actually, it would be more accurate to say that while gods sometimes partook of the feasts of mortals, no mortal would ever again sit at the table of the gods.

On Olympus banqueting was the gods' favorite pastime: "They feasted all day until sunset," Homer tells us, "and ate to their heart's content." The immortals' repast consisted of ambrosia and nectar. Besides eating, the gods also listened to music, talked among themselves, and forgot the woes unleashed upon the world by man. The banquet symbolized the immortals' carefree existence, which the Greeks liked to compare to an endless feast.

By contrast, the human banquet was a symbol of man's mortal condition—that is, his need to work in order to eat. The sacrificial ritual also symbolized continuing communication between the human and the divine, for the gods were symbolically invited to join the human guests at every banquet. In other words, the banquet defined what it meant to be human.

Banquets of Greeks

To the Greeks, the fact that many non-Greek peoples did not have banquets indicated either a total absence of communal existence or a nomadic way of life. Without banquets, civilization was impossible. For example, Strabo (15.1.53–54) tells us that Megasthenes admired many things about the Indians but had one reproach to make: "Now these [Indian customs] tend to sobriety; but no man could approve those other habits of theirs—of always eating alone and of not having one common hour for all for dinner and breakfast instead of eating as each one likes; for eating in the other way is more conducive to a social and civic life."[3]

For Greek writers, shared meals arose at the same time as the laws that constituted communities, as in the days of King Minos in Greece or, to borrow an example from Aristotle, when the Oenotrians abandoned the pastoral way of life and took up agriculture.[4] Banquets and blood sacrifices developed simultaneously, we are told, and both served to strengthen communal bonds. This refrain is common to any number of third- and fourth-century writers, from Plato and Aristotle to Theophrastus and others.

The basic point is clear. Banquets play an important role in the cultural history of the community. Their inception coincides with the institution of communal relations and the constitution of a political identity.

Banquets of Citizens

There were many kinds of banquets in ancient Greece, but all shared certain common features. Every banquet was preceded by a blood sacrifice and comprised an eating phase and a drinking phase (*symposion*). The guests, stretched out on covered sofas alongside movable tables, lay propped up on one arm supported by a cushion under the elbow. A stool next to each sofa was reserved for sandals. Dishes were few in number, and the fingers were used for eating. Scraps were tossed to the ground. Slaves served the food. In private homes dinner was served in a room called the *andron,* indicating that all the guests were men. There were also banquet rooms in temples and other places, but a banquet could be improvised almost anywhere so long as the space was large enough to receive the guests. Indeed, some feasts were held in public squares and gymnasia.

Most banquets were gatherings of families, friends, or adherents to a cult. Few traces of these relatively modest banquets have survived, however, because their simplicity was such that no elaborate protocol was necessary. By contrast, Greek cities typically organized vast public banquets to which some or all members of the civic community were invited. On these occasions edicts adopted by the civic assembly were proclaimed to the population as a whole. Records of these events have survived, so we can say who was invited and who was not, how the authorities viewed these festive gatherings, and what sort of relationship existed between the organization of the banquet and the social structure of the city.

In the archaic period, the guests at civic banquets were the same people who wielded power in the community, namely, the aristocracy. Aristocratic families took turns in organizing these banquets, which fostered solidarity. The expenditure lavished on these meals demonstrated the wealth of each family, a wealth based of course on land.[5] The *aristoi,* or "best people," were represented not only at banquets but also in military expeditions, religious rituals, and possibly also in some sort of communal assembly.

Major banquets were held in connection with civic holidays such as the Panathenian Games or Great Dionysian Festival. The city organized these dinners and in some cases obliged its wealthiest citizens to absorb their cost under the liturgical system. To be named a public host (*hestiator*) was both an honor and a heavy burden. We have little information about the precise nature of these important ceremonial dinners; surviving inscriptions are more concerned with the sacrificial rituals and distribution of meat. The banquets were apparently held in an area near the city gates on the fringes of the Ceramics Quarter. There, a building called the Pompeion contained a series of banquet halls large enough to hold not the entire population of the city but a significant number of magistrates and notables, and outside there was open space for additional temporary structures—huts covered with branches and tents—in which additional guests could dine. By analyzing postholes found at the site, archaeologists have deduced this hierarchical division of the banquet space for public occasions.[6]

The best description we have of the atmosphere of these festive occasions can be found in Euripides' *Ion,* in which we read of the banquet that the eponymous hero stages for the people of Delphi. To be sure, the action is supposed to take place in Delphi, but there can be no doubt that the description draws heavily on Athenian tradition. The banquet is held in a tent whose decor features themes from Athenian myths. Euripides' text is one of the few descriptions of a public banquet in classical Greek literature:

> The boy knew just what to do.
> He set up a framework of poles,
> A hundred feet by a hundred feet—
> Or so they say who measured it—
> Across the whole town square,
> Big enough to shelter everyone in Delphi
> At noon, when the sun's unendurable,
> At evening, when Heaven's lamps burn low.
> . . . .
> Inside the marquee he put tables, gold drinking-cups.
> He sent a crier round the town, tiptoe with eagerness,
> Calling anyone who wanted to join the feast.

Soon the square was full. Garlands, laughter,
Good food and drink. Plenty for everyone.

(Ion 1132–42, 1165–70)

Like Ion, a number of fifth-century Athenian politicians invited fellow citizens to join them in banquets. Indeed, such generosity on the part of leaders as different as Cimon, Nicias, and Alcibiades was so appreciated by the citizens of Athens that a democrat like Pericles, who opposed such patronage by the wealthy as a potential threat to democracy, did what he could to end it. Although political change affected the nature of Greek banqueting, the feasts themselves remained a persistent feature of public generosity in Greece; the *euergetes,* or benefactors, of the Hellenistic and Roman periods derive from this tradition.

These *euergetes* paid for civic banquets, for which they were thanked by public assemblies. Because these proclamations of gratitude were inscribed in stone, we possess detailed information about these events. Scrupulously precise accounts have been found in the temple at Delos, for instance. Not only was the quantity of meat prescribed for each guest, but so was the way the meat was to be cooked, whether grilled on a spit or boiled in a cauldron. The type and amount of wine to be served were also indicated. The menu varied with the occasion. At Priene, for instance, a benefactor offered his guests a light meal in his home to mark the beginning of one holiday, but that evening there was a genuine banquet.[7] Although the men could look forward to a glass of old wine, women, who in an exception to the general rule were invited on this occasion, were offered only sweet wine or barely fermented grape juice. Sometimes banquet followed banquet for several days running, although it is difficult to say whether this was a way of accommodating the entire population in batches or whether everyone attended each and every dinner.

As a general rule, banquet invitations in the classical period went to men of quality, although one does begin to see hesitant signs of change. Except for rare occasions, women, children, and slaves were excluded. Guests were generally citizens, especially prominent citizens. In some cities, however, one does find invitations being issued at certain times to freemen who were not citizens. The higher their status, the more likely they were to be invited. Resident aliens were more likely to receive invitations than transients or residents of nearby cities. Romans, increasingly a presence in the Greek world, crop up on guest lists with increasing frequency.

NOTES

1. See Marcel Detienne and Jean-Pierre Vernant, eds., *La cuisine du sacrifice en pays grec* (Paris: Gallimard, 1979), with a bibliography by J. Svenbro.

2. For further information, see Pauline Schmitt-Pantel, *La cité au banquet* (Rome: École Française de Rome, 1992).

3. Strabo, *Geographia* XV.1.53–54.

4. Aristotle, *Politics,* VII.1329b.

5. E. Stein-Holkeskamp, *Adelskultur und Polisgesellschaft* (Stuttgart, 1989).

6. W. Hoepfner, *Das Pompeion und seine Nachfolgerbauten* (Berlin: De Gruyter, 1976).

7. I *Priene,* 108, 109, 111.

CHAPTER 8

The CULTURE *of the* SYMPOSIUM

Massimo Vetta

The beginnings of the symposium can be traced back to the dawning of the archaic period. The Homeric poems, whose composition spans various periods of the Greek Middle Ages, recount not only meetings in which people both eat and drink but also occasions on which wine drinking is a distinct activity following the meal. In the first book of the *Iliad* (457–76), after the mass sacrifice in Apollo's honor to celebrate the restitution of Chryseis to her father and the subsequent banquet, the young men fill their mixing bowls, or kraters, with wine and pass them around. Then, after singing hymns of praise, they fall asleep by the stern cables. This episode is no less significant for the fact that it follows a sacrifice and takes place in the open. In Homer's world, councils of war overlapped with commensality and entertainment, often enlivened by storytelling and heroic songs accompanied on the lyre.

Unlike in later phases of Greek history, the Homeric banquet and its continuation after the tables had been cleared was an expression of hierarchy. The participants consumed food provided by the mass of soldiers, celebrated a right to sit at the table acquired through their prowess in combat, and recognized a higher *kratos* than that of the others. Commensality was a private spectacle compared with the public one offered on the battlefield to fellow warriors; it was a representation of wisdom and rhetorical ability.

There is clear evidence of the fact that wine drinking took place as a separate activity in many places. In the Homeric world, however, greater social value is attributed to the consumption of food and the time devoted to it. Although allusions seem to be made to archaic symposia, the Homeric feast encompasses behavior and situations that would be anomalous at a later date. When the contemporaries of Archilochus listened to the rhapsodist tell of the banquet at which the Phaeacians welcome Odysseus, they were entertained by a combination of events that was already extraneous to their culture (*Od*.VII.182–85). Insufficient importance has been given to the fact that Odysseus, the guest, eats while the others drink to Zeus and, liberally, to one another, and that Odysseus himself describes his ideal notion of entertainment, saying that the best that life can offer is for the bard to entertain the banqueters from the very beginning of the meal (IX.2–11).

The term *symposion* appears for the first time in the work of Alcaeus, although the practice to which it refers was already common in the islands and Asia Minor at the beginning of the seventh century B.C.E. In this period, unlike in the late Greek Middle Ages, entertainment based on wine drinking alone was codified to the extent that it had its own genre of monodic poetry. The sources are more or less contemporary with the oriental practice of reclining on a *kline* rather than sitting. From its very first appearance, the symposium can be defined by certain constants to which other ingredients were sometimes added. It was a meeting of men that only took place following a meal. It had a ritual introduction with libations to the gods and the choral singing of the paean. It was not an everyday event but was linked to private or civic celebrations. The participants were related in various ways, rarely based merely on family ties, sharing the same lifestyle and behaving according to norms that they regarded as specific to their ethnic group.

Among its other ingredients, the most frequent and significant was poetry. Apart from the extensive but relatively unvaried data provided by vase paintings, we can understand much of the evolution of the symposium from the archaic age to the Hellenistic age thanks to the uninterrupted and invaluable information provided by poetry. Other important ingredients were games, courtship, the education of youths, and the continuation of the symposium in the form of the *komos,* when the participants left the dining room as a group.

Up to the rapid transformations that took place as a result of the Peloponnesian wars, the symposium in this form was the most significant moment of social aggregation in Greek culture. It was based on membership of the aristocracy, on a common intellectual and poetic culture, and on a shared vision of the ways and means of political struggle. The enduring value of the symposium was that it was a private expression of a harmonious commingling of religious significance, pragmatic function, and simple pleasure. Wine established contact with Dionysius, although at a later date the ritual also involved Zeus, Apollo, and other divinities, depending on the specific context. The symposium was an occasion for libations and hymns, at first traditional and later improvised by those present. Compared with the solemn sacrifices of public festivities, it was a private moment of religious symbolism based on a circumscribed relationship with the gods. Libation was at times accompanied by a vow (*synomosia*), which transformed the group of drinkers into a fraternity.

Preceded, as we have seen, by the commensality of Homer, which had its own rules, the Hellenic symposium was primarily an *ethical* experience inspired by the need to create an ideal emotional condition. The basic principle of being together was a recurrent theme in poetry (which accurately reflected changing social circumstances) and survived unaltered to the imperial age. *Hesychia* excluded conflict, suspended material acts, and invoked the serenity needed to establish a correct relationship with the gods. *Euphrosyne,* on the other hand, expressed a state of delight produced by wine and by the pleasure of the occasion, generating the appropriate mood for constructive dialogue and the appreciation of poetry. The gradual effect of wine, producing euphoria, a sense of unusual lucidity, and then oblivion, accompanied the symposium as it moved from seriousness to heightened perception to the free play of courtship and recreation.

Throughout the archaic period, meeting around the krater was a frequently repeated identification ritual, a liturgy of brotherhood without hierarchies, the narration of a dialectic between the political ideal of a group and the actual life of the city. Often illustrated on vases, the krater occupied a central position to symbolize equality and equilibrium (*dike*). It structured the space of the *andron*, the room in which the symposium was held, just as the statue of a god organized the emblematic spaces of the city. Equidistance was the essence in these cases, as in others; it governed the position of Homer's warriors around the booty of war, of hunters who meted out the centrally placed prey into equal parts, and of participants in a sacrifice who divided up the meat of the victim into equal parts.

The krater, in which wine and water were mixed in varying degrees, was specifically Hellenic. The Greeks, who drank undiluted wine only on rare occasions, regarded the mixing of wine as an act that distinguished them from barbarians, uniting those who practiced it and excluding others. A well-known verse by Anacreon (fr. 33 G.) compares these opposed concepts. The symposium was a symbol of Greek hospitality. Since foreigners had both to learn and to make themselves known, the banquet was a moment for memory, knowledge, and truth. Each guest brought as a gift his own story, his family history, and often his poetry. He committed himself to welcoming in his own house at a later date all those who had listened to him around the krater. Symbolizing both integration and exclusion, hospitality was the means by which the fraternity expressed itself politically, often in a way that was different from, and even antithetical to, official city policy. For the foreign guest, the ceremony surrounding the drinking of wine was a test. Despite being an outsider until that moment, he had to show that he was capable of respecting the traditional *kosmos,* or worldview.

The vision that the Greeks had of the symposium complemented their vision of the hunt and of war. For archaic man, the use of arms and resting after meals represented constructive inaction following activity. This idea already existed for Homer, and its finest example can be found in the fourth book of the *Iliad* (231–64). Inspecting the Greek army, Agamemnon pauses before Idomeneus. He praises him highly, declaring that he honors him both in battle and at the feast, where the wine of honor is mixed with that of kings. To symbolize Achilles' withdrawal from the war following the embassy's visit, Homer depicts him as being involved in something akin to a symposium, entertaining his companion, Patroclus, with a hymn to heroic deeds.

Later, Greek lyric poetry established a convention according to which meetings involving wine and the activity of war were counterposed. War itself, even tales of war, became inappropriate themes in the context of symposial *euphrosyne.* Wine provided a way of forgetting war and death. The importance of this correlation is testified by numerous vase paintings. In a red figure cup by the Scheurleer painter, datable to the end of the sixth century B.C.E. (Louvre G 70), a banqueter rides a leather bottle and plays a *rhyton* as if it were a trumpet. This image parodies the warlike gesture depicted on the other side of the cup. A banquet scene on an Attic *dinos* is placed beside that of a battle and a group of ephebes on horseback (Louvre E 876).

Although the inspiration behind the symposium appears to be the desire to constitute a *kosmos* and partake in a constructive and yet moderately ludic ritual, the reality of these meetings around the krater was also one of repeated transgression. Poetry says little of this aspect. Like other festivities, the ceremony of wine often transformed itself into an occasion for intemperance and excess. The image of the banquet interrupted by debauchery and violence was a frequent motif in myth and epic. A common theme in vase painting stressed the origins of the war between the Centaurs and the Lapiths, triggered by the outrageous drunkenness of Eurytion in the halls of Pirithous (*Od.* XXI.295–304).

The symposium was also the place in which conflict took the form of verbal skirmish. There is evidence from vase painting, albeit slight, of the existence of symposia without *hesychia,* or poetry, in which the effect of wine was welcomed simply to give free rein to competitiveness and erotic play. However, when drinking cups show scenes of unruliness, they are transposed into the lawless world of the satyrs, the iconography of which is based on the uncontrolled use of wine. In contrast to the world of culture represented by the symposium, the ambiguous court of Dionysius symbolized the barbaric, nonceremonial use of wine. Groups of ithyphallic satyrs were often the protagonists of an intemperate and fantastic symposial eros, apparently far removed from the nonviolent seduction that involved adults and adolescents. It seems clear that courtship around the krater was unknown during the Greek Middle Ages. The handmaids of Odysseus joined Penelope's suitors only after the banquet, when the men had gone to their beds (*Od.* XX.6–8, XXII.461–64).

Ceremony and History

Throughout its long history, the ceremony surrounding the drinking of wine followed an almost unchanging code of prescriptions that governed the objects used and the order in which events took place. If a Milesian nobleman of the seventh century B.C.E. had found himself at an Attic banquet held by Cimon, he would not have felt out of place. The uninterrupted testimony of vase paintings has provided us with an almost complete record of the ceremony.

Although the event was occasionally, particularly in the archaic period, held outside (for example, *Il.* I.467–74; Hes. *Op.* 688–96), those symposia that were not held in the nobleman's or tyrant's dining hall took place either in tents set up in the field or in public buildings, above all temples. An idea of the architecture of these places can be obtained by looking at the rooms annexed to large sanctuaries discovered in various parts of Greece, since sanctuaries were among the places used for the sacrificial meal preceding the symposium. They were small rooms, holding an average of seven *klinai,* one on the wall to the right of the door, which appears to have been placed off center. The first *kline* on the right was regarded as the place of honor. The cup was traditionally passed from left to right, and banqueters took turns singing following the same order. The reason for the meeting could be entirely private, such as a wedding, the presence of a guest, or a family event, or linked to a public occasion, such as victory in the games, a political appointment, or a civic celebration. Frequently, for fraternity symposia the only reason was the need to make a political decision.

The separation between the preliminary phase devoted to eating and the symposium itself was marked by the fact that the tables were cleared, the floor was purified, and the banqueters, after washing their hands, received garlands for their heads, chests, and cups. The crown, a symbol of initiation, was the physical sign of membership representing the link created by drinking together. As in the theater, once the scene had been set, the sacred phase of the meeting could begin. It can be imagined that this was marked by silence, or *euphemia,* which predisposed those present to make contact with the gods. Before mixing water and wine in the krater, each banqueter received a cup of undiluted wine from which to pour a few drops in honor of the good spirit (*agathos daimon*). This religious act formalized a communal link and sealed an eternal bond. Wine and water were mixed according to proportions dictated by the type of entertainment that would take place (Plu. *Quaest. conv.* 657d). The almost barbaric mixing of two parts of wine to one of water, mentioned by Alcaeus, must have been very rare and was certainly intended for an exceptional occasion (fr. 346 V.). A krater in which equal parts of water and wine had been poured was considered dangerous and bound to lead to drunkenness in a very short time. Such a mixture was reserved for symposia in which entertainment was more important than serious matters, as repeatedly mentioned by playwrights. Less alcoholic mixtures, of two or three parts of water to one of wine, were recommended by Hesiod (*Op.* 696) and regarded by Plutarch as the mixture of perfect balance.

Before the servants started mixing the wine, the symposiarch was appointed. Apart from the distinction between young and old men, this is the only sign of hierarchy to be found in symposia, and it is not clear when the practice began. The position of symposiarch did not necessarily reflect official power, indicating the independence of the meeting from the rules governing public life. The symposiarch established the ratio of wine to water, the number of kraters to set out, and the forms of entertainment to amuse the group. He was the only person who could violate the rules of equality, obliging some to drink more than others or to demonstrate their abilities.

Once the wine had been prepared, the servants filled the cups from a jug (*oinochoe*) or ladle. With the wine from the first krater, libations were made to Zeus and the Olympic family. The second was dedicated to the spirits of heroes, while the third was drunk in honor of Zeus Soter. The sacrificial part of the feast was accompanied by a double flute and the choral singing of a paean, which could be followed by poetry or the recital of brief sections of hymns to those divinities that had some connection with the purposes of the meeting. After this liturgical introduction, the entertainment began, its form depending on the reason behind the symposium. Appetizers were then served to stimulate the thirst—cheeses and different types of bread (*traghemata*) can be seen on archaic vases and are mentioned on numerous occasions by playwrights (Ath. XIV.640c–658). In its later, more festive part, known as the *komos,* the symposium often moved out into the streets. The krater was carried outside by the dancing participants in a drunken parade, more or less unruly, accompanied by the flautist. Scenes of this type can be seen on vases from the end of the fifth century B.C.E. on.

The immutable nature of the rite was accompanied by an evolution in the function and symbolic values of the symposium. This can only be reconstructed in approximate terms. Indeed, on the same evening in the same city, various symposia could coexist to welcome a guest, celebrate a family event, or conspire politically—not to speak of symposia in which these three functions were fulfilled simultaneously.

The Symposium and Poetry

Until the beginning of the Hellenistic age, much of the significance of the symposium derived from the presence of poetry, which provided the ceremony with a constantly renewed relationship to tradition. The Homeric hero waited for the evening, when the bard would release the poetic spell that transformed his heroic deeds into myth.

Most monodic lyric poetry, including elegies and iambics, was uniquely destined for symposia. As well as being a unique opportunity for composition, the symposium also provided a context in which specific aspects of the Greek poetic heritage were preserved until the arrival of the Alexandrian scholars. Flute and kithara players were a constant feature in the iconography, as was the banqueter who sang with a cup in his hand. The musical instruments appear on the walls as a symbol of an indissoluble bond between the seduction of wine and the fascination of images and sounds. The *megaron* of Odysseus and the court of Alcinous show that heroic and mythological kithara playing was the earliest lyric genre practiced during banquets. The sung epic then became the object of an interesting phenomenon in which poetry had a twofold use. In archaic Sparta, during the reign of Terpander, pieces composed for accompaniment by the kithara or flute in musical contests were later reused for festive banquets. Private performances by poets who competed in the most important pan-Hellenic and local competitions were a common feature in the age of Stesichorus.

Apart from providing an opportunity for listening to professional bards, the symposium allowed banqueters to improvise their own poetry according to the mood of the moment. The opening ritual was followed by general conversation, and personal stories readily became the subject for song. One of the most delightful fragments by Alcaeus, a welcoming song for the return of his brother Antimenides from the East, transformed the story of survival into poetry, just as the Homeric bards had done for guests (fr. 350 V.). Reciting poetry was an important sign of equality within the group. It united its members to the exclusion of others and expressed a communal act of creation. According to the testimony of Dicaearchus and Aristoxenus, one meaning of the term *skolion* was the kind of poetry that the most skilled banqueters offered to the symposium, indicating whose turn it was to sing by passing a twig of myrtle among themselves. The term derives from the irregular path taken by the twig, which traced an ideal line among the best singers. The best contributions stayed in the memory of those present, becoming part of their tradition. Athenaeus preserved a collection of twenty-five anonymous examples of these scolions from archaic and classical Attica, and they still possessed political relevance a century after their composition.

Ever since the dawning of oral epic poetry, the banquet was the exclusive site for verse improvisation. A precious collection of fragments of extemporaneous verse, often anonymous, can be found in the elegiac anthology attributed to Theognis. Containing material that by and large can be dated to the sixth century B.C.E., it contains the most genuine examples of sympotic verse in our possession. In the symposium of Theognis, any of the banqueters could take the myrtle twig from the most skilled performer among the group, according to a variable practice of poetic improvisation. The anthology provides traces of a kind of competitive improvisation that took the form of a "chain" of poetic interventions on a single theme. An opening utterance could stimulate others by a process of accumulation or correction (*metapoiesis*), often reusing the same verbal material. The opening, or the appropriate addition, could be a quotation from well-known poets; this explains the presence in the anthology of verses by Mimnermus, Solon, and Tyrtaeus.

In addition to the elegiac symposium, inspired by tradition and commemoration, there existed—and at times even coexisted—the iambic symposium, devoted to invective and the playful, unruly telling of stories. The iamb and epic poetry were linked to burlesque improvisations at agricultural feasts in honor of Demeter and Hermes. For those who listened to Archilochus and Hipponax, iambic poetry was none other than the channeling of the village feast into the symposium. At the end of the open-air celebrations, during which grotesque and satirical figures were presented, the meeting of a few friends represented both the offshoot and reflection of the earlier celebration. It was the time for conjuring up imaginary presences, giving voice to absent friends, and creating an event that seemed to prefigure a theatrical performance.

Between the sixth and fifth centuries B.C.E., the great poetry of professionals such as Ibycus, Anacreon, Simonides, Pindar, and Bacchylides was linked to the symposia of tyrants or the richer aristocratic *ghene*. The poet was a resident of the court and created poems for particular celebrations. He possessed an inexhaustible stock of images to be used in describing the multitude of gestures, fantasies, and desires of those present at the banquet. Poems to celebrate great sports victories were closely linked to banquets in the later archaic period. There must have been an extraordinary atmosphere in those symposia held on the very night of the competition when the contemporaries of the athlete celebrated his victory in a tent or the halls of a sanctuary. The epinicia of Pindar and Bacchylides were certainly composed as poems for banquets to follow up those that had been heard by the entire city.

In the Athens of Pericles and Critias, the poetic repertoire continued to be interwoven with the splendid creations of sympotic improvisation. Dionisios, Euenus of Paros, Ion of Chios, and Critias himself invented a new elegiac language based on the imaginative metaphorization of entertainment based on wine. With the fourth century, the function of spectacle prevailed, and the banquet became the occasion for listening to poetry that had originally been intended for other ends. Gradually, theater took over: professional actors were engaged to sing monodies and to recite particularly significant monologues and even whole scenes. The most gifted among the banqueters often contributed to this kind of performance. The repertoire included the great fifth-century tragedies, with a preference for Euripides and, later, Menander. According to Plutarch, the plays of Menander were so well suited to the mood of the symposium that one could more easily do without wine than without the writer's verses (*Quaest. conv.* 712b–e). Alexandrians introduced mime and other kinds of short poetry suitable for recitation, such as the *Idylls* of Theocritus.

By this time, however, banquets without any poetry at all had become common. In intellectual and philosophical circles, committed discussion, rhetoric, history, and sophistry took place to the accompaniment of wine. Plato provides the earliest evidence for phenomena of this kind. The habit of simple singing continued in more backward outlying regions and among the lower classes, as Polybius testifies, in his lifetime, in Arcadia; two papyrus fragments provide textual support for this (IV.20, 8 ff.; *P. Berol. inv.* 13270; *P. Teb.* 1). As time passed, reading together began to predominate. For this practice, sites other than the symposium became established. These were gymnasia, libraries, and the seats of philosophical schools.

BIBLIOGRAPHY

Bowie, E. L. "Early Greek Elegy, Symposium, and Public Festival." *Journal of Hellenic Studies* 106 (1986): 13–35.

Dentzer, J.-M. *Le motif du banquet couché dans le Proche-Orient et le monde grec du VIIème siècle avant J.-C.* Paris: Diffusion de Boccard, 1982.

Fabian, K., E. Pellizer, and G. Tedeschi, eds. *Oinepa teuche: Studi triestini di poesia conviviale.* Culture Antiche, Studi e testi, no. 3. Alessandria: Edizioni dell'orso, 1991.

Figueira, T. "Mess Contributions and Subsistence at Sparta." *Transactions of the American Philological Association* 114 (1984): 87–109.

Fisher, N. R. E. "Drink, Hybris, and the Promotion of Harmony." In *Classical Sparta: Techniques behind Her Success*, ed. A. Powell, pp. 26–50. London: Routledge, 1989.

Gentili, B. *Poesia e pubblico nella Grecia antica*. Rome, 1995. [*Poetry and Its Public in Ancient Greece: From Homer to the Fifth Century*. Trans. A. Thomas Cole. Baltimore: Johns Hopkins University Press, 1990.]

Lissarrague, F. *Immaginario del simposio greco*. Rome, 1989.

Lombardo, M. "Pratiche di commensalità e forme di organizzazione sociale nel mondo greco: 'Symposia' e 'syssitia' " *Annali della Scuola Normale Superiore di Pisa* 18 (1988): 263–86.

Murray, O. "Symposion and Männerbund." In *Concilium Eirene XVI: Proceedings of the 16th International Eirene Conference*, ed. P. Oliva and A. Frolíková, 1:47–52. Prague: Kabinet Pro Studia Recká, Rímská a Latinská CSAV, 1983.

Murray, O., ed. *Sympotica: A Symposium on the Symposion*. New York: Oxford University Press, 1990.

Murray, O., and E. Tecusan, eds. *In vino veritas*. London: British School at Rome/American Academy at Rome, 1995.

Pretagostini, R. "Anacr. 33 Gent. = 366 P: Due modalità simposiali a confronto." *Quaderni Urbinati di Cultura Classica* 10 (1982): 47–55.

Rossi, L. E. "Feste religiose e letteratura: Stesicoro o dell'epica alternativa." *Orpheus* 4 (1983): 5–31.

Schmitt-Pantel, P. *La cité au banquet: Histoire des repas publics dans les cités grecques*. Rome: École Française de Rome, 1992.

Slater, W. J., ed. *Dining in a Classical Context*. Ann Arbor: University of Michigan Press, 1991.

Tedeschi, G. "Solone e lo spazio della comunicazione elegiaca." *Quaderni Urbinati di Cultura Classica* 10 (1982): 33–46.

Vetta, M. "Identificazione di un caso di catena simposiale nel 'corpus' teognideo." In *Lirica greca da Archiloco a Elitis: Studi in onore di F. M. Pontani*, pp. 113–26. Padua: Liviana, 1984.

———. "Il simposio: La monodia e il giambo." In *Lo spazio letterario della Grecia antica*, 1:177–218. Rome, 1992.

———. "Poesia e simposio." *Rivista di Filologia e di Istruzione Classica* 109 (1981): 483–95.

Vetta, M., ed. *Poesia e simposio nella Grecia antica: Guida storica e critica*. Universale Laterza, no. 621. Rome: Laterza, 1983.

Vickers, M. *Greek Symposia*. London: Joint Association of Classical Teachers, [1978].

CHAPTER 9

The DIET *of the* ETRUSCANS

Giuseppe Sassatelli

"The Tyrrhenians prepare sumptuous repasts twice a day on carpets of many colors and with silver goblets of all kinds, and a crowd of beautiful slaves, dressed in precious garments." This is how the philosopher Poseidonius of Apamea described the Etruscans. Poseidonius had traveled extensively in the West, albeit at a relatively late date—the second and first centuries B.C.E. His presentation of Etruscan dining habits has reached us in the work of Athenaeus (IV.153c), an even later writer and sworn enemy of luxury, and is echoed by Diodorus Siculus (V.40) in a longer passage. The latter description of the two main meals of the Etruscan day is part of a series of observations on the almost unlimited fertility of Etruria. Diodorus suggests that this was a contributing factor to the decadence of the Etruscan people. In the view of these, and other, ancient writers, the Etruscans' fondness for good living, partly the result of the abundance and quality of agricultural produce, had led to their diminished vigor as a race.

Writing in the first century B.C.E., an era in which the Etruscan civilization had already disappeared, all Poseidonius and Diodorus could do was to repeat a series of already historical clichés regarding the self-indulgence and excess of the Etruscan people, clichés that were dear to such Greek writers as Aristotle and Theopompus. Traditionally, the Etruscans had always been considered a people devoted to unbridled luxury and pleasure and were thus associated with other "barbarian" peoples, especially those in the East.

Poseidonius' description of the banquet stressed not only the sumptuousness of the surroundings and the finery of the slaves' attire but also the fact that such banquets took place twice a day. This becomes relevant if one considers the fact that the Romans (like the Greeks) had only one proper meal a day. After breakfast (*ientaculum*), the Romans had *prandium*, which was normally eaten standing up and without tables or utensils (that is, *sine mensa*). The *coena,* which started in the early afternoon, was the one real meal of the day.

Unlike the Greeks and Romans, no Etruscan historian provides us with information on the features of the Etruscan diet. The very scant information offered by Greek and Latin writers pertains almost exclusively to agriculture and the breeding of animals, whose produce must inevitably have provided the basic Etruscan diet. Only a small part of this information touches on food and its preparation. Archaeology, however, has added more pieces to the picture. Pollen and the remains of animals and plants allow us to make assumptions regarding which animals were eaten, which plants were grown, and, therefore, which products generally reached the table.

Cereals

Greek and Latin writers all agreed that Etruria was famous for the high quality and quantity of its agricultural produce when compared with the rest of ancient Italy, including Latium, and that Etruscan agriculture was highly advanced.

This is exemplified in a famous passage by Livy (XXVIII.45) that gives a list of foodstuffs provided by Etruscan cities to Scipio for his African expedition. Despite the blows received during the recent Roman conquest, the Etruscan cities were able to offer a wide range of foods, especially *frumentum,* for the provisions of the Roman army. The picture that emerges is one of an Etruria that is still at its peak in this type of production, confirmed by other sources, such as Varro in a well-known passage from *De re rustica* (I.44.1). In a list of rules for sowing, in which he gives the amount of seed required to produce a certain yield, Varro says that in some areas the yield can be tenfold, while in other areas, such as parts of Etruria (*in Etruriae locis aliquot*), it can be up to fifteenfold.

The greater quantity and higher quality of cereals depended not only on the fertility of the soil but also on the more advanced tools and techniques possessed by the Etruscans. An original crop system had been used very early on in Etruria. This was based on a two-year crop rotation: one year of growing cereal and one year during which the field could be used for grazing or growing pulses. This system, which enriched the land for the following year's cereal crop by providing the soil with nitrogen, had important repercussions on the social structure of the groups that adopted it. Earlier, more rudimentary techniques such as burning the stubble after harvest or leaving the land to grass had been linked to the collective ownership of land. The introduction of two-year crop rotation represented an important advance in the rationalization of agriculture, with significant results in terms of yields. It also laid the foundations for new forms of land use and production relations based on a regime of defined individual ownership.

Pulses

Pulses played an important part in the human diet as well as being used at times for animals. Broad beans and chickpeas, in particular, were ground into flour, although they were often eaten boiled as well according to Pliny (XVIII.118), who mentions broad bean soup (*puls fabata*) among the uses of this type of bean.

In the Etruscan diet carbohydrates were provided by cereals, especially different varieties of wheat, and vegetable protein by pulses, which, when dried, were a better source of protein than meat. This dietary balance between carbohydrate and protein perfectly reflected the two-crop rotation system in the fields, where cereals were grown alternately with pulses.

Olives

Although olive-based products had less impact on the everyday diet, they played a significant role in the economy of the various Etruscan centers, especially in the south, where surpluses were used for trade. Nonetheless, there is evidence that olives were eaten. Olives stored in brine in Etruscan amphorae were found in the wreck of the *Giglio*, dated 600 B.C.E. In the Tomb of the Olives in Caere (575–550 B.C.E.), olive pits, considered an offering to the dead, have been found. Cato (*Agr. Orig.* 58) mentions olives among the foods to be supplied to slaves and describes them as a good source of protein.

Animal Breeding and Hunting

It is clear that most of the protein in the Etruscan diet came from pulses. Nevertheless, the use of meat protein and fats is indicated by evidence of animal breeding and, to a lesser degree, of hunting.

Once again, a significant number of written sources testify to these practices, although most of the evidence comes from archaeological discoveries that are richer and more revealing than those regarding vegetable remains. The first fact to emerge clearly from the written sources is the absolute predominance of pigs (Polyb. XII.4). Unlike cows and sheep, pigs were bred exclusively for food. Among other things, pigs were ideally suited to the geography of Etruria, whose many woods and oak groves provided them with acorns.

There is less specific information regarding the breeding of sheep and goats. According to certain sources, these were raised in large numbers in Pisa and Caere (Lycoph. *Alex.* X.4.7–8) and in the country of the Volsinii (Plin. *Ep.*VIII.20). Apart from providing meat, both sheep and goats gave wool, milk, and other dairy products such as cheese. Some types of Etruscan cheese were very famous. The two-crop rotation system encouraged the coexistence of arable and livestock farming on the same *fundus,* although it was not always easy to maintain a balance between these two activities. This was particularly true in the case of goats, whose grazing habits devastated the fields.

Cattle raising was common but insignificant in terms of the Etruscan diet since oxen were bred to plough the fields and do similar work.

The fact that hens were raised in large numbers, primarily for their eggs, can be seen from banqueting scenes in many tomb paintings where they appear alongside other domestic animals such as dogs, cats, ducks, geese, pigeons, blackbirds, and partridges. Many of these were almost certainly bred to be eaten.

Hunting was an eminently aristocratic activity and, as such, was "disinterested and prestigious" (Milet, *Hecatée*). Nonetheless, it had concrete—albeit limited—repercussions on the Etruscan diet.

Etruria, which was full of game such as wild boar, deer, hare, and marsh fowl, was ideally suited to hunting. The Etruscans were famous for their hunting skills, using nets, weapons like swords, javelins, and spears, or more specialized tools such as hare snares, as is testified by numerous paintings. The most commonly hunted animal was the wild boar, although deer, wild goat, hare, and—more rarely—fox were also pursued. Finally, the Etruscans organized bird hunts, particularly for marsh fowl (Strabo V.2.9), which they captured using nets or slings, as we can see in the Tomb of Hunting and Fishing in Tarquinia.

Fishing

Fishing was a well-organized activity, to judge from the archaeological remains of fairly large fish and of crustaceans (limpets, mussels, scallops, and razor fish). How-

ever, although there is no doubt that fishing played an important role in the Etruscan diet, evidence for this conjecture is scarce.

Cooking and Banquets

The picture of the main vegetable and animal resources used by Etruscans in their
diet is thus fairly clear. All our information about the characteristics of food and its
preparation, however, comes from written sources since—despite the existence of
many paintings of banquet scenes—they hardly ever provide us with information
about this aspect of the Etruscan diet.

In the first place, the banquet was a ceremonial event with numerous ideological and social meanings, and representations of the event rarely had a purely narrative function. In the second place, the scenes represented are not real banquets
during which food was eaten (*deipnos*), but symposia, convivial meetings that
could even coincide with the final part of the *deipnos,* in which the banqueters
drank wine to the accompaniment of music and dancing.

Archaeology has revealed a substantial number of utensils used in the preparation of food: small ovens, *foculi,* skewers, grates, various types of containers and
pans, cheese graters, funnels and filters for wine, meat knives, and mortars and pestles. Some of these utensils can also be seen in the stuccoes in the Tomb of the Reliefs in Tarquinia, which represented the interior of a sumptuous aristocratic home
of the fourth century B.C.E.

But the most complete representation of a banquet, including the various
phases of preparation, can be found in the Golini I Tomb in Orvieto, dating from
the first half of the fourth century B.C.E. The tomb belonged to a powerful family
of the late rural aristocracy that had left the town and invested its resources in the
countryside. The interior of the tomb is divided into two parts by a wall. In the
space to the right, a series of paintings show the preparations for a banquet. On
the entrance wall we can see the slaughtered animals, both raised and hunted,
ready to be cooked and hanging from hooks in the open air: an entire quartered
ox, with its head on the ground beneath it, a roe deer, a brace of small birds, and
another brace of larger birds. On the left wall someone is cutting the meat into
pieces with a kind of cleaver, and four tables have been laid and are ready to be
taken into the nearby banqueting hall. Each table holds two portions of flatcakes
(one for each banqueter on the same triclinium), two bunches of grapes, some
eggs, and, at its center, a pomegranate. Beside the tables, a servant is accompanying
on a double flute the work of his companions, particularly that of one figure who

is using two pestles to crush some sort of vegetable in a mortar with a spout. The act of crushing not only cereals or pulses but also seeds, herbs, and spices was a basic element in the preparation of condiments for meat (Apicius V.9.1; VIII.1). On the far wall, a man is putting a kind of frying pan onto the fire, watched closely by another figure who seems to be supervising the entire organization of the banquet. On the dividing wall, other people work busily around a table bearing containers of all types and sizes, some for liquids and some for solids. The latter are full of a yellowish substance that appears to be *puls*.

The food and drink that had been prepared with such care was then taken into the nearby banqueting hall where the tomb's owner, his illustrious guests or his ancestors (all with *cursus honorum*), and the underworld divinities of Hades and Persephone would soon be taking part in the sumptuous banquet.

The high rank of the participants, the fine quality of the banquet and the way in which it was conducted, and the perfect organization of its preparation all contributed equally to exalt the rich way of life enjoyed by this small rural aristocratic community in the countryside near Orvieto, a wealth that was also reflected in their diet.

BIBLIOGRAPHY

Ampolo, C. "Le condizioni materiali della produzione: Agricoltura e paesaggio agrario." In *La formazione della città nel Lazio, Dialoghi di Archeologia,* special issue 3 (1980): 15–16.

Barbieri, G. "On Meat." In *L'alimentazione nel mondo antico: Gli Etruschi,* pp. 49–53. Catalogue. Rome: Istituto Poligrafico e Zecca dello Stato, [1987].

Blanck, H., and G. Proietti. *La Tomba dei Rilievi di Cerveteri.* Studi di Archeologia, no. 1. Rome: De Luca, 1986.

Camporeale, G. *La caccia in Etruria.* Rome: G. Bretschneider, 1984.

Cristofani, M. "Il banchetto." In *L'alimentazione nel mondo antico: Gli Etruschi,* pp. 59–93. Catalogue. Rome: Istituto Poligrafico e Zecca dello Stato, [1987].

———. "Duo sunt liquores." In *L'alimentazione nel mondo antico: Gli Etruschi,* pp. 37–40. Catalogue. Rome: Istituto Poligrafico e Zecca dello Stato, [1987].

———. *Rasenna: Storia e civiltà degli etruschi.* Milan: Libri Scheiwiller, 1986.

Cristofani, M., and M. Gras. "Agricoltori, artigiani e mercanti." In *Gli etruschi: Una nuova immagine,* pp. 68–77. Florence: Giunti Martello, 1984.

D'Agostino, B. "L'immagine, la pittura e la tomba nell'Etruria arcaica." *Prospettiva* 32 (1983): 2–12.

De Grassi Mazzorin, J. "Reperti faunistici dall'acropoli di Populonia." *Rassegna di Archeologia* 5 (1985): 131–71.

De Marinis, R., ed. *Gli etruschi a Nord del Po.* Catalogue. Mantua: Galleria E Museo di Palazzo Ducale, 1986.

Gianfrotta, P. A. "On Fishing." In *L'alimentazione nel mondo antico: Gli etruschi,* pp. 5–58. Catalogue. Rome: Istituto Poligrafico e Zecca dello Stato, [1987].

Heurgon, J. *Vita quotidiana degli etruschi.* Uomo e Mito 37. Milan, 1986.

Östenberg, C. *Luni sul Mignone e problemi della preistoria d'Italia.* Lund: Gleerup, 1967.

Pairault Massa, F. H. "Problemi di lettura della pittura funeraria di Orvieto." *Dialoghi di Archeologia* 3 (1983): 19–42.

Sassatelli, G. "Cibo, alimentazione e banchetto presso gli etruschi." In *L'alimentazione nell'antichità,* pp. 211–36. Parma, 1985.

CHAPTER 10

The GRAMMAR *of* ROMAN DINING

Florence Dupont

The Cognitive Value of the Roman Diet

Like many other Mediterranean civilizations, ancient Greece in particular, Rome was a sacrificial culture: a domestic animal could be transformed into edible meat (i.e., slaughtered and butchered) only if ritually sacrificed. The Romans used the blood sacrifice as an opportunity to define their identity as civilized men and members of a community. They situated themselves with respect not only to the gods and the animal kingdom but also to other human beings. In addition, they confirmed the legitimacy of their ties to the soil. Eating meat in Rome was therefore intimately associated with the fundamental rite of Roman religion, the sacrifice.

To be sure, meat was not the only food eaten by Roman citizens, which is to say, by civilized men. Indeed, any people that subsisted on nothing but meat and animal by-products was by definition barbarian: the Germanic tribes, which primarily consumed milk, meat, and cheese, are a prime example.

Meat, a necessary but not sufficient part of the civilized man's diet, was a central part of every festive Roman meal, no matter how simple. The master of the household might make a personal sacrifice, usually to the household gods, and then offer a portion of the sacrificial meat to his guests, or he might purchase his meat from a butcher shop that sold meat from public sacrifices. This meat was referred to as a *caro,* or share, and the banquet at which it was consumed was referred to as a *cena,* or place of sharing. The Roman banquet was thus, above all, a sharing of meat. In polytheist Rome, the sharing of bread had no symbolic value. More than that, if the host of a banquet had tried to serve nothing but products of the earth, his guests would have perceived his action as an insult.

Although the culture of Rome was a sacrificial culture, like that of the Greeks, it was not a banquet culture. The Romans never adopted the Greek *symposion,* in which the drinker, possessed by wine, welcomed into his body divinities such as Eros, Dionysus, and the Muses. In fact, Roman civilization had no tradition of religious possession, whether erotic, prophetic, or poetic, hence no place for the Dionysiac rituals and banquets of the Greeks. Indeed, the Romans did not believe in Dionysiac possession and looked on it as a form of charlatanism. Guests at Roman banquets were served meat and wine at the same time. The wine was simply a drink—a special kind of drink, perhaps, but not a sacred drug.

Rome was thus different from classical Greece in that it lacked any form of social ritual based on convivial drinking. Roman banquets were not unlike the banquets of archaic Greece: *dais,* the word for "banquet" in Homer, derives etymologically, like the Latin word *cena,* from the root for sharing sacrificed meat. One important difference, however, was that the Homeric banquet was an occasion for celebrating communal memories, during which a bard, possessed by the Muse, chanted an epic. There was nothing like this in Rome, where banquets were not ordinarily an occasion for the cultivation of language.

ROMAN FOOD SYMBOLISM The Romans took a great interest in all matters connected with eating, including the customs of others as well as themselves. Philosophers, historians, satirists, comic poets, orators, and encyclopedists obsessed with food tirelessly applied the well-known maxim: "Tell me what you eat and I will tell you who you are." To this they added: "Tell me with whom you eat." Transgressing the Roman dietary code classified a person as "other"—that is, outside civilized Roman norms. Among those so categorized were not only Germans and Numidians but also tyrants and would-be tyrants, professional philosophers, wealthy freedmen, and gladiators. Constant reminders of dietary norms were built into political institutions and regulative social practices. Censorial edicts and sumptuary laws regulated the luxury of banquets, and violators were threatened with social and political disgrace. People addicted to splendid dining or guilty of overindulgence became the butts of satiric poetry, graffiti, and gossip.

For a noble Roman, the concept of honor involved both personal frugality and generous hospitality. The princely ethic, by contrast, was one of gourmandism and self-indulgence. Vitellius was a monster who devoured the gods' share of sacrifices and downed the previous day's leftovers in the most wretched of taverns. Augustus betrayed his plebeian origins and his pettiness by his inability to participate in a banquet and his constant nibbling; when it came to food, he lacked generosity.

Like other peoples, Romans "ate symbols." Indeed, symbolism was one of their paramount concerns. They therefore formulated countless ethical precepts concerned with eating (see table 1), just as other cultures formulated rules governing sex. Eating was one of the languages of "distinction" by means of which Romans situated themselves in time, space, and society. For them, food was "good to think with" (to borrow a phrase from Lévi-Strauss).

SYMBOLIC REASON AND UTILITARIAN REASON This symbolic aspect of Roman eating is one reason why the subject cannot be studied solely from an economic standpoint. If symbolic logic governed the Roman alimentary economy, the reverse was not true. An example will help to make this point clear.

There is general agreement that grain growing and indeed agriculture in general yielded little profit in Roman society, whereas livestock made people wealthy. From a purely economic standpoint, this makes no sense. Indeed, the growing urban population should have led to rising prices and a brisk and profitable trade in grain. This was not the case, however, because wheat was considered necessary for survival. Hence to make a profit selling grain was frowned upon: wheat was exempted from the laws of the market, unlike foods regarded as luxury items. Grain had to be sold at cost or even distributed free of charge (the *annona* was a free annual grain distribution to Roman citizens, paid for out of public funds). The city did not, however, impose on itself a duty to feed the indigent one by one. In fact, the citizen-farmer remained the Roman ideal: every Roman was supposed to own enough land to supply his family's daily needs. Romans used the term *paupertas,* the root of our "poverty," to refer to this idea of self-sufficiency without excess. Loss of self-sufficiency was sharply distinguished from poverty by the word *inopia* (misery), which was regarded as a moral failing resulting in social disgrace because it implied a failure to manage one's patrimony in a proper manner. Misery made a person an outcast. Such an individual was seen as physically repellent (*sordida*). Even if not threatened with starvation, the miserable wretch ceased to be culturally a free man. In times of drought or war, when free grain was distributed to Roman peasants and unemployed city dwellers, *inopia* became a communal event, a *pestilentia,* or scourge, which lifted the burden of moral culpability from the shoulders of individuals. Citizens, it was felt, must not be allowed to endure the economic and social consequences of shortages due to a breakdown of the *pax deorum.*

By contrast, sacrificial meat and other banquet items, including wine, were free to vary in price. When Sulla ordered the price of meat reduced so that the people of Rome could celebrate a certain holiday, for example, he was accused of pandering to the plebs. Thus it is fair to say that two economic systems coexisted in Rome, each corresponding to a different symbolic function of food: the nourishment of free citizens and the celebration of religious holidays.

LANGUAGE AND UTTERANCE Historians have been able to trace the evolution of the Roman diet in sufficient detail to propose a periodization. The changes they have noted are essentially quantitative in nature, however. For nearly a millennium food symbolism in Rome remained stable. It must therefore be analyzed as an enduring structure: the symbolic significance of bread, meat, and vegetables did not change from Cato's *De agricultura* to the *Historia Augusta*. No doubt this was because Roman food symbolism was inextricably intertwined with the blood sacrifice and agriculture, which were integral parts of Roman identity. Only after the major cultural revolution brought about by the advent of Christianity did food customs truly change.

This symbolism can be studied as a language in which each meal can be considered an utterance. Meals, whether solitary or communal, had both a physiological significance (the survival of the individual) and a symbolic significance (expression of affinity to Roman culture). The two were inseparable.

Typology of Roman Foods: Fruges *and* Pecudes

In describing a food system, one can focus on either production or consumption. The Romans did both, and in so doing they elaborated two homologous representations, classifying food according to where and how it was produced and where and how it was consumed (see table 1).

With respect to production, the basic distinction was between *fruges*, products of the cultivated soil, and *pecudes*, foods derived from animals raised for meat on uncultivated land (fallow fields and woodlands). In Roman parlance there were two broad categories of agricultural land (*ager romanus*). The first consisted of plowed fields (*arua*) together with vineyards and orchards (*horti*). These terms evoked a sedentary occupation of the soil (economic aspect) as well as the construction of cities and roads (political aspect). Agriculture—especially plowing, which transformed the soil from an uncultivated to a cultivated state—was thus an eminently civilized occupation in both the technical and religious senses. The second category consisted of uncultivated land in which wild animals (*ferae*) as well as domestic herds and flocks were free to roam; it included forests, mountains,

TABLE 1. SYMBOLOGY OF THE ROMAN DIET

Oppositions within Roman Civilization

FOOD PRODUCTION

Fruges (products of the soil):	*Pecudes* (edible animals):
cultivated land	uncultivated land
cost-free	costly
farmer=civilized	shepherd, hunter=savage
hard	soft
cooked	rotten
inanimate	animate
digestion=blood, muscles, bone	corruption=excrement

FOOD CONSUMPTION

Prandium (snack):	*Cena* (banquet):
vegetables	meats
cold	hot
upright	reclining
outside	inside
war and politics	peace
effort	relaxation
restoration	pleasure
stomach (*venter*)	gullet (*gula*)
frugality	luxury
rusticity	civility
country	city
solitude	sociability
routine	holiday
greed	generosity

Oppositions between Rome and the Outside World

Rome:	*Outside World:*
Roman soldiers	barbarians
bread	meat and dairy products
settled	nomadic
farmers	shepherds
sacrificers	nonsacrificers

Intersection of the Two Kinds of Oppositions

Civilized:	*Uncivilized:*
citizens	shepherds
bread	wild plants
city	periphery

rivers, lakes, and the sea (*silua, saltus, amnes, lacus, mare*). It is worth noting that the Romans applied the term *pecudes* to both domestic and wild animals. Roughly speaking, it meant "herd" or "flock" and was used in speaking of fish and birds as well as land animals. The Romans did not have artificial pastures, lands cultivated for use by animals. Their *prata* were not pastures but fallow or wasteland in which animals were allowed to graze. To the Romans, *prata,* covered with brambles and unappealing to the eye, were "mournful" lands.

These untamed spaces were inhabited by shepherds and hunters. This type of exploitation did not, in Roman eyes, establish any relationship between man and the soil. Shepherds and hunters were nomads, not unlike the most savage barbarians. They were troublesome people, often slaves without wives or homes and all too likely to become bandits or mercenaries. They were neither citizens nor civilized. Yet these savages tended their herds not outside the territory of the city but on its fringes. They played an essential role in Roman civilization since they provided meat for sacrifices and banquets, thereby ensuring convivial relations both among Romans and between Romans and their gods.

FRUGES: FRUITS AND VEGETABLES Cultivated land was of two kinds: plowed land and gardens. Implicit in the legal and religious status of each type of land were other, symbolic differences.

Gardens (*horti*), including vineyards and orchards, were the more civilized type of cultivated land. Roman gardens were expected to produce vegetables all year round. Many different crops were grown using a variety of techniques for irrigation, fertilization, and cultivation.

Gardens supplied the Romans with *holera,* a category that included many green vegetables, colza, tubers, and edible bulbs but not beans, peas, and other pod plants, which were called *legumina.* The list of *holera* was a lengthy one: it included various kinds of cabbage, varieties of cardoon (*Cynara cardunculus,* a Mediterranean plant related to the artichoke and cultivated for its edible leaves and roots), salad greens, leeks, herbs, turnips, carrots, parsnips, garlic, and onions, to name a few.

Like other Mediterranean cultures, Rome lived on vegetables. Every Roman wanted a garden of his own, even in the city. The typical garden was inside the walls that surrounded the household, or *domus,* whence the term *hortus,* meaning "enclosure." Like the household and crossroads gods, the garden gods were *lares,* a type of tutelary deity that symbolized permanent human occupation of a piece of land.

As far as products of the earth were concerned, garden vegetables, together with fruits and grapes, were thus the most civilized type of food and therefore edible raw or barely cooked (in salads or in the form of wine). Indeed, the term "raw" was a misnomer, since these foods were partially or totally "cooked" (*cocta*) by the sun. So when fruits and vegetables were harvested, they were, unlike meat, never in a raw state and subject to immediate spoilage.

FRUGES: CEREALS AND BEANS Cereals (*frumentum*, most notably wheat) and leguminous, or pod-bearing, plants (*legumina*) were quite another matter. These came from less civilized pieces of land, which each year had to be rescued by plowing from the ravages of winter. As such, they were considered to be less "cooked" by the sun than fruits and vegetables. Nevertheless, the Romans did not look upon harvested grains as "raw," for they believed that such grains remained alive and capable of giving rise to new plants. Hard wheat was roasted whereas soft wheat was not; then the grains were milled or more commonly crushed to yield flour. This process nipped the incipient young plant in the bud, as it were, so that the resulting flour was considered to be "uncooked" and thus apt to decay, hence subject to the same taboos as dead flesh. That is why wheat was stored as grain, milled only when ready for use, and immediately baked into bread or boiled.

Legumina were like cereals in that once the seed was "killed," it began to rot. Indeed, the Romans apparently believed that leguminous plants decayed even more rapidly than wheat. That is why the Jupiter's priests (*flamines*) were forbidden to eat broad beans as well as flour and flesh.

Two things were economically significant about the fruits of the earth: they cost nothing other than manpower, and growing them did not add to a man's wealth. And they also differed from animal herds in another respect. The land and its products were heterogeneous: one did not eat soil or amass capital in the form of grain.

PECUDES: A LUXURY OF THE WILD Edible animals were classified according to their natural habitat: air, land, or water. Land animals were of two kinds: domesticated herds, which were raised for eventual sacrifice, and wild animals, which were hunted. In Rome sacrifice and hunting were the two sources of meat.

The main victims of public sacrifices were cattle, sheep, and pigs. Sacrificial animals could be male or female, old or young, or even nurslings. Rituals were designed to provide the gods with appropriate victims. Domestic sacrifices generally used young animals: lambs, kids, piglets, and pullets. These supplied most of the meat for home banquets. Pigs were the most common sacrificial victims, so pork was a central feature of most banquet meals.

The ancients believed that every domestic species had a counterpart in the wild, and they hunted accordingly. The boar, or wild pig (*porcus siluestris*), was therefore a prime quarry, suitable for the most sumptuous banquets.

When it came to "heavenly flocks," or birds, the same distinction was made between domestic and wild species. Chickens, geese, pigeons, and peacocks were raised on farms, while wild birds were trapped with birdlime.

Only the "schools of the sea," or fish, were all wild. They were caught with lines or nets. Various shellfish were also eaten, most notably oysters.

The nice distinction between domestic and wild animals was spoiled, however, by the existence of an intermediate group of *semiferae,* or "half-wild animals." Hunting and fishing were seasonal activities: there was no fishing in winter and no hunting in spring or summer. Wealthy Romans therefore kept and bred game animals on their farms. They might breed boar and raise fish in hatcheries. The resulting animals were *semiferae.* Yet there was nothing hybrid about the manner of their slaughter: these half-wild animals were hunted or caught and never sacrificed.

Whether taken from wild, half-wild, or domestic animals, meat was always a luxury item, although the saddle of a Lucanian boar was hardly a dish to compare with an old hen marinated in wine to soften up its flesh. To sacrifice an animal from one's herd was to spend a portion of one's capital to please the gods, whereas to kill an animal just to eat its meat was considered wasteful.

PECUDES: ON THE FRINGES OF THE CITY Though produced on the fringes of the city's territory, the flesh of *pecudes* (especially fish and meat from adult animals) was usually sold in urban markets. Hence the Romans considered such flesh to be an urban product, or in any case a product "sold in town," which made it even more of a luxury item.

The path that meat followed from source to market reveals certain interesting features of Roman culture. Some meat came from the wildest reaches of Roman territory to be sold at the heart of the most civilized place in the Roman world, the city of Rome itself, while other meat came from forests on the fringes of Roman estates to be sacrificed in the master's household. This established a close relationship between two sharply contrasting parts of Roman territory or of the rural estate: the center and the periphery. The structure of the ancient city-state of Latium reflected this duality, as did the Roman estate, and it was duplicated on a larger scale in the *imperium romanum,* whose "periphery" included much of the known world. Gold, perfume, and exotic game (giraffe, bear, antelope, pheasant) came to Rome from India, Africa, and the forests of Germania. No doubt this explains why luxury was identified with the exotic in Rome and why the city was transformed into a vast world market, as we know from the third-century C.E. writer Aelius Aristides.

THE SYMBOLIC ECONOMY The territory of Latium and the Roman Empire thus consisted of a series of civilized and uncivilized regions. At the heart of the empire was the *Urbs,* Rome itself, the center of Roman political and religious life. The soil of Rome was entirely "cultivated" by urban development, but except for perhaps a few small gardens, it produced no food. Yet the city was filled with markets and shops selling luxury goods. Meat from cattle sacrificed on major occasions was sold at the *forum boarium* while other sacrificial meat was sold at the *macellum,* and fish and other seafood could be found at the *forum piscarium.*

Ringing central Rome was the Roman countryside, or *rus,* with its gardens, cultivated fields, and country houses (*villae*). This was the only fertile part of Roman territory. The work done here was honorable, worthy of a Roman citizen.

Beyond the *rus* lay the true periphery of uncultivated, hence sterile, land: forest, mountain, and swamp. Rome never developed a "naturalist" ideology or celebrated spontaneously fertile land. Wild plants (*herbae*) were not deemed fit for human consumption: leaves, seedlings, roots, and wild herbs were seen as fodder for animals. The only exceptions were medicinal plants such as nettles and a few luxury foods such as wild asparagus and mushrooms. Wild plants were substituted for vegetables and grains only in the diet of the miserably poor, and when this happened it was a scandal because human beings were reduced to the level of herbivorous beasts. Not surprisingly, shepherds were among those in this condition. Exploiting the wasteland on the periphery was a fit occupation only for slaves and the poorest peasants. Even hunting was a servile occupation.

FRUGES AND *PECUDES:* THE HARD AND THE SOFT, THE COOKED AND THE ROTTEN The dichotomy between products of the cultivated soil and edible animals was part of a general classification of animate and inanimate objects involving a distinction between the cooked and the rotten (see table 2). As we have seen, vegetables and grains were seen as partially or wholly cooked by the sun while still in the field. Hence there was little or no danger of corruption after the harvest. Cooking continued inside the human stomach and then the liver, which the Romans believed transformed digested food into blood, muscle, and bone.

By contrast, animals began to rot while still alive, for life was a process of gradual corruption that could be slowed or suspended by the presence of *anima,* the hot, dry, vital breath of life. With death, however, the *anima* departed. The body of the animal then decayed into a cold, foul-smelling liquid. To slow this process, one drained the freshly killed animal of blood and removed its viscera, which were mere concretions of blood, for the spilled blood (*cruor*) was the first part of the animal to be transformed into rot (*sanies*). This blood was offered up to the gods while still hot, along with the roasted viscera. The *pecudes* were then roasted and transformed into meats (*carnes*), but these did not undergo further cooking in the body (through digestion) and were therefore not transformed into muscle or

TABLE 2. THE COOKED AND THE ROTTEN: CULTIVATED
PLANTS AND EDIBLE ANIMALS

	Preparation	Transformation in the Body
Fruges (products of the soil)		
planting=cooking	cooking optional	digestion by cooking
Liminal foods		
broadbean= animalized vegetable	death=corruption	
bacon=vegetized animal	boiling	
Pecudes (edible animals)		
life=slow corruption	death=rapid corruption + cooking=slow corruption	total corruption

bone. Instead, meat continued to rot in the human stomach, from which it was evacuated in a putrid form (*stercus*) whose religious status was the same as that of carrion. Unlike *fruges,* meat offered no nourishment to the civilized man.

This characteristic corruption of animate creatures was connected with their mobility: life (*anima*) was incapable of animating wood or stone, which were incorruptible, to be sure, but also inflexible. Romans called these "hard," in contrast to animals, which were "soft." These terms referred not so much to an external quality perceptible to the touch as to an internal solidity. Otherwise it would be hard to understand why a boiled turnip or lettuce would have been deemed harder than a boar joint. "Hard" meant unlikely to disintegrate whereas "soft" was applied to things likely to decompose into heterogeneous elements, like a sauce that goes bad. Culture hardened; savagery softened.

If we apply Claude Lévi-Strauss's culinary triangle to Roman foods, we find that edible animals fall along a scale running from hard to soft, raw to rotten, bacon to oyster. The Romans classified the oyster as soft, moist, and cold. It was already so corrupt that many ate it roasted and peppered in order to prevent serious damage to the liver and stomach. Bacon, hardened by salting, drying, and smoking, was the only form of animal flesh that could be preserved and eaten boiled. The desiccation of the meat not only halted the corruption process but "cooked" it to produce incorruptible bacon or ham. Hence for the Romans the pig was not an animal but meat on four legs. Similarly, the products of the cultivated soil could be arranged on a scale from rawest to most cooked, from broad bean to grape. The best grapes were actually so full of life that the juice obtained from them continued to "cook" after being sealed in a barrel, thus yielding wine. The grape remained alive. And the wine itself, if not doctored or diluted with water, remained a living being against which the man who drank it had to struggle. By contrast, the broad bean resembled a dead animal.

We find the same thought structure in Roman medical texts on food. Celsus, for example, employs the same complementary categories, which transformed the spatial divisions of Roman territory into a dietary code: *fruges* build the body, *carnes* purge the body. Both undereating and overeating were believed to have deleterious consequences.

Roman Meals: The Location and Symbolism of Eating

Food production, then, was organized around a basic opposition between *fruges* and *pecudes*. This developed into a further series of oppositions related to consumption: there were two types of meals, the *prandium* and the *cena;* two purposes for eating, nourishment and pleasure; two parts of the body involved in the act of eating, the stomach and the "gullet"; two social forms of eating, isolation and conviviality; and two emblematic figures in satirical literature indicative of two harmful perversions, avarice and parasitism.

The Roman diet was a diet of extremes, ranging from everyday frugality for people of all social ranks to great orgies of wine and meat consumption on special occasions, when overindulgence was de rigueur. Banquets staged by the state, civic leaders, and provincial dignitaries and always associated with sacrifices served as pretexts for all sorts of prestige expenditures. Aristocrats spent lavishly, and at times ruinously, on public banquets—to the point of tossing whole sides of beef into the Tiber. The center of the civilized world was not only the world's greatest marketplace but also the scene of vast festivals of consumption: the Roman people enjoyed the fruit of victory. Over time the lavishness of these celebrations increased, as world conquest enriched the Romans. Yet one should not make the mistake of imagining the citizens of the early Roman republic as Romans of a later period liked to imagine them—as bearded, half-naked rustics chewing vegetables in smoky huts. In the fifth and fourth centuries B.C.E., Rome was a city within the ambit of Etruscan-Greek culture, and it shared the refinements and techniques of that culture.

CENA AND PRANDIUM The *cena* brought together a group of men to celebrate a special occasion in a covered space (a house, portico, or garden sheltered by a *velum*). These men always reclined while eating (if women were present, it was traditional for them to sit upright). Usually the company consisted of a well-defined social group: a family, patron and clients, friends of roughly equal age, professional or sacerdotal colleagues, or neighbors. The number of guests in each dining room was limited to a dozen or so, but there could be many dining rooms. Sometimes the company consisted of no more than a farmer, his wife, his sons, their wives, his grandchildren, and perhaps a few farmhands, but still the *cena* was always a celebration, no matter how limited the fare. It was never a routine meal. A *cena* of substantial proportions might be called a *conuiuium*. If it was a ritual banquet, the word was *epulum*.

Romans generally ate just enough to satisfy their hunger, however, without ceremony, often alone and just about anywhere and anytime. But not just anything: they ate only "frugal," fortifying dishes made from *fruges*. A meal of this sort was called a *prandium*.

Days were not organized around mealtimes. Romans ate whenever they felt hungry. Banquets marked breaks in the daily routine. Furthermore, the *cena/ prandium* distinction coincided with certain other distinctions concerning time and space.

The *cena,* for example, belonged to what was called *otium,* meaning both leisure time and peacetime. *Otium* comprised inactivity of two kinds: the *otiosus* was not a soldier, and he was not active in civic life. A typical *cena* might take place on a winter afternoon in the dining room of a Roman house or country villa. The guests would arrive at around two or three o'clock, well scrubbed, relaxed, and clad in robes or tunics. The banquet would end at nightfall.

By contrast, the *prandium* was the meal of Romans engaged in war, politics, or any activity that required effort (*labores*). It might be a breakfast or lunch, but there were no fixed times. For bachelors and soldiers in the field, dinner was also a *prandium;* for families in mourning, it was the single daily meal.

Since the *prandium* was purely a response to individual need, it reflected each person's character and moral qualities. Seneca was proud of taking a journey during which he ate nothing but dried figs, with or without bread. To endure a lack of food and live on virtually nothing was considered a mark of the grandeur of a man's soul, but only if such extreme frugality in daily life was regularly compensated by a joyous banquet.

BANQUET MEATS: THE IMPERATIVES OF PLEASURE By definition, a *cena* was an occasion at which sacrificed meat was consumed—and not just sacrificed meat but other foods included in the term *carnes* (that is, foods not digested by the body, upon which they had a "softening" effect). Meat was called "rotten" yet considered delicious, soft, and tasty. Through sacrifice, men shared the pleasure of eating meat with the gods at the *cena*. In every respect, the *cena* was tailored to the pleasures of the guests: the food, the sumptuous service and table settings, the couches, and the beautiful slaves—all were designed to enhance the pleasure of the diners. The *cena* was to the *prandium* as pleasure was to effort, as superfluity was to necessity (see table 1).

The *prandium* nourished; the *cena* entertained. To be sure, banquet guests consumed some nourishing food, such as bread and vegetables. But the dinner consisted mainly of meat, which was "indigestible" and eaten only for pleasure. Even the "real" foods, those that truly nourished, were supplied in such quantity that they further added to the pleasure of the experience, as did the ingenuity of the preparation: wild asparagus and mushrooms gathered in the forest might be served along with vegetables grilled like meats. Even bread became a delicacy: the bread of Picenum, for example, was made of crushed wheat that was soaked for nine days, then kneaded with grape juice before being baked in pots.

For the enjoyment of the *cena* the Roman possessed a special organ whose sole function was to experience culinary pleasure: the *gula,* located between the throat and the beginning of the esophagus. Because pleasure was not experienced in the mouth, one could not spit out a piece of meat after tasting it. The delicious rottenness had to be ingested in order to be savored.

The *cena* menu consisted of three courses combining pleasure with nutrition. The first was the *gustatio,* which included two symbolic foods, eggs and olives, accompanied by bread and honeyed wine. These appetizers may well have been intended to appease the hunger of the guests, for the verb *gustare* meant "to have a bite to eat" and referred to the *prandium*. Only after this did the true eating for pleasure begin. A more sophisticated version of the *gustatio* might nevertheless include sample "meat" dishes, such as oysters and other shellfish, dormouse, and thrush. Next came the *cena* proper, which was organized around a sacrificial meat (*caro*). At the most sumptuous banquets this might be some delicacy from a pig, possibly a pregnant sow (the nipple and vulva were especially prized, along with dozens of other select parts). With this, game animals and birds were often served, as well as fish either minced or accompanied by sauce. The dinner ended with the *secundae mensae* (second course), for which fruit (*pomum*) was favored. Walnuts, dried figs, and grape preserves were common. These fruit dishes constituted the most "civilized" portion of the banquet as well as the sweetest. Again, shellfish, small birds, and other animal delicacies sometimes accompanied this final course, along with quantities of wine.

To organize a successful *cena* was a complicated matter, requiring considerable art. Too much pleasure provoked disgust; not enough provoked frustration. The master of the house had to adapt to the occasion and to the personality of his guests while seeking to preserve his own reputation by appearing neither stingy nor pretentious. Success called for an ability to make one's guests feel closer to one another through the culinary pleasure they shared.

THE FARMER-SOLDIER: SYMBOLIC WHEAT Bread, olives, onions, wine, vegetables drenched in olive oil and cooked, salad, and figs—the *prandium* was supposed to be a cold, frugal, vegetarian meal for consumption by a single individual. A person who feasted alone on a sow's nipple or tripe stew, whether in his own home or at an inn, could only be a social outcast: a servile gravedigger, an insolent freedman, or an impudent noble (Lucullus never dined at home).

Such a meal, offering just the bare minimum necessary for survival, was the nourishment of active citizens, of people engaged in projects that required effort. Among such people, one can make a further distinction between the soldier and, say, the farmer. In civilian life, a man who ate alone, even a worker, normally ate vegetables. He might also eat bread, but bread was not an essential part of the peasant *prandium* as normally represented. Curius Dentatus, who was consul in 290 B.C.E. as well as a hero of the Samnite wars and a model of ancient frugality, contented himself with barely cooked colza when Campanian ambassadors surprised him one night with a visit. The historical accuracy of this anecdote is unimportant. What matters is that a Roman noble could eat such things without descending to the level of the herbivores. In peacetime, garden vegetables—civilized foods—were the only meal that a rural Roman required.

In wartime, however, this was not the case. Soldiers were bread eaters. Even if they took their bread with olives, onions, figs, and oil, the bread was essential, and soldiers who were served nothing but *legumina*—or, even worse, meat—protested. If they were fed colza, they turned it into herb bread that drove them wild. The phrase "herb bread," used by Caesar's soldiers confined in Dyrrachium, spoke volumes. Why didn't they cook their colza like Dentatus? Because for soldiers the only civilized food was bread. The soldier's *prandium* centered on wheat, whereas the farmer's centered on vegetables.

Bread was thus the symbolic food of the citizen-soldier. If a Roman peasant never went to war, did he need to grow wheat? In the very early days of Rome, the mobilized citizen provided not only his own equipment but also his own provisions for the duration of the campaign, or at any rate until he was in a position to take his subsistence from the enemy (a soldier consumed 1.7 to 2.2 pounds of wheat per day). Wheat was easily stored and transported in the form of grain. In Mediterranean countries wheat, along with dried fruit, was the food of travelers in remote regions. Once transformed into bread, moreover, wheat was the "hardest," most compact of cooked foods. Over time it hardened without rotting. It made the soldier's body, already heavily armored, hard and compact like itself. Agility was not a Roman martial virtue. The legionnaire was expected to display stamina, resistance to hardship, and imperviousness to fear. He was expected to stand firm in the face of enemy blows. When the army needed mobile soldiers, it relied on Rome's barbarian allies.

Because a Roman peasant did not become a citizen until he was inscribed on the rolls of the army, bread symbolized citizenship despite the fact that Romans actually consumed little wheat in peacetime. Wheat was eaten when other foods were scarce, but otherwise Romans preferred vegetables. The garden was the "poor man's farm." Only people who had achieved a certain wealth, who belonged to a higher class in the censitary (or propertied) hierarchy, raised wheat. To do so was a mark of ease, indispensable to the citizen. Although it is true that the state, in practice, soon took it upon itself to supply soldiers with food as well as arms, wheat was still the crop that allowed a Roman to leave his garden and be more than just a peasant (*rusticus*).

Wheat was symbolically significant for another reason as well: it served as a buffer against famine and scarcity, allowing peasants to survive without eating wild plants. It was an honorable substitute for vegetables. Grain was distributed whenever the poorest citizens would otherwise have been forced to "graze" for acorns and nettles or eat animal fodder such as vetch. Plebeians demanded such distributions as a right of free men—the right to a civilized food, a soldier's nourishment. In Rome famine was not so much a threat to the lives of the poorest citizens as to their civic liberty.

"Bread, cabbage, and sacrifice"—such was the Roman diet, reduced to a motto that sums up three spatial and temporal aspects of Roman civic life: war, countryside, holidays.

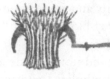

CHAPTER 11

The BROAD BEAN *and the* MORAY

Social Hierarchies and Food in Rome

Mireille Corbier

Was there a difference between the food of the rich and the food of the poor? In trying to answer this question, one faces two difficulties: the first has to do with sources, the second with the fact that the Romans, while not unaware of the difference between rich and poor, primarily classified individuals in terms of status rather than wealth.

Nevertheless, a satirical author such as Martial (first century C.E.) did not shrink from using the terms "rich" and "poor" in speaking of food: in Book 14 of his epigrams, no food items per se figure among "the various gifts of rich [*diues*] and poor [*pauper*]," but we do find a serving dish for mushrooms—a dish that "complains" of being used not for mushrooms as intended but only for a less prestigious vegetable, namely, broccoli. Similarly, in Book 13, certain foods such as the broad bean and the beet are described as being exclusively for poor people or "workers" (indeed, there is a play on words between *faba,* or broad bean, and *faber,* or worker). In the same vein, a decorated lamp from Aquileia depicts a basket containing a pitcher of wine, a round bread, and a radish with the legend "*Pauperis cena: pane uinu radic*" (Poor man's dinner: bread, wine, and black radish). Tell me what you eat and I will tell you who you are: food is an important token of social status. Artifacts like the lamp just mentioned, in which a text is combined with an image, are rare, however. For the most part, historians of Roman eating must work with sources of three kinds: normative, descriptive (sometimes merely by allusion), and archaeological.

Production and Distribution

A MEDITERRANEAN DIET Before we can appreciate social differences with respect to food, however, we must first describe the typical Roman diet, which was more or less the same as the diet of other Mediterranean peoples. It included grain, wine, oil, dried and fresh vegetables, dried and fresh fruits, sugar obtained from those same fruits as well as from honey, nuts (walnuts, almonds, hazelnuts, pinenuts, and chestnuts), together with foods rich in animal protein (milk and cheese, meat, and fish). There was also room for such gathered items as mushrooms, asparagus, laurel, wild fruits, and snails.

Food-producing regions formed concentric circles around Rome: truck farms and vineyards near the city, then wheat, and finally livestock. But this geographical distribution, captured in the well-known von Thünen model, changed in response to massive imports of grain and oil by sea.

Although the Roman diet began as a version of the basic Mediterranean diet, Rome's conquest of the entire Mediterranean region, including its desert fringes, along with half of Europe, broadened it in two ways. First, the Roman Empire came to incorporate a substantial portion of what Fernand Braudel called "carnivorous" continental Europe. No longer were meat eaters found solely on the periphery: they had joined the empire, and the Gauls and others supplied the capital with smoked meat and ham. Semiarid regions to the south and east were also incorporated into the empire and became rich sources of birds (such as the guinea fowl, also known as the "African chicken," and the ostrich) and exotic fruits (such as dates). Pepper and other spices from India arrived by way of Egypt and Arabia and found their way into costly culinary creations. Second, the Roman diet was transformed by expanding commerce in primary foodstuffs. In Rome, for example, the plebs consumed quantities of wheat imported from Egypt and Africa and oil from Betica (Andalusia) and Tripoli, while the wealthy set themselves apart by opting for more exotic imports. Not everyone ate the same foods. Some people could not afford the more expensive imported items. Others, however, were not permitted to eat certain things. Such restrictions created social divisions different from those defined by wealth. Last but not least, food was not always purchased on the market for cash.

ACCESS TO FOOD Rome, the quintessential city and surely the place with the densest concentration of money in the empire, was fed, from republican times onward, largely through taxation in kind and redistribution. This system reflected a certain apportionment of political power: 200,000 specially entitled plebeian citizens received the lion's share of public distributions of wheat (which is why this group was referred to as the "frumentaceous" plebs). From the third century C.E., they also received oil, bread, wine, and pork. The system worked only because aristocrats felt themselves bound by certain obligations. Wealthy Romans drew supplies from their estates and, with them, directly subsidized substantial numbers of servants (slaves and freedmen) and clients.

But the system also involved reciprocity, a sign of equality. Food was one of the gifts that friends exchanged with one another. Such gifts ranged from a brace of thrush or chickens to the two thousand moray eels that a wealthy breeder "lent" to Julius Caesar for a banquet celebrating one of his victories. The man, we are told, "did not wish to be repaid in money or in kind": he expected the same number of eels in return.

While "negating" monetary exchange, redistribution and reciprocity tended to reproduce the categories of rich and poor. Certain gifts were appropriate for people "below" one's own station, while others were suitable for one's "betters" and "equals."

At both the top and bottom of the social hierarchy people ate what they produced. Peasants had nothing else, whereas wealthy landowners who lived in town obtained part of their food from their own estates. Taxation profited the city, where people ate better than in the country and had first choice of what was grown elsewhere.

Urban markets were large enough to justify permanent oversight in regard to quantities and prices. Columella blamed the fact that "the poor can no longer afford expensive foods and have to settle for the cheaper ones" on the growth of the cash economy and rising prices. According to him, "In the past . . . rich and poor both lived on milk, game, meat from domestic animals, water, and wheat." In Rome, as in many later societies, money tended to increase dietary disparities. The urban poor had barely enough to scrape by: "But for a single two-as coin that I'm keeping for chickpeas and lupine, my pockets are empty," one of Trimalchio's less wealthy guests reported in Petronius' "The Banquet of Trimalchio" (first century C.E.).

In a society that exhibited inequalities of status as well as fortune, distributions of food always reflected the social hierarchy. During one public banquet to celebrate a religious holiday, the emperor Domitian ordered that meal baskets of different sizes and contents be distributed to senators and equestrians on the one hand and common people on the other. When generous donors gave public dinners in Italian cities, rank was always respected: municipal councilors received full dinners while commoners were simply served a glass of wine.

At private dinners the hierarchy was reflected not only in the seating arrangement but also in the quality of the food served. In satirical literature one often finds the second-class guests at the foot of the table excluded from the better food (such as white bread) and wine reserved for the guests at the head. But some aristocrats liked to distinguish themselves by serving everyone the same thing. Lucullus (as Plutarch tells us) adjusted the sumptuousness of his banquets to the rank of his guests. And when he dined alone, he insisted on being treated at his own table in a manner befitting a man of his quality: "Lucullus is dining with Lucullus."

The state played a role in standardizing eating habits, especially of two groups whose food was, if not provided entirely by the state, at least guaranteed by its authority: the plebeian citizens of Rome and the army. Both groups enjoyed a privileged status relative to the rest of the imperial population.

In the first century C.E., Roman soldiers took Roman customs with them wherever they went. Many were Mediterraneans who, when they settled in the north of Europe, continued to insist on olive oil and wine. These customs were adopted by new recruits from the provinces. The military diet, like the Roman diet, thus consisted of baked bread, meat, olive oil, and wine. Soldiers commonly drank *posca*, water mixed with a little vinegar, which both disinfected the otherwise insalubrious liquid and gave it a sharp acidic taste. It was with such a solution that a Roman soldier, moved to pity, moistened the lips of the crucified Jesus. If dilute vinegar was the Coca-Cola of the Roman army, soldiers and officers alike nevertheless preferred wine, which was believed to be a source of fortifying energy. Cato's rural slaves were given wine to drink after the grape harvest.

Slaves also ate standard fare, provided by their masters, who had a personal stake in their well-being. Their diet may have improved along with that of plebeians and soldiers. Cato's slaves received, in addition to their daily bread, what was called a *pulmentarium*. This consisted of oil, salt, and vinegar along with other foods that varied with the season, the place, and the nature of the work to be done—olives after the harvest, and when those were gone, *hallec* (the fish skin left over from the making of *garum,* a kind of fish sauce), as well as figs for those who toiled in the vineyards as the grapes reached maturity. Although Cato's recommendation of a vegetarian diet was not accepted at the villa of Settefinestre, slaves were not given top-quality meat. Diets at all levels of society improved, and disparities diminished: two centuries after Cato, Seneca's slaves received a monthly ration of five bushels of wheat, exactly the same as the imperial distributions to Roman citizens.

Choice of Foods

In Roman Italy a diet based on grains, increasingly consumed in the form of bread, gradually became standard, along with wine. Within this common diet, however, there were differences involving the preparation of food, the contents of the *pulmentarium,* the quantities and qualities of servings (especially of foods eaten fresh), and seasoning.

PREPARING GRUEL, FLATCAKES, AND BREADS The Romans of the third century B.C.E. were seen as "gruel (*puls*) eaters." In modest households the tradition of eating grain mixed with water to make gruel or baked into unleavened flatcakes continued. Soldiers in the field consumed their grain ration in the same way. In late republican and imperial Rome, which erected a monument to bakers—the tombstone in the shape of a colossal oven at Eurysaces—bread was baked at home only in aristocratic households. When wheat was distributed to plebeian citizens in the form of grain, the standard practice was to turn it over to professional bakers; soldiers did the same. Later, when Rome began distributing bread in lieu of wheat in the third century, the change represented more than just an improvement in diet. It also enabled the state to tinker with quantities and qualities: flour could be baked into smaller or blacker loaves.

PREPARING MEAT Although the Romans, unlike the Greeks, apparently did not expound on the relative merits of boiled versus roasted meat, Varro's idea was that the different techniques for cooking meat were discovered one after the other, first roasting (*assus*), then boiling (*elixus*), and finally stewing (*ex iure*), and to many contemporaries this sequence represented qualitative improvement. As for *frigere* (loosely, "frying"), the word had two meanings: it referred on the one hand to the toasting of grains and on the other hand to vigorous cooking in a hot liquid other than water, a liquid which, unlike the *ius*, was not consumed with the prepared dish. This "frying" was similar to our cooking in fat when oil was used but different when other liquids or mixtures were involved (*garum* alone; wine and *garum;* oil, wine, and *garum;* oil, honey, and *garum*; etc.). Where such mixtures are used, Apicius speaks sometimes of *coquere* ("cooking"), sometimes of *frigere.* Longer cooking times seem to have been related to the quality of the dish: meat was often boiled before roasting.

THE *PULMENTARIUM* Meals were generally composed of three main elements, one of which depended on the occasion and social level of the diners. An inscription from Isernia now in the Louvre speaks of a triad consisting of bread, wine, and *pulmentarium*. In the case in point, the *pulmentarium* was clearly the main dish, a stew, which the traveler ate with his bread. Any grain-based diet needs something to supplement the basic staple, and modern nutritional science has corroborated the wisdom of certain ancient customs. For instance, the protein not available from grain alone could be found in dried legumes, which the ancients saw as the poor man's meat, as well as in cheese, other dairy products, eggs, and of course fish and meat. According to the celebrated physician Galen, "Legumes are those grains of Demeter that are not used to make bread." He recognized their value as a source of energy and served them to the gladiators in his charge. Our best information is that Roman soldiers in Egypt primarily ate lentils, moreover. Martial tells us in *Xenia* that in frugal meals cheese took the place of meat. If the triad bread, wine, and *radix* (roots) was the "poor man's dinner," plebeians looked upon a dinner of bread, wine, and meat (with or without beans) as special.

QUALITIES, QUANTITIES, AND PORTIONS It was not uncommon for the wealthy to eat just a small part of a costly animal. When Seneca wished to criticize the "monstrous sybaritic excesses of those who select only certain portions of an animal out of disgust for the rest," he singled out the practice of eating the tongues of flamingoes. By contrast, ordinary people ate everything: tripe, blood sausages, leftover meat ground into meatballs, even the heads of sheep (which Juvenal called a "feast fit for a cobbler"). The same Juvenal remarked that a chained fieldhand (a slave of the lowest possible social condition) might dream of the sow's womb he once ate in a tavern.

A feast without meat was inconceivable. In one of Horace's *Satires*, the arrival of a guest serves as the pretext for a small farmer to forgo his usual frugal meal in order to serve a goat or chicken from the farm. Such a feast, featuring homegrown specialties, was seen as superior to a meal made with ostentatious, costly market items such as fish. In Roman times people did not distinguish between meat and fish, as they would have done in the Middle Ages. To the Romans, fish was a variety of animal flesh, served with the meat course. In what was basically a peasant society, saltwater (and hatchery) fish were an expensive luxury, reserved for the rich.

If Varro and Pliny the Elder sang the praises of pork, Cato provided the counterpoint with his praise for cabbage, which was eaten raw as well as cooked. For Pliny, however, the most important crops for the human diet after wheat were the broad bean, or fava, which was consumed primarily in the form of a puree, and the turnip, which was grilled or boiled. These two examples point to two categories of plants between which the Romans drew a clear distinction: the *legumina,* pod-bearing plants of which one ate the seed pods, including the broad bean, chickpea, lentil, and lupine, and the *(h)olera,* of which one ate the root or green stem (*holus;* the singular of this collective noun, in fact, meant "cabbage"). Lettuce was eaten as an appetizer, as it is today in some Mediterranean regions. Quality foods were not infrequently identified by their place of origin: Pliny mentions rape from Nursia and turnips from Amiternum. Oil was often used as a condiment with beans.

CONDIMENTS "Crush together some pepper, lovage, oregano, bay leaf, coriander, and onions; moisten with honey, wine, *garum,* and a little oil, heat, and thicken with starch [from wheat]." This recipe for boar sauce is one of 468 in Apicius' cookbook, which relied on ten basic ingredients. In order of frequency of use, these were pepper, *garum,* olive oil, honey, lovage, vinegar, wine, cumin, rue, and coriander. The average dish took eight or nine ingredients. Even the poor had their special recipes. According to Columella, one skillful cook used common garden herbs to season his fava beans: chervil, chicory, lettuce, garlic, and onion. Garlic had plebeian overtones and does not figure in Apicius' cookbook. Usually the ingredients of a dish were blended with mortar and pestle, a tool found in every Roman kitchen.

Food and the Social Hierarchy

UNEQUAL ACCESS TO HOT MEALS For peasants, urban plebeians, and soldiers in the field, accustomed to a monotonous daily regimen dominated by uncooked or at any rate cold dishes, the ultimate dining pleasure was a hot meal, preferably including meat and oven-baked bread. These people also liked hot or at the very least warm drinks (like our grogs) or wine diluted with hot water (*calda*), which could be bought not only in Roman cities but wherever Roman soldiers went. The sixth-century monastic rule known as the Rule of the Master prescribed a mixture of hot water and vinegar for the monks to drink after dinner, attesting to the durability in Italy of the twin traditions of the *calda* and the *posca*. A similar practice exists in China, where hot water is sometimes served to guests in lieu of tea, especially among the lower classes.

At one extreme, the poor, the peasantry, and the miserly (a favorite target of satirists) lived on *puls,* or gruel, plus broad beans and lentils, cabbage and turnips, and greens. At the other extreme, we know a good deal about luxury foods. For Cicero, oysters, fish, and home-baked bread were marks of high social status. Elite and populace nevertheless shared a taste for such soft animal parts as the nipple and uterus of both the domestic and wild sow. These were also served at banquets, but as appetizers.

Puls in its simplest form was nothing more than wheat flour mixed with water or milk. Cato gives a fancier recipe that combined semolina from high-grade wheat with cheese, honey, and eggs—a complete meal. The wealthy always served gruel made from semolina but only as a garnish for seasoned meat or brains. Although the elite did not disdain plebeian dishes, they set themselves apart by the manner in which those dishes were prepared and eaten. When they ate broad beans, for example, they added a costly, refined sauce that completely disguised the beans' taste.

Roman high cuisine was essentially an art of complexity and transformation. Surprising combinations were also favored: one aristocrat bestowed his name upon a stew of cockscombs and goose feet. A few gourmets shared sophisticated tastes: the frequent combination of *garum* and honey in the cookbook attributed to Apicius suggests a distinctive taste for a combination of the sweet and the savory, and the mixing of vinegar and honey indicates a predilection for the sweet and sour. Fruit was used as an ingredient of many dishes for the same reason.

It was not enough to be wealthy to be a gourmet, however. The wealthy but uncouth freedmen portrayed by Petronius did not eat refined dishes. One of Trimalchio's guests tells a humorous story about a funeral repast at which a variety of ordinary fare was served. In the story the plates are all mixed up. A real funeral dinner would have had three courses, in the Roman style: appetizers (*gustatio*), a meat and fish course (*primae mensae*), and dessert (*secundae mensae*). The meal would have begun with bread, snails, tripe, liver, beets, turnips, mustard, eggs, and cheese, followed by meat, including pork topped with blood sausage, with pork sausage and gizzards on the side, and perhaps, if there were no costly boar meat, some bear (purchased at cut rates after a gladiatorial contest) and ham. Finally, for dessert, there would have been pie served with honeyed wine, chickpeas, lupine, walnuts, and apples—quantity but not quality.

Ovid tells the tale of the peasant couple Philemon and Baucis, who served dinner to a visitor whom they failed to recognize as Jupiter in disguise. As the main dish they served cabbage, garnished with a thin slice of salt pork. For appetizers they served olives, wild chicory, black radish, cheese, and eggs cooked in the ashes of the fire. Dessert consisted of walnuts and figs, dried dates, apples and plums, grapes, and of course a honeycomb.

INFRASTRUCTURES By our modern standards, the kitchens in the spacious homes that archaeologists have excavated in Pompeii, Herculanum, and other Roman cities were quite small, but the fact remains that a specific room was set aside for cooking and equipped with the necessary utensils. Some houses had ovens in the courtyard for baking bread or roasting large pieces of meat. Unlike these individual dwellings, the *insulae* (apartment blocks) of Ostia, which have been preserved up to the second story, gave short shrift to cooking and other chores. Apartments were generally without fireplaces, ovens, or dedicated kitchens. In the few that did contain kitchens, the space was generally shared with the privy. Food was normally cooked on a portable brazier set near a window. The use of the *clibanus* (a sort of covered brazier) made it possible to do without an oven.

In Roman slave society one did not have to be wealthy to have a cook, and the cook role was well developed in the comic plays of the time. The rich nevertheless sought out cooks of talent and also employed a whole panoply of other servants to serve wine diluted with warm water, carve meat, and so on.

DINNER SETTINGS The sources tell us most about the dinners of the elite— not the ordinary ones but the banquets, which were probably rare even among the wealthy. Before going any farther, we must first pause to dispel the persistent myth of wealthy Romans indulging in lavish banquets at which they consumed dishes whose splendor (or rarity) was rivaled only by the crudeness of their table manners. For contemporaries, what stood out about banquets was that they were meals eaten in company—dining among one's friends. Listen to Cicero's definition of *convivium:* "To sit down to dinner with friends because they share one's life." The importance of conviviality was extended to the Latin word for dinner, *cena*, for which ancient authorities invented an etymology linking it to the Greek *koinon*, meaning "in common."

For plebeian men, social life was virtually synonymous with dining outside the home. *Tabernae* and *popinae* were inextricably intertwined, and for the common people both symbolized the pleasures of the city. The *taberna* was primarily a place where beverages were served and food was an afterthought; while drinking wine people also ate chickpeas, turnips, and salted foods, according to a sign found in Ostia. The *popina* was our bar and grill, a restaurant where dinner was served along with drinks. It catered to a plebeian clientele. Here social rank ceased to matter. The reputation of the *popina* was rather dubious, however. As in the cities of the Middle Ages, in Rome the tavern was the antechamber to the bordello. It was also a place were men gambled with dice.

In every *popina* thick vapors emanated from the stewpot and kettle that were always kept boiling on the stove. What people liked about such places was that the food was not just cooked but served hot. We hear of "steaming plates" and "smoking sausages." Drinks were also served hot.

Dietary Restrictions

TABOOS Taboos on food were uncommon. The fact that a flamen of Jupiter was forbidden to touch or even name raw meat or leavened dough was a sign of the importance attached to the transformation of raw foodstuffs into edible foods. But the Jews' abstention from eating pork was something that the Romans—who believed, as Varro put it, that "nature made the pig for the banquet table"—could not understand. Among the Romans there was no generally prescribed ritual fasting, although individuals did restrict their diets in various temporary or permanent ways.

THE ELITE The Romans did, however, encourage frugality, even among the wealthy. "Good" emperors were praised for their observance of this rule, which could be violated for ritual occasions. It was not always respected, though: among the signs of abuse were the frequency and timing of meals, the places where meals were taken, the quantity of food eaten, the consumption of rare and especially exotic dishes as well as of foods bought on the market rather than produced at home, wasted portions of meat, and certain cooking techniques (such as the excessive use of pepper, an exotic spice that tended to make dishes expensive and disguise what was being served). Republican sumptuary laws restricted the consumption of certain types of food. Simple cookery was honored for respecting the ideal of frugality.

SOLDIERS Dietary restrictions in the military essentially concerned the cooking of meat. Scipio, after ridding his bivouac of prostitutes and soothsayers and disposing of inessential baggage, limited his troops' authorized mess kit to a spit, a copper pot, and a drinking cup. For lunch his soldiers were ordered to eat raw foods standing up, while for dinner they were allowed to sample roasted or boiled meat. Such orders suggest that the troops were apt to supplement their meals by cooking other foods or buying prepared dishes from camp-following merchants.

A Sociology of Food

The historian of diet has hard information about what only a small fraction of the population ate and very little detailed data even about the rations of soldiers or Cato's slaves. The medical literature does, however, make it possible to discover dietetic principles that were to some extent actually applied. Anthropologists concerned with the symbolic aspects of eating have little in the way of taboos to work with in the case of Rome, but the rituals of sacrifice do offer a field of study characteristic of Mediterranean societies. Nevertheless, the richest vein in the study of Roman cookery, table manners, and dining customs doubtless belongs to the sociologist. In this realm the sociologist is concerned not so much with "distinction" as with the opposition between the licit and the illicit, which crops up repeatedly in Roman discourses about food. To be sure, the sources still afford only limited understanding of Roman eating, cooking, and gastronomy. Despite this, sociological study can shed clear light on urban behavior with respect to food.

The categories of analysis may at times seem rather simplistic: rich and poor, aristocrat and plebeian, citizen-soldiers and slaves, nouveau riche and old elite, including senators and other prominent men, even emperors, who at times conducted themselves with dignity while at other times deliberately acting in degrading ways. These distinctions remind us of Rome's conquests and their consequences. Roman society was profoundly transformed, right down to its eating habits, by the growing cash economy and the spectacular increase in the income and expenditures of privileged groups. Yet Romans for the most part continued to see the growing disparity in terms of traditional status hierarchies, even if they were only too well aware that the new hierarchies of consumption were undermining not only the rules on which their civilization was based but their own self-image.

BIBLIOGRAPHY

Ampolo, C. "Il pano quotidiano delle città antiche fra economia e antropologia." *Opus,* 1986, pp. 143–52.

André, J. *L'alimentation et la cuisine à Rome.* 2d ed. Études et Commentaires, no. 38. Paris: C. Klincksieck, 1981.

L'animal dans l'Antiquité romaine: Actes du colloque de Nantes (1991). Tours, France: Centre de Recherches A. Piganiol, 1995.

Apicius. *L'art culinaire [De re coquinaria].* Trans. and ed. J. André. Paris: Belles Lettres, 1974.

Bats, M. *Vaisselle et alimentation à Olbia de Provence (v. 350–v. 50 av. J.-C): Modèles culturels et catégories céramiques.* Revue Archéologique de Narbonnaise, suppl. 18. Paris: Editions du Centre National de la Recherche Scientifique, 1988.

Bettini, M. "Del fritto e d'altro." *Opus,* 1986, pp. 153–66.

Blanc, N., and A. Nercessian. *La cuisine romaine antique.* Grenoble, 1992.

Clemente, G. "Le leggi sul lusso e la società romana tra III e II secolo." In *Società romana e produzione schiavistica,* 3:1–14. Bari: Laterza, 1981.

Corbier, M. "Le statut ambigu de la viande à Rome." *Dialogues d'histoire ancienne* 15, no. 2 (1989): 107–58. ["The Ambiguous Status of Meat in Ancient Rome." *Food and Foodways* 3 (1989): 223–64.]

———. "Sociabilités populaires à Rome." In *A tavula è trazzera: Convegno internazionale sulla cultura dell'alimentazione nei paesi del Mediterraneo* (Trapani, 13–15 décembre 1990).

———. "Trésors et greniers dans la Rome impériale." In *Le système palatial en Orient, en Grèce et à Rome: Actes du colloque de Strasbourg, 19–22 juin 1985,* ed. E. Levy, pp. 411–43. Travaux du Centre de Recherche sur le Proche-Orient et la Grèce Antiques, no. 9. [Leiden]: E. J. Brill, 1987.

Cuisine antique. Les Dossiers d'archéologie, special series, no. 3, 1992.

D'Arms, J. H. "Control, Companionship, and Clientela: Some Social Functions of the Roman Communal Meal." *Échos du monde classique/Classical Views* 3 (1984): 327–48.

———. "The Roman *Convivium* and the Idea of Equality." In *Sympotica: A Symposium on the Symposion,* ed. O. Murray, pp. 308–20. Oxford: Clarendon Press, 1990.

Davies, R. "The Roman Military Diet." In *Service in the Roman Army,* ed. David Breeze and Valerie A. Maxfield, pp. 187–206. Edinburgh: Edinburgh University Press, 1989.

Dupont, F. "La consommation du pourri et la sociabilité alimentaire à Rome." In *La sociabilité à table: Commensalité et convivialité à travers les âges. Actes du colloque de Rouen (14–17 novembre 1990),* ed. Martin Aurell, Olivier Dumoulin, and Françoise Thelamon, pp. 29–33. Publications de l'Université de Rouen, no. 178. Rouen, 1992.

Étienne, R. "Les rations alimentaires des esclaves de la *familia rustica* d'après Caton." *Index* 10 (1981): 66–77.

Février, P.-A. "À propos du repas funéraire: Culte et sociabilité." *Cahiers archéologiques,* 1977, pp. 29–45.

Flobert, P. "À propos de l'inscription d'Isernia (CIL, IX, 2689)." In *Mélanges de littérature et d'epigraphie latines, d'histoire ancienne et d'archéologie: Hommage à la mémoire de Pierre Wuilleumier,* pp. 121–28. Collection d'Études Latines, Scientifique fasc. 35. Paris: Belles Lettres, 1980.

Gabba, E. "Ricchezza e classe dirigente romana fra III e I sec. a.C." *Rivista Storica italiana,* 93, no. 3 (1981): 541–58.

Garnsey, P. "La fève: Substance et symbole." In *La sociabilité à table: Commensalité et convivialité à travers les âges. Actes du colloque de Rouen (14–17 novembre 1990),* ed. Martin Aurell, Olivier Dumoulin, and Françoise Thelamon, pp. 317–23. Publications de l'Université de Rouen, no. 178. Rouen, 1992.

Goody, J. *Cuisines, cuisine et classes.* Paris: Centre Georges Pompidou, Centre de Création Industrielle, 1984. [*Cooking, Cuisine, and Class: A Study in Comparative Sociology.* New York: Cambridge University Press, 1982.]

Hanoune, R. "Le dossier des *xenia* et la mosaïque." *Recherches franco-tunisiennes sur la mosaïque de l'Afrique antique.* Vol. 1, *Xenia,* 7–42. Collection de l'École Française de Rome, no. 125. Rome: École Française de Rome, 1990.

Kleberg, T. *Hôtels, restaurants et cabarets dans l'Antiquité romaine: Études historiques et philologiques.* Bibliotheca Ekmaniana, no. 61. Uppsala: Almqvist & Wiksells, [1957].

Lepetz, S. *L'animal dans la société gallo-romaine de la France du Nord. Revue archéologique de Picardie,* special issue, no. 12 (1996).

Mrozek, S. "Caractère hiérarchique des repas officiels dans les villes romaines du Haut-Empire." In *La Sociabilité à table—Commensalité et convivialité à travers les âges: Actes du colloque de Rouen (14–17 novembre 1990),* ed. Martin Aurell, Olivier Dumoulin, and Françoise Thelamon, pp. 181–86. Publications de l'Université de Rouen, no. 178. Rouen, 1992.

———. *Les Distributions d'argent et de nourriture dans les villes italiennes du Haut-Empire romain.* Brussels: Latomus, 1987.

Pavolini, C. *La vita quotidiana a Ostia.* Bari: Laterza, 1991.

Sabban, F. "History and Culture of Food and Drink in China." In *The Cambridge History and Culture of Human Nutrition.* Forthcoming.

Scheid, J. "Sacrifice et banquet à Rome: Quelques problèmes." *Mélanges de l'École française de Rome: Antiquité* 97, no. 1 (1985): 193–206.

Settefinestre: Una villa schiavistica nell'Etruria romana. 3 vols. Edited by A. Carandini and A. Ricci. Modena: Panini, [1985].

Tchernia, A. "La formule *pane et uino adiecto* et l'inscription du collège d'Esculape et d'Hygie (CIL, VI, 10234)." *Epigraphica* 44 (1982): 57–63.

———. *Le vin de l'Italie romaine.* Rome: École Française de Rome, 1986.

CHAPTER 12

DIET *and* MEDICINE *in the* ANCIENT WORLD

Innocenzo Mazzini

In the ancient world a great deal was written on the relationship between diet and health, and many of these works—though probably a fraction of what was written at the time—have survived to the present day. The literature can be divided into two categories: strictly medical texts and "profane" contributions.

The medical works can in turn be divided into three further categories according to the extent to which food was at the heart of their subject matter: treatises dealing exclusively with food or diet—from the fifth- to sixth-century B.C.E. Hippocratic corpus (*De diaeta*, *De diaeta in acutis*, *De salubri diaeta*) to the works of Galen (second century C.E.), Oribasius (fourth century C.E.), and Anthimus (sixth century C.E.); herbals by Dioscorides, Pliny, P. Apuleius, and others; and medical works belonging to the various specializations that took diet into consideration for therapeutic reasons, in particular, Celsus' first-century work *De medicina*.

Food and Daily Regimens

In the classical world, the term "diet" referred not simply to food but to an entire way of life, or regimen. Dietetics was one of the three main branches of ancient medicine, along with surgery and pharmacology. Their primary objects of identification and, at the same time, forms of cure were eating habits, gymnastics and sports, work, baths, sleep, sexual activity, vomiting, and purges. Their aim was not merely to cure illness but also—even primarily—to prevent ill health.

In its widest sense, then, diet—as a means of preventing and curing illness—was a branch of medicine reserved for the rich, who were able to spend time and money on their health. The other classes had to make use of medication and surgery, which either rapidly restored health or, more often, led to death. In the best of cases, for the poorer classes, generalized dietary rules compatible with their working lives were suggested.

> Now first of all I shall write, for the great majority of men, the means of helping such as use any ordinary food and drink, the exercises that are absolutely necessary, the walking that is necessary, and the sea-voyages required to collect the wherewithal to live—the persons who suffer heat contrary to what is beneficial and cold contrary to what is useful, making use of a regimen generally irregular. . . . But when a man is favorably situated, and is convinced that neither wealth nor anything else is of any value without health, I can add to his blessings a regimen that I have discovered, one that approximates to the truth as closely as is possible.   (Hippoc. *De diaeta* 68.1, 69.1)

In the ancient world, food science was a significant and all-encompassing branch of medicine because of a number of widely held convictions: the causal relationship between food and a balanced state of health; the fact that food and drink possessed both natural and artificial features; the links between food science in relation to health and the other branches of medical knowledge; and the absolute primacy of food for survival, in both the healthy and the sick.

Health as Balance

Health and illness are, respectively, the expression of balance and imbalance of the elements that make up the human body, such as the humors. Equilibrium, upset or compromised by causes that may be independent of an individual's will, can be preserved or regained by means of a balanced relationship among these elements. Alternatively, it can be compensated for by means of food, work or gymnastics, and with tools from the other medical branches, surgery or medicine. More specifically, food adds while work subtracts. The right food, chosen specifically for the complaint, preserves or reestablishes balance. It is transformed into liquid in the stomach and absorbed through the veins, thus compensating where necessary for deficient or corrupt humors.

I maintain that he who aspires to treat correctly of human regimen must first acquire knowledge and discernment of the nature of man in general— knowledge of its primary constituents and discernment of the components by which it is controlled. . . . For food and exercise, while possessing opposite qualities, yet work together to produce health. For it is the nature of exercise to use up material, but of food and drink to make good deficiencies.

(Hippoc. *De diaeta* II.1–2)

The Natural and Artificial Features of Food and Drink

Food and drink could preserve or restore health only if they contained the features—or, rather, potentialities or virtues—enabling them to combat the excess or integrate the lack that had produced imbalance, and therefore sickness, in the human body. Given the absolute predominance in classical times of the concept of the humors—blood, phlegm, and yellow and black bile, each with its characteristics (hot and dry, cold and dry, hot and moist, cold and moist)—it was essential to identify the same characteristics in food and drink. These characteristics could be single or combined, exclusive or prevalent, innate or acquired, natural or artificial. They could also be distributed according to different levels of intensity (usually four) of dryness, moistness, heat, and cold.

Since food and drink act through the digestive system, it was also important to identify the digestive and nutritional features of each foodstuff in relation to the prevailing concept of digestion at the time. Digestion was regarded as a form of cooking, by means of which food was transformed into juices and liquids that were more or less dense or viscous. Moist and hot foods, which were soft and not very dense, were thus considered more digestible but less nutritious in the sense that they were more rapidly "cooked," absorbed, and evacuated.

These basic characteristics—dry, moist, hot, cold, digestible, indigestible, and so on—were established empirically or rationally, either on the evidence of the senses, primarily taste and touch, or on the results of experiments carried out by oneself or others.

But above all things everyone should be acquainted with the nature of his own body, for some are spare, others obese; some hot, others more frigid; some moist, others dry; some are costive, in others the bowels are loose. It is seldom but that a man has some part of his body weak. So then a thin man ought to fatten himself up, a stout one to thin himself down; a hot man to cool himself, a cold man to make himself warmer; the moist to dry himself up, the dry to moisten himself; he should render firmer his motions if loose, relax them if costive; treatment is to be always directed to the part which is mostly in trouble.   (Celsus, *Med.* I.3.13–14)

On the other hand, none of their species [varieties of chicory] is known to all, because they do not grow in all places; thus, in general, in order to acquire a notion of their effectiveness, both a classification and a specific description are required. If the plant gives a spicy, pungent or hot sensation to the taste or sense of smell it is likely to be soluble and slimming. Following this criterion, whenever the plant has the pleasing scent of an aromatic plant and gives the same impression when it is tasted, it is likely to have a warming power.

(Gal. *De victu attenuante* 16–17)

The natural virtues of foods were not necessarily constant. They could be artificially accentuated, weakened, or transformed by the environment, their preparation, or by culinary processes. In the case of animals, they also varied according to which anatomical part was eaten and so on.

The powers of foods severally ought to be diminished or increased in the following way. . . . Take away their power from strong foods by boiling and cooling many times; remove moisture from moist things by grilling and roasting them; soak and moisten dry things, soak and boil salt things, bitter and sharp things mix with sweet, and astringent things mix with oily.

(Hippoc. *De diaeta* 56.9)

Food Science and the Other Branches of Medical Knowledge

Classical physicians were well aware of the need to sustain the preventive and therapeutic effects of food by using the other branches of medical knowledge. This was deemed necessary because of the classical concept of diet, the variability and adaptability of food in relation to different characters and ages, the objective limits of food as a cure for certain disturbances or illnesses, and so on. Physicians who were expert in food matters thus had to know about the effects and virtues of gymnastics, the human nature and its temperaments, surgery, and pharmaceutics.

I maintain that he who aspires to treat correctly of human regimen must first acquire knowledge and discernment of the nature of man in general— knowledge of its primary constituents and discernment of the components by which it is controlled . . . the power possessed severally by all the foods and drinks in our regimen. . . . For it is necessary to know both how one ought to lessen the power of these when they are strong by nature, and when they are weak to add by art strength to them. . . . And it is necessary to discern the power of the various exercises, both natural exercises and artificial . . . and not only this, but also to proportion exercise to bulk of food, to the constitution of the patient, to the age of the individual, to the season of the year, to the changes of the winds, to the situation of the region in which the patient resides, and to the constitution of the year. A man must observe the risings and settings of stars.   (Hippoc. *De diaeta* II.1–2)

The absolute importance accorded to food by classical physicians can be explained by the following: it was essential for both the healthy and the sick; good digestion or bad digestion were the premises, respectively, for all states of health or illness; and a cure was often obtained more effectively through a correct diet than through medicines. "We do not need the other means of support at all times, but without nourishment neither the healthy nor the sick can live" (Gal. *De alimentorum facultatibus* I.1).

Food for the Healthy

The most important basic features of a healthy diet were variety, personalization, flexibility, moderation, and the preference for cooked foods, which were considered more digestible.

The fact that variety was considered important can be seen in the explicit recommendations made by classical writers and in the huge range of meats, fruits, vegetables, and cereals they considered—practically all the food products available at any given historical time. Variety was extended by further distinctions, evaluating each foodstuff according to its geographic provenance, the way it was cultivated, and the climate and environment in which it grew.

Things coming from the waterless, dry and torrid regions are all drier and warmer and provide the body with more strength. It is necessary to know the property, not only of foods themselves . . . but also of the country from which they come. So those who wish to give the body stronger nourishment, without increasing the bulk of food, must use corn, drink and meat from waterless regions.   (Hippoc. *De diaeta* II.56.4)

It is well to avoid . . . no kind of food in common use.   (Celsus, *Med.* I.1.2)

To be effective a diet had to be personalized, taking into account the individual's age, constitution, activity, and gender. It was important for a physician to know his patient's job because of the basic principle of the interaction between work and food. Since treatises and dietary regimens were usually aimed at the upper classes, however, the kinds of activity taken into consideration were primarily sports of varying degrees of violence and contemplative acts such as listening, thinking, and observing.

Age had to be taken into account when prescribing a regimen since different states were thought to prevail at different ages. Children were considered hot and moist; youths, hot and dry; adults, dry and cold; and old people, moist (or dry) and cold. It is thus clear that dry, cold foods were recommended for children while cold, moist foods were prescribed for youths, and so on.

Apart from activity and age, each individual had his or her own balance of elements, an idiosyncrasy to be taken into consideration. Thin people were told they should eat moist foods, for example, while fat people were supposed to eat dry foods.

Gender was also an element that the physician could not afford to overlook when prescribing a dietary regimen. Women were considered moist and cold while men were seen as dry and hot. It is clear, then, that dry, hot foods were recommended for women whereas men were given diets containing moist, cold dishes.

Only after all these elements had been considered could a dietary regimen be prescribed *ad personam*.

> The various ages stand thus in relation to each other. A child is blended with moist, warm elements, because of them he is composed and in them he grew. Now the moistest and warmest are those nearest to birth, and likewise those next to it, and these grow the most. A young man is composed of warm and dry elements. . . . The man, when his growth is over, is dry and cold, because the onset of the warm no longer has the mastery. . . . Old men are cold and moist, because fire retreats and there is an onset of water.
>
> (Hippoc. *De diaeta* I.33.1–2)

> Those with physiques that are fleshy, soft and red, find it beneficial to adopt a rather dry regimen for the greater part of the year. For the nature of these physiques is moist. Those that are lean and sinewy, whether ruddy or dark, should adopt a moister regimen for the greater part of the time.
>
> (Hippoc. *De diaeta salubri* 2)

The males of all species are warmer and drier, and the females moister and colder, for the following reasons: originally each sex was born in such things and grows thereby, while after birth males use a more rigorous regimen, so that they are well warmed and dried, but females use a regimen that is moister and less strenuous, besides purging the heat out of their bodies every month.   (Hippoc. *De diaeta* I.34)

Numerous specific diets have survived to this day, differing according to the age, profession, or lifestyle of the individual. They are often highly detailed, catering to children, old people, pregnant women, wet nurses, athletes, long-distance travelers, and so forth. The following is a diet for old people, prescribed by Galen.

Old men must not eat much of starches, or cheese, or hard-boiled eggs, or snails, or onions, or beans, or pig-meat for food, and still more that of snakes or ospreys; or all those having hard flesh difficult to digest. On this account, therefore, they should not eat any of the crustacea, or mollusca, or tunnies, or any of the cetacea, or the flesh of venison, or goats, or cattle. These also are not useful for anyone else; but for the young, mutton is not a bad food, but for old men none of these, and still less the flesh of lambs, for this is moist and viscid and glutinous and phlegmatic. But the flesh of fowls is not unsuitable for an old man, and of those birds which do not live in swamps, rivers, and pools. And all dried foods are better than fresh. Therefore, as has been said, it is necessary to abstain from all obstructive foods. . . . It is clear that it is necessary also to eat bread, neither lacking in salt, or leaven, or baking, nor the substitute praised by all, or the preparations made from it. . . . And unless an abundance of honey were mixed with the cakes made of butter and bread-substitute, no food would be more antagonistic to everybody, not merely to old men.   (Gal. *De sanitate tuenda* 5, 6)

The personalized regimen, however, could not remain constant over time; it had to be adjusted gradually at least four times a year according to the seasons: in winter, foods could be hotter, stronger, drier, and more nutritious, such as grain, meat, and undiluted wine; summer called for cold, moist foods, which were lighter and more digestible, such as wholemeal bread, vegetables, and water. In the intermediate seasons, intermediate foods were preferred.

The season of the year also merits consideration. In winter it is fitting to eat more, and to drink less, but of a stronger wine, to use much bread, meat preferably boiled, vegetables sparingly. . . . In spring food should be reduced a little, the drink added to, but, however, of wine more diluted; more meat along with vegetables should be taken, passing gradually from boiled to roast. Venery is safest at this season of the year. But in summer the body requires both food and drink oftener, and so it is proper in addition to take a meal at midday. At that season both meat and vegetables are most appropriate; wine that is much diluted in order that thirst may be relieved without heating the body; laving with cold water, roasted meat, cold food or food which is cooling. But just as food is taken more frequently, so there should be less of it. In autumn owing to changes in the weather there is most danger. Hence it is not good to go out of doors unless well covered, and with thick shoes, especially on the colder days; nor at night to sleep in the open air, or at any rate to be well covered. A little more food may now be taken, the wine less in quantity but stronger.   (Celsus, *Med.* I.3.34–38)

A call for moderation, the correct amount of food and drink, accompanied dietary recommendations throughout the classical period—from Hippocrates to Anthimus—but it became all the more insistent in periods when general economic conditions encouraged excess, especially during the early centuries of the empire. The link between medicine and ethics, especially in the field of dietary regimens, was reinforced, particularly under the influence of Stoicism. Health was also a question of controlling the instincts, including those that governed eating; it was the result, in other words, of virtuous living.

Coming to food, a surfeit is never of service, excessive abstinence is often unserviceable; if any intemperance is committed, it is safer in drinking than eating.   (Celsus, *Med.* I.2.8)

First of all, one must reiterate that which was said by Hippocrates who, when proposing a healthy diet, affirmed: exercise, food, drink, sleep, and the pleasures of sex, all in moderation.   (Gal. *Adhortatio ad artes addiscendas* XI.17)

Cooking food was regarded as a development in terms of health and had already been identified with the discovery of medicine itself in one of the oldest texts of the Hippocratic corpus, *De antiqua medicina.* The various ways of cooking food became tools for modifying their natural properties to the benefit of people's health. It is clear that the praise of cooking was closely linked to the concept of digestion as a "cooking" of the food that had been eaten. Physicians also stressed the importance of eating food that had been prepared in some way or that had been rendered more digestible, in order to avoid the risk of premature aging, damaging to the health of even the most robust.

> Hence arose the necessity for seeking a diet adapted to [the ancients'] nature, and by degrees they were led to what we now employ. After having thrashed out and washed the grain, ground and sifted it, it was kneaded and made into bread and cakes, or boiled and roasted with other things. A mixture was formed by food of different strength, in order to accommodate it to the constitution. . . . Now, what more fitting name could be given to this discovery than that of medicine? (Hippoc. *De antiqua medicina* 3)

The Diet of the Sick

Throughout medical tradition, from *De antiqua medicina* on, physicians were aware of the differences and correspondences between the diet of the healthy and that of the sick. The differences consisted, above all, in its aims, times, and quantities. Most of the basic principles of a healthy person's diet—variety, moderation, flexibility, and personalization—remained valid for someone who was sick.

The aim of a sick person's diet was to restore health. This could be accomplished primarily in combination with other dietetic tools as well as drugs and surgery. In some cases, food was the only medicine prescribed.

A number of personalized diets have survived, mainly in classical clinical treatises dealing with such illnesses as dropsy, fever, various forms of madness, kidney complaints, convalescence after surgery, and so on.

For the sick, food was administered under the strict control of the physician. On the one hand, it was important that food be given to help the patient resist disease. On the other hand, it was equally important that the food not nourish the illness. The best time to feed the patient was when the illness was in remission. At the beginning of the illness, when the patient still had sufficient strength, food was eliminated or reduced; in periods of convalescence, it was gradually reintroduced.

> What is the best moment to give food to the sick? When it is clear that the least affected parts are the chest and parts of the stomach. And what is the worst? When these parts are the most affected. When are they most affected? At the onset of the climax of the illness. When are they least affected? When the illness is in remission. It is thus evident that the best time to give food to the sick is when they begin to recover.
>
> (Gal. *In Hippocratis de acutorum victu liber commentarius* I.45)

The quantity of food given to the sick was as important as when it was given, precisely because of the reason mentioned above. On the one hand, it had to prevent the patient from becoming excessively weak and falling victim to new illnesses; on the other, it had to avoid making things worse. In short, it had to be neither too much nor too little.

> Now moderation in food is also to be observed: for the patient ought not to be surfeited lest it madden him, and he should certainly not be tormented by fasting lest he collapse through debility. The food should be light, in particular gruel, and hydromel for drink, of which three cups are enough, given twice a day in winter, and four times in summer.   (Celsus, *Med.* III.18.16)

Innovations over the Centuries

Throughout the ancient period—from the *De diaeta* of Hippocrates to the *De observatione ciborum* of Anthimus—no substantial evolution seems to have occurred in general dietetic principles. What did change with the passage of time and the diversification of populations was the variety of foods considered. In some cases, differences in detail also occurred, between one author and another, in the evaluation of certain foods or the diet prescribed for certain illnesses.

Rare and exotic products, for example, appeared in Celsus' *De medicina*—meats such as crane, peacock, thrush, and snails; fruits such as dates. In his *De alimentorum facultatibus* Galen referred to such previously unheard-of delicacies as the udder of milking sows, the liver of animals fed on figs, and the testicles of roosters nourished on milk-based mash. In *De observatione ciborum* Anthimus devotes a large amount of space in such a short work to different kinds of meat, various types of cooking, and, above all, dairy products and other drinks and foodstuffs that had been less widespread at an earlier date, such as beer and lard.

The dietician effectively carried out his research within the limits of the food that was available and the people who became his patients. Throughout the entire period, the latter remained the same, those with time and money to spare.

BIBLIOGRAPHY

Ackerknecht, E. H. "The End of Greek Diet." *Bulletin of the History of Medicine* 45 (1971): 242–49.

Alfageme, I. R. "Higiene, cosmética y dietética en la comedia ática." *Cuadernos filología clásica* 9 (n.d.): 241–74.

Celsus. *De medicina*. 3 vols. Trans. W. G. Spencer. Loeb Classical Library. Cambridge: Harvard University Press, 1935–38.

Edelstein, L. "Antike Diätetik 'Die Antike' = Diaetetic in Antiquity." In *Ancient Medicine: Selected Papers of Ludwig Edelstein*, ed. O. Tempkin, trans. C. L. Tempkin, pp. 303–16. Baltimore: Johns Hopkins University Press, 1967.

Galen. *De bonis malisque sucis*. Ed. A. M. Ieraci Bio. Naples, 1987.

———. *De diaeta in morbis acutis secundum Hippocratem: On regimen in acute diseases in accordance with the theories of Hippocrates*. Ed. M. Lyons. Berlin: Akademie-Verlag, 1969.

———. *La dieta dimagrante*. Ed. N. Marinone. Turin, 1965.

———. *Opera omnia*. 20 vols. Ed. C. G. Kühn. Leipzig, 1821–33. Reprint, Hildesheim: G. Olms, 1964–65.

———. *Opere scelte*. Ed. M. Vegetti. Turin, 1978.

———. *A Translation of Galen's Hygiene (De sanitate tuenda)*. Trans. R. M. Green; ed. H. E. Sigerist. Springfield, Ill.: Thomas, 1951.

Gourevitch, D. "Le menu de l'homme libre: Recherches sur l'alimentation et la digestion dans les oeuvres en prose de Sénèque le philosophe." In *Mélanges de philosophie, de littérature, d'histoire ancienne offerts à Pierre Boyancé*. Rome: École Française de Rome, 1974.

Grant, M. D. "Food and Diet in Later Antiquity." Ph.D. diss., St. Andrews University, 1988.

Harig, G. "Die Diätetik der römischen Enziklopädisten." *NTM: Geschichte der Naturwissenschaften, Technik und Medizin* 18 (1976): 14–23.

Harig, G., and J. Kollesch. "Gesellschaftliche Aspekte der antiken Diätetik." *NTM: Geschichte der Naturwissenschaften, Technik und Medizin* 13 (1971): 13–24.

Hippocrates. *Del regime salutare*. Ed. A. Lodispoto. Rome, 1961.

———. *Du régime*. Ed. R. Joly. Paris, 1967.

———. *Du régime des maladies aigües. Appendice. De l'aliment. De l'usage des liquides*. Ed. R. Joly. Paris: Belles Lettres, 1972.

———. *Oeuvres complètes*. Ed. E. Littré. Paris: J. B. Baillière, 1839–61. Reprint, Amsterdam: A. M. Hakkert, 1962.

———. *On Humours, On Nutriment*. Trans. and ed. J. N. Mattock. Arabic Technical and Scientific Texts, vol. 6. Cambridge: Middle East Centre, 1971.

———. *Regimen in acute diseases*. Ed. M. Lyons. Cambridge 1966

———. *Testi di medicina greca*. Ed. A. Lami; intro. by V. Di Benedetto. Milan 1983.

———. *The Writings of Hippocrates and Galen*. Trans. John Redman Coxe. Philadelphia: Lindsay and Blakiston, 1843.

Joly, R. *Le niveau de la science hippocratique*. Paris: Belles Lettres, 1966.

Jouanna, J. *Hippocrate*. Paris: Fayard, 1992.

Kulf, E. "Untersuchungen zu Athenaios von Attalea: Ein Beitrag zur antiken Diätetik." Ph.D. diss., Göttingen University, 1970.

Marinone, N. *Il riso nell'antichità greca*. Bologna, 1992.

Mazzini, I. "Alimentazione e salute secondo i medici del mondo antico: Teoria e realtà." In *Homo edens: Regimi, miti e pratiche dell'alimentazione nelle civiltà del Mediterraneo. Atti del II*

Colloquio Interuniversitario Regimi, miti e pratiche del bere, Torino 8-9 settembre 1989, ed. O. Longo and P. Scarpi, pp. 257–64. Milan: Diapress/Documenti, 1991.

Michler, M. "Das Problem der Westgriechischen Heilkunde." *Sudhoffs Archiv: Zeitschrift für Wissenschaftsgeschichte* 46 (1962): 137–52.

Oribase. *Oeuvres d'Oribase.* 6 vols. Ed. C. Bussemaker and C. Daremberg. Paris: Imprimerie Nationale, 1851–76.

Romano, E. *Medici e filosofi: Letteratura medica e società altoimperiale.* Palermo, 1991.

Smith, W. D. "The Development of Classical Dietetic Theory." In *Hippocratica: Actes du colloque hippocratique de Paris, 4–9 septembre 1978,* ed. M. Grmek. Paris: Éditions du Centre National de la Recherche Scientifique, 1980.

———. "Erasistratus's Diaetetic Medicine." *Bulletin of the History of Medicine* 56 (1982): 398–409.

von Tralles, A. *Original-Text und Übersetzung nebst einer einleitenden Abhandlung,* ed. T. Puschmann. Vienna: Braumüller, 1879. Reprint, Amsterdam: A. M. Hakkert, 1963.

Wörle, G. *Studien zur Theorie der antiken Gesundheitslehre.* Stuttgart: F. Steiner, 1990.

CHAPTER 13

The FOOD of OTHERS

Oddone Longo

Human Beings and the Gods

There is no doubt that, for the Greeks, the fundamental distinction between the human world and that of the gods was that the former was mortal and the latter immortal. However, it should be recognized immediately that there existed an equally rigid distinction regarding the food and drink each group consumed. We need only recall those "foods" that, denied to human beings, were reserved for the gods: substances that gave life and that were destined to renew, day by day, divine immortality. Among these were nectar, which held violent death at bay, and ambrosia, whose immortalizing function was expressed as the negation of *moros,* the fate of death that inexorably awaited all mortal creatures.

No less necessary than the first two substances, inasmuch as it expressed human worship of the gods, was a third "food," useless to human beings. This was the smoke that rose from the altars on which were burned those parts of animals—cows, goats, and pigs—that were destined for the gods, the other parts of which were periodically eaten by human beings.

The "otherness" of divine nourishment, when compared with that of people, was expressed by dividing the body of the sacrificial victim into edible and inedible. The edible parts were eaten at the banquet that was considered an integral part of the sacrifice, while the inedible parts, once they were burned and transformed into smoke, provided the gods with the extra nourishment they needed.

The distinction between parts for humans and those for the gods (bones, fat, and some entrails) was sanctioned in Greek tradition by the myth of Prometheus, who tricked Zeus by sharing out the "sacrificial victim" to the advantage of human beings (Hes. *Theog.* 535 ff.). The fact that the sacrificial smoke was considered an integral and indispensable part of the divine diet was stressed in a comic vein by Aristophanes in *The Birds,* where he describes how the Olympian gods would risk starvation if the birds succeeded in their plan to intercept the sacrificial smoke.

"One is the race of men, and one of gods," as Pindar said. The division between their two natures is made concrete, as we have said, in the opposition between mortality and immortality, strictly linked in its turn to their respective food codes—one for men and one for gods. A god who was so tempted by the smell of grilled meats at a banquet that he partook of them as men did would lose his divine nature by doing so. He would be demoted to the ranks of men, a risk that Hermes ran in Homer's Hymn to Hermes (l. 287), where the young god, "desirous of meat," is forced to abstain.

By the same token, if a human being were, by some extraordinary circumstance, allowed to eat the food of a deity—even that of a minor god or nymph, such as Calypso—he or she would acquire immortality and thus a similar, if not equal, nature to that of the gods. This is why Odysseus, whose only desire was to return to Ithaca, rejected the deity's offer of immortality and, despite sharing her bed and table, ate only "human" food that had been specially laid out for him (*Od.* V.194 ff.).

This separation and alimentary dualism is reinforced by a further opposition within the human condition: food for the living and food for the dead. Whoever ate the food of the dead would automatically enter the kingdom of the dead and be forbidden to return to the land of the living. Likewise, any human being who failed to eat the food of the dead would not be admitted to the underworld. This happened to the companions of Odysseus when they ate the lotus in the land of the lotus eaters. The rule was also valid in the world of the gods, as can be seen in Homer's Hymn to Demeter, when Hades offers the food of the dead to Persephone in order to be able to marry her. Once swallowed by the unknowing Persephone, the pomegranate seeds allowed her to spend half of her life with the god of the underworld.

These distinctions between human beings and gods and between the living and the dead are no more than generic, however. "Humans," in the simplest sense of the term, have never existed outside a specific cultural context. Every culture, at whatever stage it might be (and even more so at a rudimentary stage), tends to identify "humans" with the members of its own group and to attribute to those who do not belong to that group "nonhuman" characteristics. We shall now consider the extent to which this is true, as far as food is concerned, in Greek culture. For the Greeks, "humans" were, first and foremost, "bread eaters"—that is, consumers of cereals (barley, grain) that had been cooked in some way. This basic cereal-based diet distinguished Greeks not only from nonagricultural peoples but also from those who cultivated and ate different cereals. In the eyes of the Greeks (who ate barley), spelt, for example, was considered the staple of Italic peoples.

This "ideological" position was the product of the basic Greek diet throughout the Hellenic peninsula and the Aegean islands: 80 percent of a Greek's daily calories came from cereals, primarily barley and grain. The proteins and fats in their diet were provided by secondary agricultural produce (pulses and olive oil) and by the rare, and thus sacralized, consumption of animal flesh. The comic poet Philemon (fr. 105K.) described how the "most just" possession for a Greek (in a significant shift from an alimentary code to an ethical one) was a small plot of land that would offer him everything that "human nature" required: "grain, oil, wine, dried figs, and honey." What else could one desire? The choice offered by Philemon was the "Mediterranean triad" of grain, olives, and wine, with its restricted use of foods with a high sugar content (honey being the only sweetener adopted). What was missing from the poet's list were pulses (an essential source of calories as well as enzymes and vitamins), dairy products (especially those from goats, which enriched the diet with protein and animal fats), and fish, both fresh and preserved, much appreciated by the Greeks whenever circumstances allowed.

Diet and Lifestyle

In light of these considerations, it should come as no surprise that dietary "otherness"—that is, "the food of others"—does not concern only the gods and the dead. It is primarily, though not exclusively, a feature of descriptions of an ethnographical and anthropological nature (whether "real" or "imaginary"). Within the Greek world as a whole, diets inevitably varied a great deal in relation to economic and social differences. Literary sources include such examples as the robustly meat-based diet of the Homeric heroes (both Greek and non-Greek) in the *Iliad* and the endless banquet of the suitors in the *Odyssey*. But it is largely in comparison with other cultures that the Greek diet ("diet" as "life" or *bios*) acquired its specificity.

Greek anthropology had two moments of glory. The first was the work of the historians, geographers, and doctors of Asia Minor, whose work—with the exception of Herodotus, the Hippocratic corpus, and fragments from other authors—

has been mostly lost. The second coincided with Greek-Macedonian expansion under Alexander and continued with the establishment of his powerful successors.

Both these moments were times of intense cultural interaction between Hellenic and non-Hellenic peoples. During the former, this interaction occurred between highly civilized Greek cities in Asia Minor, such as Miletus, Smyrna, and Halicarnassus, and the recently established Achaemenid empire, with its similarly Indo-European matrix and undoubtedly high level of culture. This interaction, later to become dependency, led to more or less direct contact with the ethnic groups and cultures belonging to the empire, apart from the Medians and Persians.

During the second period, Greek-Macedonian expansion over a vast empire stretching to the borders of India, and the establishment after Alexander's death of his various successors, obliged those holding political power to obtain as detailed a knowledge as possible of their subjects' lands, both geographically and ethnographically. Journeys of discovery, with the aim of drafting reports for the Hellenic rulers, were carried out. Some of their material has survived in the form of extracts and paraphrases such as those found in the works of Diodorus Siculus and Photius dealing with the expeditions made by Agatharchides for the Ptolemaic kings. Although these are incomplete, they provide us with a picture of the cultures (and, above all, the diets) of "barbarian," or even "savage," peoples both inside and outside the boundaries of the various kingdoms.

Let us begin with the Ionic age and Herodotus, who, apart from being "the father of history," was also the father of anthropology, or, if one prefers, ethnography. In contrast to the work of his predecessors and contemporaries—the historians, travelers, and "ethnographers" of Ionia—that of Herodotus had the fortune of surviving intact to this day, a fortune it probably deserved.

An episode in Herodotus provides us with a significant example of the profound interaction between the culture of the Greek cities of Ionia and the Achaemenid civilization, an interaction that the ideological interpretation of the "Persian wars" as "wars of independence" has blurred. When describing Cambyses' failed campaign in Egypt (III.22 ff.), Herodotus does not hesitate to offer the Persian diet as a model of civilization and, above all, of Mediterranean alimentary civilization, contrasting it with the exotic diet of the Ethiopian kingdom. In an imaginary dialogue between the messengers of the king of Persia and the king of Ethiopia, Herodotus makes a cultural comparison between the two kingdoms (for the Greeks, the Ethiopians were halfway between history and myth). An essential part of the dialogue is the contrast between two different dietary regimens. The Ethiopian king expresses a mixture of surprise and disgust when he discovers that the Persian diet is based on wheat bread, given that Ethiopians lived on milk and boiled meat. When he then learns that dung is used to fertilize wheat, he concludes that bread eaters are neither more nor less than dung eaters.

The other section in Herodotus that deserves consideration for the quality of the information it provides regarding food is the ethnographical description of Scythia and the lands around its farthest borders. This is almost certainly the region of western Asia that is farthest from the civilizations of the Mediterranean, even though the lands that correspond to modern-day Ukraine were known as "the granary of Greece" (and of Athens!).

The Scythians known as nomads were horse breeders and clearly knew nothing about agriculture. They lived almost entirely on horse milk and its by-products (IV.2.19), a diet that for the Greeks was, to say the least, unusual. Alongside these were another group of Scythians known as farmers or plowers. Although this group grew cereals, they did not eat the produce themselves but sold it, probably to the Greeks. Herodotus does not describe the diet of these farmers, but it is likely that they too lived on milk products.

Finally, Herodotus describes a third group of Scythians curiously known as Greco-Scythians, or Callipidae, occupying the river basin of the Borysthenes (now the Dnieper). Although they shared most of the customs of the other Scythians, they grew cereals and ate them. They were also therefore bread eaters, and it was probably this characteristic that earned them the epithet "Greek," which, despite its incompatibility with "Scythian," simply referred to their diet. Apart from bread, these people also ate other agricultural produce, such as millet, lentils, onions, and garlic, just as the Greeks did (IV.17).

Beyond the farthest borders of Scythia we find populations whose dietary codes shifted dramatically from human to inhuman—populations, in other words, among which cannibalism was a more or less widespread practice. In these borderline cultural areas, Scythians and non-Scythians overlapped. The original Androphagi, who lived beyond the desert at the edge of Scythia, were, naturally enough, also nomads (IV.18). They dressed like Scythians but spoke a different language. Like the Homeric Cyclops, they knew neither justice (*dike*) nor law (*nomos*), and their habits were more savage than those of other men. Despite these characteristics, however, Herodotus is uncertain of their ethnic identity, claiming that they are "the only Scythians to eat human flesh" (IV.106).

In other places, we find examples of occasional, ritualized cannibalism. Among the Issedones, when a man's father died, his sons brought sheep to his house as a sacrificial offering. The sheep and the body of the dead man were jointed and sliced and the two meats, mixed together, were cooked and offered to the guests (IV.26). In other respects, the Issedones had a strong sense of justice (they were *dikaioi*). The Massagetae had a similar custom. Animal breeders and fishermen, these people generally lived on milk and fish and clearly knew nothing about agriculture. When one of their number became very old, he was sacrificed along with his sheep. The meats were then mixed, boiled, and eaten as part of a funerary banquet (I.216).

In the "Scythian ethnography" of Herodotus, therefore, we move from a positive extreme, represented by the Greco-Scythians of the Borysthenes, both cultivators and consumers of cereals, to the negative extreme of the Androphagi, habitual cannibals. Between these two extremes were the farmer Scythians, who did not eat the grain they produced, and the nomadic Scythians, who raised horses and lived on milk and its by-products.

The first moment of glory in Greek anthropology was therefore that of Herodotus and his culture. The second was the Hellenistic age. We shall now consider some examples of the way in which the "food of the others" was described by an ethnographer such as Agatharchides (whose work, as we have seen, has reached us in the summaries of Diodorus Siculus and Photius).

In the center of Africa, at the farthest borders of the desert, lived the Acridophagi, or locust eaters, who caught their prey by lighting fires as the insects approached. The fires not only killed the locusts but also smoked them. In order to make them more digestible, the Acridophagi dipped them in brine. These marinated locusts were then eaten immediately or set aside, not to be eaten until the next "harvest" (Diod. Sic. III.29).

Ethiopia, beyond Egypt, was the home of the Rhizophagi, root eaters who pulled up roots from the marshes, crushed them with stones, and then mixed them with water to make a kind of meatloaf that was baked in the sun. This was the only food they knew, but they had such quantities that they were never reduced to fighting among themselves or against other peoples (Diod. Sic. III.23). The image is one of a primitivist Eden.

Hylophagi, or leaf eaters, climbed up trees with great agility to pluck the tenderest shoots. They were able to digest any kind of bark or branch as long as it was fresh and juicy. They lived in bands that could not be qualified as families since, as in other "savage" populations, women and children were held in common. Not only their diet but also their physical characteristics, such as the ease with which they swung from tree to tree using both hands and feet, marked them out as beings that were closer to animals than humans. They went naked and defended their territory using branches as weapons. Their lives were short, and they almost always died of starvation. The frequency with which they were struck by glaucoma and became blind made it impossible for them to find their food (Diod. Sic. III.24).

These three examples are enough to indicate the nature of this type of ethnography. Nevertheless, one might also consider the more complete description given by Agatharchides (and, before him, by Nearchus) of the population of Ichthyophagi, or fish eaters, who lived along the African and Adriatic coasts from the Red Sea to the mouths of the Indus.

Throughout this "primitive" (or "primitivist") ethnography, the model is approximately the same. The populations described are situated at a lower level, particularly in a cultural sense, to the point of exhibiting indisputably bestial characteristics. What all these descriptions have in common is the exclusive nature of the diet. That which defines these people, usually to the point of providing them with their name, is what they eat. These foods are usually considered inedible or, at the very least, exotic, just as the way in which they are prepared (baked in the sun, etc.) is considered extravagantly primitive. It is only in the case of the Ichthyophagi that the diet was based on a type of food that was not only well known but also appreciated among the Greeks. Indeed, when available, fish was one of the main sources of animal protein for the Greek world.

However, what really distinguishes both the Ichthyophagi and the other peoples is the fact that they were all *monophagi*—that is, they depended on a single food source. The most extreme case of this was the group of Ichthyophagi known as Apotoi. Having no source of fresh water, these people ate their fish raw in order to obtain the water they needed to survive. In this way, the fish they ate was a substitute for something they did not even know existed.

We shall conclude our rapid "ethnographic" survey by looking at the description Arrian gives us of eating habits in distant India. According to a traditional scheme (already codified in Plato), humanity passed through a "primitive" period (for Arrian, preceding the arrival of Dionysius, the hero-god who civilized India) during which men (Indians) lived on tree bark or devoured the raw flesh of animals they had been able to capture. In such a wild land, Dionysius introduced not only city life and laws but also the consumption of wine and grain, instructing the local people in how to cultivate their fields. However, populations that knew nothing of agriculture remained at the borders of civilization. These included mountain dwellers, who lived on the flesh of wild animals, and Indian shepherds and hunters. But even the first of the seven castes listed by Arrian, that of the Brahmins, continued to follow a primitive pre-Dionysian diet (either as a cultural rejection or as an ascetic exercise); they lived exclusively on fruit and tree bark, described as "tasty and nutritous as dates." The members of the caste never wore clothes and led a life of misery, spending the winter in the sun and the summer in the shade of large trees (Arr. *Ind.* VII.4–5, XI.11, XII.8).

The conceptual framework, that of Alexandrian and subsequent ethnography, could have come from Aristotle's *Politics*: "There are many different kinds of food, and that means many different ways of life, both of animals and humans; for as there is no life without food, differences of food produce, among animals, different kinds of life" (1256a).

This is undoubtedly the most effective expression in the classical world of the strict interdependence between culture and diet. Aristotle then distinguishes three cultural models: that of "nomads" (migrating breeders of domestic animals), that of "hunters" (including fishermen and raiders), and "the third and largest class [which] lives off the earth and its cultivated crops." This three-part division was not as rigid as it seems, and various combinations existed.

Even before Aristotle, an "evolutionary anthropology," not contemplated by Aristotle, had located the most barbaric forms of appropriation and consumption, such as cannibalism, in the earliest and most primitive phases of human history. To restrict ourselves to a single example, the pseudo-Platonic *Epinomis* regards the first stage in the cultural evolution of humanity as the rejection of cannibalism and the selection of edible animal species, followed by the cultivation of barley and grain, the building of houses, the construction of tools, and so on (947 ff.).

We cannot conclude this survey of the ways in which the Greeks considered the "food of the others" without examining one of the seminal texts of classical Greek literature—Pericles' funeral speech (Thuc. II.38.2). "Because of the size of our city, there come to us all the goods of every land, and it is our fortune to find our own native products no more familiar to us than are those of the rest of the world." Although the habitual austerity of Thucydides' style (as well as that of Pericles) does not allow the historian to say what these goods are, it is nonetheless clear that they occupy first place in Pericles' encomium of Athens.

In his elegy to the *optimus princeps,* Pliny the Younger simply echoes the words of Pericles (*Pan.* 29.2). Pacifying the Roman Empire and reinstating traffic and trade, Trajan allowed for such constant interaction between its various peoples that "any produce from *one* region becomes the produce of *all* peoples" (*ut quod genitum esset usquam, id apud omnes natum videretur*). The cultural and dietary "cosmopolitanism" no longer converged on the capital as it had done on Athens. In Rome, on the other hand, at least within the ideological context of the Trajan elegy, we find a diffusion and distribution of resources, an equal fruition of natural produce throughout the entire universal empire. Apart from literary and ideological representations, it would appear that, for Romans, the "food of the others" posed no problems. Rich Roman tables, in both the capital and the provinces, must have offered an extraordinary variety of both homegrown and exotic foodstuffs.

Those people who did not remain outside the Roman sphere of influence gradually assimilated the ways of the empire, especially its diet. In a civilization based on agriculture and raising livestock, the dietary regimen was nothing other than the last stage of an entire productive process. At its source were the forms of appropriation and exploitation of the means of production (primarily the earth itself) and of techniques of production in the context of the vast and uniform expansion of Roman conquest and colonization.

The overall uniformity and homogeneity of agriculture in the Roman Empire has been stressed. It was based, once again, on the "Mediterranean triad," despite the considerable climatic differences between the Mediterraean basin and central Europe. This uniformity of production and consumption developed alongside the settlement of retired centurions in the provinces, followed by the spread of "capitalist" *villae*. Both these reflected specific political and economic policies. They formed part of the process of urbanization and Romanization throughout the empire, which included the diffusion of a particular way of life, one of the most important aspects of which was diet.

This is indirectly confirmed by the lack of interest shown in the "food of others" by such Roman "ethnographers" as Pliny the Elder, who rarely refers to "alien" diets among primitive peoples, even in his habitual references to Greek sources, and by historians like Tacitus in his descriptions of barbaric populations such as the Germans and the Britons.

In Periclean Athens, the "imperial city" was said to have appropriated the food of others, regarding it as its own. In the Roman Empire, on the other hand, it was the "capital of the world" that imposed its own diet on its subject peoples, gradually pushing other foods, customs, and practices aside. Although, like Athens, the city of Rome was the "showcase of the world" in food, as in everything else, the empire as a whole based its expansion and centuries-long domination on a process of conquest that was also one of cultural expansion. Within these processes, homogeneity of diet was an element of absolute importance.

BIBLIOGRAPHY

Amouretti, M.-C. *Le pain et l'huile dans la Grèce antique, de l'araire au moulin*. Paris: Belles Lettres, 1986.

André, J. *L'alimentation et la cuisine à Rome*. Paris: Belles Lettres, 1980.

Burkert, W. *Homo necans: Interpretationen altgriechischer Opferriten und Mythen*. Berlin: De Gruyter, 1972. [*Homo necans: The Anthropology of Ancient Greek Sacrificial Ritual and Myth*. Trans. Peter Bing. Berkeley: University of California Press, 1983.]

Detienne, M., and J.-P. Vernant. *La cuisine du sacrifice*. Paris: Gallimard, 1979. [*The Cuisine of Sacrifice among the Greeks*. Trans. Paula Wissing. Chicago: University of Chicago Press, 1989.]

Fentress, E. "Agricoltura, economia rurale e trasformazione del paesaggio agrario." In *Civiltà dei Romani*.Vol. 1, *La città, il territorio, l'impero,* ed. S. Settis, pp. 139–52. Milan: Electa, 1990.

Foxhall, L., and H. A. Forbes. "Sitometreia: The Role of Grain as a Staple Food in Classical Antiquity." *Chiron* 12 (1982): 41–90.

Gallo, L. *Alimentazione e demografia della Grecia antica.* Salerno: P. Laveglia, 1984.

Lazzeroni, L. R. "Il bere e il mito dell'immortalità fra India e Grecia." In *Homo edens: Storie del vino. Atti del II Colloquio Interuniversitario Regimi, miti e pratiche del bere, Torino 8-9 settembre 1989,* ed. P. Scarpi, 2:29–34. Milan: Diapress/Documenti, 1991.

Lo Cascio, E. "Forme dell'economia imperiale." *Storia di Roma* 2, no. 2 (1991): 313–65.

Longo, O. "I mangiatori di pesci: Regime alimentare e quadro culturale." *Materiali e discussioni per l'analisi dei testi classici* 18 (1987): 9–55.

———. "Una teoria aristotelica della cultura." In *Le forme della predazione: Cacciatori e pescatori nella Grecia antica,* pp. 11–20. Naples: Liguori Editore, 1989.

Page, D. *Folktales in Homer's Odyssey.* Cambridge: Harvard University Press, 1973.

Pucci, G. "I consumi alimentari." *Storia di Roma* 4 (1989): 369–88.

Raffaelli, R. "Il convito di pietra: Il cibo dei morti da Odissea a Don Giovanni." In *Mondo classico: Percorsi possibili,* pp. 175–94. Ravenna: Longo, 1985.

Scarpi, P. *Letture sulla religione classica: L'inno omerico a Demeter.* Pubblicazioni della Facoltà di Lettere e Filosofia, Università di Padova, vol. 56. Florence: L. S. Olschki, 1976.

PART THREE

From the LATE CLASSICAL PERIOD *to the*
EARLY MIDDLE AGES
(5TH—10TH CENTURIES)

LUTTRELL PSALTER, England, 1320–1340
(London, British Library, Add. MS 42130, f° 208).

The Luttrell family at dinner. The master of the house, at the center of the long table, is flanked by his wife and children; the house chaplain and his clerk are seated at the end of the table. (COL. RRITISH LIBRARY)

LAWS OF THE ORDER OF THE HOLY SPIRIT. Naples, 1353
(Paris, BNF, MS Français 4274, f° 6v°).

An outcast takes his solitary meal of bread and wine before a group of dining knights.
Portrayed in black (signaling mourning and affliction), he sits isolated at his table, his back
to the other diners. They are grouped together at separate tables for men and for women.
(COL. BNF)

CODEX DE NOBILITATE, France, end of the fifteenth century
(Lisbon, Archives Torre Tombo).

A picnic. A couple, rich bourgeois or members of the minor nobility, are seated near a well,
a sought-after spot for a picnic. A napkin draped over her lap, the woman and man share
bread and wine as well as cloves of garlic, medlar fruit (?), and cherries. (COL. LAUROS-
GIRAUDON)

HEURES D'USAGE DE TOURS, Touraine, beginning of the sixteenth century
(Paris, BNF, MS Latin 886, f° 4v°).

A hearthside meal in winter. The diner sits with his back to the fireplace, as was the custom for the master of the house or the guest of honor; wine accompanies his salt-cured
game birds. (COL. BNF)

HUNTERS BREAKING BREAD, *Book of the Hunt,* Paris, beginning of the fifteenth century (Paris, BNF, MS Français, 616 f° 67). (COL. BNF)

DETAILS OF THE PREVIOUS ILLUSTRATION.
The mechanics of a forkless meal. The fowls are deboned by hand (confirming the findings of medieval archeologists); then the pieces are pinched between two fingers and delicately sliced.

HISTORY OF ALEXANDER THE GREAT, fifteenth century
(Paris, Petit Palais, coll. Dutuit).

The poisoning of a prince at his table. In a banquet hall hung with silk, the prince, alone on the dais, sits on his throne under a canopy—all indications of his dignity. He is served more fowl on a larger platter than any other diner, another sign of his power. Facing him across the room is a sideboard displaying the house's most precious dishware. (COL. LAUROS-GIRAUDON)

MIRROR OF HUMAN SALVATION, Flanders, fifteenth century
(Chantilly, Musée Condé).

Above. Entertainment at mealtime—the fool and the musicians. The king (Ahasuerus) sits with his back to the hearth. His favorite dogs are always present, under the table if not on it. *Below.* Job and his family are crowded around a table, with women seated at the lower end. (COL. LAUROS-GIRAUDON).

WEDDING OF ORPHEUS,
Works of Ovid,
France, fourteenth-century
(Lyon, BM, MS 742, f° 165).

The wedding dinner. In the seat
of honor at the center—a rare
position for a woman—the
bride, wearing her wedding
crown, poses with crossed arms.
(COL. BM LYON)

MISSAL, France, end of the fifteenth century, beginning of sixteenth century
(Lyon, BM, MS 514, f° 1, January).

Above. The meal service. In a chateau with frescoed walls, consistent with reality, diners are attended by an army of solicitous servers while a valet in blue, white, and red livery (a color ensemble that does not date from the French Revolution!) tips his hat as he brings wine. (COL. BM LYON)

THE ROYAL BANQUET, Germany, fifteenth century
(Paris, BNF, MS Latin 511, f° 43).

Left. At a long table, the most frequent setting in depictions of eating, the diners are separated by status and sex. Those on the side of the powerful have more space to eat; the other diners are cramped. The men have been placed to either side of the king, the women relegated to the lower end of the table. Musicians and a dwarf (a fool?) entertain them. On this German table, shaped or round breads, onions, radishes, and turnips (?) accompany the fish. (COL. BNF)

CHRONICLES OF FROISSART,
France, fifteenth century
(Paris, BNF, MS Français 2646, f° 1250).

Places are uniformly set on the dressed
table that awaits summertime diners. An *al
fresco* ambience is being created by affix-
ing tree branches to the walls. Bundles of
grasses, which were sometimes scented,
are scattered on the floor. (COL. BNF)

TACUINUM SANITATIS, Southern
Germany, fifteenth century, after
an Italian manuscript from the
fourteenth century
(Paris, BNF, MS latin 9333, f° 60).

At peasant tables, few are seated. A woman
prepares the ricotta in an immense bell-
shaped cauldron. Red wine and bread are
on the table. A cheese drainer evokes
the cheese-making process. The pewter
tankard, wooden spoon, and iron ladles
are plausible cooking utensils in this context. The small dogs of the seignorial
chateaux are replaced here by an enormous black and white mastiff, protector
of the home. (COL. BNF)

INTRODUCTION

ROMANS, BARBARIANS, CHRISTIANS
The Dawn of European Food Culture

Massimo Montanari

As the bearer of a universalistic ideology and political practice, the Roman Empire extended a uniform culture over a range of local traditions and customs, including eating habits. These were not eradicated but absorbed and reduced to a series of common denominators in the many provinces of the empire around the Mediterranean and in continental Europe. The notion of the "other," which had been so strong in the Greek tradition and was rooted in the distinction between the civilized and the barbarian world, thus took second place to the imperial Roman ideology, which aimed to assimilate rather than to exclude.

It did not, however, disappear. Descriptions of "barbarians" in the writings of Caesar and Tacitus covered well-trodden ground when they touched on the feral aspects of these peoples, whose food culture was based on the exploitation of natural resources through hunting and livestock-raising in the wild rather than by the cultivation of fields and vineyards. Cultures based on bread, wine, and oil were opposed to those based on meat, milk, and butter. Naturally, there were exceptions. "Barbarians" grew and ate cereals (from which they brewed their ale, culturally opposed to wine), while Roman raised animals and ate meat. Yet the food myths of Mediterranean civilization—the classical triad of bread, wine, and oil—continued to feed imperial ideology, an ideology that, although it claimed to be universal, not only looked back to its roots but imposed them as a model throughout the empire. The traditional mythology surrounding the city and the country—in which the land fed the city's inhabitants—continued to characterize the Roman world and its civilizing mission toward the "wild" inhabitants of the forests and villages.

This distinction between different cultures and food models became particularly evident in the third and fourth centuries when the power relationship between the empire and the "barbarians" was gradually inverted. Assimilation became increasingly difficult and Roman tradition suffered a crisis of identity when confronted by a different culture that could no longer be domesticated and would soon seize the reins of power. The dramatic tension of these events, which shortly led to the collapse of traditional political and social structures in the western part of the empire, was accurately reflected in the contrast between the two food cultures. The biographies of third- and fourth-century emperors in the *Storia Augusta* present "true" Romans as being proudly fond of the food of the land: cereals, pulses, vegetables, and fruit. "Barbarians," on the other land, are described as carnivores who despise all vegetables. Didius Julianus "was happy to eat vegetables and pulses without meat," and Septimius Severus "adored the vegetables of his own land and often didn't even try the meat on his plate." Maximinus the Thracian, on the other hand, the first emperor-soldier to be born of "barbarian parents, his father a Goth and his mother an Alani," is described as having a huge appetite and as being able to eat from between forty and sixty pounds of meat a day. It is even said that "he never touched vegetables." These portraits reveal not only the tastes of individual emperors but ideological models that exemplified the clash of food cultures that was taking place.

A symbiosis developed between the two worlds for two reasons. On the one hand, the "barbarians," despite gaining control over medieval Europe, were fascinated by the Roman model and gradually absorbed its values in all walks of life, including diet and modes of production and consumption. But bread, wine, and, to a certain extent, oil, became the fashion for an additional reason. The arrival of Christianity as the official religion of the empire and its suppression, violent or otherwise, of the traditional Germanic beliefs made a decisive contribution to the widespread success of these Mediterranean foodstuffs. It is clear that Christianity, in food as in many other aspects, was the heir to the Roman world and its traditions. Bread, wine, and oil were the food products that became sacred in the Christian liturgy, essential tools of the trade for propagators of the new religion. The hagiographic stories of the early Middle Ages present bishops and abbots intent on sowing wheat and planting vineyards around their newly founded churches and monasteries. The "barbarian" aristocracy was rapidly captivated by such powerful images.

But there is another side to this picture. The exploitation of forests and other natural resources, so closely linked to the "barbarian" way of life, became increasingly popular during the early Middle Ages. The relationship that the Germanic peoples had with the land around them made a notable contribution to their political and social success. The use of forests, natural pasture, streams, lakes, and rivers for such activities as hunting, raising livestock, gathering, and fishing was no longer seen as a sign of poverty and marginalization, as it had been by the Romans. Exploiting the forest became a popular and profitable activity, conferring social prestige. The swineherd, for example, was attributed the highest value among all serfs by Longobard laws. Woods were seen with different eyes: no longer a symbol of incivility and inhumanity, they acquired the status of productive land. In early medieval inventories of land and incomes, which, in the typically concrete way of the time, measured fields in terms of sheaves of wheat, vineyards in amphorae of wine, and meadows in cartloads of hay, the pig became the unit of measurement for woods. The pig was dear to Germanic culture, as it had been to the earlier Celtic civilization, not only as a source of food but as a mythological figure. It is no accident that the legends of these cultures assigned to the figure of the Great Pig the perpetual regeneration that Mediterranean fertility rites attributed to Mother Earth.

Cultural factors were not alone in changing modes of exploitation of the land and dietary models at the beginning of the Middle Ages. There were also demographic and environmental factors at play. The collapse of the imperial Roman system led to a drop in population and a migration to towns. The countryside was abandoned, uncultivated areas increased, and forests became more important as a result. Nonetheless, the deliberate construction of an alternative economy based on the exploitation of uncultivated land was a sign of a culture undergoing transformation.

The early Middle Ages saw the development of a new system of production and consumption, based on the complicity and mutual support of an agrarian and a silvipastoral economy. This brought about a dietary regimen characterized principally by the variety of resources and types of food consumed. It is clear that this variety provided security and balance to the daily diet for most people during a period that is too often regarded in haste as dark and tragic.

CHAPTER 14

PRODUCTION STRUCTURES *and* FOOD SYSTEMS *in the* EARLY MIDDLE AGES

Massimo Montanari

In the early Middle Ages, the production and consumption of food were closely linked. Although the presence and influence of the market cannot be ignored, it was more concerned with luxury goods, such as spices, or with marginal aspects of production. As time passed, the market became more important, but until the eighth and ninth centuries, most products were eaten directly by the producer. This form of self-sufficiency thus dominated the food system of the period. It should not be forgotten that, in this context, self-sufficiency was part of an integrated social and economic system, within units of varying sizes—either the village and its appurtenances or the manor with its lands and the people who depended on it. Once again, it should be remembered that the latter unit of food production rarely worked in isolation. It was usually part of a network of farms, belonging to a single owner, that formed a productive whole. Nevertheless, it was rural land, with its complex articulation into cultivated and uncultivated, that gave this epoch its character, taking over the dominant position that had been held by the town in Roman times. The very landscape of the town was ruralized: fields, vegetable gardens, grassland, and woods penetrated urban settlements according to the logic of self-sufficiency that pervaded the early Middle Ages.

Woodlands, interspersed with clearings and natural bodies of water, surrounded human habitations. People not only carved strips, fields, vineyards, and vegetable gardens out of previously uncultivated woodlands (in inventories of the time, tools for working the land no more than complement those used by woodcutters to saw trees and cut back branches). They also exploited the uncultivated land as it stood. The diffusion of an "untamed" economy based on woodlands and grazing accompanied the expansion of cultivated areas and rural settlement strategies everywhere. Fields and grasslands, vineyards and woods, vegetable gardens and marshes all lived together; descriptions of manors and small holdings reveal the coexistence of differentiated and yet complementary resources. This coexistence was systematic—that is, the fruit of precise, premeditated choices.

A Varied Diet

The diet of the period was similarly differentiated. The produce of cultivated land (cereals, pulses, and vegetables) was widely integrated with the resources obtained from uncultivated land (game, fish, and livestock raised in clearings and woods). This variety appears to be the basic feature of the daily diet in the early Middle Ages at all social levels. There were certainly qualitative and quantitative differences between various social groups, differences that possessed a particular symbolic value in the culture of the time. Nonetheless, variety was guaranteed, as was a significant intake of both animal and vegetable products among the lower orders that made up the mass of the population. This fact should be stressed because it is so anomalous in the history of food. The European peasants of the Middle Ages enjoyed a diet that was certainly more balanced than those of other periods, both before and after, which were based on large amounts of cereal and very little meat. It is difficult to say whether this varied diet led to greater life expectancy, given that the period was plagued by numerous natural and social disasters, but there are many indications that this was the case.

Within this context of dietary variety, however, there were important regional differences connected to both cultural factors and the specific environmental situation. Pig breeding, a distinctive trait of the early medieval economy, was linked to the wide presence of oak groves as well as to the cultural preferences of the Celtic and Germanic peoples. It played a dominant role almost everywhere, although in Mediterranean Europe it was flanked and sometimes relegated to second place by sheep and goat raising. This was closer to the Roman tradition and more suited to the arid southern landscape. These differences had obvious repercussions on diets. Whereas the pig provided a formidable supply of meat (which was particularly suitable for preservation), both sheep and goats earned their keep while still alive as producers of milk and wool. This was primarily an opposition between meat and milk products rather than an opposition between different types of meat.

Pigs, sheep, and goats were, in any case, by far the most popular animals, as can be seen from early medieval documents. According to inventories, these "small animals" represented up to 80 percent and more of all animals recorded in rural properties (such as those in the Po Valley in Italy). They were small animals of a very different size and shape from those we know today. Archaeozoology has been able to establish, on the basis of animal remains found in early medieval sites, that the weight of a pig could vary considerably but was always three or four times less than the current average, with the smallest weighing 30–35 kilos (66–77 pounds) and the largest 70–75 kilos (154–165 pounds). Sheep at the time were less than half the size of their modern counterparts. In other words, a good pig could provide no more than 45–50 kilos of meat (99–110 pounds), while a sheep provided no more than 25–30 kilos (55–66 pounds).

In their appearance, too, these animals were different from those of today. Medieval iconography (dating from a few centuries later but no less revealing) shows us pigs with dark or reddish skin and stiff bristles, short, erect ears, and a pointed muzzle with tusks clearly visible. They were, in other words, half wild and resembled more closely wild boar than the domesticated pigs of modern times. This is hardly surprising, given the similar habits of pigs and boars, which both foraged in the woods and had ample opportunity to interbreed. The color, flavor, and texture of the meat must also have been different. In the Middle Ages, pork was regarded as a dark, or "red," meat. The fact that the animal roamed around the woods kept it slim. This was why it was taken from its pasture in late autumn to be fattened up at the farm. However, before being killed and salted, most pigs managed to survive more than one winter. According to archaeological data, animals were never killed before their first year was out, and sometimes after two or more years. Criteria of economic value and taste were also influenced by the conditions of the animals' existence. The hind parts of the pig (now fattened by a sedentary existence compared to the free roaming life of the Middle Ages) were not preferred to the fore parts, as they are now. At that time the fore parts were appreciated as much as, if not more than, the rump. In farming contracts of the time, peasants were often obliged to hand over a shoulder of pork to the landowner.

The raising of cattle also appears to have acquired increased importance during the early Middle Ages compared with that of Roman times, when they were considered almost exclusively beasts of burden. Destined to pull carts and plows, they were kept alive up to a very advanced age (ten or fifteen years) and only slaughtered when they were no longer of any use. Their contribution to the Roman meat diet was, in any case, negligible. According to medieval documents, cows were rare in manors and were used primarily as working animals. Archaeological excavations, however, which have discovered ox bones among kitchen remains, sometimes to a notable degree, present another picture. This is all the more surprising if one considers the average age of these slaughtered animals. They were never young (and had obviously been used in the fields), but neither were they old and "useless." Generally the age at which they were slaughtered ranges from three to five years, revealing an attempt to find a compromise between the needs of the fields and those of the table. Cattle, raised in a semifree state in forest clearings or in the forest undergrowth, thus played a part in both agricultural activity and the "untamed" economy. They too were small, much smaller than their modern counterparts (and those in Roman times, which were killed only at an advanced age). However, each cow still provided 200–250 kilos (440–550 pounds), according to archaeological estimates based on the bones that have been found. This meat ended up on peasants' tables. This is worth mentioning since it is perhaps the first time in history that beef became an important food source—although it must be said that medieval recipe books, right through to the end of the fifteenth century, pay little attention to beef, which was considered vulgar and of little dietary value. Farmyard fowl—poultry, ducks, and geese—were another source of animal protein.

Finally, there was hunting and fishing. Although few archaeological traces have been found, these activities almost certainly filled out the peasant diet to a significant degree and provided the basis for the aristocratic table (hunting) and that of the monastery (fishing) as well. Animals like the deer, wild boar, and bear were anything but exotic beasts in the forests of the early Middle Ages. Even the wild ox (the legendary auroch) would continue to roam the woods for some centuries. Hunting rights were open to all classes and would remain so until the ninth and tenth centuries, when they became a privilege for the few. Village communities, whether free or dependent, continued to exploit them to the full. Even the king's forests, during the age of Charlemagne, were open to all, although lords had already begun to create "reserves" for their exclusive use.

Fish played a large part in the "untamed" economy since it came from rivers, ponds, and marshes interspersed among the forests of the plains. In some cases, though, they were artificially farmed. Most fish eaten were freshwater. The sturgeon was particularly highly prized, while the eel was appreciated because it could survive for days out of water and thus be kept fresh. Trout, pike, tench, lamprey, barb, and carp are the most frequently mentioned in recipes from the early Middle Ages. Unlike meat, however, fish did not enjoy a good reputation. It was considered less nutritious than meat by many doctors, who regarded the latter as nutrition par excellence. Furthermore, the church used it as a penitential substitute for meat, in line with the existing monastic practice.

Cheese was almost exclusively made from the milk of sheep or goats, which were raised for that purpose. Cow's milk was used to make cheese in very few regions (for example, the Alpine valleys). In any case, cheese production was the most usual way of transforming and preserving milk, which was rarely drunk in its original form. Drinking milk was a sign of "barbarism," to which very few people still clung. It was almost anachronistic to find in the ninth century a table such as that of Ilispon, a Breton noble, at which it was normal to drink milk.

Vines and Wine

Food culture in the European early Middle Ages was characterized by the triumph of wine as something to be drunk not only on special occasions but every day. A kind of dense ale (which later, flavored with hops, became the clear liquid we know as beer) was, for a long time, a sign of "nationalist" Germanic culture. It was also used in pagan rituals as a deliberate alternative to wine, sacred to Christianity. In the long run, however, it could not compete with wine, which was universally recognized as a prestigious drink, not only for its taste but also for its image. The wine-drinking area extended throughout Christian Europe, with different social connotations in different regions. According to the quality of the product, it was considered an everyday or luxury drink. In the northern part of the continent, however, it was, by definition, a drink for the elite. The dense ale mentioned above was characteristic of peasants' tables in the northern regions, although it later spread to the Mediterranean and, in particular, to the Iberian Peninsula, where Germanic food culture was strong, perhaps owing to preexisting Celtic traditions. The consumption of cider was rare in Europe as a whole, even though it was regularly produced in the imperial domains during the Carolingian age.

In all cases, however, people drank alcoholic beverages, with water being remarkable for its absence. The whole of medieval literature is marked by a profound diffidence toward water, which was recognized as a carrier of germs and diseases. The custom of constantly mixing water with wine should thus be interpreted as a rule of hygiene rather than taste. Wine, in its turn, was usually diluted with water to reduce its density and acidity. The Italian verb *mescere*, meaning both "to pour" and "to mix," is emblematic of the period.

Cereals and Pulses

Work in the fields produced mainly cereals. However, in this case too, the early Middle Ages marked a rupture with Roman agricultural tradition, which centered on wheat as a high-quality product destined for the urban market. The success during the Middle Ages of lower-quality grains, more productive and easier to cultivate than wheat, is the sign that the economy based predominantly on self-sufficiency, as we have seen, was more influenced by immediate dietary needs. In place of wheat, people grew rye, oats (genuine medieval "inventions," these wild grasses were selected and cultivated from the fourth and fifth centuries on), barley, spelt, millet, and sorghum, along with pulses—broad beans and beans, primarily, followed by chickpeas, yellow peas, and, later, green peas. Pulses were not only cultivated beside cereals but were also used in the same dishes. Local variations (with rye, oats, and spelt preferred in north-central Italy, barley and millet in the south-central regions) should not disguise the fact that there was a basic uniformity in the choice of more rustic cereals. Another common feature was the number of different types of grain cultivated on each farm or small holding. This was also a kind of "insurance." Diversifying growing times and harvests offered greater protection in cases of climatic adversity, against which the technology at the time was almost powerless.

Vegetables were a basic complement to cereals and pulses. They were cultivated intensively in the gardens that could be found beside all houses, rural and urban alike. The most common were turnips (also grown over large areas in open fields) and cabbages (kohlrabi, white cabbage, and kale, with cauliflower becoming popular only at a later date). Onions, leeks, and garlic played an essential part in the peasant's daily diet, along with many types of salad plants (lettuce, chicory, endive, chard, and so on) and numerous other leaves and roots (carrots, fennel, radishes, and parsnips), not to speak of a multitude of herbs. The particular importance of these items in the peasant's diet was also due to the fact that, unlike other cultivated land, the private garden was considered a sort of "duty-free" area for which the tenant paid no dues to the landlord. If one then considers the extraordinarily high yield of these gardens, thanks to the availability of human and animal manure (unlike the fields, where cereal yields were no more than three to four times the seed sown), it is hardly surprising that vegetables played such a decisive role.

Cooking

Carefully stored in dry places that ensured their conservation throughout the year, cereals were used whole or ground into flour. When boiled, they provided soups (made primarily from barley and spelt) or polenta (made with millet or sorghum). Pulses, too, were often ground and used as flour. Mixed into a dough with water, they were made into a type of bread, cooked under the ashes of a fire or on terracotta slabs, and formed into flatcakes. Real bread—that is, leavened and then cooked in the oven—was rare. Few people had ovens, which would later become a lordly prerogative, with peasants being obliged to use them and to pay for their use. Furthermore, the cereals most commonly available, unlike wheat, were low in gluten and therefore did not leaven easily. These flatcakes quickly became hard and needed to be dipped into something like water, wine, or soup before they could be eaten. In this sense, bread was the "natural" complement to those soups and broths, which, in their turn, were the most common way of eating meat.

In peasant homes meat, normally salted, was boiled. This not only reduced the taste of salt but also tenderized the often leathery texture of the meat. Above all, it preserved and exploited to the full its nutritional juices, which went into the stock that was then used as a base for other dishes. The basic tool in the peasant's kitchen was the cooking pot, hanging on a chain over the fire or placed directly onto it. Inside the pot, meat, cereals, vegetables, and pulses were boiled and reboiled. Evidence of this has been found in archaeological remains of cooking receptacles in early medieval sites, almost all of which are forms of stockpots made of terracotta or fire-resistant stone.

Soups and *pulmentaria,* with or without meat, also formed the basis for the monk's diet, which, albeit with numerous contradictions, shared with that of the peasant the spirit of humble poverty symbolized by the pot over the fire. Roasting, on the other hand, and all those direct cooking techniques that did not make use of water or stock, belonged to a different cultural and dietary sphere: the minority world of the warrior nobility.

A Stable System

We have seen that the peasant sphere is the most relevant in evaluating the early medieval productive system. We now need to consider whether—and, if so, to what extent—the system described above, based on a mixture of cultivation, exploitation of woodlands, and grazing, was sufficient to guarantee enough food for day-to-day survival.

There is no doubt that the answer is affirmative. By all appearances, the system worked, allowing the rural population not only to survive but also to grow, inverting, from the seventh century on, a decline that had begun in at least the third or fourth century. However, this is not the most significant fact, for we are well aware that population growth and living standards (above all, those related to food) do not always go hand in hand, the current situation in developing countries being a case in point. One might even claim that it was precisely the low demographic pressure during the first centuries of the Middle Ages that allowed people to organize a system of subsistence largely based on such activities as the exploitation of forests and natural pastures. Although these were not very productive on a strictly economic level, they offered considerable food security by ensuring diversified supplies and thus a varied diet.

Integration between animal and vegetable resources guaranteed the European population of the time a substantially balanced diet as is confirmed by archaeological studies of human remains found in early medieval sites. The physiological development and growth rates of individuals generally appear to be normal, as does the chemical composition of their bones. Malformation seems to have been rare, and teeth show few signs of wear (a sign of a diet based predominantly on coarsely ground cereals). The satisfactory nature of the diet can also be seen in written documents, which make no particular references to that curse of later generations, famine, except in a handful of exceptionally dramatic cases.

This does not mean that there were no crises in production at a local or more general level. What it does mean is that "agricultural" famine could be overcome by drawing on other resources. During the famine of 779 in France, the poor sought succor at the monastery of Aniane, where they were fed daily—a hagiographic text of the time assures us—on lamb, beef, and sheep's milk until the new harvest restored the situation to normal. It is significant that in the early Middle Ages "forest famines" had as much impact as agricultural famines. A lack of acorns or grass, a dearth of game, a drought or severe cold spell, which prevented the fish from breeding and men from fishing, were all events worthy of note. Just as much as a shortage of cereals or a plague of insects in the garden, these events attracted the attention of chroniclers.

Within such a system of production and consumption, it was unlikely that everything should be lacking at the same time. This state of affairs was prevented by the variety of available resources—a variety that, for the lower classes, would tend to decline in successive centuries, eventually producing cases of pure and simple monophagism. The clearest example of this is the role played by corn and potatoes in eighteenth- and nineteenth-century Europe.

Was this a period of unexpected well-being, then? Not by any means. However, we should not confuse low life expectancy, the familiar presence of pain and death, and the terrible impact of infectious diseases (constantly referred to in hagiographic sources, where people wait faithfully for the magic touch of a saint) with dietary instability. All this had very little to do with diet, and relative food security could easily be accompanied by adverse living conditions. We only have to think of wars, sackings, and the violence of the powerful to understand why people feared for the fate of their laboriously accumulated stores. The early Middle

Ages does not seem to have experienced illnesses related to famine or malnutrition, as later generations would. Nevertheless, there were limited episodes of mortality during epidemics produced by careless food habits. Rotten meat and moldy cereals were clearly no stranger to the peasant's table.

And what about cannibalism and the blood-curdling episodes that can be found in the chronicles of the time? Although we cannot assume that these are all mere literary inventions, they are clearly exceptions, the likes of which can be found in more recent times and up to the present day. It is true that, in the early Middle Ages, such practices seem to have been regarded as less perturbing. Eating human flesh was a sin that was embraced—without too much scandal—by the case histories of penitential works. In some instances, such as accounts of Turks being devoured by Christians during the first Crusades, cannibalism was no longer regarded as a necessity but acquired a clearly ritual character.

However, images such as these do not enable us to understand the normality of everyday life during an epoch that offered far more food security than has generally been acknowledged. The very chronicles that tell of "bread" made during periods of famine from ingredients gathered in the fields and woods (herbs, fruit, acorns, ferns, even certain types of edible clay), then mixed with small residues of flour, also present us with a picture of a food culture that was rich and strongly rooted in the land. They reveal an awareness of plants and animals that was exploited in every possible way to ensure daily survival.

BIBLIOGRAPHY

Andreolli, B., and M. Montanari. *L'azienda curtense in Italia: Proprietà della terra e lavoro contadino nei secoli VIII–XI*. Bologna: CLUEB, 1983.

Audoin, F. *Ossements animaux du Moyen-Age au monastère de Charité-sur-Loire*. Histoire Ancienne et Médiévale, no. 18. Paris: Publications de la Sorbonne, 1986.

Baruzzi, M., and M. Montanari. *Porci e porcari nel Medioevo: Paesaggio, economia, alimentazione*. Bologna: IBC/CLUEB, 1981.

Bolens, L. "Pain quotidien et pain de disette dans l'Espagne musulmane." *Annales: Économies, sociétés, civilisations* 35 (1980): 462–76.

Bonnassie, P. "Consommation d'aliments immondes et cannibalisme de survie dans l'Occident du haut Moyen Age." *Annales: Économies, sociétés, civilisations* 44 (1989): 1035–56.

Camporesi, P. "Il formaggio maledetto." In *Le officine dei sensi*, pp. 47–77. Milan: Garzanti, 1985. [*The Anatomy of the Senses: Natural Symbols in Medieval and Early Modern Italy*. Trans. Allan Cameron. Cambridge, England: Polity Press, 1994.]

Doehaerd, R. *Economia e società dell'alto Medioevo*. Rome, 1982.

Fomaciari, G. F. Mallegni. "Alimentazione e paleopatologia." *Archeologia medievale* 8 (1981): 353–68.

Livi Bacci, M. *Popolazione e alimentazione: Saggio sulla storia demografica europea.* Bologna. 1987. [*Population and Nutrition: An Essay on European Demographic History.* Trans. Tania Croft-Murray. Cambridge Studies in Population, Economy, and Society in Past Time, no. 14. Cambridge: Cambridge University Press, 1990.]

Messedaglia, L. *Il mais e la vita rurale italiana.* Piacenza: Federazione Italiana del Consorzi Agrari, 1927.

Montanari, M. *L'alimentazione contadina nell'alto Medioevo.* Nuovo Medioevo, no. 11. Naples: Liguori, 1979.

————. "Bere acqua (e vino) nel Medioevo." In *Letture d'acqua,* ed. O. Longo and P. Scarpa, pp. 231–35. Padua, 1994.

————. *Campagne medievali: Strutture produttive, rapporti di lavoro, sistemi alimentari.* Turin: G. Einaudi, 1984.

————. *La fame e l'abbondanza: Storia dell'alimentazione in Europa.* Rome: Editori Laterza, 1993. [*The Culture of Food.* Trans. Carl Ipsen. The Making of Europe. Oxford: Blackwell, 1994.]

————. "Vegetazione e alimentazione." In *L'ambiente vegetale nell'alto Medioevo,* 1:281–322. Spoleto: Presso la sede del Centro, 1990.

Muzzarelli, M. G. "Norme di comportamento alimentare nei libri penitenziali." *Quaderni medievali* 13 (1982): 5–80.

Zug Tucci, H. "Il mondo medievale dei pesci tra realtà e immaginazione." In *L'uomo di fronte al mondo animale nell'alto Medioevo,* pp. 291–360. Spoleto: Presso la Sede del Centro, 1985.

CHAPTER 15

PEASANTS, WARRIORS, PRIESTS

Images of Society and Styles of Diet

by Massimo Montanari

Medieval sensibilities were very strongly attuned to the correspondence between diet and "lifestyle," understood as the concrete expression of a specific social status that had to be clearly demonstrated by its possessor. Dietary behavior had an immediate significance, since it was the first way in which differences of rank were communicated and displayed. The manner in which the produce of the earth and the woods—both cultivated and uncultivated resources—was approached, therefore, varied considerably according to rank and cultural choices.

Meat, Strength, and Power

For peasants, the forest was essential for daily survival and a balanced diet (and indeed the term "peasant" does little to suggest the multiplicity of productive activities in which medieval peasants were actually engaged). For nobles, it was even more essential since it also defined their identity. Apart from their interest in tithes and taxes, early medieval aristocrats cared little about agricultural work and the way in which cultivation was carried out. Their real "productive" interest lay in hunting, the only activity other than war to which they devoted themselves with passion. Hunting was the true image of war, on a practical and technical level as much as on a metaphorical one. Riding after the prey in the thick of the forest, studying strategies with one's companions to surround and capture the beast, confronting it with only a sword in hand—what better preparation for war could there be? Hunting fully expressed the culture of strength and violence that was consecrated in the practice of war. From a dietary viewpoint, the result was the absolute primacy of game. In the noble diet *venationes,* or game, occupied an inevitably central role, as Einhard, Charlemagne's biographer, tells us when he writes that the emperor's supper was made up of four other courses, "in addition to game, which the hunters usually skewered, and which he ate with greater pleasure than any other food."

There was another difference—of a more gastronomical nature—between the diets of peasants and nobles. While peasants almost always boiled their meat, owing to their desire to extract every drop of goodness from it, nobles preferred roasts, the meat being cooked directly above the fire on long skewers or wide grills. Quite apart from individual tastes, the preference for roasted meat was the expression of precise cultural values. According to a well-known and anthropologically widespread tradition, the use of fire without the mediation of water and household vessels implies a greater intimacy with the "raw"—that is, with nature in its wild state. This confirmed the profoundly feral image that the warrior nobility possessed and liked to project. Roasted meats expressed the very close link between the notions of meat-eating and physical strength, a link that pervades all facets of medieval culture. The dietary science of the time, informed by ancient tradition but adapted significantly to the social and nutritional valorization of meat consumption, confidently asserted that meat was the best food for a man's physique, his muscles, and—effectively—his "meat." The great Roman medical writer Aulus Cornelius Celsus had written, in accordance with the cultural tradition of the Greek classics, that bread was the food most suited to man "because it contained more nutritional matter than any other food." However, medieval medical writers, such as Anthimus in his sixth-century treatise *De observatione ciborum* (dedicated to Theodoric, king of the Franks), emphasized the exceptional nutritional value of meat. Aldobrandino of Siena, some centuries later, would reiterate this cultural shift by saying that "among all the things that provide man with his nutrition, meat provides him with the most. It fattens him and gives him strength."

In the case of game, the basic concept of strength deriving from the eating of meat was enhanced by the bellicose and indisputably "military" techniques that nobles employed to obtain it. Meat then was an expression of strength. And since, in the warrior mentality, there was an inevitable equation between strength and power (with the right to command being legitimized by physical strength and military prowess), an equally inevitable third link developed between meat and power.

In the peasant's diet, meat appeared to be a simple complement (albeit, in the early Middle Ages, both regular and important) to polenta and soups made from cereals and vegetables. In the diet of the powerful, however, it acquired a very different value and status. It was the symbol of power itself. Thus, in Carolingian times, the misdeeds of the powerful were punished by the obligation to abstain from meat for short or long periods. In the most serious cases, they were denied meat for life. Significantly, this obligation was flanked by the requirement to lay down arms—to relinquish, in other words, their social status.

A further difference was quantitative. The powerful ate a great deal. Strength, that indispensable attribute of power, was seen not only in terms of the type of food eaten (primarily meat) but also in terms of the amount. Celtic and Germanic literature, where examples of this kind of dietary behavior are most commonly found, offer some interesting cases of "competitions" in which the ability to eat more, and more rapidly, is regarded as a sign of nobility. We need only look at Snorri Sturluson's *Prose Edda,* which describes the competition between Loki and Logi to eat their way to the center of a tray laden with meat. The competition seems to end in a draw, but victory smiles on Logi, who manages to eat not only the meat but the bones and even the tray itself (evidently made of hard bread, as was the custom of the time). This kind of mentality appears to have been very common in the early Middle Ages, although there are also traces of different attitudes to food among groups of nobles who were less influenced by northern European culture. A significant case in point might be the "Mediterranean" extraction of a figure like Guido, duke of Spoleto, who—according to Liutprando of Cremona—was rejected in 888 as the last king of the Franks because of his frugal eating habits, thus bringing the Carolingian dynasty to a close. The archbishop of Metz is said to have exclaimed: "No one who is content with a modest meal can reign over us." This episode reveals, above all, a desire to confirm Frankish nationalism (which was victorious with the election of Count Eudes of Paris). It is equally significant that a hefty appetite should have been perceived as the expression of such nationalism. In any case, Guido's dainty appetite was an exception to the rule in the early Middle Ages.

Working and Fighting

The contrast in lifestyle and diet between peasants and nobles became clearer mainly after the beginning of the Carolingian period in the eighth and ninth centuries. Before that time, it was less evident owing to the existence of a mixed social class of farmer-warriors. They represented by far the most important element in the political system both in France during the Merovingian dynasty and in Italy under the Lombards. The "free people in arms," small or medium-sized landowners and members of the king's army, continued to hold considerable political sway up to the beginning of the Carolingian period. Following that time, the class rapidly declined. Large-scale landowners took over from small holders; many farmer-warriors lost their independence, rights, and public duties; and a professional military caste emerged. From that point on, it became easier to divide society into two distinct groups: those who fought and those who worked. Within the so-called tripartite society—an ideological construction first elaborated in the ninth century and destined to have considerable success in later centuries—the world was divided into the monastic and the lay, while the lay was further subdivided into *laboratores* and *bellatores*. It was the task of the monastic world to pray for the souls of the other two categories, while the *bellatores* protected society from its enemies and the *laboratores* provided it with its food.

Rural people were thus relegated to the role of mere producers. Furthermore, from the ninth century on, everything was done to exclude them from activities that exploited the forest and open land and to imprison them in the role of "peasant." The forest—which, as we shall see, now began to be cut down to make room for new areas of cultivation—became increasingly seen as a space reserved for the powerful to hunt in, with attempts being made to keep rural communities outside. Legal records of the period are full of clashes between lords and peasants (sometimes individuals, more often entire groups) regarding the use of woodlands and the right to graze and hunt. These liberties, which had previously been enjoyed without restriction, were now being seriously challenged. Although the marginalization of the peasantry was still to come, the trend was already clearly visible. The very term *laboratores,* which began to be used to define the class of rural people, was clearly intended to indicate not simply "workers" but, far more specifically, "peasants"—those who worked in the fields. In the terminology that became predominant at that time, *labor* referred essentially to agricultural labor, or even the fruit of that labor: cereals. The peasant thus became defined as the producer and consumer of products of the soil; his foods were cereals, pulses, and vegetables—not, however, wheat, which would continue for considerable time to be regarded as a high-quality product reserved for the tables of the rich and powerful. It must be repeated that this picture only partly reflects daily life: meat would continue to play a part in peasants' diets for some centuries. Nonetheless, it expressed a tendency, or desire, to reserve meat for those who were worthy of it. Vegetables symbolized the peasant world to such an extent that their bodies smelled of them. John, the biographer of Odo, Abbot of Cluny, did not hesitate to confess—although he was ashamed of it later—that he had moved away from his mas-

ter during a visit to Rome because he could not bear the stink of onions and garlic coming from the sack of a peasant who had joined their company.

The Quality of the Person

The type of food, the amount that was eaten, and the way in which it was prepared—these three factors together symbolized the social class or, as was said at
the time, "quality" of the person. This expression had already been used in classical texts to indicate the individual character of the consumer and his or her subjective dietary needs, influenced at different times by the environment, the climate, the season, and the task performed, not to mention age, gender, and physical
constitution. However, in the Middle Ages (specifically in that period between the
eighth and ninth centuries described above, during which the aristocracy acquired the upper hand), the notion of a person's "quality" changed dramatically. It
no longer referred to the physiological identity of the individual but to his or her
social class. Dietetics thus began to acquire, alongside its traditional character of
health and hygiene precepts, a new role—that of establishing social norms and
codes of behavior. These codes became increasingly rigid as time passed, reflecting
a similar process in the social order.

We shall see below the paradoxical results of this social regimentation of eating
habits, but for now we shall merely observe that the trend had already clearly begun in the Carolingian age. Frankish capitularies of the ninth century were concerned with nothing but social rank when they established that the provisions for
the imperial tables while traveling should be fixed "according to the quality of the
person." Alcuin, in his turn, when illustrating the various forms that the sin of
greed can take, does not fail to deplore those who prepare dishes that are more refined than their personal quality would justify.

Power and Humility

The third social order, that of priests and monks, was suspended between the other two. From the point of view of social class, it was closer to the noble world,
from which the members of the ecclesiastical and monastic hierarchies generally
came. It is therefore no accident that in the tripartite scheme mentioned above,
prayer and work were functionally distinct activities in contrast to the dictum of
the Benedictines (*ora et labora*). Socially and culturally, the process is identical to
that which we have already identified when looking at the distinction—both fac-

tual and conceptual—between *labor* and *militia*. In this case, too, the blurring of the two activities (which was normal during the first centuries of the Middle Ages, when monks and peasants tilled the earth together in a context of material poverty and spiritual humility) gradually disappeared. Churches and monasteries became centers of power and landowning wealth, surrounded by troops of servants and dependent peasants. The monks of the Carolingian age no longer enjoyed working with their hands and preferred to define themselves simply as *oratores*. On a strictly ideological plane, the choice to enter the church (in particular, a monastery) implied a rejection of the world and its struggles for power; thus, a person's diet hinged—albeit somewhat ambiguously—on peasant poverty rather than on noble plenty. At a dietary level, the rejection of worldly strength and power (in exchange for a much more beneficial strength and power) implied renouncing meat and sumptuous banquets, symbols of a noble lifestyle, in favor of vegetables and "peasant" frugality. The very value of hunger, a true obsession (if not material, certainly psychological) for the poor, was sublimated in the ascetic practices of fasting and abstinence. Of course, this was a matter of choice. Hunger imposed by circumstances, the real hunger of famine and daily deprivation, could not be regarded as possessing such high value. This is what made the choice ambiguous. Peasant culture had no intrinsic sense of the value of frugality that many attributed to it; rather, if anything, it was pervaded by a fear of hunger and by the desire to eat as much as possible whenever possible. From this point of view, it was much closer to the ideals and practices of the noble world than to the choice of renunciation made by the clerical and monastic world.

Humility and the Model of the Powerful

The Christian predilection for vegetables (and thus for a presumed peasant model, which, especially in the early Middle Ages, did not correspond in any way to everyday reality) went back a long way. Although the Gospels made no distinction between foods and recommended that all food should be accepted as a gift from God, renouncing meat—a symbol of violence and death, physicality, and sexuality—was a cardinal point of monastic spirituality from the dawn of Christianity. Roots and leaves were the favorite food of hermits, who found in the forests of the West the equivalent of the eastern "wilderness." For Europe in the early Middle Ages, their diet was a new and original way to approach the wilderness and its resources. The food they ate, ideally raw to indicate their rejection of the world and civilization (and thus of fire and cooking), was the image of a paradise lost and regained. With the development of organized monasticism, a sort of "taming" or institutionalization of the eremitic urge, the choice of diet remained firmly anchored to vegetarianism, but shifted toward cultivated produce. It is no accident that the Rule of St. Benedict repeatedly prescribed a dietary model based on cooked foods: soups of vegetables and pulses and *pulmenta,* to be accompanied by bread, as in the peasant diet.

In monasteries, however, the bread was made of wheat, and this was already a sufficient indication of its failure to respect the presumed peasant model. Furthermore, in its anxiety to renounce meat and its consequent need to find substitutes, monastic culture ended up by developing highly refined gastronomic strategies, which provided polemicists in later centuries with the stereotyped image (not entirely unfounded) of the greedy monk. What kind of renunciation, commented St. Bernard in his attack on the monks of Cluny, can there be in a cuisine that possesses dozens and dozens of different ways to cook eggs? What kind of penitence, noted Peter Abelard, can there be in the search for refined and skillfully prepared fish, far rarer and more expensive than simple meat? Meat itself frequently continued to appear on monastic tables, either as a form of indulgence or as an exception—for illness, for example, or debilitation (meat was still seen as providing physical strength)—or simply because discipline was slack. Hagiographic sources are full of meat-eating (and sometimes punished) monks, and these cases cannot simply be regarded as individual deviations from the rule. It was difficult to renounce entirely the aristocratic dietary code. The culture and mentality of the monastic world was deeply imbued with the lifestyle of the powerful.

Among priests, however, no such conflict existed. Living in the world, they accepted its rules and, for them, meat played a normal role in the everyday diet. Abstinence during Lent existed for them, as it did for all other members of Christian society as a whole. More than a way of purifying the individual, it was a mark of religious identity and social conformity. It is no accident that imposing fasts during Lent was, in the Carolingian era, the first method used to control those pagan populations that had been converted, more or less against their will, to Christianity.

In sum, numerous correlations existed between dietary custom and a person's social identity (not to speak of his or her economic, religious, and political identity). They provided the basis, still to be made explicit, for an ideological distinction that would become increasingly rigid and constrictive in later centuries.

BIBLIOGRAPHY

Andreolli, B., and M. Montanari. *L'azienda curtense in Italia: Proprietà della terra e lavoro contadino nei secoli VIII–XI.* Bologna: CLUEB, 1983.

Andreolli, B., and M. Montanari, eds. *Il bosco nel Medioevo*. Bologna: CLUEB, 1988.

Eginard. *Vita Karoli Magni*. Ed. G. H. Herz. Hanover, 1863.

Fumagalli, V. *Terra e società nell'Italia padana: I secoli IX e X*. Turin: G. Einaudi, 1976.

Galloni, P. *Il cervo e il lupo: Caccia e cultura nobiliare nel Medioevo*. Rome, 1993.

Landouzy, L., and Pépin, R., eds. *Aldobrandino da Siena: Le régime du corps de maître Aldebrandin de Sienne*. Paris, H. Champion, 1911.

Lévi-Strauss, C. *Le cru et le cuit*. Mythologiques 1. Paris, 1964. [*The Raw and the Cooked*. Trans. John and Doreen Weightman. Introduction to a Science of Mythology, vol. 1. Chicago: University of Chicago Press, 1983.]

Montanari, M. *Alimentazione e cultura nel Medioevo*. Rome: Laterza, 1988.

————. *L'alimentazione contadina nell'alto Medioevo*. Nuovo Medioevo, no. 11. Naples: Liguori, 1979.

————. *Campagne medievali: Strutture produttive, rapporti di lavoro, sistemi alimentari*. Turin: G. Einaudi, 1984.

————. *La fame e l'abbondanza: Storia dell'alimentazione in Europa*. Rome: Editori Laterza, 1993. [*The Culture of Food*. Trans. Carl Ipsen. The Making of Europe. Oxford: Blackwell, 1994.]

————. "Vegetazione e alimentazione." In *L'ambiente vegetale nell'alto Medioevo*, 1:281–322. Spoleto: Presso la Sede del Centro, 1990.

Montanari, M., ed. *Convivio: Storia e cultura dei piaceri della tavola dall'antichità al Medioevo*. Rome: Laterza, 1989.

Prinz, F. *Klerus und Krieg im früheren Mittelalter*. Stuttgart: Hiersemann, 1971.

Tabacco, G. 1966. *I liberi del re nell'Italia carolingia e post-carolingia*. Spoleto: Centro Italiano di Studi sull'Alto Medioevo, 1966.

Zug Tucci, H. "La caccia da bene comune a privilegio." In *Storia d'Italia: Annali* 6 (1983): 397–445.

PART FOUR

WESTERNERS *and* OTHERS

INTRODUCTION

FOOD MODELS *and* CULTURAL IDENTITY

Massimo Montanari

When Vladimir I, prince of Kiev, decided to abandon paganism and embrace the new faith for himself and his people in 986, he summoned to his palace representatives of the four main religions—Christians from Rome and Byzantium, Muslims, and Jews—in order to gauge the validity of each. Among the long theological disquisitions that were made, considerable attention was devoted to the dietary prescriptions of the four faiths, according to the twelfth-century Russian chronicle that describes the event.[1] The Jewish and Muslim ban on pork was viewed with disfavor by Vladimir, who also disliked the fact that alcohol was forbidden, telling the envoy of the Bulgarian Muslims: "We Russians like to drink, and there is no way we can live without it." Nor was he impressed by the Roman Christian observance of fasting as a form of purification, reportedly quipping: "Our forefathers would not approve."

These were clearly not the only reasons why Vladimir chose Byzantine Christianity, adopting both its doctrine and rituals. But the text stresses the value of diet as a sign of religious, ethnic, and cultural identity. Thus, before continuing our journey through the dietary culture of western Europe under the Church of Rome, we need to focus on the religions with which it came into conflict from the Middle Ages on—Greek Orthodoxy, Islam, and Judaism. The relationship between these religions involved hostility and exchange, osmosis, and the reaffirmation of difference.

Cultural specifics, nationalist claims, and religious conflict were frequently expressed by means of food and behavior at table. Blessing food indicated faith and conferred upon it a specific identity, excluding others from its consumption. Gregory of Tours tells the story of two priests, one Catholic and one Aryan, who, when invited to lunch by a married couple of different faiths, competed to see who could bless the food first as it arrived at the table, thus preventing the other from eating it. Even eating at the same table as people of a different faith was regarded with suspicion, when not explicitly prohibited, during the Middle Ages. Eating together was a sign of communion and identity, of belonging to the same group. Whether a Muslim should or should not eat with non-Muslims was discussed at length.

However, it was primarily among the Jewish community that dietary prescriptions and proscriptions functioned as a powerful cultural bond, indicating both the identity and the otherness of the group. This worked both ways. Just as Jews distinguished themselves by means of dietary rules, so Christians attempted to define them from outside. Jews were forbidden to use Christian butchers while, in Valencia in 1403, "Jewish" meat was banned from Christian market stalls. These norms were evidently dictated primarily by the desire to define cultural identity with easily recognizable social markers. But there must also have been a more or less conscious "magical" awareness of food, according to which it transmitted metaphorical or symbolic qualities. There is no other way to explain a curious episode described by the fourteenth-century English chronicler Walter Map in which Patarine heretics put a precise food strategy into practice in order to "capture" reluctant proselytes: they "offered special dishes to convert those they could not approach through words."[2]

There were many points of contact between the different religions and cultures in medieval Europe and beyond. These links reflected common biblical roots and a basic complicity that was most solid—despite appearances to the contrary—in the early Middle Ages. The language and spirit of the Old Testament was more pervasive in early medieval Christianity than those of the New Testament. Food taboos from Leviticus (such as a ban on meat "soiled by blood") persisted in apostolic writings and penitential texts. Monastic rejection of meat revealed a perception of it as impure, a marked contrast to the message of the New Testament. This excessive proximity to the Jewish cultural model was one of the accusations made against Roman Catholicism by the Greek Orthodox Church following the schism in the eleventh century. Once again, food symbolism was a central issue. The unleavened bread of the Jewish tradition (similar to the host of the Roman Catholic tradition) was in marked contrast to the "real" leavened bread of early Christianity, proudly preserved in the Orthodox ritual as the symbol of a distinct religious identity.

Meat played a central role in mechanisms of cultural and religious differentiation during the early Middle Ages, when the subsistence-based economy was silvipastoral and forests were measured in terms of the number of pigs they contained. In this context, it is hardly surprising that pigs were regarded as both a symbol and a guarantee of otherness. The remains of St. Mark were smuggled out of Saracen territory hidden beneath salted pork, a technique that was redolent with symbolic implications. Furthermore, in the medieval iconography of the pig's patron, St. Anthony, it was the only "real" animal (that is, without a symbolic function) to appear above the altar.

In relation to the Islamic world, the pig played an absolute symbolic role, representing Christian Europe in its entirety. (This was less true with regard to Judaism, where the ban on pork was one of many such prohibitions.) Another basic distinction concerned wine, a feature of Christian tables that was specifically excluded—ideologically, if not always in practice—from the Muslim diet. From this viewpoint, the arrival of Islam on the Mediterranean scene played a decisive role in defining European food culture. Under the Roman Empire, the countries around the Mediterranean had been considered a largely homogeneous area, held together by geographical contiguity and uniform political domination around a central point. The Arab invasions of the seventh century turned the Mediterranean into a dividing line. This shift has been regarded as the moment at which the center of the world moved northward to become the Holy Roman Empire of Charlemagne. The foods that represented the new Europe—pork and wine—were confined to areas north of the Mediterranean, a paradox when one considers that wine had always been part of the traditional Mediterranean triad. Even bread, as basic a food in Islamic as it was in Christian culture, acquired an additional sacred role in Europe, becoming in one sense an exemplary element of Christianity. Bread and wine, which had previously defined Mediterranean culture, now defined, along with meat (especially pork), the diet of medieval European Christians.

Islam not only defined medieval Europe's dietary identity by exclusion but also—and equally significantly—by introducing new elements, often from Persian culture. Many aspects of Islamic cooking turned up in Christian Europe. Even though spices had been adopted in Roman cuisine, their use was extended in variety and quantity (saffron, for example, was actually grown in Europe for the first time). New vegetables, such as eggplant and spinach, were introduced alongside new fruits, including citrus fruits. The arrival of cane sugar led to such delicacies as candied fruit, marzipan, and nougat, along with a taste for creamy textures, scents, and contrasting flavors. Even more substantial contributions to European cuisine were rice and pasta, introduced by the Arabs of Sicily and Spain. These significant additions helped to strengthen those bonds around the Mediterranean that Arab invasion had weakened. Although there were evident northern influences in European cooking, even in Mediterranean countries such as Catalonia and southern and central Italy, these were overlaid and interwoven with equally strong influences from the Arab world.

The extent to which these developments were the result of new influences or a revival of Roman culinary traditions continues to be a subject for debate. There is a good case for both arguments. The Arabs certainly contributed to the development of medieval European culture, while the classical tradition clearly provided its foundation. This is true for gastronomy and even more so for dietetics, which developed during the Middle Ages on the basis of classical authors mediated by Arab writers and doctors. The two sciences shared the same basic interests. Spices, for example, made food more flavorsome and also more digestible.

Classical heritage was even more direct in the food culture of Byzantium, the heir to the Roman Empire and its productive models, based on commerce and the town market. Specific foods were handed down, such as *garum* (fish sauce), described by Apicius and produced in Greece and on the eastern coasts of the Adriatic up to and beyond the Middle Ages, to be sold in the West. A more general influence was the taste for saltwater fish and lamb (as opposed to pork and beef in the West). Symbols and images of food often mediated the complex political and cultural relationship between Byzantium and the West. The Holy Roman Empire's ambassador to Byzantium, Liutprand, bishop of Cremona, described his disgust at the fatty lamb served at the Byzantine court, as well as the excessive oiliness of the other food and the fetid stench of the *garum*. He may not have been familiar with these foods. Alternatively, he was emphasizing his otherness from those foods and that culture. In either case, the description was a way of expressing disdain toward his political adversary.[3]

Food, therefore, frequently played a symbolic role in political and religious disputes. It should not be forgotten, however, that it was precisely these exchanges between different cultures that enabled medieval Europe to forge its own complex and original identity. The people of the time were well aware of this, as is demonstrated by the legend claiming that the school of medicine in Salerno— one of the centers for the diffusion of dietetic and gastronomic medieval culture—originated in the meeting of four doctors of different nationalities and cultures: a Latin, a Greek, an Arab, and a Jew.

NOTES

1. For the episode concerning Vladimir I, see I. P. Sbriziolo, *Racconto dei tempi passati* (Turin, 1971), pp. 49 ff.

2. Walter Map, *De nugis curialium,* trans. and ed. M. R. James, rev. C. N. L. Brooke and R. A. B. Mynors, Oxford Medieval Texts (Oxford: Clarendon Press, 1983).

3. See Liutprand, *Relatio de legatione constantinopolitana*, in *Liudprandi opera,* ed. J. Becker (Hannover-Leipzig, 1915), pp. 181–82. [*Relatio de Legatione Constantinopolitana*, trans. and ed. Brian Scott, *Reading Medieval and Renaissance Texts* (London: Bristol Classical Press, 1993).]

CHAPTER 16

CHRISTIANS *of the* EAST
Rules and Realities of the Byzantine Diet

Ewald Kislinger

Constantinople, the great city on the Bosporus, symbolizes the fusion that took place in the fourth and fifth centuries between the Roman concept of the state and Christianity. New Rome, the heir to the empire, was bound by its imperial heritage. At the same time, however, it was strongly influenced by Greece and the East. Despite the ideological and spiritual foundations that it shared with a Latin-Germanic West, the city nevertheless developed its own civilization, now known as Byzantine, from the old name of the city, Byzantion.

The Land and Its Produce

During its thousand-year life, from the late classical period to the fall of Constantinople in 1453, the territory ruled over by the Byzantine Empire varied considerably. Up to the Arab advance in the seventh century, it covered the entire eastern Mediterranean. Before that, under Justinian I (525–65), it had gained control over Italy, North Africa, and part of Spain. At a later date, during the reign of Basil II (976–1025), it grew once again, stretching from Calabria to Syria. The core territory—that with which we are most concerned—remained the Balkan Peninsula (more or less to the east of present-day Belgrade and south of the Danube), the Aegean Isles, including Crete, and Asia Minor as far as the Caucasus.

Climatic factors and the lay of the land clearly influenced agricultural production (and, indirectly, population density). The fertile lowlands of Thrace and Thessaly, the floodplains of the Axios and the Aliakmon near Salonika, Bithynia, the river valleys of western Asia Minor with their estuaries on the Aegean, and the coasts of Pontus made it possible to grow cereals (wheat, barley, and millet), olives, fruit and nut trees (apple, pear, plum, apricot, peach, pomegranate, fig, and hazelnut), and many varieties of vegetables, especially pulses. The empire's woodlands also provided an ideal place to raise pigs. The arid high-lying lands of central Anatolia and the mountainous regions of the Balkans—from the Rhodope massif to the Pindus range—were well suited to a developed pastoral economy. Fishing was carried out in all coastal areas. The sea salt extracted in Macedonia and the Black Sea was used to preserve fish in brine (an activity carried out on a large scale, particularly in the Crimea). Islands like Crete, Euboea, Lesbos, and Rhodes produced good-quality wine, but even areas on the mainland, such as Phrygia, grew vines up to 1,500 meters above sea level, while the merchants of Cilicia (c. 500) exported wine as far as Constantinople. In short, the empire offered a full range of basic agricultural produce, typical of the Mediterranean diet. Issues regarding the use of land (and any damage caused to fields and pastures) were dealt with by the *nomos gheorghikos,* or peasant law.

Politics and the Food Market: Supply and Demand

The devastating appearance of the plague in 542–45 and successive epidemics, together with Arab invasions of Asia Minor and the Slav occupation of the Balkans, radically transformed the population distribution of these areas in the sixth and seventh centuries. Vast tracts of land were depopulated or fell under foreign domination, while late-classical cities (*poleis*) were reduced to fortified settlements (*kastra*). But people's diets achieved an equilibrium. The reduction of cultivated land (and thus produce) did not create problems for an equally reduced population. A few annual fairs were enough to ensure the volume of regional trade needed. The categories of producer and consumer were, for the most part, one and the same, or at least increasingly similar. It is no surprise that an Avar attack on Salonika should have found its inhabitants outside the city, working in their fields (*Miracula Demetrii* 2:1). Patras was supplied with food by the slaves living in the surrounding countryside.

By the end of the ninth century, the political situation in the Byzantine Empire had already stabilized. External enemies had been repelled while numerous lands within the empire, which had previously evaded state control, had been reconquered. Great landed estates, or latifundia, increased dramatically in the tenth and eleventh centuries, producing surpluses in areas where harvests had previously yielded no more than three or four times the seed sown. Buyers for the surplus were found in Italy, where increasing food demands could not be met by local supplies. The relative safety of movement between East and West (partly owing to the decline of Arab power, with the loss of Crete in 961 and of Sicily from 1061 on) made it easier for the Marine Republics, above all Genoa and Venice, to develop their trade. Previously restricted to luxury items from the East (spices and silk), trade in these cities became increasingly comprehensive.

To start with, not only the producer benefited from this trade, but also the Byzantine state through taxes and tributes. As time passed, however, western traders began to take over the domestic market to such an extent that they controlled the retail sales of foodstuffs. The account books of a middleman (c. 1360) in Heraclea, on the Black Sea, contain numerous references to Venetian cheese imported from Crete and caviar from the Venetian colony of Tana on the Sea of Azov. Between 1436 and 1440, in the Constantinople suburb of Pera, many Byzantines bought everyday items from the merchant Giacomo Badoer. The Byzantine *oikumene*, or world, had been economically undermined and fragmented, primarily as a consequence of the Fourth Crusade, into a series of small political entities. As a result, they were unable to resist the immense political and economic power of Venice and Genoa. In the best of cases, they were relegated to the role of junior partners and thus easily subjugated. In 1348, for example, Genoa reacted to the Byzantine policy of dumping in Pera, the independent Genoese colony within the capital, by withholding supplies of grain and wine (Alexis Macrembolites, *Logos historikos*, 147). It was not until the Ottoman conquest (or *pax turcica*) that the market became unified and balanced once again.

THE SPECIAL CASE OF CONSTANTINOPLE: SUPPLYING A METROPOLIS
Constantinople inherited not only Rome's historical role but also its incredible size and urban structure. The area inside the Theodosian walls was approximately 1,400 hectares while in the same epoch Salonika and Trebizond covered only 270 and 90 hectares, respectively. At almost all times, then, the city par excellence had hundreds of thousands of mouths to feed.

During the earliest centuries, Byzantium continued to follow the Roman custom of importing grain from Egypt. A special fleet left Alexandria three times a year to transport the 800,000 units of grain requested by Emperor Justinian's edict (XIII.8).

Without even considering bad years, the distances that had to be traveled made the entire food supply system unreliable and subject to crises. Contrary winds often blocked ships at the entrance to the Sea of Marmara. At the mouth of the Hellespont on the island of Tenedos, a grain warehouse made it possible to unload supplies so that the fleet could be rapidly prepared for further voyages. Despite this, crises in supply occurred more than once. When it became impossible to buy wheat bread in 582, the emperor ordered barley from the imperial reserves to be used. The situation remained desperate, and ground pulses were mixed with the barley flour. Nevertheless, people continued to die of hunger and only a miraculous catch of tuna saved the city from starvation (Michael Siros, X, 19).

The victims of disasters of this kind accentuated Constantinople's population decline, which was already dramatic following the epidemics mentioned above. At the same time, however, they had the secondary effect of making it easier to feed the city. Already during the Sasanian occupation of Egypt (which began in 616 and lasted several years), it was possible to find a rapid substitute for Egyptian grain. Thrace and Bithynia soon supplied the city with its needs, later to be supplemented by grain from the northern regions of the Black Sea. Supplies from Egypt were interrupted even before the country was finally lost to the empire (641–42).

State control covered almost all basic Byzantine foodstuffs. It is significant that the term "meat" was limited to the flesh of pigs, sheep, and goats. Cattle did not provide meat but were regarded as working animals. The gourmet who, in a twelfth-century satire inspired by Lucian, dictates a shopping list from the afterworld, would have been satisfied by the array of goods offered in Constantinople: "Send me then a five-month-old lamb, two fattened three-year-old chickens, like the ones the poultry sellers (*ornithopolai*) have at the market, where the fat of the breast hangs down to the legs, a month-old suckling pig, and, finally, a pig's udder, the fattest you can find" (Timarion). In the fifteenth century a similar wealth of produce could be found at seaside markets, where—according to a contemporary source—butchers, dried-meat vendors, fishmongers, and fruit and vegetable sellers (*lachanopolidai*) all had their stalls.

Fruit and fresh vegetables do not appear in the Book of the Prefect, although they were widely grown in the surrounding countryside and in the city itself. It was probably their abundance that made it possible for market regulations to ignore them. The *Gheoponika,* a sixth-century collection of rules concerning the cultivation of fields and gardens that was then revised in the tenth century, provides an idea of the variety available in its list of the seasonal products permitted by the climate of Constantinople: "In February, sow: parsley with leeks and onions, carrots, beets, beans, salads of various types, and also green cabbage, sprouts, coriander, dill, and rue. Transplant: salads, chicory, lettuces, Phrygian salads. In May, sow: beets, orache, as well as mint. In September, sow: beet mallow, late endives, and wild beet. Transplant: turnips, winter endives, coriander, and horse-radish. In October, sow: salads, chicory, lettuces. Transplant: rape, beets, endives, watercress, rocket, cabbages. In November, fenugreek. Transplant: beets and, separately, mallow."

The last state interventions to be made in the supply and demand relationship occurred during the reign of the Palaeologi (1259–1453). These interventions were mainly prompted, however, by the state's desire to raise income through taxes. In the middle of the fourteenth century, for example, Venetian taverns boomed in Constantinople, since the exemption from sales tax, established by their contracts, enabled proprietors to sell wine from Crete and other places at lower prices, thus attracting Greek customers. The imperial authorities repeatedly threatened to block imports and to impose special duties in order to increase the volume of business—and of taxes—in Byzantine inns. In 1363, after long negotiations, a compromise was reached. The number of Venetian taverns permitted to sell draught wine (*ad spinam*) was reduced to fifteen, while the number allowed to sell tax-free wine in bottles remained the same. Groups of customers thus had the choice of buying a bottle to share outside the tavern or drinking their wine on the spot. Watered down to this extent, the agreement made little difference to Byzantine tax returns.

SUPPLYING THE ARMY A soldier's rations depended, above all, on the extent to which specific products could be preserved. Instead of fresh bread, he received *paximadion* (in Latin, *buccellatum*), a kind of rusk, baked twice to make it light and dry. During marches, meat and bacon were available in salted form and, during campaigns, in salt water. When soldiers were in the camp, they had fresh meat provided by the animals they took with them. The quality of drinking water was carefully controlled. Mixed with wine vinegar, it became *phouska* (in Latin, *posca*). Repeated warnings in military writings that water bottles should be filled with water and not with wine, however, clearly reveal the soldiers' preference.

Cooking Methods

The Byzantine cuisine did not always offer hot, cooked food. Apart from ideological and sociological restrictions, the working day of the peasants restricted their diet to bread, cheese, olives, and fruit. Moreover, in the bigger cities there was a shortage of fuel. Reinhold von Lubenau, who traveled across the Ottoman Empire in 1587–89, noticed that in thousands of houses in Constantinople fires were never lit from one year to the next and that nobody cooked food at home because of the price of wood. People found it cheaper to eat in taverns.

These taverns had replaced the ancient Roman *popina* and the Byzantine *kapeleion*. They offered mostly pulses and vegetables, cooked and kept simmering in the pot with water and oil to form a kind of soup. This was followed by pieces of lamb or pork cooked on a spit, familiar to readers of Homer as the "meat dripping with fat" and to today's tourists as the *souvlaki* of Greek tavernas. Undoubtedly, with its spit-roasted meat, fried fish, and frequent use of garlic, onions, and leeks, Byzantium respected a centuries-old tradition, although it would be unwise to assume that this was entirely unbroken. *Garum* (*garos*), for example, a kind of liquid extracted from macerated fish that had been very popular since ancient times as a condiment, is now the name of a salt solution used in modern Greece to preserve fish with no culinary value of its own. The main sweetener today is sugar whereas in Byzantium honey was used—spread, for example, on flatcakes fried in oil. Citrus fruits for dessert, such as limes with honey, were rare up to the nineteenth century, when they appear to have been imported from the West. In their drinking habits, too, the Byzantines differed from modern inhabitants of the region. Wine was not drunk neat but rather diluted with warm water (the modern Greek word for wine, *krasi*, comes from the Byzantine *kerannymi*—"to mix"). Both the addition of resin to ensure that the wine would keep and the mixing of the must with rose petals, fennel, or celery gave the wine an unusual flavor.

Dietary Rules

THE INFLUENCE OF CHRISTIAN ASCETICISM Basil the Great of Caesarea, in his *De legendis gentilium libris*, said: "You shall not be a slave to your body, but you shall do all you can to procure that which is best for your soul, which we free, so to speak, from a prison if we separate it from the passions of the flesh."

One of the main tools available for weakening the bondage of this prison and freeing the soul was fasting (*nesteia*). While greed was the first step toward a total surrender to the blandishments of the senses, fasting worked as a remedy: *contraria contrariis*. By fasting, the flesh, susceptible to wayward passions, could be rendered powerless, the influence of the devil curtailed, and the sin of Adam cleansed. Most people chose the wilderness, far from luxury and abundance, for this spiritual exercise (*askesis*), which had already been prescribed by Judaism and the Cynic philosophers. The act of dietary asceticism held extreme renunciation and the preservation of God-given life in a precarious balance. It was in the desert wilderness that the hermits (*eremos*, or "solitary") of the third to fifth centuries endeavored to acquire *apatheia*, indifference to the senses and earthly passions. Having achieved their aim, some of these hermits returned, less "earthly" than before, to a world that was, in its turn, becoming increasingly detached from paganism. These victorious pioneers of faith had the new task, in a world that was by now largely Christian, of being instructive and stimulating examples for others, advisers who were both within society and yet outside it. After the emperor, the saint was the second guiding figure in Byzantine society, and, at the same time, an unreachable model for normal citizens. He had to be unreachable because a society made up entirely of saints could never function. Other ways, more practicable from a social and economic view, to tear the people away from earthly temptation and lead them toward redemption thus had to be found.

As members of a pious community, the faithful could effectively compete to save their souls. Independently of their social class, a good 10 percent of the population chose this path. The first monasteries in Egypt and the area of Syria and Palestine grew up out of the local community of hermits and were still regarded as rigorously alternative worlds. The monastic community of Mount Tes Nitrias, to the west of Alexandria, comprised 5,000 men with "diverse life styles: each does what he can and what he wishes, to the extent that one can stay alone or in the company of another or of many others. There are also seven bread ovens that serve these men and the anchorites of the desert . . . There is a big church . . . and, next to the church, a hostel (*xenodocheion*). . . . On the mountain there are also doctors and pastry-makers. Wine is used and even drunk" (Palladius, *Lausiac History,* fifth century). The large monastic centers, such as those on Olympus in Bithynia, on Latmos near Miletus, or the *haghion oros,* still in existence, on Mount Athos, were organized along the same lines.

Although the monastic system was originally conceived as being in opposition to the rest of society, like the figure of the hermit himself, it soon settled into a form of coexistence, becoming part of the local economic and social fabric. Founded in 1088 on the then deserted isle of Patmos, the monastery of St. John already owned four ships by the end of the twelfth century, using them to transport goods from one of the monastery's Aegean possessions to another. Despite its imperial role as an "island of monks," Patmos also provided a home for lay people. These men worked five days a week for the monastery before returning to their families. The diet offered by the monastery was the basic minimum—one meal a day of uncooked food. According to the statutes of other monasteries, however, both the number of meals and the amount of food varied considerably from one monastery to another.

Thanks to the weekly days of fasting and four other periods of abstinence (Lent, Pentecost, the first half of August for the Feast of the Virgin, and the forty days following November 15 for Christmas), eastern Christianity reached far beyond the walls of the monastery, influencing everyday diets by offering laypeople another, less demanding way to achieve saintliness in life.

The fasting prescribed by the faith, however, was not simply a question of voluntary renunciation. It was often used as a form of punishment by ecclesiastical trials. The sinner had to make up for his shortcomings by subjecting himself to a diet that was more or less that of a monk. Penitence through renunciation implied that the object of renunciation was normally available and appreciated. These rules thus shed light on everyday diets.

The Christian attack on alcohol and, in particular, on wine—since the Byzantines considered beer to be barbaric—was highly effective. Sigurd of Norway, during his time in Byzantium in 1111, realized that his men were dropping like flies. The reason for this seemed perfectly clear, and Sigurd ordered them to drink less wine or to dilute it. But the intemperate drinkers were later absolved. It was not so much the amount they had been drinking as the quality of the wine itself: when a pig's liver was immersed in undiluted wine, it immediately dissolved. *In vino veritas*. As a monk said centuries earlier, enlightened after a couple of glasses as to the nature of the liquid: "Stop, don't you know that this is the devil himself?"

SOCIAL DIFFERENTIATION The table of Isaac II Angelus, emperor of Byzantium (1185–95), overflowed with bread, game, fish, and wine (Nicetas Choniates, 441). Wholegrain bread (*psomos pithyrodes*) and fresh cheese (*asbestotyron*), however, were the only things available in the cupboard of a simple woman (Theophanes Continuatus, 199). At first sight, the king and the peasant woman would appear to come from two different worlds. Yet they both belonged to the same Byzantine society. The quality and quantity of produce available was correlated to the social position and economic possibilities of the consumer. In other words, the supply was inversely proportionate to the social pyramid, at whose apex stood the emperor and his court.

The successors to the throne of Constantine remained faithful to the food culture of an Apicius. In homage to the self-representation of imperial dignity, the table at court was laid with a boned chicken filled with almonds in honey sauce, or even an entire roast sheep whose belly was opened to reveal a flock of live sparrows (Theodoros Prodromos, *Rodanthe and Dosicles,* twelfth century). Fishermen from Tembros (today's Porsuk Çayi) in Phrygia cast their nets in the service of the court. Carp (*kyprinos*) and other freshwater fish were also part of this lavish imperial diet, independently of the restraint of numerous sovereigns. Measure (*metron*) and a sense of economy (*prosekon*), two typical virtues of the *basileus*, must have ensured that the solemn feast did not degenerate into debauchery and that these Christian rulers behaved in a manner befitting that of kings whose power was granted by God. Moreover, even during feasts, no opportunity was wasted to demonstrate toward subjects ostentatious philanthropy and charity (*phrontis, euerghesia*) by inviting the poor to certain banquets.

The upper classes tried to demonstrate their closeness to the throne through external aspects of their behavior, such as a fondness for fine food. Nor should we forget the efforts made by the wealthy to alleviate poverty through charitable acts. The network of benevolent foundations (*euagheis oikoi*) included not only hostels, hospitals, and homes for the aged but also public soup kitchens. The hospice for the poor run by Michael Attaleiates fed six needy people daily, offering them a piece of bread as well as meat or fish, cheese, pulses, and cooked vegetables.

The fourteenth-century *Book of Fish* (*Opsarologos*) reflects, on a smaller and highly specific scale, this kind of social differentiation. The role played by fish in Byzantine cooking, which had fifty everyday ways to prepare it, here takes on a literary form as the protagonists in a trial for high treason are represented as fish. Gray mullet (*kephalos*), perch (*labrax*), and sole (*psession*), all excellent fish to eat, represented high functionaries. The smaller, cheaper, and less tasty sardines (*engraulis*), scorpion fish (*skorpios*), and other less prestigious sea fish (*smaris*) were the minor dignitaries, while the accused was represented by a dried mackerel, and the emperor—which comes as no surprise—was a sturgeon.

MEDICAL RULES Byzantine medicine, anchored in the tradition of Hippocrates and Galen, was based on the pathology of humors. Illnesses were attributed to the unbalanced mixing of the four bodily humors: blood, phlegm, and yellow and black bile. These imbalances were, in their turn, caused by mental disturbances, seasonal and other external influences, and, last but not least, a bad diet. The choice of the right food on a day-to-day basis made an essential contribution to maintaining a healthy psychosomatic equilibrium. Each foodstuff was associated with the qualities of hot, dry, moist, and cold, with each of the four humors possessing two of these qualities.

Academic treatises such as Simeon Seth's *Compendium of the Effects of Different Foodstuffs* (eleventh century) certainly existed, but monthly diet and health calendars were far more accessible to the lay person. One of these suggests: "May: wash your hair frequently. Eat warm foods, fennel, and drink its juice to eliminate bile. June: drink undiluted wine [*akraton*], a glass in the morning, and make sure that it is white. Eat lettuce with vinegar because it is good for the stomach. July: abstain from venereal commerce, do not let blood or vomit, eat sage and rue and drink fresh and pure water."

As far as eating was concerned, diet-sheets known as Hierophilos contained even more information. For example, they warned against drinking "moist" drinks in November and advised eating "dry" meats such as venison, roe deer, boar, and hare. It is worth noting that game was mentioned far more frequently in these texts than in other sources. Since hunting was a pastime for the powerful, it is likely that these sheets were aimed at people in these circles. The fifteenth-century doctor

John Kaloeidas wrote a letter to an illustrious Byzantine suffering from gout. The letter contained a series of dietary recommendations. The patient was to avoid fatty meat, pulses, raisins, and pine kernels, but could eat soup with lamb's meat, partridge, and thrush. John Cortasmenos blamed marrow, eaten in a state of physical prostration, for cases of shivering and headaches, while he believed that grapes and caviar from Pontus, eaten for breakfast at an inauspicious moment, caused breathing difficulties. It is very doubtful, however, whether an average and possibly illiterate Byzantine, when faced by a plate of salted pork in a sauce of Phrygian cabbage, would have thought for one second about the balance of his humors. Even Psellus devoted a whole letter (no. 233) to the delights of a plateful of truffles (*hydnon*); warnings that they caused bad humors were completely disregarded.

Food and Drink: The Image of the Other

The best-known book written by a foreigner on Byzantine life was *Relatio de Legatione Constantinopolitana,* the work of the tenth-century bishop and diplomat Liutprand of Cremona. He was disconcerted by what he found on his travels. He disapproved of the frugal meals of his Greek counterparts (*insipit et claudit cenam lactuca tenacem*) and of the food at court, which was, in his view, dripping with oil and steeped in a disgusting fish sauce. He was equally unimpressed by some fatty mutton dressed in garlic, which the emperor himself had eaten. According to both Nicetas Choniates, in an account written in 1204, and Eustace of Salonika, a Latin would sell his soul for a fillet of beef or salted pork and pureed beans, dressed in a garlic sauce.

When considering these reciprocal attacks, a question comes to mind. Was Liutprand a precursor of *nouvelle cuisine* or did Byzantine tastes change rapidly between 1000 and 1200? There can be no way of knowing.

BIBLIOGRAPHY

Balard, M. *La romanie génoise (XII–début du XV siècle).* 2 vols. Genoa-Rome: École Française de Rome, 1978.

Battaglia, E. *Artos: Il lessico della panificazione nei papiri greci.* Milan: Vita e Pensiero, 1989.

Brandes, W. *Die Städte Kleinasiens im 7. und 8. Jahrhundert.* Berlin: Akademie-Verlag, 1989.

Bryer, A. "The Estates of the Empire of Trebizond: Evidence for Their Resources, Products, Agriculture, Ownership, and Location." *Archeion Pontou* 35 (1978): 370–477.

Chrysostomides, J. "Venetian Commercial Privileges under the Palaeologi." *Studi veneziani* 12 (1970): 267–356.

Dagron, G. *Naissance d'une capitale: Constantinople et ses institutions de 330 à 451.* Bibliothèque Byzantine—Études, no. 7. Paris: Presses Universitaires de France, 1974.

Dalby, A. *Siren Feasts: A History of Food and Gastronomy in Greece.* London: Routledge, 1996.

Dar, S. "Food and Archaeology in Romano-Byzantine Palestine." In *Food in Antiquity,* ed. John Wilkins, David Harvey, and Mike Dobson, pp. 326–35. Exeter, England: University of Exeter Press, 1995.

Dembinska, M. "Diet: A Comparison of Food Consumption between Some Eastern and Western Monasteries in the 4th–12th Centuries." *Byzantion* 55 (1985): 431–62.

Eideneier, H. *Ptochoprodromos: Einführung, kritische Ausgabe, deutsche Übersetzung, Glossar.* Cologne, 1991.

Garzya, A. "Diaetetica minima." *Diptycha* 2 (1980–81): 42–52.

Haldon, J. F., trans. and ed. *Constantine Porphyrogenitus: Three Treatises on Imperial Military Expeditions.* Vienna: Verlag der Österreichischen Akademie der Wissenschaften, 1990.

Harvey, A. *Economic Expansion in the Byzantine Empire 900–1200.* Cambridge: Cambridge University Press, 1989.

Hendy, M. F. *Studies in the Byzantine Monetary Economy, c. 300–1450.* Cambridge: Cambridge University Press, 1985.

Herz, P. *Studien zur römischen Wirtschaftsgesetzgebung: Die Lebensmittelversorgung.* Stuttgart: F. Steiner, 1988.

Hiestand, R. "Skandinavische Kreuzfahrer, griechischer Wein und eine Leichenöffnung im Jahre 1110." *Würzburger medizinhistorische Mitteilungen* 7 (1989): 143–53.

Hirschfeld, Y. *The Judean Desert Monasteries in the Byzantine Period.* New Haven: Yale University Press, 1992.

Hunger, H. "Allzumenschliches aus dem Privatleben eines Byzantiners: Tagebuchnotizen des Hypochonders Johannes Chortasmenos." In *Polychronion: Festschrift F. Dölger,* pp. 244–52. Heidelberg: C. Winter, 1966.

Ieraci Bio, A. M. "Testi medici di uso strumentale." In *Akten XVI. Internationaler Byzantinistenkongreß.* II, 3: 33–43. Vienna, 1982.

Jacoby, D. "La population de Constantinople à l'époque byzantine: Un problème de démographie urbaine." *Byzantion* 31 (1961): 81–109.

Jeanselme, E. "Le régime alimentaire des anachorètes et des moines byzantins." In *Comptes rendus du IIᵉ Congrès Int. d'Histoire de la Médecine, Paris 1921,* pp. 106–33. Evreux, 1922.

Jeanselme, E., and L. Œconomos. "Aliments et Recettes Culinaires des Byzantins." In *Proceedings of the 3rd Int. Congress of the History of Medicine. London 1922,* pp. 155–68. Antwerp, 1923.

Kalleres, I. "Cibi e bevande nei papiri protobizantini." In *Epeteris Hetaireias Byzantinon Spudon* 23 (1953): 689–715.

Kaplan, M. *Les hommes et la terre à Byzance du VIᵉ au XIᵉ siècle: Propriété et exploitation du sol.* Byzantina Sorbonensia, no. 10. Paris: Publications de la Sorbonne, Université de Paris I-Panthéon-Sorbonne, 1992.

Karpozelos, A. "Realia in Byzantine Epistolography X–XII c." *Byzantinische Zeitschrift* 77 (1984): 20–37.

Kislinger, E. "Pane e demografia: L'approvvigionamento di Costantinopoli." In *Homo edens: Nel nome del pane,* ed. O. Longo and P. Scarpi, 4: 279–93. Bolzano, 1995.

———. "Retsina e balnea: Consumo e commercio del vino a Bisanzio." In *Homo edens: Storie del vino,* ed. P. Scarpi, 2:77–84. Milan, 1991.

———. "Taverne, alberghi e filantropia ecclesiastica a Bizanzio." In *Atti della Accademia della Scienze di Torino: Classe di scienze morali, storiche e filologiche* 120 (1986): 83–96.

Koder, J. *Der Lebensraum der Byzantiner: Historisch-geographischer Abriß ihres mittelalterlichen Staates im östlichen Mittelmeerraum.* Graz: Verlag Styria, 1984.

———. *Gemüse in Byzanz: Die Versorgung Konstantinopels mit Frischgemüse im Lichte der Geoponika.* Vienna: Fassbinder, 1993.

Kolias, T. "Essgewohnheiten und Verpflegung im byzantinischen Heer." In *Byzantios: Festschrift für Herbert Hunger zum 70. Geburtstag,* pp. 193–202. Vienna: E. Becvar, 1984.

Köpstein, H. "Zu den Agrarverhältnissen." In *Byzanz im 7. Jahrhundert,* pp. 1–72. Berlin: Akademie-Verlag, 1978.

Kukules, P. *Life and Civilization of the Byzantines* [in Greek]. 6 vols. Athens, 1948–55.

Lefort, J., and J.-M. Martin. "L'organisation de l'espace rural: Macédoine et Italie du sud (X^e–XIIIe siècles)." In *Hommes et richesses dans l'Empire byzantin,* ed. V. Kravari, J. Lefort, and C. Morrisson, 2:11–26. Paris, 1991.

Leven, K.-H. "Festmähler beim Basileus." In *Feste und Feiern im Mittelalter,* ed. D. Altenburg et al., pp. 87–93. Sigmaringen: J. Thorbecke Verlag, 1991.

Lilie, R.-J. *Handel und Politik zwischen dem byzantinischen Reich und den italienischen Kommunen Venedig, Pisa und Genoa in der Epoche der Komnenen und der Angeloi (1081–1204).* Amsterdam: A. M. Hakkert, 1984.

Mango, C. "Il santo." In *L'uomo bizantino,* ed. G. Cavallo. Rome, 1992. [*The Byzantines.* Trans. Thomas Dunlap, Teresa Lavender Fagan, and Charles Lambert. Chicago: University of Chicago Press, 1997.]

Montanari, M. *Alimentazione e cultura nel Medioevo.* Rome: Laterza, 1988.

Moutsos, D. "Prodromic droubaniston oxygala." In *Byzantion* 54 (1984): 586–92.

Œconomos, L. "Le calendrier de régime d'Hiérophile d'après des manuscrits plus complets que le Parisinus 396." In *Actes VIe Congrès Int. Et. Byzantines,* 1:169–79. Paris, 1950.

Oikonomidès, N. *Hommes d'affaires grecs et latins à Constantinople (XIIIe–XVIe siècles).* Montreal: Institut d'Études Médiévales Albert-le-Grand, 1979.

Ostrogorsky, G. *Storia dell'Impero Bizantino.* Turin, 1973.

Papagianne, E. "Monaci e mercato nero nel XII secolo: Osservazioni su alcuni problemi nel libro del prefetto" [in Greek]. *Byzantiaka* 8 (1988): 61–76.

Patlagean, E. *Pauvreté économique et pauvreté sociale à Byzance: IVe–VIIe siècles.* Civilisations et Sociétés, no. 48. Paris: Mouton, 1977.

Paviot J. "Cuisine grecque et cuisine turque selon l'expérience des voyageurs (XVe–XVIe siècles)." *Byzantinische Forschungen* 16 (1991): 167–77.

Schmalzbauer, G. "Medizinisch-Diätetisches über die Podagra aus spätbyzantinischer Zeit." *Jahrbuch der österreichischen Byzantinistik* 23 (1974): 229–43.

Schreiner, P. "Die Produkte der byzantinischen Landwirtschaft nach den Quellen des 13–15 Jh." *Bulgarian Historical Review* 10 (1982): 88–95.

———. *Texte zur spätbyzantinischen Finanz- und Wirtschaftsgeschichte: Handschriften der Bibliotheca Vaticana.* Vatican City, 1991.

Sirks, B. *Food for Rome: The Legal Structure of the Transportation and Processing of Supplies for the Imperial Distributions in Rome and Constantinople.* Amsterdam: J. C. Gieben, 1991.

Strazzeri, M. V. "Drei Formulare aus dem Handbuch eines Provinzbistums." *Fontes Minores* 3 (1979): 323–51.

Teall, J. L. "The Grain Supply of the Byzantine Empire, 330–1025." *Dumbarton Oaks Papers* 13 (1959): 87–139.

Thiriet, F. *La romanie vénetienne au moyen age: Le développement et l'exploitation du domaine colonial vénetien (XIIᵉ–XVᵉ siècles).* Paris: E. de Boccard, 1959.

Tinnefeld, F. "Zur kulinarischen Qualität byzantinischer Speisefische." In *Studies in the Mediterranean World: Past and Present,* 11:156–76. Tokyo, 1988.

Volk, R. *Gesundheitswesen und Wohltätigkeit im Spiegel der byzantinischen Klostertypika.* Miscellanea Byzantina Monacensia, no. 28. Munich: Institut für Byzantinistik und Neugriechische Philologie der Universität, 1983.

Weber, T. "Essen und Trinken im Konstantinopel des 10. Jahrhunderts nach den Berichten Liutprands von Cremona." In *Liutprand von Cremona in Konstantinopel,* ed. J. Koder and T. Weber, pp. 71–99. Vienna: Verlag der Österreichischen Akademie der Wissenschaften, 1980.

CHAPTER 17

ARAB CUISINE *and* ITS CONTRIBUTION
TO EUROPEAN CULTURE

Bernard Rosenberger

In the empire that the Arabs built from the Indus to the Ebro, the climate, vegetation, fauna, and ways of life were similar to those found in the cradle of Islam. The cultural traditions of Byzantine Syria, Egypt, Africa, the Sassanid Empire, the Maghreb, and Visgothic Spain could not have been more different, however, from the culture of Arabia. Yet in all these places a civilization steeped in the precepts of the Koran and based on the Arabic language was created in the space of less than two centuries. So "Arab cuisine" will refer to the cuisine of countries that adopted Arabic as their language and whose recipes in that tongue have survived.

The cultural synthesis in question took place in cities, new as well as old, which thrived on trade. The disintegration of the empire did not hinder the flow of people, goods, or ideas that typified the Muslim world from the eighth to the fifteenth century. Despite political divisions and the persistence of distinctive local traditions, which were more pronounced in rural areas remote from the political center than elsewhere, a remarkable cultural unity was achieved. Islam left its mark on food as it did on every other aspect of life. Arabs who became wealthy by virtue of the conquest retained some of their old customs but at the same time adopted the style of the aristocrats they had defeated. Subjugated peoples adapted to new laws and customs while clinging to many of their own traditions.

Christians, fascinated by the wealth of their enemies, frequently borrowed from them. It was not so much the Crusades as the reconquest of Spain and Sicily that introduced first the countries of the Mediterranean and later those of western Europe to classical Muslim foods and tastes.

Islamic Norms

The Revelation, in a break from both pagan Arab and Jewish traditions, had established its own definitions of the licit and the illicit, the pure and the impure. Islam imposed fewer prohibitions than did Judaism. As in the latter, forbidden foods included pork, animals sacrificed to idols, and animals not slaughtered in accordance with certain prescribed rules. Hence we may speak of a blood taboo. Drinking fermented beverages was also prohibited in order to keep Muslims from praying while intoxicated. It was not as widely respected as the prohibition on pork, which continued to induce a powerful revulsion.

Muslim fasts lasted longer and were more arduous than Jewish ones. During the month of Ramadan, Muslims were expected to abstain from food and drink during daylight hours. This was a difficult ordeal when the period in question coincided with the longest and hottest days of the year. But relatively sumptuous nocturnal meals took on a festive character that helped the faithful endure the daily privation. The mealtime ritual began with an invocation and ended with a prayer of thanksgiving. Sitting cross-legged, the guests served themselves from a tray placed on a low table or a leather pad. They used only three fingers of the right hand, which had previously been purified. Food was prepared in such a way that utensils were not necessary. Spoons were used only for liquids.

Islam looks upon food as a gift from God that is to be used sparingly and shared with people in need. Involuntary transgressions of the Law, or transgressions made necessary by circumstances, are forgiven. These rules were well suited to the milieu in which Islam was born, although later legal-religious schools and sects interpreted the dogma in various ways of their own. One area of controversy concerned whether it was proper to eat with non-Muslims. Some authorities held that it was permissible to share meals with other "peoples of the Book"—that is, Jews and Christians. But this left open the question of what foods served by these non-Muslims could be eaten. The fear of ingesting something impure led the strictest interpreters of the Law to prohibit all contact with outsiders.

The Arab Legacy and the Persian Model

The Arab legacy is more important than one might suspect from the frugal circumstances in which it originated. The nomadic shepherds of the pre-Islamic period lived on dairy products, a small amount of meat, and dates. In the oasis and the southern part of the peninsula, where the climate was less arid, the food was more varied. Grains, vegetables, and fruits were eaten. In poorer, harsher environments, people were obliged to eat what they found, including grasshoppers and roasted lizard. But hospitality was the law of the desert: the best food was served to travelers.

A dish known as *tharid* is illustrative of the scarcity of resources and simplicity of Arab taste: it consisted of slices of bread soaked in a spicy meat stock. This simple dish, which the Prophet had praised, was a complete meal, a luxury for a small banquet or great occasion.

Even after migration and acculturation, Arab cuisine continued to favor dairy foods, dates, mutton, and camel hump, which shows that Bedouin tastes had survived. In nineteenth-century Morocco, camel's milk was still a drink fit for a sultan. Does this attachment to a symbolic, ritualized, almost sacred food suggest nostalgia for an idealized, mythified Arabia and affinities with the first Arabs? Although such preferences may have been a mark of pride for aristocrats keen to evoke their real or imagined past, they also made converts of others who wished to identify with them. And then, too, the shepherd's life was hardly peculiar to Arabia but common throughout the Middle East and Maghreb.

Persia's culinary traditions deeply and permanently influenced Arab cuisine. Under the Abbasid dynasty, which inherited many of the projects of the Kings of Kings, Iranian converts often attained the highest offices. Persian fashions triumphed. Too little is known about Sassanid cuisine to determine its exact influence on the cooking of the Baghdad caliphate, but we do know that the meat of young animals, either roasted or fried in butter or oil, was much appreciated in the palaces of Persia. Meat was sometimes sweetened with sugar or syrup. Meat and organs were also marinated in a mixture of sour milk and spices. Stews, pâtés, and aspics were common, and rice and spinach were often served on the side. Crushed walnuts and almonds featured in a number of sweet desserts. Fruit occupied a prominent place in many meals, accompanied by a selection of wines. This tradition was probably the source of the many thick, creamy dishes and sweets found in Arab cookbooks. Numerous recipes have Persian names, some of which have passed into the Romance languages.

Owing to the Arab world's ease of communication and cultural unity, plants from the tropics already acclimatized in Persia soon became common throughout the empire: among them were sorghum, rice, sugarcane, eggplant, spinach, citrus fruits, and bananas.

REGIONAL VARIETIES AND SOCIAL DIFFERENCES The factors that promoted unity within the Arab world should not be allowed to hide the great diversity that persisted over its vast extent. The very nature of the sources tends to distort our view: cookbooks were used by only a small segment of society, whose comfortable lifestyle varied little throughout the Muslim world. What common people ate was rarely discussed in these texts. Yet the popular diet was more dependent on local resources and customs than was the diet of the elite. For example, steamed semolina was traditional in the Maghreb, and people from that region were so fond of it that they missed it when they traveled to the eastern part of the empire. When one of them fell ill, a plate of couscous was enough to restore him to health. Egyptians to this day have a marked taste for the fava bean. Substantial migrations led to the introduction of new foods, such as yogurt and bulghur, which the Turks imported into the Middle East.

Diet and taste also depended on ambient conditions. If nomadic shepherds were not particularly fond of fruits and vegetables, people in the cities ate a lot of them, a fact that struck European travelers, along with the quality of the white bread, which only the wealthy ate. Doctors believed this bread was particularly well suited to people who did not have to do much physical labor. Workers could easily digest a less refined loaf. Science justified socioeconomic categories by treating them as natural. The poor were expected to make do with dark bread made from barley, sorghum, millet, and other seeds that could be turned into flour, including grape seeds and acorns.

The difference between the cities and the countryside was thus quite considerable. Peasants consumed more soup, porridge, and flatcakes than bread. They had barely enough to eat, and their diet was poorly balanced and subject to seasonal variations in local production. Their menus were limited and monotonous. Often the preparation was so rudimentary that one hesitates to call it cooking. In the lavish and varied diet of the aristocracy, pleasure counted as much as concerns about health. Many recipes took account of the dietetic theories of the time. Cooking techniques were complex, and service was elaborate. Ostentatious display was an obvious motive, as is evident from the lavish use of rare and expensive ingredients, especially spices.

CONSERVATION, PREPARATION, AND SALE OF FOOD Arab food preservation techniques were inherited from earlier civilizations, certain of whose methods became widely known. Grains were often stored in underground silos. This was an efficient method of storage as long as proper precautions were taken in building and filling the structure. It was essential for the air inside the silo to prevent the growth of parasites and microorganisms. Hay stored in lofts had to moved about to prevent heating. Those who could afford it maintained their own private stockpiles. The authorities stored grain received as payment of taxes; this stockpiled grain was used both for the rulers' own needs and in times of scarcity.

In the climate that prevailed in the Arab world, drying was the simplest way to store meat and fruit. Fish was salted; smoked fish was rare. Food was protected from contact with air by coating it with fat, honey, or sugar or by pickling it in brine or an acidic solution whose effectiveness was enhanced by the addition of herbs. This type of preservation was generally done at home.

Producers processed some foods before selling them. Milk was transformed into butter and cheese, for example—a simple task that did not require expensive equipment. But making sugar in large quantities was beyond the capacity of a single family or small shop. It took a substantial plant to press the cane, cook the juice in order to thicken it, and then crystallize and refine it. All of this required a major investment, and it was one of the few food-related activities that developed into an industry in the modern sense of the word. Fishing and tuna packing were two others.

In some cities where water power was readily available, milling also developed into something like an industry. There were several mills in Fez, for instance, that ran virtually nonstop. Animal-driven mills were more common, however, and in many homes milling was done by hand. Kneading dough was generally still a family activity, even in the cities, where baking, on the other hand, was entrusted to professionals. The baker took a portion of the dough in payment for his services and from this made bread that he then sold to other customers. The *muhtasib* kept an eye on food prices and quality. He inspected fruits and vegetables, dairy products, fowl, meat, and fish and visited the shops of roasters, doughnut makers, pastry makers, and confectioners. City dwellers bought a substantial proportion of their food already prepared.

KITCHENS AND COOKS Cooking was often done outdoors in an area some distance away from any dwelling. The major piece of equipment was the fireplace, which in some cases was little more than a brazier. Charcoal was preferred to wood because it produced less smoke and was easier to transport. Next to the open hearth there might be an oven (*tannur*). Essential water came from wells, springs, or rivers and was piped into city fountains.

Kitchen equipment was similar to that found in Christian Europe with a few exceptions. Cookbooks recommended cooking food in new clay pots. If glazed, a pot could be used as many as five times. Beyond that, grease impregnated the porous material and gave the food a bad taste. It is doubtful that everyone was in a position to follow this advice. In families of modest means, the mother or other females did the cooking. In large households we do not know whether men or women were in charge of the kitchen. At court a master chef commanded a large hierarchy of subordinates, each with a different specialty. The master chef was responsible for preventing theft and waste and for monitoring the quality of ingredients and dishes: the health, not to say the life, of the prince depended on his vigilance. An obsession with poisoning, a real danger not always clearly distinguished from food poisoning, made finding a trustworthy master chef essential and all but turned the job into a political office. Egyptian women were reputed to make excellent cooks. Some kitchens were staffed by slaves, and the price of a skilled cook could be quite high. The art was often passed from generation to generation. Recipe books emphasized the need for strict cleanliness of both the person and the workplace. When preparing meat, it was essential to remove all bits of bone and to wash the meat in cold water to eliminate any trace of blood; pans and utensils had to be washed after every use. These rules reflect a concern with ritual purity as much as with hygiene. Other recommendations had more to do with taste: cooks were urged not to slice meat with a knife that had been used to cut onions, leeks, or carrots, for example.

Cooking Is the Art of Seasoning

The distinctive features of Arab culinary art derive from the use of certain ingredients, cooking techniques, flavorings, and consistencies. Let us begin our survey of classical Arab cooking by looking at flavorings. One author from this period suggested a surprising yet revealing classification. He began with fragrances, the noblest of all food additives in the Arab repertoire. Heading the list were musk and amber, whose high cost limited their use to the wealthiest diners. Next came rose water, which was readily available, followed by saffron, cinnamon, galanga, clove, mastic, nutmeg, cardamom, and mace. A second group of flavoring ingredients consisted of dried fruits and nuts: dates, raisins, almonds, walnuts, hazelnuts, pinenuts, and pistachios. A third group comprised fresh fruits, both sweet and sour, such as apples and pomegranates. Fourth came sugar and honey. The next group included stimulants such as *morri* (a fermented sauce something like soy sauce or Vietnamese *nuoc mam*) and *bunn* (believed to be coffee berries, but we have no idea how these were used). Then came grains and beans, which were used as thickeners, followed by herbs and vegetables (onion, garlic, leek, celery root, fresh coriander, mint, bitter orange leaf, thyme, marjoram, sumac berries, fennel, carrots, cabbage, and spinach). Only at the end of this long list did our author see fit to include such common ingredients as salt, pepper, coriander seed, cumin, caraway, ginger, vinegar, and dairy products. He then discussed wine, which was thickened by being allowed to sit in the sun for an extended period: we do not know how this was used, however. And finally he mentioned colorants such as saffron and spinach, which he had discussed previously in other contexts. Clearly, a wide range of ingredients was used to control the consistency and appearance as well as the taste of each dish, and we must extend our notion of spices and flavorings accordingly.

"Understanding spices is the cornerstone of the art of cooking," maintained the anonymous author of one Andalusian cookbook. "Spices distinguish one dish from another, define flavor, and heighten taste." More than that, they "promote well-being and prevent harm." To promote the good and fight evil—a Muslim ideal. The medicinal properties of certain spices compensated for the harmful properties of some foods. In order to use spices well, therefore, the cook was advised to heed the advice of the physician. In this way the gourmet, regardless of his age or state of health, could eat what he liked without risk to his physical "temperament."

Fats played an essential role in Arab cooking. In frying, for instance, it was deemed wise to use a strongly flavored fat from the tail of the sheep. Recipes explained how to extract the fat from the tail, clarify it, store it, perfume it, and color it. Less expensive fat from around the animal's kidneys and other parts of its body was also used, as was fat from other animals (but not pigs). Most common of all was olive oil. Andalusia, the Maghreb, and Syria were noted for their olive oil and supplied the needs of places like Iraq and Egypt, where olive trees were few and far between. In regions without olives, oil was made from sesame seeds, whose neutral taste was well suited to frying fish and chicken. Oil made from cartilage, walnuts, and almonds was used for special purposes. Butter also played an important role after clarification for storage (clarified butter was called *saman*). Fresh butter was spread on bread. Other dairy products were also used in cooking. Fresh milk was used for cooking rice, while sour milk figured in any number of dishes. Cheese, both fresh and dried, added flavor and could be used to thicken sauces; so could eggs, which were rarely eaten as such.

The extensive use of vinegar is somewhat surprising, since it was made from wine, which was prohibited. Other acidic liquids such as cider vinegar, citrus juice, and sour fruit juices were also widely used, especially for preserving olives, capers, and various vegetables, which were then used to make tasty appetizers. The same liquids were also used for marinating meat and fish and making a variety of sauces, especially for meat dishes.

MEATS The most common recipes in the cookbooks are for meat dishes, including meat from domestic animals, fowl, and game. Animals were slaughtered by having their throats slit according to prescribed rules, but we do not know how they were butchered after that or which cuts were favored, although recipes do generally indicate which cut was considered best for each dish. Broadly speaking, Arabs liked their meat tender and well marbled with fat. Organ meats were cooked separately. The head of the sheep was (and still is) highly prized.

Beef was not much liked or widely eaten, as was the case in Europe before the revolution in European taste. Cows and oxen that gave milk or labored in the fields had tough, dry flesh. When young, they were of some gastronomic interest, but people were reluctant to sacrifice them. Many recipes called for camel meat: this was an Arab tradition, and the Prophet himself was partial to it. Of course, it was mainly the younger animals that were slaughtered. Most meat came from vast flocks of sheep, however. People liked the taste of mutton and the abundant fat that it provided, and its price put it within reach of even modest pocketbooks. Physicians looked upon the flesh of the yearling lamb as being close to perfection. As a food that balanced heat and moistness, it was, according to the medical thinking of the day, suitable for people of all ages and temperaments.

Goats, which mingled with flocks of sheep, were less widely eaten. Castrated males were not highly prized. Although horse meat was not taboo, no one ate it. Mule and donkey meat was despised, and only in times of absolute need would anyone eat it. Nevertheless, we do find recipes for the meat of the onager, or wild donkey. The meat of the gazelle was considered the most healthful of all game meats, as well as the tastiest and most natural. Rabbit and hare, common in Spain, were not well liked. The boar was hunted, but eating its meat was generally considered illicit.

Most prized of all was fowl, which people raised even in the city—hens first and foremost, then roosters and pullets, but these needed to be cooked in fat if they were to acquire a good taste. The price of chicken was low, it was easy to cook, and it could be prepared in any number of ways (one oriental cookbook contains seventy-four recipes). Although pigeons were as well liked as hens or pullets, geese were preferred to ducks. Partridges were plentiful, easy to trap, and the object of much praise. Francolin and quail were similarly prized. Small birds were commonly eaten as well, but the sources rarely bothered to distinguish among thrushes, blackbirds, starlings, and the like.

Meat, raw or cooked, was often marinated at least overnight in order to imbue it with the flavor of herbs and spices. The basic marinade might consist of sour milk, vinegar, or *morri*. Recipes for roasted meat are relatively rare, despite a widespread taste for *shuwa* (roast lamb). There was a well-stocked roasters' souk in Fez known as the "smoky market." Since foul odors were frowned upon, roasting was done outdoors, even in large houses. It also tended to dry out the meat. In order to avoid these two drawbacks, many cooks preferred the *tannur* (bake oven). Grilling was rarely used because people liked to eat meat that fell apart after lengthy cooking. Sometimes meat was chopped or crushed with a mortar to make *banadiq*, or meatballs, or to serve as a stuffing or to make dishes such as the very popular *harissa*, a mixture of pounded meat and soaked, crushed grain cooked for a long time in a moderate oven. It was common to boil meat in a casserole with salt, onions, herbs, and spices such as pepper, fresh or dried coriander, cinnamon, and ginger. A wide range of other ingredients was often added, along with vegetables, which could be thrown into the pot at different times depending on the type of vegetable and the effect desired. Stews were frequently thickened by adding soaked or peeled chickpeas, lentils, or fava beans. Rice and noodles were also used to absorb some of the stock.

Many dishes derived their name and character from their acidic ingredients: sour milk or whey, vinegar, cider vinegar, lemon juice, bitter orange, pomegranate, crabapple, orange, apricot, or sumac berry. If the acidity seemed excessive, sugar could be added to correct it; honey was also used, but not as often, sometimes with thick grape must, in order to obtain a sweet-and-sour taste. Dates, raisins, almonds, walnuts, and hazelnuts, shelled and chopped, not only sweetened the pot but thickened it as well. Sometimes meat was fried before boiling. Often the stock was reserved, and the meat was simmered in its own fat mixed with a little of the stock to produce, once again, a sweet-and-sour taste. On occasion boiled meat was fried in fat from a sheep's tail. Or it might be chopped (along with whatever cooked in the same pot) and then thickened with eggs, spiced, and fried in a frying pan. But such dry, browned preparations were less common than dishes that aimed for a mixture of creamy smoothness (from fat), tenderness, and a sweet-and-sour taste. Meat was almost always the main ingredient of a complex creation.

Fowl, especially small birds and pigeons, were more commonly roasted on a spit, often stuffed with butcher meat. The combinations of ingredients used with fowl were not the same as those used with meat. The flesh of birds was sometimes used to make sweets (*halawat*); it was mixed with fruit, from which each specialty took its name: *rummaniya,* from *rumman* (pomegranate), or *tuffahiya,* from *tuffah* (apple), or *mishmashiya,* from *mishmash* (apricot), and so forth. According to Persian tradition, chicken was also served in an aspic of plums or blackberries. There are recipes for chicken cooked with almonds, pistachios, hazelnuts, poppy seeds, and so on. Some of these appear to be quite sophisticated. In one, the skin of the chicken is carefully removed and filled with a stuffing of chicken, bread, almonds, herbs, and spices. Then it is sewed back up and cooked. The best *isfidbadj,* whose name is a mark of its Persian origin, was made with the white meat of the chicken slowly cooked in a stock carefully flavored with herbs and spices until the chicken was ready to fall apart. To this was then added crushed almonds and simmered over a very low flame until ready to serve, at which point ground cinnamon was added to taste. This delicate dish may well have been the ancestor of our blancmange, which it so strongly resembles.

Just before serving meat or chicken, it was common to add a little rose water and garnish the plate by arranging, for example, hard-boiled eggs, either whole or sliced in half, in a pattern reminiscent of the narcissus. For that reason the dish in question was known as *nardjisiya;* in this case the eye mattered more than the palate.

FISH In some areas fish was a basic staple. It was sold at markets in Cairo, Seville, and elsewhere. Yet cookbooks contain few fish recipes because fish was not considered a food of great value from either a dietetic or a gastronomic point of view.

Fatty fish were the best liked—carp and shad from fresh water and tuna and sardines from the Mediterranean. Sardines and anchovies were packed for preservation on the Spanish coast and in the Maghreb. They had to be de-salted before use. Fresh fish had to be carefully cleaned. Sometimes it was marinated. Because it was thought to be "cold" and "moist," it was often grilled, baked, or fried to dry it out. Poaching, though rarely practiced, was invariably followed by baking or frying. In the oven the fish was laid out on a glazed dish, its belly filled with herbs or a stuffing made from bread, almonds, and walnuts in a sour sauce. Some cooks used grape juice as a binder, however. A well-known eastern dish was made with *tirrikh,* a small fish from Lake Van, which was salted and chopped and made into a sort of omelette.

VEGETABLES Vegetables could be purchased at urban markets all year round. Some came from gardens while others, such as wild mallow, asparagus, and artichoke, were gathered wherever they grew. Regional variety was great. Vegetables made up an important part of the diet of people of relatively modest means. Often combined with meat, they were cooked in ways designed to improve what was thought to be their insipid taste. Vegetables were often pickled in vinegar to make appetizers that many people loved to eat. The role of beans was particularly important. When grain was in short supply, they served as a replacement, and for poor people they were a staple. Lentils were the most popular in the Middle East, and fava beans in Egypt. Chickpeas were eaten everywhere. People also ate green beans, though not the sort we now tend to think of, which originated in America. Fava, peas, and green beans were also eaten raw.

A number of vegetables proved particularly successful and quickly spread to Spain, where they enjoyed a place of honor in twelfth- and thirteenth-century cookbooks. At the head of the list was the eggplant (*badindjan* in Arabic, *berenjena* in Spanish). Despite its black color and reputedly toxic juice, it owed its success to its low price and culinary advantages, for it was easy to prepare sumptuous dishes with it. Once its bitterness was removed with salt and boiling water, its neutral taste allowed it to combine with any number of other ingredients. It was often served with meat and used as a stuffing for chicken. It could be fried, stuffed, or baked. It could be disguised to look like meat. Or it could be seasoned with vinegar, *morri,* coriander, mint, thyme, garlic, and the like. It was sometimes combined with walnuts, almonds, and other vegetables. In short, it was used in much the same way that we use potatoes today.

Spinach (*isbanakh* in Arabic, *espinaca* in Spanish), though very different from eggplant in consistency, became popular because of its supposed dietary value. Beets, sometimes called "Yemenite vegetables," were also favored and figure in many dishes. Carrots—white, yellow, and red—keep well and found favor where green vegetables were not plentiful. Their mild taste made them a good accompaniment for meat as well as an attractive garnish.

Of course vegetables that were already being eaten continued to be eaten even after these newcomers arrived. Of the roots, the turnip is mentioned most often. The cookbooks have nothing to say about radishes because they were eaten raw. The cauliflower is mentioned as often as the cabbage. Lettuce was eaten in mixed salads as well as combined with meat. Onions were a basic ingredient. Raw, they caused bad breath, and the Prophet's poor opinion of them must be taken into account. The same can be said of garlic. Leeks were used in much the same way as onions. Poor people ate them in Syria and Iraq. Squash (the Old World species, gourd and calabash) was popular. According to one Andalusian recipe, it was possible to treat and comfort the sick by preparing squash in such a way that it resembled fish. Cucumber, abundant everywhere, was sometimes lumped together with melon. It was served in dishes containing other summer vegetables. Asparagus was a delicate accompaniment for meat. The vegetable known as *kharshaf* (*al-cachofa* in Spanish) was actually a relative of the artichoke, cardoon, the petioles of the leaves of a plant whose capitulla had been eaten since earliest antiquity. In making soups and sauces in Egypt and the Middle East, much use was made of *mulukhiya,* a mucilaginous fruit of a tree of the mallow family. The *kulkas,* a tuber known since ancient times, was first scalded and then fried.

Fennel, celery root, wild celery, and parsley were all used to add flavor to a variety of dishes. Some mushrooms and other fungi were eaten, including white and black truffles, which were reputed to be aphrodisiacs. The *muhtasib* of Seville tried to forbid the sale of truffles in the vicinity of mosques on the grounds that they were a food for debauchery.

SOUPS If one were to go by European tradition, a compilation of this sort should begin with soups, but in my view they were a derivative of cooking meats and vegetables. Making soup was a way of taking advantage of rich meat-cooking stock and of using leftovers. Although soups were simple and popular, we find numerous soup recipes in cookbooks destined for use in wealthy households. As the reputation of *tharid,* mentioned earlier, shows, people liked foods whose thick consistency did not alter their taste. A wide variety of ingredients were used to make soup: chopped meat, pounded meat, and vegetables. Flour and rice were used to thicken the mixture, and eggs were used as a binder.

GRAINS Flour was mixed with bouillon, milk, or water to make porridge, which was generally eaten in the morning. The large number of surviving recipes shows that this simple dish, which could be enriched at will, was appreciated by the wealthy as well as those not so wealthy. Making bread was not really the business of cooks, so cookbooks rarely give recipes for it, with the exception of the Andalusian one by Tujibi. Perhaps the custom of making bread at home was more deeply rooted at this extreme western end of the Arab Empire than it was in the eastern end.

There were many sorts of bread. The best kind for making certain *tharid* (stuffings) was fine flour or semolina of wheat, well leavened and cooked in a sort of baker's oven (*furn*), which had been known since antiquity, or else in a *tannur.* Poorly leavened white or black bread baked in a rudimentary oven or in the ashes of the fire in rural households was just good enough, the doctors said, for people whose constitution and habituation to hard labor enabled them to digest this gross type of food, which looked more like a pancake or crepe than a bread.

Two types of noodle were discussed: long, thin ones, similar to spaghetti, called *rishta* in the eastern regions and *itriya* in the western regions (from which we get the Catalonian *aletria*), and little ones, similar to vermicelli, which were called *sha'riya* in the east (from *sha'r,* "hair") and *fidawsh* in the west (from which came the Spanish *fideos*). Cookbooks described how to make these noodles and how to cook them in meat stock. They were served with meat and lentils in the east. Rice could be cooked in the same way, or in milk, or in the oven. It was often sugared and flavored with spices. The making of couscous was not described in detail because it was fairly well known. Recipes were more likely to describe cooking techniques involved in producing regional or local variations. Grains played only a limited role in making pastry.

FRUITS There is good evidence for the abundance, variety, and quality of fruit as well as its importance in cooking. Arab princes ordered fruit brought to Baghdad from afar: melons packed in ice and shipped in lead containers, along with prized Damascus grapes and plums. The Middle East was apparently the original home of a number of species known to the Greeks and Romans. The Arabs played the important role of improving these species and making them known over a wide area. These include the apricot (*barkuk* in Arabic, from which we get the Spanish *albaricoque* and the French *abricot*), and the peach, which was soon acclimatized in Iran.

What information we have about the diffusion of citrus fruit is unreliable. The melon, known since antiquity, was joined by the watermelon, which came from India. Both were widely cultivated as sweet, refreshing treats. Vineyards withered because of the ban on drinking wine, but table grapes and especially raisins (*zabib*) were extensively exported to Europe, where they gained a considerable reputation. Nevertheless, many people believed that fruits were not good to eat except for very sweet grapes and figs. Perhaps they felt that the negative properties of fruit diminished when the fruit was cooked and sweetened. Fruit was often served with meat—quince, apples, and sour fruits that were artificially sweetened. Fruit and sugar were also used to make jelly and syrups.

SWEETS Many dishes were sweetened with sugar, which was obviously much appreciated. Cookbooks contained numerous recipes for pastries and confections. European travelers in Arab lands were amazed by the quantity and quality of their sweets. They were also delighted by the variety of delicious drinks (*sharab*) made with fruit and sugar, which they referred to as syrups and sorbets, and they especially liked the sophisticated touch of adding shaved ice, which was brought down from high mountaintops and preserved in basements. Various medicinal salves were made from apple, quince, and walnuts mixed with sugar. Thus the confectioner also served as an apothecary. The subject of sweets deserves further study based on the available cookbooks and other sources.

The biscuits carried by travelers had the same name, *ka'k,* as a sweet pastry ring, but recipes show that the ingredients and preparation were different. Most cake recipes called for relatively few eggs, semolina, quantities of almonds, walnuts, pistachios, dates, and lots of sugar and honey as well as spices such as cinnamon or saffron and, less often, spikenard or camphor. From these ingredients a thick batter was made that could be shaped into various geometric forms and then baked in a moderate oven. Various sorts of doughnuts were also made from a soft or semiliquid batter consisting mainly of flower and water, which in some cases was allowed to rise before deep-frying in oil. Andalusians were very fond of doughnuts stuffed with white cheese (*majabbanat*). Many cakes and doughnuts were dipped in honey after baking and then sprinkled with rose water, which was also used by confectioners to flavor sugar and almonds. With crushed almonds and sugar one made a kind of marzipan, which was sometimes cut into diamond shapes. Finally, there was a candy made of starch and sugar not unlike what is nowadays known as Turkish Delight.

CHARACTERISTIC CONSISTENCIES AND FLAVORS Cookbooks did not discuss raw foods, which smacked of animality and savagery. The demand for fresh, high-quality products coincided with the religious insistence on purity and a cultural sensitivity to odor. Salting food to preserve it was not widely used, in contrast to the Christian west; the climate probably had a great deal to do with this. The recipes suggest a preference for very well cooked food of thick consistency and with pronounced flavors. No doubt the predilection for lengthy cooking over a slow fire or in a moderate oven was related to the type of fuel used and the design of fireplaces. The purpose of cooking was to make food tender or to thicken it or dry it if it was moist. The ideal was to achieve a consistency that was neither too thick nor too thin.

Many dishes combined meat with a variety of other ingredients that would not be mixed today. Seasoning also relied on a combination of flavors that might nowadays seem incompatible. This cannot be satisfactorily accounted for by the supposed necessity of cooking everything together. It would be astonishing if the large households for which these recipes were intended had only one cookpot. It is more likely that the mixture of ingredients, especially those intended to achieve a thick consistency, along with eggs and crushed, dried fruits as binders, was meant to satisfy a predilection for food that was soft, creamy, sweet, and fragrant. The popular *harissa* and the more refined *isfidbadj* typify these preferences, as do many other dishes. Similarly, many foods were chopped or crushed with a mortar "so as to obtain the consistency of marrow," according to one recipe. A more pragmatic explanation might stress the fact that Arabs ate not with utensils but with their fingers.

Luxury and ostentation certainly do not explain why so many different ingredients and spices were combined. The purpose was in fact dietetic. It is no accident that Razes, one of the greatest Arab physicians, wrote a treatise entitled *Correctives for Various Foods*. By studying the ingredients used to make various dishes, we might be able to grasp some of the rules for combining one thing with another.

Arab cuisine also aimed at achieving other than gustatory effects. Certain "deceptive" dishes were intended to surprise the diner: vegetables and fish were sometimes prepared to look and taste like meat. The desire to surprise is evident in a dish that was served to an Almohad emir: a vealer was roasted in an oven and then stuffed with roast lamb, inside of which was placed a goose, and inside the goose a chicken containing a pigeon stuffed with a small bird. Presentation was a paramount concern. Every dish had to please the eyes first of all, which is why saffron, which lent a pleasant color to food, was used so often.

Arab Contributions to European Cooking

Opinions differ as to what European cuisine owes the Arabs, although there is general agreement that they introduced into Europe a number of tropical plants—including rice, sorghum, sugarcane, spinach, eggplant, watermelon, apricot, lemon, and bitter orange. There is doubt about the artichoke and the shallot, despite their names. These might have been new varieties of plants already known in Europe. Rice and sugar were used well before they were grown in limited areas of Italy, Sicily, and re-Christianized Spain. Sugarcane did not become widespread until later, and its propagation was a complex phenomenon in which Arabs did not play a significant role. Until the sixteenth century most spices were imported by way of Muslim countries. Many of these, especially pepper, were known to the Greeks and Romans. In the late Middle Ages a broader range of spices was used in greater amounts than ever before, but the precise role of the Arabs in this development is not easy to ascertain. Saffron, however, did enter Europe through Spain.

We also know next to nothing about how certain Arab dishes entered the cuisine of various European countries. Direct contact with the East had only a limited effect. Scholars often cite the case of a Frankish knight in Syria who ate as the Muslims ate and employed Egyptian cooks. Yet even if some individuals appreciated Arab cooking, few managed to bring it with them upon returning from the Crusades, which in any event did not detain them long. As for the Franks who settled in the Latin kingdoms, few returned to their native lands. In Sicily and Spain, however, things were different. The Norman court in Palermo adopted many Arab customs. On the Iberian peninsula there were constant contacts between Christians and Muslims, and in the eleventh century the kingdoms of the north, which already counted Mozarabs among their populations, conquered true Muslims. In the fourteenth and fifteenth centuries, it became fashionable to dress, play, and probably eat like an enemy who no longer inspired as much fear as in the past and whose way of life Europeans aspired to emulate. In wide circulation at the time were almanacs of a sort known as the *Tacuinum sanitatis,* which contained translations of Arabic works on dietetics, as the title indicates (*tacuinum* comes from the Arabic *taqwim*) and certainly played a part in communicating Arab ideas about food.

By studying cookbooks one might be able to gauge the extent of Arab influence, the path it followed, and the dates at which it was felt in one place or another. But no such research has been done, and caution is in order, for the vocabulary turns out to be misleading. The adjective "Saracen" may simply refer to a dark color, for example. It remains to be seen whether Saracen gruel actually derived from an Arab source. Camel sauce contains enough cinnamon to give it a camel color, but it may be a simple misspelling of the French *cannelle* (cinnamon) that is responsible. In any case, its sweet-and-sour taste and use of crushed almonds as a binder are not uncommon in oriental sauces. In one thirteenth-century *liber de coquina* as well as in fourteenth-century Italian cookbooks, we find recipes whose names cause us to raise an eyebrow: *romania,* a dish made with chicken and pomegranate; *somacchia,* made of sumac and almonds; and *lomonia,* made with lemon juice. In these cases it seems clear that both the name and the recipe have Arabic roots: "pomegranate" is *rumman* in Arabic, while the second recipe is for *summaqiya* and the third for *laymunia* (from *laymun,* lemon). And in the first book mentioned above, there is a *mamonia,* which comes from *ma'muniya,* a dish mentioned earlier. Later, in the sixteenth century, we come across a *riso all turchesca,* whose origin is obvious.

In Iberian cooking souvenirs of the Muslim era abound. But here things get complicated, because al-Andalus continued to observe certain customs that date from Roman or Roman-Visigothic times. Two well-known books contain recipes for dishes that may have been regional derivatives of Middle Eastern recipes but that also might have developed out of native traditions. It is possible that the Arab heritage helped to preserve practices not very different from those of neighboring countries that did not live under Muslim domination. To this day, for example, one finds a meatball dish known as *albóndigas,* which comes from the Arabic *al-banadiq.* Although recipes for this dish from the Middle East and Muslim Spain have survived, we also know that something quite like it was prepared in ancient Rome.

To measure the extent of Arab influence on European cooking, one might look at the earliest European cookbooks to see if their recipes contain ingredients and flavors typical of Arab cooking (certain spices, sugar, almonds, rose water, fruit and citrus juices, sweet flavors, spicy flavors, etc.). Caution is called for in interpreting these findings, however. Only recipes containing several of these elements should be considered, and then one still must check to make sure these were specifically Arab. Pepper, saffron, and cloves, for example, were already known in antiquity, so their use is of little significance. And the sweet-and-sour combination, inherited from Persia, was known in Rome. In any case, Arab influence in Europe certainly existed from the thirteenth to the fifteenth century, after which it diminished but without disappearing altogether. By then there were new exotic influences to contend with, however, and the world was being transformed.

CHAPTER 18

MEDITERRANEAN JEWISH DIET
and TRADITIONS *in the* MIDDLE AGES

Miguel-Ángel Motis Dolader

Among the most obvious distinguishing traits of medieval Jewish communities in the West was their continuing adherence to biblically inspired culinary and dietary tradition and practices. Despite their essential culinary otherness, the Jews were not impervious to neighboring Mediterranean cultures, though the core of their distinctive culinary taboos and imperatives remained intact.

This essay traces the main currents of Hebrew dietary practices, with particular emphasis on Spain, the epicenter of High Jewish culture through 1492. Food, its interdicts and exhortations, informed the daily life and special holy days and festivals of the Jews, revealing much about the cultural uniqueness of this embattled minority as a religious, even racial, island within a sea of Christian political, economic, and doctrinal power.

The partaking of food is, in large measure, a socializing practice, not a mere act of subsistence. So, in such a dispersed and endangered species as the Hebrews of the Diaspora, food codicils, even for the *conversos* (Jews in Spain converted to Christianity) became a means, at times clandestine, of strengthening ties of solidarity.

Religious Festivals of the Jews

The Sabbath, commemorating the Lord's day of rest after creating man in His own likeness, is one of Judaism's most important institutions. Its observance is codified in the Pentateuch. To symbolize physically the impending spiritual renewal, special dishes and tablecloths were used and attention paid to rituals illuminating the home. The lighting of candles, a task performed exclusively by women, could not take place until a white cloth had been placed on the table. Once lit, with a pinch of salt applied to the wick to keep the flame burning longer, the candles were allowed to burn down until they burned out.

The Mishnah lists thirty-nine activities prohibited on the Sabbath, including cooking food, butchering and salting animals, kneading flour, and lighting a fire. Strict observance would prevent preparation of the Sabbath meal, hence the *de apparatio,* the preparation of food the evening before. The typical dish for this holy day was *hamín,* or Jewish stew, also called *adafina* ("something hot"). The basic ingredients, hard-boiled eggs, chickpeas, and meat, were often accompanied by cabbage and other pungent vegetables, hence the need to mask the special odors emanating from the *hamín* by burning wool or heads of garlic at the door of the house; a grilled sardine or two also proved helpful at times in this thankless task.

ROSH HASHANAH   In the Hebrew lunar calendar, Rosh Hashanah is observed on the first day of the new moon in the seventh month, Tishri (hence usually in September). Known as the Feast of the Horn, the sounding of the *shofar* (ram's horn) within the precincts of the synagogue symbolizes the descent of Moses from Mount Sinai, where he received the Tables of the Law. Rosh Hashanah marked the beginning of the new year.

For Rosh Hashanah Jews ate apples covered with honey (to symbolize a "sweet year"), accompanied by comestible symbols of fertility: dates, pomegranates, nougat, leeks, and other vegetables.

YOM KIPPUR   This highest of holy days, the culmination of the ten penitential days that began with Rosh Hashanah, was observed with rigorous fasting as a sign of expiation and reconciliation. Known under various names as Feast of the Great Pardon, Fast of the Good Day, Greater Fast, Fast of Pardon, the Good Day, and the Great Smoked Kipper, Yom Kippur commemorates the Jewish people's identification with God and their calling as His chosen people. It usually coincides with September or early October (the tenth day of Tishri), the time of the grape harvest.

Houses were decorated with *tovajas* (new tablecloths) and additional illumination. Among the numerous prohibitions, regulated by the books of Leviticus and Numbers, was the ingestion of food.

The celebration began with supper the evening before, which had to take place before dusk and after careful religious preparation. Foods had to be easy to digest (hence poultry was preferred, mainly hens and chickens), and alcoholic drinks and spices such as saffron or pepper were not served because of their caloric content and their tendency to cause dryness of mouth. During this meal bread was usually spread with honey to symbolize the wish to begin a happy year.

The supper that broke the fast, after stars appeared in the firmament, tended to be succulent. Meats figured as a central dish, though poultry was prominent, and more rarely fish (a casserole of tuna or perhaps hake with eggplant). Grapes, figs, almonds, and eggs were also served.

SUKKOTH Sukkoth began five days after Yom Kippur and was popularly known as Passover of the Huts (Sukkah) or Feast of Tabernacles. This celebration, which took the name of the huts made with boughs or foliage like those that, for forty years, the Israelites built in the desert after the flight from Egypt, commemorated Yahweh's protection of his people. Thanksgiving was offered with the fruits of the earth because it was the period of harvest.

The streets and plazas of the Jewish quarters formed a very adequate backdrop for the huts' construction; if this was not possible, some families chose the dining room or interior courtyards of their houses, setting up large tables with food and sweetmeats for seven days. All visitors were invited to partake of them. As at Passover, they ate cakes, nougats, dried fruits, and drank white or red kosher wine.

An Inquisition prosecutor described the ceremony as follows: "The said accused person was accustomed to observing and solemnizing the Passover, popularly known as 'the huts,' in which he caused to be made huts of fennel and other green things in his house, within which he ate in the Jewish fashion and his household with him, and if he could not make the said huts secretly, he went to the houses of relatives and friends of his who were converts and sometimes to the Jewish quarter, to make the said huts with them . . . to observe the said feast he ate on new plates and platters, in the Jewish fashion."

PURIM Purim, or the feast of Queen Esther, was celebrated in the month of Adar, and its genesis went back to the freedom that King Ahasuerus granted to the Jewish people against the wishes of his minister Haman. The reading of the Megillah gave rise to several local traditions. In the Sephardic communities of Turkey, Greece, and Morocco, an effigy of Haman, made of wood or stuffed with rags and straw, was dragged through the streets and then hanged or burned. Anthropologists have seen certain resemblances with Judas Iscariot or other scapegoat icons.

The fast was broken, as usual, at dusk; a very common dish was one made of chicken and hard-boiled eggs with parsley. Wine was consumed in large quantities, sometimes to the point of intoxication. Games of chance were played and masks—like those of Carnival—were worn. It was the customary moment to exchange gifts of pastry or sweets (*miskloaj manot*).

PASSOVER (PESSACH) The feast, which began on the fifteenth day of Nisan—usually in March or April—and lasted a week, celebrated liberation from the Pharaoh's yoke and the ten plagues that fell upon Egypt.

Typical foods for this occasion were "unleavened" or "thin" bread—made without yeast—and macaroons, toasted chickpeas, and various pastries. Abstention from leavened bread commemorated those loaves that the Children of Israel carried on their shoulders when they crossed the Red Sea. Dietary laws banned possession of yeast in homes, even in tiny amounts.

Preparation of the house was carried out by women, and it consisted of arranging the platters, plates, and new dishes the night before as well as placing lamps for their illumination.

While unleavened bread and celery were eaten as a sign of sadness, lettuces were a symbol of joy. Hence, after Passover came to an end, the Jews gave their families and friends—especially converts—unleavened bread, pastries, "tipsy" cakes, and celery, receiving in return cheese, eggs, sweets, lettuces, yeast, radishes, green onions, almonds, and other foods.

The Passover banquet began on the first night with a supper composed of a salad of celery and lettuce with vinegar, or, in Spain, vegetable dishes like the one customarily eaten in the Kingdom of Aragon, composed of chickpeas, bread with sauces, eggs, and honey.

Life's Journey: Ars vivendi atque ars moriendi

For the Jewish people, life's major rites of passage were invariably accompanied and consecrated by communal dietary traditions and restrictions.

BIRTH INTO LIFE AND SOCIETY: SWEETS One of the most joyous events was the birth of a child, particularly if the child was a male, which ensured perpetuation of the race. In Spain, the new mother was regaled with little gifts (*albricias*), such as capons, money, kerchiefs, rings, pattens, swaddling cloths, sashes, cradles, nursing bottles, and diapers. Special foods were prepared. For example, in Catalonia "they eat wafers and doughnuts, and rice with oil and honey, and then they welcome the child." In the Jewish quarters of the Near East, women who had just given birth were served "new mother's toast" or fritters.

The ceremonial of *hadas* was a party (*besorah,* or "glad tidings") in honor of newborns on the seventh night after birth; for males, it preceded circumcision. Young women and relatives gathered in the new mother's room to partake of celebratory cakes, sweetmeats, and slices of bread with honey. The infant was placed in a basin, and gold, silver, and various grains were tossed in. While the baby was being washed, chants were sung to frighten off the evil eye and attract the "good star." Often (especially in Castile) the baby's palms, armpits, and soles of the feet were anointed with myrrh. Male circumcision took place on the eighth day, consecrating the newborn to the God of Israel. It also marked the child's incorporation into the community. It was performed in the synagogue or at home and was the occasion for a meal.

THE NUPTIAL BANQUET: FISH AND FERTILITY Jews were endogamic, tending to marry among blood relatives whenever the family's circle of friends permitted it. Otherwise, it was necessary to call on the good offices of marriage brokers (*shadkan*). Once each member of the couple had been accepted by the respective parents, the dowry and trousseau were agreed upon and the marriage agreement signed some three or four years before the wedding. Arrangements were completed before the girl came of age, at around thirteen or fourteen. Her husband was usually about eighteen, although in second marriages the difference in age was more obvious, generally in favor of the masculine partner.

The festivities began in the bride's house with the *almosama* (as it was known among the Sephardic Jews of Salonika), which took place on the Saturday afternoon preceding the week of the wedding. On this happy occasion, in which the feminine presence predominated, drinks and sweets were distributed.

The future husband had the task of finding a place to celebrate the religious ceremony (*kiddushim*), hiring the musicians, and arranging for the banquet. Among the lower classes, it was customary for the bridegroom's family to send small loaves of sesame bread to their relatives and to the bride's family prior to the wedding. The purpose of this gift, known as the *gorban* (sacrifice), was to free the groom from the evil eye.

The nuptial banquet took place at nightfall with friends and relatives and those who had presented gifts, even though large quantities of sweets such as doughnuts and cakes had already been served. Music and dancing seemed indissolubly linked to eating and drinking. After partaking of the meal, the bride and groom retired to their bedroom, where, before retiring, they received the paternal blessing, exhorting the God of Abraham, Isaac, and Jacob to give them happiness, peace, wealth, and many descendants. A custom still preserved among the Sephardim is to have the mothers of the bride and groom place pastries and candies under the pillow of the bridal bed to "sweeten" the spouses' mouths.

After the wedding, the week of nuptial rejoicings began. The husband offered the stream of visitors doughnuts and *tarales*—large bracelet-shaped biscuits made of flour, oil, and sugar that had been prepared days before by the bridegroom's mother. Some communities celebrated the "day of the fish" as a conclusion to this week of festivities. The husband went to the market very early in the morning to buy a fine string of fish. This was placed on a tray that was set on the floor. The bride stepped over it three times in the presence of her family and neighbors, who wished her the same degree of fertility as the fish. Before the tray was carried away, those present put money on it for the cook who had been in charge of providing dishes for the couple and the wedding party.

It was the bride's filial duty to maintain her ties with her mother's house. According to an ancient ritual, the mother placed sugar or a sweetmeat on her daughter's tongue before the bride crossed the threshold.

FUNERALS: THE EGG, SYMBOL OF ETERNITY After a death in the family, the water jars and pitchers in the house were emptied in the belief that, if this was not done, the soul would bathe in this water during the first seven days or the Angel of Death would clean his sword there. In some areas, a glass of water was placed on the windowsill on the ninth day and on the Sabbath and during the mourning period so the soul could take refreshment. In any case, water jars turned upside down in the street were an external sign of grief.

Mourning, strictly observed by the nearest relatives, was reflected in food. During the first week, the diet was very restricted, consisting of fish, hard-boiled eggs, greens, fruit, olives, and vegetables (*cohuerzo*). Among orthodox Jews, only milk and eggs were consumed. Meat was strictly prohibited. Meals were served on the floor, with or without tablecloths, or on low stools. As for beverages, only water was drunk, and it had to be brought from the fountain or from other houses at least seven blocks away.

The Food Pantry

There were extremely detailed rules about foods that were prohibited and those suitable for consumption.

MEAT AND FISH In a Europe that was essentially carnivorous, where meat was eaten daily and abundantly and wine was consumed like water, Jews had to deal with intrinsic problems that were sometimes hard to solve in view of the strictness of their dietary rules. Indeed, there was a wide range of prohibitions about animal food. Certain flesh was considered abominable because of "impure" genetic origins; however, poultry and such animal parts as blood and abdominal fats could, by rabbinical law, be bought and sold despite impurities of origin. Among invertebrates there were no exceptions, with all reptiles excluded. The classification of mammals was rigid, according to their zoological taxonomy: only cud-chewing animals with cloven hooves could be eaten.

There were also laws relating to certain animal parts that could not be eaten. In the case of poultry and mammals, the blood had to be drained before it was eaten (Deuteronomy stated that "blood is life" because it contained the soul). Nor was consumption permitted of the suet and lard (*heleb*) of sheep, cattle, and other bovines, not to mention wild birds and game or the tendon of the thigh (*guid hanashé*). These prohibitions were associated with sacrificial laws: because these animal parts were destined for the altar, they could not be eaten.

Such extensive restrictions on the consumption of meat meant that sources of energy and proteins had to be derived from fresh or salt fish, even on the Sabbath. Fish could be eaten if it had scales and two fins, according to a biological classification into creatures with bones and with cartilage.

CEREALS AND VEGETABLES Cereals and vegetables formed a very important part of the diet: bread was one of the fundamental foods, and vegetables and greens, often cooked together in the form of soups, were widely eaten, as were fruits.

On medieval Jewish tables the cereals most often eaten were wheat, barley, oats, and rye, consumed not only in the form of bread but also as noodles. In times of scarcity bread compensated for the lack of meat in the diet. The importance of bread can be seen in the fact that, for ordinary people with limited economic resources, the daily ration in the early Middle Ages was about four pounds. As a point of comparison, an average family of converts sent about a bushel and a half to the Jewish quarter to provide unleavened bread baked for Passover.

The kind of bread depended on the type of flour used. The bread was mostly wheaten, and two kinds were distinguished for ritual reasons: unleavened bread (which some converts used quite assiduously and which was often employed as liturgical bread) and bread made with yeast.

At the end of the fifteenth century, the expression "fine bread" was a common way of referring to ordinary bread as opposed to the unleavened kind used at Passover. According to Hebrew tradition, there were three kinds of unleavened bread: *torta,* which was round; *laganum,* a very light bread of ancient origin; and *crustulum,* a crusty bread that was very thin and baked on a plate or grill. Thin loaves with a hole in the center were called *pan cenceño* (flatbread), described as "a thin loaf, white, like paper, all painted and decorated with a thimble."

As a caloric supplement to cereals there were dry legumes, and it was not uncommon to use them in making bread. Those consumed most often by Mediterranean Jews were chickpeas, lentils, broad beans, and white beans. These legumes played an important role in providing seasonal variety and in the preparation of vegetable stews.

Eating fruits and vegetables was, of course, essential for maintaining a balanced diet. Among kitchen-garden vegetables we can name several kinds of cabbage, chard, spinach, eggplant, and celery. Fruits varied with the seasons and local production.

Dried fruits were very nutritious, which gave them a certain importance. The following description of a dish made in Zaragoza, Spain, to celebrate the end of Yom Kippur gives some idea of the typical ways in which dried fruits were used: "Last night they boiled two dozen eggs in water until they were hard, then they chopped up part of them and then chopped the others all together and mixed them with honey, almonds, raisins, pinenuts, dried chestnuts, and sauces that had been ground up, with oil and other things, and caused all this to boil in a kettle for two or three hours."

BEVERAGES Among beverages, in Spain at least, wine held undisputed first place. The wines that were drunk reflected regional differences, depending on raw materials and cultural biotypes. Consumption of wine was two or three times that of bread, for wine was drunk at any hour of the day, while bread was reserved for mealtimes.

The *responsa* of Isaac ben Sheshet Perfet tell us how impossible it was to preserve the kosher quality of Jewish wine. In a letter written around 1396, Rabbi Amram Efratí ben Meru'am of the Oran community responded that neither the converted Jews of Mallorca nor those of other regions could properly oversee their vineyards and that, furthermore, they could not avoid contact with Christians.

Problems also arose in the importation of wine because of the rights of tax collectors. In Játiva the Jewish governing body forbade the importing of wine unless the right to place it in vats had been guaranteed. The community agreed to drink no other wine, treating it as impure, unless it had been introduced with the consent of the rabbinical court or the members of the council.

Jewish wine, both red and white, was made, we are told, "so as to be good and perfect and better aged" than the other kinds of wine bought and sold in the marketplace; hence it was insisted upon by clergy and chaplains.

We have proof of the serious problems faced by the Jewish communities when the harvest was scarce and wine made in other districts had to be imported, or, on the other hand, when the harvest was excessive. Occasionally conflicts arose between communities. Thus, when in 1288 the community of Monzón passed a law banning the drinking and buying of wine made by the Jews of Barbastro, the decree had to be repealed by the king.

The grape harvest was an annual event that involved that part of the Jewish population who made wine either in their own homes or in houses that possessed a wine vat. It must be remembered that after the grapes were picked, the Jews had to trample them and prepare the wine, put it in vats, and store it in locked wine cellars—all without any Gentile participation in its preparation.

Water's lack of nutritive value in comparison with wine relegated it to a secondary place, at least during meals. Jewish homes usually got their water from streams or from artesian wells. Wells were closed to Jews at times of strict regulation and during periods of plague and social upheaval. Jews were even accused of poisoning wells. It was not uncommon for Jews to have cisterns of their own, as in Trapani, Termini, or Corleane. Other more privileged Jewish communities, Palma de Mallorca, for example, had a carefully maintained water system.

Dairy products occupied an important place in the diet. Milk and cheese, by Talmudic law, had to have their own receptacles. To judge from comparative studies, dairy products were not stored for any length of time.

There were some very famous and tasty specialties among the Sephardim, such as the *pepitada* prepared in Smyrna. This was a type of orgeat made with the flesh of melon seeds, resulting in a milky color and texture. Its refreshing character made it very appropriate in the heat of summer.

The Kitchen

The kitchen was situated on the second floor, on the same level as the rooms used for sleeping, and above the area occupied by the "palace" or public rooms (those on either side of the porch where the entrance to the house was located). The kitchen had a separate door and a ceiling in which beams and strips of wood alternated, supported on pillars, while the floor was whitewashed. Its central feature was the hearth or chimney, around which the furniture was placed. A long bench ran along two or three of its sides. It served as a dining room if the house did not have a special room for this purpose.

Utensils are very important in explaining culinary processes and dietary habits. Many utensils were not used exclusively for food preparation. Numerous inventories, which form the basis for documentary investigation of domestic culture, do not mention even the simplest of the instruments necessary for preparing, cooking, and serving dishes.

Preparing food for cooking began with washing the raw materials. In Sicily, where every household had large basins, there were numerous ceramic, wooden, or metal plates (*bremi, laviczi*) while in Provence bowls or other types of dishes (*grazali, gravede*) were used. The absence of sinks indicates that dishes were washed in earthenware or copper basins.

Kitchen knives are mentioned from time to time, and the mortar seems to be a basic utensil. Most utensils were made of wood, horn, or stone. Indispensable pieces of kitchen equipment included the grill and the frying pan, which were used for cooking directly over the fire and for broiling, along with the cooking pot, employed for cooking over an indirect flame.

The Universe of the Table

The table is one of the ultimate expressions of ritual practice, and the settings required careful preparation for holy day special occasions and ancestral celebrations.

As for table service, inventories mention the dishes, the cutlery, and the dining furniture. Cloths and napkins (both collective and individual) existed in abundance, along with perhaps one or several *longerie* (long tablecloths measuring more than two meters), which may have served for two or more diners. In the dining rooms of Aragonese Jews we find numerous tablecloths and napkins that were referred to as "drapes" or "mouth cloths."

As for utensils, it is surprising not to find wooden spoons in the inventories, although silver spoons were very common in merchants' houses. The knife was for personal use, and each person brought one to the table; only very large knives are inventoried: "*cultelli grandi di taglari in tabula.*"

Dinnerware was composed of collective dishes such as wooden or bronze trays (*tafaria*) and deep platters of undecorated wood (*virnicatu*). The ceramic plate (*lembu*) appeared in the fifteenth century and proved to be very durable. Plates both large and small (*platus, platellus*) came even later, as did objects made of tin, wood, and clay, a reflection of the growing prosperity of the Jewish urban upper class.

Provençal practice was based on three elements: the bowl (*paraxis* or *stanhada*), the cutting knife (*talhador*), and the pannikin or deep platter (*grazale* or *grazelectus*). The knife was used by two persons, each of whom had an individual platter and sauceboat.

Clay or tin vessels, or bowls or glass receptacles (*gottu*), probably conical in shape, were used for drinking. The presence of bottles with long narrow necks (*botelhus*) suggests that wine or water may have been drunk directly from the bottle. There were many jars and pitchers, usually made of materials other than glass; clay and tin pitchers appeared after the end of the thirteenth century.

Butcher Shops and the Oven

In the Jewish quarters, besides services of public or social interest, there were minimal facilities relating to culture, teaching, social services, religious activities, or hygiene. In general, the urban space was divided up in three ways: private residential space, civic/social and religious space, and commercial space. Although it would be anachronistic to expect the medieval Jews to possess a well-defined territorial model and an organized structure in the modern sense of the term, they did have, within the area dedicated to commercial transactions, their own means of producing and distributing food.

Some groups owned a supply center called "the shop of the Jewry," rented to either a Christian or a Jew under a one-year, renewable lease that began on the first day of Lent and ended during Carnival, dates corresponding to the fiscal year. One of the contracts signed by the Jewish community of Epila contained the following stipulations: "You must have the said shop well supplied with sardines and with hake, candles, oil, and cheese which you must sell at the same prices as the Christians' shopkeeper is obliged to offer during the present year, and must observe all the conditions that the said shopkeeper is obliged to observe."

Among the independent establishments that guaranteed supplies of basic products were the butcher shop (*macellum*), which, after the synagogue, was one of the most typical buildings of public use. In principle, the attitude of the Christians was tolerant, allowing the Jews to purchase meat.

The clients of butcher shops were not exclusively Hebrews, for converts and Christians also patronized them. In this respect, the trial records of the Inquisition are very eloquent, showing that butcher shops produced more than their basic needs and even supplied the entire city with mutton, beef, veal, and kid. It appears that Jewish butcher shops sold higher-quality meat, especially during Lent, and that conditions were more hygienic, the shops better supplied, and the prices more competitive. Thus the authorities' insistence that prices be the same as those in the Christian market proved futile.

Sometimes Jews did not possess their own butcher shop and there was a common one, shared with Christians and Mudejars, the Muslims living under Christian rule. As an example of discrimination, in 1312 the authorities of Elche banned the town's Jews from slaughtering in Christian shops, citing the fear that the meat would be contaminated, an attitude similar to that maintained by the Mudejars. Similarly, after 1403, the Jews of Valencia were also banned from slaughtering meat in Christian butcher shops. At the end of the century, the Jewish quarter disappeared after a series of assaults, aimed at repressing the small Hebrew colony that remained in the city.

Medieval canon law was unanimous in condemning Christian consumption of meat coming from Jewish butcher shops, for it implied an offense against religion. In Castile some local statutes limited the sale of meat by Jews at certain periods of the year; Sepúlveda banned it for three days before and after Easter, Christmas, and Pentecost, except for kid. The statute of Salamanca fined any Christian butcher who sold Jewish meat and forced him to burn the merchandise; and if someone slaughtered meat for Jews during Carnival or Lent, municipal authorities threatened to shave his head.

In fact, meat was the chief source of conflict with the majority. As we indicated above, meat had to fulfill a set of standards; the so-called *terefah* could not be eaten because the pleura were swollen. Nor could the animal that had blood in its body, as a dying animal usually did. The problem arose, in this case, when, after an animal's throat had been cut, it had defects that made it unsuitable for consumption, or when, through an error by the rabbi, the meat was impregnated with blood. Then it was sold to Gentiles at lower prices, violating the economic preconditions for market prices.

Jewish communities usually had privileges that assured them their own oven, where they baked the unleavened bread (*matzoh*) consumed during Passover. Royal or seignorial authorities tended to limit private ownership of grist mills, for it meant they could not impose the corresponding taxes and fees. Permission for these establishments was accomplished by issuing the appropriate privilege.

When they had to share this infrastructure, either through public or private ownership, and in order to guarantee ritual correctness, the rabbis stated that it was sufficient for a Jew to participate symbolically by tossing a log or branch on the fire from time to time or at regular intervals, even if the baking was done by a Christian.

Kneading the dough, an operation usually performed at home once a week, required its own implements. Of the inventories that have been preserved from the Kingdom of Aragon at the time of the expulsion, the "kneading place" is referred to as a separate location only twice, both times in the Jewish quarter of Calatayud. But it is true that a third of Jewish homes had "kneading basins" or troughs, usually in the porches, the wine cellars, or the kitchen.

The Domestic Scene

The kitchen is essentially a feminine area where men play a secondary and passive role confined to butchering animals or buying supplies in the market; they have no part in kneading bread and degreasing or bleeding meat, which is women's work. A family's social standing was closely related to domestic service, and it was common to hire women—the great majority of them unmarried—from the Jewish quarter or nearby towns. Evidently a certain degree of specialization existed, for sources distinguish several different categories: housekeepers, nurses, cooks, and maids. More generically, the term *moza* was used to designate the woman who took part in household duties like general cleaning or laundry and who also helped in the kitchen.

The wars, violence, and pogroms that occurred in the thirteenth, fourteenth, and fifteenth centuries shook the foundations of society, promoting uncertainty and leading to the reassembling of Jewish families around compact nuclear groups. The terrible epidemic of 1347–48 spread the ravages of bubonic and pneumonic plague, which did not disappear from the West until the fifteenth century. At the outset of the fourteenth century, the working population was reduced by two-thirds or half, suspending any expansionist tendencies and frustrating the great promise of the thirteenth century.

In Mediterranean Judaism, always patrilineal, the lineage was identified with the *bayt*—the father's house—and with a hereditary surname. Children were not automatically emancipated with marriage, and their dependent condition could last until a greatly delayed majority, certainly until their father's death. Inbreeding was almost an official rule and was praised in literature as well as folk wisdom, which invited a man to take a wife on the same street where he lived.

In this context, the table was not a mere piece of furniture where food was displayed and eaten; it was the axis around which the family life revolved. Despite the importance of the domestic family unit, living in the same house and around the same hearth, composed of the husband and wife and their unemancipated children plus domestic servants and apprentices, there was an extended family made up of the children who had left home and, up to a point, the sons- and daughters-in-law as well as other assorted relatives.

The inheritance system formed a strong link among these patriarchal, extended families in a society whose growth rate did not allow the children to live outside the economic unit until marriage (dowry) and the death or decline into old age of the parents (inheritance) made them administrators of a productive unit. This explains the importance of in-laws and grandparents, since the new conjugal society formed after marriage was enfolded into the family of one of the marriage partners.

Specific features of the art of cooking occurred only when religious components converged at certain festive times. The Jews' daily menu hardly differed from that of their Christian neighbors, except in some methods of preparation and in certain raw materials of animal origin.

FOOD PREPARATION The cleaning and preparation of meat after butchering was extremely important because it was linked to rabbinical precepts. According to dietary law, no Jew could eat blood, the source of life. Before being eaten, meat and poultry had to be submerged in a solution of salt water (*melihah*) to expel the blood. This requirement, which was unnecessary when meat was broiled, did not apply to fish.

Another preliminary step consisted of quartering or otherwise cutting up the animal, which involved utilization of choppers, cleavers, and knives. Strokes were administered at the joints; shallow cuts were made, never complete ones. Use of a knife generally meant that the rest of the operation had to be performed by hand, while smaller animals, especially poultry, were skinned and broken apart manually. The bones were usually cut during the meal, as is shown by scratches made by the blade of a knife to separate the flesh from the bone.

The pieces of meat were cut into little chunks, according to domestic needs and to make them suitable for being cooked in pots. Whatever the kind of animal, the method of carving was apparently unimportant and simply meant that boiled meat was eaten. There was no real selection of pieces; everything was consumed.

GENETIC KEYS OF THE GASTRONOMIC TRADITION: RECIPES Like cooking elsewhere in medieval western Europe, Jewish cooking reflects a taste for spices, a preference for acidic flavors (like those of vinegar, sour wine, lemon or orange juice, green apples, etc.), and a lack of differentiation between salty and sweet dishes.

Butter was employed infrequently. Throughout western Europe, oil was used on days of abstinence and animal fats on other days. Church regulations standardized culinary practice in this respect, although this uniformity did not survive the Reformation. As for the Jews, they used olive oil exclusively, recovering the Graeco-Latin tradition, and this resulted in fried dishes of better quality.

We rarely know in detail all the ingredients of dishes or the method of preparation; however, thanks to their survival in tradition, we can make a partial reconstruction. Indeed, Jewish recipe collections, especially those preserved by Sephardic Jews of our day, recreate the most outstanding dishes, which involve a grammar of taste dating back many centuries.

Culinary elements do not conform to present-day standards; for example, celery and lettuce could be served at any point in the meal. Nor was there the same distribution of dishes into first course, main course, and desserts, so we have to think in different terms while remaining mindful of the fundamental dishes, based on vegetables, meats, and so forth.

Stews constituted a special chapter, owing to their prominence both on feast days and ordinary days. *Hamín* was omnipresent and was an essential element in the diet owing to its high protein value. Its customary ingredients were legumes (primarily chickpeas) and seasonal green vegetables (like cabbage and leeks), hard-boiled eggs, meat (goose, beef, mutton, or ox), onions, and different kinds of spices (like saffron, pepper, and salt). Its composition was as varied as the ethnographic geography of medieval Jewry, the products of the land, and the season of the year when it was consumed, though it maintained its fundamental character. Thus, in Catalonia *hamín* consisted of spinach, chickpeas, mutton, salt meat, and eggs; in Toledo, of chickpeas, beans with meat, coriander, caraway, cumin, pepper, and onion. In Murcia it was more austere: a pot of chickpeas without meat but with abundant oil; in the Canary Islands goat's meat was used, cooked with oil and onions in abundance and accompanied by little cakes made of unsalted barley flour.

Preparation was not complicated, for all the ingredients were placed in a pot and cooked together until the dish was finished. Eggs were "haminized" by placing them in earthenware pots and boiling them in the shell with oil and ashes, which gave them their typical dark color.

Other dishes that merited the description of "Jewish foods" or "Jewish stews" were fricassees, meat pies, and meatballs. Meatballs were just that—balls of veal or beef and spices browned in olive oil. The following descriptions indicate that meatballs could be prepared in two ways—either fried and then seasoned with sauce or simmered in broth: "She minced the meat and made little balls of the said meat with sauces and fried them in oil, and they ate"; "she took the said meatballs and stuffed them into mutton tripes and tied them with string and put them to cook in the broth." As for meat pies, there were both sweet and salted varieties. They were eaten either as dessert or a main course and were extremely popular. They were cooked in a vessel known as a *padilla,* a large pot described as "taller than a handbreadth."

The kinds of salads served depended on the season. At Passover a salad of celery, lettuce, and vinegar was indispensable. Another popular vegetable on medieval Jewish tables was eggplant, cooked as an accompaniment to stew or stuffed with meat and spices.

The commonest fried dishes were those made with squash, spinach, or leeks, although they could also be made with pumpkin or onions. In all these dishes, except those with pumpkin, breadcrumbs were added for thickening. The fried dishes based on green vegetables were served as a first course on Pessach, when unleavened bread replaced the breadcrumbs. Vegetables were used profusely as an accompaniment to meat and fish.

There are few references to dishes containing fish, which were fried or broiled. There was considerably greater consumption of mutton, veal, lamb, and poultry. Meat was usually roasted or braised, with oil and spices. Chickens were roasted; the bird was covered with oil after it was cleaned and roasted whole, or it was stewed with sauces.

Sauces, an essential complement of meat and vegetables, were seasoned with aromatic herbs or prepared with oil and the spices available in city markets. The preferred sauce to accompany boiled fish was made with eggs, flour, lemon, and the broth from cooking the fish.

Eggs were prepared either hard-boiled or in the form of omelettes; they could also be eaten seasoned and combined with meat, greens, or sauces. One Aragonese convert explained that she "broke eggs into an iron frying pan, and after they were cooked tossed in some ground meat fried with onions, and then beat more eggs and added them and took another frying pan with coals in it and covered them."

Among the spices most frequently cited are garlic, saffron, pepper, and, less often, coriander, not to mention the seasoning in the oil as well as salt.

Of the ample and varied desserts and sweets, we may mention nougat, rye-flour biscuits, quince paste with honey, salted almonds, cheese crullers, and sweets made with hempseed.

According to Jaume Riera, the daily diet of a typical middle-class Jewish family during the fourteenth and fifteenth centuries consisted of bread, cabbage, salad, olive oil, and wine.

In general, people ate a great deal and drank in large quantities. The daily intake of food may seem quantitatively excessive, but it was of inferior quality because of the relative lack of glucose, proteins, fats, and certain vitamins. In contrast, the meals of the European nobility, while theoretically better tasting and composed of foods rich in calories, were notably lacking in certain vitamins, especially Vitamin A. This resulted in low resistance to infections and a consequent incidence of bladder and kidney ailments. In this regard medieval Jewish cuisine might be said to be more balanced than Christian cuisine.

Sacrificial and Symbolic Ceremonies

The slaughtering of animals was a complicated matter in rabbinical Judaism, requiring particular skills in cutting the animal's throat (*shehitah*) as well as exploration of the animal once it was opened (*bediqah,* or ritual inspection). These acts were performed by a special official, who received the name of *shohet* and *bodeq.*

The *shohet,* or butcher, was hired by the community; he was paid a fixed salary and could have no other employment. By law no other professional was allowed to perform the sacrifices. It sometimes happened that the concession of a monopoly on meat was stipulated in the clauses of the contract, as in Borja and Barbastro, but only when there was a guarantee of regular supplies to the citizens.

The butcher had to cut the arteries and trachea with a single stroke of the knife, and this was followed by a very careful inspection to make sure that the animal suffered from no illness. If it had died from natural causes or if it had been killed by a wild animal, its flesh was prohibited (*nevelah*).

To acquire sufficient skill, the butcher had to complete elementary rabbinical studies and be accredited by a certificate of expertise (*kabbalah*), some texts of which have survived to the present day. From the thirteenth century onward, his professional development, owing to its religious nature, was supervised by a rabbi—the rabbi of butchering—in matters such as bleeding the animal, cutting the internal organs, boning, castration, and so forth, as well as dietetic laws in general.

Another ritual concerned the extraction of the challah, a portion of dough tossed into the oven before baking. This ceremonial act represented the tithe owed to the Lord. This practice, very widespread among converts, persists today as a cult element of the collective unconscious in many parts of Mediterranean Europe.

THE CADENCE OF TIME AND THE CLOCK OF LIFE Distribution of the principal meals throughout the day occurred in relation to the vital cycle. The existence of a morning meal (*yantar*) seems proven, and another at twilight, the supper. Both meals were referred to with the verbs *disner* or *souper,* and the other meals between those two were indicated by the verb *boir.*

In addition, people probably ate on arising at daybreak, but the fact that not all members of the family were present explains why there was no specific term to indicate the meal. Documents reflect only the practice of a meal structured around the table, with the presence of a minimum number of diners.

The main meal took place at midday, after the day's work was done. Some Inquisition records give more details. Hence one witness describes a meal that took place between twelve and one o'clock in the afternoon in a convert's household in Calatayud: everyone was sitting at the table and eating rye bread, the bowls with the last of the *hamín* were being removed from the table, and the diners were preparing to eat some capons or roast fowl.

It was a common practice that, when a successful business transaction had taken place, if one of the participants went to the home of a third person who was at table, he would be invited to join in the meal.

Supper was eaten at the end of the day to coincide with the last rays of twilight. The Hebrews were influenced by the Sumerians and Babylonians in their measurement of time, so their calendar was governed by the phases of the moon. Fasts were broken after seeing the moon in the firmament.

SACRALIZATION OF THE PROFANE: ABLUTIONS AND BLESSINGS

Presence around the table had its own liturgy, for the table was not simply a place for the mere act of eating. The table was also a small public space where different participants, linked to one another by kinship or friendship, came together.

Purification and ablution before pronouncing the blessing (*berahah*) reveal Islamic influence. To preside over the preliminary blessing as well as the one at the end of the meal, which every pious Jew pronounced each time he participated in a pleasurable activity, a minimal quorum (*mezumah*) was needed. This was similar, to some degree, to the *minyan*. The documents make a distinction between the "blessing in the Jewish fashion" and that pronounced by Christians; the Jewish blessing required a particular setting, in which a proper garment, the *tallit*, was worn.

In the blessing spoken before the meal, bread and wine are the sacred elements—adopted by the Christians as a sacramentalization of the Last Supper, representing transubstantiation of the body and blood of Christ: "He performed the blessing at the table by taking a cup of wine in his hand, and said certain words over the wine in Hebrew, which this witness did not understand, and then he took a sip of wine and gave all the others sips of it, and then he took a loaf of bread and cut it in seven pieces, but not completely cut through, saying seven words in Hebrew which this witness did not understand, and then he took that bread which he had blessed and cut, and took a mouthful and gave mouthfuls to all the others, and said that it was blessed bread, and then they had supper, and afterward, when they had supped, he spoke the benediction and they stood up."

Another no less beautiful blessing began with the prayer "Let us bless Him, for we have eaten of what is His, and by His favor we live," to which the other diners replied, "Blessed be He, for we have eaten of what is His, and by His favor we live." After this formula, the sacral circuit was closed and was followed, at least on festive days, by animated after-dinner conversation, which could last for hours, sometimes in the Romance tongue and sometimes in Hebrew.

BIBLIOGRAPHY

Apfel, J. "The Service for Yom Kippur Kattan." *L'Eylah* 24 (1987): 34–36.
Avery-Peck, Alan J. "Law and Society in Early Judaism: Legal Evolution in the Mishnaic Division of Agriculture." *Religion, Literature, and Society in Ancient Israel* 1 (1987): 69–87.

Bahloul, J. "Le Culte de la 'table dressée': Étude du rituel alimentaire chez les Juifs d'origine algérienne vivant en France." In *The Sepharadi and Oriental Jewish Heritage: Studies,* ed. Issachar Ben-Ami, pp. 517–28. Jerusalem: Magnes Press, 1982.

Beinart, Haim. *Los conversos ante el tribunal de la Inquisición.* Barcelona: Riopiedras, 1983.

Benayoun, Joëlle Allouche. "Les pratiques culinaires: Lieux de mémoire, facteur d'identité." *Rassegna Mensile di Israel* 49 (1983): 615–37.

Brin, Gershon. "The Firstling of Unclean Animals." *Jewish Quarterly Review* 68 (1977): 1–15.

Cantera Burgos, Francisco. "Carne trifá." *Sefarad* 14 (1954): 126–27.

Cantera Montenegro, Enrique. "Solemnidades, ritos y costumbres de los judaizantes de Molina de Aragón a fines de la Edad Media." In *Actas del II Congreso Internacional: Encuentro de las tres culturas,* pp. 59–88. Toledo, 1985.

Dobrinsky, Herbert C. *A Treasury of Sephardic Laws and Customs: The Ritual Practices of Syrian, Moroccan, Judeo-Spanish, and Portuguese Jews of North America.* New York: Yeshiva University Press, 1986.

Espadas Burgos, Manuel. "Aspectos sociorreligiosos de la alimentación español." *Hispania* 131 (1975): 537–65.

Estrugo, José María. "Tradiciones españolas en las juderías del Oriente Próximo (Reminiscencias y apuntes)." *Sefarad* 14 (1954): 128–47.

Feliks, J., and H. Rabinowicz. "Dietary Laws." *Encyclopaedia Judaica* 6:26–45. Jerusalem, 1971.

Freudenstein, Eric G. "Sabbath Fish." *Judaism* 29 (1980): 418–31.

Grant, R. M. "Dietary Laws among Pythagoreans, Jews, and Christians." *Harvard Theological Review* 73 (1980): 297–310.

Gutwirth, J. "Les pains azymes de la Pâque chez les hassidim." *Oriente Moderno* 16 (1976): 137–48.

Hershman, Abraham Moses. *Rabbi Isaac ben Shéshet Perfet and His Times.* New York: Jewish Theological Seminary of America, 1943.

Herzog, Mikhl. "The Culinary Treasures of the Language and Culture Atlas of Ashkenazic Jewry." *Jewish Folklore and Ethnology Review* 9 (1987): 6–12.

Jordan, W. C. "Jews on Top: Women and the Availability of Consumption Loans in Northern France in the Mid-Thirteenth Century." *Journal of Jewish Studies* 29 (1978): 39–56.

———. "Problems of the Meat Market of Béziers, 1240–1247: A Question of Anti-Semitism." *Revue des Études Juives* 135 (1976): 31–49.

Kirshenblatt-Gimblett, Barbara. "The Kosher Gourmet in the Nineteenth-Century Kitchen: Three Jewish Cookbooks in Historical Perspective." *Journal of Gastronomy* 2 (1986–87): 51–89.

Kriegel, Maurice. "Un trait de psychologie sociale dans les pays méditerranéens du Bas Moyen Age: Le juif comme intouchable." *Annales: Économies, sociétés, civilisations* 31 (1976): 326–30.

Lacave Riaño, José Luis. "La carnicería de la aljama zaragozana a fines del siglo XV." *Sefarad* 35 (1975): 1–33.

Leibovici, Sarah. "Títulos de nobleza de la adafina." *Maguen-Escudo* 57 (1985): 7–12.

León Tello, Pilar. "Costumbres, fiestas y ritos de los judíos toledanos a fines del siglo XV." In

Simposio Toledo Judaico, 2:67–81. Toledo: Publicaciones del Centro Universitario de Toledo, Universidad Complutense, n.d.

Levine-Melammed, Renée C. *Women in Spanish Crypto-Judaism, 1492–1520.* Ann Arbor: University of Michigan Press, 1986.

Manger et boire au Moyen Age: Cuisine, manières de table, régimes alimentaires: Actes du Colloque de Nice, 15–17 octobre 1982. 2 vols. Centre d'Études Médiévales de Nice, Publications de la Faculté des Lettres et Sciences Humaines de Nice, no. 28. Nice: Les Belles Lettres, 1984.

Molho, Michel. *Usos y costumbres del los Sefardíes de Salónica.* Biblioteca Hebraicoespañola 3. Madrid: Consejo Superior de Investigaciones Científicas, Instituto Arias Montano, 1950.

Montanari, M., *Alimentazione e cultura nel Medievo.* 2d ed. Rome, 1989.

Motis Dolader, Miguel-Ángel. *Ordinaciones de la alcabala de la alhama judía del Huesca del año 1389.* Zaragoza, 1990.

———. "Régimen alimentario de las comunidades judías y conversas en la Corona de Aragón en la Edad Media." In *Coloquio sobre la alimentación en la Corona de Aragón en la Edad Media.* Lleida, 1990.

Motis Dolader, Miguel-Ángel, et al. "Ritos y festividades de los judeoconversos aragoneses en la Edad Media: La celebración del Yom Kippur o Día del Perdón. Ensayo de etnología histórica." *Jerónimo Zurita: Cuadernos de Historia* 61–62 (1990): 59–92.

Sánchez Moya, M. "El ayuno de Yom Kippur entre los judaizantes turolenses del siglo XV." *Sefarad* 26 (1966): 273–304.

Neuman, Abraham. *The Jews in Spain: Their Social, Political, and Cultural Life during the Middle Ages.* 2 vols. Morris Loeb Series, no. 3. Philadelphia: Jewish Publication Society of America, 1942.

Paul, S. M. "Classifications of Wine in Mesopotamian and Rabbinic Sources." *Israel Exploration Journal* 25 (1975): 42–44.

Raphael, Freddy, and Martine Weyl. "Trois 'chants du Séder' des juifs d'Alsace." *Ethnologie française* 11 (1981): 271–78.

Rehfeld, Manfred. "Was heisst das eigentlich—'Kascher' und 'Kaschrut'?" *Tradition und Erneuerung* 47 (1981): 20–32.

Riera i Sans, Jaume. "La conflictivitat de l'alimentació dels jueus medievals (segles XII–XV)." *Alimentació i Societat a la Catalunya Medieval. Anuario de Estudios Medievales* 20 (1988): 295–311.

Romano Ventura, David. "Creencias y prácticas religiosas de los judíos de Valencia (1467–1492): Propuestas metodológicas a base de documentos inquisitoriales." *I Congreso Internacional Luis de Santangel i el seu temps.* Valencia, 1987.

Romero, Elena. "Algunas recetas de repostería sefardí de Bosnia [por Gina Camhy]." *Estudios Sefardíes* 1 (1978): 161–88.

Rosner, Fred. "Milk and Cheese in Classic Jewish Sources." *Hototh* 9 (1987): 517–32.

Santa María, Ramón. "Ritos y costumbres de los judíos españoles." *Boletín de la Real Academia de la Historia* 22 (1993): 181–88.

Santamaría, A. "Sobre la Alhama de Mallorca: El impuesto 'size del vin juheuesch': 1400–1435." *La España Medieval* 1 (1980): 467–95.

Sanz Egaña, C. "Matanza por el rito judío (Schechitah)." *Revista de la Biblioteca, Archivo y Museo del Ayuntamiento de Madrid* 21 (1929): 75–82.

Schuhl, P. M. "Tracce di costumanze elloenistiche nel 'Säder' di Pasqua." *Rasegna Mensile di Israel* 34 (1968): 138–42.

Segre, R. "Gli ebrei e il mercato delle carni a Casale-Monferrato nel tardo Cinquecento." *Miscellanea di studi in memoria di Dario Disegni*, pp. 219–37. Torino, 1969.

Shaul, J. *El destierro y la simiente*. Colección Cocina en el Mundo Entero, Cocina sefardí. Palafrugell, Spain: Orión Editores, 1989.

Shatmiller, J. "Droit féodale et législation rabbinique: La cuisson du pain chez les Juifs du Moyen Age." In *Manger et boire au Moyen Age: Cuisine, maniéres de table, régimes alimentaires: Actes du Colloque de Nice, 15–17 octobre 1982*, 1:68–69. Centre d'Études Médiévales de Nice, Publications de la Faculté des Lettres et Sciences Humaines de Nice, no. 28. Nice: Les Belles Lettres, 1984.

Shaftesley, J. "Culinary Aspects of Anglo-Jewry." *Folklore Research Center Studies* 5 (1975): 367–400.

Silver, Daniel Jeremy. "Considering Candles and Cake." *Journal of Reform Judaism* 26 (1979): 11–19.

Siporin, Steve. "The Table of the Angel and Two Other Jewish-Venetian Food Customs." *Lares: Rivista di Studi Demo-Etno-Antropologici* 50 (1984): 357–65.

Toaff, Ariel. *Il vino e la carne: Una communità Ebraica nel Medioevo*. Bologna: Società Editrice Il Mulino, 1989.

Woolf, M. "Prohibition against the Simultaneous Consumption of Milk and Flesh in Orthodox Jewish Law." *The Psychodynamics of American Jewish Life: An Anthology*, ed. N. Kiell, 4:287–306. New York: Twayne Publishers, 1967.

PART FIVE

LATE MIDDLE AGES

(11TH — 14TH CENTURIES)

INTRODUCTION

TOWARD A NEW DIETARY BALANCE

Massimo Montanari

Traditionally the Middle Ages are considered a homogeneous historical period, endowed with an intrinsic unity. However, for the purposes of this book, the period has been divided into two distinct parts to reflect the marked differences in modes of production and models of consumption between the two epochs. The tenth and eleventh centuries were a turning point. Balances that had been established with such difficulty during the early Middle Ages were overturned; instead we encounter new historical phases that laid the foundations for many aspects of the modern world.

The most significant factor in this shift was that most people started to depend on an agrarian economy for their sustenance. The silvipastoral system, which had been possible in the early Middle Ages owing to low populations, gradually declined and became, with the exception of a few predominantly highland areas, ever more insignificant. This was the result not only of an increase in population throughout Europe, and thus a greater demand for food, but also of changes in economic and social structures. Decisive factors in this transformation included the shift from a subsistence economy to one based on the market and an increase in commercial activities, initially in the country and later in the towns. More land was cultivated, and this trend was the consequence of two distinct but linked developments: the growth of demand as populations grew and the pressure put on peasants by landowners—feudal lords and, in Italy, the urban middle classes—to exploit their property to the full in order to accumulate surplus produce for the market.

In the early Middle Ages the silvipastoral system had played an essential role in integrating the meager harvests, providing food for immediate consumption. The development of an agrarian economy, which enabled such products as grain to be accumulated and stockpiled, paved the way for the revival of trade routes in the centuries that followed. This had already begun toward the end of the early Middle Ages in the context of courtly landholdings. It was, however, from the tenth century onward that landowners became a significant social force, sustained by the administrative and judicial powers that they had wrested from centralized authorities. The typically feudal distribution of power that took place in rural areas from the tenth century to the twelfth century was mirrored, especially in the towns of central and northern Italy, by a shift in political and economic control favoring the urban middle classes.

These factors radically transformed the European landscape from the eleventh century on. Forests were cut down to make room for fields—in the plains, the hills and, finally, in the mountains. At first, small holdings nibbled away at the edge of woodland. This was followed by systematic plowing to create collective farms over large areas and by large-scale farming ventures encouraged by people in power, such as those established in Germany to the east of the Elbe. In all cases, these developments helped to define the epoch, introducing the understanding that—as a twelfth-century chronicler noted—"we cannot survive without farming the land."

The concept of "dearth" underwent a significant change. In the early Middle Ages it had referred to many things—from a shortage in agricultural products to a lack of natural resources. Later the meaning shifted to indicate a bad harvest or a limited availability of cereals. The monetary connotation of "dearth" also developed as market deficiencies forced prices up. Cereals became a staple of the peasant diet as natural resources became harder to find: wooded areas declined and hunting and grazing reserves were the domains of the powerful. Now that peasants could no longer gather or hunt, the meat in their diet was replaced by cereals, pulses, and vegetables, widening the gap in diet between the rich and the poor.

From the mid-1300s to the mid-1400s, the population fell dramatically once again, following the Black Death (1348–50) and the famines that preceded and accompanied it. As a result, forms of silvipastoral economy returned, although common land continued to be enclosed by the rich. There is evidence that meat production increased considerably and that the peasant's diet improved as a result. The urban middle classes, however, were the ones to benefit most since the market satisfied their dietary needs. Following this period, however, the situation returned to normal. Peasants went back to eating vegetables, and the divide between rich and poor continued to widen.

By the end of the Middle Ages, two main social groups enjoyed a privileged diet. The first was the aristocracy, which continued to see itself—both in practice and symbolically—as a class of meat eaters, treating the vegetables and pulses of the poor with disdain. The second was composed of town dwellers of all classes who were guaranteed the presence of foodstuffs on the market as a result of the local authorities' food policies. Unlike the three traditional orders (the aristocracy, the church, and peasants), the fourth "urban" order continued to develop, becoming a protected and privileged social group. This contrast between rural and urban models of food consumption has been, in both concrete and symbolic terms, the biggest novelty in the European diet since the Middle Ages. It first appeared in countries with a developed urban culture, such as Italy, becoming more generalized as time went by.

A subsistence economy versus a market economy was not the only distinction. Another contrast was the domestic preparation of food (typical of rural areas) compared to the specialization of trades that characterized urban society in food as in other sectors. The opposition between city and country was symbolized gastronomically by wheat bread, on the one hand, and the dark bread, polentas, and cereal-based soups, on the other. This distinction was already present in the early Middle Ages, when it served to indicate the identities of the aristocrat and the serf. In the same way, fresh meat from the city markets was in contrast to the salted meats found in the countryside. It is no accident that salted meats played no part in the town dweller's diet, which was based on spicy, sweet, and sharp flavors rather than salt, as can be seen from the recipe books of the later Middle Ages. The unexpected popularity of lamb in the urban diet of this period (despite the fact that it was not recommended in the food literature of the time) seems to indicate a desire for novelty and an explicit opposition to the rural fondness for pork. This and other dietary fashions reveal, above all, the will to reject the rural world in favor of new models of consumption. This is confirmed by the fact that, in those regions where lamb played an integral part in the traditional rural diet, it failed to make any headway in the towns.

The pride that town dwellers felt in their new identity (especially among the lower orders) was such that any risk of being forced to return to rural conditions was seen as a sign of social regression, immediately provoking waves of protest. When there was no wheat and the town markets offered only inferior cereals, the people rose in fury and the authorities were forced to find some way to placate them—by importing grain from afar, requisitioning local markets, and so on. These revolts were caused less by hunger than by humiliated pride.

The development of table manners, which occurred at the height of the Middle Ages in both cities and courts, played a part in the cultural establishment of privilege, defining its style as much as its content. Courtly and urban manners were defined, first and foremost, by exclusion—a rejection of anything rustic—and nowhere was this more evident than at table. Tableware, and the way the table was laid, also served to distinguish one class from another, as did the art of cooking itself.

In the final centuries of the Middle Ages, this became increasingly refined. Its social significance was due not only to the greater care taken in food preparation or the "quality" of the food but also to the powerful link that was forged between gastronomy and dietetics. In the Middle Ages, as in the classical world, these two bodies of knowledge advanced hand in hand, with the preparation of food being regarded primarily as a way to meet the need for nutritional balance. Medieval culture, however, interpreted this need in an explicitly social sense, defining it not as an attribute of the person—as Greek dietetics had done—but as an attribute of class. The aristocracy had their own dietetics, gastronomy, and etiquette, as did peasants. Food and table manners became the most effective way to confirm and consolidate the established order.

CHAPTER 19

SOCIETY, FOOD, *and* FEUDALISM

Antoni Riera-Melis

Between approximately 1080 and 1280, a small group of armed landowners took control to the detriment of rural peasant groups and the old public administration. This seignorial order of things, whose chief feature was a total juridical and economic inequality of persons, proved to be effective, dynamic, and innovative. Under its aegis there was a demographic expansion as well as economic growth, a transformation of family structures and the use of manpower, a technological and scientific renewal, and a change in food production systems.

The Socioeconomic and Cultural Context

In a world that was still profoundly rural, like the Europe of the year 1000, important transformations were occurring in the countryside. It was in the rural areas that the first signs of change began to appear, the beginning of a long phase of economic expansion. While in some particularly advanced peripheral regions signs announcing a new situation were already perceptible in the second half of the tenth century, growth would not reach all of the West until the second half of the following century after the famines of 1005–6 and 1032–33.

Beginning in the middle of the tenth century, in Latium as in Catalonia, a number of phenomena presaged an imminent economic renewal: small settlements were established, infrastructure that had been destroyed was rebuilt, exchange of various kinds increased, booty was coined, and the circulation of money expanded. Once the panic that had prevailed during the first half of the century had passed, a growing recovery of life and hope unmistakably replaced death and pessimism.

SIGNS OF GROWTH The most obvious sign, though not necessarily the first, of a change of period took the form of a slow but sustained rise in population, which would continue for almost three hundred years—until the end of the thirteenth century. This demographic increase was the result of a rise in the birthrate and a drop in infant mortality (although life expectancy remained about the same). Between 1000 and 1350 the population of France, the Low Countries, Germany, England, and Scandinavia tripled, and in Italy it doubled. Rates of increase were somewhat lower in Poland, the Iberian peninsula, Russia, Hungary, and the Balkans. Demographic totals rose from 12 million to 35.5 million in western and central Europe, from 17 million to 25 million in the south, and from 9.5 million to 13 million in eastern Europe. In some places on the continent the population reached figures so high that they would not be surpassed until the end of the Modern Age.

After 1080 a wave of young people overflowed the old walls of the cities and flooded the countryside, creating new villages and taking over unplowed land and forests. This new injection of vigor brought land under cultivation; rural exploitation of land increased, and urban workers became more active.

The result of this demographic increase was a more flexible extended family, the basis of communal living. The conjugal nucleus, composed exclusively of parents and children, became individualized within the bosom of the clan, the lineage; the large huts of the Carolingian era in which thirty to fifty persons lived, at least in southern Europe, were replaced by small houses built around a hearth. The weakening of blood ties permitted the gradual establishment of other ties; initially vertical ties (clienthood, dependence, and devotion) later became horizontal (brotherhood, association, common interests). The nuclear families that resulted from the breakup of the old extended domestic groups became integrated into a new organization within the framework of the seigniory in an environment controlled by a member of the aristocracy, a professional warrior.

With this increase in manpower, fields were cultivated, marshes and swamps were drained, canals and roads were built, and forests were cut down. Direct evidence of this activity is often found in documents of the twelfth and thirteenth centuries, revealing feverish activity in the expansion of cultivated fields in the bogs and marshes. Initially land was cleared in already existing agricultural areas; a second stage of utilization gave rise to new and independent farms.

In old fields as well as new, bread cereals prospered: the different varieties of wheat, rye, and even millet as well as those grown as feed for livestock—barley and oats. There was also a close connection between the economic and social progress of the feudal period and the rise of vineyards. "Prestige" grape-growing by monastic establishments and nobles was replaced by suburban or rural wine production, given impetus by peasants who enjoyed considerable autonomy and by lords who wanted a high, regular, and easily marketable source of income. Contracts of *complantatio,* which guaranteed the tenant, in exchange for assuming all the costs of preparing the soil, almost complete ownership of half the resulting vines and usufruct (subject to tax) of the other half, played a decisive role in the expansion of vineyards during the central period of the Middle Ages. Greens and vegetables, which before the tenth century had been regularly cultivated only in the kitchen gardens of monastic and seignorial establishments and in peripheral or interstitial areas of fields and small freeholds, now became grouped around the peasant house. The work of women and children, systematic manuring, irrigation, and constant care changed these small family plots into small areas of intensive production, where broad beans, garlic, onions, leeks, cabbage, and spinach were grown.

The rapid expansion of cultivated fields was not the automatic result of an increase in available manpower; it derived also from other, very different causes, notably the spread of various technical advances that profoundly altered the relationship of man to his surroundings. It was not a question of a simple accumulation of different innovations, but rather the creation of a real technological system whose elements were interdependent on each other.

Gristmills, a legacy from antiquity, multiplied rapidly everywhere in the West from the eleventh century onward; their millstones were no longer moved by animals or slaves but by the power of canal water or wind, with the resultant saving of energy. The working capacity of draft animals was increased considerably through more advanced harnessing systems—the frontal yoke (for oxen) and the rigid shoulder collar (for horses and mules)—and by the spread of the practice of shoeing. The expansion of metallurgy, to the degree that it made iron available to large segments of society, increased the strength and variety of agricultural tools. In fact, one of the period's most important technical inventions was the wheeled plow (*carruca*), which differed from the old Roman plow (*aratrum*) in its metal share, blade, and moldboard. The traditional plow, lightweight and made almost exclusively of wood, opened only superficial furrows; it continued to be used on the fragile soils of the Mediterranean slopes. The new and much more solid plow, pulled by one or several yoke of oxen or horses and capable of turning over the earth at greater depth, was especially effective in the deep, moist soils of the Atlantic plains.

Savings in manpower resulting from the new agricultural tools permitted a considerable improvement in systems of cultivation. The multiplication of agricultural tasks, as the regeneration of soils improved, made possible a gradual reduction of fallow land. Except in the driest or least populated areas, this was reduced to one year out of two. In some especially fertile areas, such as Picardy, Île-de-France, or the basin around London during the thirteenth century, more intensive models slowly began to appear. Certain rural communities, eager to increase their harvests, now tried rotations with shorter fallow periods in these areas of fertile soils and an Atlantic climate. As a result, the fallow period was restricted to one year in three after two successive plantings of cereals—winter wheat at the end of autumn and a quick-growing cereal like oats or barley shortly before the spring equinox of the second year. The transition from a biennial to a triennial rotation permitted an increase in the surface planted annually on each plot, which rose from one-half to two-thirds of tillable lands.

Despite the process of "agriculturalization" undergone by the rural economy during the central centuries of the Middle Ages, woods, pastures, and moors continued to play a considerable role in the daily life of both lords and peasants. The importance of reserves of wooded areas (for construction material and firewood, grazing areas, hunting preserves, and gathering zones) was particularly evident during failures of cereal crops, when they became emergency food sources, places of last resort, for the lowest levels of rural society. The desire to have nearby hunting areas and to preserve the supply of good timber for their numerous construction projects and for fuel led the lords, beginning in the early twelfth century, to minutely regulate the utilization of forests. As new settlements reduced available forest resources and the penetration of Christianity into rural areas stripped the woodlands of the magical aura they had possessed during the early Middle Ages, the ruling classes either limited or carefully designated peasants' rights to use the resources of these areas. Many of the forests reserved by the feudal aristocracy had initially been communal, and their use had entailed no limitations other than those assigned by local assemblies in the surrounding villages. This privatization of uncultivated areas and the establishment of guards (*forestarii, gruarii,* or *saltarii*) led to peasant uprisings in Normandy and other regions of western Europe. Hence deforestation had negative consequences for the agriculturalists themselves and for society as a whole, such as the growing expense of utilizing the woods that remained and the increased flooding due to the amount of alluvial material carried by rivers.

FEUDAL AGRARIAN STRUCTURES Changes of such magnitude obviously had a great influence on production. The great Carolingian domains, unable to adjust to change, continued to evolve toward a new structure that spread all over western Europe: the territorial seigniory. This eleventh-century creation, which had very effective mechanisms of expansion, did not differ from the previous large landholdings in its internal organization (which was also binary, based on the co-existence of reserves and tenancies), but rather in the adoption of certain procedures that were much more dynamic and open.

The warrior aristocracy, increasingly consumerist and demanding in the face of the difficulty of replenishing the supply of slaves with which it directly exploited the reserves, took advantage of the surplus manpower generated by demographic expansion both inside and outside their domains to parcel out the *terra indominicata* and to grant exploitation of the resulting plots in exchange for rents. The great Carolingian *mansos*, which had been split up by the proliferation of peasant families, were replaced by tenant holdings of varying size. The lord, proprietor of the land, leased them in exchange for a fixed rent in cash, for part of the chief crops (typically cereals, wine, and oil), and for a certain number of farm animals and poultry, ham, cheeses, and eggs. He also required payment of an entrance fee at the time of concession and reserved to himself certain fees for any change of leaseholder, including inheritance of the lease by his children. To balance these seignorial guarantees and fees, concession of the lease soon became perpetual and its holder could even transfer it. During a period of demographic expansion and advances in agricultural techniques, the lords could increase their incomes through constant establishment of new farmers on their domains, without having to subject them to too much pressure, to frequent labor service, or to tie them to the land. Peasant families could concentrate their efforts on working the land they had received, participating in the increase in production generated by their labor but without entering into servitude.

The collapse of public structures and the aggressive potential of their retinues offered the nobles other sources of income that complemented what they received from leasing their lands. These were derived from private jurisdictions and from the right of judging, protecting, and requiring taxes and services to particular rural groups. Territorial seigniories were superimposed on the network of jurisdictional ones; though different at first, both tended to mingle in the course of time. Almost all the jurisdictional nobles were originally large landowners, and the same was true of territorial nobles. The usurpation of public functions and their hereditary linkage to their own families allowed the military aristocracy to increase participation in the distribution of the crops produced by agricultural growth. In exchange for effective protection and justice, the nobles demanded new taxes from their peasants and the small free proprietors under their protection, which those who had to pay them did not hesitate to describe as *malae con-*

suetudines (bad usage). Modest juridical barriers, such as "old customs," collective memory, and active resistance, based on fraud, evasion, and delaying tactics, were employed by humble folk in opposition to the nobles' increasing fiscal demands. However, usage was manipulable, and it was hard for peasants to resist the pressures of those who held power. A tax structure created for the military aristocracy managed to eat up the profits of rural families and reduced the differences between free peasants and dependents, leveling them from below and deepening the moat that separated the nobles from the working classes.

Peasant freeholds—the *predia, propietates,* and *hereditates* that were scattered over the countryside in Carolingian times—gave way around 1050 to territorial seigniories. The gradual insertion of these small free parcels of land within much larger and more important landholdings was not merely an economic phenomenon; it was also a mechanism for control and domination. The concentration of peasants in permanent villages during the central years of the Middle Ages conferred on the European countryside the features that were to characterize it up to the agricultural renewal of the nineteenth century.

At the end of the thirteenth century, the dominant western landscape was very different from that of the early Middle Ages. The human imprint on the landscape had become much more visible. Numerous villages dotted the countryside, composed of a group of stone or wooden dwellings huddled around the church and cemetery, surrounded by garden plots, threshing floors, sheepfolds, vineyards, orchards, and fields of grain, whose respective boundaries were usually indicated by narrow and carefully marked pastures or wooded areas. The great forests had become residual woodlands guarded by agents of the nobles, who restricted the peasants' access to them. Fields lay adjacent to other fields, villages to other villages, and seigniories to other seigniories. Expansion of plowed areas and the growing compartmentalization of fields had almost completely eliminated the intervening areas of natural vegetation. Here and there, protected by stockades or masonry walls, were the dwellings of the nobles' agents, along with the storehouses where products extracted from the peasants were temporarily stored awaiting the lord's instructions, along with the oven, the forge, and other services for nearby peasant communities. On a hilltop, and very visible, loomed the castle, which guarded and controlled the whole seigniory. It was always well provisioned, and behind its mighty walls was kept an important part of the wealth generated by the peasants' labor—for use by a military aristocracy that lived off its property and that had assumed the power of judging, protecting, and requiring taxes and services from the rural population in its vicinity. A capillary network of land and river routes joined the villages together, connected them with the castles, and linked these with the cities. Markets prospered at crossroads, where the peasants disposed of their small agricultural surpluses and acquired a few manufactured articles sold by merchants from the cities.

INCREASE IN COMMERCE AND URBAN REBIRTH Feudal society was supported by the agricultural production of peasants, who, in addition to meeting their own needs, had to turn over part of their crops to the owners of the lands that they cultivated. For these owners, extravagance was the chief indicator of power. Hence the logic of the system consisted in effectively stimulating the peasant families to extract from their lands more than they needed for mere subsistence, encouraging continuity of production, and enforcing payment of seignorial taxes. All this led tenants to work increasingly hard to achieve a surplus that they could exchange in local markets; this desire, though widespread, encountered a technical or human ceiling that not everyone could break through. However, feudal structures generated a mercantile potential of considerable volume, overlooked by historians until quite recently. Income not spent by the nobles and the occasional surpluses from the more-active or better-equipped peasant families stimulated exchange. At first internal and later external, this exchange soon led to the coining of money, more traffic on the roads, and the rise of urban craftsmen.

In a second phase the system broke out of the narrow urban framework and gave rise to a reopening of interregional and even international connections. In this context of broadened and diversified supply and demand, the nobles made great efforts to increase their liquidity: they tried to get their hands on immediate cash, and the more intelligent producers tried to concentrate their efforts on cultivating the land or making their workshops more efficient. A result of these new interests, which were not necessarily conflicting, was the adoption of more refined techniques and release from labor services and petty obligations.

Demographic momentum, increased agricultural production, renewed commercial activity, and a change in the relationship between nobles and peasant families accentuated, during the course of the twelfth century, the social division of labor, which was more rapid in the cities than in the countryside. This division increased social pressures within the urban population, so the less efficient members of society became impoverished at a faster rate. It also ushered in the appearance of a small group of great professional merchants, businessmen rich enough to become promoters of manufactured goods. The nobles, who controlled the rural population, had to come to an agreement with this new elite—their equivalent in urban society—in order to meet the obligations of increasing consumption.

The rise in agricultural production, besides enriching the aristocracy, stimulated the development of cities. The old *urbes*, to the extent that they were frequented by nobles who sold their agricultural surpluses there and bought articles of high quality that could not be found in the country, recovered their former role of chief market and manufacturing center of the region. After the end of the eleventh century, city and country, as they developed differently, ceased to be concurrent realities and became two complementary economic environments.

Chief Nutritional Systems

All these changes gradually altered living conditions among the different classes of western society. In particular, important nutritional consequences arose from the "agriculturization" of the rural economy as well as from the powerful feudal aristocracy's restrictions on the utilization of woodlands, the proliferation of rural markets, and the increasing connection between rural and urban markets.

Foods of vegetable origin gained ground over meat in the lower social strata. Between 1050 and 1280 the diets of the different social classes lost the variety that had characterized them during the earlier Middle Ages. Bread and wine eclipsed other foods and relegated them to the position of accompaniments. Especially in the cities, their absence was almost intolerable: after two hundred years of agricultural growth, chestnuts, acorns, and alternate foodstuffs had almost disappeared except in mountainous regions. On the plains, gathering and hunting decreased as a means of obtaining food and, for most peasant families, became marginal activities, reserved for the poor (gathering) and the nobles (hunting) in normal times.

Each social class assumed an unequal portion of the agricultural and hunting-pastoral resources of society as a whole, gave them a different value, and combined them in different ways. As pointed out in earlier chapters, each constructed its own nutritional system. During the Middle Ages the table had become a powerful element of collective identity, one of the most important indicators of rank; together with his dwelling and his clothing, it gave witness to the place that a person occupied in society and the function he assumed.

THE ROYAL AND NOBLE MODEL According to a report of 1157–58, the queen of Catalonia and Aragon ate wheaten bread and drank wine every day, even during Lent. At about that same time, in a dietary regimen drawn up by members of the school of Salerno for the king of England, the monarch is advised against drinking water exclusively, for it is said to cause intestinal upsets and block digestion; wine is deemed the best drink, especially sweet white wine. The criteria for selecting a good wine, according to the Italian diet specialists, are smell, taste, color, and transparency—in that order.

The shopping list is notable for repeatedly mentioning the finer meats (hens, chickens, capons, and geese), followed by mutton, fresh and salt pork, and lamb. These foodstuffs, well seasoned with spices (pepper) and less exotic condiments (onions and garlic) were combined in several ways to produce abundant and varied menus. The total absence of game is surprising, for it was a food that was prominent among the gastronomic preferences of western European nobility.

After meat, bread, and wine, which constituted the central nucleus of the nobles' diet, eggs and cheese appear, though much less frequently. These two foodstuffs, with a high protein content, were combined with meat on normal days and alternated with fish on penitential occasions. In the dietary regime mentioned above, the doctors of Salerno recommended that eggs always be fresh and accompanied with wine to aid digestion. When cheese and meat were to be served at the same meal, they specified that meat should always precede cheese.

In the aristocratic dietary regime, greens and vegetables occupied a secondary place, and the absence of fruit is total. So popular today, it raised serious doubts among the doctors of the time, who counseled restricting the use of fruit, especially in autumn.

In the kitchens of palaces and castles, the vast and heterogeneous variety of foods that composed the diet of members of the royal family and western European nobles were combined and manipulated by specialized domestic servants. The key element of these establishments was the hearth, where the fire was built. The oven—along with the kneading trough, indispensable for making bread—played a secondary role in cooking other foods.

Boiling meat in water—with spices and aromatic herbs along with other condiments—to make it tender and increase its flavor became a very ordinary culinary practice in the Middle Ages. To prepare tough meats like game and beef, the technique of several boilings was used, which consisted of scalding or boiling the meat before subjecting it to further treatment in pots, frying pans, or on a spit.

Boiling coexisted with braising, frying, and roasting. Meat and vegetables were fried with lard, fish with olive oil. Roasted meat continued to be very popular; it was prepared by threading the pieces, either boiled or raw but always well seasoned, onto a skewer that was then rotated over the fire on the hearth.

Once prepared, foods were served on platters (or some other receptacle) in the dining room, a large space that was the center of intense social activity. The centerpiece of this room was the table. On normal days the dishes were made of tin, pewter, copper, glazed pottery, or fine wood; dishes of precious metals were reserved for banquets. As for cutlery, spoons, knives, and ladles, made of the same metals as the dishes, are most frequently mentioned in contemporary documents.

Drink was almost entirely restricted to wine and wine derivatives; it appeared on the table in glass pitchers or metal jugs. The frequent libations were drunk from cups made of precious metals, fine decorated wood, or glass.

In a society presided over by professional warriors, which exalted physical strength, income levels were demonstrated at table. Important men ate to satiation, and the man who ate a great deal dominated the others; he was big-boned and burly like the warriors in the epics—brave as a lion, strong as a bull, swift as an eagle, and more than human, like the angels, the four symbols of the Evangelists. So there is nothing surprising about the fact that the law hewed to these specifications and accepted (with the somewhat reluctant approval of the church) the ordeal and the judicial duel—two trials in which the strongest man won—as systems to establish a criminal's innocence or guilt. Some have linked the violence that impregnates feudal society, the propensity not to retreat before the blood that the great ones boasted about, to an excessive, heavy, and perhaps stimulating diet. To eat a great deal, especially a great deal of meat, continued to be a sign of power, a source of physical energy and sexual potency, and one of the chief manifestations of *joie de vivre*.

THE DIETARY SYSTEMS OF ECCLESIASTICS   The great Burgundian abbey at Cluny provides fertile ground for examining foods at the monastic table of this period. What was the diet of these Cluniac Benedictines like in the first third of the thirteenth century? Udalric's *Consuetudines* contains much information, both direct and indirect, about the diet that prevailed at the abbey.

From October 1 to Lent, the season of short, cold days, the community gathered in the refectory once on working days and twice on feast days. Dinner, which took place at the hour of sext (noon), consisted of two hot dishes—a vegetable soup usually made with beans and a plate of green vegetables, according to the rule of Benedict of Nursia—and one supplement, either the "general" or the "pittance" of fruits and garden vegetables, which provided the third dish. The "general," which was served on one plate for each monk on Tuesdays, Thursdays, Saturdays, and Sundays, consisted of five eggs or some cooked cheese. On Sundays and Thursdays, if it could be procured at reasonable prices, fish replaced the eggs or cheese of the "general." These dishes were always accompanied by a pound of wheaten bread and about half a pint of undiluted wine, which each diner received in a large cup.

From Easter to the end of September, the monks had two meals daily as compensation for the output of energy necessitated by the heat and long hours of the days. These two meals (also the custom on feast days in winter) were served at sext and after vespers. Supper, much more frugal than dinner, consisted of what was left of the bread and wine uneaten by each monk at noon, along with seasonal fruit or wafers.

In the morning on normal days, after the first prayers, a small breakfast was served to the monks on duty, the sick, the old, children, and other members of the community who wanted it; it was called the *mixtum* and consisted of a piece of bread and a glass of wine. At night any thirsty monks could have their last drink of the day before going to bed.

Penitential days at Cluny saw some changes in the operation of the kitchen and refectory. The community fasted during Advent, Lent, and on all established holy days throughout the year in accordance with canonical institutions. Dietary restrictions, which were not obligatory for the old or ill, covered approximately a third of the year.

On fast days the monks had only one meal, served at the hour of nones (around three o'clock in the afternoon). The composition of this meal, except from Septuagesima to Easter and on ember days, was identical to that of ordinary days and included the ration of wine. During Lent and the penitential exercises at the beginning of the four seasons, austerity was accentuated: vegetables were cooked in oil. Removing lard from the diet was compensated by an increase in the ration of bread. The mortification of penitential days, therefore, rather than consisting of qualitative changes in the diet, merely meant a delay in serving dinner and, in summer, eliminating supper.

In the Burgundian abbey the frequent dietary restrictions were compensated by celebrating certain dates with an extraordinary meal, exactly as was done in palaces and castles. Once a year, on the feast day of the Benedictine order's patron saint, members of the community received the "general" and the "pittance" at the same time. On the great feasts of the liturgical year the daily vegetable soup was replaced by more attractive dishes, and, in addition to ordinary bread, the diners received a cake made with eggs. It must have been on festive days that meat, which is not mentioned in Udalric's *Consuetudines,* was served at the monastic table. As was logical, extraordinary meals also involved a special drink, *pigmentum,* or hippocras, a type of mulled wine prepared with honey, pepper, and cinnamon.

By about 1100 the dietary regime of the Cluny monks, which their detractors thought was excessive, overrefined, and more suitable for lords than for monks, was composed of a large variety of ingredients. Foods of vegetable origin still predominated, at least in daily meals, over those of animal origin, despite the increased consumption of meat in the course of the century as more and more members of the feudal aristocracy entered the order. The repeated criticisms of a sector of the clergy that favored a stricter asceticism, as well as budgetary problems, obliged the Burgundian community to moderate its consumption during the last third of the twelfth century.

The preparation of menus suitably varied for a large and demanding monastic community was possible only with adequate supplies and equipment. Cluny had two kitchens: the ordinary one, where the monks prepared the daily soup and vegetable stew, and the normal one, where servants, directed by monks, prepared the other dishes served in the conventual refectory and all those intended for the dining room for servants and guests. Four monks, taking strict weekly turns, controlled the operation of the regular kitchen. Their task was considered so important that it could not be interrupted by any other task, not even prayers.

The structure of collective meals obliged the monastic communities to create a particular space, the refectory, and to subject its operation to an almost liturgical ritual. Each diner sat at his own place and ate in strict silence, listening to pious readings. Unlike the royal or noble dining room, the refectory was not a place of relaxation but a space—like so many others in a monastery—of isolation, an area where the community contemplated itself, with its internal hierarchies, and the monks interacted in accordance with a rigid code of customs.

How did the monks of Cluny obtain the many ingredients in their diets, both ordinary and extraordinary? According to Udalric's *Consuetudines,* such a community ought to be able to satisfy all its material needs with what its own lands produced. The expansion and dispersion of the domain, the monks' minimal dedication to manual tasks, and the increase in cash rents, both inside and outside the monastic property, led its administrators to go beyond the former closed models. Even before 1100, money and commercial exchange played an important role in the Cluniac economy. Cluny's spiritual influence was translated, among other things, into an increasing flow of assets toward the abbey. The flow of precious metals, in a climate of economic expansion, caused the community to apply to basic foods the same economic standard that, until then, had been reserved for equipment: to tie food supplies more closely to cash income than to the products in kind that had formerly been collected in the monastic lands. Gradually, the practice of buying daily supplies of wheat and wine in the marketplace became established.

After a prosperous period in which the community had become accustomed to an easy life, difficulties arose, with lack of money in the till and a scarcity of food in the storehouses. This change of economic climate, perceptible after 1120, led to a gradual drop in cash income and a parallel increase in expenses as the result of rising prices. Emergence from the crisis therefore required cuts in expenses and changes in administration of the property.

The person charged with planning and carrying out corrective measures was the abbot Peter the Venerable. To balance the budget, the reformer banned the use of paid employees in the infirmary and shifted onto the lay brothers— monks whose intellectual limitations kept them from attaining the cultural level demanded of the clergy—responsibility for almost all the monastery's internal tasks. Reduced consumption and increased workloads were not enough, however, to wipe out the deficit. In a second phase, Peter the Venerable and his fellow administrators, in view of the monks' limited appetite for sacrifice, opened a new course of action; it was meant to complement previous changes, to reinforce links between the community and its property, to reinstate direct exploitation of the land, and to improve provisioning of the reserve. The community was to buy only those articles that could not be produced or gathered on the monastery's domain. The reformers' chief objective was to restore its previous self-sufficiency in cereals and wine.

In a period when consumption of wheat was rising everywhere in Europe, bread was dark—a mixture of cereals and dried vegetables, normally barley, millet, and peas. White bread was reserved for invalids and for guests of high social status. For the monks who had eaten the portion of bread reserved for supper and for penitents and the poor, a third type of even coarser bread was made with barley or oat flour. The vegetable stew, which in some cases contained only gleanings, beech leaves, or grasses, was prepared without any type of fat, not even olive oil. In Cistercian monasteries of the time, fish, eggs, cheese, and milk were forbidden to monks, even at monasteries with surpluses of these products. Thus they were considered exquisite delicacies, reserved for celebrating great events.

Five centuries of Benedictine experience allowed the Cistercians to apply a very rational structure to their buildings. Their monasteries had two kitchens equipped with running water, one for the monastery and one for guests; they had two large refectories—one for the professed monks and another for the lay brothers—and a dining room for visitors. The monastery kitchen was the exclusive domain of professed monks; all of them, in weekly turns of two, assumed the task of preparing the community's daily meals. The dietary regime had too important a role in the ascetic life to be entrusted to lay brothers. The operation of both refectories, despite the suspicion aroused in the new monks by the Cistercians' excessive ritualism, was also subjected to a rigid discipline. The monks and lay brothers ate their austere meals rapidly and in unbroken silence while listening to pious readings. Speaking at table was punished by eliminating wine or, if it was not on the table, taking away one of the two dishes of greens or cooked vegetables.

THE DIETARY PRACTICES OF PEASANTS To reconstruct the dietary practices of peasants and small proprietors from the eleventh to the thirteenth centuries is a task a good deal more complicated than that of analyzing the diets of nobles or clergy. Because there are no direct sources, historians have to rely on the scraps of information contained in very different sorts of documents, such as tax records, lists of donations, wills, household inventories, and funeral banquets.

What was the ordinary diet of the rural lower classes? The daily ration of a couple subject to *corvée*, or forced labor, in the domain of Beaumont-le-Roger in 1268 consisted of a large loaf and two smaller loaves of bread weighing about 2.25 kilograms (almost 5 pounds), a gallon of wine, half a pound of meat or eggs, and a bushel of peas. Many small proprietors and peasants would have thought it a privilege to eat such a diet, offered by a lord to his dependent peasants in exchange for their labor, on a regular basis.

The advance in cereal cultivation had placed bread at the center of rural diets, and it was present at every meal. While consumption of the bread called *ros*, made of hard wheat, became more common among the working classes in the cities, the peasants' loaf was a good deal darker and made of secondary cereals like barley, rye, spelt, or, in the best cases, a mixture of grains. Most rural families reserved for the market a good part of the "noble" grain that they had left over after paying taxes. In rural areas the color of the bread also represented a status symbol, an unmistakable indication of the consumer's social class.

The second component of rural diets was wine. This drink possessed a number of advantages that made it particularly attractive to the rural lower classes: considerable nutritive value, a slightly antiseptic character, and its intoxicating effects. During the twelfth and thirteenth centuries, as a result of the constant increase in grape-growing, almost all rural establishments had vineyards and small wine cellars, along with a vat, pails, funnels, and barrels. The quality of the wine depended as much on the district's soil and climate as on the equipment and experience possessed by the family who made it. In Catalonia at this time the peasants already distinguished several types of wine: white, red, and aged. The frequent mention of wine in wills offers evidence that, for the peasant class, wine had become a very accessible and widely consumed product.

Proteins were contributed by meat—for the most part, from small farm animals. On almost all family farms, in addition to a pair of oxen for plowing, there were a few sheep, pigs, goats, chickens, and geese. Despite the fact that the gradual disappearance of woods with acorn-bearing trees made raising pigs on a large scale difficult, this animal continued to play an important role in peasant diets; its flesh was eaten fresh in winter and salted or in the form of sausage throughout the year. Lard, the ordinary fat in many regions of western Europe, was also obtained from the pig. Most of the bones found in excavations belonged to young animals, indicating that they were killed when they weighed between 40 and 80 kilograms (88–176 pounds). Sheep and goats, on the other hand, were eaten when old, after their capacity for producing wool and milk had been exhausted.

The need to maintain a supply of eggs, and the payment of a good many chickens as seignorial taxes, obliged peasants to restrict the consumption of poultry as much as possible; it was reserved for invalids or for banquets on important feast days.

Hunting, a very widespread activity among the peasant class during the early Middle Ages, gradually declined after 1080 as a result of increased settlement. Rabbits, hares, grouse, partridge, and woodcock became less frequent in peasant diets during the twelfth and thirteenth centuries, as fire and the axe thinned the forests and access to them was restricted by the nobles.

Cheese, another nutritious food, was used as a substitute or complement for meat, especially in mountainous regions. In view of the frequency with which this product appeared in lists of in-kind taxes, it must have been a rare rural home that did not have the indispensable equipment for cheese-making.

The expansion of cultivated fields at the expense of wilderness made vegetables and greens two types of food that were easily obtainable for all of rural society. Broad beans, peas, lentils, and chickpeas as well as tares, vetches, and flat peas, almost unknown in western diets today, appeared frequently on peasant tables. In the family kitchen gardens women, children, and old folk grew a broad selection of vegetables—cabbage, onions, garlic, leeks, turnips, spinach, and squash. This supply was supplemented with the systematic gathering, in meadows and woods, of asparagus, watercress, mushrooms, and some aromatic plants like thyme, marjoram, basil, laurel, fennel, and sage.

With vegetables and greens, small quantities of fresh or salted meat, lard or olive oil, and sops of dry bread or flour, peasant women prepared soups and stews, two hot dishes that, together with bread and wine, were almost daily fare in many rural homes. A monotonously unchanging presentation was relieved by ingredients that varied from one season to another.

On penitential days, with a regularity that is difficult to assess, meat was replaced by cheese, dried fruits, eggs, or fish, and lard by olive oil; these were foods that aroused little enthusiasm among the peasants of the twelfth and thirteenth centuries. But on certain rare occasions, almost always coinciding with the great feasts of the liturgical cycle, peasant families bolstered their diets to compensate for the penitential days and to break the monotony.

During the central period of the Middle Ages, funeral banquets were a widespread custom in many regions of western Europe. After the funeral rites had taken place, family and friends, along with the clergy who had officiated at the ceremonies and the poor folk who had attended them, met at the deceased person's home to celebrate a ritual meal. This banquet symbolically reconstituted the community following the loss of one of its members. The instructions for the banquet left by many testators in their wills suggest what was served on these occasions; the main foods were bread, wine, and meat.

The Limits of Growth

In a society where bread was at the center of ordinary diets, and where only poor folk, beggars, and outcasts went hungry in normal years, a poor harvest of cereals became a serious problem, if not a tragedy, for the urban and rural lower classes. They had to await the arrival of grain from outside while searching for alternative foods, foods of last resort, in the ever diminishing woods and wastelands. Despite the expansion of cultivated fields and the increase in commercial exchange, four great food crises affecting all of Europe occurred in the central years of the Middle Ages (1005–6, 1032–33, 1195–97, 1224–26). Even during a century and a half when the menace of famine relented slightly, there were regional crises every twenty-five years or so.

Widespread lack of fertilizer, the inefficiency of agricultural tools, and the reduction of fallow fields owing to the peasants' need to provide surplus crops for market affected the soil's fertility and resulted in a gradual drop in harvests. After the middle of the thirteenth century many peasant families began to have serious subsistence problems and were forced to request reductions in taxes from their overlords. On the properties of the Pia Almoina of the cathedral of Barcelona, a decrease in taxes owing to "sterility of the land" began around 1270 and intensified early in the fourteenth century.

After the turn of the century, bad harvests were repeated with a rapidity and intensity hitherto unknown. Two great famines occurred: that of 1315–17, which struck the Atlantic coasts, and that of 1346–47, which affected the entire continent. The appearance of the Black Death in 1348 decimated a population that had recently passed through a time of great scarcity. It marked a change of era, the beginning of a period of adversity.

BIBLIOGRAPHY

Alexandre, P. *Le climat en Europe au Moyen Age: Contribution à l'histoire des variations climatiques de 1000 à 1425, d'après les sources narratives de l'Europe occidentale*. Paris: École des Hautes Études en Sciences Sociales, 1987.

Bisson, T. N. *Fiscal Accounts of Catalonia under the Early Count-Kings (1151–1213)*. Berkeley: University of California Press, 1984.

Bloch, M. *La société féodale*. Paris: A. Michel, 1968. [*Feudal Society*. Trans. L. A. Manyon. Chicago: University of Chicago Press, 1961].

Bredero, A. H. *Cluny et Cîteaux au douzième siècle*. Amsterdam: APA-Holland University Press, 1985.

Brooke, C. *Europe in the Central Middle Ages, 962–1154*. 2d ed. A General History of Europe. London: Longman, 1987.

Conde, R. "Alimentación y sociedad: Las cuentas de Guillema de Montcada (1189)." *Medievalia* 3 (1982): 7–21.

Fossier, R. *Enfance de l'Europe: Aspects économiques et sociaux, X^e–XIIe siècles*. 2 vols. Paris: Presses Universitaires de France, 1982.

Laliena, C. "Sicut ritum est in terra aragonensis." In *I Colloqui d'Història de l'Alimentació a la Corona d'Aragó*, 2:665–91. Lleida, 1995.

Montanari, M. *Campagne medievali: Strutture produttive, rapporti di lavoro, sistemi alimentari*. Turin: G. Einaudi, 1984.

———. *La fame e l'abbondanza: Storia dell'alimentazione in Europa*. Rome: Editori Laterza, 1993. [*The Culture of Food*. Trans. Carl Ipsen. The Making of Europe. Oxford: Blackwell, 1994.]

Poly, J.-P., and E. Bournazel. *La mutation féodale, X^e–XIIe siècles*. Paris: Presses Universitaires de France, 1980. [*The Feudal Transformation 900–1200*. Trans. Caroline Higgitt. New York: Holmes & Meier, 1991.]

Riera-Melis, A. "Alimentació i ascetisme a Europa occidental en el segle XII. El model cluniacens." In *I Colloqui d'Història de l'Alimentació a la Corona d'Aragó*, 1:39–105. Lleida, 1995.

———. "Alimentació i poder a Catalunya al segle XII: Aproximació al comportament alimentari de la noblesa." In *Revista d'Etnologia de Catalunya* 2 (1993): 8–21.

———. "Pobreza y alimentació en el Mediterráneo Noroccidental en la Baja Edad Media." In *La Mediterrània, àrea de convergència de sistemes alimentaris (segles V–XVIII)*, pp. 39–72. Palma de Mallorca, 1996.

———. *Senyors, monjos i pagesos: Alimentació i identitat social als segles XII i XIII*. Barcelona, 1997.

Russell, J. *Medieval Demography*. New York: AMS Press, 1987.

Sesma, A. "Aproximación al estudio del régimen alimentario del reino de Aragón en los siglos XI y XII." In *Homenaje a don José María Lacarra en su jubilación*, 2:55–78. Zaragoza: Anubar, 1977.

CHAPTER 20

SELF–SUFFICIENCY *and the* MARKET

Rural and Urban Diet in the Middle Ages

Alfio Cortonesi

Wheat and Other Cereals

In the first few centuries of the second millennium the role of bread gained ever greater importance in the daily diet. The growth in population between the tenth and thirteenth centuries led to a notable increase in the amount of land under cultivation and, consequently, a decline in the exploitation of pastures and forests. Bringing new tracts of land under cultivation, which was destined to radically transform the European landscape, led to an analogous growth in the number of "bread-eating lands." Cultivation expanded and, at the same time, wheat began to dominate the scene, replacing such cereals as rye, spelt, and barley, which had predominated during the early Middle Ages.

Wheat, of course, never became the only crop. Recent studies have shown that rye bread was very popular in medieval Piedmont, in the towns as well as in the country, while millet bread was common in Lucca and, more generally, in the northwestern part of Tuscany. Nonetheless, wheat continued to dominate town dwellers' tables.

The situation in the country was very different. Various sources suggest that, in many cases, peasants used a variety of minor cereals rather than wheat. These cereals were easier to grow and gave larger and more guaranteed yields, providing peasants with greater food security. Owing to their rapid growing cycles, spring cereals, like millet and sorghum, were of considerable help in emergencies. The quality of bread made from millet and, in particular, rye was also highly appreciated.

This clearly does not mean that wheat was not the main cereal in vast areas of the Italian countryside. Throughout the south, white bread was the rule, even for the humblest peasants, just as it was in much of the country surrounding the communes of northern and central Italy. In Latium, small and medium-sized landowners tended to prefer wheat to the minor cereals, despite the fact that they depended for survival on their own production.

Cereal consumption in rural areas reflected social differences far more than it did in the city. The more vulnerable families in the countryside, who depended solely on what they grew themselves, were more likely to grow the hardier minor cereals than wheat. Producers with access to the market, albeit intermittent, behaved differently. Anyone who could afford not to worry about day-to-day survival—a class that obviously included nobles—preferred wheat.

Cereals were not just used to make bread. Small-grained cereals were widely used to make soups and porridges, together with the smaller pulses. Flatcakes and polenta, dressed in various ways, were also produced. Among peasants, this kind of food was particularly widespread and often completely substituted for bread. As confirmed by several written sources referring to the Po Valley, this situation was still prevalent at the beginning of the modern age, when the arrival of corn almost completely swept away minor cereals.

Not all cereals were produced for human consumption, especially in Mediterranean economies, where the almost total absence of forage made it difficult to raise livestock. Barley and spelt and, whenever present, oats made an essential contribution to animal fodder. Sorghum was used for cattle and pigs, while farmyard poultry ate millet. This helps us understand the importance of the minor cereals in the medieval rural economy.

Recent studies have shown that the situation in Italy—which differed considerably from one region to another—was only partially reflected in other European countries. In medieval France wheat was grown on all cultivated land, and both urban and rural consumers preferred it. The bread was not always of the same quality, however, and social hierarchy was reflected in the demand for bread using flour that was more or less refined. In 1273 in Marseilles three kinds of bread were baked: *albus* (white), *medianus* (mixed grain), and *panes cum toto* (whole grain). In other towns, such as Manosque, Tarascon, and Apt, only two qualities were available, but bread made with wheat was still the most popular.

In Germany, during the same period, the regular consumption of white bread was the privilege of the rich, while the poor ate mostly rye or spelt bread. The latter, which occupied a marginal role in Italy, played a much larger part in the southern German diet, whereas rye was more frequent in the central and northern regions. On the tables of the poorer peasants—where, according to Werner Rösener, "bread and good quality meat were rare"—both oats and barley could be found, although neither grain could be transformed into decent bread.

Chestnuts

Chestnuts played an important part in the diet of people who lived in mountainous and hilly regions. Whether fresh or dried in order to preserve them, they were a constant presence on the table in these areas. Chestnut flour was used to produce not only polenta and savory tarts but also bread, which, despite its modest quality, was invaluable in times when cereals were in short supply. This was the norm, given the relative scarcity of cereal-growing in high-lying areas.

In the early and late Middle Ages, numerous mountain communities in Italy depended on chestnuts for sustenance for large portions of the year. They were also one of the main economic resources for the peasant populations in the siliceous areas of France. The landscapes of Périgord, Limousin, the Auvergne, and the mountains around Lyons were dominated by chestnut trees, as were the regions of Vivarais and the Cévennes. The sixteenth-century chestnut groves of the Cévennes were the main source of income for the whole region.

Throughout this period, chestnuts were cultivated almost exclusively to satisfy the demands of producers, but this does not mean that the higher-quality nuts were not taken to town markets, especially those in proximity to the chestnut-growing areas.

Pulses and Vegetables

Broad beans were an important item in the peasant's diet and were present all over Italy. Peas, chickpeas, and beans—the only type known in the Middle Ages being the lima bean with its "eye"—were also cultivated, albeit to a lesser extent. In Germany, however, beans, peas, and lentils were the most common pulses, while in England beans and peas were the most frequently documented. At the end of the fourteenth century and for the whole of the fifteenth century, in fact, peas occupied 30 percent of the vegetable garden at Leicester Abbey. As early as the end of the thirteenth century, in the gardens at the manors of Brent and Zoy in Sedgemoor, beans were one of the most important crops.

What northern and Mediterranean countries share is the fact that pulses were grown in open fields as well as in closed vegetable gardens. In the latter case, they were destined for home consumption. The vegetable garden was usually adjacent to the house, and no country dwelling was complete without one. Anything produced in one of these private gardens was exempt from dues.

When the garden was near a town or within its walls, vegetable growing took on a different role. The force of attraction of the market meant that produce was no longer strictly for home consumption but was destined for commercialization, both at nearby markets and much farther afield. In the thirteenth century, in fact, Picardy onions and garlic, as well as Brittany onions, were sold in the street markets of London.

Fruit

Fruit became more popular in the late Middle Ages. Sources document an increase in the cultivation of fruit trees from the beginning of the thirteenth century, largely on the part of landowners. This increase is a mark of a more demanding and refined dietary regimen.

Limes, lemons, and bitter oranges were grown in the Italian Mezzogiorno in larger and larger quantities throughout the thirteenth century, as were hazelnuts. These were traded not only among southern merchants but also in Rome, Pisa, and Genoa. The orchards surrounding Lake Nemi, admired by Pope Pius II, provided a wide variety of produce for the markets of Rome. A common denominator of this new demand was the emergence of a wealthier social class able to afford products that were still considered superfluous (and therefore tokens of privilege). Peasants in the country, living at subsistence level, ate very little fruit throughout the Middle Ages.

Oil

In Mediterranean Europe, olive trees were more widely cultivated than any other fruit tree from the twelfth and thirteenth centuries on. Olives grew almost everywhere in Italy, with regional variations owing to the climate; in contrast, there are no records of olive cultivation in France farther north than Vivarais and the Dauphine province. In those areas where olives did not prosper and therefore olive oil could not be produced, animal fat took its place in the diet. Walnut oil was also used in some regions.

Wine

The importance of wine during this period is well known. Recent research has shown that vines were planted and cultivated to varying degrees on almost any strip of available land, even in semiurban environments. This phenomenon can be explained by the fact that wine was increasingly in demand and yet it was difficult to transport and therefore market. The obvious, and necessary, consequence of these two factors was a considerable degree of small-scale self-sufficiency in wine production.

Available data regarding town dwellers in the Italian communes register decidedly high per capita wine consumption. Residents of Florence, it has been calculated, drank between 260 and 270 liters of wine a year, and similar figures have been estimated for Genoa and Venice. In Bologna consumption in the late Middle Ages was not twice but three or four times today's level. With these figures in mind, wine drinking can no longer be considered a privilege of the few. The emergence of "bourgeois" viticulture went hand in hand with an expanding market that catered not just to the privileged but to all. Significantly, almsgiving to the poor included the public distribution of wine. It was thus by no means considered superfluous; rather, it was seen as being "nutritious for the life of man."

Although wine supplies were generally plentiful, social status was reflected both in the quantity and quality of the product served at table. Without oversimplifying, it would be reasonable to say that light, watered-down wine typically washed down the meals of laborers (and was often served in taverns or at the workplace), while finer wine with a higher alcohol content was the prerogative of the wealthier classes—at least as far as day-to-day consumption was concerned. The numerous small or medium-sized growers produced wine mostly for their own consumption, but this does not mean that it never reached the market. The prospect of profit was often enough to convince producers to sacrifice at least some of their better-quality wine.

In many regions of central and northern Europe, the supremacy of wine was challenged by cider, mead, and beer (*cervisia* or *malta*). At the beginning of the twelfth century, cider was popular in Normandy, the Basque country, and the kingdom of Galicia. Beer—brewed from barley and oats and flavored, from the late Middle Ages on, with hops—was commonly drunk in northern and central Germany. It took over from wine except in the southern regions of the Rhine Valley, Moselle and Alsace. In numerous areas both wine and beer were drunk by peasants and laborers while mead declined in popularity, as it was difficult to keep.

Meat

Increasingly drastic deforestation and the progressive privatization of the right to use forest resources during the early and late Middle Ages led to another transformation in eating habits, especially among rural populations. Peasants were no longer able to supplement their diet by freely exploiting common land.

People in the late Middle Ages consumed less meat than their counterparts in the early Middle Ages. Nevertheless, a considerable amount of meat was still eaten, and often in greater quantities than in the modern age. People in towns ate differently from people in the country, however, both in terms of quantity and quality. Lambs, kids, and veal calves, all finer-quality meats, found their way to market and thence to the town slaughterhouses, while the older animals, worth less at the market, were eaten by their breeders.

Peasants raised farmyard poultry and, above all, pigs to increase their meat intake. Despite the reduction in open forest, pigs—bred mostly in sties—played a vital role in peasants' diets throughout the period. Salted pork was an important food source in winter months, and lard was the most commonly used fat in central and northern Europe as well as in those Mediterranean regions where olive oil was not plentiful.

It is clear that changes in production systems—during which so much land was brought under cultivation, and common land, previously used for grazing, free-range livestock raising, and the gathering of wood and wild fruit, was reduced—dealt a blow to the rural population, to peasants in particular. The gradual expropriation of hunting rights in the forests—which became, by the end of the Middle Ages and especially in those areas subject to manorial landlords, an exclusive reserve for the privileged—also had a lasting effect on the rural population. Peasants were often no longer able to ensure their own food security because of the expansion of privately owned property. It is thus easy to imagine how vulnerable they were and how their situation worsened dramatically every time a crisis in production threatened self-sufficiency and caused them to seek refuge in the towns.

BIBLIOGRAPHY

Cherubini, G. *L'Italia rurale del basso Medioevo*. Rome: Laterza, 1985.

Comet, G. *Le paysan et son outil: Essai d'histoire technique des céréales (France, VIIIe–XVe siècles)*. Rome: École Française de Rome, 1992.

Cortonesi, A. *Terre e signori nel Lazio medioevale: Un'economia rurale nei secoli XIII–XIV*. Naples: Liguori, 1988.

Desportes, F. *Le pain au Moyen Age*. Paris: O. Orban, 1987.

Drummond, J., and A. Wilbraham. *The Englishman's Food: A History of Five Centuries of English Diet*. Rev. ed. London: Pimlico, 1991.

García de Cortázar, J. A. *La sociedad rural en la España Medieval*. Mexico City: Siglo Veintiuno Editores, 1988.

Gibault, G. *Histoire des légumes*. Paris: Librairie Horticole, 1912.

Grand, R., and R. Delatouche. *Histoire agraire du Moyen Age*. Paris: E. de Boccard, 1950.

Le Roy Ladurie, E. *Les Paysans du Languedoc*. Paris: Flammarion, 1969. [*The Peasants of Languedoc*. Trans. John Day; ed. George Huppert. Urbana: University of Illinois Press, 1974.]

Licinio, R. *Uomini e terre nella Puglia medievale: Dagli Svevi agli Aragonesi*. Bari, 1983.

Mazzi, M. S. "Note per una storia dell'alimentazione nell'Italia medievale." In *Studi di storia medievale e moderna per Ernesto Sestan*, 1:57–102. Florence: L. S. Olschki, 1980.

Messedaglia, L. *Il mais e la vita rurale italiana*. Piacenza: Federazione Italiana del Consorzi Agrari, 1927.

———. *Per la storia dell'agricoltura e dell'alimentazione*. Piacenza: Federazione Italiana del Consorzi Agrari, 1932.

Montanari, M. *Alimentazione e cultura nel Medioevo*. Rome-Bari: Laterza, 1988.

———. *L'alimentazione contadina nell'alto Medioevo*. Nuovo Medioevo, no. 11. Naples: Liguori, 1979.

———. *Campagne medievali: Strutture produttive, rapporti di lavoro, sistemi alimentari*. Turin: G. Einaudi, 1984.

———. *La fame e l'abbondanza: Storia dell'alimentazione in Europa*. Rome: Editori Laterza, 1993. [*The Culture of Food*. Trans. Carl Ipsen. The Making of Europe. Oxford: Blackwell, 1994.]

Nada Patrone, A. M. *Il cibo del ricco e il cibo del povero: Contributo alla storia qualitativa dell'alimentazione: L'area pedemontana negli ultimi secoli del Medioevo*. Turin: Centro Studi Piemontesi, 1981.

Pini, A. I. *Vite e vino nel Medioevo*. Bologna: CLUEB, 1989.

Pinto, G. *L'alimentazione contadina nell'Italia bassomedievale*. Pistoia, 1986.

———. *La Toscana nel tardo Medioevo: Ambiente, economia rurale, società*. Florence: Sansoni, 1982.

Postan, M. M., ed. *The Agrarian Life of the Middle Ages*. 2d ed. Cambridge Economic History of Europe, vol. 1. Cambridge: Cambridge University Press, 1966.

Rösener, W. *I contadini nel Medioevo*. Rome, 1989. [*Peasants in the Middle Ages*. Trans. Alexander Stützer. Urbana: University of Illinois Press, 1992.]

Stouff, L. *Ravitaillement et alimentation en Provence aux XIVe et XVe siècles*. Paris: Mouton, 1970.

CHAPTER 21

FOOD TRADES

Françoise Desportes

In Chartres, in the first third of the thirteenth century, merchants in the food trades, together with artisans in textiles, leathers, metal, and wood, financed a substantial number of the stained-glass windows intended to fill the wall openings that gave the newly constructed cathedral its remarkable feeling of lightness. Like other donors, these tradesmen were keen to sign their offerings, and the cathedral's master glaziers obliged by depicting them with the tools of their trade in unobtrusive locations on the windows they subsidized. Thanks to this practice, we can still see the bakers, butchers, fishmongers, grocers, and tavern keepers of that time engaged in activities typical of their respective professions. At the end of the same century, during which time urban life in the medieval West reached its apogee, the Lombard poet Bonvesino de la Riva, celebrating the splendors of the powerful city of Milan, included the many tradesmen who contributed to its renown. At the head of the list he mentioned the city's 300 bakers, 440 butchers, 500 fishmongers who caught and sold fish from the region's lakes and rivers, and more than 150 tavern keepers.

From the Ancient City to the Medieval City

As the western Roman Empire gave way to medieval Europe, the food trades changed in various ways across the continent. Outside of Italy, where urban life continued relatively unperturbed, many cities shrank in size as wealthy families fled to their country estates and the poor gradually moved beyond city walls. As new patterns of social and political power emerged, two groups became the principal clients of those who traded in food and drink. The first of these groups was made up of the entourage of clerics and soldiers surrounding the bishops who wielded power in most cities; the second consisted of skilled artisans whom these privileged individuals employed. Tradesmen either found places in the kitchens and pantries of the powerful or found other lines of work.

Two trades survived these difficult centuries fairly well, however—the tavern keepers and the bakers.

Tavern Keepers

From Cologne and Trier to Nîmes and Barcelona, from London to Paris and Lyons, to say nothing of the streets of Naples, Rome, and Milan, the keepers of taverns, cabarets, and inns continued to supply the merchants and peasants of the diocese, the intimates and servants of the great, and even the poorest members of the clergy with food and drink in a convivial setting. ("Tavern," "inn," and "cabaret" were interchangeable terms throughout the Middle Ages, as we know from the *fabliaux* and other literary sources, which often used such places as settings.) Although they dispensed mainly wine, barley beer, and mead, many also sold bread and cheese and served foods prepared in their kitchens.

Later, in the tenth and eleventh centuries, taverns appeared in the towns that sprang up around crossroads, fortifications, and monasteries, as well as at the gates of episcopal cities and of the new towns that proliferated in various European principalities after 1100. Because of the extensive range of their acquaintances, many tavern keepers became personages of note. When Guibert de Nogent discusses the beginnings of the communes of Laon and Amiens in a well-known passage of his autobiography, the only artisans he mentions, other than butchers (*macellarii*) and cobblers, are tavern keepers (*caupones*), whom he found notable for both their wealth and their foul tempers. Significantly, the pious monk does not use the adjective "base," a label that the church attached at that time to most of the food trades, especially the two that concern us here. In 1147 Count Thibault IV of Chartres recognized the social influence of tavern keepers by issuing a set of rules that established and governed their guild.

Bakers

Even more indispensable to the life of the city were the men who tended its ovens. Their job was to bake bread brought to them in the form of dough. They loaded their ovens with loaves and removed them when done, ovens being dangerous pieces of equipment that only authorized bakers were allowed to use and maintain. Their work relied on age-old know-how and a long practical tradition: there was as much of a hierarchy of privilege at the door of the oven as at the gate of the mill, and disputes were common.

Until at least the end of the twelfth century there was little distinction between oven tenders (*fornarii*) and bakers (*pistores*), who, according to the consecrated expression, "knead and shape dough for sale." It was primarily the latter who fell under the clause of Charlemagne's edict of 793, which stipulated that henceforth one denier would be the price of twelve wheat breads, fifteen rye breads, twenty barley breads, or twenty-five oat breads, each loaf to weigh, according to the new standard, two "pounds" (804 grams). The confusion between bakers and oven tenders arose from the fact that the latter also sold bread—namely, loaves left by users of their ovens, including both private individuals and other professionals, as payment for their services. As the demand for bread increased, oven tenders were more and more tempted to make and sell loaves of their own. The *fornarii* of Piacenza had sufficient wealth and influence to sponsor a column capital in the nave of the cathedral, on which one sees a man tending his oven and surrounded by clients. These were the men who, in the first half of the twelfth century, baked bread from dough prepared by the servants of the wealthy and executed special commissions with grain or flour provided by clients. This specialty persisted through the end of the Middle Ages and often much later in the cities of Italy, Provence, and reconquered Spain. Along with the bakers, the *fornarii* put bread on everyone's table.

Outside the Mediterranean region, bakers quickly began to resist the competition from *fornarii*. Between 1150 and 1200, in a number of cities under French royal dominion, bakers petitioned the king for the exclusive right to make bread, which was granted in return for an agreement to make a regular payment to the royal treasury and submit to inspection by royal officials. Soon thereafter the bakers also won the right to build their own ovens. English bakers, who were governed by John Lackland's edict of the early thirteenth century regulating the weight of loaves, already owned their own ovens; the same was true of bakers in most German cities. Nowhere did private ovens totally supplant public ones, and the fact that, in the fourteenth and fifteenth centuries in southern Europe, people of all stations regularly bought bread from bakeries did not mean that baking at home was no longer practiced.

Millers

At the same time, many millers who were paid in grain for their services tried to use that grain for baking bread. They soon encountered opposition from municipal authorities as well as customer resistance. The millers' reputation for dishonesty, laziness, and fecklessness worked against them. Although their services were indispensable, their social position remained somewhat marginal. The number of millers in cities and suburbs rose dramatically after the year 1000, but the only service they were asked to perform was that of grinding grain between properly adjusted millstones and extracting an equivalent weight in flour. Nothing else was to be done at the mill. The chore of sifting raw flour, aptly termed "flour as milled" or "as it comes from the mill," was for the private kitchen or bakery. Millers in regions where malt-based drinks were consumed—beer in northern Germany and ale (made without hops) in England—were also called upon to crush malt for professional and home brewers.

Other Trades in Middle-Sized Towns

Some decades after the founding of Montauban in 1144 by Alphonse-Jourdain, the count of Toulouse, the anonymous author of the *Chanson des quatre fils Aymon* credited Renaud, the eldest of Aymon's four sons, with building the town and bringing people to it. No sooner did Renaud call for settlement within the town's walls than five hundred wealthy bourgeois settled there: "One hundred are tavern keepers, one hundred are bakers, there are one hundred butchers, one hundred fishermen and fishmongers, and one hundred are merchants whose business ventures extend all the way to the greater Indies." Three hundred other residents worked in trades that the poet did not see fit to mention. Was this account notable for placing food at the center of its description of the new city, or was it an expression of satisfaction, rather surprising for this particular literary genre, at the prospect of being well nourished on the part of a man of middling station? In any case, these lines are of great interest for their catalog of the various trades that were apparently necessary to sustain a small town in the late twelfth century: bread, meat, fish, and wine (from grapes that grew within the walls or were imported from elsewhere), supplemented on occasion by small amounts of costly spices, the most readily available of which were probably already pepper and saffron. Local gardens and chicken coops could be readily tapped for the rest, which consisted of vegetables and herbs, eggs, and cheese, along with other dairy products now and then.

The same trades crop up a half century later in the vitriolic sermons that the Franciscan monk Berthold of Regensburg delivered not only in his native city but also in Munich and Constance. Using examples taken from life, he vilified the principal vices of each of the estates that constituted the workaday world as ordained by the Creator. The fourth of the six estates in Berthold's classification consisted of "those who sell food and drink. Their job is to bake our bread, sell us meat, brew our beer, prepare our mead, and catch our fish. Some supply cheese and eggs, others oil, herrings, and other foods. We absolutely depend on these trades. One roasts, the other boils." Elsewhere, the Franciscan did not fail to include millers, "who have more than one trick up their sleeves," as well as those egregious swindlers, the grocer and his wife.

Big Cities

Berthold's description of the food trades in middle-sized towns omitted none of the many food-related specialties. The sources, which include both official regulations (already numerous in the thirteenth century, which was an age of organization in all areas and a prolific promulgator of both economic regulations and guild by-laws) and a few surviving fiscal documents, mention none that Berthold does not cover. Things were different, however, in great metropolises such as Paris, Venice, Genoa, Milan, and Naples and in big cities like London, Cologne, Rouen, Toulouse, and Barcelona.

Consider, for example, Étienne Boileau's *Livre des métiers* (Book of Trades), which deals with Paris. This volume, established in 1268 under the auspices of the royal provost responsible for supervising the trades, included the statutes of 101 Paris "communities" in the order in which they were submitted to the Châtelet. All branches of the food trades are represented, with the exception of the butchers, who failed to file their guild regulations. It appears that in each sector of the food business there was room for two or three different specialties, each with its own guild. In the case of fish, for example, there was a guild of freshwater fishmongers, another of saltwater fishmongers, and a third consisting of "fishermen in royal waters," who took pike, mullet, eel, and carp from boats anchored in the Seine and Marne from the tip of the Île Notre-Dame all the way upstream to Saint-Maur-des-Fossés. And the bread peddlers (*regrattiers et regrattières de pain*), who had a guild of their own, were authorized to sell not only bread, which comprised the bulk of their business, but also small amounts of saltwater fish, cooked meat, salt, fruit, eggs, cheese, and certain common spices (such as pepper, cumin, and cinnamon). This privilege set them apart from other hucksters who traded in garlic, onion, and shallots, for which there was a demand in every kitchen; their additional wares were limited to butter, eggs, cheese, vegetables, and "local" fruits.

In the big cities of both northern and southern Europe, butchers left the viscera of slaughtered animals to specialized organ-meat dealers, who prepared their merchandise for sale in communal markets. Europeans generally, and Italians in particular, had a decided taste for these inner organs. In one of the superbly illuminated manuscripts of the *Tacuinum sanitatis in medicina,* compiled in the fourteenth century for the Cerruti family of Verona, eight of nineteen illustrations depicting the butcher trade are devoted to the sale and home preparation of brains, hearts, udders, livers, spleen, and other organs, while two or three others feature the head and feet. Or, to take another example, consider the *Three Hundred Stories,* written by the Florentine Franco Sacchetti at the end of the fourteenth century. One of the best-known of these stories features tripe from a heifer that has been simmered for a Sunday dinner. Two groups of friends, Florentine merchants living in Venice, quarrel over this tasty dish. The butcher in the story sells both meat and inner organs. The citizens of Palermo, especially the poor, were also fond of *malcuchinatu,* which included tripe and other variety meats.

The Emergence of New Food-Related Trades

New food-related trades did not begin to appear until the first half of the fourteenth century in many cities, the fifteenth in a few others. The new trades did not deal in new products, however. Artisans banded together to form guilds, which nearly always succeeded in persuading the authorities to approve and register their statutes—or in some cases even to draft them. Their purpose was simply to secure an exclusive right to prepare and sell some type of food that had previously been prepared and sold without regulation by local journeymen.

Several factors contributed to the proliferation of new food-related specialties. First, there was a general tendency toward greater specialization in all sectors of industry, from textiles and leathers to metal and woodworking. Artisans were prohibited from working in trades related or complementary to their primary activity. Second, there was a long-term improvement in the standard of living, coupled with the emergence, toward the end of the Middle Ages, of distinctive big-city tastes.

THE BAKERY The evolution of the bakery trade is illuminating in many respects. Wheat flour had been widely used by bakers throughout Europe since the thirteenth century. Indeed, in many places no other kind of flour was used for bread: "good wheat bread" had become a touchstone of urban civilization. Nevertheless, there were two or even three varieties of such bread. The best was made of top-quality white flour and baked to a golden crust; this was called *pain de bouche* or *pain mollet* in France, *Semmelbrot* in Germany, and *pandemain* or *white bread* in England, and it was prized by people of privilege. Bread of somewhat lower quality was eaten by a larger group of people consisting of government officials and others with regular sources of income. In France this category of bread was represented by loaves known variously as *bis-blancs, jaunets,* and *bis* (brown bread). In Paris and Reims in the fourteenth century people also ate a loaf known as the *pain à bourgeois*. A third type of loaf, whole-wheat bread (*pain à tout, pain de tout blé*), was generally eaten by the poorest people and used in a variety of dishes.

Whenever there was a major religious holiday or grain prices were low, bakers used some of their flour for cakes and pastries. They made wafers and waffles by heating light, unleavened pastry dough between two red-hot pieces of iron. Or they plunged balls of dough into boiling water and then dried them in the oven, a technique that required adding yeast and kneading the dough until it was almost hard before plunging it into the water. Bakers sometimes added milk, eggs, and herbs to bread dough or made pastry baskets that they filled with minced meat, fish, or cheese. These delicacies generally could not be sold without the permission of the municipal authorities, and in northern Europe the authorities sometimes regulated their weights and prices, as they did everywhere for bread.

Wealthy individuals ordered their bakers to use some of the flour they supplied to make pastries all year round. These were served after dinner or supper or consumed with wine as a morning snack. Soon the demand for pastries was so great that bakers could not keep up with it, and the authorities found it difficult to limit production to Christmas, Easter, and processional holidays. The cookie trade was about to be born.

In Paris, where cookie makers (*oubloyers*) were granted privileges as early as 1270, King Charles VI reaffirmed their status by issuing new guild regulations in 1397 and 1406. From these we learn that the trade was "very dangerous and difficult to learn." A journeyman cookie maker needed to be able to make at least five hundred large wafers (*oublies*) in a day, along with three hundred *supplications* and two hundred *esterels*. Only small wafers could be sold in the street. *Supplications* and *étriers* were varieties of *oublies*. The former took their name from the fact that they were originally eaten only on certain religious holidays and some were placed on the altar as offerings. *Étriers* were probably named for their shape (the word means "stirrup").

The bakers appear to have retained control of the fabrication of pâtés and similar "products of the oven" for a longer period of time. Although the Paris pastry guild did not record its first constitution until 1440, there may well have been pastry specialists before that date. Once their guild was recognized, they began to expand the range of their production: in addition to meat pastries and tarts, they also created pastries out of milk, eggs, and cream, usually sweetened, such as *darioles, flans,* and *dauphins.* In order to become a master pastry maker in Le Mans in the early sixteenth century, one had to be able to use sugar loaves to make *hypocras,* a sweet, spiced wine used as an aperitif and after-dinner drink. It was not until 1566 that the king joined the Paris cookie makers' guild to that of the pastry makers, and the two would be wedded frequently thereafter. Meanwhile, the candy makers, who consumed vast quantities of sugar and sweet syrups, began to form their own guilds in Valencia in Spain, in Sicily, and in the cities of northern Italy after splitting off from the guilds of grocers, who had previously monopolized the production of dragées, pignolats, marzipan, and nougat.

THE DELICATESSEN Another special case, about which much less is known, was the delicatessen. In various Mediterranean cities in the fourteenth century, some butchers began to specialize in the sale of pork. They apparently did not form a distinct guild, however.

Nevertheless, in Bologna around 1380 the authorities designated an area around the Ravenna gate for the skinning of hogs, a particularly polluting and foul-smelling activity that must have been carried on previously in streets closer to the slaughterhouse. In Provence, meanwhile, stalls laden with pork butchered that day or the day before occupied a special place in the *mazel,* or market. In other cities we find, as early as the middle of the thirteenth century, a range of trades whose names—*porcatores, salaterii, salaroli, lardaroli*—indicate that they were involved with the meat of the pig. Their job was to cut up the animal's flesh, salt it, and separate out the lard. These workers apparently did not slaughter the animals themselves but were obliged to purchase carcasses from butchers. Nor were they permitted to enter into private contracts with farmers. The first regulations of the *arte dei salaroli,* recorded in Bologna in about 1250, granted them the right to sell not only salt pork and lard but also olive oil, cheese, vegetables, seeds, suet, and candles. Strangely enough, the statutes make no mention of other items that we know to have been in great demand, including the mortadella, salami, and sausages with which the pork peddlers of Carpentras, Arles, and Marseilles filled their stalls.

In northern Europe, especially in the north of France, *charcutiers saucissiers* were late to appear on the scene. In Paris the first regulations governing this trade were issued by the royal provost, Robert d'Estouteville, early in 1476. At that time there were only a dozen or so merchants involved in the business of "cooking pork and making sausages" as well as selling lard "and other butcher products." By giving their trade a distinctive name, they hoped to set themselves apart from the many itinerant vendors who sold cooked meat illegally. Their intention was probably to reclaim the title of *cuisiniers de chair,* or "cookers of flesh," as opposed to "roasters," a distinction dating from the end of the reign of Saint Louis. Like the roasters, they promised to buy meat only from guild butchers, to use only fresh, unspoiled meat, and, from September 15 to the beginning of Lent, to make sausages only from "well-minced pork—well salted with fine salt and [with nothing but] good, clean, well-chosen fennel or other fine spices." As the etymology of the word *charcutier* suggests, these northern dealers sold both fresh and cooked meat, mostly pork sausages along with smaller quantities of mutton and veal stew. In Italy and Provence, *salumerii* sold pieces of salted meat, ham, and salami, usually along with cheese and olive oil.

PASTA Finally, we must not neglect the development in Italy, toward the end of the Middle Ages, of an industry with a great future in store. Pasta, inspired by an Arab tradition and first prepared in the kitchens of wealthy Sicilians, was already being produced by artisans in Sicilian towns as early as the twelfth century. By the middle of the thirteenth century there were pasta makers in Naples as well as in various Ligurian cities, most notably Genoa, which imported large quantities of durum wheat and, later, semolina for making macaroni and lasagna. Not exactly a luxury item, pasta was still a quality food, reserved for the tables of the wealthy. Before long, Tuscany and other regions of Italy began manufacturing a food whose long shelf life was not the least of its advantages. Despite this, its consumption was not democratized until the seventeenth century. Similar products were developed in the cities of the Spanish Levant around the same time.

Where Food Was Processed and Sold

Food workers plied their trades in all parts of Europe's cities, not simply in the many taverns, inns, and hotels, often located near city gates or crossroads or close to crowded markets, ports, or schools. In France, at least, these were among the few establishments marked with signs indicating not the building but its function. Similarly, in winemaking regions of southern Germany, wine makers who wished to sell their own wine retail placed a piece of vine or a straw "cork" over their doors. Many taverns were just rooms that opened directly onto the street. Others were located in cellars or half-basements equipped with benches and tables where customers could serve themselves directly from the barrel.

Food and other shops were intermingled along city streets. A baker might sell his wares next door to a goldsmith, a grocer next to a cobbler, or a candy maker next door to a barber. In the foreground of Ambrogio Lorenzetti's famous fresco *The Effects of Good Government* in Siena's city hall is a delicatessen located next door to a classroom in which pupils hang on their teacher's every word.

In medieval vernaculars, the workplace of the artisan who was both the maker and seller of his own wares was never named for the type of work done there. In other words, the baker's shop was referred to not as a bakery but as the baker's "house" or "establishment" or simply "workshop." Other generic terms, such as *botiga* in Occitan or *bottega* in Italian, but in northern France *boutique,* were relatively uncommon until the end of the Middle Ages. By contrast, the room in which bread was baked in monasteries, schools, and *maisons Dieu* as well as in aristocratic houses was called the bakery (*boulangerie*), and fruits and vegetables were kept in the *fruiterie*.

A SPECIAL CASE: THE BUTCHER While most food shops were located for the convenience of their customers in different parts of the city, butchers and fishmongers had long been confined to specific areas by decision of the authorities. In regard to butchers, a number of different policies were adopted. Italian city governments restricted their *macellarii* to locations on the outskirts or even outside the city walls along roads used for bringing livestock to town. Farther north, in France and along the Baltic coast, butchers were allowed to set up shop in the center of town, close to the major market, which often revolved around the meat business. In still other cities butchers were scattered around town, mainly because more than one authority had jurisdiction over them.

In any case, animals were inspected for good health before being slaughtered on an open killing ground, sometimes surrounded by a fence and preferably located close to a stream. After slaughter, the animals were gutted and skinned. By regulation, blood, viscera, and other "filth" had to be packed in sealed containers and disposed of in the countryside or dumped in a stream at a suitable distance from town. Such was the law, at any rate. Nevertheless, many butchers throughout Europe persisted in killing livestock, especially smaller animals, in the street right in front of their shops, or in small, private killing grounds, which sometimes received grudging authorization (for example, in Orléans in the fifteenth century). Carcasses were then either taken whole to the market or cut up and sold on the spot.

There were two sorts of meat markets, and it is not clear why one was preferred over the other in any particular case. The most common seems to have been the large market shed in which vendors specializing in different types of meat tended stalls of prescribed dimensions. Whenever the sale of meat was authorized, the vendor would open his stall, which he purchased or rented for an amount that depended on various factors. In surviving images, however, it is more common to see small open shops with butcher blocks for cutting and slicing meat, racks of cleavers and knives, meathooks, and bins for waste with dogs always hanging about. Meat that remained unsold at the end of the day and had "passed its prime" was often salted for resale by the butcher himself or by a peddler.

ANOTHER SPECIAL CASE: THE FISHMONGER The authorities also prescribed the locations of fish markets. Ocean and freshwater fish were packed in seaweed or grass in baskets, hampers, or barrels and kept cool with periodic infusions of fresh water for transport to market stalls. Saltfish, most notably herring, were sold in the regular markets. Only the city's own fishermen were entitled to sell fish from their own private establishments. Some even maintained fish hatcheries along riverbanks.

Shops

Shops, which also served as warehouses, were invariably small, and sales usually took place "at the window." A sort of shutter opened outward to form a counter over the sidewalk. At night it could be raised to cover the lower part of the window and secure the shop.

Late medieval iconography features numerous representations of these "windows." One of the finest such images, from the Rhineland, appears in the fifteenth-century *Tacuinum sanitatis,* mentioned earlier. It depicts a sumptuous German bakeshop whose counter holds a basket brimming with small rolls, while the baker can be seen in the background removing another batch of rolls from the oven. Many shop windows had a second shutter that could be raised to serve as a kind of awning to protect the merchandise from dust, rain, and sun.

A celebrated miniature from Giles of Rome's *De regimine principum,* a late-fifteenth-century work now in the Bibliothèque de l'Arsenal in Paris, illustrates a somewhat different system. On the left side of this picture one sees a candy and pastry shop that was entirely open. A heavy wooden sideboard with three panels projected into the street and prevented clients from entering the shop itself, but in the background one can see pots and bottles arrayed on shelves, a large vessel with handles that may contain the "good *hypocras"* advertised on a placard affixed to an awning, several tarts, and a large sugar loaf. A bulky chest similarly restricted access to the minuscule Sienese *salumeria* in Lorenzetti's fresco. It was only in the north of Europe, and probably at a later date, that one began to find closed shops that clients were allowed to enter. Although these shops had doors, they were always kept open to allay the suspicion of fraud that inevitably arose when merchants hid themselves from the gaze of passersby.

Last but not least, one should not neglect the men, women, and children who, with or without official permission, peddled food on the street. A baker's apprentice might be sent out to sell rolls, flans, miniature pies, and cookies. On the streets he would be likely to rub shoulders with shadier peddlers, often unscrupulous youths out to earn a little cash by unloading inferior goods on unwary buyers. These were a constant concern of the police. A peddler's wife might fill a basket with eggs, cheese, and fruit and try to hawk her wares on the streets. Or a fishwife might try her luck with a pail of fresh fish. Interestingly, women, though ubiquitous when it came to selling food other than meat, had very little to do with food processing. Thus until the end of the fifteenth century, we can be sure that Margot the pork butcher, Jehanne the baker, and Marie the grocer were widows who, with the assistance of a devoted male employee, had taken over their late husband's business.

The Status of the Food Trades

The numerous urban food workers of the Middle Ages were by and large of low economic status. The food trades were closely supervised by local authorities and often treated with an understanding and toleration appropriate to a group on which everyone relied. The welfare and reputation of a city depended on its bakers, butchers, and fishmongers. Magistrates were governed by one paramount concern: to ensure an adequate supply of "good and honest" food.

The same fundamental principles reigned across Europe. All food and beverages sold on the market were required to be "worthy to enter the human body," to be of good odor and flavor, "neither putrid nor stinking," and free of adulterants and additives intended to conceal shortcomings. Manipulation of foodstuffs was particularly frowned upon. As Berthold of Regensburg put it, the deceptive practices of a shoemaker, tailor, or blacksmith "affect only property" whereas those of the butcher who blows on old meat to improve its appearance or of the innkeeper who perfumes his wine and beer "harms life itself"; the perpetrators of such crimes were guilty of murder and risked their very souls. Regulations were similar everywhere, as were the punishments for infractions, which included destruction of the offending goods together with fines and humiliating penalties as well as possible revocation of the right to continue in the trade.

The authorities' concern with maintaining a regular supply of food had an economic as well as a moral basis. Although they treated food workers as partners, civic leaders never relaxed their oversight of this fundamental activity.

CHAPTER 22

THE ORIGINS *of* PUBLIC HOSTELRIES IN EUROPE

Hans Conrad Peyer

Public hospitality—in the form of inns that were always open and provided meals and temporary lodging to travelers and local residents for a price—first evolved in Europe in the thirteenth and fourteenth centuries out of various older models of hospitality. Their history reaches back as far as earliest human accounts. Social groups in primitive cultures that had no contact with the outside world and often turned away strangers or killed them appear to have developed a primitive form of hospitality for magical-religious and practical reasons. On the one hand, strangers were received as guests because it was presumed they had magical powers or were gods. On the other hand, contact was made possible with other groups through merchants and messengers. In cultures where money was either unknown or only known in a rudimentary form, strangers could find lodging, protection, and food for only a limited period, usually for three days. With the act of hospitality, a close bond was forged between host and guest, and hosts were obligated to assist guests with their affairs in any way possible; this obligation even extended as far as blood vengeance. They became mediators between their guests and the world around them. Hosts could also become their guests' heirs if the guests died while in their care.

Hospitality in Antiquity

As early as prehistoric times, however, hospitality manifested itself in several different forms. These subsequently merged in a variety of ways, and a distinction apparently existed relatively early between an unconditional, basic form of hospitality and a second form of hospitality with conditions. Unconditional, basic hospitality included lodging, water, fire, and horse fodder, but no food. Hosts could also choose to provide hospitality with conditions, which made food, drink, and other comforts (such as a woman for the night and departure gifts) available to guests following the formal greeting upon their arrival.

In the Middle East, by comparison, a more general form of charity was emphasized and strangers were automatically entitled to this charity when they entered a house or tent. When it was joined with the dictum to love one's neighbor, this charity became a fundamental principle throughout Christian times. Restrictions on hospitality, such as a time limit and the refusal of provisions, served to protect hosts and their generally restricted and costly food supply. As more people from all walks of life began to travel, however, this limited private hospitality sufficed less, and more advanced, sovereign-state political entities developed additional, supplementary forms of hospitality. To these belonged the dreaded compulsory or coerced hospitality for traveling rulers, dignitaries, and their retinue. At each place of rest, vassals had to provide lodging, provisions, and horse fodder, often on an oppressive scale. This kind of hospitality was evident in many different parts of the world and played a significant role in Europe from the Hellenic age, via Rome, until the end of the Middle Ages. Indeed, the last remnants of this form of hospitality existed until the eighteenth century.

To ensure both lodging and provisions for strangers and to ease the strain on private hospitality, various kinds of public inns emerged during the post-Homeric Hellenistic period; in fact, Greek cities and temples often maintained these houses. After the fifth century B.C.E., cities frequently provided foreign merchants with directions to special commercial and waterfront areas where inns and warehouses were located. At the same time, commercial hospitality for a price developed in all regions of the Greek world, together with a developing monetary economy, in the form of public houses, eating establishments, and inns with lodging and stables. Around 400 B.C.E. these establishments were accepted as everyday businesses and they were spread throughout port cities, commercial towns, temple districts and bathing resorts, and along important highways.

Throughout the expanding Roman Empire, wine taverns and eating establishments (*taberna, caupona, popina*) as well as inns with lodgings and stables (*taberna, hospitium, diversorium, mansio, stabulum*) appeared in cities and, in time, at rest and horse-changing sites along the major imperial roads. As a rule, the Roman inns were equipped with a kitchen and restaurant that opened toward the street; they also had sleeping rooms with beds, washrooms, toilets, and often horse stables. For meals they generally provided simple fare, such as bread, fish soup or a small amount of meat, and, above all, wine. They all had a conspicuous tavern sign and the name of the inn on the outside wall of the establishment. At smaller road-houses, the name of the inn often became the name of the town.

In Greece and Rome, however, the commercial taverns and inns were regarded, without exception, as disreputable. They were seen as thieves' dens and brothels and were frequented primarily by the lower classes—porters, sailors, prostitutes, and others. They were not located in the better city districts because the upper classes often had sufficient opportunities for lodging, provisions, and social entertainment in the city and country and in the provinces, thanks to the hospitality of their social equals. Only on longer journeys did the aristocracy occasionally have to stay in inns. Because of their unfavorable reputation and yet their indispensability, innkeepers were subject to strict regulations under Roman law. Along with slaves, gladiators, and sexual procurers, both male and female innkeepers belonged to the maligned vocations. Senators could not marry innkeepers or their daughters. Tavern and stable owners were liable for the possessions that their guests entrusted to them, although theft and robbery often occurred in their establishments. For regulatory purposes, innkeepers were forced to become part of guildlike associations, and as places of criminal activity and disturbances, inns were officially monitored. For this reason, the early Christian church warned against taverns and prohibited clerics from staying at them. This was one reason for the construction of religious and monastic inns (*xenodochia, hospitia*) for Christian travelers, pilgrims, and especially the poor. However, the church could not avoid creating an exception clause, which allowed clerics to enter a tavern in emergency situations, nor could it ever completely keep taverns from springing up near churches and places of pilgrimage. At the end of Greco-Roman times, the original forms of hospitality, especially among the upper classes, existed side by side with imperial hospitality, state and religious inns, merchant quarters, and, finally, the despised but widespread and indispensable commercial taverns and *diversoria*.

Taverns and Guest Houses

With the renewed prevalence of basic hospitality and the rising popularity of hospitality for a price, the European medieval era repeated, to a certain extent, the development of hospitality during classical antiquity. Only in the late Middle Ages, however, did the inn create completely new, socially acceptable forms of public hospitality, which forever shaped the world of hospitality. Following the collapse of the Roman Empire and its monetary economy, the archaic hospitality that closely bound hosts and their guests and included a pledge of blood vengeance once again predominated in the kingdoms that existed during the "barbarian" invasions and in the kingdom of Charlemagne during the eighth and ninth centuries, and it continued to do so until the eleventh century. This type of hospitality included unconditional, basic hospitality, primarily among the aristocracy, and simple hospitality without board, usually for merchants, pilgrims, and other travelers. Those who did not receive a meal from their host had to carry their own provisions while traveling, or they had to shop in marketplaces, which were becoming scarcer, or eat in the even fewer taverns. As traffic slowly increased again following the Carolingian era, travelers and pilgrims faced a growing shortage of rooms and opportunities for provisions. Rulers, civil servants, and independent proprietors made do by expanding commercial hospitality in their areas of influence. During their administrative trips, their rural subjects were required to make increasingly greater contributions toward lodging and provisions. Rulers and the larger monasteries attempted to provide relief for pilgrims and ordinary travelers with the construction of monastic and travel hospices. However, these efforts were, for the most part, unsuccessful prior to the eleventh century. To survive, even large monasteries were repeatedly forced to check the heavy flow of poor travelers, despite the hospitality provisions in the Rule of St. Benedict.

Taverns, which had become increasingly rare during the era of the barbarian invasions, gradually began to reappear throughout western Europe. Rulers, monasteries, and the nobility built these taverns in cities, places of pilgrimage, and at rest sites to function as retail locations for wine, beer, and the most necessary provisions—and, in some instances, as overnight shelter. Not infrequently, at imperial toll sites they developed into a kind of everyday mini-marketplace under one roof. Because taverns provided owners with considerable income, they became a popular sovereign right, even though they continued to be regarded as places of ill repute. Yet they were visited by peasants, dealers, and carters, among others, though strictly condemned by both the clergy and nobility.

Strongly reminiscent of classical times, these conditions began to change very quickly. Between the eleventh and the fourteenth centuries, under the pressure of a general economic upswing and especially a sharp increase in international trade, the older forms of hospitality were no longer adequate. Monasteries, cities, and villages increasingly resisted coerced sovereign hospitality, and it gradually disappeared. Even the numerous hospices along major trade, overland, and pilgrimage routes could not handle the demand. Particularly where important roads passed through sparsely populated areas, a shortage of accommodations existed. This situation hastened the transition from a private, barter-based form of hospitality to a public, money-based one, a development that occurred throughout Europe and is supported by documentary evidence from the eleventh to the thirteenth century.

Despite the growing number of travelers, however, peasants could not refuse them the necessary board and lodging. On the other hand, travelers could not force the peasants to provide room and board. They had to pay the peasants prices that were established through arbitration by several residents in the village. These regulations, which were difficult to enforce, made additional taverns necessary along well-traveled roads. In fact, in 1279 the Norwegian crown ordered arbitration as a temporary solution to replace Norway's renowned simple hospitality; in 1335 the Norwegian king arranged for the construction of taverns in cities and along important travel routes. Thus peasants were no longer burdened by travelers, and travelers did not face a shortage of accommodations.

From the eleventh century until the late Middle Ages, taverns began appearing everywhere—in cities, villages, and along major routes. They provided provisions and lodging, and in some cases entire villages, even cities, developed around these taverns. The old, unconditional, and often deliberately lavish hospitality that was frequently used to humble guests existed only among aristocrats and princes. In contrast, long-distance merchants and occasionally other travelers began to stop regularly at commercial houses in cities, where hosts not only provided provisions but also assisted with business transactions. For this, merchants paid their host a commission and performed similar services at home. At the same time, the old intimate ties between host and guest that existed with private hospitality loosened in general; the obligation of hosts to avenge the death of their guests disappeared, and their rights as heirs to the possessions of their guests were increasingly restricted. Regional rulers, states, and communities assumed the protection of travelers, and many private homes in the city became a kind of commercial inn for better-class guests, while inns and taverns began more and more to resemble each other. In fact, at the end of the thirteenth century, city councils in Italy, France, and, somewhat later, southern Germany created a single type of public inn. This new inn spread gradually over all of Europe and eventually influenced taverns in rural areas. With this, the general distinction between public, commercial hospitality and private, archaic hospitality began to give way to a social distinction between reputable inns, less reputable ones, and inns that should be avoided.

Hotels and Inns

The public inn (*hospitium, honestum, publicum*) provided room and board for strangers and local inhabitants. For this reason, commercial innkeepers often could not act as middlemen or engage in any secondary businesses, in contrast to merchants and many other rural innkeepers who provided similar services. Instead, they had to leave these activities entirely to a broker or other businesses in the city. Accessibility distinguished the inn from the private house, which was open only to those whom owners permitted to enter. While the house rules of private owners prevailed in their homes, the public inn was open to everyone, and these commercial inns were subject to regulations determined by public, city, and feudal authorities that could use their power at any time. In this sense, innkeepers were representatives of public authority and, therefore, had to attach unique, recognizable signs to their establishments for strangers. These did not resemble Roman tavern signs, but rather the general pub and peace signs that were common after the early Middle Ages. Green boughs, wreaths, barrel hoops, and banners were quite popular emblems. However, these were often inadequate for most inns in the city; hence, special signs, which were forever linked with the tavern, were hung up. The names and images of saints and biblical figures were preferred, such as St. Jacob and the Three Wise Men, who represented long journeys or pilgrimage routes; legal symbols, fabulous creatures, various animals, and other special objects could be found in the coat of arms of the tavern owner or local ruler.

The city and sovereign regulations that applied to commercial taverns obligated the innkeepers to accommodate guests until no vacancies existed, when the inn sign was removed. Until then, inns could not turn away anyone who obeyed their rules. They were also prohibited from luring guests into their establishments and were required to provide directions to other inns. As of the fifteenth century, the documentary evidence confirms that inns were inspected by the city watchman on his rounds, and it was his duty to report overnight guests to the city council.

The sale of wine and beer was the most important service performed by tavern owners, and they often carried on an extensive wine trade. As the local authorities benefited greatly from the beverage tax, the price and quality of wine and beer, as well as amounts, were officially established and often controlled. The provisions offered by taverns and inns were only the most basic ones—bread, cheese, some meat, and horse fodder—until well into the late Middle Ages. Only then did the better inns begin to prepare abundant, higher-quality meals, especially when travelers ordered them ahead of time through an advance party. However, as of the fourteenth century, larger meals were apparently prepared even in the most primitive pubs. In these cases, guests either transported their own provisions, live animals, dishes, and other essential items, or they bought the necessary items in a nearby market and then let their attendants prepare the meals.

After their establishment in 1300, inns at public rest stops provide accommodations for many different groups of guests. For example, judicial court hearings and the subsequent meals, which for the most part took place outdoors or in private houses in the central Middle Ages, were relocated to inns. The same was true for the meals of the ruling class, which were relocated from private homes to inns at the expense of cities or villages. In addition, many princes sent less important guests to inns and bore the expense. Thus, with this increasing importance of guest establishments, privacy was once again possible in private homes. Prisoners of war and hostages were often housed in inns, and by the end of the thirteenth century, criminals could find temporary refuge in taverns rather than in churches and other locations, as was customary earlier. The same was true for the unique medieval stockade (*hostage, obstagium, otage*), a holding area that bondsmen used at the debtor's expense to guarantee the payment of a debt to a creditor. While hostages stayed in a castle or cloister during the central Middle Ages, after 1300 they often stayed for weeks in an inn at the expense of the debtor and until the debt was paid. In the country, animals and other items used as surety for outstanding bills and debts were kept in the stalls and barns of inns, which were considered neutral areas. Finally, in the late Middle Ages disaffected individuals and conspirators met in inns and made them centers of civic and rural unrest.

The design of the inns differed according to social class. The simplest inns were one-room stone or wooden houses where people, animals, and goods were placed next to the fireplace. As a rule, however, most inns were ordinary city or rural homes, some better than others. Some houses were specifically designed as inns, with a courtyard, stalls, and storage space on the ground floor; the top floor often had lounges and sleeping quarters for guests. The best inns of the fourteenth and fifteenth centuries could be found in France, England, and Italy. They often had individual rooms with beds and closets, doors equipped with a lock, and well-stocked lounges and restaurants. Until the sixteenth century, more modest inns with a restaurant and mass sleeping quarters were common in German-speaking territories. Until the nineteenth century, only the most primitive inns existed in Poland and Spain, and even these were completely unknown in the Balkans. In fact, in these outermost areas of Europe archaic forms of hospitality still prevailed. Everywhere the capacity of inns was relatively modest.

The small inns could accommodate between ten and twenty guests, the large ones sixty at the most. The number of inns in an area varied from a single house along a road to as many as ten inns in larger villages and small cities, twenty in medium-sized towns, and between forty and one hundred in large cities. As a rule, the ratio was one tavern for every 200–500 inhabitants. In settlements they were often located along the major routes or near gates, market squares, and docks.

After its inception at the end of the thirteenth century, the public inn soon offered not only lodging and provisions for strangers and local residents, but also other kinds of provisions and accommodations in the city and country. During the central Middle Ages such accommodations generally existed outdoors or in castles, churches, and private homes. The expansion of public inns throughout Europe was a sign of increasing traffic and the growing importance of money as well as an indicator of an important structural change in public life.

CHAPTER 23

MEDIEVAL COOKING

Bruno Laurioux

Because the subject of medieval cooking has not been extensively investigated, misleading assertions and misguided approaches abound. Hence we would do well to pause a moment at the outset to consider what sources are available and what methods are likely to add to our knowledge of fourteenth- and fifteenth-century cooking practices.

From Kitchen Accounts to Cookbooks

Although numerous kitchen account books have survived, they are unfortunately scattered in many locations and highly uneven in quality. Most daily expense records have vanished, and what annual summaries have survived are obviously less detailed. The richest series of documents, such as the accounts of the dukes of Savoy and the pontifical records *Introitus* and *Exitus,* have not yet been published or thoroughly studied. One exception is the highly detailed record kept by Humbert II of Viennois from 1333 to 1349. This is at once an account book, a collection of menus, and a book of household regulations, and it contains a remarkably detailed compilation of the dishes served in a typical week to the dauphin and members of his household.[1]

For a special dinner or banquet a separate service or household account might be maintained, and the clerk responsible for this chore sometimes allowed himself to include a description of the occasion, thus affording us a glimpse of the dinner menu.[2] This was often just a list of dishes copied from the recipes used in their preparation, but on occasion the banquet chronicle might be more elaborate. The menus of such memorable banquets were designed to exhibit the power and prestige of the prince who staged them.

Few literary works dwelled on the composition of meals and dishes. Historians who place undue confidence in unrepresentative literary sources have given misleading accounts of medieval dining customs. It is true, however, that the most detailed descriptions we have of medieval dinners come from satirical and comic literature. In the thirteenth century, for example, Raoul of Houdenc uses a description of the tortures of hell as an excuse to present a veritable catalog of culinary techniques: defeated champions are sautéed in garlic, whores are roasted in a tart sauce, "black monks" are fried in fat, and "perjurers" have their tongues fried in butter. The carnival tradition is full of such purple passages, no doubt inspired by regional culinary customs. In Italy, for instance, it comes as no surprise to find stories featuring macaroni and ravioli atop mountains of grated parmesan cheese.

Stained-glass windows, frescoes, and illuminated manuscripts tell us a great deal about dining customs and rituals, but identifying the food on the tables or on the platters carried by servants in these images is often a difficult task. If we see a bird, how can we tell what kind it is? As for the accompanying sauce, identification is made all the more difficult by the fact that the artist may have chosen his colors more for aesthetic reasons than for accuracy of representation.

Archaeological evidence is more useful. The study of bones found at various European sites has already demonstrated that beef was the primary meat consumed throughout the Middle Ages, thus refuting conventional wisdom about the "family pig." Thanks to traces of carving, flesh-stripping, and combustion, we can also describe how animals were prepared from the slaughterhouse to the kitchen. Study of the evidence from Ligurian sites suggests a shift at the end of the Middle Ages in the preparation of pork: rather than strip all the meat from the bone and preserve it by smoking or salting, small pieces of fresh meat were cooked on the bone.[3] In addition, the pots, pans, and other implements that turn up in the course of excavation offer evidence of preparation and cooking techniques. Systematic comparison of archaeological findings with estate inventories and iconographic images is one of the most promising avenues for the study of medieval cookery.[4]

Ultimately, however, one is forced to turn to cookbooks. More than a hundred manuscript collections of recipes have survived, constituting a series of documents attesting to culinary practices across Europe from Denmark to the heel of the

Italian boot and from England to Bohemia. The earliest of these date from the beginning of the fourteenth century, and manuscripts continued to be produced at an increasing rate until the end of the fifteenth century. Precisely identified as to date and place of origin, these compilations are useful for comparative purposes in both time and space, provided that certain precautions are taken.[5]

How to Read Medieval Recipes

A culinary manuscript cannot be taken at face value as evidence of how food was cooked at the time and in the place of the document's origin. For one thing, many cookbooks are based to one degree or another on earlier models, in some cases models that are several centuries old. Rarely do they simply reproduce those models verbatim, however. If historians are to interpret cookbooks correctly, they must first carefully examine textual traditions and separate the various layers of each manuscript. This work is tedious but indispensable. In order to understand medieval French cooking, for example, one has to follow the development of the *Viandier,* the "best-selling" cookbook of the day, which evolved as French cooking evolved in the fourteenth and fifteenth centuries—so much so, in fact, that the version that was finally printed in 1486 has little in common with earlier manuscript versions.

Historians have much to learn from a careful study of recipes. Each manuscript can be approached in a number of ways. Recipe titles define what one might call a cookbook's repertoire. Each compilation called for a distinctive range of ingredients. Finally, every cookbook promoted certain flavors, colors, and fragrances. Although a dish with a particular name might be prepared in several different ways, the repetition of a name is already a valuable piece of information. Recipe names sometimes reveal traditional influences and evolving patterns. In the late fifteenth century, for example, when southern Italian cooking was dominated by an Italo-Aragonese style, the words *potagio* and *suppa* were used for what Venetian and Tuscan cookbooks always called *brodetto* (soup). Also worth noting, though not always to be taken literally, are dishes named for people or places. Thus what was called Saracen gruel, generally prepared with bacon and wine, most likely owed its name not to any Arab influence but to its dark color.

It is not enough to look only at the names of dishes, however. The content of recipes must also be studied. To date, we have only scratched the surface in this area, so in what follows I will limit my discussion to just a few ingredients of particular significance. If the choice of ingredients constitutes the "vocabulary" of a recipe, we must also consider the "syntax"—namely, cooking techniques. Terms for techniques and implements can tell us a lot about how things were done in the kitchen. Because of the complexity of this type of analysis, it has been possible only to sample the available sources.

Spices

The taste for spices predates the Middle Ages. Imported from India and the Far East since antiquity, spices appear in nearly all the recipes attributed to Apicius by a fourth-century compiler. In the medieval period, however, pepper, which had figured in 80 percent of Apicius' recipes, lost favor.[6] By the late Middle Ages it had been supplanted in western cooking by other spices, most notably ginger. Later, however, from the sixteenth to the eighteenth century, pepper again became the dominant spice, indeed virtually the only one utilized. This change was particularly noticeable in France, where the older techniques were rejected by the *nouvelle cuisine* that developed after 1650.

Sweet and Sour

Medieval cooking relied on a palette of three fundamental flavors: pungent (from spices), sweet, and sour. Bitter ingredients are rarely mentioned. One Anglo-Norman cookbook recommended a pinch of sugar to take the bitter edge off the taste of walnuts. About half the recipes in this collection call for an acidic taste to be obtained with vinegar made from grapes or apples; the use of citrus juices (lemon and bitter oranges) was confined mainly to the Mediterranean countries. Although wine itself was not classified by physicians as an acidic substance, it was clearly used as one in medieval cooking. People long preferred light, low-alcohol wines such as the acidic whites that were a specialty of the Île-de-France region. The malmsey that English cooks favored was something else entirely, a kind of sweetener, as were the concentrated musts and thick wines that were produced and used in Italy.

The taste for acidity seems to have been particularly prevalent in France. The oldest manuscript in the *Viandier* calls for a sour ingredient in more than 70 percent of its recipes. Sour ingredients are combined with spices in more than half of the dishes in this collection, and the combination of pungent with sharp—particularly wine or cider vinegar with that favorite French spice, ginger—was typical. In England and Italy, by contrast, the predilection for sour foods was less pronounced, and acidic ingredients were almost always tempered by some sweet-and-sour combination.

Indeed, the Italians and English generally had a sweet tooth. If one were to establish a map of sugar usage based on cookbooks, it would coincide with the taste for sweet dishes made with other ingredients such as honey, dates, and raisins. Thus, as long ago as the thirteenth century, the European "sugar bowl" included much of the southern continent from Languedoc to the boot of Italy together with the British Isles. But French cookbooks rarely mention sugar, and then almost always as a medication. Neither the *Viandier* nor the early-fourteenth-century *Enseignements* evinces much interest in honey, dates, figs, prunes, or raisins, either. The plain fact is that the fourteenth-century French simply did not like sweet foods.

There is no economic or commercial reason for this contrast. It is true that sugar began to be produced in the western Mediterranean region, whereas previously it had been necessary to import it from the Levant. But the "boom market" in sugar that one finds in the fifteenth century in Sicily, the Valencia region, and the Atlantic islands, only recently recaptured by Spain, was a response to rather than a cause of increased demand. In any case, English consumers of sugar were no closer to the producing regions than were the French. This was primarily a matter of taste, as subsequent developments would make clear.

By the end of the fourteenth century sugar had made modest inroads into Parisian cooking, perhaps under the influence of recipes and customs from regions to the north: England, Flanders, Hainault, and Brabant were all consumers of sugar. The transformation of the repertoire of French cuisine continued and even accelerated in the fifteenth century, and sugar was the beneficiary. It became such a well-established ingredient that it began to be included in the most classical dishes. Nevertheless, purely sweet or sweet-and-spicy dishes remained rare, and it was the growing popularity of the sweet-and-sour combination that accounted for the increased use of sugar. Thus it was because French palates had lost some of their fondness for sour flavors that the French began to consume sugar.

Sugar's success in France was still quite modest, however, compared with its popularity in areas where it had been used for ages. Its use continued to increase in the fifteenth century in places such as England and the Aragon-dominated Mediterranean rim. In southern Italy and Portugal one finds that up to two-thirds of the recipes in late-fifteenth-century cookbooks called for sugar. This was partly because of the Iberian custom of sprinkling sugar and cinnamon as a finishing touch even on dishes that were already sweet to begin with. Furthermore, the Italians and English, who had traditionally used sugar to take the edge off strong spices, now began to use it in sweet-and-sour dishes as well, just as in France. Thus the fifteenth century witnessed a certain homogenization of European culinary customs, a process in which sugar was just one of many factors.

Cooking with Butter

Just as there was a European "sugar bowl" in the late Middle Ages, there was also a "butter dish"—that is, an area in which butter was used in cooking, although it is not easy to determine its contours.[7] How often a particular fat was used in the kitchen depended on the proportion of recipes that called for browning or frying, and this varied widely from one cookbook to another. We cannot even be sure how much fat was used, although it does seem that, contrary to conventional wisdom, medieval cooking was less given to fat than was later cookery, particularly in the preparation of sauces.

Furthermore, ecclesiastical regulations on the use of fat varied widely with time and place. In some regions the use of butter was permitted during Lent, while in others it was limited to meatless days in non-Lenten periods, for which the rules were traditionally relatively lax. Yet certain books still insisted that butter could be used only on meat days. Although fats were a daily necessity, their use was strongly influenced by geographical and economic constraints, which in part shaped the regional preferences reflected by the cookbooks.

The use of butter in the Middle Ages was not limited to those regions that we commonly associate with butter. It was used, for instance, in southern Italy and Catalonia. Although the substance was ubiquitous, it was not dominant, for it is mentioned in barely more than 15 percent of all recipes and was still much less common than olive oil, bacon, and lard. Butter was most frequently used along the North Sea and English Channel from Denmark to Flanders and Normandy.

English culinary treatises contain relatively few discussions of butter. Although this may seem surprising, the social, cultural, and religious status of butter can help us to understand why it was so. Butter was not consumed in England during Lent except by children and the elderly. Only meatless recipes for such things as doughnuts, pancakes, and eggs called for it. By contrast, it was a regular part of the Welsh diet: Caxton described the Welsh national dish as a thick soup known as *cawl*, made with grain, leeks, butter, milk, and cheese. The Welsh were of course not only geographically remote from the center of English culture but also a poor people known for their sobriety. The increased use of butter in the sixteenth century might have something to do with growing Welsh influence in public affairs, whereas the reticence of medieval cookbooks on the subject might be a reflection of elitist disdain for the Welsh.

In the second half of the fifteenth century, French cookbooks switched to describing butter as a fat that could be used during Lent, especially as an accompaniment to fish. In the new cooking repertoire that gained favor in Paris and the Île-de-France, a taste for butter is apparent, no doubt in response to the influence of nearby Flanders. One can point, for example, to *beurre frais frit* (fresh-fried butter), which is also found in Flemish and German cookbooks. More surprising, however, was the conversion to butter in southern Italian cooking in the same period, for which there is abundant evidence.

Nevertheless, the vogue for butter did not sweep all of Europe. Southern France, from the Auvergne to the Toulouse region and Savoy, was one pocket of resistance. No stranger to the mountains of Auvergne, butter was replaced in Limagne by walnut oil, of which the supply was plentiful. In Provence olive oil was favored, while northern and, to a lesser degree, central Italy also refused to switch. To judge by the evidence of cookbooks, there is something paradoxical about the geographical distribution of butter use in Italy: olive oil and lard were used in the north, butter in the south. Despite, or rather because of, the difficulty of obtaining and preserving butter, southern elites favored it as a way of distinguishing themselves from the rest of society.

NOTES

1. See Bruno Laurioux, "Table et hiérarchie sociale à la fin du Moyen Age," in *Du manuscrit à la table*, ed. C. Lambert, pp. 87–108 (Montreal-Paris, 1992).

2. See Bruno Laurioux, "Les menus de banquet dans les livres de cuisine de la fin du Moyen Age," in *La Sociabilité à table: Commensalité et convivialité à travers les âges,* ed. M. Aurell, O. Dumoulin, and F. Thélamon, pp. 173–82 (Rouen: Publications de l'Université de Rouen, 1992).

3. P. Audoin, "Les ossements animaux dans les fouilles médiévales de la Charité-sur-Loire: Conclusions relatives à l'alimentation du XIe au XVIe siècle," in *Comptes rendus des séances de l'Académie des inscriptions et belles-lettres,* January–March 1984, pp. 199–217.

4. F. Piponnier, "Equipements et techniques culinaires en Bourgogne au XIVe siècle," *Bulletin philologique et historique du Comité des travaux historiques et scientifiques (histoire jusquen 1610), année 1971,* 1977, pp. 57–81.

5. Bruno Laurioux, "Entre savoir et pratiques: Le livre de cuisine à la fin du Moyen Age," *Médiévales* 14 (1988): 59–71.

6. Bruno Laurioux, "Spices in the Medieval Diet: A New Approach," *Food and Foodways* 1 (1985): 43–76.

7. See Jean-Louis Flandrin, "Le goût et la nécessité: Sur l'usage des graisses dans les cuisines d'Europe occidentale (XVIe–XVIIIe siècles), *Annales: Économies, sociétés, civilisations* 38, no. 2 (1983): 369–401.

CHAPTER 24

FOOD *and* SOCIAL CLASSES *in*
LATE MEDIEVAL *and* RENAISSANCE ITALY

Allen J. Grieco

According to a medieval commonplace, human beings were believed to survive by drinking wine (or ale and beer in northern Europe), eating bread, and
eating "all those other things" that could be eaten with bread. This third category of foodstuffs was usually referred to by a highly significant Latin term: *companagium* (*companatico* in Italian, *companage* in French). When dealing with medieval food history, this ubiquitous trio turns out to be both a useful and a
fundamental way to subdivide human fare, especially when examining the diets
of the poor. Economic considerations, but also economic imperatives, limited
both the choice of what people ate and how much they ate. This was particularly true in a society where the surplus produced tended to be very limited indeed. Furthermore, even slight price differences seem to have put certain food
items beyond the reach of the lower social classes, thus making these products
appear as something more linked to the realm of the desired than to what was
actually eaten. These very reduced margins within which to make choices, encountered by economic historians whenever they compare the incomes of the
working classes to the cost of wheat, would seem to have brought about a very
different price structure in the realm of foodstuffs than the one we are familiar
with at present.

Grain Consumption and Social Hierarchies

By present-day standards, it might come as a surprise to know that in late medieval and Renaissance Italy the cost of wheat flour—from which bread, the real staff of life, was made—seems to have been abnormally high, especially if we compare its cost to that of meat products. In late-fourteenth-century Florence, for example, one pound of the cheapest meat (pork) cost only twice as much as the best-quality flour, whereas the most expensive meat (veal) cost only two and a half times as much as wheat flour. Today, of course, we are used to a much greater price differential since meat is usually ten to fifteen times more expensive than flour, depending on the kind of meat and the cut. What might seem to have been only a slight price difference must not, however, be underrated since, as I have suggested, it constituted a major discriminating barrier in the eating habits of a large segment of the population, especially in those areas of Europe where wheat and other grains either were used to make bread or were boiled to make a dish of gruel.

It is a commonplace to point out the clear link between bread consumption and social rank. The lower a person's social rank, the greater the percentage of income spent on bread. For example, historians have found that the percentage of the dietary budget devoted to bread on one of King René's properties in 1457 varied from a minimum of 32 percent for the overseers to a distinctly higher figure (47 percent) for the cow herders and mule drivers; it reached a maximum of 52 percent among the shepherds, who were considered the lowest-grade workers. The percentage devoted to wine, on the other hand, was less variable, ranging from a minimum of 28 percent for the overseers to a maximum of 34 percent for the shepherds. The most radical discriminant was, however, the percentage devoted to the *companagium,* the various kinds of food that brought a bit of variety to what was otherwise a diet consisting of vast amounts of bread or gruel. Only 14 percent of the lowly shepherds' dietary budget was devoted to this item, whereas the overseers, responsible for managing the property, were able to devote as much as 40 percent of their budget to something other than bread and wine. In short, bread occupied an increasingly conspicuous percentile share of the diets of the lower social classes; inversely, this proportion shrank as one rose through the social hierarchy.

This state of affairs does not seem to have been limited to Mediterranean Europe. Christopher Dyer, in *Standards of Living in the Later Middle Ages,* has shown that the importance of grains (wheat, barley, and oats) was just as fundamental in English peasant diets, even though these were integrated, as in most other European countries, with large quantities of vegetables (onions, garlic, leeks, and cabbage being the most often mentioned) and small quantities of meat and cheese.

In a society where social distinctions were made manifest in a variety of ways, food was an important distinguishing element not only between the different social classes but also between rural and urban culture. Literary texts are particularly sensitive indicators of the social value attributed to different foods and therefore allow us to penetrate the social code with which foodstuffs and meals were invested. For example, any number of literary texts can be found that underscore the fact that the daily use of white bread distinguished the city dwellers from the rural populations, who were more likely to eat bread made with a mixture of grains (wheat or millet, for example) or who, more simply, boiled their grain and ate it in this less refined form. That this distinction was not a purely literary one can be seen from the fact that social and dietary differences were also recognized in the confined spaces of fifteenth-century ships, where at least two different tables existed. According to Benedetto Dei's report to the Consuls and Masters of the Sea of Pisa in 1471, there was a strict scale of salaries respecting the hierarchy of the men on board ship, just as there were distinctions made in the food served. The owner of the ship and the "officers" were served white bread whereas the rank and file had to be satisfied with rations of dry biscuit.

Literary texts also draw attention to the importance given to the proper choice of foods, especially on public occasions when banquets and meals commemorated an important event linking a given family to the community at large (birth of a child, marriage, knighthood, death). There was, in fact, a fine line between what was considered to be good enough and yet not excessively lavish and, on the other hand, food that could only be considered too poor and therefore not becoming the status of the family and the occasion on which it was being served. An excessive display of wealth was controlled and sanctioned by sumptuary laws promulgated not only by the Italian city-states but also elsewhere in Europe. These laws, an interesting source for food historians, fixed with great precision what foods could be served, how much at a time, and to how many guests. The opposite extreme, too poor a meal, seems to have been a rare occurrence that was usually condemned by the community (only morally speaking, of course) and was considered as reprehensible as excessive luxury.

The diets of the wealthier members of the community, a rather complex but interesting problem, have to be examined using a more sophisticated approach than that of calculating the percentile incidence of bread in their general intake. In fact, for the classes other than the laboring ones, it would seem that social distinctions on the basis of diets became apparent primarily in their choice of foodstuffs other than bread. In this case, however, it is not advisable to use literary texts as a source since they can always be suspected of enunciating rules and regulations that were not observed. There are many other sources—such as letters, travel accounts, and private memoirs—that allow us to penetrate into an everyday world where the direct link between food quality and social status moves from a more theoretical plane to a perfectly explicit one.

An excellent example of this link between food and social status can be found in a letter written in 1404 by Ser Lapo Mazzei, a Florentine notary known to us for his voluminous correspondence with his friend and mentor Francesco de Marco Datini, a rich merchant who lived in the city of Prato. In one of these letters, he wrote thanking his friend for what was meant to be a handsome gift of partridges, but reminding him in no uncertain terms that those birds were not food for his sort of person. In fact, Lapo complains to his friend, saying, "You will not leave me in peace with your partridges and God knows I do not like to destroy so many all at once, considering their price, and I would not give them to the gluttons, and it would grieve my soul were I to sell them." He then proceeds to explain that, were he still a servant of his people (a euphemism by which he meant sitting in the governing body of the city of Florence), it would then have been his duty to eat such fowl. This statement might seem curious to the present-day reader, but his comment should be taken quite literally. The Signori of Florence were, in fact, *required* to eat great quantities of partridges and fowl in general, since this was seen as an outward sign of the civic and political power they wielded. Such food, however, was not considered fit for normal people, both in a moral and in a medical sense.

Morally and medically speaking, it was dangerous to eat food that was thought to produce excessive overheating in the human body and therefore lead those who were imprudent enough to eat this way directly from the sin of gluttony (*gula*) to the closely associated and even more dangerous sin of lust (*lussuria*). This was something that Lapo must have believed to be true, as most of his contemporaries did, since in another letter to Francesco he only needed to remind him of the partridges he had eaten in Avignon in order to allude to a mistress he had had in that city as a young man. Even a great theologian and preacher like Bernardino of Siena believed that eating fowl could be dangerous; he made a point of telling the assembled crowd in the Piazza del Campo that widows, the subject of this sermon, had to be careful in choosing their food. He reminded them that they had to avoid foods that "heat you up since the danger is great when you have hot blood and eat food that will make you even hotter." In particular, he pointed out: "Let me tell you, widow, that you cannot eat this or that. . . . Do not try to do as you did when you had a husband and ate the flesh of fowl."

In any case, Lapo made it clear that such presents were not welcome, but that if his wealthy friend wanted to give him some coarser foods, fit for working people, this he would accept with pleasure. Lapo, it must be said, had not changed much over the years; in a letter he wrote some fourteen years earlier, when he first met Francesco, he told his new friend, "I like coarse foods, those that make me strong enough to sustain the work I must do to maintain my family. This year I would like to have, as I once had, a little barrel of salted anchovies."

The nutritional guidelines followed by Lapo did not apply to everyone. In fact, his friend Francesco was quick to break these rules, and his diet continued to be, even after the Avignon interlude, the diet of a man who was anything but temperate. From the study by Iris Origo, *The Merchant of Prato,* it is quite obvious that for Francesco di Marco Datini, as for many of his contemporaries, food was not a neutral matter and that his social status was seen to be closely linked to the kind of food he managed to buy. Thus, meat that was not worthy of him could unleash what seems to us to have been an excessive reaction. On one occasion he was sent some veal that was not up to par (probably from an animal that was too old). His reaction was to write to the agent and tell him, "You should feel shame to send such meat to as great a merchant as I am! I will come and eat it in your house, and only then shall we be friends again!"

The notion of "good" meat being fit mainly for the higher social strata and lower-quality meats being fit for the less elevated members of society (considered to be a "scientific" fact even by the doctors writing about diets) is borne out by another of Datini's letters. In this letter he asks a man by the name of Bellozzo to go to the market "where there are most people and say, 'give me some fine veal for that gentleman from Prato,' and they will give you some that is good." For a man that was so conscious of his status and the food that went with it, it became a matter of some importance if he managed (or, for that matter, did not manage) to buy the same food that was allotted to the priors of Florence whose high table (*mensa dei signori*) saw the best food to be had in Florence. On various occasions he either complained that the Signori of Florence had bought up the best fish available or was able to boast to his wife that he had bought the same veal that was reserved for the priors.

Even literary texts bear out the fact that it was considered quite normal for items of exceptionally large size, as long as they belonged to what was considered a noble food such as fish or fowl, to be destined for exceptional people, usually the local ruler. According to one of these stories, probably more than just a literary topos, a pair of exceptionally large capons appeared on the market in Milan where they were immediately bought up by a gentleman who, far from having them cooked for his own table, thought it fitting to send them as a present to Bernabò Visconti, the ruler of Milan.

At times hierarchical distinctions were observed in an even more extreme way—to the point of seeming an overdetermined mechanical exercise. A particularly good example of this is seen in the meals served to two Bavarian princes who visited Florence with their retinue in 1592. This group of visiting dignitaries and their hangers-on were offered a diversified meal that was meant to respect the social hierarchies at play. Thus, the two princes were served a dish with five different fowl (fowl being the noblest food possible). The "second table" (the one for the nobility accompanying the princes) was served dishes with only four different fowl. The cupbearer and the other top-ranking "servants" were also given dishes with four different fowl, but they were to eat their food in a private room separate from the banquet hall. Then came the lower-ranking servants (thirty in all) who had to share five dishes with one fowl each. These servants ate in the *tinello*, a kind of antechamber used for this purpose. The document then specifies that the horses and mules of the visitors were to be taken care of. The last to be mentioned in the list, even after the animals, were the very lowest ranking servants (a total of 140), who were put up in two different hostels in the city. Hierarchies were thus expressed not only in terms of the diversity of food served but also in terms of where the food was consumed (the distance from the master seeming to be the measure).

Food and Worldview

These distinctions through food, whereby the upper classes were meant to eat more "refined" foods, leaving coarser foodstuffs to the lower classes, were commonplace. Sixteenth-century treatises on the nobility examined this problem and reminded their readers that the "superiority" of the more refined part of the society was due, at least in part, to the way in which they ate. Thus, Florentin Thierriat in his *Discours de la préférence de la noblesse* asserted that "we eat more partridges and other delicate meats than they [those who are not of the nobility] do and this gives us a more supple intelligence and sensibility than those who eat beef and pork."

All of the examples cited above suggest that there was something like a code that made a meal noble or poor and that this code was not a personal one but rather one known and shared by most people. The idea that the rich and poor were meant to eat in very different ways may seem more or less senseless to us today, but in the late Middle Ages and the Renaissance the idea was grounded in a set of theories that were believed to be objective. According to the prevailing worldview, there existed a series of analogies between the natural world created by God and the world of human beings. It seemed self-evident that God had created the world as well as the laws that governed human society, both being structured

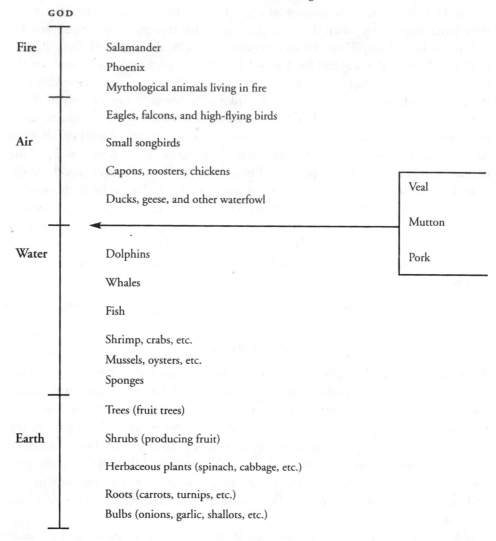

The Great Chain of Being

GOD

Fire
- Salamander
- Phoenix
- Mythological animals living in fire
- Eagles, falcons, and high-flying birds

Air
- Small songbirds
- Capons, roosters, chickens
- Ducks, geese, and other waterfowl

Veal

Mutton

Pork

Water
- Dolphins
- Whales
- Fish
- Shrimp, crabs, etc.
- Mussels, oysters, etc.
- Sponges
- Trees (fruit trees)

Earth
- Shrubs (producing fruit)
- Herbaceous plants (spinach, cabbage, etc.)
- Roots (carrots, turnips, etc.)
- Bulbs (onions, garlic, shallots, etc.)

INANIMATE OBJECTS

by a vertical and hierarchical principle. Human society was, quite obviously, sub-divided in a hierarchical way, but it was also thought that nature itself had been created as a kind of ladder, usually referred to as the Great Chain of Being (see above). This great chain was thought to give a particular order to nature since it not only connected the world of inanimate objects to God but also linked all of creation together in a grand design. Between the two extremes of the chain were to be found all the plants and animals created by God (including even mythological animals such as the phoenix). Furthermore, God's creation was thought to be a perfectly hierarchical entity in which everything respected an ascending or descending order. Each plant or animal was thought to be nobler than the one below it and less noble than the one above it, so no two plants and no two animals could have the same degree of nobility.

The Chain of Being subdivided all of creation into four distinct segments that represented the four elements (earth, water, air, and fire), to which all plant and animals (both real and mythological) were linked. Earth, the lowest and least noble of these elements, was the natural element in which all plants grew, but even within this segment of the chain there was a perfectly hierarchical system at work. According to the botanical ideas of the time, the least noble plants were those that produced an edible bulb under ground (such as onions, garlic, and shallots). After these came slightly less lowly plants whose roots were eaten (turnips, carrots, and many root crops no longer in use). The next step up in the plant world was to all those plants whose leaves were eaten (spinach and cabbage, for example). At the top came fruit, the most noble product of the plant world. Fruit was considered to be very much superior to all other plant products and therefore more fit for the upper classes. The supposed nobility of fruit was due to the fact that most of it grew on bushes and trees and thus grew higher off the ground than all of the previously mentioned produce.

Moreover, plants were thought to actually digest the terrestrial food they absorbed with their roots and turn it into sap, which continued to improve as it rose in the plant and produced leaves, flowers, and, best of all, fruit. It was even thought that the taller the plants grew, the more the rising sap "digested" and transformed the cold and raw humors of the earth into something more acceptable. Even on the same tree the fruit that was higher off the ground was thought to be better than the rest. This rather mechanical application of a theory led people to think of strawberries and melons as very poor fruit, a consensus that was further confirmed by the informed opinion of dieticians.

The second segment of the Chain of Being (the segment associated with water) produced the lowly sponges that seemed more plants than anything else; nevertheless, they were considered somewhat sentient since they responded to touch. One step up from them, but still at the low end of this category, were the mussels and other shellfish that could not move on their own and seemed, because of their shells, to be partially inanimate. Higher up, and therefore more "noble" than the previous group, were the various kinds of crustaceans (such as shrimp and lobsters) that crawled on the floor of the sea. Somewhat more elevated were the various kinds of fish, even though they were distinctly overshadowed by another group of aquatic animals at the top of the category—all those animals that, like dolphins and whales, tend to swim on the surface of the water and, at times, even reach out of this element into the next highest one (air) as if they were striving upward to some kind of perfection. It might well be that these ideas about the nobility of dolphins and whales contributed to their being hunted and eaten in this period of European history more than any time after.

The third segment of the Chain of Being, the one connected with the element air, contains yet another hierarchy of values. It begins, at the bottom, with the lowest kinds of birds—those that live in water (ducks, geese, and wild birds living in or near water, such as the cormorant) and were thus thought to reveal their lowly status by being associated with that lower element. Chickens and capons were considered to be much better fare since they were more obviously aerial animals; in fact, any respectable banquet had to include such fowl. The next step up was occupied by songbirds, a very late medieval and Renaissance culinary passion, and at the top of the category were the highest-flying birds, such as the eagle and falcon. The latter were not really considered to be food but rather were kept as companions and were used primarily by the upper classes for hunting. The story in Boccaccio's *Decameron* (day 5, novella 9) concerning the unrequited love of Federigo degli Alberighi reveals an interesting use of these ideas. Federigo, who has been reduced to poverty in his efforts to win over his beloved monna Giovanna, ends up living in a little farm outside Florence with his last earthly possession, a falcon whose hunting talents manage to keep him fed. Many years later Giovanna comes to see him because her son is convinced that the only thing that will cure him from his sickness is to own Federigo's falcon. Unfortunately, the noble Federigo has no food on the day that he receives Giovanna, and, although he is in the throes of anguish, he decides that the falcon is a "*degna vivanda di cotal donna*" (a worthy dish for such a woman). The pathos of the story is developed around the idea that the falcon is both a companion and a noble food and that Federigo has no other choice than to transform him from a faithful companion into a dish for his beloved.

The Great Chain of Being, as it was understood in the late Middle Ages and during the Renaissance, did not manage, like most general theories, to account for everything. One of its main problems was to classify quadrupeds since they were hard to assign to any element in particular. While they obviously were earthbound, they could hardly be considered in the same way as plants. On the other hand, quadrupeds could not be linked to the element air and thus compared to birds. In practice they were not introduced in the general scheme. However, these animals can be inserted somewhere in the middle of the chain: they were considered, quite obviously, nobler fare than what the plant world produced and yet less prized than fowl.

The meat of quadrupeds, like everything else, was ordered in a strict hierarchy.

At the very top was veal, always the most expensive meat on the market, and second only to fowl. At banquets, such as the one that was held in honor of the marriage of Nannina de' Medici to Bernardo Rucellai in 1466, veal was given to the people who came from the country properties of these two families, whereas the most important guests were served capons, chickens, and other fowl. In the hierarchy of meats, mutton (very much the everyday fare of the merchant classes) was placed below veal, and pork occupied the lowest rank. The latter was looked down upon, especially when salted, probably because it was also the meat that was most available for the lower classes.

The hierarchical structure of both society and nature suggested that these two worlds mirrored or paralleled each other. As a consequence, it was believed that society had a "natural" order whereas nature had a kind of "social" order. One of the outcomes of this parallelism between the natural and the social worlds was the general view that the upper strata of society were destined to eat the foods belonging to the upper reaches of the realm of nature. In fact, the idea that the produce of nature was not all the same (since it was hierarchically ordered) and that specific foodstuffs were associated with specific sectors of society became increasingly plausible. It seemed to make perfect sense that fowl be considered the food, par excellence, for the rich and mighty of the earth who, it was thought, needed to eat birds precisely to keep their intelligence and sensibility more alert as the previously quoted Thierriat would have had it. Doctors like the Bolognese Baldassare Pisanelli, whose treatise on diet was first published in 1583, could say without a hint of irony, "*Le pernici non nuocono se non a gente rustica*" (Partridges are only unhealthy for country people). They also pointed out that fowl was suited to the upper classes whereas the meat of quadrupeds, which was, according to the ideas of the times, heavier and more substantial, seemed more suitable for the merchant classes since their type of life called for somewhat more sustenance. Pork and old animals in general (sheep, goats, and oxen) that were no longer useful otherwise provided the meat for the lower classes that needed yet more sustenance.

The working classes might have been destined some meat, but they were considered best off eating vast amounts of vegetables. There is no doubt, of course, that vegetables had a prominent part in the poor man's diet in western Europe from the fourteenth to the sixteenth century, primarily for economic reasons. In fact, vegetable gardens all over Europe produced relatively cheap and abundant quantities of edibles. However, this kind of diet was also invested with a strong class bias that surfaces in all kinds of documents. The link between vegetables and the lower social orders is always very evident to the extent that it sometimes constituted a quasi-symbiotic relationship. Doctors, dieticians, and the authors of *novelle* are often guilty of a significant inversion when they affirm that the great quantities of vegetables eaten by the poor are the result of a physiological necessity rather than a diet imposed on them for economic reasons. A well-known example of this is to be found in the late-sixteenth-century tale of Bertoldo by the Bolognese author Giulio Cesare Croce. In this story, a peasant from the mountains, accustomed to eating turnips and other lowly food, is adopted by a king and lives at his court. As time passes, the peasant Bertoldo becomes increasingly sick; since the doctors do not know his social origins, they give him the wrong remedies. Bertoldo, who knows what is really wrong and the remedy required, asks for nothing more than some turnips cooked in the ashes of the fire and some fava beans (also associated with the diet of the peasantry). Unfortunately, nobody sees fit to provide him with this simple fare and he finally dies a miserable death. The ironic epitaph on his tomb reminds everyone that "He who is used to turnips must not eat meat pies."

The Great Chain of Being can thus be said to have had a double function. On the one hand, it ordered and classified the natural world in ways that could be understood; on the other hand, it provided a social value for all the foodstuffs used by man. This double function of classifying and evaluating created a code that could be used to communicate social differences in a subtle way. Every foodstuff had a specific connotation, and even the diets prescribed by doctors respected social differences as one of the most important variables. As a consequence, all foodstuffs were invested with an outward and apparent value, very much like clothing, that communicated social differences. Little wonder that sumptuary laws give so much attention to what was served on everybody's plate, as if it were possible to calculate an exact equivalence between different dishes while staying within the limits of what was still considered an acceptable display of luxury. In Florence, for example (but one could look elsewhere and find the same phenomenon), a city statute passed in 1415 specified that the course of roasted meats served at wedding banquets could consist of only one capon and a meat pie on each trencher. However, it was also possible to serve a duck and a pie, or two partridges and a pie, or two chickens and a pigeon, or two pigeons and a chicken, or a duck and two pigeons, or even just two chickens. These laws and their obsessive attention to details tried to anticipate all the possible combinations and permutations of an alimentary system that was highly codified. However, just as the lawmakers did not manage to foresee new inventions that allowed people to circumvent the rules in the realm of clothing, so did organizers of banquets seem to find loopholes in the laws. In the end, food and social differences were too deeply rooted in a society where even a subsistence diet was anything but ensured.

CHAPTER 25

SEASONING, COOKING, *and* DIETETICS
in the LATE MIDDLE AGES

Jean-Louis Flandrin

More than anything else, it is spices that draw our attention to the question of seasoning. At no time in European history did spices play as great a role as in the fourteenth, fifteenth, and sixteenth centuries, and at no time were they as important in cooking, to judge by their variety, frequency of use, and the quantities utilized. This is true of all European aristocratic cuisines, even though they differ greatly in other respects. Moreover, spices achieved their height of importance in international trade at this time, whether we measure that importance in terms of the value of merchandise transported or the efforts of the great maritime powers to monopolize this traffic. It was in the search for spices—as much as gold and silver—that Europeans went out to conquer the Seven Seas and the other continents and thus changed the course of history.

Why Spices?

What justified such an expenditure of energy? Little attention has been paid to this question, and no satisfactory answer has been forthcoming. To begin with the least convincing explanation: spices were used to preserve meat or to hide the foul taste of poorly preserved meat. On close inspection, this answer does not hold up.

First of all, the substances used in the preservation of meat and fish were mainly salt, vinegar, and oil, not spices. Although some sources are unclear on the matter and although pâtés prepared for shipment to distant places were indeed more highly spiced than those intended for immediate consumption, spices were never really in competition with salt, and it was not for their preservative powers that people were willing to pay much more for them than for salt.

Second, leaving salted meats aside, meat in general was consumed sooner after slaughter than it is today. As evidence for this, we have municipal regulations prohibiting the sale of meat slaughtered more than one day previous in summertime and three days previous in winter as well as statistics concerning the number of animals slaughtered daily. Louis Stouff has compiled and graphed these data for an entire year for the city of Carpentras in the fifteenth century, and from his work it is clear that animals were generally killed not three days before their meat was sold or two days or even one, but on the very same day. If medieval gastronomy is to be criticized, it has to be for consuming meat that was insufficiently aged rather than rotten.

Finally, if anyone did eat preserved meat or meat that had gone bad, it wasn't the wealthy nobles and bourgeois, who consumed spices, but the hapless poor, who couldn't afford such luxuries. Indeed, salted meat turns out to be quite rare in the recipes found in treatises on cooking; they frequently mention salted fish, especially for Lent (eel, herring, cod, trout, salmon, sturgeon, whale, dolphin, shad, whiting, mackerel, mullet, and even pike), but salted meat and fowl (pork, boar, beef, venison, goose, coot, and, very rarely, mutton and marmot) occur much less often than fresh meat and fowl. Furthermore, salted meats were almost always eaten with mustard and almost never with spices.

Other explanations, though not as egregiously misguided, are nevertheless unsatisfactory. Several good historians have argued that the use of spices was a means of achieving social distinction. It is true that people lower down on the social ladder could not afford to buy these expensive luxuries, and it is also true that as wealth and social rank increased, so did the use of spices in terms of both quantity and variety. Nevertheless, the argument does not take us very far because spices were certainly not used primarily as a status symbol. Indeed, the rarity of a commodity has never been enough by itself to make people covet it or treat its possession as a mark of distinction. In order to serve that purpose, the commodity in question must also be perceived as superior to other commodities capable of fulfilling the same function. Beer may have been as rare in grape-growing regions as wine was elsewhere, yet nowhere was beer more coveted than wine, which was seen as an "aristocratic" beverage. In fact, for complex cultural reasons, beer was everywhere regarded as inferior to wine. Likewise, the fact that exotic spices were rarer than domestic herbs is not enough to account for the higher price of the former or for their value as a status symbol. Before people could covet imported spices, they first had to learn of their existence and have reasons for believing them superior to garlic or parsley.

A third argument takes us a bit farther than the first two. It holds that the West learned about spices from the Arabs, whose civilization they came to admire during the Crusades. Recent proponents of this thesis, such as Toby Peterson, maintain that the cookbooks that popularized spicy cooking in the West were all inspired by Arabic precursors.

Indeed, the sophistication of Arab civilization is well known, and there can be no doubt that it enjoyed considerable prestige in medieval Europe: the West learned from the Arabs in many areas. Furthermore, Arabic cooking is indeed spicy, and Maxime Rodinson has shown that certain western dishes borrowed directly from Arab recipes. Finally, Arabs controlled the trade in spices between the places where they were produced and the Egyptian and Syrian ports to which Venetian, Genoese, and Catalan traders came to buy them. Stated succinctly, the argument is that what accounts for the use of spices in western Europe in the Middle Ages is the cultural and commercial dominance of Arabic civilization.

The trouble with this argument is that spices were used well before the Crusades (in the tenth to thirteenth centuries)—even before an Arab empire existed (that is, before the seventh and eighth centuries). We know from Apicius' culinary treatise that Roman high cuisine already used spices: 80 percent of the recipes it contains employ pepper. Although the range of spices used in the Middle Ages was wider, Bruno Laurioux has shown that the basic pattern was set by the end of antiquity, and Europe continued to import spices throughout the early Middle Ages.

Medicinal Virtues of Spices

Traditionally, the word "spices" referred not to just any aromatic substance used in cooking but only to exotic substances imported from abroad. Many of these oriental imports were used for therapeutic purposes rather than cooking. All the spices used by cooks also had medical uses. For example, according to *Le Thresor de santé* (1607), pepper "maintains health, fortifies the stomach, . . . [and] eliminates winds. It facilitates urination, . . . cures chills from intermittent fevers, and also heals snake bites and hastens the expulsion of stillborn infants from the womb. If drunk, [it] is good for coughs. . . . Ground up with dried grapes, [it] purges the brain of phlegm and stimulates the appetite." Cloves were good "for the eyes, liver, heart, and stomach." Oil of clove was "excellent for treating toothaches. . . .

It is good for stomach fluxions due to cold and for cold maladies of the stomach. . . . Two or three drops in bouillon of capon will cure colic. It is of considerable help in digestion if boiled with fennel seed in good wine."

Every spice was supposed to possess analogous virtues. Not only were spices more commonly used for medicinal purposes than as condiments, but the former use also predated the latter historically. Bruno Laurioux has shown that every spice used in the medieval kitchen was originally imported as a medicine and only later employed as a seasoning.

The question remains whether these pharmaceutical products were employed in the kitchen for medicinal purposes or purely as flavorings. This is a question worth asking, since most of the drugs that we nowadays abuse against medical advice were originally used on the advice of physicians for medicinal purposes. Included under this rubric are sugar, coffee, tea, tobacco, and alcohol, to name a few. In the fourteenth century Magninus of Milan warned readers of his *Opusculum de saporibus* against abusing sauces specifically because of their medicinal value: "Sauces . . . have a medicinal nature, hence the wise man excludes them from a healthy diet, for in order to preserve health one should abstain from consuming all things medicinal."

Be that as it may, physicians from the thirteenth to the beginning of the seventeenth century repeatedly recommended using spices to make meat more digestible. Aldobrandino of Siena wrote in his *Regimen corpus* (1256) that cinnamon was good for "fortifying the liver and the stomach" and "cooking meat thoroughly." Similarly, ginger was "good for fortifying a cold stomach . . . and cooking meat well," while cloves "fortify the stomach and body, . . . eliminate flatulence and evil humors . . . due to cold, and help to cook food thoroughly."

In this period everyone conceived of digestion as a form of cooking. The essential agent in this process was animal heat, which gently cooked food in the stomach, a sort of natural cookpot. Accordingly, spices that were used as seasoning, all of which were considered to be "hot" (and for the most part dry), had the virtue of counterbalancing the "coldness" of the foods with which they were served, thereby assisting the digestive cooking process. Pepper was said to be "of the fourth degree" of hotness and dryness. Cloves, galanga, cardamom, and curcuma were of the third degree; cinnamon, cumin, cubebe, and nutmeg were of the second degree; and so on.

In fact, numerous native flavorings and condiments were also thought to be hot and dry. As noted in Aldobrandino's book, garlic and mustard were of the fourth degree, just like pepper; parsley, sage, pennyroyal, leeks, garden watercress, and mountain hyssop were of the third degree; fennel, caraway seeds, chervil, mint, roquette, and river watercress were of the second degree; and so on. In general, all aromatic plants were considered hot. But spices, which came from the hot countries of the East, had been seen since antiquity as more refined and subtle and therefore medically more reliable than indigenous aromatic plants.[1]

A condiment's degree of hotness was not its only virtue. Beyond the third degree, foods and spices were considered dangerous. The fourth degree of coldness included the poisonous mushrooms. As for the fourth degree of hotness, garlic was thought to be suitable only for the crude stomachs of peasants. And pepper, the strongest of spices, vanished from French aristocratic cookbooks in the fourteenth and fifteenth centuries, when its use was confined to lower levels of society. When cooking for the delicate stomachs of the social elite, French chefs used only "long pepper" (a hot spice of the third degree), and they always took the edge off by mixing it with other, less searing spices.

Cooking for Digestibility

In general, seasoning served two broad purposes: it made food more appetizing by improving its taste, and at the same time it made food more digestible. While some cookbooks presented themselves as manuals of practical dietetics, most treatises on dietetics included recipes along with medical explanations of their health benefits.

For example, Magninus of Milan's *Opusculum de saporibus* dealt systematically with the major meats, fowl, and fish. It began by summarizing the "physical" characteristics of each food—its degree of hotness or coldness, dryness or moistness, crudity or subtlety—and then explained the best way to cook it together with recipes for the most appropriate sauces. For example, beef, a dry meat, was only to be eaten boiled, and because it was crude and "cold," it called for a "hot" sauce to warm it up and tenderize it: a saffron pepper sauce, a sauce made with roquette, or a white garlic sauce. The fact that indigenous spices are prominently featured in two of these sauces probably indicates that beef was still an unsophisticated food eaten by people of low status.

The same was true of goose, whose meat, according to *Le Thresor de santé*, was "highly excremental . . . and hard to cook. . . . There is no other domestic bird whose flesh is as crude, cold, and moist." The author recommends eating it "with a sauce made of bread roasted in the oven, soaked in good bouillon, and strained with six cloves of crushed garlic (to taste), mixed with ginger, and all boiled together on a stove. . . . It is also good to lard and stuff the goose with sage, which should not be eaten. On the fire this draws off some of the excess viscosity. Crushed pepper may also be added."

The flesh of the crane was another matter. Like beef, its meat was "hard, cold, dry, and stringy, and its crude juice is hard to digest and can lead to congestion of the blood and melancholic humor." Since the meat of the crane was served to aristocratic diners, however, *Le Thresor de santé* recommended that it be eaten "with cloves, salt, and powdered pepper." Aldebrandino of Siena recommended serving it with "black pepper sauce," a preparation that involved a number of precious spices.

Aldobrandino, perhaps because he was writing for a princess, also prescribed spices for more common dishes such as brains and tongue. Brains were said to be "cold and moist . . . [and] viscous . . . producing abomination and corrupting easily in the stomach," which was why they were to be eaten "before all meats" and "flavored with vinegar and pepper and ginger and cinnamon and mint and parsley and other things of the same nature." Tongue was a "mixture of cold and hot, but . . . stands closer to coldness than to hotness," so it was to be eaten "flavored with pepper and cinnamon and ginger and vinegar and other such spices."

As for salt, the most common condiment, Joseph Duchesne, writing early in the seventeenth century, gave an apt description of the dual function of seasoning, gastronomic as well as dietetic: "Salt is hot and dry by nature, hence its virtues are cleansing, dissolutive, purgative, constrictive, and astringent; and that is why, by consuming the superfluous and excremental moisture in many things, such as flesh, fish, and fruit, it preserves them from corruption. As such, salt is among the things most necessary to human consumption, which no one can do without. . . . Salt alone is useful as a seasoning for all meats, which would otherwise have an unpleasant taste or flavor and be more subject to corruption in our bodies."[2]

Two and a half centuries earlier, Magninus of Milan had pointed out salt's dual virtues in his *Regimen sanitatis:* "Salt . . . adds goodness of flavor to comestibles and removes the harmful influence . . . of a certain aqueous and indigestible moisture. Hence these foods are cooked and digested more fully with salt than without it." But not all foods required it: "Foods that are moist and excremental as well as crude [such as pork] need salt more," whereas "foods that are dry or without excess moisture and delicate [such as chicken and partridge] need very little salt when seasoned."[3] Later he notes that when cooking legumes and other herbs, "salt and water are not sufficient: we need oil, butter, or fat. Because legumes and other herbs are by nature melancholy and earthy, it is good to season them with something fatty, which tempers their earthiness and makes them smoother and more delectable and therefore more digestible and nourishing." Cold condiments such as wine and cider vinegar also had dietetic value. In *De saporibus* he recommends that "summer sauces be made with cider vinegar or juice from grapes taken from the top of the vine, vinegar, lemon juice, orange juice, or grenadine." The same "cold" ingredients could be used in any season to moderate the heat of other spices so as to transmit their beneficial effects to all parts of the organism, thereby allowing their "aperitive virtue," or sharp, biting taste, to reach into the body's tiniest conduits.

In the early seventeenth century Duchesne, commenting on the "qualities of vinegar," noted that "it is one of the primary stimuli of the appetite" as well as

> useful for cutting into and opening up the liver [and] dampening the ardor of the bile. It also prevents corruption and aids digestion in stomachs . . . which are too hot . . . but it should be used with discretion, if necessary correcting and moderating its effects with sugar and other things. Cider vinegar may also be used to stimulate the appetite and moderate the blood and bilious humor and is therefore useful in treating choleric complexions and people afflicted with maladies of heat.

Cooking techniques were also designed to make meats more digestible. Fatty (and therefore moist) cuts were roasted to "dry" them out, whereas lean and "dry" pieces were boiled. Thus suckling pigs and fresh pork were roasted, as were leg and shoulder of lamb, quail, and fatty capons; beef was always boiled. Pork was also salted to lessen its "moistness." This was the theory, at any rate, but some recipes seem to contradict it: *Platine en français,* for example, recommends boiling breast of veal and roasting its spine as well as roasting hare and pheasant on a spit. But these exceptions only confirm the rule.

Le Thresor de santé recommends numerous ways of eating oysters, some of which were better than others from a dietetic point of view. Oysters, we are told, "are difficult to digest . . . if one swallows them raw with their water in the manner of the Ancients," for "their flesh is very soft and not very nourishing and yields a raw, moist juice that does not go down easily." It was better "to cook them in the shell over coals with butter and crushed pepper." Since "their salty juice makes them hard to digest," though, "a better method is to boil them with correctives. Remove them from the shell, wash them well in their own water filtered through cloth, and boil them with butter, spices, and Corinthian grapes. When half-cooked, add finely chopped marjoram, thyme, parsley, and savory, along with onions, saffron, and cider vinegar." All things considered, however, "oysters roasted over a slow fire are even healthier, because the heat corrects their excessive moisture."

Tastes

Dietitians generally offered several recipes for cooking each type of food they discussed, and cooks and consumers no doubt chose among them based not only on dietetic considerations but also on availability of ingredients and taste. Indeed, physicians themselves considered the gastronomic function to be just as important as the dietetic function: improving the taste of food was also a matter for dietetics.

Magninus of Milan explains this at several points in his *Regimen sanitatis*. The condiments and sauces used in seasoning foods "are of no small value in a healthy diet, because condiments make food *more delectable to the taste and therefore more digestible. For what is more delectable is better for digestion.* Condiments add nutritional value and correct for harmful properties." He discusses this theme in connection with each of the most common condiments: salt, oil, lard, and butter.

Physicians complained that achieving sophisticated tastes sometimes took precedence over medical considerations. It would be a mistake, however, to assume that gastronomy and dietetics were systematically opposed. On the contrary, medieval tastes were largely shaped by dietetic beliefs.

Although physicists and physicians did not always agree about the number of simple flavors, all acknowledged nine basic tastes that were distinguished from one another by quality, substance, and relation to the four elements as summarized in the chart opposite.

Each flavor could be transmuted into the one above it in the table by the action of heat, as Ambroise Paré pointed out in the sixteenth century:

> Nature generally . . . adheres to a certain order in the coction of flavors.
> . . . The first to appear is the acerbic flavor, which is still quite crude; then with a certain amount of concoction it becomes austere and then acidic. With still greater concoction it becomes mild and oily, and if the heat is increased still further it will turn salty, after which the salty becomes bitter, until finally, if the heat is increased too much, it becomes acrid, the flavor whose nature is entirely that of fire.

There was no shortage of examples of such transmutations. Green fruits, for example, tasted acidic or even acerbic, but as they ripened under the action of the sun, they acquired a sweet or oily taste. Honey and sugar, which tasted sweet, turned bitter when caramelized by the effects of heat. Finally, it was the action of the tropical sun that gave pepper and other spices the hottest of all flavors—acrid, or, as we say nowadays, "hot" or "spicy."

Any food that was nourishing was supposed to have something of "sweetness" in it, implying that it contained at least some degree of heat. Substances that had only cold flavors (austere, acerbic, or acidic) or hot flavors (bitter, salty, or acrid) were useful not as foods but only as medications or condiments. They were also quite useful for balancing the flavor or temperament of foods that were too hot or cold or insufficiently sweet.

THE NINE BASIC FLAVORS BY QUALITY, SUBSTANCE, AND RELATION TO THE FOUR ELEMENTS

Quality	Flavor	Fire	Air	Water	Earth	Substance
	Acrid or pungent	x			x	Subtle
Hot	Bitter	x			x	Gross
	Salty	x			x	Medium
	Oily	x	x			Subtle
Temperate	Sweet	x	x			Gross
	Insipid		x			Medium
	Sour or acidic				x	Subtle
Cold	Austere				x	Gross
	Acerbic				x	Medium

Recommendations for Eating Fruits

To what extent did actual eating practices conform to the prescriptions of the dietitians? To judge by what they themselves said, the answer is "not entirely," since they were quick to denounce the slightest transgression, much as preachers denounced moral failings from the pulpit. Nevertheless, medieval dietary prescriptions, like Christian moral preachings, left an indelible trace on European customs.

According to *Platine en français,* Galen is supposed to have said that he never had a fever because he never ate fruit. Yet we know that fruits were consumed in large quantities by the social elite. Gourmet fashions (or social conformism) thus had an impact, but when it came to the way in which fruit was eaten, all the recommendations of the dietitians were scrupulously observed in order to counteract the deleterious consequences.

One recommendation had to do with when fruit should be eaten. Those fruits that were considered "cold" or "subject to putrescence," such as sweet cherries, plums, apricots, peaches, figs, blackberries, grapes, and especially melons, reputed to be the most dangerous of all, were to be eaten at the beginning of the meal. Others, including apples and pears, quince, chestnuts, and medlars, were better eaten at the end of the meal because they had the virtue of preventing other foods from "coming up"; indeed, they had the opposite effect, hastening what was consumed toward the exit in the manner of a press.

Physicians also recommended that certain fruits be eaten in conjunction with other foods and condiments. In *Le Thresor de santé,* for example, we read that "it is recommended that melon be followed by a mild cheese or a small amount of meat seasoned with either salt or sugar in order to keep the melon from putrefying." This is probably the basis for the current Italian custom of eating melon with pro- sciutto. The French tradition, for which we find evidence from the sixteenth cen- tury to the present day, was rather to season melon with salt and pepper and to drink a glass of clear wine along with it.

Pears, "being quite windy," according to *Le Thresor de santé,* were to be "braised with anise, fennel, or coriander" before eating, and afterward it was recommended that one "immediately drink a good glass of old wine." Indeed, pears became "good and beneficial when cooked in good red wine, larded with cloves, sugar, and cinnamon, and served hot with quantities of fresh butter and creamy cheese with sugar on top." They were often served cooked with sugar and spices.

What the Cooks Tell Us

In the preface to *Le Cuisinier françois* (1651), we read that the recipes in the book are designed "to preserve and maintain a healthy condition and good disposition by teaching [cooks] to corrupt the vicious qualities of meats by contrary season- ings." The editor concludes by saying that, like *Le Médecin charitable,* his book be- longs in the library of everyone concerned about health since "it is much more agreeable to spend a modest amount . . . on ragouts and other meaty delicacies in order to preserve life and maintain health than it is to spend vast sums on drugs, herbs, medicines, and other unwelcome remedies in order to regain health once lost."

We need not take the editor at his word. Nevertheless, his sales pitch proves that even at this late date a cookbook could be presented as a practical treatise on dietetic hygiene. Furthermore, a statistical analysis of recipes shows that, in prac- tice, cooks by and large conformed to the recommendations of the dietitians.

While a treatise on dietetics such as the *Opusculum de saporibus* gave precise in- dications about what sauces to use for each type of meat, fowl, and fish and in- cluded detailed recipes for each sauce, few cookbooks of the period, like *Le Viandier de Taillevent,* went into such matters. This may have been because meats such as boiled beef and port were too vulgar for Taillevent to concern himself with. Often it seems that we are dealing with two different cuisines, no doubt be- cause of the nationalities of the authors.

Nevertheless, Taillevent and other cookbook authors were by no means cava- lier about matters of dietetics. To begin with, they respected the taboos laid down by the dietitians. For example, the taboo against mixing milk with fish, which we find in the Spanish physician Petro Fagarola's *Regimen conditum,* is honored in all eighty-five fish recipes in *Le Viandier de Taillevent,* where only almond milk is ever mentioned in connection with fish. The same is true of *Platine en français.*

Furthermore, while the sauces discussed by Magninus of Milan and other dietitians are not totally identical to the sauces that we find in medieval cookbooks, the overlap is significant. For instance, *De saporibus* asserts that "roasted turtledove, partridge, pigeon, and quail need no sauce other than salt and lemon juice," whereas Taillevent, a fourteenth-century French chef who was not yet familiar with lemons, recommends seasoning roast partridge, pigeon, turtledove, pheasant, plover, woodcock, and other birds with salt only. Magninus recommends camelina (a type of mustard plant) for roast rabbit and small chickens, while Taillevent suggests using it not only for these meats but also for roast rabbit, kid, lamb, mutton, and venison. Finally, the way in which, say, *Le Ménagier de Paris* recommends preparing camelina sauce (with vinegar during the summer and wine during the winter) follows exactly the recommendations of Magninus and other dietitians.

In general, the "coldest" and "crudest" meats were the ones served with the hottest, spiciest sauces. With chicken all that was necessary was *jance,* a mixture of white wine, cider vinegar, and ginger, along with cloves and burnt rather than white bread. *Jance* was also used on fried fish kept hot with boiling oil. With boiled fish, which was always cold and moist, green sauce made of vinegar, cider vinegar, ginger, and various hot herbs was served, or else camelina, which was more stimulating and penetrating. The latter sauce, served frequently with the "crude" flesh of quadrupeds, was made with vinegar or red wine or both, toasted bread, and a mixture of four or five spices, including ginger, grain of paradise, clove, and even "long pepper" along with the dominant cinnamon. Cinnamon was supposed to be the "subtlest" of the spices, hence it was no accident that it figured prominently in a sauce that was served with "crude" meats. Hot sauce included the same spices, but the dominant ingredient was cloves, to which long pepper was sometimes added. The solvent was vinegar uncut by wine or cider; burnt bread, hotter than browned bread, was used as a binder. It will therefore come as no surprise that this very stimulating sauce was served with venison and boar, which were particularly hard to digest, as well as with "viscous" fish such as the lamprey and large eels and "crude" fish like "sea hogs," dolphin, and porpoise. These "gross" meats were also served with black pepper sauce, another very hot sauce made of ginger, pepper, burnt bread, vinegar, and cider.

The total absence of spices from recipes intended for the sick is as significant as their presence in recipes for the healthy. Anyone suffering from a fever was forbidden to eat spices, because these, being hot and dry, could only make the fever worse. Food for the sick was still cooked, however, but it was always boiled—never roasted. Instead of spices, two-thirds of these dishes were seasoned with sugar, the most "temperate" of condiments.

We are now in a position to sum up the relation between dietetics and cooking in the Middle Ages. Then, as now, snobbery and ostentation drove some wealthy people to eat dangerous foods such as fruit, venison, river fish, lamprey, and porpoise. These abuses were denounced by hygienists and moralists alike. Nevertheless, dangerous foods were seasoned and cooked so as to correct their "vices." This was typical of medieval and Renaissance cooking, and not only of the recipes found in dietetic treatises (which may or may not have been used in practice) but also of those in ordinary treatises on cooking.

Dietetics and Oral Culture

Does this mean that cooks were founts of scientific knowledge and preoccupied above all with dietetics, as the editor of *Le Cuisinier françois* suggested? Or that they worked closely with physicians, as Terence Scully has argued? Perhaps, but the main point lies elsewhere. Because the concepts of ancient medicine were not far removed from common experience, the principles of dietetics could be propagated by means other than books. Everyone in medieval society learned those principles by eating, as we see even today in various societies where spices are eaten from the Antilles to China.

What is more, venerable proverbs attest to this oral circulation of certain prescriptions of the old dietetics. Many such proverbs warned against the danger of eating fruit—not just green fruits ("Mauvais est il fruiz qui ne meüre," late thirteenth century) but all fruits ("De bon fruit, méchant vent et bruit"). Pears were a particular target: "Après la poire, le vin" (fifteenth century); "Sur poyre vin boire" (1577); "Après la poire, prestre ou boire" (1578); "Après la poire, le vin ou le prestre" (1579, 1611); "After a pear, wine or a priest" (1584, 1607, 1611, 1659); "Water after figs and wine after pear" (1659, 1666). Peaches, too, were sometimes included, and even that comparatively well-balanced fruit, the fig: "La pêche aime le vin"; "The peach will have wine, the fig water" (1573, 1577, 1629, 1659); "Al fico l'acqua ed alla pesca il vino." As for the melon, although it caused physicians more worry than any other fruit, we find no mention of it in proverbs before the sixteenth century, no doubt because it was a latecomer to non-Mediterranean regions.

By contrast, ancient proverbs warn against salad, which, like raw fruit, was believed to be cold and difficult to "cook": "De la salade et de la paillarde, si tu es sage donne t'en garde" (Meurier, 1578); "A good salad is the beginning of an ill supper" (1659, 1664, 1670, 1732); "Qui vin ne boit après salade est en risque d'être malade" (1578); "Qui vin ne boit après salade est en danger d'estre malade" (1579); "He that drink not wine after salad is in danger to be sick" (mentioned fourteen times between 1552 and 1755). To counter the coldness and moistness of salad, people relied on salt ("Salade, bien salée") and oil, which was thought to be hot like salt, rather than on vinegar: "Salade bien lavée et salée, peu de vinaigre et bien huilée."

Old cheese, deemed to be hot but heavy, was also thought difficult to digest. It was used as a kind of medicine to facilitate the digestion of other foods: "Cheese digests all things but itself" (1566, 1584). In this it was like the pear, and it was recommended that the two be eaten together: "Oncques Dieu ne fit tel mariage comme de poire et de fromage" (God made no better marriage than pear with cheese; thirteenth century). As much as the pear, if not more, cheese was thought to make a fitting end to a dinner: "After cheese comes nothing" (1623, 1639).

The third type of dangerous food was salted meat: "De chair salée, de fruit ni de fromage nul ne s'en fie tant soit prudent et sage." To be sure, salt improved cold meats such as beef and especially moist meats such as pork. But salted meats were blamed as a cause of scurvy and therefore regularly served with a seasoning believed to protect against scurvy—namely, mustard, as both proverbs and cookbooks attest: "De chair sallée sans moutarde/Libera nos Domine." "De plusieurs choses Dieu nous garde/de toute femme qui se farde/d'un serviteur qui se regarde/. . . et d'un boeuf salé sans moutarde" (sixteenth century).

Proverbs also warned against fish, which was believed to be cold and moist, like water ("Tout poisson est flegme"), and therefore dangerous: "Chair fait chair et poisson poison" (1578). If some ancient proverbs recommended not eating fish in months ending in *r* (as for oysters today), the reason was that fish were difficult to keep during the summer. But other sayings recommended eating fish only during the summer, probably because it was too "cold" a food for winter: "Si les mois sont errez, le poisson ne mangerez." "Poisson au soleil et chair à l'ombre." Since the peak month for fish was March, during Lent, these proverbs went unheeded, but they are nonetheless significant. Another reason why fish had to be well cooked, preferably by frying, was its "phlegmatic temperament," which also called for serving it with wine and following up with dried fruits: "Veau, poulets et poissons crus font les cimetières bossus." "Le poisson qui naît dans l'eau doit mourir dans l'huile." "Poisson, goret, cochon ou cochin, la vie en l'eau, la mort en vin." "Après poisson, noix est contre-poison" (1578). "Après poisson, noix en poids sont"—this meant, according to Gabriel Meurier, that walnuts were "esteemed and prized" after fish.

To sum up, cooking, then as now, was a matter of preparing foods so as to make them taste their best—but best in the terms of a particular culture whose taste differed from ours because it was shaped by different dietetic beliefs and culinary traditions. Because every flavor had a precise dietetic significance, anything that was done to enhance flavor also had implications for the digestibility of the food in question. Every cook might have his own style, just as artists and writers had theirs. But the cook exercised his creativity within the bounds of rules defined by the complementarity of temperaments and flavors, rules that were at once gastronomic and dietetic. We find the same duality today outside of Europe in many cultures with spicy cuisines, such as China and other countries of the Far East as well as in the Caribbean, where popular thinking about diet is directly inspired by the western medicine of yesteryear.

NOTES

1. See Marcel Détienne, *Les Jardins d'Adonis: La mythologie des aromates en Grèce* (Paris: Gallimard, 1972). [*The Gardens of Adonis: Spices in Greek Mythology,* trans. Janet Lloyd. Mythos: Princeton/Bollingen Series in World Mythology (Princeton, N.J.: Princeton University Press, 1994).]
2. J. Duchesne, *Le pourtraict de la santé.*
3. Magninus of Milan, *Regimen sanitatis.*

BIBLIOGRAPHY

Aldobrandino da Siena. *Le Régime du corps.* Ed. L. Landouzy and R. Pepin. Geneva: Slatkine, 1978.
Braudel, F. *Civilisation matérielle, économie et capitalisme, XVᵉ–XVIIIᵉ siècles.* Paris: A. Colin, 1967–79. [*Capitalism and Material Life, 1400–1800.* Trans. Miriam Kochan. New York: Harper and Row, 1973.]
Bruyerin, Jean Baptiste. *De re cibaria libri XXII omnium ciborum genera, omnium gentium moribus, et usu probata complectentes.* London, 1560.
Céard, J. "La Diététique dans la Médecine de la Renaissance." In *Pratiques et discours alimentaires à la Renaissance: Actes du colloque de Tours, mars 1979,* pp. 21–36. Paris: G.-P. Maissonneuve et Larose, 1982.
Duchesne, J. *Le pourtraict de la santé: Où est au vif représentée la règle universelle & particolière, de bien sainement & longuement vivre.* Saint-Omer, 1618.
Fagarola, P. *Regimen conditum.* In L. Thorndike, "Advice from a Physician to His Sons." *Speculum* 6 (1931): 110–14.
Grieco, A. J. "The Social Politics of Pre-Linnean Botanical Classification." *I Tatti Studies: Essays in the Renaissance,* no. 4 (1991): 131–49.
Jansen-Sieben, R. "From Food Therapy to Cookery-Book." In *Medieval Dutch Literature in Its European Context,* pp. 261–79. Cambridge: Cambridge University Press, 1994.

Laurioux, B. "Spices in the Medieval Diet: A New Approach." *Food and Foodways* 1 (1985): 43–76.

López, R. *The Trade of Medieval Europe, the South*. Cambridge Economic History of Europe. Cambridge: Cambridge University Press, 1952.

Magninus of Milan. *Opusculum de saporibus domini M. Mayni de Mayneriis*. In L. Thorndike, "A Medieval Sauce Book." *Speculum* 9 (1934): 183–98.

———. *Regimen sanitatis Magnini mediolanensis medici famosissimi*. London, 1517.

Miller, J. I. *The Spice Trade of the Roman Empire 29 B.C. to A.D. 641*. Oxford: Clarendon, 1969.

Patni, R. "L'assaisonnement dans la cuisine française entre le XIVe et le XVIe siècle." Thesis, Écoles des Hautes Études en Sciences Sociales, 1989.

Peterson, T. "The Arab Influence on Western European Cooking." *Journal of Medieval History* 6 (1980): 317–40.

Platina, Il (B. Sacchi). *De honesta voluptate*, Venice, 1475. [*De Honesta Voluptate: The First Dated Cookery Book*. Trans. Elizabeth Buermann Andrews. St. Louis: Mallinckrodt Chemical Works, 1967.]

Platine en françoys tresutile & necessaire pour le corps humain qui traicte de honneste volupté et de toutes viandes et choses. Ed. D. Christol. Lyons, 1505.

Riddle, J. M. "The Introduction and Use of Eastern Drugs in the Early Middle Ages." *Sudhoff Archiv* 49 (1965): 185–98.

Rodinson, M. "Recherches sur des documents arabes relatifs à la cuisine." *Revue des études islamiques* 17 (1949): 95–165.

Scully, T. "The Opusculum de saporibus of Magninus Mediolanensis." *Medium Ævum* 54 (1985): 178–207.

Stouff, L. *Ravitaillement et alimentation en Provence aux XIVe et XVe siècles*. Paris: Mouton, 1970.

Le Thresor de santé ou Mesnage de la vie humaine. Lyons, 1607.

Weiss-Amer, M. "The Role of Medieval Physicians in the Diffusion of Culinary Recipes and Cooking Practices." In *Du manuscrit à la table: Essais sur la cuisine au Moyen Age,* ed. C. Lambert, pp. 69–80. Montreal: Presses de l'Université de Montréal, 1992.

CHAPTER 26

"MIND YOUR MANNERS"
Etiquette at the Table

Daniela Romagnoli

Ethics and Etiquette

The history of good table manners is closely intertwined with that of manners in society as a whole. It is a history that concerns ethics and etiquette—that is, both internal moral values and the external formal aspect of people's relations with others. All societies have developed norms governing behavior among groups and individuals. The links between ethics and etiquette have thus existed everywhere and at all times, and the assonance between the two terms is more than a play on words; it reflects the inseparability of the two spheres. It is hard to imagine a code of good manners, however superficial it might be, that does not depend, albeit indirectly, on a series of moral choices. Of course, good manners, in themselves, are no guarantee of morality or civility, precisely because their role is simply to structure the conduct of social relations. But while manners alone cannot ensure genuine civility, a disorderly society that disregards all codes of behavior cannot consider itself civilized.

The table is the place for social relations par excellence. It is the point at which body and soul, matter and spirit, the external nature of etiquette and the internal nature of ethics meet. Table manners are thus underpinned by two concerns: the control of the body and its gestures, and the bridling of the soul and its motions.

The body is inevitably conditioned by its context. It may be required to sit at a table using cutlery, as is the norm in modern Western society. It may be expected to eat in a semireclining position or seated on rugs or cushions, using only the hands to eat or, more commonly, a single hand. The material surroundings dictate specific techniques for eating, which reach their most refined and codified levels at the banquet, the shared meal with the highest social or religious significance.

A Long Story

It is normal for us to talk about the "table." We commonly use such expressions as "sitting around the table" or "getting down from table." We have "table manners," "tablecloths," and "tableware"; we even have music specifically written to accompany banquets, as music written for the Renaissance courts testifies. For example, Adriano Banchieri (1568–1631) wrote a madrigal comedy called *Festino nella sera del Giovedì grasso avanti cena,* which was to be performed at mealtimes. But perhaps the best-known example was the *Tafelmusik* (table music) composed by Georg Philipp Telemann in 1732–1733. This term is important because it gave rise to a serious misunderstanding: the term "table music" did not mean that it was to be performed as mealtime entertainment but that it was written for "table" instruments—that is, instruments that musicians could play sitting around a table. The term thus referred to an early form of chamber music. The widespread misunderstanding is significant because it shows how natural the idea of music during meals was at the time.

Other societies had and still have different customs. In Western culture today, there are many social occasions that do not necessarily take place at the table. These occasions certainly cannot be called "banquets," nor can they be referred to with the less momentous terms "lunch" and "dinner." They often revolve around drink rather than food (a cocktail party, for example) or involve eating informally and hurriedly, perhaps with a plate balanced on the knee and a glass in the hand. Events of this kind express a different form of sociality. They neither envisage nor allow the calm exchange of views that takes place at a genuine banquet, in which the centrality of the table helps to create the mood of mutual serenity and receptiveness. The complex codes governing good table manners—elaborated through the centuries and handed down from generation to generation, adapting to changing lifestyles and dominant social groups—could never have developed in a fast food culture.

For roughly one thousand years, at banquets in the ancient Greek and Roman worlds as well as in the whole of the Mediterranean East, people ate while reclining on specially made couches. In ancient Greece they leaned on their right elbows, and each couch (*kline*) had its own table. In ancient Rome the couches were arranged in a special room (*triclinium*) around a central table on which the food was placed. The reclining position was a princely privilege and was reserved for the upper strata of rich societies. Jews, who traditionally ate seated, gradually adapted to the customs of their neighbors, the Syrians—the Last Supper, in fact, probably took place in a room very like a Roman *triclinium*. The reclining position made it impossible to use both hands to maneuver cutlery, such as knives. It was perfectly compatible, however, with the habit of eating food with the fingers of one hand.

When the Roman Empire split into east and west, each to follow its own destiny, the way of life in the western regions changed radically, transforming the style of banquets with it. Guests now sat around a table. In the New World—born from the transformation of the empire, with the contribution of a vast influx of "barbarians," who began to settle in western Europe from the fourth and fifth centuries on, and with the strong imprint of the church—a division of roles gradually took place. A military aristocracy almost completely took over from the old Roman aristocracy, while culture slowly became the almost exclusive domain of the church and was used to interpret and disseminate the word of God. The church played an important role in civilizing the warrior-cavalry class by polishing its rough manners. So-called courtly literature, in particular romance—which flourished from the twelfth century on as feudal dynasties multiplied—offered a model of behavior perfectly suited to that world. The concept of "courtesy" (a way to behave at court) was born, together with that of *urbanitas* (urbanity) and *civilitas* (civility). The latter two concepts have a long and complex history. They were already used in classical times, and they interest us here for their inextricable link with the city (*urbs*, *civitas*). At the other end of the scale, the concepts of *vilainie* (villainy, from the Latin *villa*) and *rusticitas* (rusticity) were associated with the countryside (from the Latin *rus*) and with uncultured peasant behavior.

As far as the table was concerned, courtly literature stressed the importance of being hospitable, by means of banquets, among other things. It described the entertainment that could be laid on for the pleasure of guests as well as the beauty of the tableware, clothes, and people involved. It described the quantity and quality of food being served, which was exhibited as a status symbol. The abundance and richness of the food offered was associated with the capacity to eat and drink vast quantities—with the result that prodigality and excess were transformed into positive qualities.

Early Normative Documents

Numerous normative texts devoted to good manners began to appear at the beginning of the twelfth century. Of course, good table manners played an important part. The earliest texts were written in Latin, but they were soon followed by translations or by works written directly in the various vulgar tongues (German, French, Italian, Catalan, and so on). Some of these tracts achieved lasting success and reached an incredibly wide audience—far beyond their initial geographic or social spheres—even playing an essential role in establishing the rules of civil society; so good manners became vital to the complete education of a model citizen.

> . . . a tavola che s'è, lassass servì,
> no fa l'ingord, no slongà i man suj tond,
> no sbatt la bocca, no desgangheralla,
> no metess a parlà denanz vojalla.
>
> Tegnì giò i gombet, no fa pan moin,
> no rugass in di dent cont i cortij,
> no sugass el sudor cont el mantin,
> infin, nissuna affatt di porcarij
> che hin tant fazil lor sciori a lassà corr,
> come se el mond el fuss tutt so de lor.

(At table, wait to be served, do not be greedy, do not stretch out your hands toward the serving dish, do not lick your lips, do not open your mouth too wide, do not speak before you have emptied it. Keep your elbows down, do not dip your bread in your wine, do not pick your teeth with a knife, do not dry off your sweat with your napkin—in short do not do any of those things that lords are allowed to do, as if they were the lords of the earth.)

An early-nineteenth-century Milanese poet, Carlo Porta, thus lists the most elementary rules of good table manners. But he presents them as the words of a butler addressing a group of poor folks who aspire to the position of private chaplain (a position that was much sought after because it guaranteed regular and plentiful meals). The butler advises the peasants on the basic rules for living in the house of a marchesa. Porta's verses seem to echo norms established more than five hundred years earlier. The difference, however, lies in the fact that these norms were originally developed to train adults and children—primarily of the upper classes—in the difficult art of social relations. In Porta's time, these rules were so widely accepted that only the very poor, who had had no access to polite society, needed to be instructed in them. At the same time, however, they formed part of every child's education.

Normative Tradition and the "Civilizing Process"

Although many norms have retained their validity, it should be noted that many others have languished with changes in the lifestyles and attitudes of social groups. This process—referred to by the sociologist Norbert Elias as "the civilizing process"—took centuries, evolving differently in varied political and social contexts in western Europe. A significant example of the length of time this process could take is provided by the history of the fork, which arrived in the West from Byzantium in the eleventh century. In the fourteenth century it was used in Italian cities as both a serving and an eating utensil. At the beginning of the seventeenth century—according to the account of an English traveler in Italy—forks were made from gold and silver as well as from humbler materials such as wood and tin, evidence of their diffusion and daily use among the middle classes. In the same period, however, the use of forks provoked a sarcastic reaction in England; even by the end of the century, at the court of Louise XIV of France, the fork had still not been fully accepted.

The history of good table manners is marked by the gradual abandonment of both indiscriminate behavior and openly exhibited physicality. From the norms dictated in the twelfth century to the enormously influential handbooks produced in the sixteenth century—such as *De civilitate morum querilium,* a tract on bringing up children by Erasmus of Rotterdam, or *Galateo,* written by Giovanni della Casa—the same prohibitions are constantly repeated: do not blow your nose at table, do not spit in your plate, do not put chewed bones or food that has been tasted back on your plate.

Indiscriminate Behavior

When the first texts on table etiquette appeared, tableware, with the exception of knives, was not intended for individual use. People did not have their own plates and glasses; food was placed on a board, or even a large piece of bread, that was usually shared by two diners. Similarly, houses did not devote specific areas exclusively to eating. In manors and castles, the only separation between public and private space was that between the bedroom and the hall, where all daily activities were carried out. Space was precious and, in such a sparsely furnished environment, there was no room for a fixed dining table. Boards were laid on trestles when needed, a practice that gave rise to the expression "to set the table." Going down the social scale, the absence of differentiated space and the promiscuity of living conditions went as far as the sleeping arrangements. Beds were rarely intended for individuals or couples, but were used by parents and children, brothers and sisters, regardless of gender. Even worse, from a modern viewpoint, the same rules applied in public places, such as inns.

As the table boards had no intrinsic value, clean tablecloths were used to cover them, reaching the ground. By the end of the meal they must have looked like a battlefield. It is no surprise, then, that people were constantly invited not to dirty the cloth more than necessary. Napkins were introduced to save the tablecloth, which was harder to clean. Della Casa expressed contempt for people who reduced the tablecloth to a state in which "latrine cloths were cleaner." A host who was worthy of the name should offer water for washing hands at the beginning and end of the meal, changing napkins at least once. Although the practice of washing one's hands at the end of the meal was obviously a necessity, washing before the meal might have been more than symbolic. In the first half of the fourteenth century, Francesco da Barberino suggested that the bride of a king should come to the wedding banquet with her hands already washed so as not to dirty the water that was offered. This suggests that clean hands were not the rule but the exception.

A fixed table, usually accompanied by a sideboard, was gradually introduced, starting with the wealthier houses of the great Italian and Flemish merchants. It won a place in the all-purpose living room, which began to be divided into specific areas.

The increasingly influential concept of privacy—perhaps more bourgeois than aristocratic—produced profound social changes, culminating in the middle of the nineteenth century in Victorian England with greater segmentation of domestic space. Some rooms were thus reserved for private use; others, like the drawing room and, at times, the dining room, were devoted to social occasions. The only examples of this kind of specialization during the medieval courtly period could be found in monasteries. Conceived as terrestrial images of Jerusalem, they were themselves cities, bustling with activity and allotting space to each function. Alongside the parlor, the dormitory, and the scriptorium was the refectory, reserved for the monks' meals.

This transition from a movable table in a large communal hall to the fixed table in a bourgeois dining room is reflected by a gradual proliferation of increasingly specialized tableware, mainly for individual use. The most obvious examples are cutlery (for fish, meat, fruit, desserts, etc.) and glasses (for water, white wine, red wine, dessert wine, aperitifs, spirits, and even different types of spirits such as whisky and cognac). This inevitably led to a proliferation of norms and a prevalence of etiquette over ethics, of *savoir faire* over *savoir vivre*.

Good manners in general, and good table manners in particular, were not limited to notions of mere physical decorum to legislate the ability to discern and adapt to different circumstances (times, places, people) and to practice self-awareness, self-control, and restraint. References to these abilities were already clear in some twelfth-century texts produced by ecclesiastical and lay writers.

Controlling the Body

From the numerous texts devoted to table manners, let us look at one of the most significant and long-lasting medieval examples: *Da quinquaginta curialitatibus ad mansam* (The Fifty Rules of Table Courtesy) by Bonvesin de la Riva, still used three centuries later in the version adapted by Giulio Cesare Croce (*Cinquanta cortesie overo creanze da tavola*). At the time of its composition in the thirteenth century, Italian city-states were at the height of their glory, and lords and artisans, aristocrats and the middle classes, typically coexisted. This was also the period in which norms of social behavior proliferated throughout most of western Europe. Not surprisingly, works by contemporaries of Bonvesin dealt with similar issues in other countries. Examples include the German text known as *Tannhäuser* and, a century later, the writings of the Catalan priest Francesco Eiximenis, who was keenly interested in table manners.

Born in Milan, Bonvesino (c. 1240–1314) was a *magister gramaticae,* or Latin teacher. Although the religious tone of his precepts are clear (before sitting down, think of the poor, because he who feeds a poor man feeds the Lord; at the end of the meal, thank Jesus Christ for what you have received), ethics is not his main concern. The aim of the work is clearly to dictate norms that instill a full awareness of the meaning and social value of eating together: the ability to control the motions of the soul and their external manifestations as gestures and words.

Inevitably, it is through physical acts of serving oneself, lifting food to the mouth, chewing, cutting, offering, and receiving that the relationship with food and drink is expressed. Norms governing speech were another way of regulating the social aspect of eating: do not speak with your mouth full; do not ask questions when someone is drinking; do not disturb others at table with useless or unpleasant noises or with incessant or irritating chatter. Above all, certain subjects should not be broached during meal times:

> Tanfin ke i oltri mangiano, no di' nove angoxose
> ma tax on di' parolle ke sian confortose

(Do not refer to upsetting things while people are eating, but keep quiet or use comforting words.)

There is no room at table for sadness, suffering, disgust, coarseness, vulgarity, or incivility. In other words, *guarda no sii vilan* (mind your manners):

> sta' conzamente al desco
> cortes, adorno, alegro e confortoso e fresco

(Behave correctly at table: courteous, elegant, cheerful, and lighthearted.)

As Giovanni Della Casa was to say in the middle of the sixteenth century, the table should be a place "of merriment and not of scandal." Respect for other people's sensibilities is present in all fifty of Bonvesin's rules of courtesy.

"Disgust" is a recurrent term in these works. The glutton who gulps his drink before having swallowed his food disgusts his drinking partners; the person who grabs food from the table "is ugly and disgusts his fellow diners"; he who dips too much bread into his soup "can cause disgust" in his neighbor. A polite man should not stroke cats or dogs, which appear in numerous paintings and miniatures where they are portrayed not only under the table but actually sitting on it during meals. Coughs and sneezes that spray saliva over the table should be avoided. By the same token, there are prescriptions designed to guarantee the diner's deportment: no slouching, no leaning, no crossing of legs, no elbows on the table. Even the precepts that constantly stress the need for personal cleanliness, both in serving and in eating, reflect the same disgust for vulgar, unseemly conduct—do not dip your bread in wine if someone is drinking from the same glass; if you pick your teeth with your fingers, you will not be welcome at the table.

Respect for fellow diners is frequently expressed and applied to a variety of circumstances—offer the tastiest morsels when your good friend eats at your table; do not complain about the food being offered by saying that it is badly cooked or too salty; hide any "fly or dirt" found in the food. The exercise of self-control goes so far as to disguise pain or discomfort and to avoid saddening fellow diners. Finally, as an example of extreme delicacy, every effort should be made by the host to eat as much as the guest, to put him at his ease, and to encourage him not to stop eating until he is full.

The Presence of Women

Women were also present at the bourgeois table of Bonvesin. Their participation, which had an important role in the banquets of courtly society, remained significant. In numerous works dedicated to women in the thirteenth and fourteenth centuries, especially in urban bourgeois and mercantile circles, women lost their role as "queens of the feast" to become "queens of the house." When present at table, women were treated with courtesy and deference (for example, it was the man's job to carve the meat and offer the woman the best cuts). However, this did not mean that they were excused from respecting the rules of etiquette. According to Bonvesin, any man or woman who sucks noisily from the spoon behaves like an animal at the trough.

Francesco da Barberino, who also compiled rules of behavior for both men and women, asked the former to treat the latter with discretion in order not to upset their "natural" bashfulness: "Be sure that you are not immoderate with them. . . . Do not look them in the face, especially when they are eating, because they might be ashamed."

A few decades later, Eiximenis, the author of a long treatise that provided a portrait of feminine virtue, described the perfect wife as a wise administrator, thrifty, and a skilled housekeeper: "*la casa ès perduda si la dona no retèn*" (the house is lost if the woman does not save). At the same time, however, she must be a generous and, above all, cheerful hostess, since no feast, however abundant, can succeed "*si la dona fa cara trista*" (if the woman has a long face).

Prodigality

Clearly, the quantity and quality of food has more to do with ethics than etiquette. Handbooks of manners have always been against excess in its various forms, from greed to fussiness. As usual, however, the boundaries are not clear-cut. A thirteenth-century author known as the Anonimo Veronese explains in his *Insegnamenti a Guglielmo* (Teachings for William) that eating too much is unbecoming, not on a moral plane, but because it suggests a constantly unsatisfied need for food more associated with the poor than with the wealthy.

Hands or cutlery? Complicated rituals or simple tastes and ways? The choices that societies make are linked not so much to a presumed high or low level of civility as to the greater or lesser complexity of their structures. Such codes of behavior serve to differentiate social groups and to allow an individual to emerge from the mass (as the term "distinguished" clearly expresses). However, they also act as an indispensable tool for communication, for that continuous process of mediation that is human coexistence.

Alberti, L. B. *I libri della famiglia*. Turin: Giulio Einaudi, 1969. [*The Family in Renaissance Florence*. Trans. Renée Neu Watkins. Columbia: University of South Carolina Press, 1969.]

Aresty, E. B. *The Best Behavior: The Course of Good Manners—from Antiquity to the Present—as Seen through Courtesy and Etiquette Books*. New York: Simon and Schuster, 1970.

Bertelli, S., and G. Crifi, eds. *Rituale, cerimoniale, etichetta*. Milan: Bompiani, 1985.

Biadene, L. *Cortesie da tavola in latino e in provenzale*. Pisa, 1893.

Brunet, J., and O. Redon, trans. *Tables florentines: Écrire et manger avec Franco Sacchetti*. Paris: Stock, 1984.

Certaldo, Paolo di Pace da. *Libro di buoni costumi*. Ed. A. Schiaffini. Florence: F. Le Monnier, 1945.

Contini, G., ed. *Le opere volgari di Bonvesin de la Riva*. Rome: Presso La Società, 1941.

———. *Poeti del Duecento*. 2 vols. Milan: R. Ricciardi, 1960.

Croce, G. C. *Cinquanta cortesie overo creanze da tavola*. Bologna, 1609.

Della Casa, G. *Galateo*. Turin, 1975.

Elias, N. *Über den prozess der Zivilisation. Soziogenetische und psychogenetische Untersuchungen*. Vol. 1, *Wandlungen des Verhaltens in den weltlichen Oberschichten des Abendlandes*. Basel: Haus zum Falken, 1939. [*The History of Manners*. Trans. Edmund Jephcott. The Civilizing Process, vol. 1. New York: Pantheon Books, 1982.]

Eiximenis, Francesco. *Dotzé libre del Crestià*. Vol. 2. Ed. C. Wittlin et al. Girona: Collegi Universitari de Girona, 1986.

———. *Lo libre de les dones*. 2 vols. Ed. F. Naccarato. Barcelona: Curial Edicions Catalanes, 1981.

Francesco da Barberino. *Documenti d'amore*. 3 vols. Ed. F. Egidi. Documenti di Storia Letteraria, no. 3. Rome: Presso la Società, 1905.

———. *Reggimento e costumi di donna*. Ed. G. E. Sansone. Collezione di Filologia Romanza, no. 2. Turin: Loescher-Chiantore, 1957.

Franklin, A. *La civilité, l'étiquette, la mode, le bon ton, du XIIIᵉ au XIXᵉ siècle*. 2 vols. Paris: Emile-Paul, 1908.

———. *Les repas. La vie privée d'autrefois: Arts et métiers, modes, moeurs, usages des Parisiens, du XIIème au XVIIIème siècles, d'après des documents originaux ou inédits*. Paris: Plon, Nourrit, 1894.

Furnivall, F. J. *The Babees Book*. Early English Text Society, no. 32 (o.s.). London: N. Trübner & Co., 1868.

Glixelli, S. "Les contenances de table." *Romania* 47 (1921): 1–40.

Jaeger, C. S. *The Origins of Courtliness: Civilizing Trends and the Formation of Courtly Ideals, 932–1210*. Philadelphia: University of Pennsylvania Press, 1985.

Le Goff, J., and M. Lauwers. "La civilisation occidentale." In *Histoire des Moeurs*, vol. 3, *Thèmes et systèmes culturels, Encyclopédie de la Pléiade*. Paris: Gallimard, 1989–91.

Lévi-Strauss, C. *L'origine des manières de table*. Mythologiques 3. Paris: Plon, 1968. [*The Origin of Table Manners*. Trans. John and Doreen Weightman. Chicago: University of Chicago Press, 1990.]

Merker, P. "Die Tiszuchtenliteratur des 12 bis 16 Jahrhunderts." In *Mitteilungen der Deutschen Gesellschaft zur Erforschung Vaterländischer Sprache und Altertümer in Leipzig*. I, 1:1–52. 1913.

Petrus Alphonsi. *Disciplina clericalis*. Sammlung Mittellateinische Texte, vol. 1. Heidelberg: C. Winter, 1911.

Romagnoli, D., ed. *La città e la corte: Buone e cattive maniere tra Medioevo ed Età Moderna*. Milan: Guerini, 1991.

Ugo di San Vittore. *De institutione novitiorum*. In ed. P. Migne. *Patrologiae Cursus Completus: Series Latina,* vol. 176. Paris, 1878–1904.

Vincent de Beauvais. *De eruditione filiorum nobilium*. Cambridge, Mass., 1938.

CHAPTER 27

From HEARTH *to* TABLE

Late Medieval Cooking Equipment

Françoise Piponnier

Archaeologists excavating Mediterranean villages have discovered a small number of outdoor hearths. Generally, however, each cottage contained a single indoor hearth, usually situated on the packed-earth floor itself, much like the hearths found at prehistoric sites, although the dwellings themselves were of course much more substantial than any prehistoric shelter. In virtually every case the hearth was open rather than closed. Virtually no medieval cottage contained a fireplace.

Some cottages had more elaborate hearths, which were designed to confine the fire within a well-defined area. These might be dug down into the earth or raised slightly above it, or they might be lined with stones or bricks set on edge atop stone or clay tiles or with bits of flagstone driven into the ground at an angle. Peasant hearths were generally small. In the Burgundian village of Dracy, even the largest were barely more than sixty centimeters (less than two feet) on a side. The hearth was nearly always placed against a wall and close to a door.

The nearby home of a minor nobleman, also unearthed by archaeologists, demonstrates the stark contrast between the life of the peasant and that of his lord. It contained a large rectangular hearth nearly two meters (more than six and a half feet) on a side. Lined with bricks, this hearth was located in the center of a room whose packed-earth floor still bears traces of several smaller hearths. The house also included a number of other rooms, at least one of which was equipped with a relatively small fireplace. In this comparatively lavish dwelling, the chore of cooking evidently merited a room of its own. By contrast, in most rural and some urban homes, the room containing the hearth was the only room in the house. Other spaces might exist under the same roof, alongside or above this single room, but these were used for storage or as shelters for animals. In town, fireplaces were more common, but their presence in rooms identified as bedrooms suggests that they were used exclusively for heating.

In the north of France the *four banal,* or communal oven, was still the rule in the countryside, although certain Burgundian charters granted peasants the right to build small ovens for baking pastry. In town the homes of the wealthiest citizens contained ovens of their own, but most townsfolk took their homemade dough to professional bakers or purchased their bread and pastry already made.

To be sure, rural hearths were less well equipped than urban fireplaces, but their equipment was less rudimentary than their quite primitive construction might suggest. Estate inventories list many objects that archaeologists rarely come across. Although iron tripods were ubiquitous, trammels were still rare in rural Burgundy in the fourteenth century, although more common in towns. Some trammels came with iron rings to hold earthenware cooking pots with the aid of chains looped around handles designed expressly for the purpose. Andirons were apparently used only in fireplaces, never in open hearths, as were heavy firedogs and bellows, which were, in any case, quite rare. Servants and housewives must have been quite skillful at managing fires without special tools, because iron shovels and picks were uncommon.

Even when equipped with a tripod or slightly elevated, hearths were set low to the ground, forcing those who used them to bend or crouch in ways that modern kitchens have made us forget. Cooks tended their fires and pots from a squatting position or perhaps seated on a low stool.

Cooking Utensils

The most common archaeological find—ceramic cookware—is rarely mentioned in textual sources, but it does appear often enough to suggest that it was used by people of all stations for simmering vegetables and making soup. Findings from the most comprehensive archaeological sites suggest that cooking pots were frequently acquired in pairs of similar type but different capacity. Round pots were used both for cooking and storing such commodities as grain, dried vegetables, eggs, and lard. Round pots equipped with beaks for pouring were used not for cooking but for transporting liquids, especially water. Earthenware pots were much more fragile than metal cookware and required frequent replacement. Although it is common to find fragments of such pots, it does not follow that boiled foods dominated the medieval diet.

Surviving inventories indicate that rural homes in fourteenth-century Tuscany as well as Burgundy often contained metal utensils. Iron skillets were the most common, along with copper pots and kettles. Excavation has turned up a wide variety of containers and fragments of containers ranging from simple pots made from a single sheet of copper to heavy cauldrons of molded bronze embellished with decorative motifs. Some documents indicate that the latter may have been made of the same alloys used to make bells. Hence many households had the ability to fry, fricassee, and braise. Porridge for children and probably also for the sick was cooked in saucepans.

By contrast, such grills and spits as have been found were almost exclusively in the homes of the well-to-do, whether in town or in castles and fortified dwellings in the countryside. Some spits had mechanisms for rotating them. Spatter pans of copper or glazed tile were placed under the roast to collect the drippings. Roasting was apparently reserved for substantial cuts of good-quality meat. A boiling pot would have been located nearby, for we know from various culinary treatises that meat was frequently boiled before roasting.

Pastry-making was mainly left to professionals. Nevertheless, we do find molds for pâtés, tarts, and flans in private homes. Only professionals and the wealthiest private kitchens possessed waffle irons and griddles. The numerous waffle recipes contained in medieval cookbooks suggest that waffles were a savory pastry often made with cheese. This probably accounts for the cheese graters found at a few sites.

The cookbooks also tell us that grills were used for toasting bread, which often served as a binder for sauces. The mortar was an essential implement for crushing the various ingredients that went into these sauces. Mortars, found nearly everywhere, came in many sizes and were fabricated out of many different materials. Those used for grinding mustard seeds resembled millstones. A well-equipped kitchen would have boasted several. The inventories, not very helpful on this score, tell us that these were made of "milling stone." The precise type of stone employed probably varied with the intended use. Pieces of some very crude mortars have been found in the village of Dracy. These may be fragments of homemade implements or scraps from partly finished items that the craftsman for one reason or another rejected as unsuitable. They bear only a faint resemblance to the artfully shaped receptacles we find elsewhere, equipped with beaks for pouring, pivots, and even decorative motifs. Only apothecaries possessed the large bronze mortars with iron pestles that were designed for crushing spices. By contrast, turned wooden mortars with wooden pestles were ubiquitous, even in homes where it is unlikely that much use was made of spices. Here these implements served to prepare seasonings from local ingredients such as vinegar, cider, and aromatic herbs.

Wherever heat-resistant containers were not required, wood played a substantial and often underestimated role in the preparation and preservation of food. It was used for salt cellars and salting tubs, vinegar bottles, water pails, kneading boards, sieves, cookie cutters, cheese boxes, oven paddles, pot covers, bowls, ladles, and stirring spoons. From excavations in damp regions where wooden objects were able to survive for long periods, we know that many different species of wood were used. Both buyers and sellers had their preferences for one kind of wood over another: for some purposes hardwoods were better than soft, or an artisan might prefer to work with wood that was easy to split or rip. It is scarcely imaginable, moreover, that in the eyes of their owners wooden objects did not take on some of the symbolic attributes of the trees from which their wood was derived.

Metal implements, more commonly included in inventories than wooden ones, were good for putting the finishing touches on many dishes. The range of implements suggests the range of dishes prepared. Sauces and soups were strained through tin strainers. Boiled and fried foods were drained with perforated spoons. Pieces of meat were snagged with iron meat hooks. Boiled foods and sauces were scraped from saucepans with copper spoons. Such diverse implements suggest a wide variety of cooking methods involving relatively large pots and pans made of metal, since metal spoons and hooks could easily crack earthenware vessels. Furthermore, many earthenware pots had fairly small openings, too small to admit the large implements that archaeologists have turned up.

Where Did People Eat?

Burgundian cottage inventories do not indicate how the various items listed were distributed around the house. Archaeologists, however, have unearthed a number of burned dwellings, and their findings tell us something about how living space was apportioned.

The main room, containing the main entrance to the home, generally had a hearth located next to the door as well as a sleeping area (indicated in the excavations by the presence of charred textiles). A few animal bones are the only sign that meals may also have been eaten in the main room.

Off this main room was usually a pantry containing a substantial number of earthenware pots, along with iron-ringed wooden containers, copper cups, pewterware, a stock of beans, and probably wine in barrels. A second storage area, which normally did not communicate with the main room of the house, held the family's most precious possessions: large cooking pots, engraved copper drinking cups, and perhaps some pewter.

More detailed inventories of urban dwellings suggest a similar arrangement: the main room, which contained the hearth, was generally not the only place where food was stored, prepared, and eaten. Wine, whether for sale or home consumption, was kept cellared. So were salted meats and fish, whereas dried meats were often kept in the attic, along with salt, cheese, and a small keg for aging vinegar. Only small quantities of dried vegetables, flour, and lard were kept in the kitchen. It was not unusual for oil and grain to be stored in a bedroom.

Cooking utensils were often distributed around the house in a similar fashion, especially in spacious dwellings amply equipped with various kinds of implements. Items in daily use were kept in the kitchen: ropes, iron-ringed buckets, and copper ladles for fetching water from the well, equipment for the hearth, and a few pots, pans, and kettles for cooking, along with perhaps a spit for roasting. Other utensils were scattered around the house, from the cellar to the attic to the various recesses of the barnyard or courtyard, waiting for an unusual occasion to serve a particularly fancy meal or out-of-the-ordinary dish.

Households large enough to have an oven of their own sometimes had a special room, as in a bakery, for sifting grain and kneading dough. More often there was a breadboard in the kitchen, along with oven paddles and other equipment for making bread. Kitchens rarely contained cabinets for storing utensils. The only storage facilities mentioned with any regularity in the inventories are shelves "for storing pots." By contrast, trestle tables and "buffets" that served as small individual tables appear frequently in urban inventories. If no such furniture is mentioned, we must assume that meals were taken in the kitchen, especially in the smaller homes of the poor. Even in homes large enough to have a "dining room" equipped with its own table and chairs, one has to remember that the servants did not dine with their masters and spent much of their time in the kitchen.

Finally, in some urban homes tables and chairs were stored in the attic, courtyard, or cellar and set up as needed inside or outside for special occasions. Trestle tables were easily moved and could quickly be set up against a wall in a space normally used for other purposes.

Levels of Dining

In noble households it was traditional to have a servant pour water over one's hands before dining. This tradition accounts for the presence of pitchers and basins as part of every aristocratic establishment's household equipment. In the fifteenth century buckets with beaks were hung in a convenient location in well-to-do urban households for the same purpose. Such amenities remained rare among the other social classes, however. Peasants, laborers, and artisans had to make do with crude washtubs for their comparatively brief preprandial ablutions.

Dinner seating naturally depended on whether one was taking one's meal in a vast seignorial dining hall, a bourgeois dining room, or a single-room peasant dwelling. In a château or wealthy urban home, a trestle table might be set up close to a fireplace so that honored guests could be seated with their backs to the fire, either on chairs with high backs and armrests or on comfortable benches equipped with backrests and pivoting seats that could be swiveled around to face the fire. Benches without backrests were provided for the less important guests. When the number of diners was small, the trestle table might be replaced by a four-legged table. Widespread in southern Europe, tables of this type became increasingly common in northern France over the course of the fifteenth century.

Among the peasantry and the urban lower class, tables were a rarity, as were lamps, candles, and other sources of light. Depending on the season, meals were probably taken either close to the glowing coals of the fire or near the door, which was often the only source of natural light and ventilation. Where inventories do not mention a table, many sources indicate that meals were eaten on a small bench or "buffet." Obviously not everyone could be seated around such a small surface, and in many homes there was only one dinner chair, reserved for the master of the household or an honored guest. Others sat on low stools or other, less comfortable seating, perhaps nothing more elaborate than a pile of straw.

In the late Middle Ages, table linen was still a costly luxury. Although many peasant families owned a tablecloth, it was not for daily use. A relatively wealthy townsman might have a hemp tablecloth for everyday use and a linen one with a woven or embroidered pattern for more festive occasions. A townsman of more modest means might make do with a serviette both to cover the small buffet on which he placed his dinner in lieu of a table and to wipe his hands, as the rich man wiped his hands on the tablecloth.

From written sources we know that even in peasant households each diner had his or her own dishes and utensils. Forks were still unknown, but knives with handles of carved wood or bone turn up frequently in excavations. These were indispensable for slicing bread, which was the main staple. If there was a quarrel, the table knife all too readily became a weapon. Wooden spoons with handles shorter than the spoons used in the kitchen also turn up frequently at certain excavation sites. There was even a wooden spoon in the meager baggage of one Burgundian beggar whose contents we happen to know, and there is reason to believe that wooden spoons and dishes were more common than the inventories suggest.

Throughout the Middle Ages the typical dinner setting in Burgundy as well as in central and northern Europe consisted of articles made of wood or metal. Along the Mediterranean, however, terra-cotta, porcelain, and glass were common at all levels of society.

Although drinking vessels came in a bewildering variety, Burgundians probably drank directly from the glazed earthenware and pewter pitchers that figured among their possessions. Indeed, in the region around Dijon these items turn up in such great numbers in the inventories of well-to-do households, often together with *cimarres,* or large bottles for serving wine, that we are justified in assuming that people drank from them. In any case, peasants took drink to the fields in earthenware flagons. Urban travelers preferred leather-encased tin "bottles." Because people drank in so many different settings, drinking vessels came in many shapes and size. This profusion reminds us of the importance attached to drinking as both a daily custom and a festive ritual.

Serving dishes also came in many shapes and sizes. These generally matched the other dinnerware, being made of pewter in wealthier homes and of wood in more modest households. One wealthy woman from Dijon owned an unusual dish made of "clay of Damascus." We cannot tell from this description whether this was an imported dish or one that imitated oriental ceramics, a fairly common commodity in the Mediterranean region in the fifteenth century. Even more modest materials were sometimes decorated: one isolated source mentions a serving dish with an ornamental pattern "in red paint." Little is known about the precise shape of these wooden serving dishes. No doubt they were quite similar to the ceramic dishes in use in the Mediterranean countries, which resembled a very shallow cup atop a circular base.

On aristocratic tables one was apt to find not only dishes and drinking cups but elaborate accessories designed to resemble ships and castles. Bourgeois diners settled for simpler settings, often including a salt cellar, sauce boat, and pewter pots and dishes. Social differences were reflected in table settings even more than in kitchen equipment. Both the quantity and quality of table articles varied widely.

From chroniclers' accounts we know a great deal about princely feasts, at which music and entertainment vied with unique and delectable dishes for the attention of the pampered guests. Cookbooks reveal the secrets of aristocratic and bourgeois kitchens and how they were equipped and used. We are far less well informed about the cooking and eating habits of the less privileged, however. From the so-called Bourgeois de Paris, who compiled a compendium of advice for his young wife, we learn what implements were required to prepare certain dishes and what it took to serve a multicourse banquet. The sources that tell us about more modest households, such as wills and estate inventories, are generally little more than lists of kitchen implements and tableware, leaving everything else to the imagination.

Nevertheless, such sources abound, and when we combine the meager information they contain with the results of archaeological investigation, it is sometimes possible to gain new insight into the eating habits of vast sectors of the medieval population. The medieval kitchen may have been rudimentary, but its relatively simple equipment lent itself to a variety of uses. Hierarchies were strict, even within the home, and meals were simple—though perhaps not quite as frugal as we sometimes think. Dinner was served close to the hearth, sometimes on a table, sometimes not. For soup there would have been a wooden bowl and a spoon. For cutting bread, the main staple, there would have been a knife. And for water and wine perhaps a couple of pitchers and some cups. What emerges from archaeological research, then, is not the swashbuckling Middle Ages of Hollywood romance perhaps, but neither was it the age of wretched, barely human misery that we sometimes imagine.

PART SIX

The EUROPE of NATION-STATES
(15TH—18TH CENTURIES)

DAVID TENIERS THE YOUNGER, *The Five Senses,* 1640–1650, Musée d'art ancien, Brussels. Allegory and bourgeois genre scenes were often combined, as in this depiction that is primarily concerned with customs and manners and also strongly evokes the human senses. (COL. HANFSTAENGL–GIRAUDON)

VINCENZO CAMPO, *Fruit Merchant,* around 1580, Pinacoteca di Brera, Milan.

In the foreground fruits are being divided by type into containers used for transportation, storage, and table display. An earlier moment, the picking of fruit, is shown in the left background. (COL. ALINARI-GIRAUDON)

PIETER CORNELISZ VAN RYCK, *The Cook,*
around 1628, Museum voor Schone Kunsten, Ghent.

The foodstuffs—meat and fish, vegetables and fruits—are displayed in no clear order on a table. These and the dressed carcasses hanging behind suggest a variety and abundance that the cook, who looks directly at the viewer, seems to be demonstrating. (COL. GIRAUDON)

REMBRANDT, *The Flayed Ox,*
1655, Musée du Louvre, Paris.

Rembrandt uses foreshortening in his portrayal of the skinned animal, which occupies the center of the painting. The trajectory of the forward protrusion of the carcass is echoed in the silhouette of the barely sketched cook. The light that falls on the carcass creates a dramatically intense form. (COL. GIRAUDON)

DIEGO VELÁZQUEZ. *Kitchen Scene with Christ in the Home of Mary and Martha,* 1618, National Gallery, London.

Velázquez inserts a sacred scene into a genre scene. By means of these two highly synthetic views the artist represents the dialectic themes of "the active life"—the women tending to household tasks—and "the contemplative life"—the women listening to words of salvation. (COL. GIRAUDON)

LOUIS LE NAIN, *Rustic Meal,* 1642, Musée du Louvre, Paris.

This depiction of a "humble" meal takes us back to the traditional values of spontaneity, moderation, and equilibrium that an advanced, artificial society has nearly lost. Themes of admonition and nostalgia blend in this celebration of honest sentiments. (COL. LAUROS-GIRAUDON)

LUIS PARET Y ALCAZAR, *Charles III de Bourbon, King of Spain, Lunching While His Court Looks On*, around 1778, Museo del Prado, Madrid.

The grand ceremony is the ultimate form of the meal. The art decorating the walls represents timeless allegories, and the cortege of courtiers provides the decorum appropriate to the meal of the sovereign, who, curiously, is the only person seated at the table amidst this imposing crowd. (COL. GIRAUDON)

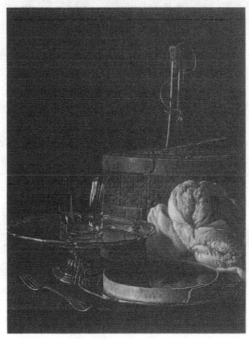

DANIELE CRESPI, *Saint Charles Borromeo Dining*, beginning of the seventeenth century, Church of S. Maria della Passione, Milan.

This painting is one of the finest representations of self-mortification by fasting. Notice in particular the signs of penitence and meditation and, in the background, the attitude of the spectators who come in on the saint unawares. (COL. ALINARI ANDERSON-GIRAUDON)

LUIS MELÉNDEZ, *Still Life, Afternoon Tea*, second half of the eighteenth century, Museo del Prado, Madrid.

The artist brings together various kitchen utensils, emphasizing bulky items that contrast with the organic quality of the food and the artificial nature of the tableware. (COL. LAUROS-GIRAUDON)

MARTEN VAN HEEMSKERCK, *Family Portrait,*
around 1530, Staatliche Kunstsammlungen, Cassel.

The association of food and flowers with portraiture is common in Nordic imagery. In this
family portrait the food ends up occupying the entire table, with signs that the products of
nature have been disarranged by human activity. (COL. LAUROS-GIRAUDON)

BARTHOLOMEUS VAN DER HELST, *Banquet of the Civil Guard on July 18, 1648,*
1648, Rijksmuseum, Amsterdam.

Left, above. In celebration of the Peace of MÅnster the militiamen abandon themselves to
the joys of the banquet. They have left war and combat behind and now celebrate the
renewal of brotherhood as well. As a banquet scene, Van der Helst's rendition distinguishes itself in that it constitutes a sort of document or chronicle of the event. (COL. HANFSTAENGL-
GIRAUDON)

JEAN-BAPTISTE SIMÉON CHARDIN, *Dessert,* or *Brioche,* 1763, Musée du Louvre, Paris.

Left, below. In the last phase of his career Chardin consistently favored simple composi-
tions—ordered, linear arrangements and a subdued palette. The expressive atmosphere
bathing the objects is dominant in the painting. (COL. LAUROS-GIRAUDON)

EDOUARD MANET, *Luncheon in the Studio,* 1868, Neue Pinakothek, Munich.

In an ambiguous fashion, Manet surrounds his figures with articles and furnishings from his studio—the armor and the laid table, for example. *Luncheon* is a representation of the painting life but also of a place of human interaction. (COL. BRIDGEMAN-GIRAUDON)

INTRODUCTION

THE EARLY MODERN PERIOD

Jean-Louis Flandrin

The most striking historical fact of the early modern period (1400–1800)—namely, the European conquest of the Seven Seas and the subsequent integration of the other continents into Europe's commercial network—had an impact on the European diet that has continued to the present day. Not until the nineteenth and twentieth centuries did the tomato, potato, corn (maize), and other American crops transform European agriculture and cooking. Nevertheless, while it took three centuries for these new crops to be fully assimilated (and then only as a result of a gradual deterioration in the popular diet), other exotic crops entered the European diet much more quickly. The pimiento was accepted in some countries, for example, while the turkey was adopted almost everywhere; three new beverages—coffee, tea, and chocolate—soon accounted for a substantial portion of global trade; and sugar, which had long been known in Europe, began to be produced in vastly greater quantities under European control.

Other major historical changes of the early modern period also had important dietary implications. The Reformation put an end to ecclesiastical regulation of what many Europeans ate, with the result that the relative uniformity of the medieval regimen gave way to a diversification along national lines. The domination of the economy by northern countries encouraged the production and consumption of alcohol in both wine-drinking regions and elsewhere. Advances in printing technology allowed print culture to flourish, thereby transforming the function of the cookbook and extending the influence of certain national cuisines while curtailing that of others. And scientific progress, especially seventeenth-century advances in chemistry, temporarily disrupted the traditional relationship between cooking and dietetics.

Steady urban growth continued to favor the transition from subsistence agriculture to market agriculture. The resumption of demographic growth in the sixteenth century and then again in the eighteenth century led, in the absence of notable advances in agricultural technology and yield, to an increase in the amount of land planted in grain and, as in the eleventh, twelfth, and thirteenth centuries, to a growing proportion of cereals in the popular diet and a shift in the perceived status of various foods. The acquisition of farmland by the social elite in various European countries increased the wealth of both the nobility and the bourgeoisie and fostered a more refined gastronomy and more sophisticated table manners while at the same time leading to increased malnutrition among the peasantry. And in some countries, such as France, the growth of a modern state greatly increased the tax burden in the seventeenth century, driving peasants from the land, turning them into proletarians, and accelerating the transition to a market economy. Meanwhile, the state took charge of organizing food distribution, just as it had done in the Roman and Byzantine empires.

Demography and Daily Bread

The demographic growth that was so apparent in Europe from the eleventh century to the beginning of the fourteenth century was definitively halted by the Black Plague. It resumed in some parts of the continent before the end of the fifteenth century and elsewhere by the early 1500s and continued until the end of the 1800s, despite a slowing of growth in many countries during the 1600s. The European population, estimated at 90 million in the mid-1300s and at 125 million by the early 1700s, increased from that point forward extremely rapidly, to 145 million by 1750 and 195 million by 1800. In France, during the thirty years prior to the French Revolution, the amount of land under cultivation rose from 47 million to 60 million acres. Similarly, in England, hundreds of thousands of acres were enclosed and plowed under in the second half of the eighteenth century. In Ireland, Germany, and Italy vast expanses of swampland were drained and planted.

In new territory, such as the North American colonies and the great plains of eastern Europe, new farmland was carved out of virgin territory, and there was no disruption of established dietary patterns. In western Europe, however, where the land was "already full," the increase in the amount of land devoted to grain came at the expense of land reserved for grazing, hunting, and gathering. This had the effect of increasing the proportion of grain in the popular diet, with a corresponding decrease in variety and meat consumption.

A few figures drawn from various parts of Europe will help to drive this point home. In Berlin the average per capita daily meat consumption at the end of the nineteenth century had dropped to less than a quarter of a pound compared with three pounds in 1397 (a twelvefold decrease). In Naples in 1770, 21,800 head of cattle were slaughtered to feed a population of roughly 400,000, whereas two centuries earlier some 30,000 head had been slaughtered to feed a population of roughly 200,000 (a threefold decrease). In Languedoc, in the countryside around Narbonne, the daily ration of farmworkers began to deteriorate as early as 1530 or 1540, especially where meat was concerned: on one farm three heads of cattle had been raised to feed six workers until 1540 but just two to feed the same six workers from 1549 to 1562. Elsewhere, the amount of meat allocated to each farmworker fell from 40 kilograms (88 pounds) between 1480 and 1534 to just 20 kilograms (44 pounds) after 1583. This deterioration probably worsened over the next few centuries in various parts of Europe. Height statistics bear out this hypothesis: over the course of the eighteenth century, the average height of Hapsburg army recruits apparently decreased, as did that of Swedish conscripts. Moreover, the average height of London adolescents appears to have decreased in the late eighteenth and early nineteenth centuries, while that of Germans in the early nineteenth century was significantly less than it had been in the fourteenth and fifteenth centuries.

Unfortunately, the available statistical data are too meager to allow a genuine quantification of the deterioration in the common man's diet or a sketch of its chronological evolution, which probably varied from region to region. Yet without a genuine agricultural revolution, which by the end of the eighteenth century had truly begun only in England, such a deterioration was an ineluctable consequence of demographic growth in the old agricultural countries. Fernand Braudel has proposed a very persuasive mathematical argument: given the technology available at the time, one hectare (2.471 acres) planted with wheat yielded five quintals (one quintal equals 100 kilograms equals 220.5 pounds) of grain, or 1,500,000 calories, whereas one hectare used for grazing yielded at best one and a half quintals of beef, or just 340,000 calories. In order to sustain the rapid rate of demographic growth, pasture had to be sacrificed to grain fields, and bread largely replaced meat in the popular diet.

Paradoxes

The grain sold on the open market came essentially from the ecclesiastical tithe and ground rents paid to noble landlords, while most dairy products, eggs, meat, wine, and vegetables—all the rest of the diet, apart from game—came from small peasant farms. People sold what they did not consume, and it was only logical for the growing of cash crops to increase as the market expanded.

The greater the proportion of grain in the popular diet, the greater the impact of grain shortages on the mortality rate. The seventeenth and eighteenth centuries suffered a series of major grain shortages (in 1662, 1693–94, and 1709–10 in France, 1739–41 in Germany, 1741–43 in England, 1764–67 in Spain and Italy, and 1771–74 in northern Europe, for example). It is often asserted that these crises were no different from the earlier crises that had afflicted the premodern agricultural system periodically over the entire history of its existence, just then coming to an end. In all likelihood, however, these final crises were far more severe than any the preceding centuries had witnessed.

A strange geographical paradox tends to support this hypothesis. The Sologne region of France was a poor and unhealthy place in the late seventeenth and early eighteenth centuries, and its inhabitants had barely enough to eat, whereas the neighboring Beauce region was one of France's richest breadbaskets. During grain crises, however, the proud Beaucerons sought refuge with the poor Solognots, whose comparatively old-fashioned and therefore more varied diet enabled them to hold out better in time of famine.

One finds a similar contrast between the wealthy Limagne region and the impoverished mountainous areas of Auvergne. Because Limagne's peasants, blessed with soil that was ideally suited to wheat, grew and consumed little else, they not only were more vulnerable to grain crises but also suffered from certain chronic dietary deficiencies, reflected in their small physiques and poor health. Many of their highland neighbors, born in a region whose poor soil and harsh climate made farming difficult, left to seek their fortunes elsewhere. Although the resources of the Auvergne could not sustain a rapidly expanding population, they were sufficient to allow a varied diet based on raising livestock, hunting, gathering, and fishing as well as farming, so highlanders suffered fewer dietary deficiencies than did their lowland neighbors and were therefore taller and healthier. According to Abel Poitrineau, these dietary differences might even explain why the one group was so much more dynamic and enterprising than the other.

Dispossession of the Peasantry

The upheaval in rural landownership, which in countries such as England was a prerequisite of the agricultural revolution, also contributed to the impoverishment of the peasant diet, especially in the more prosperous regions strategically located with respect to the market. In these areas, nobles, royal officeholders, and bourgeois had, by the end of the sixteenth century, gained possession of most of the land—land that at the end of the Middle Ages had still been in peasant hands.

In England, the enclosure movement was well under way by 1516, if Thomas More's *Utopia* is to be believed. In Île-de-France the pace of change picked up after 1530, and by the eve of the Wars of Religion (1562–98) the results were already impressive: one study of more than 6,000 hectares spread across seven villages of the Hurepoix shows that only 33.75 percent of the land was still in peasant hands. The Wars of Religion accentuated the contrast: in Wissous in 1600, only 21 percent of the land was owned by peasants, and in Gentilly in 1620 the figure was only 29 percent. By the mid-1600s, peasant ownership was more or less a thing of the past. In Avrainville, for example, where 47 percent of the land had still been owned by peasants in 1550, the figure for 1688 was just 17 percent. In Brie peasants owned less than a fifth of the land. In Burgundy, in the aftermath of the Thirty Years' War (1618–48), it was not unusual to find entire villages deserted.

In France and other western European nations, the degree and rapidity of the dispossession of the peasantry were greatest in the regions that were richest, closest to big cities, and most advanced in the use of agricultural technology. In regions where small farms dominated (in the mountains, in vine-growing areas, and in copse or hedgerow country), and in poorer, less populous regions generally, where land was less attractive to noble and bourgeois landlords, peasant ownership held up better.

In eastern Europe (Bohemia, Hungary, Poland, Muscovy, and so on), where the economic and social system was very different, the nobility also managed to appropriate a much larger share of the harvest than in the fourteenth and fifteenth centuries, not so much by taking possession of the land (which was less densely populated than in the West, hence not as scarce and therefore less expensive to purchase) as by subjugating the peasantry and markedly increasing compulsory labor requirements. This subjugation of the peasantry of northern and eastern Europe between the sixteenth and eighteenth centuries made for a sharp increase in the amount of grain sold to the more populous and economically advanced countries of the West.

Imported Wheat and Royal Wheat

In the absence of an agricultural revolution, it was primarily wheat from the Baltic, transported at first by Hanseatic shippers and later by Dutch merchants, that fed the growing urban population of western Europe, and not only in times of crisis. Shipments of "sea wheat" had already proved a saving grace in the Middle Ages when the local harvest fell short of what was required, or even in normal times for supplying commercial cities with no local breadbasket, such as Genoa. What changed was that, first of all, imports from the Baltic now outstripped imports from the Mediterranean; later, toward the end of the eighteenth century, there would be a further influx of wheat from the Black Sea and North America. In addition, the quantities shipped increased dramatically. Finally, the international grain trade now revolved around Amsterdam, which set prices for all of Europe from the seventeenth century on.

Finally, in France at any rate, there was a new investment by the state in solving problems of food distribution that had previously been the responsibility of individual cities and to a large extent still remained so. French monarchs in the eighteenth century became increasingly concerned with the possibility of popular uprisings due to bread shortages. To forestall that possibility, they stocked wheat and promulgated new laws governing the sale of grain. Both responses appear to have improved the situation, but not everyone agreed that this was the case. In *The Bakers of Paris and the Bread Question, 1700–1775,* Steven Kaplan has shown that when merchants followed the king's orders to stockpile grain, their actions were often interpreted as attempts to corner the market in order to drive up prices. Large-scale wheat purchases did in fact raise prices on local markets and force some people to go hungry, and critics saw this as evidence of a "famine conspiracy." Furthermore, laws promoting free trade in grain, which ultimately stimulated new cereal production, had to be withdrawn or modified on several occasions in the face of vehement protests by various groups: the best known of these episodes was the "flour war" of 1775.

Everything for Bread

Was the French government right to intervene in the food distribution system rather than leave it, as in the past and as in some other countries, in the hands of municipal governments and private interests? It would have been difficult to have acted differently: whereas popular protest in the seventeenth century had been directed mainly against taxes, in the eighteenth century it was directed mainly against shortages of bread. Although these disturbances were not as severe as in previous centuries, they could not be neglected.

Thus the bread question became the paramount political issue of the day, just as wheat came to dominate agriculture and the popular diet. Various academies organized competitions to elicit answers, and "enlightened" thinkers suggested ways of dealing with the problem that may not always have been well founded but whose orientation nonetheless remains significant. In 1793, for example, A. P. Julienne Belair proposed that grain fields should be cultivated not with plows and draft animals but with hoes—by hand, as in a vegetable garden. From this he expected to obtain not only an increased yield per acre but also—probably with greater justification—the use of fields otherwise devoted to raising feed for the animals.

Another essayist, Antoine Augustin Parmentier, suggested making bread with flour from potatoes, which could be grown in fallow fields between grain harvests and with yields two to three times greater than that for wheat. But in many parts of Europe people did not yet feel miserable enough to accept such fare, which was considered fit only for hogs, even if it could be turned into bread. It was not until the nineteenth century that the potato was universally accepted, but not in the form of bread.

New Food Crops

The potato was just one of the new food plants that helped feed the population of Europe in the nineteenth century, if not earlier. There was also rice, which had been known since the Middle Ages and was much appreciated by the social elite, but not acclimated to the Po Valley until late in the fifteenth century. Buckwheat, from northeastern Europe, spread in the sixteenth century to the Netherlands, Germany, France, and northern Italy, as did maize, or Indian corn, from America. These plants, which to some extent competed with one another, generally became established in different regions for reasons that had as much to do with culinary as with agricultural traditions.

Pure buckwheat is edible only in the form of gruel, porridge, pancakes, or gray polenta, which in northern Italy came to rival the yellow polenta traditionally made with millet. In order to make bread, buckwheat must be mixed with other grains. Its advantage is that it grows in very poor soil, where the yield of ordinary wheat would be very low. It could also be concealed between rows in regular wheat fields, a technique that allowed peasants to evade the tithe. First introduced into the poorer parts of Brittany and the Alps, where wheat was hard to grow, buckwheat may also have become established in other regions, where its smaller impact on the market means that its presence has left less of a trace in the historical record.

Maize had an even greater impact. Imported into Europe by Christopher Columbus in 1493, it quickly became acclimated. It was grown in Castille, Andalusia, and Catalonia in the early 1500s. By 1520 we find it in Portugal. It subsequently made its way into southwestern France (reaching Bayonne in 1523) and northern Italy (reaching the Veneto sometime between 1530 and 1540) and from there to Pannonia and the Balkans. At first it seldom replaced traditional grains but was grown on fallow land and used as fodder. Peasants also raised it in their gardens and ate it, especially in areas where the diet was traditionally based on millet or panic grass, poor grains from which it was difficult to make bread. In southeastern France, maize was often called "Spanish millet" or "fat millet." The same was true in Portugal, northern Italy, and Albania.

The historian of maize is somewhat hampered by the fact that it was initially grown in peasant gardens and therefore exempt from the tithe and seignorial dues, so there is little record of its early use. As the population grew, however, eighteenth-century agronomists, philanthropists, and landlords took a real interest in the plant because of its reputation for miraculous yields. In Pannonia those yields ran as high as eighty to one, compared with six for rye and even less for wheat. Impressed by these results, landlords cleared large fields for planting in corn and compelled peasants to eat greater and greater quantities of this relatively inexpensive food. Only then did resistance to its spread develop, especially since the crop was now subject to seignorial dues and resented by some as a less palatable substitute for wheat.

That resistance proved justified, moreover, for as barley cakes and millet gave way to polenta and cornbread, epidemics of pellagra broke out. This disease, a consequence of niacin deficiency, can cause skin eruptions, nervous disorders, and even death. First noted in Asturias in 1730, it spread as the prevalence of corn in the popular diet increased, soon afflicting southwestern France, northern Italy, and the Balkans, where it continued to wreak havoc into the nineteenth and even the early twentieth century.

In parts of France, Italy, and other southern European countries, chestnuts formed a part of the daily diet. In fact, inhabitants of these areas were not so bad off, since those who were obliged to eat the "bread of the forest" were also likely to consume substantial quantities of pork from the hogs that thrived in the same areas. For instance, one sixteenth-century observer reported that people in the Cévennes mountains regularly ate pork fried with chestnuts. But these people ate real bread "only on Sundays" and were condemned the other six days to make do with chestnuts. To contemporaries this made the Cévenols the most wretched of souls, as low as the radish eaters of Savoy and the Limousin.

Such prejudices explain why people who lived in grain-growing regions so steadfastly resisted the potato. If they grew potatoes on the sly, as people elsewhere grew buckwheat, it was generally to feed their livestock. And if travelers had nothing but praise for pork from pigs fed on "truffles," as in northern Italy, for example, such praise did nothing to encourage the peasants themselves to eat the same fare until the late eighteenth or early nineteenth century.

The timing of potato adoption varied widely from region to region, however. In 1573 potatoes figured among the purchases of the Sangre hospital in Seville. Charles de l'Écluse, who introduced the potato into the Netherlands in 1580, wrote that Italians liked to eat potatoes in lamb stew in the last decades of the sixteenth century. In 1600 Olivier de Serre reported that potatoes were eaten at various places in the Alps. In all these cases, however, it is hard to know how many people were involved. Things were different in Ireland: soon after the potato was adopted there in the seventeenth century, it became the major staple of the Irish diet. It also established a presence in England (in Lancashire and West Yorkshire, for example), in Prussia (where Parmentier discovered it as a prisoner in the eighteenth century), and in France and other countries.

Other American Species

Edible species did not await the arrival of Christopher Columbus to begin their travels. New crops arrived in Europe, mainly from the East, throughout antiquity and the Middle Ages. But when America was discovered, a whole range of new species arrived in a short time. Many of these were relegated to culinary purgatory for several centuries before achieving amazing success in the last two centuries. The tomato, for example, may have appealed to Italians, Spaniards, and southern Frenchmen as early as the 1500s or 1600s, but it was not widely eaten in Europe before the late 1700s or the early 1800s. In some northern countries people continued to turn up their noses at it during the nineteenth century, and German botanists denounced it as toxic. Even in Italy, although tomatoes were eaten in salad ("with salt, pepper, and oil, much as cucumbers are eaten," according to the *Dictionnaire de Trévoux* of 1704), the use of tomato sauce on pasta came later: no such thing is mentioned in any eighteenth-century cookbook or traveler's account.

The eggplant, which was often confused with the tomato because both were referred to as "gilded apple" (*pomodoro*), came not from America but from Asia, imported by Arab traders as far back as the Middle Ages. In the fourteenth century it was mentioned in a number of Catalonian recipes. It took longer than the tomato to gain acceptance in France and northern Europe, however; when ceiling prices were set on many foods during the Revolution, the eggplant was included only in a few southern districts.

The Jerusalem artichoke was served at fine Parisian dinners in the seventeenth century, no doubt because it tasted like artichoke at a time when the latter was all the rage. It never really caught on, though, and according to the *Dictionnaire de Trévoux,* it was eaten mainly by the poor, who referred to it as *pomme de terre* (earth apple, today the French term for "potato").

A more significant development was the rapid yet unobtrusive acceptance of the lima bean. This replaced the *phasol* or *phaséol,* a similar bean that had been eaten in antiquity and the Middle Ages and of which a black-eyed variety is still eaten in Africa today. This older bean can be seen in the bowl of Annibale Carracci's *Bean Eater* (painted in the seventeenth century). Not only did the new bean discreetly replace the *phaséol* in the European diet, but in many countries it also took over the latter's common name (*fasoulia* in Greek, *fasule* in Albania, *fayot* and *flageolet* in French), and everywhere it usurped its scientific name (*Phaseolus*), as scientists now applied the Latin term *Dolichos* to what had formerly been the *Phaseolus.* In France the new bean was sometimes called *fèverolles* and sometimes *haricot,* which is believed to derive from *ayacótl,* the word for the bean in Mexico. Supposedly, the French misunderstood the Spanish pronunciation of this Indian word and turned it into *haricot* as a result of a confusion with *haricot de mouton,* an old medieval stew. Curiously enough, this dish was until quite recently prepared with turnips, not beans.

Today it is hard to imagine what the African diet was like before the introduction of American species: that is, without manioc, peanuts, and red pepper. In fact, red peppers did not exist anywhere in the Old World prior to the sixteenth century, which means that the cuisine of Thailand, Korea, and many other countries was quite different from what we associate with those places today. In Europe the red pepper quickly gained success in Spain, both as an ornamental plant and as a substitute for pepper, compared to which it was deemed to be "hotter," tastier, and much less expensive. It also gained a foothold in southern Italy, the Balkans, and Hungary, whose paprika is today widely appreciated. Was it for climatic reasons that it was less successful in central and northern latitudes? Perhaps, because wherever it became a regular part of the diet, it was only after acclimatization, unlike the usual medieval spices, which were in fact distinguished by the fact that they came from exotic climes. But it may also have had something to do with the fact that it arrived in a period when many European countries, especially France, were turning away from spicy cooking. And if red pepper is eaten in France today, it is mainly in the mild variety known as sweet pepper or pimiento.

The slow rate at which American foods were generally adopted is typical of the process of culinary change in early modern society. Yet some species gained acceptance much more quickly than others, or more quickly in certain regions than in others. Indeed, the turkey caught on with amazing speed. Discovered by Cortés and his men in Mexico about 1520, the "Indian chicken" was mentioned by Rabelais in his *Gargantua* (1534). And we know that Marguerite d'Angoulême contracted with a farmer in Navarre to raise turkeys for her table. At a banquet given by Catherine de' Medici at the bishopric of Paris in 1549, seventy "Indian chickens" costing twenty sols apiece and seven "Indian roosters" costing thirty sols were served. The most surprising thing is that these prices were already markedly below the prices for native birds such as peacock and heron (forty sols), pheasant and bustard (seventy sols), crane (eighty sols), swan (a hundred sols), and so on. The turkey was accepted almost from the moment it arrived because all sorts of large birds were already served on aristocratic tables, including some that we consider inedible, such as cormorant, stork, heron, crane, swan, and peacock. Hence there was no problem with introducing the turkey, which was large, decorative, and tasty in the opinion of satisfied consumers both then and now.

Similar arguments can be advanced to explain the relatively rapid acceptance of corn by millet eaters and of string beans by those already accustomed to the old European variety. If the pace of change in these cases was slower than in the case of the turkey, it was not because common folk were less open to new foods than were members of the elite; it may be quite simply that the sources paid less attention to what the poor ate than to what the rich ate.

Exotic Spices and Colonial Beverages

The conquest of the Seven Seas, which led to European domination of the rest of the world, began as an effort to control the spice routes. First the Portuguese, then the Dutch, and finally the English commanded the lion's share of the lucrative trade in exotic seasonings, but it was not until the seventeenth century that the last Levantine competitors were finally eliminated.

Pepper was by far the dominant spice. The amount of pepper imported and consumed throughout Europe increased by as much as 50 percent in the fifteenth century but rose only 27 percent in the sixteenth century, suggesting an actual decline in per capita consumption. Imports of other spices are estimated to have increased by 177 percent in the fifteenth century and roughly 500 percent between 1500 and 1620. In the seventeenth century competition between England and Holland led to lower prices for pepper and a slow expansion of the market. Later, in the late 1700s, as American smugglers undermined the English and Dutch monopolies of the East Indian trade, consumption increased rapidly.

Despite the virtually steady rise in imports, spices henceforth played a less prominent role in both European cuisine and European commerce than in the Middle Ages. By contrast, the modern period was the heyday of such colonial beverages as chocolate, coffee, and tea, which became a regular part of the regimen and accounted for an important share of overseas trade.

After discovering chocolate in Mexico, the Spanish had the idea of mixing it with sugar rather than with chili as the Indians did. Cortés sent some to Charles V in 1527, but it was not until the end of the sixteenth century that Spaniards wholeheartedly accepted the new beverage. It took much longer to catch on in other countries, with the possible exception of Italy, and did not become a major component of world trade until the nineteenth century.

Coffee, which came originally from Ethiopia and Yemen, was introduced into Europe by the Turks. Having gained a foothold in Venice by 1570, it subsequently conquered all of Italy. By 1644 it had reached Marseilles, and from there it moved northward to Paris, where it subjugated the social elite in the second half of the century. *Café au lait* even became a working-class drink in the eighteenth century. Germany, England, and various other countries had already begun drinking it a century earlier. Rising consumption encouraged a proliferation of coffee plantations in Dutch colonies (such as Ceylon, Java, and Surinam), British colonies (such as Jamaica), the French Antilles, Portuguese Brazil, and elsewhere.

Tea, the last of the three colonial beverages, came to Europe from China. Although used sparingly in Holland and France as early as the seventeenth century, it became truly popular only in England, where it supplanted coffee after 1730 and soon became the national beverage. Tea accounted for half the value of the cargo shipped by the East India Company between 1760 and 1797. Russians also began drinking tea in the eighteenth century, but other European nations preferred coffee.

All these colonial beverages were sweetened with sugar. Muslims had always sweetened their coffee, but sugar traditionally had not been used with either tea or chocolate in their native lands. In other words, the sharp rise in sugar consumption was linked to the success of these colonial beverages across the continent. But sugar consumption began to rise as early as the fourteenth century, so obviously there were also other reasons for its use. By the seventeenth century the growth of sugar consumption had led to the establishment of vast sugar plantations in tropical countries colonized by Europeans: Madeira, the Canary Islands, the Azores, Brazil, the Antilles, and other "sugared isles." These plantations depended on slave labor and the importation of Negroes—and slavery is of course the ugly side of the history recounted here.

New Foods

Innovation in food choice was not limited to the introduction of exotic new species into the European diet. Many local foods that the elite of medieval society had formerly disdained now returned to favor.

Study of French cookbooks and of the records of food purveyors has supplemented knowledge gleaned earlier from kitchen account books. The evidence suggests that the elite's preference for fowl over meat lessened. This may have been a consequence of reduced beef consumption by the lower classes: the opposition between "gross" and "delicate" meats diminished as that between bread and meat increased.

From the kitchen accounts of wealthy households we know that bread consumption by the elite decreased in the early modern period. (In the absence of other evidence, this decrease may be interpreted as a consequence of the replacement of thick breadboards by flat plates in the sixteenth century.) Cookbooks reflect an even more marked distaste for gruel and other forms of boiled grain (barley, millet, oats, wheat, etc.), which had been in favor in the Middle Ages. As elite consumption of bread and other cereal-based foods declined and popular consumption rose, not only did the status of meat and fish change, but so did that of legumes.

In the Middle Ages, legumes other than fresh and dried peas had been left to the lower classes, especially in France, and the dietitians had approved. But in the sixteenth and seventeenth centuries legumes became fashionable, owing no doubt to Italian influence and perhaps also to the Counter-Reformation. Mediterranean artichokes, cardoon, and asparagus vied with melons, oranges, and lemons for the hearts of gourmets, and mushrooms, truffles, and numerous native legumes could be found on wealthy dinner tables and in countless cookbooks. Recipes abounded for everything from sugared peas to chickpeas, fava beans, and lentils, to say nothing of the lima beans from America that were supplanting the *Phaseolus* across Europe. There were also all sorts of roots, ranging from carrots and parsnips (and even certain kinds of radish) to caraway, Chinese artichokes, salsify, scorzonera, and, among the more delicate roots, asparagus (which was much in fashion), tender vine tendrils, and their competitor, shoots of hops. Also in favor were countless herbs and greens, from lettuce and purslane to watercress, chicory, endive, and chard—as were cucumbers and pickles of the traditional sort as well as squash and pumpkin. And the early seventeenth century saw a vogue for truffles, morels, agaric, and other mushrooms—wild as well as cultivated—which had once been disdained by laymen and experts alike. Until recently most studies of shifting food preferences have concentrated on the French elite, but similar changes apparently occurred elsewhere as well, sometimes a bit sooner (as in Italy), sometimes later.

Despite the doctors' traditional warnings, fruit was greatly appreciated by the medieval elite, especially in Italy, and even more appreciated in the early modern period. In a French meal dessert stood out from the other courses and generally consisted of a number of fruits served in a variety of ways: raw (either whole or coarsely chopped to make fruit salad) as well as cooked (in compotes, marmalades, and both "liquid" and "dry" preserves). Indeed, it was considered more refined to refer to the last course of dinner simply as "fruit." "Dessert" was a more "vulgar" term, relegated to the bourgeoisie.

Orchards adjacent to country houses were enlarged and often became the pride and joy of the master, whether noble or bourgeois. Herb gardens, also expanded, were another source of pride. Amateur horticulturists devoured books on gardening, such as Nicolas de Bonnefons's *Le Jardinier français,* while their wives consulted any of the numerous treatises on the making of preserves. Throughout the seventeenth and eighteenth centuries gentleman farmers proudly showed off their orchards to friends and bred new varieties of fruit. By 1700 their efforts had succeeded in making fresh fruit available in all seasons: pears, for example, could be had at all times except in the month of June. Physicians, impressed by what they took to be an improvement in overall quality, stifled doubts about the effects of fruit on physical well-being.

The New Cooking and the New Taste

From the study of cookbooks we learn that, in the upper reaches of society at any rate, there was a great deal of culinary innovation, not only in the choice of ingredients (such as legumes, fruits, dairy products, and beef) but also in seasonings. In France the "strong" (vinegary and spicy) sauces that had been in vogue in the Middle Ages gave way to sauces based on fats or sugar (and thus richer in quickly absorbed lipids and starches). The new sauces were said to be more "delicate" and more respectful of the intrinsic flavors of other ingredients. The same tendency can also be observed in other European countries, such as England to the north, Poland and Germany to the east, and Italy and Spain to the south, although in these countries the search for smooth consistencies (provided by fats) and sweet flavors did not lead to as firm a rejection of spices as in France.

Attitudes toward fruits also began to change in early modern France. In legal terms, up to the time of the French Revolution, the word "fruit" had referred to any product of the soil: in charters specifying the extent of the church's tithe, for example, we find the phrase *gros fruits* (gross product) used in this sense. In another sense, it was not uncommon in the 1500s and early 1600s to classify such things as olives, truffles, and artichokes as "fruits" suitable to be served as dessert. At some point in the seventeenth century, however, these "fruits" began to be reclassified as "vegetables." This change took place because a new distinction, "sweet" versus "savory," gradually emerged as a basic principle of classification.

This happened in the seventeenth century, and its effects continue to be felt to this day. As early as 1674 we find one chef expressing skepticism about the equivocal nature of meat served in sweet sauce. Even before that, we note a migration of fruits and other foods containing sugar toward the final courses of dinner. The triumph of sweet and savory did not come quickly, however. At the beginning of the nineteenth century, three fruits were still served as hors d'oeuvres: melons, figs, and blackberries (all three served with salt). Until the middle of the century, it was common to serve entremets, or side dishes, that combined sweets and savories. And ripe cheeses were not relegated to the dessert course until the twentieth century.

In France changes in dietary preferences appear to have gone hand in hand with changes in literary and artistic tastes. In the seventeenth century, for example, when fat-based sauces replaced spicy sauces, proponents of the "new cuisine" were fond of arguing that the modern sauces were more respectful of the natural taste of ingredients. This argument obviously has much in common with the cult of the natural in French art and literature of the classic period. Resisting this French neoclassicism, other cuisines, which continued to use spices and to serve meat in sweet sauces or garnished with fruit, were linked to the baroque.

Dietetics and Gourmet Dining

The situation can also be looked at from another angle, however. Many of the changes that affected first France and then the countries that remained hostile to neoclassicism can perhaps be explained as the result of a relaxation of the connection between cooking and dietetics. During the Middle Ages and in fact as late as the beginning of the seventeenth century, the diet of the elite closely followed the recommendations of the physicians in regard not only to choice of ingredients but also to cooking techniques, seasoning, and eating. When it came to choosing ingredients, members of the elite left "gross" meats such as beef and pork as well as most vegetables to the common people, whose stomachs were supposedly more robust. The elite ate only "delicate" fowl, relatively "light" fish, and soft wheat bread. Cooking techniques were adapted to the nature of the meat: beef was never roasted, for example, because it was too "dry," whereas quail was never boiled because it was too fat, and anyone incautious enough to eat suckling pig, which was dangerously "moist," always roasted it first. As for seasoning, pork was almost always eaten salted, because in its fresh state it was too "cold and moist," and other hard-to-digest meats were always highly spiced. And, finally, while many people were willing to run the risk of eating fruit, they usually spiced it well or ate it at the beginning of the meal in accordance with the dietitians' recommendations.

Under the banner of "changing tastes," all these hygienic precautions began to disappear in the seventeenth and eighteenth centuries, as did all references to the old dietetics. Cooks and gastronomes spoke only of "harmonizing flavors" and forgot that in times past flavor had been of concern as much to physicians as to aficionados of fine dining. Scientifically classified on a scale of temperature ranging from hot to cold, flavor had once been accepted as a reliable indicator of the nature and digestibility of any food. Now, however, it became common to disparage the outdated wisdom of the "old physicians." In the *Dictionnaire de Trévoux,* for example, we find that whenever digestion is mentioned, allusion is made to various chemical principles: acids, salts, tartars, and so on.

Was scientific progress ultimately the fundamental reason for the changes in taste that gastronomes of the period saw as a mark of progress in the culinary arts and sensibilities? A third interpretation is also possible: namely, that the relaxation of the links between cooking and dietetics in a sense liberated the gourmet instincts. No longer did culinary refinement aim at maintaining health. Now it could be directed at flattering the tastes of gourmets. But gourmets did not yet call themselves gourmands: in French the word *gourmandise* became a synonym for gluttony, whereas *friandise,* or the love of good food and the art of recognizing it, became a refinement of the civilized individual.

Interestingly, the status of the sense of taste, with which nature had endowed both humans and animals in order to enable them to distinguish between the edible and the inedible, rose noticeably in the middle of the seventeenth century. The word "taste" was used figuratively in discussions of literature, sculpture, painting, music, furniture, clothing, and so on. In all these areas taste was the faculty that made it possible to distinguish between good and bad, beautiful and ugly. It was the characteristic organ of the "man of taste," a variant of the *honnête homme,* or gentleman. Such a promotion suggests a certain degree of indulgence toward the *friand-gourmand.*

Literature for Lovers of Food and Drink

It was not until after the Revolution, when Grimod de La Reynière published his famous *Almanach des gourmands* (1804), that it became possible to admit without shame to what once had been considered the deadly sin of gluttony. The new spirit did not last long, however, and it may well have contained an element of provocation, for the word *gourmand,* still associated with gluttony, was replaced by newer euphemisms: *gourmet* and *gastronome.* Nevertheless, even before the debut of what we would now consider to be "gastronomic literature," we witness a proliferation of texts devoted to the arts of eating and drinking—indeed, the emergence of a literature of *friandise* suggests a certain liberation of *gourmandise.*

Culinary treatises, or at any rate compilations of recipes, appeared even before the invention of printing, circulating in manuscript in various European countries as early as the end of the thirteenth or the beginning of the fourteenth century. Unlike the treatises of ancient Greece and Rome, China, Persia, and the Arab world, these compilations were technical rather than lyrical and were the work of professional cooks—even if written on orders of their noble employers and with the aid of professional scribes, as was the case with Master Chiquard, cook to Amadeus VIII of Savoy.

Printing increased the variety as well as the number of such technical works about food. Significantly, such works soon narrowed their focus, specializing on one or another of the increasingly distinct aspects of the culinary arts. Sixteenth-century Italian culinary treatises were impressive for the number and sophistication of their recipes: among them were works by Scappi, cook to Pope Pius V (published in 1570), and Messibugo (published in 1540). Before getting into culinary matters proper, Messibugo describes the sumptuous banquets he prepared for the Estes, not omitting a single ingredient of each dish and including information about the musical accompaniment for each course. Their only rival anywhere in Europe was a book by the German Rumpolt, which gave recipes from many countries, especially the Hapsburg provinces of central Europe, and, three centuries before French gourmets, specified which wines were to be drunk with various dishes.

Vittorio Lancellotti's *Lo Scalco prattico* (1627) was not a cookbook but simply a compilation of menus, more numerous than those in Messibugo's book yet every bit as sumptuous. Once again, the dishes in each course are described in such detail that they are almost as good as recipes. In France Pierre de Lune published *Le Nouveau et Parfait Maître d'hôtel* (1662), which included many menus and table layouts. A number of books were published in England, Italy, and France on the subject of carving, with illustrations of various fowl indicating where each cut was to be made. In France there were manuals for wine stewards, waiters, and the like, all combined in the *Escole parfaite des officiers de bouche* (1662), with illustrations showing how to fold napkins and peel fruits. All the food service professions were arts whose techniques were now set forth in treatises written by professionals.

Another type of work that proliferated in the sixteenth century was the compilation of "useful secrets" covering subjects such as medicine, cosmetics, practical jokes and tricks, and so on. Some were intended specifically for women and dealt with an interesting conjunction of subjects—cosmetics and jams, for example. Among these were the *Bâtiment des recettes* and the *Excellent et moult utile opuscule* by Nostradamus (1555). In France and Italy these books of secrets never contained recipes for cooking, but they did sometimes include recipes for making jam, preserves, electuaries (powders mixed with honey or syrup), and the like, all varieties of sweets used for therapeutic purposes of one sort or another. The reason for this was probably that cooking was a menial activity in these two countries, whereas beauty treatments and the confection of preserves were at that time considered worthy of the interest of "ladies" and "damsels" of the elite. By contrast, in England one finds books containing recipes along with techniques for making preserves and other sweets as well as formulas for medication. These were supposedly written by the mistresses of aristocratic households for their peers. Such ladies needed to master these arts in order to perform the duties associated with their station in society, duties that involved both hospitality and the care of the sick.

Such books by aristocratic ladies had to contend, in England as in France and Italy, with competition from culinary treatises by professionals employed in the homes of the well-born and well-to-do. In England some of these professional treatises were adaptations of French cookbooks or works by French-born chefs claiming to be experts on French cuisine. In part, this reflects the fact that European cooking was dominated by certain national cuisines: in the sixteenth century the dominant cuisine was Italian. Later, toward the end of the sixteenth century and at the beginning of the seventeenth, Spain took the lead. But by the middle of the seventeenth century, even before the French monarchy achieved political dominance, French cuisine had triumphed, as can be seen from the fact that *Le Cuisinier français* was translated into English in 1653, in the middle of the Fronde, at a time when the luster of the French monarchy was greatly diminished. The influence of French cookbooks extended far beyond England—to Denmark and Sweden, for example, where the first cookbooks were adaptations of French works, as well as to Holland and even Italy in the eighteenth century.

Paralleling the proliferation of the "arts of the palate" and of the technical literature dealing with those arts was an outpouring of works of various kinds defending the pleasures of good food and drink, not to say gluttony and bibulousness. The first of these was a work of the Italian Quattrocento, *De honesta voluptate* by the humanist Bartolomeo Sacchi, known as Platina. Platina was neither a chef nor a physician (neither was "Le Ménagier de Paris," for that matter), and what he offered his readers was a mix of culinary and dietetic information with nostalgic memories of the pleasure that he and his friends had experienced in savoring the creations of Master Martino, the great Roman chef of the mid-fifteenth century. What is more, he used his recollections to defend the genteel pleasures of refined yet simple cooking, pleasures that we would be hard-pressed nowadays to characterize by any word other than "gourmet."

In the centuries that followed, Platina's work enjoyed international success: by the early sixteenth century his Latin treatise had been translated into Italian, French, German, and other languages. He also had disciples (not all of whom were aware of being his disciples), who took pleasure in eating well-cooked food and drinking good wine and who liked to write about their experiences. Among them were a number of professionals, such as the mysterious "L.S.R.," the author of *L'Art de bien traiter* (1674). Not content merely to record recipes that explained how to prepare good dishes and pastries and how to select and serve good wines so as to derive the greatest possible pleasure from what one ate and drank without damage to one's health, L.S.R. was also an ardent champion of proper cooking techniques. He defended the rather vulgar taste for eating rare meat straight from the spit and piping hot with no sauce other than its natural juices. He also recommended wrapping meat with well-browned bacon before broiling so as to enrich the drippings. A quarter of a century earlier, Nicolas de Bonnefons had published *Le Jardinier français* (1651) and *Les Délices de la campagne* (1654), in which he vigorously advocated simple methods of cooking designed to preserve the "natural" flavor of various ingredients. Some professionals who wrote cookbooks made room for commentaries by "intellectuals" such as the two Jesuits who wrote the preface to *Les Dons de Comus* (1739), who not only sang the praises of the book but also extolled the recent refinement of French cooking, discussed its debt to early Italian masters, argued the merits of their gifted and created pupils, the chefs of France, and praised the enlightened French aristocrats whose love of good food was the sine qua non of perfecting the arts of the table.

In fact, it was the European aristocracy generally that provided the enlightened amateurs and patrons of the culinary arts, and it was the English, including Lord Chesterfield and many others, who led the way. But whereas aristocratic gourmets in France worked effectively to advance the national cuisine, there is reason to think that in other countries, especially England, their exclusive love of the dominant French style prevented the colloquy of popular, bourgeois, and aristocratic cooking from which great cuisines are born.

Returning to gourmet texts by nonprofessionals, we cannot omit either John Evelyn's invaluable treatise on salads or Arthur Young's informed commentary on dinners he ate at inns in France. Indeed, in the comments of early modern travelers about the food they encounter on their journeys we read a clear sign of the liberation of the gourmet instinct. The Dominican gourmet Father Labat was one of a number of writers who tapped this vein, and he made no secret of his desire to appeal to contemporary readers by giving his blessing to their fondness for food.

Before leaving this subject, finally, we must say a word about the flourishing of drinking societies in this period. Drinking songs were of course a medieval tradition that continued to flourish. And another traditional genre, that of ribald literature with its depiction of heroes much given to drink and other forms of debauchery, achieved perfection in the work of Rabelais. The "good-humored companion," a figure much in vogue in the sixteenth century with young and not-so-young aristocrats, was essentially a "jolly toper." The seventeenth century witnessed the emergence of various types of drinking societies: while the Société des Coteaux (whose members prided themselves on their ability to identify not just the estate on which a wine originated but the precise hillside on which the grapes had ripened) may have been imaginary, the Société de la Méduse, a gambling and drinking society whose members included women as well as men, was quite real, as we know from bylaws that have survived to this day.

To sum up, then, the sixteenth, seventeenth, and eighteenth centuries gave rise to a wide range of books, poems, and songs dealing with the pleasures of food and drink. In the nineteenth century these provided the fertile soil in which gastronomic literature proper took root and flourished.

Meals and Table Manners

The art of dining was further refined by the invention of new types of furniture and eating utensils. The eating schedule also changed in the upper strata of society to accommodate the increased leisure time of the upper classes, whose daily routine rapidly diverged from that of manual laborers. Dinner "courses" were more clearly delineated, and the order in which courses were served was modified in keeping with the new thinking about food. Some changes in eating and drinking habits affected all of Europe, while in other respects national differences persisted or increased.

In France it was not until the eighteenth century that the dining room, equipped with a permanent dinner table, became a fixture of every aristocratic household. This change also occurred elsewhere, although the precise timing remains to be determined. Another novelty of the period was the adoption of the fork. Said to have been invented in Byzantium, the fork appeared on some Italian tables as early as the fourteenth century, as we know from various paintings. In the sixteenth and seventeenth centuries it made its way into neighboring countries.

Forks on dinner tables are depicted in French paintings of the early 1600s. Nevertheless, if we believe the dismayed reports of English writers like Tobias Smollett, it would appear that the fork was not fully accepted even in the upper reaches of eighteenth-century French society. An engraving from 1730 shows Louis XV surrounded by ranking nobles of his court, all of whom are eating with their fingers.

The shallow dish, which replaced the medieval cutting board in the sixteenth century, caught on much more quickly. It also became customary to provide each guest with a spoon, a knife, and a glass, and the custom of passing eating utensils around the table was abandoned. Only serving utensils were still shared, and these were not supposed to touch anyone's mouth, nor were morsels of food to be eaten directly from common serving plates. They were to be placed first, as we do today, on each individual diner's plate and if necessary sliced before being raised to the mouth with a spoon or fork. The indiscriminate habits of the past were henceforth banished. A sort of invisible screen now separated each diner from his neighbors, and the new utensils enhanced this isolation. All this took place, moreover, two centuries before Pasteur demonstrated the existence of microbes and their role as agents in the transmission of disease.

New Dining Schedules

Like the advent of printed books, the introduction of new utensils and new table manners had for a time the effect of increasing the distance between social classes. Changes in the dinner schedule had the same effect, moreover.

In the Middle Ages, working people ate four or five meals a day, whereas upperclass adults ostensibly took only two daily meals. But in fact women, children, elderly people, and even less ascetic adult males, whose numbers were probably substantial, regularly consumed three or four meals a day. In any case, the timing of the main meals was virtually identical regardless of one's class: dinner was served at noon or one o'clock after a nine o'clock breakfast (or at ten o'clock where breakfast was not eaten), and supper was served at nightfall. Thus to a slightly lesser extent than today, virtually everyone ate at the same time. With the passage of time, however, the dinner hour of the social elite in virtually every western European country was delayed, whereas that of the common people remained what it had been. In Paris, between the end of the sixteenth and the beginning of the nineteenth century, dinnertime was set back eight hours (by the time of the Empire it was at six o'clock in the evening), and supper was postponed by almost six hours, from dusk until eleven o'clock at night. In England, dinner, which at the end of the seventeenth century was eaten in the late morning, around eleven o'clock, was delayed until two in the afternoon in the second half of the eighteenth century. In London, fashionable hosts served dinner as late as five in the afternoon, with a late snack at around midnight. The Spanish, who continued to serve dinner at noon, were more old-fashioned in this respect, but court nobles delayed their dinner until one or two o'clock, and foreign ambassadors often waited until two or three. By contrast, the Italians were out in front of everyone else: as early as 1580 Montaigne remarked that in good households dinner was served at two in the afternoon and supper at nine in the evening, after the theater. Across Europe the eighteenth-century elite became accustomed to attending the theater every evening and to staying awake later at night. Workers, who were not at liberty to turn night into day and day into night, increasingly lived on a different planet from people of fashion.

Dining and Conviviality

Among the upper classes, however, certain hierarchies were less pronounced than they once had been. In the eighteenth century, all a person needed in order to be invited into good society was a rudimentary level of cultivation, which could be acquired in secondary school and perfected in the salon. If a person was well turned out, had good manners, and could carry on witty conversation, he could dine anywhere. Around the dinner table, moreover, it became increasingly common to pretend that everyone was equal. Although the highest-ranking guests still enjoyed certain prerogatives, these rarely included having special dishes or wines set aside for them. Or so it was in France, at any rate: we frequently find French travelers of the period complaining that rigid hierarchies were still observed around dinner tables in Germany and Poland.

On the other hand, the French had long expressed astonishment at the familiar relations that obtained between masters and servants in those countries. Montaigne made an observation of this sort about German inns as early as 1580. In the Middle Ages such familiarity was apparently universal, with hierarchical ritual the other side of the coin. This amounted to excluding from the table all who were too obviously different—namely, those whose culture, conversation, and manners indicated that they were working people or bourgeois. This social segregation, particularly apparent first in France and later in England, is one aspect of early modern manners that persists today.

Such exclusiveness was a price that people seemed willing to pay: French dinners and especially suppers, occasions for witty conversation, friendly relations, and convivial high spirits as much as for gourmet pleasures, appear to have achieved a kind of perfection in the eighteenth century, a perfection that people who survived the Revolution admitted to feeling nostalgic for many years later.

Styles of Serving

It was also between the sixteenth and eighteenth centuries that *service à la française*—the French style of dining—assumed its classic form: soup, appetizers, and tangy sauces in the first course; a roast with salad and possibly side dishes in the second course; an optional third course; and finally a dessert or "fruit" to end the meal. Guests served themselves freely, and in order to make sure of pleasing everyone the *maître d'hôtel* saw to it that the menu included a variety of dishes. Variety was once a consequence of the idea that different people have different temperaments and therefore different dietary needs and that appetite was a sign of those needs. By the eighteenth century, however, its only purpose was to please the palate of the gourmet and redound to the glory of the household.

In Germany, Poland, Russia, England, and many other countries, each dinner course included a large number of dishes, just as in France. But slicing was done by the butler, and a tray was then passed around by waiters so that each guest was offered each dish in succession, as is commonly done today, although then the number of dishes was far greater. By contrast, in the old French system, each guest normally sampled only a small number of dishes, which were placed on the table for each course. As a result of this practice, the French enjoyed a reputation for sobriety among their neighbors to the east and north.

Some foreigners did not appreciate the fact that the French style of serving made it impossible to reach dishes located far from where one was seated unless one had a servant to fetch them. Guests without servants had to make do with dishes within reach. Among those who disliked the French custom were the impoverished Jean-Jacques Rousseau and the sharp-tongued Russian Fonvizin. By contrast, another malcontent, Hubert Vautrin, a French teacher in Poland, complained that when one wished to sample an appetizing dish there, it was necessary to wait until everyone at the table had been served in hierarchical order. And many guests who had no interest in the dish being served did not deign to answer the servants who placed it before them, thereby slowing the service considerably. Indeed, everyone acknowledged that the old serving style was slow and that countries where it remained the custom took forever to get through dinner.

Drinking Customs

Fonvizin was not alone in one of his criticisms of French customs—namely, his attack on French drinking manners. In order to prevent spillage, bottles were placed not on the table but on a sideboard where glasses were also kept. Whenever a guest wanted something to drink, he either had to get up and get it himself or send a servant if he had one or ask one of the house servants to fetch it for him, and it was usually difficult to get their attention. French writers such as Grimod de La Reynière voiced similar complaints.

In northern and eastern Europe, the problem did not arise because it was unusual to drink with dinner. As in Greek antiquity, banquets were divided into two parts: one for drinking, the other for eating. In England the women withdrew after the first or second glass. In other countries observers do not mention women. But everyone—especially the French, who found the practice revolting—agreed that by the end of a series of toasts and dares, all the guests at eastern European dinners were dead drunk. In Poland they sank beneath the table one by one, and servants then carried them off to bed.

Differences, Resemblances, Influences

What is most striking about national drinking customs is their diversity. The same is true about serving customs, although travelers generally found these less striking.

Other national differences grew more pronounced in the early modern period. This may have been due in part to the Reformation. With the advent of Protestantism there were fewer and fewer holidays celebrated simultaneously across Europe, and Calvinists were especially hostile to "the superstitious observance of dates." In England fish consumption plunged dramatically after the break with the Catholic Church. In the seventeenth and eighteenth centuries English travelers remarked that the French ate lots of fish, not just because they were obliged to but because they liked it. Such reports may be accurate only with respect to the upper classes. But some Frenchmen apparently found the obligation to forgo meat less onerous than did the English.

Other striking differences developed in regard to cooking techniques and taste. In the Middle Ages people everywhere had cooked with lard on meat days and with oil on lean days—or so we surmise from what we read in cookbooks of the time. Now, however, a geographical divide emerged between countries that cooked with butter and those that cooked with oil. Not all the countries that used butter were Protestant, because in the wake of the Reformation the Catholic Church had authorized any number of dispensations. As for the oil countries, they were not only Catholic but also, if not primarily, Mediterranean. In the seventeenth and eighteenth centuries people in these countries began cooking even meat with oil, for reasons of convenience, taste, and national identity having nothing to do with religious observance.

Furthermore, the Reformation seems to have played no part in the English rejection of garlic after the seventeenth century or the French hostility to sauces made with mint. And the French aversion to very spicy dishes, especially those made with certain spices, only heightened the difference between France and the rest of Europe for a century or two. Two points bear emphasizing, however. First, this difference was in no sense a national tradition since the French in the Middle Ages had eaten food every bit as spicy as their neighbors. Second, it was not permanent. Most European cuisines today are no spicier than the French, and some are less so. National cuisines evolved in similar directions but at different rates, thus for a time exaggerating differences between them.

By the end of the eighteenth century, however, certain convergences had begun to appear. Sugar consumption increased everywhere, people developed a taste for colonial beverages, foreign plants were acclimated and introduced into the diet, and attitudes toward certain vegetables and certain ingredients such as butter changed dramatically.

CHAPTER 28

GROWING WITHOUT KNOWING WHY

Production, Demographics, and Diet

Michel Morineau

The demographic characteristics of Europe in the early modern period (short-hand for the sixteenth, seventeenth, and eighteenth centuries) were very different from what they are today. From 80 to 90 percent of the population lived in the countryside, and the size of the harvest was the major obsession, owing to an agricultural yield that was still low by modern standards and, moveover, varied widely from year to year. Whether there would be enough to feed everyone was a constant worry. Dietary deficiencies weakened the body and increased its vulnerability to fatal disease, which was still rampant.

Yet the population of Europe increased from 80 to 180 million between 1500 and 1800. Overcoming each new crisis, Europe maintained its share of the world population—about one-fifth. But this fact does not imply that the relatively small continent that stretched from the Atlantic to the Urals possessed any unique prowess: Asia fared just as well, if not better. If we are to understand the demographics of early modern Europe, whose population growth was neither steady nor uniform, we must first look at each European nation individually.

Diversity of Growth

Like the rest of Europe, England (in the strict sense, not counting Wales or the county of Monmouth) was struck by the Black Plague in the fourteenth century and did not regain its former population until the beginning of the sixteenth century. The end of the War of the Roses inaugurated a period of growth that proved durable. Much information is to be found in parish registers, where records of baptisms, funerals, and marriages were kept.[1] After a period of rapid growth (roughly 72 percent in the eighty years beginning in 1541), the rate of increase slowed, so the population presumably grew no more than 30 percent from 1580 to 1700. This tranquil picture masks a number of painful losses (from plague in 1603–1604, from the great rebellion of the mid-seventeenth century, and from the London plague in 1664–1665), but these were soon repaired. The resumption of growth proved relatively slow but picked up in the first half of the eighteenth century (which saw an increase of 14 percent). Thereafter it accelerated to the point where the growth for the fifty years ending in 1871 (80 percent) surpassed that of any comparable period in the past.

In France (or, more precisely, the territory within France's present-day borders), careless record-keeping by parish priests has made it more difficult to reconstruct the population in the years before 1670.[2] Hence not much can be said about the earliest part of the period, which saw the outbreak of a number of epidemics, including the plague of 1529–1530 whose impact on many parts of France was severe. Nevertheless, everyone agrees that the next fifty years were a period of remarkable growth. This ended in 1580 at the latest (and even earlier in some parts of the country), only to resume in 1600 and continue until another epidemic struck in 1630, reducing the total population by approximately 20 percent. Circumstances thereafter were unfavorable to growth, and the depression continued except for brief respites followed by renewed downturns. Apparently it took a half century before the recovery that began in 1670 reached the previous high-water mark. Growth thereafter remained modest (by 1790 the increase was a mere 26 percent) and subsequently slowed once again. Thus the French population curve in the seventeenth century was much more varied than the English, and the growth rate in France was subsequently lower than in England. This imbalance would persist into the nineteenth and twentieth centuries.

The population of the German-speaking countries apparently increased by 50 percent between 1500 and 1630, but little is known about ups and downs within that period.[3] The Thirty Years' War, which broke out in 1618 and gained intensity thereafter, reduced the population substantially, owing not only to the troops' excesses but also to the famine and epidemic that followed in their wake. By 1650, after the fighting had ended, the decrease in population totaled 25 percent. Over the next century and a half, however, the descendants of the survivors proliferated, yielding a population increase of 60 percent by 1800. Emigration, though not negligible, did little to slow this growth. Subsequently, the German population grew at an astonishing rate, quadrupling from 18 million to 70 million between 1800 and 1950 in spite of two world wars.

Based on survey data from the period 1528–1536 and the census of 1594, scholars used to believe that the population of Castile experienced an uninterrupted period of spectacular growth in the sixteenth century (47.53 percent). More recently, however, the consensus has been that growth slowed and the population may have actually declined in the final quarter of the century, even before the outbreak of the so-called Atlantic plague in 1596–1602, which marked the beginning of a century-long depression.[4] Catalonia, less densely populated, continued to grow in the seventeenth century until the outbreak of another plague—this time Mediterranean—which afflicted it along with the entire Spanish Levant. The prompt recovery that followed the end of the plague was interrupted by the War of the Spanish Succession (1701–1714). In 1717 the population of all of Spain was almost 15 percent less than it had been in 1590, despite some growth in the northwest from Guipúzcoa to Galicia. During the eighteenth century, the population rose by probably about 40 percent, to judge by the census of 1795, and neighboring Portugal grew at a similar rate.

Modes of Growth

Although it is true that humankind, like other living species, is destined to be fruitful and multiply, the fact remains that the growth of the human population is subject to all sorts of threats. History amply attests to a whole host of dangers, ranging from microbes and viruses to scourges for which man himself is responsible.

To say that climatic change is of fundamental importance is in no way to deny the kind of national and local variations in population growth that we have just surveyed. The European climate cooled after 1300, and weather patterns were subsequently quite capricious. Some regions, such as England, proved to be better protected against the elements than others. Plants had to adapt to changed local conditions: in one place they might be subjected to sleet storms, while in another they might be protected by a blanket of snow. The severity of epidemics varied with time and place. A variety of obstacles impeded the spread of disease. For instance, we have maps showing the limits of the 1656 plague epidemic in Naples; the picture that emerges is like a mosaic. Nevertheless, broader influences such as war must also be acknowledged.

People did not stand idly by as misfortune after misfortune buffeted them. Each new planting after a period of famine was a humble expression of the will to live. So was the adoption of new crops, whose full importance becomes apparent in this context: buckwheat was acclimated to Brittany in the fifteenth century and rice to the Po Valley at the beginning of the sixteenth century. Peasants began growing maize from Portugal to Basque country in the late sixteenth century. Potatoes were planted in Ireland at the beginning of the seventeenth century as well as in the Netherlands, Lorraine, Alsace, and elsewhere. As war and crop failures ravaged eastern Europe and the Balkans in the middle of that century, the potato spread eastward. The availability of corn and potatoes lessened the impact of bread shortages, saved lives, and, as we have seen in studies of Galicia (where corn was grown) and Ireland and Flanders (where the potato played a similar role), helped to restore growth.[5]

Natural Resources and Demographic Growth

That natural resources also have an important influence on demographic growth goes without saying, but the question deserves a closer look. By the early modern period, the role of hunting and gathering had diminished nearly everywhere except for a few outlying areas such as northern Sweden and the forests of Russia and Transylvania. There were often feudal or seignorial constraints on such activities in any case. Nevertheless, natural conditions dictated a whole range of choices from the type of grain that could be grown to the kind of livestock that could be raised.

While Mediterranean countries were proud of their wheat (such as the Castilian *tierra de campos* and *tierra de pan*), rye dominated to the north, oats from Ireland to Norway, and barley had a northern limit. Olive groves and vineyards were also restricted to certain regions; for fear of frost, vineyards that once thrived at higher altitudes and relatively northern latitudes were abandoned.

This geographical diversity was reflected in both cooking techniques (oil, butter, or lard; bread, flatbread, or porridge) and diet. Cereals formed an essential part of the diet in all areas except those close to the Arctic Circle. Grains accounted for anywhere from one-half to three-quarters of the daily caloric intake.

From what we have been able to ascertain, that caloric intake appears to have been adequate (3,000 calories per day and even more for mature males). This is a surprising finding, and it applies of course only to prosperous years, not to times of famine. Various estimates and calculations agree that this is an accurate figure, even for Ireland in the eighteenth century, where the basic diet consisted of potatoes (5 kilograms, or 11 pounds, per day), a pint of milk, oats, and peas.[6] Some diets were better balanced than others in terms of the ratio of starches to fats and proteins, while others included only the best grains or accepted new ingredients (such as sugar and tea, which formed part of the regular diet of people in Kent in the eighteenth century). Little is known, however, about the consumption of fruits and vegetables, which are sources of vitamins and minerals. Nor do we know much about who ate garlic and onions. Half a century ago Lucie Randoin enumerated the virtues of the latter in the diet of the typical Egyptian *fellah,* and the argument no doubt holds true for the peasants of Crete and the shepherds of Provence and Rouergue as well.[7]

Modes of Production

Thus the quality of the diet alone is not enough to explain either the growth of the European population in the early modern period or the accentuation of national differences in the eighteenth century. It turns out, moreover, that the mode of agricultural production in each country was well adapted to natural conditions; otherwise it would not have endured. Biennial crop rotations were suited to the Mediterranean environment, whereas triennial rotations became common in the north.

Each nation's peasants did their best to cope with the conditions they faced. In some places land was available for cultivation or at least clearing. In other places supposedly fallow lands were secretly used for growing additional food crops, especially some of the newer crops from abroad that were reputed to produce miraculous yields.

Man proved to be persistent and ingenious when it came to overcoming obstacles in order to obtain enough food to stay alive and reproduce. But dependency on the new crops could lead to disaster. Ireland, for example, was hit hard by a plant disease that reduced the potato harvest, and by 1846 the ensuing famine had initiated a dramatic loss of population through emigration that continued long after. In countries where the imbalance between population density and resources took longer to reveal itself, the resulting downward spiral of prosperity also encouraged emigration to America. We see this in Norway, Sweden, Germany, Poland, Italy, and Portugal. In France, where the demographic pressure was not as severe, the population redistributed itself by way of a compensatory internal process of osmosis.

We come finally to England. Industrialization was no panacea, as can be seen from the fact that millions of Englishmen emigrated in the nineteenth century. Nevertheless, many scholars hold that the Industrial Revolution did much to stimulate population growth in the eighteenth century. In their view, industrial ventures provided employment for young people forced into early marriage, which led to an increase in the number of children per couple. No doubt a similar situation obtained in rural areas with decentralized industry enjoying access to external markets coupled with a local supply of food for its workers. In the vale of Trent, however, the gap between the birth rate in industrialized villages and that in villages which remained rural did not widen from 1670 to 1800.[8] Furthermore, it is too easy to attribute population growth to industrialization alone, when in fact the cultivation of the potato played just as great a role. The presence of the potato is well attested from an early date in Lancashire and West Yorkshire, two regions in the vanguard of change. The similarities with nearby Ireland are too great not to conclude that there must have been some causal overlap.

In fact, a different type of industrialization emerged, superior in technology and organization to that found elsewhere. The resulting development, very different from that of the previous century, was sustained by England's durable lead in machinery, by a certain internationalization of trade (with Australia, New Zealand, and Argentina), and by the availability of a breadbasket in the United States, which also provided a ready outlet for Britain's excess population. This led to dramatic changes in both the British way of life and the people's standard of living. The rate of population growth in the nineteenth century was far greater than in the eighteenth and is much more deserving of the appellation "demographic revolution" or "explosion."[9] Bear in mind, however, that the phenomenon was not limited to England or even Europe. It was worldwide, and in some parts of the world population growth proved compatible with older economic patterns. The facts should therefore be approached with great caution when searching for general conclusions.

Eating to Live

What did people eat? Although the question has always aroused a great deal of curiosity, the answers have often been disappointing, ranging from open-mouthed amazement at the feasts of kings to lachrymose commiseration for the meager fare of the poor. To venture to say more is risky because of the scant information available.

To be sure, it is easy to compile lists of food resources available to consumers in different parts of the continent. Along the edge of the Mediterranean from Greece to Spain was the domain of wheat, olives, cheese made from the milk of sheep and goats, lamb, fish, and octopus—supplemented on occasion with almonds, figs, and even oranges. Wine (along with water) was the main drink. Farther north we find more rye, together with barley and buckwheat in some places, beef, ham, chestnuts, apples, and beer.

No list of foods is exhaustive, and there was bound to be variety, of course, over any wide area. Owing to natural conditions and customs in the shale hills of the Rhineland and Luxembourg, for example, spelt was widely eaten there, whereas the English preferred wheat and the Scots liked oats (for porridge). One also has to take into account subtle cultural changes, such as the revival of artichokes in Italy and Picardy and the decline of Dutch carrots in the area around Nantes. Trade linked widely separated areas: cod from Newfoundland became a staple in Provence and Languedoc. Exotic new crops were introduced: in the second half of the sixteenth century people began growing rice in the Po Valley and the Spanish Levant, corn in Portugal and Galicia. Potatoes came to northwestern Europe in the seventeenth century and to central and eastern Europe in the eighteenth century. In the nineteenth century potato consumption rose sharply, along with consumption of green beans, tomatoes, and turkey.

There were also changes in the ingredients used in cooking. Classically, olive oil, goose fat, butter, lard, and walnut oil each defined distinct areas of culinary tradition. And grilling, roasting, and boiling (including stews) constituted the usual litany of cooking techniques. Into the pot one might throw a few pinches of salt (on which states found it easy to levy taxes) along with some herbs and spices (such as pepper, cloves, and nutmeg).[10] Little by little, chocolate, coffee, and tea, all sweetened, found a place as tonics and restoratives alongside spirits distilled from grain as well as wine.

This picture, however attractive, is misleading. For one thing, the colonial beverages just mentioned made their appearance quite late. And they were rare and expensive, so not everyone could afford them and it took some time for prices to drop. As for food, not everyone had regular access to all the foods itemized above. Most people's meals were in fact quite monotonous. People mostly survived on grain in the form of bread, brown rather than white, or flatcakes or porridge. The last, though deemed old-fashioned, remained on the menu in a number of countries from Scotland to Russia. Little meat was consumed. The exceptions were places not conducive to the growing of cereal crops, particularly mountainous regions where large quantities of dairy products were consumed, and countries such as Norway and Iceland where the diet was based on fish.

We should be under no illusion, moreover, as to the nature of regional cuisines. Many specialties that we nowadays think of as "regional" originated or at any rate were refined in the nineteenth century and owed little to the treasures of ingenuity that the housewives of earlier periods displayed on special occasions—such delights as gingerbread with honey, cakes for Christmas, and so on. What could be bought on the market depended not only on a family's means but also on what was available. In hard times, which were frequent, two factors conspired to force changes in the diet: instead of wheat bread, which was already rare, people ate rye bread or black bread, chestnuts, turnips (when available), and herbs (a term that covered not only garden vegetables but also plants gathered in the woods and fields). If things got worse, they ate whatever they could find or went without food; in the worst of cases they died of starvation.[11]

In light of these facts, it is clear that the problem of devising statistical indices that accurately capture long-term trends affecting the majority of the population is not easily solved. What sources should be used? Accounts of princely feasts are obviously of no use. Nor are the holiday banquets that one sees, for example, in paintings by Brueghel, even though such village festivals dotted the calendar. The archives are filled with the budgetary records of institutions such as schools, orphanages, and hospitals, from which we can learn about the rations distributed to pensioners but not necessarily about the *vulgum pecus,* since secondary schools were for nobles and ecclesiastics and the sick were often fed more than the healthy in keeping with medical beliefs about the therapeutic virtues of diet. We must be equally cautious about using records of the rations given to soldiers (both infantry and cavalry), sailors (whether naval or commercial), and galley slaves. Even when the documents deal with rations of groups closer to the mass of the population, such as laborers, vineyard workers, weavers, and so on, we must ask how representative these categories were.

Of course, we can also attempt to use data about wages and prices to see how much food people could actually afford. Vauban did just that in his *Projet de dixme royale,* in which he tried to estimate how much bread artisans and laborers could buy. What he came up with was six *livres* of bread (one *livre* was the equivalent of 489 grams) for a family of four (two and a half to three *livres* for the father, one to one and a half *livres* for the mother, and one for each of the two children). These quantities, of course, varied with the price of grain: the cost of bread consumed roughly 30 percent of the family's income in good times and up to 90 percent or more when grain was in short supply). The shortcoming of Vauban's method is that it focuses on just one item of consumption and therefore tells us nothing about the composition of the menu.

To overcome this difficulty, we can focus not on bread but on a ration about which we possess independent knowledge, such as gruel. In my view, this is the best way to proceed when studying the wage-earning population. But wage earners were a minority in the Ancien Régime, where most people were peasants who grew part of what they ate. This further clouds the picture, especially since some foods are never mentioned in our sources (whey, buttermilk, nettles, etc.). Obviously we cannot hope to arrive at an exhaustive accounting, but it seems highly probable that in the past peasants ate at least as well as workers did.[12]

No matter what method is chosen, the findings are similar: in normal years caloric rations were always above, and often well above, the level today regarded as adequate for a worker engaged in moderately hard physical labor (2,400 calories per day); indeed, they were close to the level required by a man engaged in hard labor (4,000 calories). More than half of this total caloric intake was in the form of grain. Hence there was an abundance if not an excess of starch in the diet. Fat and protein intake depended on local customs and menus but did not regularly fall below minimum daily requirements. It is almost impossible to gauge the consumption of vitamins and minerals (although we do know that, among sailors, a steady diet of salt meat and cod aboard ship often led to scurvy, due to a deficiency of vitamin C). Thus people had enough to eat—this goes without saying, or they would not have survived—but "enough" is not the same as "plenty."

NOTES

1. R. S. Schufield and E. A. Wrigley, *The Population of England, 1541–1871: A Reconstruction*, 2d ed. (Cambridge: Cambridge University Press, 1989).

2. J. Dupâquier, *Histoire de la population française*, 4 vols. (Paris: Presses universitaires de France, 1988).

3. J. Mirow, *Geschichte des deutschen Volkes vom den Anfängen bis zur Gegenwart* (Gernbach: Katz, 1990).

4. J. Nadal, *La población española: Siglos XVI a XX*, 2d ed. (Barcelona: Ariel, 1974).

5. J. M. Pérez García, "Un modelo de sociedad rural de Antiguo Régimen en la Galicia costera: La Península del Salnés," Ph.D. diss., Universidad de Santiago de Compostela, Departamento de Historia Moderna, 1979.

6. K. H. Connell, *The Population of Ireland, 1740–1845* (Oxford: Clarendon Press, 1950).

7. L. Randoin, *Vues actuelles sur le problème alimentaire* (Paris, 1937).

8. J. D. Chambers, *The Vale of Trent, 1670–1800: A Regional Study of Economic Change*, Economic History Review, suppl. 3. London: Cambridge University Press, 1957.

9. M. Reinhard, A. Armengaud, and J. Dupâquier, *Histoire générale de la population mondiale*, 3d ed. (Paris: Montchrestien, 1968).

10. Eating raw foods was not in favor, except for certain specialty items such as oysters, and even then only in certain places. Elsewhere oysters were eaten warm. It was not uncommon to eat dried or smoked meat, however.

11. Before the potato became an essential food for much of the population in the nineteenth century, it was used as a substitute for other foods. Cooks later developed a thousand regional dishes with it.

12. See my *Pour une histoire économique vraie* (Lille: Presses Universitaires de Lille, 1985). Agricultural workers were often served one or two meals a day by their employers, along with morning and afternoon snacks.

CHAPTER 29

COLONIAL BEVERAGES *and the* CONSUMPTION *of* SUGAR

Alain Huetz de Lemps

Cane sugar, which had been no more than an exotic curiosity in the ancient world, was brought to the Mediterranean by Arabs, who began growing cane in conquered lands such as Spain and Sicily. Christians, after discovering sugar in the East during the Crusades, began using it at home, but it remained a rare and costly luxury occasionally prescribed by physicians or sparingly used as a "spice" in cooking. Shrewd merchants from Venice and Geneva saw an opportunity to import sugar from the East and sell it in Germany, France, England, and other western European countries. In order to make it last longer and improve its quality, the sugar was refined in Venice, but the Venetians also sold brown sugar and even molasses.

The growth of the European trade encouraged the development of sugar plantations in the Near East, a development in which the Frankish kingdoms of the twelfth and thirteenth centuries participated. But as Turkish power expanded, and especially after the fall of Constantinople in 1453, the trade in sugar became increasingly difficult, and by the end of the fifteenth century Europe was importing almost no sugar from the Levant.

Sugar: A Prized Commodity

In the fifteenth century the European taste for sugar continued to grow. To satisfy the burgeoning market, sugar refineries sprang up in the coastal plains of Sicily, which the Normans had recaptured four centuries earlier. New plantations were also established in the Valencia region of Spain in the first half of the fifteenth century, inaugurating an active trade in sugar with the countries to the north.

As demand for sugar continued to rise, the Portuguese brought plants and technicians from Sicily to Madeira, which they had discovered in 1419. Within a few decades the island became western Europe's principal supplier. Production eventually outpaced demand despite the continent's voracious appetite.

In addition to Madeira, the Canary Islands, conquered by the Spanish in 1480, and São Tomé, colonized by the Portuguese in 1483, also proved hospitable to sugarcane.

During the sixteenth century sugar assumed an increasingly important place among the exotic ingredients sold by dealers in "spices." "Formerly," Ortelius wrote in 1572, "sugar could be found only in the shops of apothecaries, who kept it exclusively for the sick, but now people eat it gluttonously." And he added: "What once served as medicine now serves as food." Sugar-sweetened dishes became fashionable, and Valencian *dulcerías,* made with the local sugar, were highly prized. In England desserts sculpted in sugar were served on special occasions.

Given the increased demand for sugar, it will come as no surprise that one of the first projects attempted by the discoverers of the New World was importing cane plants along with technicians and equipment for manufacturing this valuable commodity. Christopher Columbus planted sugarcane in Hispaniola (Santo Domingo) on his second voyage. In 1516 Fernández de Oviedo presented the first six sugar loaves produced in America to Emperor Charles V as a gift. By 1530 there were thirty Spanish sugar mills operating in Santo Domingo. In the 1520s Cortés oversaw the building of sugar mills in Mexico, and plantations sprang up all across Spanish America. Most of the production was for local consumption, however: "The amount of sweets and marmalades consumed in the Indies is crazy," Father Acosta observed at the end of the sixteenth century. The Spanish never became major suppliers of sugar to Europe.

By contrast, the Portuguese, who discovered Brazil in 1500, established numerous plantations there after 1530, and nearly all the sugar they produced went to Europe. The sharp increase in European sugar consumption was associated with the vogue for three new beverages: chocolate, coffee, and tea, all stimulants that would come to occupy an important place alongside traditional alcoholic beverages in the second half of the seventeenth century.

American Chocolate

The Spanish "discovered" chocolate when they colonized the New World and subsequently introduced it into Europe. The Aztecs had used chocolate in their rituals and had even used cocoa beans as a form of money. With these beans, Oviedo observed, one could obtain anything one's heart desired: gold, slaves, clothing, women. The fruit of the cacao plant (*Theobroma cacao*) contained from twenty-five to thirty-five such beans, from which native Americans made a paste to which they added various other ingredients, especially ground chili pepper and *achiote* and sometimes corn, fruit, and even hallucinogenic mushrooms. Prepared in various ways, chocolate was used as a sweet beverage, a drug, an aphrodisiac, and even food. Díaz del Castillo, who along with Cortés attended the banquets of King Montezuma at Tenochtitlán (now Mexico City) in 1519, described how the drink was made: cocoa, ground up and mixed with chili pepper, was boiled and then whipped with a whisk to make a foamy beverage. The Spanish conquistadors found this drink quite spicy and bitter, "better to be tossed out to pigs than drunk by men," according to one.

Attitudes changed, however, when someone had the idea of adding sugar. No one knows when or where this discovery, crucial to the future of sugar, was made. Certain Mexican traditions attribute it to nuns living in Oaxaca, who presumably wanted to make a milder drink by replacing ground chili peppers with sugar. The necessary sugar was available from Mexican cane plantations, and sweetened chocolate proved to be immensely popular among Spanish creoles.

The conquistadors of course spread the news of this strange new drink back home in Spain. Charles V, to whom Cortés had made a gift of cocoa beans, served it to his courtiers in 1527, but the reception was apparently not very enthusiastic. It was not until 1585 that the first actual cargo of cocoa beans was shipped from Veracruz to Spain. By the end of the sixteenth century, however, "*esta preciosa y medicinal bebida*" was in vogue: people drank it either first thing in the morning or in the afternoon. Spanish aristocratic women acquired the habit of sipping a cup of chocolate with their afternoon snack. The church also took an interest in the new beverage: a controversy over whether it was permissible to drink chocolate while fasting lasted until 1662.

Meanwhile, other countries also discovered chocolate. Although we do not know precisely when this took place, we do know that by 1595 it was being drunk in Florence, in Venice, and by the early seventeenth century in Naples, from which it was evidently imported into Germany in 1641. By then Dutch ships were carrying cocoa from Venezuela to Spain. In 1657 the Dutch introduced it into England. In France chocolate seems to have made its appearance at the beginning of the seventeenth century. Anne of Austria, the daughter of Philip III, was quite fond of it. Chocolate became fashionable among the aristocracy under Louis XIV, especially after his marriage in 1660 to Maria Theresa, who had acquired the habit of drinking chocolate in Spain. In 1671 Madame de Sévigné wrote about chocolate in her letters; initially she was quite enthusiastic, but thereafter she changed her mind several times, for the new beverage had its detractors at court.

Under Louis XIV chocolate consumption remained essentially democratic. In the eighteenth century its popularity grew across Europe, and cocoa bean imports from America continued to rise. The first true industrial enterprises appeared in the 1770s. In France these included the Pelletier factories and Le Grand d'Aussy's *chocolaterie royale*. In 1819 Pelletier built a new factory, in which a steam engine was installed in 1839.

In Holland, Conrad Van Houten, after moving to Amsterdam in 1828, succeeded in separating cocoa powder from cocoa butter, an achievement that led to a major improvement in the quality of chocolate and quickly turned the Netherlands into a major supplier. The first chocolate factory in Switzerland was built at Vevey in 1819. Several others followed: Suchard in 1824, Kohler in 1828, and then Lindt, Tobler, and finally Nestlé. In the 1870s the latter two firms perfected a process for manufacturing milk chocolate.

In fact, chocolate was no longer regarded solely as a beverage. More and more of it was consumed in the form of solid tablets, which children liked, and various types of candy. Worldwide production rose from 10,000 metric tons in 1830 to 115,000 in 1900. Today it has reached 2 million. Cocoa beans have become a major item of international trade.

To feed the demand from Europe and North America, cacao plantations sprang up not only in South America, especially Brazil and Ecuador, but also in Africa, first in São Tomé in 1824, then in Fernando Poo (Bioko) in 1850, and subsequently in Ghana, Nigeria, Cameroon, and the Ivory Coast, as well as in Ceylon and the East Indies. Wild gyrations in the price of cocoa are a major concern of many Third World countries today.

Coffee from the Near East

Western Europe discovered another beverage shortly after discovering chocolate—namely, coffee. The coffee plant (*Coffea arabica*), a shrub from the mountains of Ethiopia, was apparently introduced into Yemen sometime between the fifth and the fourteenth century. In Ethiopia coffee was mixed with butter and made into a paste, which was then eaten, but in southern Arabia it became a beverage: the seeds of its fruit were roasted, ground into powder with a mortar and pestle, and then mixed with boiling water. Sufis drank the resulting dark liquor because it kept them awake during nocturnal prayers, but the initial pious intention was soon overshadowed by more sensual pleasures. By the late fifteenth century there were coffee-drinking establishments in Mecca, and by the early sixteenth century Cairo had become a great coffee metropolis despite opposition from certain religious quarters. Soon the entire Near East was drinking coffee: the first cafes were opened in Constantinople in 1554.

Turkish coffee found its way into western Europe via the Mediterranean. Merchants who had lived in the East and grown to like the beverage imported not only coffee but also equipment for making it from Constantinople. Thévenot, in an account of his travels in the East in 1664, lauded the beneficial effects of the dark liquid, and in 1669 the sultan's ambassador served coffee to Louis XIV and his court. Hoping to profit from the occasion, an Armenian dressed as a Turk set up a coffee shop in Paris the following year, but he was not very successful and moved on to England. Other Armenians and Italians followed, however. In 1672 the Sicilian Procope opened a cafe, and when the Comédie-Française was established across the way in 1688, Procope's cafe soon drew a clientele of actors and writers connected with that institution. In the eighteenth century the Café Procope became a veritable literary salon: Voltaire drank a mixture of coffee and chocolate there, and Rousseau, Diderot, and Condorcet were also frequent customers. The so-called Du Belloy filter coffeemaker made its debut in 1691.

The growth of the coffee trade naturally drew the attention of royal treasury officials, but the privilege granted in 1692 to a *bourgeois* of Paris authorizing him to sell "all coffee, teas, sorbets, and chocolate, together with the drugs of which they are composed such as cocoa and vanilla," was rescinded the following year. Thereafter coffee could be sold freely; a customs duty of ten sols was collected at the port of entry, Marseilles. Coffee shops proliferated over the course of the eighteenth century: by 1720 there were 380 public cafes in Paris, and by the end of the century there were more than 600. In 1782 Le Grand d'Aussy tells us, "there is not a single bourgeois home in which coffee is not served, not a single shopkeeper, cook, or chambermaid who does not take *café au lait* in the morning. In public markets on some of the capital's streets and byways there are women who sell the rabble what they call *café au lait,* which is really bad milk stained with used coffee grounds."

Little by little the habit of drinking coffee also spread to the provinces. In Germany a cafe was opened in Regensburg in 1686, another in Hamburg in 1690. The new beverage first found an audience with intellectuals and women. In 1727 Bach wrote a cantata whose subject was a worried father's desire to cure his daughter of her passion for coffee, a passion shared with most of the other young women of Leipzig.

Coffee made its first appearance in London in 1652. Coffeehouses multiplied thereafter, but when some became hotbeds of political protest, the city prosecutor decided to close them down in 1676. The ban was soon lifted, however, and from 1680 to 1730 Londoners discovered the pleasures of drinking coffee. British coffeehouses sold tea along with coffee, however, and the former quickly displaced the latter.

As coffee consumption grew, people in Europe began to look for new sources of supply. Meanwhile, Arab merchants attempted to hold on to their monopoly of coffee from Yemen. By sailing around Africa, it was possible to buy directly from dealers on the Arabian coast, and in 1660 coffee from Moka was sold at auction in London and Amsterdam. In 1726 Yemen exported 19,267 sacks of coffee weighing 280 pounds apiece. Of these, 54 percent were sold through Arab and Turkish dealers, 26 percent by English traders, 10 percent by the Dutch, 7 percent by French importers, and 3 percent by Persians and Indians.

Arabia was unable to meet the growing demand by itself, however. Some enterprising Dutchmen managed to get hold of coffee plants, which they planted in Ceylon and Java. Their venture quickly brought success, as large quantities of coffee began to be shipped to Europe from the Dutch East Indies. Samples of these Javanese coffee plants ended up in the botanical gardens of Amsterdam. In 1714 the city made the gift of a small coffee tree to Louis XIV, who gave it to Antoine de Jussieu for preservation at the Jardin des Plantes in Paris. In 1723 the tree bore fruit, and Captain de Clieu sailed with a plant grown from its seeds to Martinique, where it was quickly acclimatized. Seeds from this plant were distributed throughout France's colonies, especially to Santo Domingo, which became France's principal supplier in the eighteenth century.

Meanwhile, the Dutch introduced the coffee plant into Suriname in 1718 and the Dutch into Jamaica in 1730. The wife of the governor of French Guiana gave several stalks to a Portuguese officer in 1723. These were planted in Pará and became the basis of the Brazilian coffee industry. Other plants were shipped from Goa to Rio. *Fazendas* proliferated on the good soil of São Paulo, and in the nineteenth century Brazil became Europe's principal supplier.

European coffee imports, estimated at 33,000 tons annually in the middle of the eighteenth century, had doubled by the eve of the French Revolution. When the Napoleonic wars cut the continent off from its overseas suppliers, some Germans stepped forward with a beverage that their countrymen had been drinking since 1770, made from a local plant, chicory. This was not only cheap but also caffeine-free. During the blockade of the continent, people in France grew chicory as a coffee substitute. After peace was restored, this substitute did not disappear. Mixed with genuine coffee, it was found to moderate its stimulant effects, thus making it possible to drink greater quantities than before.

Over the nineteenth century coffee consumption continued to grow rapidly. Wholesale sales rose to 100,000 tons in 1835, surpassed 600,000 tons by 1880, and reached more than a million tons on the eve of World War I. Today, coffee production worldwide ranges from 5 million to 6 million tons annually. The two largest buyers are the United States and Germany. France ranks third at 378,000 tons, ahead of Italy and Japan. Although Colombia is reputed to produce the best arabica coffees, Brazil is the world's leading producer. Fluctuations in the Brazilian harvest can spell shortage or surplus for the world market, with important implications for coffee prices. This can have dramatic consequences, especially for smaller producers in Africa, where both arabica and robusta are grown.

Tea from the Far East

Of the three beverages involved in the great revolution in European taste, tea was the last to arrive. The Chinese had already been drinking it for a very long time, however. According to tradition, the idea of making a drink from the young leaves of *Thea sinensis*, a shrub native to the mountains of southern China, dates from 2737 B.C.E. Infusions made from tea leaves, stimulating to both body and spirit, were originally used in religious ceremonies, but the beverage became fashionable at court during the Tang Dynasty (618–907), and "teahouses" sprang up all over China. When Marco Polo visited the country in the middle of the thirteenth century, he was struck by the enormous quantities of tea that the Chinese consumed.

Tea was adopted by China's neighbors, the Koreans, in the seventh century, and by the Japanese, who were introduced to it in 729, as well as by the Mongols, Tibetans, Tatars, and Turks of central Asia. In the sixteenth century, Portuguese missionaries to the Far East once again described tea to correspondents back home, and it is quite likely that the first Europeans to drink tea were the people of Lisbon. In 1606 tea was mentioned in Holland, and there are reports that it was drunk there as early as 1637. Physicians—accused, incidentally, of being in the pay of the Dutch East Indies Company, suppliers of the precious commodity—lauded the exceptional qualities of the "drug."

Tea apparently arrived in France during the reign of Louis XIII. Somewhat later, Mazarin took tea "as protection against gout." In 1657 a thesis was written on the virtues of tea. As late as 1674, however, it was still not very well known in France. Supplies were scarce and prices were high. It was also in the mid-seventeenth century that tea made its debut in Saxony and England. Catherine of Braganza, the wife of King Charles II, who reigned from 1660 to 1685, allegedly introduced the British court to tea. Samuel Pepys recorded in his celebrated diary that he drank tea for the first time in 1660. In 1667 he wrote, "At home I found my wife making tea, a beverage that Mr. Pelling, the apothecary, told her was very good for her cold and bronchia." The British East India Company, which bought tea from the captains of Chinese junks in Bantam (Java), imported 4,713 pounds of it in 1678. This very small quantity shows that tea was still a mere curiosity whereas coffeehouses were numerous.

It was in the early eighteenth century that tea drinking really became popular in England. Coffeehouses found themselves serving more tea than coffee. In 1703 the directors of the East India Company observed that "tea is gaining greatly in reputation among people of all stations," and in 1718 they issued orders to load "as much tea as each ship can hold." Between 1760 and 1797 tea accounted for 81 percent of the value of all cargoes carried by the British company, far more than silk or porcelain. Other companies—in Holland, France, Denmark, and elsewhere—also claimed a share of the trade, which from 1784 was conducted directly with China. Tea imports to western Europe reportedly amounted to less than 900 tons in 1720, around 7,000 tons in 1766, and more than 14,000 tons in 1789. Most of this total went to England; some companies, including one headquartered in Ostende, sold what they imported to smugglers, who transported it across the Channel. During the wars of the revolutionary period, this trade was interrupted, but American ships sailed into Canton's River of Pearls to pick up the slack.

Tea's astonishing success in England was apparently due to a combination of factors: among these were energetic promotion by the East India Company, which advertised extensively; the custom, already established in England, of drinking coffee and spirits sweetened with sugar; a desire to restrict the use of alcohol; and a drop in prices, accelerated by a decrease in import duties in 1784. Tea drinking spread rapidly from the aristocracy to the urban population and ultimately to the countryside. In fact, tea became an integral part of the British daily routine. In the nineteenth century the popularity of tea in Great Britain continued to grow, with consumption rising from 12,000 tons annually in the decade 1801–10 to 89,000 by 1890.

On the continent, by contrast, tea drinking remained marginal, especially in France, where its devotees, mainly Parisian, were often seen as putting on airs: "He takes tea twice a week," Countess de Genlis wrote about one of her relatives, "and he thinks himself the equal of Locke or Newton." In the provinces tea was seldom drunk: one of Balzac's heroines in *Les Illusions perdues* sets out to astonish the provincial town of Angoulême in the 1820s by serving tea at a party, "a great innovation in a city where tea was still sold by apothecaries as a drug for indigestion." Tea was also little known in Italy and Germany except in literary and artistic circles.

At the opposite end of Europe, Russia followed England in embracing tea, a fact that is easily explained by the commercial relations that developed across the Asian continent. Tea came to Russia by caravan. It was first mentioned in 1618, but its use did not become common in well-to-do households until the eighteenth century, and imports at that time were still less than 500 tons annually. Tea did not become popular and did not spread to rural Russia until the following century.

Farther south, the Turks of central Asia had long been tea drinkers, and the beverage eventually made its way into Turkey proper—that is, into the heartland of coffee country. During the nineteenth and twentieth centuries, green tea became the primary beverage of the Muslims of North Africa. Two trading centers developed, one in Libya, the other in Morocco, where English traders may have played an important role in popularizing the beverage.

For a long time China was the sole producer of tea, and because of this the English found it expedient to intervene directly in the country's internal affairs. In 1827 the Dutch succeeded in acclimatizing tea in Java. The English began work on huge plantations in the Assam in 1834 and in Ceylon in 1842, and by the end of the nineteenth century these two regions had become Britain's principal suppliers.

The Triumph of Sugar

In their native lands, chocolate, coffee, and tea were drunk without sweeteners and consequently retained a certain bitterness. When these drinks became fashionable in Europe, however, sugar was also in vogue. Some Englishmen went so far as to sugar their wine. Thus the popularization of the three new beverages went hand in hand with a dramatic increase in the consumption of sugar. Sweets became more common. In England, for example, tea was served in the afternoon with sweet pastries and biscuits.

The English, according to one contemporary text, had "the sweetest tooth in Europe," and sugar consumption there rose appreciably over the course of the eighteenth century. From 4.5 pounds per person per year in the first decade of the century, it increased to 14.7 pounds in 1792 and to 19.8 pounds in the first decade of the next century. As Sidney Mintz has shown in *Sweetness and Power: The Place of Sugar in Modern History,* sugar, once an exclusive luxury of the wealthy, eventually sweetened every workingman's cup of tea. The sweet substance became the country's leading import; in 1791, of the 95,569 tons imported, only 16,186 were subsequently exported to other countries.

France also became a major sugar importer, receiving 86,584 tons in 1791. Its refineries, erected at Colbert's behest in Rouen, Nantes, Marseilles, and Bordeaux, served a domestic market smaller than that of England (per capita consumption in France was no more than 2.6 pounds per year at the end of the eighteenth century). But France exported a considerable quantity of refined sugar both to the countries along the Mediterranean and to northern Europe. Amsterdam, which had been a major sugar-refining center in the seventeenth century, was only partially supplanted by Hamburg in the following century, thus leaving the door open for the French. Overall, Europe imported 75,000 tons of sugar in 1730 and 250,000 tons a year by the end of the century. Sugar became the principal commodity in maritime trade, and by the seventeenth century it played a major role in shaping the colonial policies of the great powers.

The English occupied Barbados in 1627 and Jamaica in 1655, and the French moved into Martinique and Guadeloupe in 1635 and then into Santo Domingo at the end of the seventeenth century. Europeans set up plantations in these colonies and, like the colonizers of Brazil before them, made abundant use of slave labor. Several million black Africans were shipped overseas as a direct result of the spread of cane plantations in Brazil and the West Indies. By the end of the eighteenth century, Santo Domingo was producing 80,000 tons of sugar per year and Jamaica, 60,000. During the French Revolution, Santo Domingo became the Republic of Haiti and the plantations were ruined, making room for other Caribbean islands, most notably Cuba, to grab a share of the market.

The market expanded at an even faster pace in the nineteenth century: sugar became a basic component of an increasingly diverse European diet, especially in the cities. Annual per capita consumption reached 88 pounds in England, 33 in France, and 31 in Germany, but only 12 in Spain and 6.6 in Italy. In the United States it was 66. Since demographic growth was rapid, demand exploded: shipments of sugar rose from more than a million tons in 1850 to 8.385 million in 1900.

When the countries of continental Europe were cut off from their colonies during the Napoleonic wars, they began to rely on sugar beets, a crop that grew well in fallow plains. After a slow start, beet sugar output grew rapidly. In 1860 it accounted for only 352,000 tons of a total world sugar production of 1.7 million tons. By 1880 it was up to 1.8 million out of a total of 3.8; by 1900 it had reached 3.8 out of a total of 8.3 million. Germany, France, Austria-Hungary, and Russia were the major producers as well as consumers.

The success of the sugar beet did not mean that cane sugar production in the colonies did not also increase. Efficient new factories replaced traditional sugar mills. Cuba became the world's leading producer. To be sure, slavery was outlawed in one country after another, but the slaves were replaced by native contract workers on plantations in South Africa, Mauritius, and the Fiji Islands. While American growers in Hawaii brought in workers from China and Japan, Australian growers would hire only whites.

The scale of sugar production thus increased dramatically in the nineteenth century, but the rise in consumption that went hand in hand with this increase was in large part due to the three colonial beverages that had established themselves as a fixture of the European daily regimen long before.

CHAPTER 30

PRINTING *the* KITCHEN
French Cookbooks, 1480–1800

Philip Hyman and Mary Hyman

From 1480 to 1800 cookbooks were an important segment of French publishing. We have counted some fifty distinct texts on culinary subjects from that period.[1] It was not uncommon, however, for a successful title to be reprinted twenty or more times. Accordingly, these fifty texts appeared in 472 different editions. Some continued to sell for fifty years or more.

Printed Texts of the Renaissance

The case of the first cookbook printed in France is highly instructive, even exemplary. Known as *Le Viandier,* it was the successor to the best known culinary compilation of the Middle Ages. However, when the book was first printed, at the end of the fifteenth century, only 80 of the 230 preparations described came from medieval manuscripts; all the rest were new. Although the editor proudly proclaimed his devotion to the manuscript tradition, he did not hesitate to update this classic text. Other editors would adopt the same policy later on, publishing a new text under an old title. But one also finds old texts published under new titles. In any case, *Le Viandier* proved to be a smashing success: between 1486 and 1615 it was reprinted twenty-three times by thirteen different publishers in Paris, Lyons, and Toulouse.

For twenty years, *Le Viandier* reigned supreme. A first blow to its dominance was struck in 1505, when an Italian work, *De honesta voluptate et valetudine* by Bartolomeo Sacchi, known as "il Platina" or "Platine," was translated into French under the title *Platine en francoys*.[2] This text, which taught "the art of living," included a recipe section in its first Latin edition that accounted for just under half of the text.

Around 1540 a new series of recipe collections emerged as a direct competitor to *Le Viandier* on its own turf. Unlike that work, and even more unlike the Platina, these books were rarely attributed to a specific author but were presented rather as the work of "a number of highly expert cooks."[3] The most comprehensive and widely circulated work of this new generation was entitled *Le Grand Cuisinier de toute cuisine*. Like *Le Viandier* before it, this was a compilation of current recipes together with older ones. A careful examination of the recipes in *Le Grand Cuisinier* reveals that two-thirds were totally unknown in the Middle Ages and that the kind of cooking the work teaches differs markedly from medieval cooking.

Le Grand Cuisinier was also innovative in the way it was organized. The structure of the book followed that of a dinner with three meat courses (*en gras*), with a chapter devoted to each course. The first chapter explained how to make gruel, cabbage, stew, *haricot* (a kind of stew), soup, and sweetbreads. The second chapter dealt with preparing capon, partridge, hare, swan, cormorant, mutton, veal, and several other dishes that were either boiled or roasted or wrapped in dough. The third chapter contained instructions for preparing jellies, almonds, creams, hulled barley, sauces, and several other foods. To these chapters was added a fourth covering dealing with such nonmeat items as eggs, fish (eel, pike, carp, sturgeon, and several other kinds of fish, both freshwater and saltwater), vegetables, and several other meats. The book ends with a section of "instructions on making a banquet" and a series of menus. Although the structure of a meal has changed somewhat over the years, most present-day French cookbooks are still organized in the same way, much more rigorous than the organization of *Le Viandier*. It is worth noting, moreover, that the chapter on fish is arranged in alphabetical order by the name of the fish (*anguille, brochet, carpe, esturgeon*).

Between *Le Viandier* and *Le Grand Cuisinier* on the one hand and the Platina on the other, the sixteenth century witnessed the emergence of a voluminous specialty literature of an intermediate kind, known as *livres de confitures*, literally "books of preserves." These works, which contained recipes for preserves made with honey or sugar, preserves pickled in vinegar, spiced wines, bars of soap, perfumes, and plague remedies, were the ancestors of the so-called *livres d'office* of the seventeenth and eighteenth centuries.

From the middle of the sixteenth century on, food lovers thus had a variety of works at their disposal: the "classic" *Viandier* and the more "modern" *Grand Cuisinier* for the kitchen, specialty books offering instruction in the art of making preserves and other "healthy" recipes, and, finally, a compendium of dietetic and culinary knowledge in Platina's *De honesta voluptate.*

The Legacy of Le Cuisinier françois

Between the first edition of *Le Grand Cuisinier de toute cuisine* and the middle of the seventeenth century, a single new text with useful information about cooking appeared, *Le Thresor de santé,* written by "one of the most celebrated and famous doctors of this century." In organization and approach, *Le Thresor de santé* may be compared with the Platina: the author, not content simply to describe the most commonly used ingredients, also tells us how they are prepared and in so doing provides a substantial number of recipes.[4] In addition, it provides interesting information about the eating habits of people in the different provinces of France.

With the exception of this text, French publishers for a century confined themselves to reissuing recipes created in the late Middle Ages and the first half of the sixteenth century. *Le Thresor de santé* is the only evidence we have of the changes affecting French cooking in the second half of the sixteenth century, changes that presaged even more drastic modifications that would not be revealed until the publication of La Varenne's *Le Cuisinier françois* in 1651.

The book is divided into two almost equal parts: the first is devoted entirely to meat, the second to nonmeat dishes with a special chapter on Lent. In each part the recipes follow the same order: soups, appetizers, second course, entremets, and pastry. There are also special chapters on basic preparations such as *liaisons à conserver* (preserving sauces), *jus* (gravies), and so on. Appropriately enough, the work begins with a recipe for a stock that can be used as "nourishment for all preparations, whether it be soup, appetizer, or entremets."

As for the recipes themselves, the medieval heritage of gruel flavored with exotic spices was replaced by stews seasoned with native spices and garden herbs. Compared with sixteenth-century cookbooks, *Le Cuisinier françois* stands out for the unity of its style and the tone adopted by its author. Frequent references from one recipe to another, often between recipes separated by many pages, indicate that the text was conceived as a whole. Another rather remarkable fact is that in nine different places the author refers to himself in the first person, something never seen in any previous work. With all these innovations, *Le Cuisinier françois,* according to one contemporary, "derived honor from having bestowed rules and method" on an art that previously had neither.

Although *Le Cuisinier françois* included a treatise on preserves, this did not prevent the publication of specialized works on the subject. In 1653 Jean Gaillard published *Le Pastissier françois,* a work which, according to its preface, "seems to be the first of its kind, since no author until now has given the slightest instruction in this art . . . which was kept so very secret by the most celebrated pastry chefs of the court and of Paris that there are many very large cities and even entire countries in Europe where no one knows anything about it or is capable of practicing it."

The fact that pastry in this period included savories as well as sweets is confirmed by Antoine Furetière's *Dictionnaire universel* of 1690, which defines "pastry" as a "preparation of dough with one or more delicate seasonings of meat, butter, sugar, or fruit, such as pâtés, torts, tarts, biscuits, brioches, etc." Pastry recipes had been included in cookbooks since the Middle Ages. Yet never before had all aspects of the art been presented in such a comprehensive way, and this is what made *Le Pastissier françois* as revolutionary as *Le Cuisinier françois* some two years earlier. Its importance was such that at the end of the century Furetière would give as his example of the word *patissier* the following sentence: "*Le Pastissier françois* is a book from which one learns the art of the *pastissier*."

If *Le Pastissier françois* was the only work on pastry-making published in France between the middle of the seventeenth century and the end of the eighteenth century, this should not be taken to imply that the art of pastry-making itself was neglected. Many books dealt with all aspects of the culinary arts within the pages of a single volume.

Unlike books on pastry-making, books on *confitures,* or preserves (*livres d'office*), did not suffer from the publication of these encyclopedias of cooking. They seized the opportunity to become more comprehensive. The number of sugared preserves increased constantly. Distilled waters and cold and iced drinks were introduced, alongside flavored waters, soaps, pomades, and other hygienic products that had been included in the previous century's *Petit Traicte de confitures.*

As dessert courses evolved toward ever more spectacular presentations, the illustrations in these compendia of preserves tended to become much more lavish than those in regular cookbooks. For example, the first recipe book to include an illustration of a fully set table (as opposed to a mere plan) was *La Nouvelle Instruction pour les confitures, les liqueurs et les fruits* (1692). This was a large, foldout plate depicting a table set with pyramids of fresh and preserved fruits, biscuits, jams, and other dessert foods.

Toward a New Cuisine

The last innovative cookbook of the seventeenth century was Massialot's *Le Cuisinier roïal et bourgeois,* first published in 1691. This was the first culinary work to be presented in the form of a dictionary and to depict table layouts *in situ*—that is, in the form of drawings of a table situated in a room, covered with a tablecloth, and set with dishes and serving trays. Complemented in the following year by the publication of *La Nouvelle Instruction pour faire les confitures,* this was also the first multivolume cookbook. As it progressed through various editions and revisions, it was the only culinary treatise to follow the changes in cooking that took place in the early part of the eighteenth century. A slowdown is noticeable in the production of new titles and new publishing formulas. This period of stability, if not stagnation, lasted until 1734. During this time, *Le Cuisinier roïal et bourgeois* became *Le Nouveau Cuisinier royal et bourgeois,* and the cookbook section expanded from one to three volumes between 1712 and 1730.

The first writer to insist on a veritable rupture with the past and to characterize his cooking as modern was Vincent La Chapelle. While working in London, La Chapelle published his text first in three English volumes in 1733 and then in four French volumes in 1735. Entitled *Le Cuisinier moderne,* the work was the forerunner of a lavishly illustrated series of cookbooks that might equally well be considered art books. Three- and four-volume cookbooks subsequently became commonplace. In 1739 the first two volumes of Menon's *Nouveau Traité de cuisine* appeared, and a third volume was added in 1742, the year that saw the publication of Marin's three-volume *Suite des Dons de Comus* and the addition of a fifth volume to La Chapelle's *Cuisinier moderne.* Finally, in 1755, Menon published his four-volume *Soupers de la Cour.*

It was also Menon who, in the crucial year 1742, introduced the expression *nouvelle cuisine* in the title of the third volume of his *Nouveau Traité de cuisine,* where he declared that "the chef who works in the new style is preferable to the one who persists in the old method." Nevertheless, he went on to say that one must not "decry the old cuisine, since it must be the basis of the new." Meanwhile, *La Suite des Dons de Comus* promised readers that they would see "the old cuisine reconciled with the new."

Although the writers who published these books in the period 1743–1745 repeatedly stated that the new cuisine was "based on the old," the gap between ancient and modern cooking continued to widen as nearly everyone embraced the new cause. This mid-eighteenth-century diversification of cooking affected the substance as well as the form of cookbooks. In 1738 *Le Festin joyeux ou la Cuisine mise en musique,* the first collection of recipes in verse, or rather song, was published. In another innovation, texts began to include not just table plans but illustrations in the text itself to aid in the creation of certain dishes, such as *pigeon en tortuës* and *potage de citrouille* in Massialot's *Nouveau Cuisinier roïal et bourgeois* (1730) or the small drawings of *lièvre au gîte* and *lapereaux en vis-à-vis* in *Le Cuisinier instruit* (1758).

The transformation in the realm of desserts was no less significant, especially when it came to the development of ice creams and sherbets, to which Emy devoted an entire work entitled *L'Art de bien faire les glaces d'office* (1768). Meanwhile, the dessert table attained new heights of magnificence, and books on desserts often contained numerous high-quality illustrative plates. The five plates in Menon's *Maître d'hôtel confiseur* (1750) depicted palaces, statues, terraces, and other decorative sculptures in sugar and frosting. But this was nothing next to the thirteen large plates in Gilliers's *Cannaméliste françois* (1751), the most comprehensive treatise on desserts to that date. This work described how to construct enormous pastry tableaux on curved tables that allowed guests to "wander" among the sculptures and other decorations around which the bowls of dessert were arrayed.

Alongside this obvious taste for lavishness and luxury another tendency emerged. This new trend, which would change the culinary landscape of France forever, found its fullest expression in a modest volume published in 1746 and entitled *La Cuisinière bourgeoise*. This was also the work of Menon, and it was destined to become the unrivaled bestseller among cookbooks printed in France in the eighteenth century. In terms of longevity and number of editions published, *La Cuisinière* stands out above all other French cookbooks.

On the eve of the French Revolution we find a great stability prevailing in the small world of cookbooks and dessert books; yet at the same time we see signs of the changes that were to come. The success of *La Cuisinière bourgeoise* continued unabated, and while a few other quality cookbooks continued to be reprinted, no new cookbook appeared in France between 1758 and 1788, other than compilations such as *Dictionnaire portatif de cuisine,* published in 1767. Nevertheless, the culinary eighteenth century ended on a rebellious note with Jourdain Le Cointe's *Cuisine de santé* (1789), which criticized "all those sticky *roux, coulis,* and *sauces* which are like glues poisoned with fragrant spices." The revolutionary period proved to be a decisive turning point for culinary literature. After 1800, no pre-1789 text would be reissued by French publishers except for *La Cuisinière bourgeoise*.

Although the "culinary reality" captured by cookbooks turns out to have been quite selective and each work reflects different preoccupations, we nevertheless learn a wealth of detail about cooking technique and preparations that we could never discover in any other way. Some cookbooks, such as *Le Cuisinier françois* and

La Cuisinière bourgeoise, met the expectations of a broad audience, whereas others, such as La Chapelle's *Le Cuisinier moderne* and the more lavish pastry books, tell us about the extravagance of "dream banquets." Whatever their nature, however, cookbooks allow us to see how food was prepared according to the rules of the art. Thanks to their wide readership, these books helped to transform individual know-how into a collective possession, thereby revealing the evolution of an eminently evanescent art that might at first glance seem almost impossible to convey by means of the printed word.

NOTES

1. Included as cookbooks in our survey were any works in which at least half the text consisted of recipes or which had titles indicating a culinary intention or which are generally recognized as cookbooks (see the list of first editions in the Bibliography). Thus we have included, along with cookbooks proper (i.e., works consisting primarily of recipes), works such as *De honesta voluptate et valetudine* by Bartolomeo Sacchi (known as Il Platina), even though only about a quarter of the text is devoted to recipes, because the author was recognized as an authority on culinary matters by his contemporaries. This was made quite clear in 1584 when Jean Ruelle's widow published the book in Paris under the title *Grand Cuisinier de B. Platine.*

2. From 1539 on, the book and author were more commonly referred to as Baptiste Platine de Cremonne, *De l'honneste volupté.*

3. The works in this series are rarely dated. Nevertheless, with the invaluable assistance of the late Brigitte Moreau, former conservator of the depository of the Bibliothèque Nationale, we have been able to establish the following chronology: in about 1536 a *Petit Traicte auquel verrez la maniere de faire cuisine* was printed for Pierre Sergent, who, in about 1538, added to this brief pamphlet of 133 recipes 200 additional recipes and brought it out under the new title *Livre de cuysine très utille et proufitable.* None of these new recipes can be found in the medieval treatises, but two or three years later more than 150 medieval recipes were added to the text (some in place of more recent recipes) to create *La Fleur de toute cuysine,* which sometime around 1542 was renamed *Le Grand Cuisinier de toute cuisine.*

4. Because the recipes make up less than half the text, however, and because, in contrast to the case of the Platina, we have found no evidence that contemporaries took *Le Thresor* to be anything other than a book on dietetics, we have not included it in our list of cookbooks.

BIBLIOGRAPHY

The following is a selected list of first editions of cookbooks for the period 1480–1800. Brackets indicate attributions.

1486 Taillevent [?]. *Cj Apres Sen Suyt le Viandier*. Paris [?]. Caillot [?].

1505 Platine (pseud. Bartolomeo Sacchi). *Platyne en françoys*. Lyon: François Fradin.

1538 *Petit Traicte auquel verrez la maniere de faire cuisine*. Paris: Pierre Sergent [?].

1542 *(La) Fleur de toute cuysine* (renamed *Le Grand Cuisinier de toute cuisine*). Paris: Pierre Sergent.

1545 *Petit Traicte contenant la maniere pour faire [. . .] confitures [. . .]*. Paris: Jehan Longis.

1555 Nostradamus. *Excellent et Moult Utile Opuscule*. Lyons: Antoine Volant.

1651 La Varenne. *Le Cuisinier françois*. Paris: Pierre David.

1653 *Le Patsissier françois*. Paris: Jean Gaillard.

1654 [Bonnefons, Nicolas de.] *Les Délices de la campagne*. Paris: Pierre Des Hayes.

1656 Lune, Pierre de. *La Cuisinier*. Paris: Pierre David.

1659 *La Maistre d'hostel*. Paris: Pierre David.

1660 *Le Confiturier françois*. Paris: Jean Gaillard.

1660 *Le Cuisinier méthodique*. Paris: Jean Gaillard.

1662 *L'Escole parfaite des officiers de bouche*. Paris: Jean Ribou.

1662 Lune, Pierre de. *Le Nouveau et Parfait Maistre d'hostel*. Paris: Charles de Sercy.

1667 [La Varenne.] *Le Parfaict Confiturier*. Paris: Jean Ribou.

1668 *L'École des ragousts*. Lyons: Jacques Canier e Martin Fleury.

1674 L. S. R., *L'Art de bien traiter*. Paris: Jean Du Puis.

1689 *Traité de confiture*. Paris: Thomas Guillain.

1691 [Massialot.] *Le Cuisinier roïal et bourgeois*. Paris: Charles de Sercy.

1692 [Massialot.] *Nouvelle Instruction pour faire les confitures*. Paris: Charles de Sercy.

1714 [Liger.] *Le ménage des champs*. Paris: Beugnié.

1735 La Chapelle, Vincent. *Le Cuisinier moderne*. La Haye: printed by the author.

1738 [Le Bas, J.] *Le Festin joyeux ou la Cuisine mise en musique*. Paris: Lesclapart, Père.

1739 [Marin.] *Les Dons de Comus*. Paris: Prault Fils.

1739 [Menon.] *Le Nouveau Traité de cuisine*. Paris: Saugrain Fils.

1740 *Le Cuisinier gascon*. Amsterdam. Paris.[?]

1746 [Menon.] *La Cuisinière bourgeoise*. Paris: Guillyn.

1749 [Menon.] *La Science du maître d'hôtel cuisinier*. Paris: Paulus–du–Mesnil.

1750 [M. C. D., pseud. Briand.] *Dictionnaire des aliments*. Paris: Gissey.

1750 [Menon.] *La Science du maître d'hôtel confiseur*. Paris: Paulus–du–Mesnil.

1751 Gilliers. *Le Cannaméliste françois*. Nancy: printed by the author.

1755 [Menon.] *Les Soupers de la Cour*. Paris: Guillyn.

1758 *Traité historique et pratique de la cuisine*. Paris: Cl.-J.-B. Bauche.

1758 [Menon.] *Cuisine et Office de santé*. Paris: Leclerc, Prault Père, Babuty Père.

1759 [Menon.] *Le Manuel des officiers de bouche*. Paris: Leclerc.

1761 [Menon.] *Almanach de cuisine*. Paris: Leclerc.

1761 [Menon.] *Almanach d'office*. Paris: Leclerc.

1767 [Chesnaye des Bois.] *Dictionnaire portatif de cuisine*. Paris: Vincent.

1768 Emy. *L'Art de bien faire les glaces d'office*. Paris: Leclerc.

1782 *Essai sur la préparation des aliments*. London and Paris: Onfroy.

1783 Buchoz, J.-P. *L'Art alimentaire*. Paris: printed by the author.

1785 *Etrennes aux vivans*. Paris: Leclerc.

1789 Le Cointe, Jourdan. *La Cuisine de santé*. Paris: Briand.

1790 Le Cointe, Jourdan. *La Pâtisserie de santé*. Paris: Briand.

1795 [anno III.] *La Cuisinière républicane*. Paris: Mérogot the Younger.

1796 [anno IV.] *Le Petit Cuisinier économe*. Paris: Janet.

1796–97 *Le Manuel de la friandise*. Paris: Janet.

1798 *Manuel du cuisinier amateur* [?]. Temple du goût [?].

1799 [anno VII.] *Le Parfait Cuisinier français*. Paris: Libraries Associées.

CHAPTER 31

DIETARY CHOICES *and* CULINARY TECHNIQUE,
1500–1800

Jean-Louis Flandrin

The medieval cuisines of western Europe, insofar as we are able to reconstruct them from surviving cookbooks, share certain common characteristics that clearly differentiate them from the European cuisines of the nineteenth and twentieth centuries. By contrast, it is hard to imagine what common features (other than those linked to modern food-processing technologies) might characterize the latter in relation to the cuisines of other periods or other continents.

Clearly, the modernization of cooking was not a simple process whose broad outlines can be spelled out for the continent as a whole. Its history must be written country by country, but given the current state of research, this is unfortunately not yet possible. In Europe, national cooking styles diverged between the end of the Middle Ages and the middle of the nineteenth century, at which point the development of large-scale industry began to reverse the process, not only in Europe but to some extent throughout the world.

In this chapter, which is devoted to the cuisine of the sixteenth, seventeenth, and eighteenth centuries, I have therefore chosen a two-pronged approach. I will focus first on the culinary art of one European country—namely, France, not only because its history is for the time being better known than that of other countries but also because its cuisine was the dominant cuisine in Europe during the period in question. I will then examine the differences between French taste and the tastes of other countries and try to determine to what extent those differences were rooted in ancient traditions or had more recent origins or were simply the result of discrepancies in the pace of modernization.

French-Style Modernization

In France modernity of taste manifested itself in both the choice of ingredients and the manner of their preparation. To be sure, changes could easily go unnoticed, since meat dishes still dominated the better tables while the diet of humbler people was mainly based on vegetable matter (in the form of bread and soup). Beyond this apparent stability, however, important and complex changes were taking place.

A NEW TASTE FOR VEGETABLES In the second half of the sixteenth century and throughout the following century, the number of vegetable dishes mentioned in cookbooks increased sharply, as shown in the graph opposite. In the eighteenth century, the rate of increase slowed, but the number of species mentioned continued to increase—from twenty-four in the fourteenth and fifteenth centuries to twenty-nine in the sixteenth to fifty-one in the seventeenth and fifty-seven in the eighteenth.

Within this overall category, the prominence of three families of vegetables increased more than the average: mushrooms, artichokes and cardoons, and asparagus and other tender shoots. Cookbooks did not begin to record the success of these vegetables until after 1651, but other evidence, such as treatises on dietetics, suggests that it was already considerable in the second half of the sixteenth century.

By contrast, starchy vegetables declined steadily in relation not simply to other vegetables but also, in the case of cereals, to other foods generally. Whereas in the Middle Ages the social elites had sought the most nourishing plants, from the sixteenth century on they favored less nourishing ones, as if their goal were no longer simply to survive but rather to introduce greater diversity into cooking and indulge their appetites.

FOWL AND MEAT The one innovation in meat-eating that historians usually mention is the introduction of the turkey in the first half of the sixteenth century. This bird, imported originally from America, is mentioned with increasing frequency in cookbooks, and the fact that its price was falling suggests that it was eaten by growing numbers of people, despite which it maintained its gastronomic status. But two other changes not related to the discovery of America tell us more about the dominant trends in European taste.

First, the number of animal species served on the better tables decreased (while the number of plant species increased). Between 1500 and 1650, cormorant,

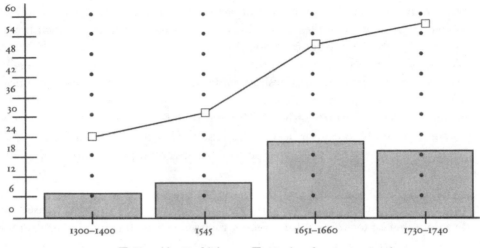

	Vegetables: % of dishes		Number of species mentioned

stork, swan, crane, bittern, spoonbill, heron, and peacock—large birds once featured at aristocratic feasts but deemed inedible today—vanished from cookbooks and markets. So did marine mammals and their by-products, ranging from whale blubber, once considered indispensable during Lent, to porpoise and seal. Of the amphibious species classified as "fish" by the church, only the scoter, a kind of diving duck that no one eats today, survived as a dish for meatless days until the end of the eighteenth century.

Archaeological investigation of animal remains has confirmed this narrowing of the range of edible species with respect to both fish and birds. At the monastery of La Charité-sur-Loire, for example, monks in the eleventh century had eaten dozens of species of fish, but by the seventeenth century they had lost all taste for species other than the carp they raised in their hatchery. Historians have concluded from this and other evidence that diet ceased to be determined by the hazards of production and began to be shaped instead by consumer preferences.

This interpretation is supported, insofar as the social elites are concerned, by kitchen accounts and butchers' ledgers. As early as the fourteenth or fifteenth century, cooks in aristocratic households turned up their noses at goats and sheep (male or female). They did on occasion serve the meat of cows (equivalent in status to steer meat) and specific parts of the animal such as the udder, as well as the meat of the kid, which was recommended by dietitians. Both of the latter meats vanished from princely tables and cookbooks in the first half of the eighteenth century. By the end of the century, the kid was still prized in only a few provinces, as we know from the schedule of price ceilings imposed by the Revolution. As for cow meat, its exclusion was the counterpart of the gastronomic rehabilitation of steer beef, which had been less costly than veal and mutton in the sixteenth and early seventeenth century but overtook these in 1639.

As the status of beef rose, so did the proportion of butcher products generally relative to other types of animal flesh in cookbook recipes. Much more attention was paid, moreover, to the particular cut of meat. With the exception of *Le Ménagier de Paris* (1493), fourteenth- and fifteenth-century cookbooks had usually been content simply to call for beef, veal, and so forth without indicating any specific cut. It was in the early modern period that specifying the cut became commonplace.

CHANGES IN COOKING TECHNIQUE As the variety of cuts increased, so did the number of techniques for cooking each one so as to bring out its distinctive characteristics. Take beef, which in the Middle Ages had been considered "crude" and dismissed as indigestible. Chefs in the aristocratic kitchens of the period made little use of beef other than in bouillons, stews, and pâtés. For roasting and even for serving with sauce they preferred the more "delicate" meat of fowl or of smaller mammals such as rabbit, hare, mutton, and veal. Only *Le Ménagier de Paris,* a bourgeois cookbook, concerned itself with the specific qualities of different cuts of beef, some of which it recommended for roasting.

In the seventeenth and eighteenth centuries, cooks used beef to make not only soup but also stock and gravy, which required roasting the beef in order to collect its juices. They also began roasting sirloin, fillet, and rump steak and serving them in their own juices. And they grilled steak and ribs. Sometimes the meat was cooked first in sauce and then grilled in buttered paper (*en papillote*) to promote complete absorption. Sirloin, fillet, hip, rump, oxtail, tongue, kidneys, brains, tripe, and eyes were also braised in a sort of court-bouillon. Slices of top round or rump larded with fat and marinated in white wine might also be baked in a sealed terrine. Cooks raised the status of the lowly stew by preparing stews with nothing but meat from the rump or breast of the animal. Stews could be reheated with onions to make *miroton,* just as roasts had been reheated in the past and served as *galimafré.* Oxtail was braised in a sauce of wine and onions or marinated, breaded, and grilled "*à la sainte menehoult,*" as this technique was known. The steer's palate was marinated and fried either in rings or croquettes. Tongue was served *en paupiettes* (wrapped around a filling) and *au gratin* (topped with grated breadcrumbs and butter) or else braised and then roasted on a spit and served with sauce.

Thus, like their medieval predecessors, seventeenth- and eighteenth-century French chefs often subjected meat to two successive types of cooking. They tried harder, however, to preserve the natural flavor of the ingredients. Before putting meat on the spit for roasting, both Taillevent's *Le Viandier* and *Le Ménagier de Paris* had generally recommended "parboiling" in water in order to firm up the meat in preparation for larding. But by 1651 La Varenne was recommending "blanching over the fire" for the same purpose so as not to dilute the meat's natural juices.

When the preliminary cooking was done in liquid, cooks were more careful about quantities. Many recommended braising or cooking in a court-bouillon, in some cases adding that the amount of liquid to be used "should be just enough to moisten the meat," as in the recipe for braised beef tongue in *La Cuisinière bourgeoise*. Sometimes the goal was to get the meat to reabsorb all the juice it had lost while being cooked in the bouillon. In cooking ribs, for example, cooks were admonished to "reduce the sauce so that all of it sticks to the rib" and then to condense it still further by grilling *en papillote*.

Unlike medieval chefs, who often boiled previously roasted meats in highly spiced sauces so as to impregnate the flesh thoroughly with the flavor of the sauce, cooks in later centuries avoided this technique for a variety of reasons. According to *Le Cuisinier français,* for example, sirloin fillets should first be roasted, then sliced, and "simmered uncovered" for a time brief enough not to darken the meat. Similarly, *La Cuisinière bourgeoise* recommended heating the meat in its sauce "without boiling" so as not to toughen its texture. But others, like the purist author of *L'Art de bien traiter,* rejected these methods, preferring instead to roast the meat on a spit and serve it rather rare in its own juices.

Fowl were also roasted on a spit and dressed with sauce only on the serving plate. Furthermore, the sauce was ladled onto the plate itself rather than over the meat. In addition to preserving natural flavors by browning the meat, cooks tried to harmonize flavors by wrapping the meat in strips of bacon or buttered paper to protect it from the heat during cooking. There was even concern to preserve natural component flavors even in stews, including the old *haricot de mouton*. *La Cuisinière bourgeoise* gave not only the usual recipe but also a second recipe for *haricot de mouton distingué,* a more delicate preparation, in which the cutlets and turnips were cooked separately and combined only on the serving plate.

In addition to new cooking techniques, early modern chefs also invented new ways of making sauces. They often used a *liaison* made of thickened almond milk or egg yolks whipped with cider vinegar, both of which were known in the Middle Ages. But they also developed the butter *liaison,* which they used to make white sauce, the equivalent of the modern *beurre blanc*. For meat sauces and stews they preferred *roux* (or "fried flour," as it was called at the time), which almost completely supplanted the old method of thickening sauce with bread. The *roux* technique, much decried nowadays, was at the time a widely applauded innovation that made it possible to make much smoother thickened sauces than in the past.

CHANGES IN SEASONING The most dramatic changes concern seasoning, and here we have evidence that what took place was nothing less than a mutation of taste. The "strong flavors" of the Middle Ages—sour and spicy—still had some adherents, but increasingly the social elite rejected them in favor of sauces made with fat. This resulted in dishes that many people considered to be subtler and more "delicate" while better preserving the "natural" taste of their ingredients. Although people continued to cook with spices and vinegar in the seventeenth and eighteenth centuries, they used much less of these strong seasonings than in the past and much more butter and cream, together with the natural juices obtained from cooking meat (sometimes reduced by boiling).

Spices still figured in 60 to 70 percent of all recipes, however, a proportion just as high as in the Middle Ages. But two changes are worth noting. First, the number of spices in common use had diminished considerably: long gone were galingale, grains of paradise, mace, "*spicnard*" (spikenard), cardamom, anise, cumin, mastic, and the long pepper, while cinnamon, ginger, and saffron were rarely used. Cinnamon was increasingly associated with sweets and ginger with charcuterie. The only spices that continued in regular use were pepper, cloves, and nutmeg, and these were much more widely used than before.

They were also used more sparingly. This statement is difficult to prove on the basis of cookbooks alone because recipes were still imprecise. From them, however, we do learn that cloves were no longer stuck into limes or (as is still done nowadays) onions. And in addition to cookbooks we have the reports of French travelers, who complained of foreign cooking so spicy that, no matter how hungry they were, they could not eat what they were served. Such complaints, which do not appear until the middle of the seventeenth century, attest to a change of Gallic sensibilities in this regard.

Acidic ingredients were somewhat more diverse than in the Middle Ages: *bigarade* (the juice of the Seville orange) and lemon juice were added to white wine, wine vinegar, and cider vinegar. In medieval sauces, which were made without oil or butter, vinegar or cider was often the only liquid component, and the bread used for thickening did little to moderate the acid's bite. This accounted for the characteristic taste of the so-called green sauce generally made of toasted bread, vinegar, and herbs, as well as the "sauce for capon or hen," described in *Le Ménagier de Paris*, which consisted of "four parts of cider vinegar and a fifth part, no more, of fat from the hen or capon." By contrast, in the seventeenth and eighteenth centuries, the acidic component was reduced. For example, the white sauce described in *L'Art de bien traiter* contained just a teaspoon of a court-bouillon prepared from one part vinegar and one part water thickened with a much greater quantity of butter. The same was true of the "piquant sauce" in *La Cuisinière bourgeoise,* where "piquant" meant not spicy but acidic: the recipe called for two large onions, a carrot, a parsnip, and various herbs browned in butter. To thicken the sauce, one added a pinch of flour moistened in stock together with a teaspoon of vinegar. Then the mixture was simmered over a low flame, which further reduced its acidity.

Unlike medieval sauce recipes, which never mention either butter or oil, the sauce recipes of the seventeenth and eighteenth centuries used these ingredients almost as frequently as we do today. Butter, which was used on lean as well as fat days, had not yet totally supplanted olive oil in aristocratic and bourgeois kitchens, much less bacon, lard, and other animal fats. It was not until the nineteenth and twentieth centuries that butter-based sauces became the characteristic feature of French haute cuisine, in contrast to popular and regional cuisines still based on animal fats and olive oil. In many recipes from the seventeenth and eighteenth centuries, moreover, butter was mixed with bacon or olive oil.

Another major change had to do with the use of sugar and with attitudes toward sweet dishes. Sugar consumption increased dramatically in France and other European countries between the beginning of the sixteenth century and the end of the eighteenth. If we look at the proportion of sweet dishes in cookbooks of the period, however, we find that it began to decline in the seventeenth century.

In the thirteenth, fourteenth, and fifteenth centuries, sugar figured at different points in the meal: in soups, appetizers, and roasted meats as well as in side dishes and desserts. Starting in the seventeenth century, however, it became increasingly common to relegate all sweet dishes to the end of dinner as well as to lunches and snacks that were consumed with sweetened beverages. In meat and fish courses sugar was not used as often as in the past, but it became more common with cakes and other flour-based confections as well as in creams and custards based on milk, butter, and eggs and in lemonades and other new drinks. Like fruits and some pastries, these were prepared by the butler in his pantry and not by the cook.

In the sixteenth century the appearance of a new type of technical literature, the treatise on making preserves, surely owed a great deal to the increase in sugar consumption. No doubt this also contributed to the growing lack of interest in sugar on the part of cookbook authors, who exemplified the modern tendency to specialize. But, more than that, there was an ever more prevalent feeling that sugar was not compatible with meat, fish, and most vegetables, as the opposition between sweets and savories continued to develop.

Other Tastes, Other Cusines

Taken together, these changes in taste and culinary practice define the French pattern of modernization. They did not occur to the same degree throughout the country, however. And in other countries we find even less evidence of them, as travelers' reports amply confirm.

TOO SWEET OR TOO SPICY In 1630 Jean-Jacques Bouchard had this to say about Provence: "Food is prepared in the Italian style, with abundant spices and extravagant, strongly flavored sauces, and as in Italy [they also make] numerous sweet sauces with Corinthian grapes, raisins, prunes, apples, pears, and sugar." This report tells us a great deal about the chronology of changes in French taste, the distinctiveness of the gastronomy and cuisine of Provence as compared with the Paris region, and French perceptions of Italian culinary practices.

Nevertheless, Italian culinary treatises of the baroque period attest to an evolution similar to that which took place in France in regard to spices. In the sixteenth century Messibugo used spices in more than 82 percent of his recipes: cinnamon, saffron, pepper, ginger, cloves, nutmeg, mace, and coriander. And Giovanni Del Turco used spices in 71 percent of the recipes in his *Epulario*. Like the French chefs of the seventeenth century, however, his palette was reduced: he used only pepper, cinnamon, cloves, and saffron, and there is no evidence that the quantities employed were larger than before. The main difference was that he used no nutmeg, whereas cinnamon was ubiquitous—and invariably combined with pasta.

The Spanish were also reputed to like their food spicier and sweeter than other nationalities. A seventeenth-century English traveler by the name of Willoughby noted that they "delight in pimiento and Guinea pepper and include them in all their sauces." And at the end of the eighteenth century, if the Marquis de Langle can be believed, the nobles of Aragon were still fond of garlic and pimiento—a "fruit as long as one's finger . . . [and] which tastes like pepper" and "leaves your mouth burning and your breath on fire for the rest of the day."

In 1691 Countess d'Aulnoy visited Spain and immediately complained about the grand supper served her for St. Sebastian's Day, which was "so full of garlic and saffron and spices" that she couldn't eat any of it. She also disliked the "very nasty stews, full of garlic and pepper," and a "pastry [which] is so peppery that it burns your mouth." At a dinner with the queen mother in Toledo, she found herself "like Tantalus, dying of hunger but unable to eat a thing. For there is no middle ground between meats reeking of perfume," and therefore disgusting, and those "full of saffron, garlic, onion, pepper, and spices," and therefore impossible to eat. The excessive sweetness of Spanish food was due not only to the craze for flavoring dishes with amber, which the countess also detested, but also for the incongruous use of sugar. The countess complained, for example, of a ham that was served to her in Madrid, which would have been excellent had it not been "covered with candies of the sort that we in France call nonpareils . . . whose sugar melted into the fat." To make matters worse, the meat was "larded with lemon rind, which considerably reduced its quality."

In 1675 Jouvin de Rochefort expressed his astonishment and annoyance at the fact that in Flanders and Ireland he was served sugared salads. In Ireland he sampled a salad that was "covered with a quantity of sugar equivalent to the snow cover on Mount Aetna" and claimed that "it is impossible for anyone who has never encountered such a thing before to eat it."

In southern Germany in 1580 Montaigne was surprised to find meat accompanied by fruit. In the inns of Basel he saw "pears cooked together with the roast." And in Lindau he declared "alien to our customs" the practice of serving "soups topped with rounds of cooked quince or apple." In Stuttgart in 1657 Coulanges was also struck by "the many unusual stews, such as gosling stuffed with cooked apples and prunes" as well as by the "black and scrawny pieces of meat dried and peppered in the local manner" and "buttered chickens festooned with cloves."

In northern Germany and Poland in 1648, Laboureur found much to criticize in the use of spices as he passed through Oldenburg, Bremen, and Danzig. But Gaspard d'Hauteville, who lived in Poland during the next twenty years, was just as struck by the use of sugar and fruit with meat. "Their sauces are very different from the French," he explained. They made "yellow ones with saffron, white ones with cream, gray ones with onion, and black ones with plums," and "they add lots of sugar, pepper, cinnamon, cloves, nutmeg, olives, capers, and raisins."

In short, from the Mediterranean to the North Sea and the Baltic, French travelers in the seventeenth and eighteenth centuries were struck by both the abuse of spices and the incongruous use of sugar and fruit garnishes with meat.

TOO MUCH SALT The chefs of central and eastern Europe evidently used more salt than the French. This is hard to imagine, given the fact that in the seventeenth and eighteenth centuries French salt consumption was much greater than it is today: seven and a half pounds per person per year at the end of the eighteenth century in regions where the salt tax known as the *grande gabelle* was collected (and this does not include salt used for salting meat and fish) and, according to estimates by the Ferme Générale, from twelve and a half to twenty pounds per year in other regions, compared with just under five pounds today. Nevertheless, there is reason to believe that Germans and others liked their food even saltier.

With the Poles the case is clear: we have the testimony not only of a Frenchman, Beauplan, who lived in Poland in 1630 and again in 1651, but also of a German, Ulryk Wedum, who visited in 1632. According to Wedum, "No other nation uses as much salt and spices of every sort as the Poles. Because food is already salted in the kitchen, they don't even put salt cellars on the table."

The evidence concerning Germany is less direct, but it suggests that the Germans, too, were accustomed to eating their food saltier than the French. In any case, the social elite in France certainly consumed a much smaller quantity of salted foods. At the beginning of the eighteenth century, a German by the name of Nemeitz alerted his compatriots to the fact that Parisians did not eat meats and vegetables preserved in salt. He admitted that "people of quality sometimes have slices of Mainz or Bayonne ham on their tables," but went on to say that "they treat these things as a great delicacy and merely sample them."

If Jouvin de Rochefort is to be believed, the Flemish also abused salt. He complained that at the Cheval-Blanc Inn in Condé he was served "a small duck which they had cooked in vinegar and in so great a quantity of salt and pepper that it was impossible for me to eat. This is done deliberately in Flemish fortress towns and other cities, because in this way they can store large quantities of food, which they cook in ovens in huge pots several times over so as to preserve the contents throughout the year."

In addition to salted meats, the Flemish, Germans, and Poles also ate sauerkraut and other vegetables preserved in salt. Because of the harsh northern winters, fresh vegetables were not always available in these countries. Salted vegetables were a solution to this problem, as Montaigne observed when he visited Konstanz in 1580: "They have plenty of cabbage, which they chop finely with an instrument designed expressly for the purpose. And thus chopped, they put large amounts of it into barrels filled with salt, from which they make soup throughout the winter." When he reached Augsburg, he noted that "throughout this part of the world they chop up radishes and turnips with as much care and urgency as we thresh wheat. Seven or eight men, armed with huge knives, carefully hack away at the vats . . . which are used to make salt preserves for the winter, as with cabbage. With those two fruits [sic] they fill not their gardens but their fields, and they harvest them."

According to the German traveler Joseph Kausch, the same salted vegetables were eaten in Poland, including the eastern reaches of the country, now part of Belorussia and the Ukraine. And Antonio de Beatis, who visited the Low Countries in 1516, had this to say: "Throughout Flanders, there are quantities of cabbage. . . . As in Germany, large amounts are stored and preserved in salt. And in winter, when the ground is covered with snow, they eat this cabbage seasoned in a variety of ways."

NATIONAL TEMPERAMENTS Building on these reports, let us try to understand the pattern underlying these apparent differences. It was out of necessity that the Flemish, Dutch, Germans, and Poles ate so much food preserved with salt. But from this habit did they perhaps acquire a taste for salty dishes? In support of this hypothesis we have the observation of Jean Le Laboureur, who claimed that at one Oldenburg banquet, "nothing was edible except the fresh eggs," not only because the pâtés were too spicy but also because "the other dishes were also seasoned *with large amounts of salt*." But only the French saw it this way: "The Polish ambassadors ate more heartily than anyone else, because Polish stews are the same . . . as we have since discovered." It was the same in Bremen: "Only the Poles ate to their hearts' content, vociferously lauding the plentiful amounts of spice and saffron and *salt* that the cooks had so lavishly laid on." Therefore, it was not only because the Poles were forced to eat preserved meats and vegetables that they consumed so much salt but also because they liked the taste, so that their chefs salted their dishes much more heavily than French chefs did.

Concerning a preserved duck that he was served in Flanders, Jouvin de Rochefort observed that it was "tasty, to tell the truth, but you couldn't eat much without succumbing to thirst." Thus there may have been a connection between the northern and eastern European taste for salt and the concomitant reputation for drunkenness. But did people drink too much because they ate too much salt, or was it the other way around? When Germans drank, they always served slices of bread sprinkled with salt and spices to stimulate their thirst, as both Montaigne (1580) and Misson (1688) observed at various points in their travels.

What is the key to understanding all this variety? Today we are apt to focus on the fact that the salt-loving tipplers of northern Europe were beer drinkers. But in the past the French and other wine drinkers were well versed in the art of stimulating thirst with salty snacks, as we know from Rabelais and many others. What is more, the wines of the past were generally much weaker than today's wines, and people customarily diluted them further with water, so what French people drank regularly was as watery as German beer.

So we have to look for other keys to explain the eating and drinking habits of the peoples of northern and eastern Europe in the sixteenth, seventeenth, and eighteenth centuries. Because the climate in the north was cold, people needed drinks that warmed them up. What struck contemporary observers was not that they drank beer but that they drank their wine undiluted, in excessive quantities, and also liked to get drunk on spirits made from grain.

Another possibility is that in the dry, cold, northern climate, it was believed that people tended to have "melancholy" and "earthy" (or "crude") temperaments. Hence they were drawn to "crude" foods. With this in mind, we can understand Neimetz's advice to his fellow Germans: "People who are accustomed to crude meats will be unable to find their fill in Paris, for there nobody eats chitterlings or salted or smoked meat or sauerkraut or rye bread or anything of the sort. Such fare is unfit for a French stomach. The Frenchman's bread is white, and all his meat is fresh." Of course, "crude" is a rather harsh word that people do not ordinarily apply to themselves; when a German or an Englishman alluded to the "delicacy" of the French, it was not without irony.

COOKING MEAT The English were very fond of their "crude meats," especially beef. They were apt to judge a country's gastronomic level by the quality of its beef, whereas the French and Italians were more likely to judge by the quality of the bread. The Englishman Townsend voiced his astonishment at the fact that in Spain beef was less expensive than mutton, a fact that would scarcely have surprised a Frenchman or an Italian.

Although the student of French markets and culinary treatises is aware that the status of beef rose in France during the early modern period, foreign visitors were not struck by this fact. To the English, in particular, the French remained chicken eaters with no idea of how meat ought to be cooked. In 1740 Horace Walpole complained of being able to find nothing but boiled beef in France. And in 1766 Tobias Smollett remarked that French beef was "neither fatty nor chewy but very good for soup, which is the only use the French make of it."

In 1656 Peter Heylin wrote that he "had heard a lot about the skill of French chefs, but they must not exercise their talent on beef or mutton." He criticized them for roasting pieces that were carved too small, which on the one hand was a mark of stinginess and on the other hand made it impossible to roast the meat properly. Conversely, when François de La Rochefoucauld visited England in 1785, he noted that the roasts served on the better tables "weigh twenty or thirty pounds." In *The Art of Cookery* Hannah Glass indicated cooking times for roasts of ten pounds (an hour and a half over a good fire), twenty pounds (three hours if the piece is thick, two and a half hours if thin), "and so forth."

In 1596 the Italian Francesco d'Ierni was also struck by Parisian meat-cutting practices: the city's butchers sold meat "not by weight but by the slice." His report should be compared with Heylin's and with the earlier discussion about the increasing variety of cuts and the adaptation of cooking techniques to the new variety. The trend toward smaller cuts, which actually reflected progress in the arts of butchery and cooking in this period, was evidently misunderstood by people from other countries.

As for cooking techniques, Peter Heylin also accused the French of placing roasts on a spit perpendicular to the fire, rotating the spit just three times and bringing the meat to the table "more grilled than roasted." Did he mean by this that it was raw on the inside and charred on the outside, as one would expect from such a technique? Perhaps, but his compatriot John Ray used the same phrase to describe a dried-out roast: "In Italy and other warm countries, meat is not only served leaner and drier than we serve ours but is also roasted until it is ready to drop from the bone and no juice remains. When they roast meat, moreover, they place the coals beneath the spit and allow the grease to fall onto them. . . . Their method of roasting is not very different from grilling or charring. I am speaking of ordinary inns and the homes of common people. In the great houses, things are different."

Arthur Young, a great admirer of French cooking, was nevertheless upset that the French "roast everything far too long." But if the tastes of the two nations were so different in this regard, why did French travelers not make the opposite complaint about the English? Why did they leave that chore to the Spaniard Antonio Ponz and the German Neimetz? The matter is all the more puzzling in that other Englishmen felt the French did not roast their meat long enough. Smollett, for example, complained that warblers, thrush, and other small birds were "always served half-raw" in the region between Lyons and Montpellier. The French "would rather eat them that way than run the risk of losing some of the juice by overcooking," he explained. He made a similar observation about the cooking in Nice, a city that struck him as virtually Italian. Perhaps the way to reconcile Smollett's comments with those of Young and Heylin is to say that in every country rare cooking is reserved for the meats people truly like, while everything else is overcooked.

All observers agreed that in France meat and fowl were larded with fat before roasting. Travelers' accounts do not tell us anything about French cooking techniques that we do not know from other sources, but they do suggest that larding was a relatively rare practice in other countries. Other evidence corroborates this: in the seventeenth century Coulanges deplored the dryness of German roasts, and a French zoologist of the mid-sixteenth century criticized the Italians for failing to lard their meat. The technique is mentioned in Italian cookbooks, however. In *Epulario* Del Turco recommends larding all roasts, with the exception of the fatty quail, which does not need it, and the pigeon, which he recommends marinating in olive oil.

Many travelers complained about the Italians' bad habit of boiling meat and fowl before roasting. In the early eighteenth century, for example, Father Labat railed against the innkeeper who plunged his roasting chickens into a cauldron of boiling water. And in the seventeenth century Gilbert Burnett remarked that "when it comes to meat, they are accustomed, in the inns at any rate, to boiling it before placing it on the spit, which makes the meat tender but quite insipid." But did the Italians boil their roasts for long periods of time in order to tenderize them and get rid of the blood, or did they just dip them briefly into boiling water in order to firm up the flesh for more convenient larding? It is the latter method that we find in *Epulario,* as well as in French culinary treatises from the Middle

Ages. In any case, the purpose of the technique is ambiguous, and it was suspected of leaching juices out of the meat, which shocked travelers from countries where it was no longer used.

The English made fun of French sauces and stews, which they said "feed not the stomach but the palate." Fancying themselves fond of simple, straightforward, nutritious food, they would never think of eating meat in any form other than boiled or roasted. La Rochefoucauld's observation corroborated this self-assessment: "Gravy is never used in English cooking, and stews are rare. All the dishes consist of meat either boiled or roasted." But English cookbooks only partially support this commonplace. In the cookbook by Hannah Glasse, who can hardly be suspected of indulgence toward French cooking, we find not only forty-five boiled beef dishes and thirty-six roasts but also thirty stews, forty braised dishes, thirty-two fried dishes, and twenty-two fricassees. What is more, most of her recipes are more complicated than comparable French recipes from the same period.

ANALOGIES The influence of French cooking on the tastes of the European social elite is particularly clear when one looks at culinary treatises: in the seventeenth and eighteenth centuries these were often simply translated from the French. Because of this, it is difficult today to study the cooking practices of other countries and how they changed. Yet even in the case of national cuisines that largely escaped the influence of the French (such as the cuisine of the Italian baroque, of Spain in the Golden Age, and of English cookbooks hostile to French techniques, such as that of Hannah Glass), we find some of the same changes that occurred in France.

In England, for example, cookbook authors began to include recipes for cooking vegetables, just as in France. The proportion of beef dishes also increased sharply, while that of fowl declined (rabbit and hare held steady). Unlike the French, however, the English retained their fondness for the large, handsome birds that were often the centerpieces of medieval banquets. In cookbooks published between 1591 and 1654 one still finds recipes for eagle, bittern, curlew, and swan (whose delicious flesh drew expressions of ecstasy from Samuel Pepys in the mid-seventeenth century), as well as crane, heron, gull, and peacock. Sea mammals (such as whale, dolphin, porpoise, and seal) fell from favor, but in England this shift was accompanied by a decline in the popularity of fish, which did not occur in France, Italy, or Spain.

Although the English continued, even after the Anglican schism, to observe Lent and meatless Fridays, it is well established that fish consumption in the British Isles plummeted. In fact, in an effort to halt the dramatic decline of the English fishing fleet, the authorities tried unsuccessfully to reinstate Saturday as a meatless day in 1548 and then Wednesday in 1563. It may well be that it was not religious obligation that kept fish consumption high in France and other Catholic countries. As Arthur Young observed in August 1787 after eating a supper of two delicious carp at an inn on the banks of the Charente:"If I were to pitch my tent in France, I should like to settle near a river capable of supplying fish like those. Nothing is more irritating than to look through one's windows and see a lake, river, or ocean yet have no fish for dinner, as is frequently the case in England." And no doubt in the rest of Great Britain as well. John Lauder, who spent a year in Poitiers in 1656, voiced his astonishment at the fact that his hosts, like "nine out of ten Frenchmen, prefer fish to meat" and "consider it more delicate in flavor." Yet these same hosts soon realized that their guest did not care for fish and, being courteous, "no longer served it more than once a month."

The rehabilitation of butter is as clear in the English treatises as it is in the French, but it comes later and more abruptly. The same is true of other northern countries such as Flanders and Sweden, where butter was virtually the only fat used in cooking. In these places, however, we have no proof that this was a novelty. In Italy butter is mentioned in the mid-fifteenth-century treatises of Martino and Platina, and in the seventeenth century it was commonly associated with pasta. Throughout Europe, but especially in the northern countries, the rise of butter appears to have been connected with the decline of the Roman Catholic church and its influence on eating.

By contrast, in southern Europe, where the church maintained its authority, the use of olive oil was more prominent in the early modern period than it had been in the Middle Ages. It was no longer reserved exclusively for meatless days. By the beginning of the seventeenth century in Provence, Italy, and Spain, olive oil was used for fricasseeing chicken, partridge, mutton, and other meats. It became emblematic of Mediterranean cooking and taste. Paradoxically, this shows that church regulation was less important than in the Middle Ages.

As for seasoning, most European countries turned away from the spicy cooking that had long been their preference. In this respect France seems to have led the way. But the English were also discreet in their use of seasoning, at least before Indian curries became fashionable. Indeed, Hannah Glasse's cookbook gives us a more precise idea of the new restraint in the use of seasoning than do most French treatises. And as we saw earlier, by the beginning of the seventeenth century, Italian chefs used no greater variety of spices than did their French counterparts, despite their reputation for a free hand in this regard. As far as we can tell from the current state of research, however, chefs in countries other than France continued to make dishes that combined sweet with savory seasonings. The separation of sweet and savory may have been not so much a sign of modernization as a distinctive feature of French cuisine.

CHAPTER 32

From DIETETICS *to* GASTRONOMY
The Liberation of the Gourmet

Jean-Louis Flandrin

The idea that the function of cooking is to make food easy to digest, and that culinary creation takes place within a system of dietetic constraints whose purpose is to balance hot against cold and dry against moist, will seem obvious today to anyone from India, China, or the West Indies. Yet Europeans find it difficult to admit that the same idea once shaped their own attitudes toward food.

When did European chefs begin to invent new recipes based solely on their imaginations, their gourmet fancies, without considering possible "deficiencies" in their ingredients? When did their clients begin to ask only for delicious and surprising new creations without regard for the "medical" properties of the food they were eating? When did both groups forget the dietetic function of seasoning and cooking in favor of the newly independent gastronomic function? When did gourmet taste declare itself as such? And when did gastronomy, the new science of eating well, replace the old dietetics? None of this happened overnight.

The Persistence of the Old Dietetics

The old dietetics continued to influence food preparation well into the early modern period. Indeed, the relationship between dietetics and cooking may never have been as close as it was in the first half of the seventeenth century. One can gain an idea of just how close by noting the number of culinary observations in a treatise on dietetics like *Le Thresor de santé* (1607) or by looking at the medical justification given by the author of a culinary treatise like *Le Cuisinier français* (1651). Still later references to dietetics can be found in countless other works about preparing and serving food and drink, but these discreet allusions often go unnoticed by readers who do not know what to look for.

In 1674, for example, the author of *L'Art de bien traiter* invoked health as a reason for resisting the growing vogue for dark or "cloudy" wines, which traditionally were spurned as "earthy," crude, and hard to swallow. He recommended drinking only champagnes, which are "among the more colorless and watery and least filling of wines, for no matter how good red wine may be, it is always heavier (*plus matériel*) than other wines because of the length of time it ages in the barrel and is never as delicious or as quick to digest; hence it is the cause of any number of indigestions and ailments." It is also for dietetic rather than gastronomic reasons that he devotes several pages to a diatribe against the fashion of drinking champagne with ice: "Ice, by nature cold and penetrating, evaporates the spirits in liquor and thus diminishes the taste, vigor, and color of the drink. More seriously, its use may be pernicious and even fatal and is apt to injure the body in peculiar ways: it is the source of colics, tremors, and horrible convulsions and by dissipating the body's natural heat causes weaknesses so sudden . . . that, owing to this miserable and lethal invention, the most splendid debauches have often culminated in death." This prejudice against iced drinks indicates the survival of an age-old belief that wine, once drunk, turns almost immediately into blood and should therefore be drunk at body temperature so as to avoid serious injury.

The same author justifies the French custom of serving many different kinds of dishes simultaneously by arguing that people have many different "temperaments." Hence what is good for one is not necessarily good for another: "One often encounters people who reject and condemn any number of good things whose taste they have never gotten used to. And since in any company it is rare that someone will not find something antipathetic to his nature, it is only proper to serve more than one kind of thing for every occasion, so that there is sure to be something compatible with each guest's dominant humor."

Traditionally, as we have seen, people believed that differences of appetite originated in nature. Taste was thought to be a matter of sympathy between the nature of the individual and the nature of certain foods; similarly, distaste was believed to be a consequence of physiological antipathy. To be sure, sympathies and antipathies could grow out of habit, or "second nature," as the physicians liked to call it, but they were mainly characteristic features of each individual's temperament—that is, of the relative proportions of the four humors: sanguine, choleric, phlegmatic, and melancholic. Since it was impossible to change a person's temperament, it was wrong to ignore the dictates of taste. French hosts therefore served a variety of dishes in every course of the meal because they believed that, for health reasons, it was important to have something that each guest would find pleasing.

As time went by, however, the dietetic justification for this manner of serving was eventually forgotten. At the beginning of the eighteenth century, Massialot was still justifying the French style of serving by invoking the diversity of individual taste. He recommended arranging the dishes so that "each person can take what suits his appetite." To that end, one should "avoid placing two dishes of the same sort next to each other without one of a different sort in between. For otherwise the service would be graceless and might offend the taste of some of the people at the table, since not everyone likes the same things." He did not, however, make any connection between the variety of tastes and the variety of temperaments. By the early nineteenth century, moreover, ostentatiousness and gluttony were no longer cited as reasons for the number of different dishes. In 1821 Archambaud simply stated that variety, now prescribed in detail as never before, "contributes to the quality of the dinner." And in 1805 Grimod de La Reynière noted that gourmets avidly devoured all the dishes in the first course. The time was ripe for harmonizing the various dishes served in each dinner, and the Russian style of service made this possible.

Violating the Prescriptions of the Old Dietetics

Grimod de La Reynière also made no allusion to dietetics to justify, in the third year of his *Almanach des gourmands,* the custom of serving figs, melon, and blackberries at the beginning of the meal. He seems to have forgotten that this centuries-old tradition was prescribed by the medicine of an earlier time.

To be sure, almost all juicy fruits had been served as appetizers from the fourteenth to the sixteenth century, in keeping with medical advice, whereas by the beginning of the nineteenth century only three remained. From the seventeenth century on, the others—grapes, cherries, peaches, clingstones, apricots, nectarines, plums, prunes, and so on—had been served at the end of the meal, along with apples, pears, strawberries, medlars, and other dessert fruits. At the time Grimod de La Reynière wrote, therefore, the prescriptions of the old dietetics had been violated daily for two centuries.

They were also violated when it came to the choice of food, as can be seen in the proliferation of vegetable dishes in the cookbooks of the sixteenth, seventeenth, and eighteenth centuries. Throughout the Middle Ages these had been left to the common people: growing in the soil (indeed buried in the soil, in the case of root vegetables), vegetables were considered "earthy," crude, base, and inedible and thus unworthy of the social elite. The fact that we find them being served on good tables in the early modern period reflects not only a change in their social status but also yet another violation of medical prescriptions. The same can be said about the increase in the consumption of the meat of quadrupeds, animals with their feet firmly planted on the ground and whose flesh had therefore been regarded for centuries as earthy, crude, and harder to digest than the flesh of fowl.

This was especially true of beef, which was criticized as late as 1607 in *Le Thresor de santé* on the grounds that it "engenders a very crude blood, which causes various diseases in individuals of a melancholy nature." Moreover, "frequent use of this meat gives rise to measles, cankers, ill temper, leprosy, quartian fever, and swelling of the spleen together with dropsy." Now such warnings were heard less and less frequently in both England and France as the number of beef dishes shot up dramatically in both bourgeois and aristocratic cookbooks.

Le Thresor de santé noted that beef "is hard to digest, but if one can digest it, because one's stomach is robust or well exercised, it provides abundant nourishment." This does not mean that it was more suitable for bourgeois consumers than for aristocrats. On the contrary, nobles, who exercised much more regularly than the bourgeoisie owing to their regular participation in hunting and military exercises, would have been expected to be more capable of digesting it. What we find in medieval cookbooks, then, is not so much respect for medical advice as a keen awareness for the vulgarity of beef. The prevalence of beef in early modern cookbooks thus indicates a waning of this social prejudice.

So much for the choice of food. Let us turn now to the manner of its preparation. If the medical prohibition against mixing milk with fish was respected in the Middle Ages by Taillevent's *Le Viandier* and in the sixteenth century by *Platine en français,* in the seventeenth century *Le Cuisinier françois* called for milk in its recipes for turbot soup, chopped carp, oyster rings, salt herring, and *harengs sorets;* in addition, cream and especially butter figured in nearly all the fish recipes. Similarly, *La Cuisinière bourgeoise* called for milk in its recipes for turbot and brill soup. Milk was also used in making stuffed cod tails, codfish pie, creamed codfish, skate with cheese, and skate and herring *à la sainte menehoult*. It is an open question whether these culinary changes came about more because the old medical prohibition dwindled or because the religious proscription of dairy products during Lent was rescinded.

Did the preparation of beef also reflect growing neglect of the principles of the old dietetics? The dietitians had insisted that beef, being dry by nature, "is healthier boiled than roasted." In the fourteenth century, however, not all beef was cooked in water or wine. When used, as it frequently was, in pâtés and thick soups, it was cooked in several different ways in succession. And some recipes in *Le Ménagier de Paris* called for roasting or grilling. A detailed analysis of French cookbooks from the sixteenth, seventeenth, and eighteenth centuries shows no significant increase in "dry" cooking of beef.

As for flavoring beef, the dietitians had always recommended seasoning in such a way as to correct the natural deficiencies of the meat. According to *Le Thresor de santé,* "Galen urged those who consumed beef out of necessity to soak it in vinegar and season it with garlic and rue to aid the digestion, but it would be very difficult to get used to such a sauce. . . . Spices and mustard might be more effective."

Garlic, rue, spices, and mustard are all "hot" spices, intended to compensate for the "coldness" of the meat. As for vinegar, thought to be "cold" and "dry" like beef itself, it was an acid, and acids were supposed to open the pores, thereby allowing the digested food to flow more easily to all parts of the body. Such assistance was particularly necessary in the case of beef, a food "so constrictive that it barely goes down at all." Unfortunately, careful analysis of the evidence does not indicate any dramatic change in the use of spices, mustard, garlic, and vinegar, as one might expect to find if the old dietetic principles were in fact being abandoned.

But did seventeenth- and eighteenth-century French chefs always use spices, garlic, and mustard because they were "hot" and in order to make beef more digestible? Or did they use these ingredients purely because they appealed to the senses? In medieval recipes, whether laconic or long-winded, hot ingredients played a crucial role. In fact, they dominated the seasoning. In *Les Enseignemens,* for example, we read: "Flesh of fresh beef, with white garlic; salted beef, with mustard." In the print edition of Taillevent's *Le Viandier,* we find this on the subject of "boiled preparations of crude flesh": "Place in water and salt to cook, and if fresh, add parsley, sage, and hyssop. Eat with white garlic or . . . cider vinegar; if salted, eat with mustard." And in the lengthy recipe that Master Chiquard gives for "beef loin in lamprey sauce," vinegar and spices stand out: "Add red vinegar . . . and then take powdered cinnamon, white ginger, grain of paradise, pepper, nutmeg, galanga, clove, mace, and other spices." The only other ingredients are wine, bread, and a little beef stock. By contrast, in the seventeenth and eighteenth centuries garlic, mustard, and spices were hidden among all sorts of other seasonings. Take, for example, the recipe for "leg of beef soup" in *Le Cuisinier françois:* "Braise in a pot until ready to fall apart and season well with a bouquet, cloves, capers, mushrooms, and truffles. Simmer your bread and garnish with your soup and seasonings." Or again, consider Pierre de Lune's recipe for "beef à la mode": "Pound the meat well, lard it with bacon, brown and place in a terrine with a glass of white wine, two glasses of water, a bouquet of herbs, salt, pepper, laurel, lemon, and a half-dozen mushrooms, cover tightly with another terrine, and cook over a low heat." In medieval recipes the seasoning of beef was as functional as in any dietetic treatise, whereas in the seventeenth and eighteenth centuries it was much as it is today.

A more sweeping change involved the use of spices, as we saw in a previous chapter. Beginning in the middle of the seventeenth century, French travelers found everything they were served in other countries too spicy for their taste. French culinary treatises of the period recommended a much narrower range of spices than in the past. They also recommended using smaller quantities and mixing exotic spices with indigenous herbs and other ingredients from neighboring countries such as lemon, capers, and anchovies. Although the proportion of dishes containing spices remained unchanged, we can still say that spices played a much smaller role in seventeenth- and eighteenth-century French cooking than in the cuisine of the fourteenth through sixteenth centuries.

It was primarily on grounds of taste that Frenchmen in the seventeenth and eighteenth centuries criticized spicy sauces. They expressed astonishment, moreover, that people in other countries continued to ascribe medicinal virtues to spices. Father Labat, for example, had this to say about saffron: "The Spanish, Italians, Portuguese, and Germans, as well as all the northern peoples—Swedes, Danes, Muscovites, and even Dutch, English, and Flemish—consume great quantities. They use it in all their sauces, stews, and pastry. They insist that it is cordial, pectoral, anodyne, alexiterous, aperitive, and somniferous and that it fortifies the memory and cures colds and bitterness of the bile. . . . They so many fine things about it that I would bore the reader if I tried to include them all."

French dictionaries of the period began to distinguish between medicinal spices and aromatic spices, and instead of indicating the dietetic utility of the latter, they warned against immoderate use in cooking. Thus in the 1704 edition of *Dictionnaire de Trévoux,* we read: "Spice, n. Any type of oriental or aromatic drug which has hot and piquant qualities, such as pepper, nutmeg, ginger, mace, cinnamon, clove, grain of paradise, etc. It is not healthy to use too much spice in sauces." The dictionary goes on to devote a second entry to "spices" in the plural: "Said also of medicinal drugs that come from the Orient, such as senna, cassia, incense, etc." Note that the qualities of "heat" and "dryness" that were still ascribed to spices at the beginning of the seventeenth century referred to distinct categories of the old physics, whereas the qualities "hot and piquant" that were invoked a century later are redundant and refer solely to sensations.

An even clearer instance of the limitation of seasoning to its gastronomic (as opposed to dietetic) function can be seen in the case of sugar. Sugar was long used as a pharmaceutical, as is illustrated by the old French saying *apothicaire sans sucre* (apothecary without sugar). In Taillevent's *Le Viandier* of the fourteenth century, 40 percent of the recipes that called for sugar were intended for the sick. And in most other cookbooks of the period, the role of sugar was to take the edge off various spices without diminishing their specific virtues, as in pharmacy. The same was true in the fifteenth and sixteenth centuries as the use of sugar in French cooking expanded. From the seventeenth century on, however, French chefs and their clients increasingly forgot about this dietetic function of sugar and began to concentrate on the need to harmonize flavors. By the end of the century it was considered a lapse of taste to use sugar on meat, fowl, fish, or vegetables. From then on, the sweetener was used only with eggs, grains, pastries, fruits, coffee, tea, and chocolate.

The opposition between sweet and savory that developed at the time in France structured not only the cooking but also the serving of food: but for a few exceptions, sugar dishes were henceforth limited to lunches, snacks, and the final dessert and side courses of dinners and suppers. Thus nearly all fruits, which for centuries had been eaten as an appetizer in keeping with the prescriptions of physicians, became dessert items in the seventeenth century.

Ambiguities in Medical Attitudes

Some early modern physicians gave their blessings to these violations of ancient medical advice. During the sixteenth and early seventeenth century, however, the power of the medical community to regulate diet was reinforced. Until the middle of the seventeenth century, dietetics remained a vital and evolving discipline, and many of the greatest physicians, including those who served Francis I, Henri III, Henri IV, and Louis XIII, took an interest in it.

Before 1550, it was a generally accepted principle that each individual should eat in accordance with his or her own nature. In the thirteenth century, for example, Aldobrandino wrote, "Whoever wishes to respect nature, which is a healthy thing to do . . . should feed each person's nature with its like, that is, hot foods for those whose nature is hot, cold foods for those whose nature is cold, and so on." In the mid-sixteenth century, however, the opposite principle triumphed. By 1607 *Le Thresor de santé* explicitly stated that foods "of moist, hot quality [are suitable] for those whose humor is melancholic [that is, cold and dry]; foods that are cold and moist for cholerics [hot and dry]; [foods that are] hot and dry for phlegmatics [cold and moist]; and foods that are dry and mediocre in nourishment for the sanguine [hot and moist].

The principle of balancing opposites was not unknown in the Middle Ages, but it was usually applied to seasonal foods and variations and to sick individuals rather than to the healthy. A passage from *Platine en françois* concerning the benefits of wine for people of different ages offers a good illustration of the way in which the nutritive function was associated with identity and the therapeutic function with opposition: "In old people wine is *like medicine* because the heat of the wine opposes the cold of the old person, and in youths it is *like meat* [that is, for nourishment], because the nature of wine is similar to their nature. But for adolescents and children it is like both meat and medicine, for how can their heat be intense in substance unless it is perfectly attuned to the quantity of their humor? And since wine gives increase and nourishment to their natural heat and dries their humor, it is as medicine to them."

During the sixteenth century, the restoration of equilibrium by balancing contrary qualities went from being a therapeutic principle to being a dietetic rule. In other words, anyone whose temperament was not sanguine was henceforth considered to be unbalanced and a potential invalid. This belief fit well with the "imperialism" of the medical profession, for now each individual needed a physician to indicate what diet was appropriate, whereas the medieval belief had been that the body itself indicated what it needed by way of appetite. Recall what Aldobrandino said in the thirteenth century: "Many things which are by no means good for engendering good blood [are] suitable for many natures, and it is better that they refrain from eating things [which are good in principle for people of balanced temperament], because, as Avicenna says, . . . [when] the human body is healthy, everything that tastes better in the mouth nourishes it."

Later, however, the appetite ceased to be seen as a reliable guide. In order to know what to eat, people now needed help from the medical profession. Not everyone chose to heed the advice of the doctors over the dictates of the appetite, however. Both the enlightened elite and the ignorant populace violated the prescriptions of the experts, as we know from countless stories, poems, and songs. What is more, a number of seventeenth-century physicians chose to justify what their illustrious clients found fashionable rather than stick with conventional wisdom. For instance, some physicians argued in favor of the practice of drinking iced wine, which the French took from the Italians and the Spanish in the sixteenth century.

Laurent Joubert, writing in 1580, did not fully accept this new aristocratic custom. Although he was willing to tolerate cooling wine during the summer by immersing bottles in well water (which one then mixed with the wine before drinking it), he refused to countenance the use of ice or snow for the same purpose. In 1659 Dr. Alziari went further in his *Conclusions sur le boire à la glace et à la neige*. Although he continued to condemn the custom of "drinking snow qua substance," and thus of putting it directly in the wine, as did Henri III and the Romans of antiquity, he sanctioned and even recommended cooling bottles in a bucket of ice during heat waves, because "well water is not sufficient to cool the beverage to the degree that nature demands" in order to compensate for the excessive heat. Of course, the French aristocracy had been doing just that since the time of Henri III: "I believe that wherever wine is cooled with ice or snow at present, no other method is used."

A similar conformism can be discerned with respect to fruits. In the *Traité de l'usage des fruits des arbres pour se conserver en santé ou pour se guérir lorsqu'on est malade* (1683), Nicolas Venette began by reminding his readers that it was the custom to eat most juicy fruits at the beginning of the meal; yet he seemed to be casting about for arguments to justify the emerging practice of serving fruits for dessert:

> Fruits with a sweet and pleasant taste are less cold than other fruits: thus, although figs, grapes, the Bon-chrétien [pear], the Rainette d'Espagne [apple], and other, similar fruits seem quite moist by nature, their coldness does not surpass the first degree. Hence they are milder and somewhat more nourishing than other fruits, and their substance is more closely related to the parts of the body. But if, along with their natural sweetness they have a smell of amber or musk, then they possess I know not what tenuous and penetrating elements which are good for the heart and brain and allow us to digest them more readily than others.

The considerable progress made in the art of growing trees in the seventeenth century seemed to have rendered pointless the age-old warnings about fruits, which, it was believed, had been quite different in the past.

Finally, advances in chemistry since the sixteenth century, some of them due to the work of French physicians, also helped to undermine the principles of the old dietetics. In *Le Pourtraict de la santé* (1606), Joseph Duchesne at first followed the medieval dietitians in pointing out both the gastronomic and the dietetic effects of all seasonings, especially spices. But in his specific comments he departed from the ancient teachings of Hippocrates and Galen. When he wrote about pepper, for example, traditionally regarded as the hottest of spices and therefore rejected by French chefs for three centuries, he had this to say:

> I shall begin with pepper of both the black and round varieties, this being the commonest spice and the one that most people believe to be the hottest, which is why many are afraid to use it. I, for one, regard pepper as the best and healthiest of spices, and one of the least fiery. The great piquant or pierc-

ing quality of pepper, which one perceives in the taste and burning sensation it leaves on the tongue, stems from what chemists call an aronic salt, which is subtle and penetrating and therefore cuts into, attenuates, and dissolves the tartars and viscidities of the stomach and other parts, and this is why the ancients found it to be good for the treatment of quartian fevers and various other maladies.

A few pages earlier, he totally demolished the accepted view of sugar: "Beneath its whiteness, sugar conceals a profound blackness, and beneath its sweetness lurks a harsh corrosiveness, as bad as that of aqua fortis. From it one can even derive a solvent capable of dissolving gold. People who have laid hands on the internal anatomy of things, and who penetrate beneath the outer skin, can say something about it, but not those who pretend to be learned without understanding a thing." If sugar was not the embodiment of sweetness, the sweetener par excellence, then the whole science of pharmacology was in doubt, as were the entire dietetics of flavor and the meaning of cooking with spices.

Although Du Chesne was Henri IV's physician, he was still a somewhat marginal figure in France at the beginning of the seventeenth century. But Louis Lémery's *Traité des aliments* (1705) was a standard reference in the eighteenth century. When Jacques-Jean Bruhier was made responsible for producing a third edition of the work in 1755, he was somewhat critical of the original, yet shared its chemical understanding of food and the digestive process. Like Lémery, Bruhier systematically referred to the "chemical principles" that each food contained. Although he still believed that cooking was an aid to digestion, he did not believe in overcooking and went so far as to insist that some foods should be eaten raw:

> Some foods require preparation, including the flesh of quadrupeds, birds, and many fish. Others are eaten as nature offers them, including fruits that have ripened to full maturity, oysters, and so on. . . . It is worth noting that if a food requires cooking, excess is nevertheless to be avoided. I am deeply convinced that for reasons of health as well as taste, it is better to err on the side of too little rather than too much. There can be no doubt that overcooking leads to loss of natural juices and thus to drying of the food's fibers, as a result of which it becomes less nourishing and more difficult to digest, because the dried-out fibers shrivel up and become more resistant to the action of the stomach.

What made such a statement possible was the fact that the stomach's action was no longer conceived of as a form of cooking but rather as a form of dissolution effected by the various gastric juices.

When Bruhier took up the matter of seasoning, he still accepted the idea that one of its functions was to correct the deficiencies of the food one ate. But in developing this theme, he used terms altogether foreign to the language of traditional medicine: "The deficiencies of each liquid must be remedied by substances with opposing qualities: in cases of alkaline intemperateness, use acids and aqueous thinners; sour and aqueous elements can also be used to combat oily and putrid excess; and so on." Furthermore, he did not believe that people outside the medical profession were aware of the need for dietary equilibrium:

> Unfortunately, seasonings are used nowadays only to flatter taste and stimulate appetite, or, rather, to create a false appetite. . . . What custom could be more pernicious? For according to the celebrated Boerhave, seasonings derived from acids, salt, and aromatic herbs are harmful to even the healthiest individuals owing to the sharpness that is their dominant quality. They injure the small vessels, which constitute the tissues of those parts of the body most necessary to life and burden the body more than they nourish it by stimulating it to consume a quantity of food in excess of what it needs. Moreover, fatty and oily substances are harmful to health when consumed to excess because they soften and weaken the solid parts of the body.

The principal danger now seemed to lie not with foods themselves but rather with seasonings: "Is it the case," Bruhier asked, "that the people with the best tables, who serve the most delicate foods, are healthier and live longer than others? No. The opposite is true. These advantages are reserved for sober people, who content themselves with simple foods and who season what they eat only to the extent required by taste." This Parthian shot was aimed at people who in the middle of the eighteenth century still believed what the editor of *Le Cuisinier françois* had believed a century earlier—namely, that good cooking preserves good health. But the number of such people was surely not as large as it once had been.

Good Taste: A New Idea?

A new concept appeared—that of taste, in the sense of "good taste." Dictionaries published in the early 1700s devoted much more space to the notion than those published a century earlier. For example, only two of the twenty-two lines about "taste" in Nicot's *Thrésor de la langue françoise* (1606) concerned metaphorical uses of the term having nothing to do with food. By contrast, the *Dictionnaire de Trévoux* (1704) devoted eighty-one of ninety-eight lines to such uses.

How are we to interpret this change? In discussing the ability to distinguish the beautiful from the ugly, writers were obliged to resort to metaphor, and the only metaphor they came up with—taste—was borrowed from the culinary realm. The seventeenth century witnessed a marked increase of interest in the fine arts—music, painting, sculpture, architecture, theater, poetry, and literature in all its forms. This increased interest manifested itself not only in a proliferation of works of art but also in an outpouring of critical writing and a new respect for art among people of quality. But the fact that in speaking of the arts they borrowed the word "taste" also suggests that the same people were interested in and talked about what they ate.

Despite the mind-body dichotomy and the moralistic condemnation of physical pleasure, the taste of food took on an importance that is hard to imagine today. According to César de Rochefort's *Dictionnaire général curieux* (1685), "Taste is not the noblest of the senses, but it is the most necessary. Saint Jerome says that without taste, man cannot live for long, but he can live without the other senses." Although we value taste today, we see it as less important to survival than sight or hearing. Even in the culinary realm, we rely on sight to read food labels, indications of safety and freshness, and so on. We no longer rely on taste to decide what might be harmful to our health, and nutritionists no longer advise us to heed our taste in deciding what to eat. By contrast, the old dietetics made taste paramount. Not only did taste indicate when a food had begun to go bad or contained some toxic ingredient, but it also told individuals what their bodies needed, given their particular temperament.

The concept of "good taste" was apparently forged in order to talk about arts and letters. In any case, it was in the context of arts and letters that the dictionaries defined the phrase. Although it was originally used in a nonfood context, it was soon applied to culinary matters, as we know from any number of seventeenth- and eighteenth-century texts and several eighteenth-century dictionaries.

For example, Voltaire, in the entry under "Taste" in his *Dictionnaire philosophique* (1764), uses the term in both culinary and nonculinary contexts:

> The taste, the sense by which we distinguish the flavor of our food, has produced, in all known languages, the metaphor expressed by the word "taste"— a feeling of beauty and defects in all the arts. It is a quick perception, like that of the tongue and palate, and in the same manner anticipates consideration. Like the mere sense, it is sensitive and luxuriant in respect to the good, and rejects the bad spontaneously. . . . As a physical bad taste consists in being

pleased only with high seasoning and curious dishes, so a bad taste is pleased only with studied ornament, and feels not the pure beauty of nature.

In 1739 two Jesuits, Guillaume-Hyacinthe Bougeant and Pierre Brumoy, wrote a preface to *Dons de Comus,* in which they discussed the concept of good taste in a culinary context. This caused them no difficulty, since they believed that cooking was one of the fine arts:

> Cooking, like any other art invented for need or for pleasure, was perfected along with the national genius of each nation and became more delicate as the nations became more polite. . . . Among the civilized nations, progress in cooking followed progress in all the other arts. . . . The Italians civilized all of Europe, and without a doubt it was they who taught us how to eat. . . . Although good cooking has been known in France for more than two centuries, it is fair to say that it has never been as delicate as it is now, or done so properly or with a taste so refined.

If cooking was an art in which progress was possible, that progress was due in part to the good taste of French aristocrats, as these Jesuit authors did not fail to point out: "We have in France a number of great lords, who, to amuse themselves, do not disdain at times to talk cooking and whose exquisite taste has done much to train some excellent chefs."

In cooking as in literature and the other arts, good taste meant classical taste for the Frenchmen of the seventeenth and eighteenth centuries. It therefore makes sense to ask whether the invention of the concept of good taste was not itself an aspect of French classicism. In order to answer this question, however, we would have to look at countries where a different conception of art was developed in this period, and space does not permit us to attempt this here.

Cooking, Gourmandise, and Gastronomy

What matters for present purposes is that the invention of the concept of good taste in France coincided with advances in chemistry and physiology that undermined the old Hippocratic dietetics long before there was any well-founded new dietetics to take its place. For three centuries this combination of circumstances seems to have distracted both cooks and consumers of food from their traditional concern with dietetics, a concern that has been revived in recent years. The effect of this was that between 1600 and 1800, cooking, once under the sway of medicine, gradually and quietly freed itself.

As evidence of this liberation, as well as how small a splash it made at the time and how potent conservative influences remained, we have only to note that dealers in rare books traditionally classified cookbooks along with works on dietetics in the "medical" subcategory of "sciences and arts." In 1764, however, in the second volume of the *Traité des livres rares,* cooking was for the first time classified as an art. Of course, this change may not have meant much because "art" at the time was still a word applied to the activity of artisans as well as artists. But in Perrot's catalog of 1776, cooking was removed from the "medicine" category, separated from books on "hygiene" and "dietetics" and from treatises on wine, tea, coffee, and chocolate, and lumped together with such other aristocratic arts as horsemanship, fencing, dance, and hunting. The two men responsible for this new classification, Née de La Rochelle and Belin Jr., made no bones about their view that the older classification was outdated and that it was time for a new one. Yet conservative forces proved too powerful, and in subsequent catalogs cookbooks were restored to their former place. Nevertheless, this reversion to tradition does not diminish the significance of the abortive revolution of 1776.

Liberated (despite the conservatism of bibliophiles) from the clutches of the medical profession, the culinary art did not immediately hire itself out to the gluttons of the day, who, after all, were still seen as guilty of a capital sin. Instead, it joined the other fine arts by aligning itself with the champions of good taste. Or so the story goes. Yet respect for good taste soon removed the taint of guilt from the passion for fine morsels of delicate flavor on the part of food lovers who preferred to call themselves *friands* rather than gourmands or gourmets so as to avoid any appearance of challenging traditional taboos (*gourmandise* is French for the sin of gluttony). It was these *friands* whom the great chefs of the day sought to please. It took the virtuous encyclopedist Jaucourt (1757) and the deliberately provocative food writer Grimod de La Reynière (1803) to restore the appellation *gourmand*. But the moral aspect of this etymological evolution is not what matters most.

What is crucial, rather, is the fact that by the end of the eighteenth century everyone accepted the idea that the quality of a dish is an intrinsic property of the dish itself, independent of the temperament of the person who eats it. From now on, each dish was held to be objectively good or bad, and this was all that mattered. National cuisines were similarly divorced from national characters. Even if good taste was not equally distributed among nations (Voltaire had a lot to say on the subject), people of good taste were capable of appreciating good cooking wherever it was to be found. Was there anything strange about the fact that in the seventeenth and eighteenth centuries it was to be found only in Europe, and particularly in France? No. The basic principle was incontrovertible. And in any case, everyone knew that the French, having learned from the Italians, had the most refined taste in the world.

Since good taste was now an objective fact, why should it not become an object of study for a true culinary science? In the nineteenth century, gastronomy, the pseudoscience of eating well, would occupy the space left vacant by the old dietetics and cloak itself in some of the prestigious garments of the discipline it supplanted. In 1825 Anthelme Brillat-Savarin would define gastronomy as a "reasoned knowledge of everything pertaining to man insofar as he nourishes himself. Its purpose is to help keep man alive by providing the best possible nutrition." Some people apparently took this definition seriously, Alexandre Dumas among them. In the *Grand Dictionnaire de cuisine,* for example, we read that "in order to make melon digestible, *some gastronomes say,* it has to be eaten with pepper and salt, and madeira, or better yet, marsala, should be drunk along with it." Obviously the author of these lines had no idea that this custom actually stemmed from a dietetic science that had long since faded from view.

PART SEVEN

CONTEMPORARY PERIOD

(19TH AND 20TH CENTURIES)

INTRODUCTION

From INDUSTRIAL REVOLUTION *to* INDUSTRIAL FOOD

Jean-Louis Flandrin

We have chosen to group the nineteenth and twentieth centuries together under the heading "contemporary period." Salient features of these two centuries include a never-ending Industrial Revolution, a rural exodus coupled with incredible urban growth (even in nonindustrial countries), a total triumph of the market economy over the subsistence economy (in the countryside as well as the city), and formidable development of international transportation and commerce.

The Industrial Revolution affected the history of food in a number of ways. The rise of the food-processing industry is perhaps the most notable of these. Today vast processing plants turn out huge quantities of such basic staples as flour, oil, sugar, and vinegar, once fabricated by artisanal methods. Other plants produce frozen TV dinners and packaged preprocessed foods. Some readily available ingredients, such as baker's chocolate and condensed or powdered milk, did not exist in the past. Others, such as mustard, butter, and cheese, were once prepared by peasants or artisans, while still others were products of the family kitchen: jellies, preserves, salted and smoked fish and meat, and prepared dishes now available in canned or frozen form.

The Industrial Revolution, together with changes in social relations and a narrowing of the income gap between rich and poor, also contributed to a drastic reduction in the number of household personnel. Increasing numbers of working-class women chose factory or office work over domestic service. As bourgeois households lost their cooks, bourgeois housewives had to learn to cook for themselves. Later a certain idea of women's emancipation, perhaps coupled with awareness that the importance of the role of mistress of the household had diminished now that there was no one left to give orders to or even to talk to, led many housewives to choose work outside the home as well.

For the lower classes, which constituted the vast majority of the population, "women's work" was nothing new: in the past women had always worked as much as, if not more than, men. But generally they worked at home: 80 to 90 percent of the population was rural, and most industrial and commercial enterprises were as much family affairs as the family farm. Women were thus able to take care of the house and children while contributing to the family income. With the Industrial Revolution and the ensuing exodus from the countryside, however, growing numbers of women found jobs in factories and offices, which made it much more difficult to combine work with household chores and child-rearing. Over the past two centuries, women have had less time for these traditional responsibilities, so as soon as they began earning enough to make it possible (in most cases not until the second half of the twentieth century), they purchased equipment designed to make cleaning and cooking easier. The increase in the number of women employed in factories and offices thus had a powerful influence on the development of both the household-appliance and processed-food industries.

Among the "ready-to-eat" industries, one should include restaurants, even though these have little in common with our usual idea of factories. It was not simply the coining of the new word "restaurant" that distinguished the modern eating establishment from the inns and taverns of an earlier era. The restaurant also served different functions. Among these was the "gastronomic function," whose innovative character has been stressed by any number of historians. Some restaurants became temples of haute cuisine, presided over by great chefs who in another era might have been employed by dukes and princes. This transformation was encouraged by the new status of gastronomy in bourgeois society, but it also owed something to a narrowing of the gap between the income of the rich and poor (although it has always taken lots of money to eat at one of these renowned establishments).

The gastronomic function was not limited to deluxe restaurants. People not wealthy enough to eat at first-class establishments could make do with all sorts of more modest eateries, where it was possible to share the pleasures of good food and good company and, for a while at any rate, to rise above one's station. Restaurants also performed another function, however: they served food to growing numbers of men and women who no longer took their meals at home, either because there was no one home to do the cooking or because the workplace was too far away to return for the midday meal. In both cases, this banishment of diners from the home was thus related to economic change—the increased number of working women and the expansion of the cities.

Last but not least, the development of international shipping and commerce greatly increased the amount of foreign foods that Europeans consumed. Not in all areas, to be sure: never again did spices play as important a commercial role as in the Middle Ages and Renaissance, nor sugar as important a role as in the early modern period. Indeed, it was between the sixteenth and the eighteenth centuries that the sugar plantations of Brazil and, later, the West Indies enjoyed a monopoly of sugar production, confiscating the market share once held by Sicily, Provence, and Andalusia, whereas in the nineteenth and twentieth centuries European beet sugar recaptured part of the market.

It was not until the nineteenth century, however, that Europe began buying most of its wheat from America, and it was not until the twentieth century that out-of-season fruits and vegetables began to find a place on European markets: green beans from Africa, grapes from South Africa and Chile, and so on. Colonial fruits first reached the market in the nineteenth century, and sales continued to increase in the twentieth century—not just tropical fruits such as banana and pineapple (joined nowadays by the avocado, mango, litchi nut, passion fruit, and the like) but also the orange, lemon, tangerine, and so on. Ever-increasing quantities of such fruits have flowed in from places such as North Africa, the Middle East, Florida, and California, to the detriment of Italy, Spain, Portugal, and Provence, which had supplied the European market since the fourteenth century. The French orange no longer exists, and the vast orange orchard that covered the plain of Hyères in the sixteenth century is no longer even a memory.

The nineteenth and twentieth centuries also witnessed a remarkable rise in oil imports from the tropics. Peanut oil, in particular, has become a strong competitor to olive oil, walnut oil, and other traditional European oils, while margarine and other products made from tropical plants have partially supplanted butter and other shortenings based on animal fats. More recently, however, European farmers have begun to reverse this trend, with colza and sunflower oil touted as substitutes for peanut oil, against which health warnings have been issued.

All of these changes were closely related and in a sense reinforced one another. In each instance, the nineteenth century heralded the twentieth, the twentieth prolonged the nineteenth. In other respects, however, the two centuries stand in sharp contrast: the evolution of foodways over the period was neither steady nor uniform.

Consider demographics, for example. The growth of the population in the nineteenth century continued and even amplified the trend that began a century earlier. In most European countries the growth rate was unprecedented, with the result that large numbers of people emigrated to the four corners of the earth. But by the end of the nineteenth century in some countries and during the twentieth century in others, the birthrate dropped below the death rate, and western Europe began attracting immigrants, at first from less developed European countries and then from outside Europe.

As for agriculture, technological advances leading to increased yields affected different countries at different times, but steady progress made it possible not only to meet the demographic challenge of the nineteenth century but also to achieve a marked improvement in the European diet. By the middle of the nineteenth century, the agricultural revolution, together with the transportation revolution and the cultivation of new land, had put an end to the famines that had periodically ravaged Europe, and in the twentieth century these benefits were extended to other regions of the world as well.

If we look at the two centuries as a whole, however, the foregoing picture needs to be modified. To begin with, the diet of many poor peasants and workers actually deteriorated in the first half of the nineteenth century. Although their meat consumption gradually rose after 1850, it appears in general to have declined until then. Furthermore, although potatoes and corn became common staples in most European countries in this period, this was not because enlightened people discovered the virtues of these imported crops but because peasants and workers too poor to buy bread were forced to eat the new foods in order to stay alive. To them, these innovations did not seem like progress.

What is more, the end of the twentieth century has seen a reversion to famine in many parts of the Third World, especially Africa, and a collapse of agriculture in any number of countries. Famine has returned because agricultural output in many places has failed to keep pace with demographic growth, the soil has been eroded, and civil wars, so common nowadays, hamper the delivery of relief supplies. Foreign aid is not an unalloyed benefit, moreover: it works against local agriculture, aggravating an already-existing crisis and laying the groundwork for future famines. Thus the past two centuries have not been a period of steady improvement in diet. There was no clear improvement in the European standard of living until the second half of the nineteenth century, and whatever improvement had occurred in the poorest countries of Africa has ended in the latter part of the twentieth century.

Nor was there any constant pattern to the evolving relationship between gastronomy and dietetics over the course of the contemporary period. The gap that developed between the two in the seventeenth and eighteenth centuries continued to widen in the 1800s, as gourmets freed themselves from the constraints of the old dietetics. In the twentieth century, however, a new, more persuasive dietetics has had a considerable impact on eating behavior, affecting not only the choice of food but also the ways in which it is prepared and served. One indication of this influence was the advent of what was called *la cuisine minceur,* made popular by the publication of Michel Guérard's *La Grande Cuisine minceur* in 1976. Long before that, however, there was a sharp rise in the consumption of fruits and vegetables. Recipes increasingly called for diced vegetables and shortened cooking times. These changes were probably related to the discovery of the beneficial effects of vitamins and dietary fiber. Similarly, the "new cuisine" banned flour-thickened sauces and called for smaller amounts of sugar in pastries and preserves in response to medical warnings about the dangers of obesity coupled with a media-induced cult of "thinness." The relative importance of gastronomic sensibility compared with concerns about health varies from country to country. The obsession with health was particularly noticeable in the United States, England, and northern Europe, where it often took on religious connotations.

The revival of a religious element in western eating habits is paradoxical in that it occurred at a time when respect for traditional religious observances was in decline (i.e., the second half of the twentieth century). Even today many people would say that the demise of dietary observances once imposed by the Catholic Church is a significant development of the period; similar changes can be observed in the eating habits of Jews and Muslims living in Europe. Nevertheless, there has been an increasingly clear tendency in the opposite direction, which is growing stronger by the day. Around the world there has been a revival of traditional Jewish and Muslim practices, including observance of dietary rules. Among Christians, new dietary prescriptions have been issued not by the Catholic Church but by various Protestant denominations, even though Protestants traditionally denounced Catholic rules in this area as superstitions.

To be sure, the new rules are very different from the old ones. Their purpose is not to prepare the soul for a period of prayer and penitence but to eliminate possibly harmful and (in one sense or another) impure foods from the diet of the faithful. Religious prescriptions of this sort, alien to strict Christian tradition, first appeared in the United States more than a century ago, and since then they have become intimately intertwined with what amounts to a sort of dietetic vulgate. In the Protestant societies of North America and northern Europe, the dietetic and the religious seem to be mutually strengthening each other.

Another paradox can be seen in a series of apparent contradictions between changes in attitude and changes in underlying realities. As the rural population dwindled in the nineteenth and twentieth centuries, people began to attach a curious value to peasant eating habits. Furthermore, as nation-states formed and unified themselves culturally across Europe, people began to develop a keen interest in local cuisines, as can be seen, for example, in the proliferation of gastronomic and tourist guides and regional cookbooks. Indeed, even as the food and hospitality industries, the tourist trade, and the media promoted a sort of globalization of taste—witness the universal popularity of hamburgers, hot dogs, ketchup, and pizza—Europeans and Americans alike have taken to highly distinctive national cuisines, as evidenced by growing numbers of Indian, Chinese, Japanese, Thai, Mexican, and Italian restaurants.

Furthermore, although the quality of many foods has declined, gastronomic literature in the nineteenth and twentieth centuries has thrived as never before. And an important tendency in twentieth-century cooking has been a move toward shorter cooking times and more discreet use of seasonings in order to allow the intrinsic quality of the ingredients to shine through.

Since many of our contemporaries see nothing but progress in the transformations of the past two centuries, we feel obliged to discuss reverses in the area of food—yet another type of paradox. The undeniable advances in European agriculture have brought problems along with benefits. The exodus from the countryside has left today's farmers in possession of much larger farms than in the past. And they obtain much better yields from the soil with less effort, thanks to mechanization, artificial fertilizers, and new species of crops. But they are at the mercy of the market economy and foreign competition, suffer from crises of overproduction, and are burdened by enormous debt. In some countries this has resulted in periodic explosions of discontent among farmers.

Strangely enough, neither farmers nor farm organizations seem inclined to question the wisdom of the continual improvements in yields that have led to the present situation of chronic oversupply and attempts to limit production by leaving some land unplanted. Nor do they seem to worry that steadily falling agricultural prices (coupled with the fact that the demand for food cannot increase indefinitely) have decreased the share of the average family budget spent on food, while an ever larger portion goes to industrial products and even more to services.

For consumers the benefits of agricultural progress are no less ambiguous. Not only has the environment been seriously polluted by modern fertilizers and intensive farming methods, but the decrease in food prices has been accompanied by a decrease in quality. The bread that is made today with new varieties of wheat is all too often tasteless. Fruits look impeccable to the naked eye because they are free from damage by insects or disease, yet they may be tainted by invisible pesticides. Harvested while still immature, they lack fragrance and flavor. Hothouse tomatoes are frequently pasty and insipid. And so on. Similarly, animals raised industrially produce lower-quality meat, especially hogs and chickens, which depend almost entirely on industrial feeds. Milk-fed veal may still be available, and decent chicken has returned to the shelves in recent years, but good bacon has been impossible to find for at least thirty years, and the same is true of sausage and fresh pork. Gourmets will often travel long distances to buy pork from specialty farmers. Is this progress?

The religion of progress has been paramount for two centuries, and for much of that time the drawbacks of progress seemed negligible. Over the past twenty years or so, however, a great deal has changed: gourmets, ecologists, and consumers worried about ingesting toxic ingredients have adopted a different line, vociferously at times, and they, too, may sometimes go too far. Only the future will tell how much truth there is in what they say. As I write these lines, Europe is in the grip of panic over mad cow disease, which has shown just how distressing uncertainty in these matters can be—not to mention the fact that the crisis has already deprived us of some delectable variety meats.

CHAPTER 33

The TRANSFORMATION of the EUROPEAN DIET

Hans Jurgen Teuteberg and Jean-Louis Flandrin

The nineteenth century stands out as a period of demographic growth that continued and in most countries exceeded that of the eighteenth century. Factors contributing to population growth included a decrease in the age of marriage, abetted by the extension of wage labor, and a decrease in the mortality rate. Not only did infant and childhood mortality diminish, but so did adult mortality, owing to medical advances, improved diet, and an end to recurrent famines, which were already less frequent in the eighteenth century. Fertility also decreased in this period. The decline in births began in most countries around 1880 and progressed rapidly: by the end of World War I, the replacement ratio had dropped to below one in Germany, Russia, and elsewhere.

France differed from other countries as to the timing of demographic change, however. There fertility dipped significantly as early as the middle of the eighteenth century, so the growth rate in the nineteenth century was much lower than elsewhere. Despite such specific differences, the pattern in all European countries was similar—first a period of exceptional population growth, followed by a period of stagnation accompanied by a marked decrease in fertility and even (in recent years) in the rate of marriage. Emigration, which had been a significant factor in many places (including England, Germany, Italy, and Poland), all but ceased nearly everywhere. In the twentieth century many countries experienced a net immigration; this was true of England, Belgium, the Netherlands, and Germany after World War II.

Paralleling the two major phases of demographic history were two distinct phases in the history of eating. Until 1880–1900 or thereabouts, the availability of traditional foods increased as production rose in response to demographic pressure; after that, the composition of the European diet changed dramatically as a new demographic regime established itself. The effect of all this on specific foods varied, however: consumption of some foodstuffs increased in the nineteenth century only to decrease in the twentieth, while others (some traditional since the Middle Ages, others only since early modern times) gained steadily in popularity.

As in the eighteenth century, one way of dealing with the demographic challenge was to experiment with new crops, especially the potato. In the long run, however, two other responses to the crisis proved even more important. The first was the agricultural revolution, which, however one defines and dates it, eventually extended to all of Europe. The other was the transportation revolution—the railroad, the steamboat, and so on—which was closely linked to the industrial revolution. Together these transformed the economic system, eliminating subsistence farming and replacing it with a system of agriculture wholly oriented toward the market.

Starches

Cereal consumption throughout Europe is much lower today than it was in the eighteenth and nineteenth centuries. Nevertheless, if statistics from France, England, Germany, and Italy are to be believed, per capita consumption peaked not in the preindustrial period but in the last quarter of the nineteenth century.

Year-to-year variations in the price of grain diminished in the industrial age as dependence on local harvests decreased. Increased storage capacity, expanded national and international commerce, and improved yields all played a part.

In addition, wheat gained market share everywhere at the expense of rye and other allegedly "inferior" grains. In northern Italy, pellagra due to overdependence on corn proved to be a problem. It was not until the first decade of the twentieth century, however, that polenta (made from corn) was displaced by wheat bread. In Calabria and elsewhere, wheat bread replaced loaves made from chestnuts and lupine. In France, by contrast, wheat accounted for 51 percent of cereal consumption as early as 1830, compared with just 39 percent for rye and buckwheat. In Germany, where rye was traditional, the chronology was different: despite a steady increase in wheat consumption up to 1902 and a steady decrease in rye consumption, rye continued to dominate until 1910, and rye consumption remained quite close to wheat consumption until the 1940s. It was only after World War II that wheat pulled ahead, and by 1975 wheat consumption stood at three times rye consumption. Even today, however, rye consumption in Germany is by no means negligible—some thirty-three pounds per person per year.

As for other cereals, only rice saw a rapid increase in consumption between 1850 and 1900. Although rice consumption has declined sharply since then, in Germany it still stands at a much higher level today than in 1850. It never reached a level comparable to that of native cereals, however. At its peak in 1898, annual per capita rice consumption in Germany was just under nine pounds.

Potatoes and Beans

The potato, which contains important amino acids and high levels of vitamin C and potassium, did not deserve either its bad reputation among early nutritionists or the label of being fit only for pigs. Although planted in various parts of Europe before the eighteenth century, it did not become a basic staple until the seventeenth century in Ireland and somewhat later in England and the Netherlands; elsewhere its popularity did not come before the eighteenth century. It was welcomed more warmly in poor areas than in the fertile plains where wheat flourished, and its adoption was long hindered by the triennial system of crop rotation, which left only the summer months for potatoes. Governments and landlords were at first hostile to the new plant, as they were to corn in Italy, because it allowed peasants to evade the tithe and other taxes. When they finally grasped how they could profit from the tuber, however, they changed their minds, as did the peasants they ruled.

No doubt culinary traditions also played a role. In northern Germany, for example, where stews were common, potatoes were accepted much more readily than in southern Germany, where gruel was the norm. In France, where the average person in the decade 1803–12 was already eating forty-five pounds of potatoes per year, consumption increased fourfold in the decade 1835–44 and nearly eightfold, to some 350 pounds annually, in the period 1905–13. Consumption remained quite high until 1939 and did not begin to drop noticeably until after World War II. In Germany, despite early introduction in certain areas, the potato was not definitively accepted as food fit for humans until the country suffered a major agricultural crisis at the beginning of the nineteenth century. Statistics show that consumption doubled between 1850 and 1900, then fell by half over the course of the twentieth century. This drop in consumption was much more pronounced than in France, but the Germans started at a much higher level: some 660 pounds per person annually in 1900.

Between 1934 and 1938, daily per capita potato consumption in France was close to the European mean of just over a pound per day. France trailed Ireland (1.2 pounds), Germany (1.1 pounds), and Finland (1.08 pounds) but led Great Britain (0.5), Austria (0.58), Switzerland (0.54), the Netherlands (0.7), and Denmark (0.73). The tuber's success in Germany was due not only to direct human consumption but also to extensive hog-rearing (the animals were fed potato peels) and to the use of potatoes in making spirits.

The potato never shed its image as food for the poor, for those who could not even afford to buy bread. Its absence from holiday menus corroborates its lowly status. From household budgets we know that the share of potatoes in the daily ration varied inversely with income and directly with family size. Still, it was the potato that made possible the demographic explosion of the eighteenth and nineteenth centuries, especially in central and northern Europe.

Dried beans, which like cereals and potatoes served as filling fare, also lost ground across the continent in the twentieth century, but initial levels and timing varied from one country to the next. In France consumption peaked in the period 1875–1914 at somewhere between 18 and 21 pounds per person annually, as compared with just under 11 pounds in the period from 1803 to 1812. By the decade 1955–64 it was back down to somewhere between 6.5 and 9 pounds. In Germany, where we lack statistics for the first half of the nineteenth century, the decline came sooner: from more than 44 pounds in 1850, consumption decreased to roughly 13 pounds from 1880 to 1910, 4.5 pounds from 1920 to 1970, and less than 2.2 pounds in 1975.

Fresh Vegetables and Fruits

Because both fresh vegetables and fruits were garden products, it is difficult to arrive at good statistical estimates for each category separately. All authorities agree, however, that consumption of these foods, rich in vitamins and dietary fiber, grew steadily from 1781 to the present. Yet all also agree that the figures for the beginning of our period are probably understated, especially for fruits, which could be eaten straight from the tree.

The countries of southern Europe were reputed to be great fruit and vegetable eaters, whereas those of northern and eastern Europe were not. Despite improvements in transportation and refrigeration, it seems likely that people clung to old habits and that those in the north and east tended to eat sauerkraut and potatoes in the winter rather than fresh vegetables. These traditional differences were less pronounced in the case of fruit, however; consumption of fruits evolved in much the same way as that of vegetables in the twentieth century. To be sure, each country had for centuries exhibited a predilection for its own fruits, adapted to its own climate. Germans even used fruits in cooking.

Sugar and Sweets

Although the upper classes became confirmed consumers of sugar in the sixteenth, seventeenth, and eighteenth centuries, it was not until the nineteenth and twentieth centuries that sugar and sweets became truly popular. The English were the exception to this rule: by the first decade of the eighteenth century they were already consuming an average of 4.5 pounds of sugar per person per year, and this rose to nearly 15.5 pounds in 1792 and 20 pounds in the period 1800–1809. Nothing like this happened in France, even though the country had become, thanks to the island of Santo Domingo, the world's leading sugar producer by the eve of the French Revolution: consumption there averaged 1.8 pounds per year between 1781 and 1790 but dropped to 1.05 in 1803–12 after the loss of Santo Domingo. With the development of beet sugar, which eventually yielded a cheaper product of quality similar to that of cane sugar, many more people began to use the substance. Consumption increased tenfold in seventy years, from 2.64 pounds per year between 1815 and 1824 to 26.4 pounds per year between 1885 and 1894. Over the next thirty years it doubled, reaching 52.8 pounds in 1920–24.

At first Germany trailed France in sugar consumption: Germans consumed from 4.5 to 6.6 pounds of sugar per year between 1850 and 1860, compared with more than 11 pounds in France, and less than 5 pounds in 1880 compared with more than 15.4 in France. But German consumption rose more rapidly than French consumption from 1890 to 1912 and again from 1952 to 1975, so that overall it led France slightly. Between 1865 and 1880, molasses, a cheap by-product of the sugar manufacturing process, enjoyed much greater success among the poor than sugar. As wages rose, however, the era of molasses came to an end. A study of household budgets for the last two decades of the nineteenth century shows that sugar had gained a foothold at all levels of society.

It is not as well known that cane sugar consumption in England in the first half of the nineteenth century decreased from 30.6 pounds in 1801 to 16.6 in 1835 to 15.3 in 1840, only to increase again to 24.9 in 1848. These changes reflected changes in the price of sugar; 1840, the year in which the price was highest, was also the year in which consumption was lowest, and the trend did not turn upward until tariffs were reduced in 1845. This evidence strongly supports the idea that by the beginning of the nineteenth century sugar was already part of the

British popular diet. Tea consumption was also more or less stagnant (it ranged from 1.27 to 1.41 pounds per person per year) during the same period.

Meat

A traditional part of the European diet, meat was also a key indicator of the standard of living; hence any increase or decrease of the share of meat in the daily ration was seen as particularly significant. There is no doubt that the average meat ration increased across Europe in the nineteenth and twentieth centuries. But exactly when did this increase begin? How much meat was being consumed initially? These are still matters of debate, especially since the answers vary from country to country.

In 1938 a number of countries were identified as major meat consumers, with a daily ration of four to eight ounces of meat per person. These included the United States, most of the non-Mediterranean European countries, and several major South American beef producers. At the opposite extreme were countries whose daily meat consumption was two ounces or less—Mediterranean nations such as Greece, Portugal, Spain, and Italy along with nearly all non-European countries outside of South America. It is worth noting that on the eve of the French Revolution, French meat consumption is estimated to have been slightly more than two ounces per person per day, or roughly the same level as that of the non-meat-eating countries in 1938.

During the nineteenth and twentieth centuries the average meat ration in France appears to have grown steadily, but this was not the case everywhere. In Frankfurt on the Oder the annual ration for the year 1308 has been estimated at 220 pounds. In Nuremberg in 1520 it was between 160 and 220 pounds. In Berlin in 1397 the average person ate three pounds of meat per day, twelve times as much as in the nineteenth century. Laborers employed on the estates of the archbishop of Mainz ate meat twice a day, and the Dominicans of Strasbourg allowed their workers a daily meat ration of 1.3 to 1.5 pounds. These figures are not accepted by all historians, however, and research in other countries on the fourteenth and fifteenth centuries generally indicates less lavish meat rations than in Germany. Be that as it may, rations for this period were higher everywhere than for the seventeenth and eighteenth centuries. Even in a Mediterranean city such as Carpentras, the average person ate nearly 60 pounds of butchered meat per year in the fifteenth century, and that total does not include chicken, game, organ meat, and salt pork that may have been obtained through channels other than the authorized meat markets. Of course city dwellers, who until the twentieth century accounted for only a small minority of the population, have always eaten much more butchered meat than the rural population. Nevertheless, most historians agree that meat consumption by both groups decreased across Europe in the sixteenth, seventeenth, and eighteenth centuries and that this decrease may have continued well into the nineteenth and perhaps even the twentieth century. In Greece, for example, the average person was still eating less than 25 pounds of meat per year in the period 1948–50, and in Spain in the period 1954–56 the comparable total was just over 30 pounds.

The English, who, like many other northern peoples, enjoyed a reputation as carnivores and who were also the most economically advanced nation in Europe, led their neighbors in meat consumption throughout the nineteenth century and the first half of the twentieth century. In the decade 1903–13, they consumed more than 130 pounds of meat per year, compared with 105 for the French and 99 for the Germans. But the British ration did not increase significantly between the two world wars, ranging from 130 to 140 pounds, whereas French consumption apparently rose fairly steadily to 127 pounds in the period 1935–38. Historians such as E. J. Hobsbawm go even further, arguing that British beef consumption decreased from 1800 to 1850. The evolution of sugar, tea, beer, and even bread consumption in England during this period may lend some plausibility to this argument.

In Germany the meat ration increased by a factor of 3.5 between 1850 and 1975. The low point occurred, however, not in 1850, when statistics began to be kept, but in 1855. Did consumption also decrease in the first half of the nineteenth century? By 1855 it was a little less than 44 pounds per year at a time when the French, never reputed to be great meat eaters, were already consuming more than 66 pounds. Moreover, after climbing steadily to approximately 104 pounds in 1899, the German ration fluctuated around that level until World War I; in the period between the two world wars, moreover, it rose above 110 pounds only twice. It was not until after World War II that meat consumption began to grow substantially and steadily, more than doubling in twenty-five years from 81 pounds in 1950 to almost 187 pounds in 1975.

The rise in meat consumption seems to have occurred relatively late in all countries except France, and it was preceded by periods of decline and long phases of stagnation. During the nineteenth and twentieth centuries, moreover, the relative proportion of different meats in the daily diet fluctuated with time and varied considerably from country to country. In France, pork, which accounted for 40 percent of total meat consumption between 1789 and 1862 (the same proportion as in 1967), represented just 33 percent of the total from 1862 to 1938, according to several estimates. Beef reportedly accounted for less than 50 percent of consumption before 1840 but for 50 to 55 percent between 1840 and 1967. Meat from sheep and goats made up 8 to 17 percent of the total.

In Germany mutton consumption declined sharply in relation to other meats, which all increased. As for fowl, consumption initially declined slightly and then stagnated between the two world wars; it was not until after 1945 that it shot up from 2.6 pounds in 1950 to 19.8 pounds in 1972. This sharp increase was due to the industrialization of chicken farming and the significant fall in prices that followed. It occurred not just in Germany but in all the developed countries. What was peculiar to Germany, or at any rate what distinguished Germany from France, was an increase in the consumption of another industrial meat—pork—which rose from 14.5 pounds per person per year in 1850 to 55 pounds in 1899 and 66 in 1937. By 1950 consumption had dropped back to 44 pounds but thereafter rose again rapidly to 99 pounds in 1975, or more than half the total consumption of meat.

Fish

Although fish played an important role in ancient gastronomy and in the history of the Christian countries in the Middle Ages and early modern period, it accounted for only a small proportion of the average daily ration. Thereafter consumption increased considerably everywhere. In France it nearly quintupled from the period 1781–89 to the period 1960–64, increasing from 5.3 pounds per person to more than 26 pounds. Consumption did not really take off, however, until the middle of the nineteenth century, when the construction of rail links made it possible for people living inland to eat fresh ocean fish and not just salted, dried, and smoked fish.

The same thing happened in Germany, where consumption rose from just 8.3 pounds in 1850 to 16.5 in 1892, 19.2 in 1913, and almost 30 in 1937. Since the end of World War II, however, the trend has been downward, dropping to below 22 pounds in 1972. Despite what these two examples might suggest, fish consumption varied widely across Europe, with geographic location an important factor. In 1938, for example, Switzerland and Austria ate less than a tenth as much fish as Portugal or Sweden. In this age of rapid transportation, this is yet another example of the power of culinary traditions.

Milk and Milk Products

Milk was rarely mentioned in nineteenth-century medical reports and working-class household budgets. Because of the difficulty of preserving milk, retail sales were traditionally confined to dairy-farming villages and were small in scale. Since no tax was levied, no record of production was kept before 1910. Historians have therefore been forced to calculate milk production from the number of cows, their estimated yield, the number of calves, their life expectancy, and so on. Such estimates are open to doubt on a number of counts, and many scholars do not find them convincing.

We have more direct knowledge of cheese consumption, since cheese had long been an important commodity in national and international trade. In France consumption apparently quintupled in a century and a half, from 4.4 pounds per person per year in the period 1815–24 to 23.3 in the period 1960–64.

Furthermore, the percentage of total milk production allotted to various dairy products varied from country to country, region to region, and period to period. These included fresh and preserved milk, cottage cheese, dry and cream cheeses, cream, and butter. Whey and buttermilk were consumed by animals as well as humans. In order to compare statistical data, therefore, one has to convert the whole range of milk derivatives into equivalent amounts of milk. For the period 1935–38 we have figures on which countries were major consumers of dairy products and which were not. Switzerland led the way (with 1.93 pounds of milk equivalent per person per day), followed by Sweden (1.49), Ireland (1.47), Norway and Australia (1.4), the Netherlands (1.4), Denmark (1.3), Austria (1.2), the United States (1.2), and Germany (1.1). At the low end of the scale were Greece (0.6), Italy (0.5), Turkey (0.4), Spain (0.4), and Portugal (0.1). France, whose consumption at that time has been estimated by one scholar at 0.85 and by another at 0.99 pounds per person per day, was in the middle range, along with Great Britain (0.8) and Belgium (0.7).

Although dairy products may have constituted a substantial portion of the traditional peasant diet in some regions, consumption at the national level has been on the rise everywhere since the late eighteenth century. In this respect changes in the image of dairy foods and in consumer attitudes are more eloquent than statistics. Fresh milk, once considered fit only for infants, came to be seen as good for adults as well. In Germany the change may have begun in 1871, when Benno von Martiny published *Die Milch, ihr Wesen und ihre Bewertung,* a book that touted the benefits of drinking milk. Shortly thereafter, in 1874, two periodicals devoted to the promotion of milk were launched. Then a number of large, modern dairies opened in the suburbs of major cities, bringing fresh milk of good quality within reach of people of all classes. But fresh milk was not embraced overnight, and despite the proliferation of "milk bars" after World War II, the acceptance of milk seems to have been more limited in the south of Europe than in the north.

Eggs

Because eggs were for so long a domestic product, data about egg consumption are fairly rudimentary, but there is no doubt that a considerable increase followed the introduction of chicken farming after World War II. In France average annual per capita egg consumption has been estimated at five dozen for the year 1790, and it had risen to just under six dozen by 1900. By 1938, however, it had climbed to a little more than twelve dozen and continued to rise to almost nineteen dozen in the period 1960–64. In Germany the average person ate perhaps one egg per week in 1850 compared with 5.5 eggs per week today (including consumption in the form of industrially processed foods). Furthermore, the average weight of an egg has increased from 1.8 to 2.1 ounces.

Egg consumption varied significantly from country to country. In the period 1934–38, the United States and most European countries consumed anywhere from 0.63 to 1.54 ounces of eggs per day, with France in the middle of the pack at 0.87. In Mediterranean countries such as Greece, Yugoslavia, Spain, and Portugal, however, consumption was just 0.35 ounce.

Oils and Fats

Consumption of both animal and vegetable fats increased significantly in the nineteenth and twentieth centuries. Nevertheless, despite pressure from major industrial interests, there is considerable variation from country to country. In France, per capita consumption of butter reportedly more than quadrupled in 150 years. Consumption of vegetable oils also increased in both France and Germany (to nearly thirty-one pounds per year in Germany compared to just over twenty-three in France), but in Germany much of this is ingested in the form of margarine rather than oil.

Beverages

Consumption of traditional fermented beverages increased relatively little overall, and everywhere there were periods of stagnation and even decline. This was especially true of the traditionally dominant drink in each country, such as wine in France and Italy and beer in England and Germany.

In France, wine production increased more or less steadily in the eighteenth century and the first half of the nineteenth century. So did consumption. In fact, it almost doubled between the end of the Ancien Régime and the Second Empire: from 24 gallons per year in 1781–90 to 42 in 1865–74. Over the next sixty years demand leveled off: consumption in the periods 1905–14 and 1920–24 was roughly the same as in 1865–74, once the great crisis due to phylloxera and other vine diseases was overcome. From 1925 to the present, however, domestic demand for wine has been in a downward trend.

The vagaries of beer consumption were similar, albeit with a different chronology, in the countries where that beverage was traditionally dominant. In England, where beer continued for a long time to be produced locally, one cannot assess consumption simply by looking at production figures for industrial breweries. Annual production figures for malt are more reliable, and they suggest that beer consumption declined from 33.9 gallons per person per year in 1800 to 19.6 in 1850, touching bottom at 18.6 in 1843 and 18.8 in 1847. This cannot be accounted for by competition from another beverage: tea consumption also declined over the same period. Both phenomena were probably a consequence of falling wages. After 1850 consumption picked up again, and after World War II it shot up from approximately 10.4 gallons in 1950 to more than 26 gallons in 1960.

Consumption of secondary alcoholic beverages generally increased. In France beer consumption, in particular, shot up at a dizzying rate after World War II. In the eighteenth century beer drinking was limited to a tiny portion of the kingdom, so in the decade 1781–90 average per capita consumption was still just over three quarts per year. The taste for beer slowly spread to other parts of the country, however, and consumption increased.

Cider consumption in France doubled between 1815 and 1938, from about 5.8 to 14.6 gallons per person per year. It started out at a much higher level than beer, for cider had been the dominant beverage in Normandy and Brittany since the Middle Ages. Elsewhere, however, cider was much less popular in the nineteenth and twentieth centuries. Because it was difficult to store and subject to significant variations in production, consumption did not increase, whereas beer, promoted by major French and foreign industrial interests, made steady gains.

Consumption of other alcoholic beverages also rose. Brandies and liqueurs began to establish a market in France in the seventeenth century. This clearly concerned a smaller segment of society than wine, however, since annual consumption in the period 1815–24 was still under a quart per person. Over the next century and a half, consumption increased more than twelvefold, climbing to just over three gallons by 1935–38.

The figures we have for Germany indicate that secondary alcoholic beverages were of much less importance there. From 1850 to 1940, wine—a secondary although traditional beverage indigenous to the southern part of the country—held steady at somewhere between 0.8 and 1.6 gallons per person per year. Only after the war did consumption rise sharply, from roughly 1.6 gallons in 1950 to more than 3 gallons in 1960 and then to almost 4 gallons in 1970 and more than 5 gallons from 1975 to 1979. As for spirits (primarily made from potatoes), consumption actually decreased from 4 or 5 quarts per person per year in the nineteenth century to less than a quart in the period between the two world wars. Since then it has risen again, to between 9 and 10 quarts in 1976.

Taken together, the total consumption of alcoholic beverages increased considerably throughout Europe. In France, where wine remained predominant, consumption stagnated after the Second Empire and then declined after 1925, but the alcoholic content of wine increased markedly with the vogue for southern wines and various techniques designed to increase alcoholic strength. A glass of wine today contains much more alcohol than in the eighteenth century, particularly since it used to be common to dilute even the weaker wines with water. Because of this, the tradition of wine drinking carried with it an increased risk of alcoholism, as did the traditions of drinking beer and spirits in northern Europe. This led to a strong backlash against alcoholic drinks.

In France one consequence of this increase in the alcohol content of wine has been an increase in the consumption of beer and cider. These beverages are today much less alcoholic than wine and are therefore chosen over wine when people drink simply to slake their thirst. But the anti-alcohol movement has gone even further, promoting the drinking of coffee and tea in preference to all alcoholic beverages, as well as a variety of industrially produced, nonfermented drinks such as lemonade and soda.

The recent increase in the consumption of nonalcoholic beverages is well illustrated by data from Germany for the decade 1970–79: in ten years consumption of such beverages there rose from 91.5 to 118.3 gallons per person per year, while at the same time consumption of alcoholic beverages varied from 42.9 to 47.0 gallons. Of the nonalcoholic beverages, tea consumption increased from 7.5 to 10.7 gallons and coffee consumption from 35.3 to 48.9 gallons, partly owing to the decline in coffee substitutes such as chicory, consumption of which fell from 4.4 to 2.1 gallons. Coffee and tea, both introduced into Europe in the seventeenth and eighteenth centuries, had long since established themselves, especially in England. Britons of all classes became tea drinkers in the eighteenth century, but consumption more or less stagnated from 1801 to 1850. It was only after 1850, as wages began to rise, that tea drinking again began to increase. As for coffee, consumption increased dramatically between 1801 and 1841, mainly because it had previously been limited to the aristocracy and bourgeoisie. In France it was in the nineteenth and twentieth centuries that coffee drinking became habitual among people of all classes: it increased twenty-four-fold between 1815 and 1938. Even tea, which in France is drunk by a much smaller segment of society, saw its consumption increase by a factor of ten. The upward trend for both beverages has continued uninterrupted to the present day.

The most spectacular development of the twentieth century, however, has been the increased consumption of industrial drinks: sodas and other sweetened beverages, fruit juices, mineral water, and so on. In Germany in the decade 1970–79, consumption increased in each of these categories, rising from 18.2 to 32.5 gallons per person per year. What is astonishing about all these figures is that per capita consumption of all beverages, alcoholic and nonalcoholic alike, increased dramatically. Do we ingest much greater quantities of liquid than did our ancestors? Or would it be more accurate to assume that much of what they drank (wine, beer, and milk) was not recorded because it never made it to market?

Given the perennial nature of the subsistence economy, the same question can be asked about fresh fruits and vegetables, certain kinds of meat (such as pork and fowl), dairy products, dried vegetables, and potatoes. Of course, we took such considerations into account in compiling the statistics, but it is impossible to eliminate all the uncertainties. Accordingly, we have made it a principle not to present figures in isolation but only in comparison with other national data. We have also limited our interpretation to only the most obvious trends.

Caloric Intake and Nutritional Balance

For the same reason we have chosen not to compare food rations calculated by different scholars for different countries at different times. Statistical estimates are in any case useful only for forming a general idea of caloric intake and dietary balance, and we prefer to comment on these matters in a more general way.

First consider caloric intake. For France, Jean-Claude Toutain estimates that the average daily diet amounted to some 1,700 calories at the end of the eighteenth century, 2,000 calories in the period 1830–40, and from 2,800 to 3,000 calories in the period 1880–1960. The ideal, Toutain points out, is about 2,800 calories. Furthermore, the gap between the malnourished and the privileged narrowed during the nineteenth and twentieth centuries. The estimate of 3,200 calories for the period 1890–1914 seems appropriate since most people were then engaged in hard physical labor (peasants made up half the population, and many others worked as manual laborers). What is more, a diet of less than 2,000 calories, typical of the period 1790–1830, is equivalent to what people ate in the 1960s in underdeveloped countries such as India, Pakistan, and Indonesia. According to Toutain, the minimum of 1,600 to 1,800 calories that has been proposed for the late eighteenth century is surpassed by all underdeveloped countries today, whereas the estimate of 2,600 to 2,800 calories for the Second Empire is higher than that for all the countries of Asia and Africa in the 1960s.

Comparison of caloric intake in various developed countries for the years 1938 and 1967 yields the following:

	1938	1967
New Zealand	–	3,400
Ireland	–	3,400
United States	3,280	3,160
Canada	3,000	3,180
Switzerland	3,140	3,150
Sweden	3,120	2,900
Norway	3,210	2,970
Denmark	3,450	3,290
Germany	3,040	2,870
Austria	3,300	3,190

Despite certain differences in the composition of the daily ration (often explicable by diverse culinary traditions), the trend in most European countries over the course of these two centuries was similar. It is useful to distinguish between two phases. In the first phase, which ended in most countries in the late nineteenth century, caloric intake increased, thanks to increased consumption of cereals, potatoes, and other starches. In the second phase, the proportion of starches in the diet decreased as the proportion of animal proteins and fats (which are more expensive sources of calories) increased, as did the proportion of calcium-rich dairy products and fresh fruits and vegetables rich in vitamins and fibers. This second phase, which came after the problem of hunger had been resolved, was greatly influenced by the recommendations of modern dietetics.

BIBLIOGRAPHY

Burnett, J. *Plenty and Want: A Social History of Food from 1815 to the Present Day.* 3d ed. London, 1989.

Drummond, J.-C., and A. Wilbraham. *The Englishman's Food: A History of Five Centuries of English Diet.* Rev. ed. London: J. Cape 1958.

Livi Bacci, M. *Popolazione e alimentazione. Saggio sulla storia demografica europea.* 2d ed. Bologna: Il Mulino, 1989. [*Population and Nutrition: An Essay on European Demographic*

History. Trans. Tania Croft-Murray. Cambridge Studies in Population, Economy, and Society in Past Time, no. 14. Cambridge: Cambridge University Press, 1990.]

Sorcinelli, P. *Gli italiani e il cibo: Appetiti, digiuni e rinunce dalla realtà contadina alla società del benessere.* 2d ed. Bologna: Lexus Club "Storia Sociale," 1994.

Teuteberg, H. J. "Food Consumption in Germany since the Beginning of Industrialisation: A Quantitative Longitudinal Approach." In *Consumer Behavior and Economic Growth in the Modern Economy,* ed. H. Baudet and H. Van der Meulen, pp. 233–77. London: Croom Helm, 1986.

Toutain, J.-C. "La consommation alimentaire en France de 1789 à 1964." *Economies et Sociétés,* vol. A, no. 11. Geneva: Cahier de l'ISEA, 1971.

CHAPTER 34

The INVASION of FOREIGN FOODS

Yves Péhaut

First came spices. Then the eighteenth century witnessed its first glimpse of the fabulous fate in store for such foreign foodstuffs as sugar, coffee, chocolate, and tea, which eventually became basic staples of the western European and North American diet. In the nineteenth century additional foreign foods appeared on the scene and quickly caught on. Some, such as tropical fruits, proved successful because of certain unique, previously unsuspected qualities. Others were "bulk goods" that soon competed with, and in some cases supplanted, similar local commodities. For nearly a century, products based on tropical oils have inundated European markets.

The Invasion of the Tropical Oils

Until the nineteenth century, people everywhere obtained the fats in their diet from local products. To be sure, there has been trade in fat-rich substances, such as olive oil in the Mediterranean, ever since antiquity. Later, Hanseatic traders did business in linseed oil from Russia and lard and suet from northern Europe, but the tonnages involved were never very large. So the countries of the south relied on olive oil, and the countries of the north relied on animal fats—lard "for the mouth" and suet "for making things." Oils derived from colza, poppy seed, linseed, and hemp were also used. Oil mills were scattered throughout the countryside. Finally, midway between these liquid and solid fats were other substances such as walnut oil, goose fat, and duck fat, all of which were used in certain regions of France especially. In the nineteenth century, however, within the space of a few decades, this neat picture was demolished.

THE EARLY YEARS (1820–70) The change was triggered, in England initially, by the Industrial Revolution, which created new needs. The supply of animal fats and fish oils proved insufficient to meet the growing demands of the soap and stearin industries (stearin, an ester found in animal fat, is used in processing textiles and in making soap and other products). Between 1801 and 1851, British soap consumption more than tripled—from 24,100 to 85,053 tons. By 1912 it had reached 366,000 tons. Meanwhile, with the advent of steam power, better lubricants were needed for machine parts milled to ever closer tolerances and required to operate at ever higher speeds. To meet these needs, Europeans turned to palm oil from Guinea and to coconut oil from India. When the slave trade was banned after the Napoleonic wars, former slave traders plying the coast of Africa were eventually obliged to look for more "legitimate" cargoes, and for English captains palm oil filled the bill nicely. British imports shot up from 887 tons in 1820 to 25,285 tons in 1845. Because of its high acid content (15–20 percent), palm oil processed right on the plantation was initially used only for industrial purposes.

In 1846 Charles Heddle, a merchant from Sierra Leone, shipped four pounds' worth of hearts of palm to England. The heart of palm is an oil-rich nugget within the palm nut, and Africans had traditionally made little use of it. But German oil processors, especially in Hamburg, began buying large quantities after 1850. They found a way to process the nut to produce an oil of low acid content that could be used for cooking, together with a high-quality feed cake that found immediate application in a country where "scientific" animal husbandry had yielded excellent results. This turn to industrial processing was further aided by the innovative work of Theodor Weber, which sparked a veritable revolution in the industry. Weber, the Samoan representative of the large Hamburg firm J. C. Godeffroy and Company, was aware of the difficulties of exporting coconut oil in barrels, so he advised the natives to dry the coconut meat instead. When prepared it in this way, the dried meat, known as copra, could easily be packed in sacks for convenient shipping. Processed in European refineries, the copra yielded an oil comparable in quality to palm-heart oil and useful for the same purposes, including cooking. Manufacturers of bath soaps also began incorporating both palm and coconut oils into their products because the lauric acid in these oils has excellent foaming properties.

In 1830 the firm of Forster and Smith shipped ten pounds' worth of peanuts from Gambia to England. But British industrialists, preoccupied with the rapidly expanding market for palm oil, showed scant interest in the peanut, whose oil had few uses at the time since the major applications were already covered. The French paid attention, however. They were familiar with peanut oil and had even experimented with peanut farming in the Landes after 1802. When the Treaty of Paris handed Senegal back to the French, the commercial centers at Saint-Louis and Gorée lay in ruins, and the outlawing of the slave trade made matters even worse. The utter failure of efforts to create plantations in the river delta upstream of Saint-Louis in the 1820s left the colony with only one commercial product—rubber—but the rubber trade along the river was constantly disrupted by skirmishes with Moorish raiders. When newly arrived merchants, mostly from Bordeaux, encouraged the local farmers to grow peanuts, Senegal at long last discovered the cash crop it needed. By the late 1830s soap makers in Marseilles had proved that peanut oil could be used to make soap, and before long it was also competing with olive oil in the kitchen. Apparently peanut oil was even fraudulently passed off as olive oil, to judge by a gibe attributed to Léon Say: "Peanut, a small nut used to produce olive oil."

A CENTURY OF MONOPOLY IN TROPICAL OILS From 1870 on, events played a key role in promoting the use of tropical oils in Europe. To begin with, there were the effects of the "agricultural revolution." Farming was intensified as fields once allowed to lie fallow were planted with crops intended as fodder for animals. Livestock producers required ever greater quantities of diet supplements for their animals, and oil cakes were often used. Most important of all, the sugar beet became a basic crop in regions with alluvial soil, where traditional crops had first been supplanted by oil-bearing plants such as colza, poppies, and rape, which, despite small yields, provided work in the slack seasons of the year. During the second half of the nineteenth century and the first half of the twentieth century, most rural oil refineries that had not been modernized shut down, thus allowing "deodorized" oil from Tunisia to gain a foothold. In Germany, the amount of land devoted to oil-bearing crops (linseed, rape, poppies, and colza) decreased by two-thirds between 1870 and 1900. These products of coastal marshlands were too costly to compete with exotic imports admitted without tariffs. In 1932, before the modest stimulus to domestic production attempted by the Third Reich, production of table oil from local raw materials had fallen to 2,000 tons, whereas consumption had risen to 150,000 tons. In 1938 western Europe consumed approximately 3.5 million tons of vegetable oils but produced only 1.1 million, mainly olive oil. By the early 1960s, after most of the former European colonies had achieved independence but before the conclusion of a Common Market accord on oils and fats in July 1967, the six member nations of the Common Market were producing only about 20 percent of what they consumed. The deficit was covered primarily by tropical oils.

In the early years of the colonial era the foreign sources of oilseed expanded, and most countries admitted these raw materials duty free in order to compensate for the shortfall of domestic production. The opening of the Suez Canal in 1869 had a dramatic impact in clearing the way for significantly increased imports from India, peanuts and sesame especially. In 1929 a record 1,770,000 tons of cargo passed through the canal. Starting in the 1880s, large quantities of cheap cottonseed oil flowed into western Europe from the United States. After special refining to remove the toxic ingredient gossypol, much of this found use in food preparation. In addition, railroad building in West Africa before World War I made it possible to extend the area in which peanuts were grown in Senegal. Later, the conquest of the French Sudan and especially northern Nigeria added still more sources of supply, which could avail themselves of the outlet to the sea provided by the opening of the Kano-Lagos rail line in 1911. The influx of additional oilseed had already led to a sharp decline in prices at the end of the nineteenth century.

New uses for imported oilseed were developed as import tonnages increased. Marseilles showed the way in the 1830s. When the supply of olive oil fell short of demand, Marseilles began importing linseed from the Levant. Liverpool became the port of entry for palm oil, Hamburg for heart of palm. Before long, however, all three major ports were receiving shipments of all types of oilseeds and oils, mostly destined for domestic markets, whereas a fourth port, Rotterdam, reexported much of what it received, apart from what was needed as raw material for local margarine manufacturers. In 1900 each of these ports received approximately 500,000 tons of oilseed along with substantial tonnages of a variety of oils. In addition, certain other ports, such as Dunkirk and Bordeaux, specialized in peanut oil.

Large technologically advanced oil-processing plants in port cities soon replaced the small rural refineries of another era, and locally grown raw materials lost nearly their entire market share to imports. After 1870, petroleum derivatives replaced vegetable oils for most nonculinary purposes other than soap and stearin. First kerosene and then gas lamps supplanted oil lamps, and by 1900 mineral oils had taken over the lubricant market as well. As local vegetable oil production steadily decreased, the population of Europe continued to grow and cities continued to expand. This led to changes in eating habits: people were increasingly likely to use dressings on fresh foods and developed a taste for fried foods, which could be prepared easily. The average standard of living also rose. As a result, demand for cooking oils increased rapidly. In the mid-nineteenth century, "direct" intake of fats (as opposed to "invisible" fats in foods) was 22 pounds per year; by 1930 this had risen in the Netherlands to 44 pounds and in Germany and Great Britain to 38.6 pounds. Table oil consumption was modest, but the manufacture of margarine, which partially supplanted butter, absorbed vast quantities of tropical oils. In France per capita consumption remained under 28.6 pounds, mainly in the form of liquid oil and, to a lesser extent, margarine. Improved refining techniques made oils once limited to industrial uses available in the kitchen, and a certain homogenization of taste made various types of vegetable oil all but interchangeable as buyers made their choices on the basis of price rather than taste. Some oils did succeed in attracting a loyal clientele, however.

Peanut oil is a case in point. Its success, particularly in France, was related to its high "smoke point," which made it especially useful for frying. New processing techniques opened up new uses for certain oils; hydrogenation, for example, could convert liquid oil into a thick, spreadable substance, and cracking made it possible to separate liquid from solid components.

The development of new products had a major impact on the use of oils and fats. In 1866 Napoleon III announced a competition to develop a healthy, economical, easy-to-preserve new fat for the working class as well as for the army and navy. The chemist Mège-Mouriés won the prize for his work on "oleomargarine," a product made from rendered beef emulsified with a mixture of water and casein prior to churning. In 1871 he sold his formula to two Dutch butter manufacturers, Jan Jurgens and his competitor Van den Bergh. The product was well received, and the margarine business thrived to the point that the two industrialists built new factories in Belgium, Germany, and England. In 1895 margarine production reached 300,000 tons, or roughly one-tenth that of butter. Success was assured by the low price of margarine, less than half that of butter, except in France, where, under pressure from cattlemen, discriminatory measures were enacted against margarine.

This technology-driven expansion of the market was very good for oilseed imports. In 1899 animal fats still accounted for 70 percent of the market, but by 1928 their share had fallen to just 6 percent. In the same period the share of hydrogenated oils and solid fractions of liquid oils rose from 23 percent to 89 percent. The triumph of margarine was consolidated in 1928 when the two Dutch manufacturers, now merged, joined with the British soap giant Lever Brothers to create the huge multinational Unilever. The margarine trust was born. With plantations in Africa and the Pacific and purchasing subsidiaries such as the United Africa Company, Nosoco, and the Compagnie du Niger Français, Unilever made sure that its vast clientele would remain loyal to its tropical-oil-derived products.

In addition to margarine, the late nineteenth century witnessed the development of another new product for the kitchen—shortening. After finding use first in the United States and India, various types of shortening eventually captured a significant share of the European market as well. The brand name best known in France was Vegetaline, which gives an indication of the composition of the substance, a mixture of nonemulsified vegetable oils with animal fats. With hydrogenation the manufacture of shortening became an important use for the less expensive oils such as soybean and cottonseed.

After World War I the supply of oilseed to Europe was restored. The supply system was reorganized during the Great Depression of the 1930s, which affected the colonies just as much as it did the mother countries. In order to rescue the economies of their colonial possession, the major powers established zones of imperial preference. France, for example, enacted a law in August 1933 imposing tariffs on "foreign" oilseeds. This was followed up by an executive order of January 1934 guaranteeing each colonial product a specific share of total metropolitan imports. For peanuts in the shell, palm oil, and hearts of palm, the quota was set at 99 percent. In other words, the French domestic market was all but closed to imports from non-French colonies. In Great Britain, the steps taken were less public, but Unilever played a key role throughout Europe. Imperial protectionism was further reinforced after World War II. In France an executive order of November 1954 created a protected market in liquid oils within the so-called franc zone.

A MODEST COMEBACK FOR TEMPERATE-ZONE OILS SINCE 1960 As the former European colonies gained independence, they lost their monopolies of certain markets and were forced to compete internationally on the basis of price. The six member states of the European Common Market, recognizing the seriousness of their shortfall in oil production, decided to admit all oilseeds duty free. This measure left the door wide open to competition from American soybeans, and livestock ranchers switched to soy-based feeds as well. The oil yield of soybeans is just 17 percent by weight, but soybean oil is a natural by-product of the manufacture of animal feed, and its low price ensured that in Europe it would become the primary oil for salad dressings and cooking. Peanut oil, being much more expensive, was used exclusively for frying. Some restaurants preferred less costly oils, however, and, as dining out increased, this further limited the market for peanut oil. Consumption of 900,000 tons in 1960 had decreased to just 250,000 tons in 1993 in the twelve countries that now make up the European Community. Meanwhile, India, faced with explosive population growth, shifted to using peanuts for food rather than export. Among African countries, only Senegal is still shipping peanut oil. Overall, African production has decreased on account of bad weather and disastrous mismanagement by "parastatal" marketing organizations.

As tropical oil imports declined, domestic European production increased dramatically. Faced with wartime shortages, lawmakers took steps to encourage the growing of oilseed plants. Later the Common Market set attractive price guidelines to encourage production still further.

On the surface it might appear that consumption of tropical oils nearly doubled in thirty years from 1,200,000 tons to 2,320,000, but much of that total went to uses outside the kitchen. The sources of palm oil have changed completely: Africa is now out of the picture, Malaysia in. But nutritionists have been highly critical of the use of these oils. They blame many common afflictions of advanced industrial societies—obesity, high cholesterol, heart disease—on excessive consumption of fat (in excess of 66 pounds per person per year). Saturated fats are thought to be especially bad, while unsaturated fats are believed to be healthier. Sunflower and safflower oil are high in the latter. Safflower, a plant native to the Orient but today grown primarily in Mexico and the United States, has a fat content that is 78 percent linoleic acid, which is unsaturated. According to today's experts, the ideal diet would consist of one-third monounsaturated fats, one-third polyunsaturated, and one-third saturated. If this goal were achieved, it would mean a reduction in consumption of animal products and fats from tropical oils. In Europe the triumph of tropical oils is definitely a thing of the past.

Imported Fruits and Vegetables

Only a few civilizations have opted for a diet based on fruits and vegetables. Coconut and breadfruit are of course important staples in the South Sea islands. Plantain plays an important role in the jungle cultures of tropical Africa. And dates are fundamental for the people of the Sahara, just as figs and apricots once were for the inhabitants of the many hilly areas bordering the Mediterranean. For temperate Europe, however, fresh fruits and vegetables were never more than supplements to a diet based on cereals, tubers, and dried beans. They were a refreshment and a treat, not a staple.

Until the middle of the nineteenth century, consumption of fruits and vegetables was essentially limited to locally produced items, and the kitchen calendar followed the garden calendar. When Nicolas Appert developed a technique for sterilization by heat at the beginning of the nineteenth century, however, it became possible to preserve vegetables so that they tasted almost fresh.

TECHNOLOGICAL ADVANCES AND THE OPENING OF THE EUROPEAN MARKET The second half of the nineteenth century was in many ways a richly inventive period. New techniques developed at that time paved the way for a considerable expansion of the area from which Europe could draw fresh fruits and vegetables. A revolution in agronomy yielded improvements in the plants themselves. Nurserymen developed new varieties that bore fruit earlier or later, yielded more, or tasted better. Advances in transportation, including ever more rapid railroads and steadily diminishing freight costs, revolutionized the geography of agriculture. No longer did fruits and vegetables have to be grown near the markets in which they were sold. Wherever the climate was propitious—in the "fruit belts" of Brittany and Cornwall, for example, but primarily in the south of France, in the Rhone and Garonne valleys and Languedoc and Roussillon—growers could take advantage of longer growing seasons and beat truck farmers to market with early spring fruits and vegetables. City dwellers rejoiced in these "first fruits" and enjoyed the extension of the season at both ends.

As transit times decreased, the center of supply moved steadily southward, even across the French border into Spain and Italy. Southern farms expanded to supply customers in the north. In the United States, growers in "Mediterranean" California and "subtropical" Florida were linked to the northeastern urban populations. Technological progress also affected ocean transport. Thanks to improvements in sailing ships, freight charges dropped by three-quarters between 1820 and 1870. The advent of the steamship extended this trend to 1935, with a brief interruption just after World War I; freight costs dropped by another half as speeds increased still further.

Shortened transit times made it possible to envision shipping products that could not have withstood long voyages. With the advent of refrigeration technology, time became even less of a factor. In 1876 the Frenchman Charles Tellier was the first to build a ship equipped with a refrigeration system, which he called *le frigorifique*. Before fruit could be shipped, however, numerous improvements were required. In the process of ripening, for instance, fruit gives off heat and various gases, especially carbonic acid, so efficient ventilation systems were needed as well. After 1890 refrigeration equipment became available for overland transportation, and freight terminals were equipped with storage and ripening facilities. Refrigerated ships, trucks, railway cars, and freight containers benefited from a whole series of technological refinements. All of these things required substantial investment, yet the overall cost of shipping fruit remained low enough not to discourage consumption. In the United States in the 1930s, the cost of shipping oranges from California to the East Coast amounted to less than one-fourth of the retail price. In France in 1924, the cost of shipping bananas by sea accounted for only 13.5 percent of the wholesale price at the point of entry.

CITRUS FRUITS, BANANAS, AND PINEAPPLES: FROM LUXURY ITEMS TO MASS CONSUMPTION Within the space of a few decades, citrus fruits, bananas, and pineapples went from being luxury goods to items of mass consumption.

First cultivated in Southeast Asia, citrus fruits were soon imported into western Asia and then brought by Arabs to the Mediterranean basin. In the fifteenth and sixteenth centuries, they were grown in Italy and Spain in the Middle Ages and in Provence, especially the Hyères region. People in Paris and other northern cities were eating them as long as ago as the fourteenth century. But for a long time they remained expensive, until new methods of transportation by ship and train brought them within reach of consumers of more modest means. At the turn of the twentieth century, oranges and tangerines were still luxury goods, and many families indulged in them only during the Christmas season. For a long time, moreover, they could be found in the markets only from November to April, when locally grown fruits were unavailable in the countries of the Northern Hemisphere.

Many factors influenced the growth of demand in Europe, which was very rapid after World War I. Europeans followed the lead of the United States, where annual per capita consumption reached 66 pounds by the 1930s, twice as much as in Great Britain and four times as much as in France. And citrus fruits are not only delicious; they are also rich in vitamins, especially vitamin C. This proved to be a decisive factor: people ate citrus fruits because they believed them to be healthy and therapeutic. Nutritionists prescribe them for people on low-calorie diets. Because it is tedious to peel oranges, most consumers preferred to get their vitamin C by drinking orange juice. Once again, the United States set the pace, and orange juice became an essential part of every American breakfast. This new fashion had two important consequences. First, eating oranges, once a winter ritual, became a year-round activity. To meet the demand for oranges during the summer, new growers set up operations in the Southern Hemisphere in places like South Africa and Brazil, which began exporting large quantities of fruit in the 1930s. Second, growers took advantage of the brisk trade to introduce new products. The grapefruit, for example, was not accepted in the United States until 1910, but from then on it was much in demand both for its juice and for the fruit itself, which was cut in pieces and served with sugar. By 1939 South Africa and Palestine had began to produce both grapefruit and pomelo, and sales have risen sharply since the late 1950s. New varieties of fruit were also developed to supply the market during the winter: tangerines and clementines both had the additional advantage of being seedless and were immediately accepted because they are easy to peel and quarter.

Eminently decorative in gift baskets, delicious to eat, full of vitamins, a good source of juice as well as fruit, and useful in making candies, pastries, ice cream, and marmalade, citrus fruits are central to the diet of western Europe, which consumes some ten million tons a year.

The banana has also become a major consumer product in industrialized countries. In 1870, Lorenzo D. Baker, the captain of the schooner *Telegraph,* was looking for cargo to fill his ship's empty hold. In Jamaica he took on a shipment of bananas and managed to deliver them in good condition to Boston, where they fetched an excellent price. By general agreement, this event marked the beginning of an international trade in bananas, which was close to a million tons in 1910, had risen to 2.3 million by 1930, and reached 9 million in 1990. Bananas account for eight-ninths of the world's imports.

An exotic fruit at first, today the banana has become commonplace throughout the temperate zone, as common as apples or citrus fruits, no doubt because it can be purchased year round. Though prized as a dessert, it is no less valued for its nutritional qualities. Indeed, at just 90 calories per 100 grams, it is the nutritious fruit par excellence, good as a quick snack or for rounding out a light meal. The old slogan "A banana is as good as a steak" is probably obsolete today now that nutritionists are recommending reduced caloric intake, but the fruit is still notable for its high energy and vitamin content (20–22 mg of glucides, 10 mg of vitamin C) and abundant minerals. Of course, not everyone who eats a banana is aware of its nutritional benefits, but another gift of nature is plain to the naked eye: the fruit is easier to eat than many other types of fruit. With so many pluses, it is easy to understand why some people look on bananas as the perfect fruit. Still, a number of banana derivatives, such as dried and pureed bananas, banana flour, banana flakes, and even banana marmalade, have failed to attract a loyal clientele.

The success of this fruit, which originated in Southeast Asia and was spread throughout the tropics by the Spanish and Portuguese in the Age of Discovery, was not due solely to its intrinsic qualities, however. It depended in large part on the enterprising spirit of a handful of pioneers and, later, on the efficiency of the "integrated" companies they created. The banana trade evolved in parallel in western Europe and North America as the first regular shipments led to a rapidly expanding trade.

Between the two world wars, however, the European market for bananas was disrupted by the protectionist policies adopted by the imperial powers. In 1926 the British government took steps to protect growers in Jamaica, which remained the world's leading banana producer in 1935. In 1928 Italy imposed heavy tariffs on foreign bananas in order to encourage production in Somalia. France also established tariffs in 1931 to encourage its colonies to produce more bananas. In 1930 the colonies were supplying only 6 percent of France's needs, but by 1938 colonial shipments of 190,000 tons all but met the demand.

World War II disrupted trade, but recovery came rapidly as the shipping fleet was rebuilt in the 1950s. When various diseases affected banana production in Central America, one variety of banana was substituted for another. Some large multinationals were reorganized because of difficulties in dealing with the authorities in the countries in which they operated (United Brands was formed in 1968). The shift from one variety of banana to another led to further changes in the method of preparing the fruit for shipment and display. Grocers no longer separated individual bananas from the bunch. Bananas ceased to seem especially exotic. Careful selection and ripening reduced losses in transit warehouses and stores, to the benefit ultimately of the consumer.

Western European consumption rose dramatically from 700,000 tons in 1950 to 3,820,000 tons in 1990, an increase of 445 percent versus just 113 percent for the United States. Germany took the lead among European nations with a per capita consumption of 30.8 pounds compared with 19.8 for the French and British. The Common Market countries have two sets of arrangements with their suppliers, and differences between these two systems have thus far prevented any agreement about how to deal with banana imports. Germany and the Netherlands buy their bananas on the open market and levy no import duties, whereas France guarantees that a certain quota of its imports will come from the West Indies; Spain does the same for the Canary Islands. The former colonies enjoy a theoretical advantage in having their bananas admitted duty free. No solution to this problem is in sight, nor do efforts by major international organizations appear to have accomplished much in the way of bringing order to world banana markets. Even if there were an agreement, its only probable effect would be that of ratifying the status quo, for the major consuming countries appear to have reached their limit on imports. The producing countries were counting on increased demand from eastern Europe, but additional imports from that quarter seem unlikely at present.

Another tropical fruit that is produced today in vast quantities and traded internationally is the pineapple (close to 10 million tons are produced annually). Anointed by Father Dutertre the "king of fruits because it wears a crown," the pineapple was probably known in Spain as early as 1535 and in France by the beginning of the eighteenth century. Louis XIV is said to have sampled the first pineapple produced in his greenhouses at Versailles. Such hothouse production was not uncommon in Europe up to the end of the nineteenth century. At elegant banquets and dinners in the middle of the century, it was customary to serve pineapple for dessert, with its "crown" intact. In Flaubert's *Education sentimentale* (1869), a woman orders a pineapple salad in a restaurant. Later in the century, however, when citrus fruits and bananas were gaining wide acceptance, the pineapple was still confined largely to the upper classes because of its high cost. The fruit was no longer cultivated in western Europe, and the needs of the continent were supplied by plants raised in unheated greenhouses on Madeira and in the Azores. Puerto Rico shipped a few tons a year to the northeastern United States, and after 1860 attempts were made to grow pineapples in Florida. But frequent frosts forced growers to give up these efforts at about the time of World War I.

Still, many people became accustomed to eating pineapple, but from the can rather than as fresh fruit. In the 1880s tests were made of the feasibility of canning sliced pineapple in a sweet juice made by squeezing the core of the fruit and adding parings from the rind. On the eve of World War I, a miraculous machine, the *ginaca,* was perfected: with this device it was possible to process fifty pineapples a minute. Mass-produced canned pineapples from Hawaii were distributed by such major firms as the Libby Company and Dole Hawaiian Pineapple. Americans liked the taste, and the fruit was soon shown to be rich in vitamins as well, especially vitamins A and E. By the turn of the twentieth century, canned pineapple was also selling well in Europe.

Today, however, people want good fresh food and are unwilling to settle for anything from a can. Canned pineapple can be served at home but never in a good restaurant. This poses a major obstacle to further expansion of the market. Europe currently imports between 600,000 and 700,000 tons, 60 percent of which comes from Thailand and the Philippines. Pineapple juice, a by-product of the canning process, is a drink that many people like but others reject as too sweet. Although often used to make cocktails, it is not really a competitor for the market share currently claimed by citrus juices. Europe consumes just over 30,000 tons of fresh pineapple juice and 40,000 tons of pineapple juice concentrate annually.

Since World War II, the big news has been the increase in shipments of fresh pineapple, which had previously been quite limited. Shipping pineapple by sea poses even more problems than shipping bananas. The fruit must be harvested several weeks before full maturity, packed very carefully, and kept at a very low temperature during transit (below 54 degrees F. and preferably around 42 or 43 degrees). Even if all due precautions are observed, the fruit is not always of uniform quality at the point of sale. In recent years, however, pineapples shipped by air have enjoyed considerable success. If harvested when ripe, handled carefully, and shipped within hours, perfect fruit can be sold for just about twice what fruit shipped by sea costs. It has been estimated that at least 30 percent of the pineapple consumed in Europe is shipped by air. Of course, the pineapple is a large fruit and, unlike a banana or orange, is not likely to be eaten by an individual on a whim. It takes a fair amount of effort to prepare it for serving. Hence there are intrinsic limits to the expansion of the market; in terms of tonnage, the pineapple ranks third among tropical fruit imports.

FRESH FRUITS AND VEGETABLES ALL YEAR ROUND Nowadays fresh fruits and vegetables imported from abroad are available on European markets all year round. Air freight, scientific conditioning, and improved shipping technologies have enabled small tropical growers to tap new export markets. Virtually anything grown in the tropics can be sold in Europe today. Just a few decades ago, who had even heard of passion fruit, guava, and avocado? Yet all are now sold in large quantities and used as basic ingredients in many dishes—to say nothing of litchi nuts, mangoes, and Cape currants. Annual avocado imports now exceed 100,000 tons, and other fruits such as mango and papaya have enjoyed a steadily growing popularity. Significantly, diversification of the market has not been slowed by the relatively high prices of many of these new fruits due to limited, poorly organized production and high air freight costs.

One reason for the popularity of imported fruits and vegetables is no doubt the fact that many Europeans and Americans have visited the tropics and developed a fondness for the bountiful gifts of nature found there. When they return from their travels, they buy things that have caught their fancy, some for the snob appeal perhaps, others for nutritional reasons (they somehow believe that fruits that have ripened under the tropical sun are richer in vitamins, say, than fruits that grow elsewhere). Immigrants are sometimes the first to import exotic fruits, and others follow their lead. For example, litchi nuts gained a following after Chinese restaurants began serving them for dessert. Because many imported products are available all year round, they attract a loyal clientele. The mango is a good example. France initially imported mangoes from its former colonies in West Africa, such as Mali and Burkina Faso. Then India and Pakistan got in on the act; after that, Peru, Brazil, and South Africa were able to meet the demand from October through March, just before the West African season, which runs from March to July. Egypt and Israel pick up the slack in the period from August to October.

The story with other tropical fruits is similar. Consumers are delighted to find fruits and vegetables "in season" throughout the year. It is no longer utopian to think of eating green beans, grapes, and strawberries at Christmastime. For many years, growing European vegetables in the tropics was considered just another of the white man's crazy ideas. But as erstwhile colonial cities grew and former colonies gained their independence, truck farms began to supply the needs of the new urban populations. Plants that grow in Europe during the summer grow in the northern tropics during the "winter." In the 1970s enterprising farmers in places like Cape Verde, which supplies the city of Dakar, saw that they could take advantage of this out-of-season pattern pattern to ship fruits and vegetables, including string beans, green peppers, zucchini, and strawberries, to France and the rest of Europe by air. Other countries, from Senegal to

Kenya to Chile and South Africa, soon copied these initiatives, making grapes, pears, and other fruits available at virtually any time of the year. To be sure, these imports cost more than similar homegrown fruits, but people seem willing to pay the price.

After overcoming many difficulties and coping with numerous failures, foreign growers were ultimately able to win customers by shipping quality products to European markets. To do this, they had to choose their seeds carefully, tend their crops judiciously, and establish farms close to ports or other transportation facilities. They then entered into contractual arrangements with exporters, who learned how to store and prepare foods for shipment by air. Air transport is costly and difficult, for there is often not enough cargo to fill a plane and there is little return traffic from north to south. But as importers and exporters have established closer ties, it has become possible to make more accurate forecasts of future harvests. Within the European Union, the special agency COLE ACP, which includes representatives of both importing and exporting countries, helps promote new products.

In western Europe, the issue of maintaining a high level of agricultural production has been a matter of recent debate, so it is important to point out that, despite the growing success of imported fruits and vegetables on the European market, local production has also increased steadily. Important restrictions do not seem necessary at the present time. Consumers can take comfort in the fact that the whole world is now their garden.

BIBLIOGRAPHY

Adam, J. *Les plantes à matières grasses*. 4 vols. Paris: Société d'Éditions Géographiques, Maritimes et Coloniales, 1941–53.

Maillard, J.-C. *Le marché international de la banane: Étude géographique d'un système commercial*. Bordeaux: Presses Universitaires de Bordeaux, 1991.

Les oléagineux dans le monde. Paris: Economica, 1986.

Péhaut, Y. *Les oléagineux dans les pays d'Afrique occidentale associés au Marché commun*. 2 vols. Paris: H. Champion, 1976.

Py, L., and J. Lacoeuilhe. *L'ananas, sa culture, ses produits*. Paris: Maisonneuve et Larose, 1984.

Robert, P. *Les agrumes dans le monde*. Paris: Société d'Éditions Techniques Coloniales, 1947.

Samson, J.-A. *Tropical Fruits*. 2d ed. Tropical Agriculture Series. New York: Longman, 1986.

CHAPTER 35

The RISE of the RESTAURANT

Jean-Robert Pitte

The origin of the restaurant can be traced all the way back to the dawn of recorded history. The business of selling prepared food began when peasants and artisans were forced to leave home for days at a time in order to sell their goods at markets and fairs. While they were away, they had to eat while meeting with friends and business associates. As cities grew, the number and diversity of restaurants increased, and the restaurant remains primarily an urban phenomenon. Nevertheless, there were, even in the Roman Empire and ancient China, inns and way stations along major roads, often far from the nearest town. These were places where travelers could change horses, rest, and restore their strength by eating and drinking while keeping company with the staff and other guests.

Street Kitchens

Throughout the world, the principal type of eating establishment has always been the street kitchen, where a person can buy a precooked dish for a modest sum. They have always existed in China and still exist throughout Asia, even in industrial and postindustrial countries such as Japan. Tokyo's *yatai,* or restaurants on wheels, are the best place to buy *lamen* and *oudon* soups and *oden* boiled in a soy- or *sake*-based broth. These establishments fulfill an important social function: office workers, students, and businessmen can often be found exchanging pleas-antries with the cook and eating together on benches protected from the street by curtains.

Street restaurants are still common in Latin America and the Middle East and Africa (the shish kebab stalls of North Africa and the *maquis* of Abijan, for exam-ple). And they are one of the charms of Papeete, where restaurant trucks park along the oceanfront in the evening and serve a variety of local and foreign dish-es. By contrast, street kitchens have all but vanished in Europe; only a few street vendors remain, but without tables where customers can sit down to eat.

The Birth of the Modern Restaurant

If most restaurants in France are permanent rather than itinerant operations, it is probably because France was the birthplace of what we now call the restaurant, which gradually replaced an older variety of eating establishments. This happened toward the end of the eighteenth century. With the exception of inns, which were primarily for travelers, and street kitchens, described above, where in Europe at that time could one purchase a meal outside the home? Essentially in places where alcoholic beverages were sold, places equipped to serve simple, inexpensive dishes either cooked on the premises or ordered from a nearby inn or food shop, along with wine, beer, and spirits, which constituted the bulk of their business. Such tavern-restaurants existed not only in France but also in other countries. In Germany, Austria, and Alsace, *Brauereien* and *Weinstuben* served delicatessen, sauer-kraut, and cheese, for example; in Spain *bodegas* served *tapas*. Greek taverns served various foods with olive oil (such as *tarama*, stuffed grape leaves, and green beans). English pubs served shepherd's pie. And French *tavernes* and *guinguettes,* located outside city walls where meals were exempt from taxes, served a variety of fortify-ing dishes such as stews, meat with sauce, and organ meats. Certain other estab-lishments, such as the *cabarets* of Paris, served only wine, however; the "blue" wines of Suresnes, Argenteuil, and Chanteloup were poured in vast quantities.

All of these places, which catered to noisy, lighthearted, occasionally disputa-tious crowds, were apt to serve plain and simple fare rather than more elaborate culinary creations. If a person wished to drink with friends in a more sophisti-cated environment, it was necessary to go to a cafe, a type of establishment that dated back to the previous century. It was in 1674 that the Neapolitan Francesco Capelli, known as "Procope," opened the first cafe in Paris on the rue de Tournon. In 1684 Procope moved to the rue de l'Ancienne-Comédie, where a restaurant still does business under that name today. Soon, in places from Venice to Vienna, from St. Petersburg to London, cafes became bastions of the Enlightenment. Clients drank not only coffee but also tea and chocolate, and along with these exotic beverages they ate cake and sorbets.

For a genuine meal one had to look either to a good inn or to a *rôtisseur* or *traiteur* (caterer, from the Italian *trattorie*). In France, these two guilds, together with the *charcutiers,* had been granted a monopoly on all cooked meat other than pâtés (chopped meat wrapped in a pastry dough, the ancestor of today's etymologically redundant *pâté en croûte*). Only common people actually ate in the *traiteur's* shop, perhaps seated at a table reserved for guests in some establishments. Even a moderately well-to-do person would have preferred to order food delivered to a private home or a room at an inn or hotel or an elegant salon rented for the occasion. Wine was supplied by the tavern or inn. (This system is still common in Japan, where hot and cold dishes can be ordered by telephone at any hour of the day or night. Small neighborhood caterers depend more on these telephone orders than on their actual restaurant clientele. In any case, the premises are often tiny, with room for no more than four or five diners.)

One city in eighteenth-century Europe stands out as exceptional, however. London had a respectable number of taverns unlike those found elsewhere in Europe. These high-class, not to say luxury, establishments served dinner together with a glass of claret, sherry, or port. Their customers were gentlemen of the upper middle class and aristocracy, especially members of Parliament. Indeed, many members of the House of Lords lived primarily on their estates and kept only modest pieds-à-terre in town. With few servants they could scarcely hold sumptuous receptions in these small apartments. When the Marquis of Caraccioli visited London in 1777, he was aghast at the ways of the English aristocracy: "Country houses aside, their lodgings are poor, and nowhere can they find better food than at a tavern, to which they commonly invite foreign friends. . . . Is this what it means to live like a lord?"

In the 1670s one of the most celebrated London taverns was run by a Frenchman, Jean de Pontac, the son of a *président* of the Bordeaux *parlement*. He took advantage of the opportunity to dispense some of the wine produced on his father's estate, the Château Haut-Brion, producer of one of the world's best "clarets."

Since the reign of Louis XIV, the cream of the French aristocracy had resided in Paris or nearby Versailles. They lived in high style in private houses (*hôtels*) in the Marais, the suburb Saint-Germain, and Versailles itself. The wealthiest rarely called on the services of caterers doing business with the general public. They preferred to employ their own *maîtres d'hôtel* and *cuisiniers*, paying astronomical sums for talented chefs and seeking to emulate the culinary extravagance of the court. This was the proving ground for the elaborate recipes that form the basis of

French haute cuisine, which already enjoyed a considerable reputation abroad. The culinary landscape of Paris was thus already in evidence: a grand luxury cuisine beyond the reach of ordinary mortals together with a large number of food and wine shops serving more common fare, together with a few places where more sophisticated creations could be purchased (such as *pâté de jambon* at Leblanc's shop on the rue de la Harpe, which in a typical year served up some 1,800 Bayonne hams). In addition to these eating establishments, there were also cafes, where one fed the spirit but not the stomach. Meanwhile, the cultivated elite kept its eyes on England. Such was the situation at the time of the Boulanger affair.

The Boulanger Affair

In 1765 a man by the name of Boulanger, also known as "Champ d'Oiseaux" or "Chantoiseau," opened a shop near the Louvre (on either the rue des Poulies or the rue Bailleul, depending on which authority one chooses to believe). There he sold what he called *restaurants* or *bouillons restaurants*—that is, meat-based consommés intended to "restore" a person's strength. Ever since the late Middle Ages the word *restaurant* had been used to describe any of a variety of rich bouillons made with chicken, beef, roots of one sort or another, onions, herbs, and, according to some recipes, spices, crystallized sugar, toasted bread, barley, butter, and even exotic ingredients such as dried rose petals, Damascus grapes, and amber. In order to entice customers into his shop, Boulanger had inscribed on his window a line from the Gospels: "*Venite ad me omnes qui stomacho laboratis et ego vos restaurabo.*" He was not content simply to serve bouillon, however. He also served leg of lamb in white sauce, thereby infringing the monopoly of the caterers' guild. The guild filed suit, which to everyone's astonishment ended in a judgment in favor of Boulanger. It was an ominous sign for the future of the guilds, which were soon swept away in the turbulence of the French Revolution, but an encouraging one for a new profession that greatly needed it.

The celebrity that Boulanger enjoyed as a result of this lawsuit ensured his success. In a letter to Sophie Volland, Diderot wrote: "I left to have dinner with the *restaurateur* on the rue des Poulies. One eats well there but pays dearly for the service." In the years leading up to the revolution *restaurateurs* set up shop everywhere. They served sophisticated dinners, no longer at an unappealing common table but at private tables covered with tablecloths and reserved for individuals or small parties. The dishes that could be ordered were listed on a framed piece of paper, and at the end of the dinner the customer was presented with a check listing what had been ordered.

Among the most renowned restaurants of the period, Les Trois Frères Provençaux on the rue Helvétius (today the rue Sainte-Anne) stood out as particularly distinguished from 1786 on. The "three brothers" exploited the exotic by serving *brandade de morue* (salt cod pounded with garlic, oil, and cream) and *bouillabaisse*—or some version of *bouillabaisse,* since it is hard to imagine how the delicate *rascasse* and *saint-pierre,* both Mediterranean fish, could have made it to the capital. Clearly, people already went to restaurants to sample exotic dishes, a habit that would become increasingly common as time went by. The "three brothers" became so well known that after the revolution the Prince de Conti hired them to head his kitchens before finally deciding to emigrate.

In 1782 Antoine Beauvilliers, another restaurant pioneer, left the service of the Comte de Provence (the future Louis XVIII) to open a restaurant on the rue de Richelieu, which he called La Grande Taverne de Londres in order to appeal to society people crazy about the English and others with fond memories of their journeys across the channel. Brillat-Savarin would later write that "for fifteen years [Beauvilliers] was the leading *restaurateur* of Paris. . . . He was the first to have an elegant dining room, impeccably dressed waiters, a select wine cellar, and superior food . . . and he seemed to pay special attention to his guests." Beauvilliers recognized regulars and addressed them by name, spoke to foreign guests in their native tongues, and moved about the dining room with a sword strapped to his side. His prices reflected these many talents. Soon Beauvilliers was so successful that he was able to move from his original location and open a new restaurant nearby, underneath the arches of the Palais-Royal, at that time a center of fashion. But no one yet used the word *restaurant* to refer to the establishment of a *restaurateur*. It was not until 1835 that the dictionary of the Académie Française recognized the word in this sense.

The revolution made the fortune of many *restaurateurs*. A number of excellent chefs suddenly found themselves without patrons, as their masters were either guillotined or fled abroad. Some chefs went into business for themselves and catered to the new princes of the day. Méot, formerly chef to the Prince de Condé, opened a restaurant on the rue de Valois in 1791. His neighbors included Bancelin, Robert (also once employed by Condé), Henneveu, and Véry. Their clients were the provincial *députés* brought to Paris by the revolution. Within the walls of the Palais-Royal, not far from where they sat as legislators, revolutionary leaders found all the Parisian pleasures they had ever dreamed of, along with other conveniences of a more prosaic sort. Louis Sébastien Mercier had this to say in 1798:

It was a very judicious fellow who, upon seeing that the Palace formerly known as Royal now housed any number of *restaurateurs glaciers* with their dining rooms and private *cabinets* packed as closely as flies on honey, had the idea of building privies for the diners at eighteen *livres* apiece. His thought was that so many truffled turkeys, salmons, Mainz hams, boar's heads, bolognas, pâtés, wines, liquors, sorbets, ice creams, and lemonades must in the final analysis ultimately find their way into a common reservoir, and that if he made it spacious enough and above all convenient enough for so many people who treated everything as a source of pleasure, the *caput mortuum* of the nearby kitchens would become his gold mine.

Here we have a fine example of a man who knew how to adapt the lesson of the emperor Vespasian to modern times.

The Restaurant in the Nineteenth Century

The revolution thus allowed haute cuisine to emerge from the milieu of the court. Customers who had never tasted truffles or *chambertin* and who might have been expected to seek to bring their actions into line with their political and social beliefs thronged restaurants in order to sample such delicacies. Before the revolution there were about 100 restaurants in Paris, but afterward the number rose to 500 or 600 under the Empire and to 3,000 during the Restoration. In 1804 Grimod de La Reynière, writing in the *Almanach des gourmands,* remarked that "the hearts of most opulent Parisians suddenly metamorphosed into gizzards. . . . In no other city in the world has the number of shops selling comestibles increased so rapidly. Paris has one hundred restaurants for every bookstore."

When the Empire collapsed, the restaurants of Paris were so renowned that officers from all the European allies flocked to them, as German officers would do again in 1940. Eugène Briffault remembered that event in his *Paris à table* (1840): "In 1814, when all of Europe rose in arms against France, the leaders of that multitude had but one cry: Paris! And in Paris they asked for the Palais-Royal, and at the Palais-Royal what was their first desire? To sit down to eat."

Throughout the nineteenth century the general level of Parisian eating establishments rose significantly, although a good number of places remained where one could buy leftovers. The cabarets disappeared, cafes became *salons de thé,* and the old appellation *café* was later taken over by the *vin-bois-charbon,* places where one could buy wood or charcoal in addition to the odd glass of wine. These were kept by the "Auvergnat diaspora," peasants who had left Auvergne for Paris and whose wives and mothers were long renowned for their lentil stews and pot roasts. The *guinguettes* of an earlier period transformed themselves into real restaurants with tablecloths and nice dishes, as can be seen in any number of Impressionist paintings. Soup kitchens and dairy shops offered home cooking at modest prices. Restaurants of this sort sprang up throughout the provinces to serve artisans, officials, and people of leisure. The *bouchons* of Lyons were the most distinguished of the lot with their saveloy and leg of lamb salads, quenelles, *tabliers de sapeur* (tripe), and *cervelle de canut* (a strong cheese), all washed down with chilled beaujolais (young rather than new).

The refinement once associated with the old aristocratic households could be found in the deluxe restaurants of the *grands boulevards* of Paris (the Café Riche and the Café Anglais), on the Place Bellecour in Lyons, and in the back streets of Bordeaux. The great restaurants relied on recipes developed and written down by Antonin Carême, the chef who presided over the *extraordinaires* (official banquets for major state occasions of the Empire and Restoration) and by his successors, Dugléré, Urbain Dubois, and, last but not least, Escoffier. Chefs prepared beautiful creations out of fish and shellfish, *foie gras* from Strasbourg (which became the very symbol of good dining in France), seasonal game, chicken, and sirloin, all buried beneath mountains of truffles and dripping with brown sauces thickened with cream or butter. Menus at these restaurants could be as long as the dinner menus for the great occasions of the Ancien Régime, but now, for reasons of convenience and price, customers picked and chose the dishes they wanted before the food was prepared and served. They also selected wines from enormous lists.

Thus the revolution, far from hampering culinary creativity or marking a step down from the heights of eighteenth-century cuisine, actually effected a transfer of the art of cooking from the aristocracy to the bourgeoisie and to some extent to the working class as well, by way of an institution—the restaurant—born of the demise of the old guilds.

Restaurants and the Tourist Trade

Toward the end of the nineteenth century came a second revolution in the art of eating well away from home, a revolution related to the development of rapid means of transportation and luxury tourism. Earlier, at the end of the eighteenth century, a few wealthy Englishmen had begun to settle on the Riviera. Later they also favored various places in Italy, Corfu, and elsewhere. At that time, however, the custom was to build or rent a substantial villa with a large staff of servants. This kind of tourism did not foster the development of restaurants. But when the middle classes began traveling across Europe in large numbers, entrepreneurs built luxury hotels to accommodate them. Food, ambiance, and service were of course part of the package.

One of the pioneers of this new type of hotel was César Ritz, a Swiss developer who formed a partnership with one of the leading French chefs of the day, Auguste Escoffier. Their first joint venture was the Grand Hotel of Monte Carlo. After that came the Savoy of London, a city noted for fine hotels since the 1820s. After making the Savoy one of the best hotels in the world, the pair opened another hotel in London, the Cecil, where Escoffier prepared his famed "Epicurean dinner," a French meal that was served to hundreds of people simultaneously in thirty-seven cities across Europe. Following Escoffier's lead, French chefs spread out across the continent, and the profession of cook became known as one of the most remunerative if difficult of the manual trades. It was, and is, also a trade that required its practitioners to move wherever their work might take them.

Here, in Escoffier's own words, delivered with the chef's customary aplomb in his remarkable memoirs, is a description of his work and influence:

> The art of cooking is perhaps one of the most useful forms of diplomacy. When called upon to set up restaurants in the most sumptuous of luxury hotels all around the world, I always made a point of insisting on French equipment, French products, and, above all, French personnel. The reason for this is that the development of French cooking has been due in large part to the thousands of French chefs who work in all four corners of the globe. These men left their native land in order to teach people in far-away places about French foods and how they are prepared. I take great satisfaction in having contributed to this development. Over the course of my career I have "sown" some two thousand cooks around the world. Most of them have settled abroad, and one can think of them as so many grains of wheat planted in previously untilled soil. France is today reaping the harvest.

The Restaurant in the Twentieth Century

Meanwhile, the word *restaurant* caught on not just in France but throughout Europe. The English took over the French spelling without change, while the Italians opted for *ristorante,* the Spanish for *restaurante,* and so on. By the late twentieth century the word had spread around the world, and one sees it today on the facades of the finest eating places in Tokyo, Hong Kong, Bangkok, Rio de Janeiro, and Cairo. One even sees it on more modest establishments in the poorer countries.

And French chefs still go abroad, much more often, in fact, than French engineers or businessmen. No other sophisticated cuisine has evolved as rapidly as the French. Today it resembles the culture of France itself, if only in its contradictions. It has become increasingly receptive to foreign influences (foods, cooking techniques, flavors, and methods of serving), particularly from the Far East. Yet it still takes a reverent attitude toward regional products and traditional presentations (or modernizations thereof). And it attaches great value to the idea of making sure that food and wine are perfectly attuned to the geographical setting, the season, and the desires of chef and diners alike.

Since World War II, French cuisine has changed in response to the demise of the grand hotels and the rise of automotive tourism. To break up the monotony of the long trip along National Highway 7 from Paris to the Côte d'Azur, wealthy Parisians got into the habit of stopping along the way to sample the gastronomic delights of the regions through which they were traveling. This phenomenon explains the success of Alexandre Dumaine at the Côte d'Or in Saulieu, of Mère Brazier in Lyons, of Fernand Point at La Pyramide in Vienne, and of Raymond Thuillier at the Oustau de Baumanière in Baux-de-Provence, among others. Never before would a great chef have dared to serve escargots, *gratin dauphinois,* or a simple herbed leg of lamb. Nowadays such dishes are demanded by clients alongside lobster and *foie gras truffé,* which remain as prestigious as ever. What is more, gourmets from around the world now think nothing of traveling from one end of France to the other in order to sample the cuisine of a renowned chef. For some years now, Japan Airlines has been organizing tours of France whose high points include a few of the major sights of Paris (the Eiffel Tower, Hermès, Vuitton) together with the restaurant founded by Paul Bocuse (even though the master himself has retired). Michel Guérard managed to attract Americans to Eugénie-les-Bains, where he set up shop. And Michel Bras, whose kitchen is in Laguiole on the inaccessible Aubrac, draws pilgrims keen to savor the rare fragrance of dishes flavored with herbs from the nearby volcanic slopes. After all, *crème de tourteau à la semence d'anis sauvage* and *langoustines à la bourrache bleue* and *foie gras aux aiguilles vertes de pin Douglas* are as exotic today as the *consommé au madère* with Parmesan that Brillat-Savarin served nearly two centuries ago to elderly gourmet relatives who could not believe their taste buds, or as the *foie gras de Strasbourg* that the Maréchal de Contades, governor of Alsace, sent to Louis XVI, who became a convinced propagandist.

Haute cuisine is thus alive and well, and it is not difficult to understand why. Its success is comparable to that of high fashion, the plastic arts, music, and literature. By contrast, what is happening to less renowned restaurants is worrisome. Everywhere the food business is turning toward the typical, the anodyne, and the insipid. And it does no good to point a finger of blame at the Americans, the pioneers of the fast food formula that is bringing in the masses from Des Plaines, the birthplace of McDonald's, to Paris, Moscow, and Peking, the home of the largest fast food restaurant in the world. If the formula has been successful, it is because it meets certain needs. Owners of more traditional restaurants may have failed to heed their clientele.

In an odd way the current situation is reminiscent of the old dispute in Paris between the *traiteurs* and the *restaurateurs*. For those who feel that the barbarian is at the gates and that all the great culinary traditions are about to vanish, it is time to get to work and come up with a way to satisfy everyone's appetites, cultural as well as physical, in a way that people can afford. The restaurant has always been the kingdom of the imagination. Without imagination it cannot survive.

BIBLIOGRAPHY

Aron, J.-P. *Le mangeur du XIXe siècle*. Lausanne: Ex Libris, 1974. [*The Art of Eating in France: Manners and Menus in the Nineteenth Century*. Trans. Nina Rootes. New York: Harper & Row, 1975.]

Bonnain-Moerdyk, R. "L'espace gastronomique." *L'Espace géographique* 2 (1975): 113–26.

Brennan, T. *Public Drinking and Popular Culture in Eighteenth-Century Paris*. Princeton: Princeton University Press, 1989.

Gillet, P. *1989 est également l'année du bicentenaire du restaurant*. Paris: Chambre Syndicale de la Haute Cuisine Française, 1989.

Heron de Villefosse, R. *Histoire et géographie gourmandes de Paris*. Paris: Editions de Paris, 1956.

Huetz de Lemps, A., and J.-R. Pitte, eds. *Les restaurants dans le monde et à travers les âges*. Grenoble: Glénat, 1990.

Ortoli, V. *Paris, capitale de la gastronomie: 200 ans de restauration*. Paris: Direction Générale de l'Information et des Relations Extérieures de la Mairie de Paris, 1984.

Pitte, J.-R. *Gastronomie française: Histoire et géographie d'une passion*. Paris: Fayard, 1991.

CHAPTER 36

The FOOD INDUSTRY *and*
NEW PRESERVATION TECHNIQUES

Giorgio Pedrocco

Food Economy and Population Growth in the Eighteenth and Nineteenth Centuries

Radical solutions to the need to provide European populations with food began to emerge in the eighteenth and nineteenth centuries alongside the rapid process of industrialization, which developed in England and other parts of western Europe. Industrial growth was based on the factory system and was accompanied by a process of urbanization, with a massive migration of population from the country to towns. The "reproduction cost" of the new urban workforce, however, was very high, owing to the difficulty of supplying food to all towns—not only industrial centers but also commercial ones.

The same period witnessed parallel growth in overall population that contributed, in those areas undergoing industrialization, to upsetting even further the already difficult balance between food supplies and population as well as between the geographical distribution of food supplies and the territorial distribution of population. The result was that living conditions for the urban working classes became particularly harsh. Food supplies were scarce and expensive, primarily because of the inadequate distribution system in the large cities. Markets and slaughterhouses were unable to absorb the increased volume of trade created by increased consumption.

It is no accident that Malthusian theories enjoyed considerable success at this time. These theories dramatized imbalances between population growth and increases in food supplies and proposed preventing both population growth and improvements in living conditions in order to avert ruinous social unrest.

The economic anxieties and political problems that emerged from this situation encouraged the transformation of the productive system in Europe. During this period, as a result of complex contractual and technological mechanisms, the agricultural sector managed to increase the volume of production of its most important food products from cereals to meat. The period also saw the birth of a new industrial sector: food processing. This developed innovative systems for the production and conservation of foodstuffs that would allow a decrease in production costs, more efficient marketing, and, finally, more rational distribution.

The Food Industry and a World Food Economy

By the middle of the nineteenth century, the growing needs of the European food markets, as a result of population growth and urbanization, revealed the basic incapacity of European agriculture to fulfil them—despite increases in production during the previous century to meet the demands of the new town dwellers.

The role of colonial and ex-colonial economies became increasingly important, since their land resources, unlike those of Europe, seemed inexhaustible. Bringing vast new areas of land into cultivation in order to provide the European market with food—especially meat and cereals—at prices markedly below those in Europe had become the most significant aspect of the world economy by the end of the nineteenth century. This revolution in food supplies was also the result of rapid new rail and sea links, which made it possible to connect urban centers with areas of production outside Europe.

The arrival of American and Russian cereals in the 1880s obliged European agriculture to transform its production, abandoning uneconomical grain cultivation in favor of more profitable activities linked to food (vineyards and livestock raising) and manufacturing (cotton, linen, and tobacco). Western Europe began to send its manufactured goods in the opposite direction, compensating for food imports in their balance of payments.

The massive development of the food industry, particularly of beef and on-the-spot butchering, made it necessary to invent ways of processing and preserving produce. This problem had always existed, and many solutions had been found through the centuries. It now became necessary to transform these traditional preservation techniques into industrial practices. In Europe especially, efforts were also made to develop packaging systems for the most common foodstuffs, from bread to wine, in order to increase productivity.

The nineteenth century was marked by important developments in the food industry, above all in the preserving and refrigeration sectors. The former enabled meat and vegetables to be kept for long periods of time, while the latter was mainly concerned with the short- and medium-term preservation of the most valued animal products from fish to beef and pork.

Bread and Wine

The first sector to be transformed was that of the staples bread and wine. For centuries these had provided the daily sustenance of the urban and rural lower classes, with other foods—such as beef and pork—being eaten only on special occasions such as feast days and festivals.

MILLS AND OVENS From ancient times, bread-making had been shared between the baker's oven and that of the home. Bakers' guilds operated in the towns; in the country, women met their families' needs by baking enough bread for up to a month in their own ovens.

Before bread could be made, the grain had to be ground into flour. From the Middle Ages on, this was done outside the home in both the country and the town. The peasant's practice of taking small amounts of grain to the mill to be ground was linked to the small size and large number of traditional mills, whose stones were moved, according to local conditions, by water or wind. Because mills had to be built near water or in exposed areas, they were often located in inaccessible or peripheral areas.

In the first half of the nineteenth century, mills were transformed by a series of innovations increasing the quantity and quality of the flour that could be obtained from grain. These innovations radically changed the structure of mills. Traditional sources of energy were now replaced by steam-driven machinery that made it possible to work throughout the year. Millstones were replaced by a system based on iron rollers. In order to store the large amounts of grain necessary to satisfy the productive capacity of these new mills, silos in various shapes and sizes were built.

At the same time, bread-making—the most common and widespread of all activities—was one of the first to be subjected to mechanization. Efforts were made to mechanize the tiresome task of kneading the dough and then baking it, which represented a bottleneck in the productive cycle. However, the complexity of producing dough continued to create problems. Eighteenth- and nineteenth-century attempts to substitute the expertise of the baker's hands in the kneading process produced dubious results. It was only in 1925 that a mixer capable of being used with all kinds of flour became competitive with manual labor. As for baking, a technique that had been developed in other areas of industry was applied: the solid fuels that had previously been used inside the oven itself were replaced by hot air.

VINEYARDS AND CELLARS Wine was the other irreplaceable element in the rural and urban diet. In the course of the nineteenth century, consumption increased considerably, despite the epidemics of blight that struck European vineyards, the only vineyards able to meet the needs of the international market. This increase in consumption confronted the centuries-old problem of preserving wine, which, after about a year, turned into vinegar.

Here, too, it was necessary to move from a fragmented rural productive system to a more articulated industrial one that distinguished grape-growing from winemaking. While cultivation and harvesting necessarily remained in the hands of the rural population, winemaking became a separate industry that was organized into a factory system during the nineteenth century, radically changing an ancient and traditional activity.

In order to satisfy mass demand, the industrialization of winemaking required new buildings. Neither the peasants' cellars nor the larger underground vaults of landowners were adequate. The original site of production—the cellar—was to lose its central role when the introduction of chemical additives into the productive process and the ability to regulate temperatures within buildings made it possible to mass-produce wine anywhere.

As a result of technical and scientific advances in the productive phases, from crushing to fermentation and aging, the winemaking cycle became more complex and exact. Two factors—chemistry and mechanics—contributed to transforming the process of winemaking into a truly industrial one and replacing many practices that had governed it, almost unchanged, for centuries.

Mechanization entered the early phases of the cycle. Crusher-stemmers and presses operated by steam rather than hand had the primary aim of reducing the labor force. Thanks to these machines, the task of pressing the grapes was shifted from the peasants to the factories. Machines could also select and classify the grapes more carefully in order to produce a more clearly defined range of wines. Chemical applications were introduced in the later phases of the cycle to stabilize the wine, which helped preserve it and facilitated its transport and marketing. A completely new operation—pasteurization—was introduced to keep the wine from turning into vinegar. In this process, developed by Louis Pasteur in the

1860s, the wine was heated in vats to a temperature of 60 degrees Centigrade (140 degrees Fahrenheit) in order to destroy all traces of colonies of microorganisms—in particular, *Mycoderma aceti* and *Mycoderma vini*. The operation rapidly brought the wine to the right temperature without damaging its characteristics.

Racking—the ancient technique of separating the wine from the lees in order to complete fermentation—was accelerated by the introduction of pumps, which made it easier to transfer wine from one barrel to another. At this stage, sodium bisulfite was added to stabilize the wine.

With the storing of wine in enormous vats, where it was aged and clarified through a slow process of sedimentation, the modern industrial plant soon replaced the traditional cellar. Producers could meet the needs of the market even in bad years by drawing on reserves. They could also guarantee that the wine maintained its "typical" features, ensuring a more consolidated relationship with the market.

The buildings that housed the new industry were large enough to provide easy access for workers and transport. They also allowed for the storage of huge quantities of wine during the aging process. The massive barrels used in this process were later replaced by cement vats lined with glass; here the wine was stored until it could be put on the market.

The Problem of Food Preservation

Industrial and commercial urban society could not be satisfied simply by the ready availability of bread and wine. Other foods, previously reserved for the upper classes, therefore had to be made accessible—albeit to a lesser extent—to the lower classes. Numerous attempts were made to provide traditionally luxury goods like meat and fish at low prices, leading to the birth of the preserving industry.

HALTING DECOMPOSITION IN ORGANIC SUBSTANCES All scientific attempts to transform preserving from a traditional activity to an industrial process depended on a better understanding of decomposition. All edible vegetable or animal organisms immediately begin to ferment and then decay as soon as they are harvested or killed. Throughout the eighteenth century, much debate had centered on whether this process was the result of "spontaneous generation" or whether it was caused by spores and ovulation. It had been observed that enzyme activity, on the one hand, and infection, on the other, were blocked by processes involving cold and heat, making it possible to preserve luxury foods on a small scale.

The French scientist Denis Papin experimented, around the turn of the eighteenth century, with preservation. He cooked and preserved foods in hermetically sealed containers or placed them raw in a sugar solution inside hermetically sealed glass jars. When Papin informed Gottfried Wilhelm von Leibniz of his discoveries, the German philosopher and scientist became the first person to suggest using food preserved in this way for soldiers' rations.

A French pastry chef, Nicolas Appert, was the first person to conceive of bottling food to preserve it for relatively long periods and then to put the idea into practice. It is not known whether he was aware of Papin's work or whether he had confronted the problem of food preservation from scratch. He ran a *confiserie* in Paris from 1789 to 1795, and it was probably during this period that he encountered the problems of preserving food and the empirical methods that were then adopted to solve them. He soon developed a method that anticipated Pasteur's ideas and techniques, based on sterilizing food in order to kill living microorganisms, *les ferments,* and their spores. Appert intuitively understood the destructive action of heat on *ferments* that modified the quality of vegetable and animal substances. Freeing the food of its *ferments* by heating it sufficiently, placing it in a hermetically sealed jar, and then immersing the jar in boiling water effectively stopped the process of decomposition. Once the jar cooled, the preserved food lasted for years.

Appert started to put his discoveries into practice on an industrial scale, setting up a food-preserving factory in 1804 at Massy and employing fifty workers. Chunks of cooked meat were placed into tin cans, meat stock was added, and the can was hermetically sealed with a soldered top. The cans were then placed into vats of boiling water for different lengths of time according to the size of the can. The cans were then cooled and kept under observation in environments of 30 degrees Centigrade (86 degrees Fahrenheit). If the can swelled (a sign that the process had not been successful), it was discarded. Those cans that showed no change in volume were put on the market.

The first to appreciate Appert's experiments were the armies of Napoleon Bonaparte, which could be provided with autonomous rations on their many campaigns, and naval crews, who were less exposed to shortages of food supplies during risky transatlantic crossings. The French navy, which directly tested these new products, was particularly impressed.

Some decades later, Pasteur formulated his theory of spores, laying the scientific foundations for a correct interpretation of Appert's methods, and developed the theory and laws of food sterilization. The process known as pasteurization is now used throughout the food-processing industry, from milk to wine.

THE EUROPEAN FOOD-PRESERVING INDUSTRY Strikingly, Appert's discoveries did not initiallly lead to the establishment of a food-preserving industry in his own country because of France's predominantly agricultural character—and the fact that Paris and the industrialized northern regions could obtain fruit and vegetable supplies almost all year round from the southern regions as well as from French colonies in North Africa. It was only after 1900 that small companies were established.

The industry had its inception in Braunschweig in Lower Saxony. In 1830 Baron Wilhelm Eberhard Anton von Campen returned from a diplomatic mission in France, where he had learned about Appert's discoveries. He tried to apply the method to game, succeeding after a few attempts. Around 1840 two local tinsmiths, Pillman and Daubert, began to experiment by preserving asparagus, which grew on the city's outskirts. They devoted part of their workshop to the new activity, which developed rapidly.

In the German port town of Lübeck, the C. C. Hahn food-preserving factory opened in 1848. Once again Appert had provided the inspiration. After Hahn had seen Appert's preserves in France, he realized their importance in providing food supplies for ships and, after a number of unsuccessful attempts, managed to make his own. By mid-century, the Hahn family was exporting preserved vegetables, primarily asparagus and peas, to Russia and Finland.

The German food-preserving industry thus began in Braunschweig and Lübeck, and it was in these towns that a parallel industry developed—supplying materials to the new food-processing industry, such as tin for canning and packaging materials. The presence of the food industry in Braunschweig also encouraged agriculture. Asparagus cultivation developed rapidly to provide the raw material.

In the last decades of the nineteenth century, food-preserving factories grew up in other German regions, numbering 224 by 1906. This encouraged the development in the 1920s and 1930s of specialized crops, mainly in Saxony and Brandenburg, where, in 1938, around 50,000 acres were devoted to asparagus, French beans, peas, and cucumbers. Innovations in agricultural labor also appeared. Modern machines were used for planting and harvesting vegetables, leading to economies in labor costs. Close links thus developed between the agricultural and food-preserving industries.

In nineteenth-century Italy, most vegetable and pulse preservation was in the hands of the Turin-based Società Anonima di Esportazione Agricola Cirio. Francesco Cirio was sometimes amusingly called "the best-known Italian abroad" because of the factory he had set up, which made it possible to export vast quantities of fruit and vegetables to countries where the climate prevented their cultivation.

Cirio's company was primarily concerned with the commercialization of preserved foods. He was the first to export large quantities of agricultural produce from the south to the north of Europe. Thanks to the collaboration of the Società delle Ferrovie dell'alta Italia, he created a network of warehouses near the railway stations from which his refrigerated carriages departed. In 1885 he founded his company with the backing of banks, financiers, and politicians.

His preserving activities took second place. In 1868 the Cirio pea-canning factory in Borgo Dora in Turin processed only 5,000 kilograms of peas and a few dozen kilograms of preserved black truffles. In the 1870s production increased, reaching a total of one million kilograms of canned peas, asparagus, artichokes, peaches, and pears.

Both in Europe and the United States, the canned milk industry developed alongside that of meat and vegetable products. Fresh milk quickly went sour and became a health hazard owing to the bacteria it contained. In England, the railway system, along with the introduction of water refrigeration and pasteurization, made it possible to set up an efficient distribution system for milk without altering its flavor or removing the cream.

To guarantee longer life and to eliminate health risks, condensed milk was developed. By the end of the nineteenth century, numerous large companies were satisfying the needs of the international market for this product, using a system designed by Malbec in 1827.

In the 1880s, the Swiss J. B. Meyenberg discovered that condensed milk lasted even longer if a method derived from Appert was adopted. This involved sterilizing the milk in a sealed container in a pressure cooker until it reached a temperature of 105–120 degrees Centigrade (221–248 degrees Fahrenheit) in order to eliminate all the spores that could trigger acid fermentation.

The largest European milk-processing factories were in central Europe, Switzerland, and Germany, while the biggest market was in England. In 1867 a German chemist living in Vevey, Switzerland, named Henry Nestlé developed a milk-based baby food. In 1905 the Nestlé and Anglo-Swiss Condensed Milk Company was founded; soon the company had seventeen plants throughout Europe and one in the United States.

THE UNITED STATES: MASS INDUSTRY AND THE FOOD BUSINESS
The pioneer of American food processing was William Underwood, who emigrated from England in 1817. He used the experience he had acquired in food preservation to open a small workshop in Boston, where he preserved fruit and

cucumbers and produced bottled sauces. During the next thirty years, only a handful of people in various parts of the country followed Underwood's example, preserving mostly fruits and vegetables.

The situation changed in 1860 in New York, when Gail Borden built the first factory for canned milk after numerous experiments and setbacks. Although the milk was not particularly good, it became very popular—as did other preserved products—when the Civil War broke out in 1861. From that moment, production rapidly expanded.

Livestock-raising became increasingly important in the United States and, in the first half of the nineteenth century, butchering was concentrated in massive slaughterhouses in Cincinnati. With the development of railways in the second half of the century, this activity moved to Chicago. These slaughterhouses were important for two reasons. They were directly linked to the corned beef industry that operated in close proximity, and they developed a mechanized butchering process involving division of labor and a nonstop production line. The complicated work of butchery was divided into numerous small operations entrusted to individual workers along a "disassembly line" of animal carcasses.

From 1860 on, in states such as Ohio, Illinois, Indiana, and California, large numbers of food-preserving factories sprang up to provide soldiers with food during the Civil War. At the end of the war, they found a new market in the urban centers, swollen by massive migration from southern and central Europe.

Economic development in the second half of the nineteenth century was further stimulated when mass production grew up alongside mass marketing. In only a few decades, thanks to contributions from scientists and technicians, new methods of fruit and vegetable cultivation were developed, and the productivity of the food industry was dramatically increased with the introduction of completely automated machinery. All this required hefty capital investment in factories and machines. Furthermore, the profitability of mass production depended on rapid processing of materials within the productive unit and equally rapid marketing.

The starting point for American power was the agricultural depression in Europe in 1873. Massive exports of foodstuffs—both fresh and processed—produced a balance of payments that was decidedly favorable to the United States.

Three canning companies, Campbell, Heinz, and Borden, began to concentrate their retailing energies on advertising (rather than on traveling salesmen) and on international marketing networks. This strategy enabled them to sell their products with greater continuity. At the same time, large networks purchased raw materials to keep factories supplied on a regular basis.

Preserving soon expanded from meat to include a whole range of other foods:

milk and other dairy products, vegetables (primarily tomatoes but also asparagus, French beans, and cauliflower), and pulses (peas and beans).

Once the agricultural crisis was resolved, European governments began to erect protectionist tariffs and to organize the exploitation of other areas, such as Russia, Argentina, and India, where the prices of cereals and livestock could compete with those in the United States.

THE REFRIGERATION CHAIN The use of snow and ice as natural preserving agents goes back to ancient times. The homes of the rich contained wine cellars and deeper underground spaces where ice and foodstuffs could be kept. Each town or village had one or more icehouses—buried structures in which the ice collected during the winter was stored for later use to preserve meat, fish, and vegetables.

During the first half of the nineteenth century, icehouses continued to offer the only solution to the problem of maintaining food at low temperatures. As the demand for ice and preserved foods increased, so did the dimensions of these structures. Even at the end of the nineteenth century, icehouses were not that different from those in use centuries before, despite increasingly refined insulating systems designed to slow down the inevitable melting of the ice.

To meet the growing demand for ice, techniques developed to produce the low temperatures required for making ice by artificial means. These techniques involved the compression and expansion of certain gases. The first refrigerator to be based on the compression and expansion of air, driven by a steam engine, was patented in 1851 in the United States by John Gorrie. It was intended to provide refreshment in hospital wards. Other refrigerators were developed in France, England, and the United States. The turning point came two decades later when Charles Tellier, an engineer and builder of meat refrigerators, managed to install them on a boat called the *Frigorifique*. In 105 days he transported meat butchered in Buenos Aires to France. This voyage marked the birth of great commercial interest in the refrigeration chain, which developed very rapidly, especially in the United States. This technique became by far the most widely used for transporting food from outside Europe to the most important European cities. "Today, fresh meat is transported from America and as far away as New Zealand in ships with holds artificially chilled by highly ingenious instruments," commented Mantegazza only a few years after Tellier's first attempts to carry butchered meat on long transatlantic voyages.

Other ships were equipped with refrigeration to make the first crossings from Australia, Argentina, and the United States to France and England. In the former countries, livestock-raising was highly developed and meat prices were therefore very low. By 1910, the trade in butchered meat from outside Europe was worth between 8 billion and 10 billion French francs.

Despite a certain reluctance on the part of the public to eat preserved food, the food-processing industry had taken off and remains an effective weapon against the Malthusian fears of the late eighteenth century.

BIBLIOGRAPHY

Agnello, L. "Francesco Cirio." In *Dizionario biografico degli italiani*, 25:807–12. Rome: Istituto della Enciclopedia Italiana, 1981.

Anelli, L. "Conservazione delle sostanze animali e vegetali." In *Enciclopedia delle Arti e delle Industrie*, 2:858–96. Turin: Unione Tipografico-Editrice, 1880.

Bottero, G. "Molini da grano." In *Enciclopedia delle Arti e delle Industrie*, 5, 2:1319–76. Turin: Unione Tipografico-Editrice, 1891.

Chandler, A. D. "Stati Uniti: L'evoluzione dell'impreas." In *Storia economica Cambridge: L'età del capitale*, 2:89–165. Turin, 1880.

Daumas, M. "La grande industrie chimique." In *Histoire générale des techniques*, 4:493–716. Paris, 1978.

Dowd, D. F. *The Twisted Dream: Capitalist Development in the United States since 1776*. Cambridge, Mass.: Winthrop Publishers, 1974.

Flick, H. "150 Jahre Konservendose." *Die industrielle Obst- und Gemüseverwertung* 45 (1960):5.

Fussel, G. E. "Incremento della produzione alimentare." *Storia della tecnologia* 5 (1965):1–28.

Gauja, P. "Nicolas Appert." In *Dictionnaire de Biographie française*, 3:140–45. Paris: Letouzey et Ané, 1939.

Giedion, S. *L'era della meccanizzazione*. Milan, 1967.

I.L.R. *Arte di conservare gli alimenti tanto vegetabili che animali impiegati particolarmente nell'economia domestica pel nutrimento dell'uomo*. Milan, 1824.

Mantegazza, P. "L'arte di conservare gli alimenti e le bevande." *Almanacco igienico popolare* 22 (1887).

Morris, T. N. "Trattamento e conservazione degli alimenti." *Storia della tecnologia* 5 (1965): 29–57.

Pedrocco, G. "Un caso e un modello: Viticoltura e industria enologica." *Annali della Fondazione Giangiacomo Feltrinelli*, 1993, pp. 315–42.

Pozzi, F. "Ghiacciaie." In *Enciclopedia delle Arti e delle Industrie*, 3:1121–30. Turin: Unione Tipografico-Editrice, 1882.

Tellier, C. *La conservation de la viande et des matières organiques alimentaires par des moyens naturels*. Paris, 1913.

CHAPTER 37

The TASTE *for* CANNED *and* PRESERVED FOOD

Alberto Capatti

Before examining industrial food preservation, the field of investigation should be defined. From a commercial viewpoint, preserved foods with strong flavors—sweet, savory, and sour—predate modern production methods by thousands of years. These flavors were produced by such agents as honey, sugar, salt, and vinegar, which ensured that preserves were both appetizing and long-lasting. They made a welcome addition to fresh foods, providing eaters with a vast range of new flavors—from candied fruit and salted fish to salamis and pickles. The preserving agent depended on the environment and its resources and defined the final product. Oils, animal fats, and honey, for example, had the twofold aim of satisfying hunger and stopping the food from spoiling.

The preserving industry inherited traditional methods of preservation, using the heat of the sun, the cold of winter, and the smoke of the hearth. In addition, it developed the physical and chemical techniques needed to regulate these processes artificially, by drying, freezing, and smoking food. Preserving became an industry only when significant quantities of food were protected from seasonal deterioration and decomposition by means of procedures that were constant, repeatable, and capable of improvement in terms of quality and price.

With the discovery of hermetic canning, the "nature" of the vegetable or meat did not change. What did change was the fact that it could be transported and kept over periods of time. Industrially preserved food gained credit because it could be stored and because it had quantifiable indices of nutrition, hygiene, and taste. The primary aim of the procedure was now to stabilize the product. A foodstuff was bought, dried, and compressed into cubes, spheres, or cylinders, then colored according to taste, gradually losing its original identity and acquiring a new one on the basis of its packaging.

The gourmet's attitude toward the food industry has always been ambivalent. Traditional preserved foods, such as *confit d'oie* and *pâté,* not only taste good but also derive their prestige from the past, while modern processed foods provide nourishment that may be tasty but is often not to be trusted. A genuine can of fish is one in which the fish do not taste of the sea or of the can. Perfectly canned sardines are cooked in oil, plump, boned, odorless, and unalterable. Only these are preferable to fresh sardines, full of bones and guts. The only way to produce a flavor-based history of preserved foods would be to compare and taste each foodstuff individually before and after the Industrial Revolution. After all, each foodstuff not only possesses its own taste but also inherits a traditional image of taste from the past.

A few comments should be added. Almost all recipe books contained a chapter on preserves aimed at restaurant owners, innkeepers, domestic cooks, and, finally, housewives. They explained how to organize provisions, economize, and create a gastronomic balance between early, current, and late produce, leftovers, and stores. At the beginning of the nineteenth century, the producer, who often possessed a "secret method," offered a choice that was wide in terms of quality, but not in number of products. From the second half of the century on, factories and shopkeepers throughout Europe divided their spheres of influence: meat and fish, fruit and vegetables, hors d'oeuvres and cakes. This did not, however, restrict the personal creativity of domestic and professional cooks.

The Origins of Preservation Techniques

It is difficult to establish the date at which research results were transformed into techniques of production. Until the Industrial Revolution, the term "preserve" was used to refer to fruits, flowers, and other foods prepared with sugar or a similar material to produce a sort of paste. These preserves were flavorful, sweet, and colored. From a technical viewpoint, they were produced by heating and cooling the flesh of the fruit, then reducing it to a paste that could be cut into squares and easily transported. Other characteristics of future preserves were already implicit in this early technique, even though it was restricted to fruit and vegetables.

The development of a standard procedure for a vast range of foodstuffs marked the passage from this simple technique to a much more varied notion of preserving. In 1810 Nicolas Appert wrote a book, which was to become famous, entitled *Le livre de tous les ménages, ou l'art de conserver pendant plusiers années toutes les substances animales et végétales.* The work described his thirty years of experience and revealed his secret: the immersion of sealed jars in a hot-water bath. He preserved a wide variety of foods: vegetables, fruit, meat, dairy products such as cream and whey, and even fish. Cauliflower and spinach, shelled peas and French beans, quartered pears, meat stock, and jellies were all treated in this way. When they were eaten, each food tasted fresh, with a recognizable flavor. If the strawberries lost their color and perfume, Appert applied the tricks of the confectioner's trade, making a paste of sugar, crushed pulp, and lemon juice to add to the preserved fruit. However, there was a clear discrepancy between the practical aims of preservation—economy (a saving in sugar, reductions in cost), philanthropy (stores for hospitals and supplies for the army), or health (protection against scurvy and food poisoning)—and the notion of consumption for pleasure. Appert's jars were appetizing and expensive. Filled with artichokes, French beans, and peas, they were studied and imitated. André Viard, in *Le Cuisinier impérial,* revealed that, among professional chefs, Appert's tricks were already known, even before they were published.

The people who preserved food in the workshop or the kitchen expressed two distinct vocations—industrial and domestic—without being aware of their incompatibility. Those in the former sphere were attracted to prestigious and profitable foodstuffs, such as early fruit and vegetables, meat, and fish, or to foods with mass appeal. The latter, on the other hand, were more concerned with preserving the produce from their orchards and gardens throughout the year. It is important to examine not only the evolution of techniques they used but also the immediate results—in other words, the quality of these prototypes. Appert insisted on the need to link up vegetable garden, workshop, and storeroom so that the vegetables, chosen for their taste, could be picked and bottled as quickly as possible. Medium-sized peas, selected among those that had "much more taste and flavor" and picked in June and July, were immersed for only one and a half hours.

Industrialists and retail tradesmen had to demonstrate that they were at least as scrupulous as chefs. This was confirmed by the author of the *Almanach des gourmands,* Grimod de la Reynière, who, in March 1806, praised the bottled fruit and vegetables in the shop of Nicolas Appert. For what reasons? Those that would become the trump cards of preserved food: price, availability, and a freshness that would deceive anyone once the food had passed through the hands of a skilled chef. "The peas above all," concluded Grimod, "prepared in this way, are green, tender and more flavorful than those eaten at the height of the season."

The bottled early vegetables and fruit recommended by the *Almanach des gourmands* were restricted to an elite. In 1811 the famous Paris restaurateur Beauvilliers suggested traditional, more economical preserves. In the appendix to his *L'Art du cuisinier,* cucumbers are preserved in brine, and precooked truffles in lard, while the tomato sauce has the consistency of apple jam.

The Development of Food Preservation

Domestic and professional cooks became the promoters of a technique that rendered their work easier every day. The aim of the preserving industry was to subject all markets, even the most elite, to French hegemony, changing the relationship between foodstuff and price by leveling out storage and transport costs. Industrialists left the first-class saloons of the transatlantic liners and the dining rooms of the rich to professional chefs and concentrated their efforts on the retail market. Soup, fish, and exotic fruit for all—that was the dream. The sardine took the lead. In Nantes, in 1851, the *Traité des conserves alimentaires,* by P. Faucheaux, reserved a special place for the humble fish.

For new consumers, no food was out of season or too expensive. For chefs, luxury foodstuffs had to be on the menu, even when they were out of season. Asparagus, beans, peas, and artichoke hearts were now offered twelve months a year. Sauces and condiments with a stock or butter base accentuated the identity of all products, fresh or preserved, "natural" or "cooked." In order to meet the challenge and extend the market, the industry had to respond with new techniques, lower prices, and additives, some of which were dangerous. Even before microbes were discovered, both trade regulations and the law kept a careful eye on the possibility of adulteration. Nevertheless, numerous risks were taken by unscrupulous preservers, some of whom used a copper sulfate solution to ensure that bottled fruit and vegetables did not lose their color.

Toward a New Century

Auguste Corthay, an industrialist who had served as chef to Umberto I of Italy, saw a bright future for preserved food: "Daily, the great factories will deliver tasty, freshly prepared and cooked food at very low prices. It will be the start of a new century!" His work, *La conserve alimentaire,* is a classic. The first edition came out in 1891 and the fourth in 1902. The following year Corthay founded and edited a monthly magazine with the same name (1903–1914). In Paris the newspaper

L'Epicier offered its readers the *Dictionnaire Encyclopédique de l'Épicerie* of A. Seigneurie, with a revised edition appearing in 1904. These professional publications, able to reach a vast readership, were matched by more academic works dealing with the art of cuisine. The first edition of the *Guide culinaire* by Escoffier, Gilbert, and Fétu is dated 1903.

The paths taken by professional chefs and the food industry continued to diverge. Corthay regarded the factory as the natural heir to the kitchen and sent his products beyond the borders of Europe, while Escoffier insisted that food should be fresh: "Peas should be very green, picked and shelled at the last minute." It is hard to disagree. Corthay, however, claimed that "the harvest starts at the end of May and continues throughout the month of June. The sooner you use the vegetables, assuming the price allows it, the better the preserves will be."

The taste and appearance of food was accompanied by other considerations: the right time to harvest, labor costs, constant availability, and the lack of seasonal barriers. In haute cuisine dishes are appreciated by the eyes, the nose, and the taste buds. They remain acceptable even if the flavor of individual ingredients is slightly diminished. In his *Le livre des menus: Complément indispensable du Guide culinaire* (1912), Escoffier suggested, for the eight menus for January, "fresh" asparagus tips, green beans, artichokes, and peas. These "early vegetables" were also suggested for the months to follow, in confirmation of the other values being offered: rarity, color, and, finally, a taste similar to the genuinely fresh product.

Research into the preserving properties of ice and steam also aimed at finding new ways to conserve food quality. The preserving industry in France tried to compete with those of Great Britain and the United States. Its failure was not the result of a lack of patented inventions, but of shortcomings in distribution and refrigeration. The very cans that allowed legionnaires to survive in the desert, and explorers at the Poles, were unable to conquer the domestic consumer front. Although traditional methods (salting, smoking, immersing in brine, vinegar, or oil) worked well for meat and some kinds of vegetables, these treatments altered the flavor of early vegetables. Jellied beef, cassoulet, and fried sardines were satisfying, but they soon became monotonous. Indefatigable experimentation by Corthay, however, yielded new industrial formulas.

Italy provides an interesting contrast to France. Judging from trade figures at the turn of the century, its preserving culture was Mediterranean rather than northern European. It exported almonds, walnuts, hazelnuts, fresh fruit (mainly grapes for wine), vegetables, and, above all, dried figs. An important part of the peasant diet, these were nonetheless an indication of Italy's backwardness in terms of diet and trade, since Italian figs were considered inferior to those of Asia Minor. Time-hallowed methods of preservation, such as the use of the sun to dry fruits and agents like oil, brine, spirits, and vinegar, were common, while canning and freezing were almost unheard of. The country took its first steps toward industrial food processing by combining Swiss and German machinery with the French model of cuisine. Among the first products to be canned were tomatoes, exports of which increased tenfold in the decade 1897–1908. The industry was seasonal and concentrated in two regions: Emilia and Campania.

Syncretism in the Food Conservation Industry

At the beginning of World War I, the food conservation industry was in full swing. Factories were working so hard that there was no time for innovation. As a result of strategic objectives and propaganda, both in the army and among a civil population subjected to rationing, a taste developed for industrially produced national foodstuffs, such as stock cubes, powdered milk, and coffee substitutes. Dried food became part of a consumer's everyday life. The rations of an ordinary soldier (formerly a peasant or laborer) included 400 grams of dry biscuits, 200 grams of canned meat, bottles of meat extract, and meat sauce for pasta.

In both France and Italy, frozen foods were politically imposed on a wary public, leading to changes in seasonal buying habits. Refrigerators were filled with cuts of meat from the United States, and the domestic market suffered as a consequence. In 1916 the first national congress of the freezing industry was held in Rome; in 1918 the first cookery book for frozen foods was produced in Paris by Joseph Bruna.

Whenever there was a distrust of raw foods and a preference for slow cooking, French gastronomy dominated. Although some of the taste and smell of the food was lost, this was made up for by condiments. Escoffier's approach was composed of a myriad of sauces to be added to the basic ingredient. In homes and humbler collective settings, things were simpler: meat in its own juices. The great novelty of rationing was the leveling out of dietary requirements (with new criteria for measuring calories) and tastes (to a standard menu for millions of consumers in allied countries). In Italy, breakfast in 1915 was dried figs, worthy of Roman legionnaires; in 1916 it became bread and coffee, in line with France and Germany.

A new dietary model was launched with refrigeration. The flavoring agent that was indispensable in canning—stock for meat, oil for sardines, brine for vegetables—was replaced by a technique that altered the food's molecular structure. The taste of the product was no longer the sum of two substances, one liquid and one solid, but the result of thermal transformation. In this process, materials that previously had to be cooked in order to be preserved were frozen raw, thus maintaining their original characteristics with only a very slight loss of color and aroma and without absorbing extraneous flavors. In France and Italy, refrigeration was available immediately after the war to such collective services as municipal slaughterhouses; it arrived in the home only in the 1950s. Freezing revolutionized the significance of raw and cooked, of fresh and seasonal. Nonetheless, food books were wary of the new technique. Questions of taste were ideological, and, throughout the nineteenth century, canning represented progress. However, by the end of World War II, the euphoria produced by a wide variety of available foodstuffs had dissipated.

New discoveries—such as vacuum packing and the use of gases like ethylene, carbon dioxide, and nitrogen—were still to come, but these did not replace traditional methods. Smoked fish and dried fruit are on sale alongside bottled vegetables in brine, oil, and vinegar. Canned tuna is not only a meal in itself but also an ingredient in more elaborate dishes. Fresh, dried, frozen, or canned beans can be used according to the time available for cooking, the season, and the occasion. Successive generations of preserves are part of our history and have contributed to our individual tastes. The sweet, savory, and acidic flavors provided by traditional preserving methods have been replaced by the odorless, flavorless gases now used to impede decay.

BIBLIOGRAPHY

Agnoletti, V. *Manuale del cuoco e del pasticciere.* Vol. 3. Bologna: Pesaro, 1832.

Appert, N. *Le livre de tous les ménages, ou l'art de conserver pendant plusieurs années toutes les substances animales et végétales.* Paris: Patrís, 1810.

Artusi, P. *La scienza in cucina e l'arte di mangiar bene.* Ed. P. Camporesi. Turin: Einaudi, 1970. [*The Art of Eating Well.* Trans. Kyle M. Phillips III. New York: Random House, 1996.]

Beauvilliers, A. *L'Art du cuisinier.* Vol. 2. Paris: Pilet, 1814.

Bruna, J. *La cuisine des aliments frigorifiés.* Paris, 1919.

Cadet-de-Vaux, A-A. *Le ménage ou l'emploi des fruits dans l'économie domestique.* Paris: D. Colas, 1810.

Chevallier, A. *Dictionnaire des altérations et des falsifications des substances alimentaires médicamenteuses et commerciales.* 6th ed. Paris: Asselin, 1882.

"Conserve." In *Dictionnaire portatif de cuisine, d'office, et de distillation.* Paris, 1767.

Corthay, A. *La conserve alimentaire.* Paris: Réty, 1902.

———. "L'exportation italienne pendant les 11 premiers mois de 1912." *La Conserve alimentaire: Bulletin mensuel de vulgarisation théorique et pratique de fabrication,* March 15, 1915.

Escoffier, A. *Le guide culinaire.* Paris, 1903. [*The Complete Guide to the Art of Modern Cookery.* Trans. H. L. Cracknell and R. J. Kaufmann. London: Heinemann, 1979.]

Fabre, J. *Dictionnaire universel de l'alimentation.* 4 vols. Paris, 1894.

Faucheux, P. *Traité des conserves alimentaires à l'usage des ménages*. Nantes, 1851.

Fournier, S. P. *L'art de préparer, conserver et désinfecter les substances alimentaires*. Paris: Barba, 1818.

Giglioli, I. *Malessere agrario e alimentare in Italia*. Portici: Della Torre, 1903.

Gouffé, J. *Le Livre des conserves*. Paris: L. Hachette, 1869.

Grimond de la Reynière, A. B. L., and J. F. Coste. *Almanach des gourmands*. 8 vols. Paris: Chez Maradan, 1803–12.

Le Cointe, J. *La Santé de Mars*. Paris: Briand, 1790.

Maigne, W. *Nouveau manuel complet des conserves alimentaires*. Paris: Librairie Encyclopédique de Roret, 1865.

Manetti, L. *Manuale del salsamentario*. Milan, 1906.

Marescalchi, A. *Le applicazioni del freddo artificiale alle industrie agrarie*. Casale Monferrato, 1912.

Rolet, A. *Les conserves de légumes, de viandes, des produits de la basse-cour et de la laiterie*. Paris: J. B. Baillière, 1913.

Seigneurie, A. *Dictionnaire encyclopédique de l'épicerie*. Paris: L'Épicier, 1904.

Vialardi, G. "Conservazione delle sostanze alimentari ad uso di famiglia." In *Trattato di cucina*. Turin, 1854.

Viard, A. *Le Cuisinier impérial*. Paris: Barba, 1806.

Willaumetz. *Des conserves alimentaires: Nouveau procédé dans la Meurthe*. Paris: Roret, 1851.

Zingali, G. "Il rifornimento dei viveri dell'esercito italiano." In *L'Alimentazione e la politica annonaria in Italia,* ed. R. Bachi. Bari: Laterza, 1926.

CHAPTER 38

The EMERGENCE *of* REGIONAL CUISINES

Julia Csergo

Foremost among the concerns of the governments that came to power in the wake of the French Revolution was the need to define what the new nation would look like and how it would be represented. To that end, the authorities redrew administrative boundaries and created new "geographies of France." Yet even as this was being done, the local diversity that seemed excluded by the new territorial order resurfaced in departmental statistics and inventories. Systematic surveys revealed differences in both local resources, dictated by nature, and regional customs, consecrated by history. The new cultural diversity of the postrevolutionary period also had a culinary dimension: *pays* and *provinces* (which for the sake of convenience we will call "regions" even though the official designation "region" did not yet exist in administrative parlance) had their distinctive dishes, and these diverse yet complementary specialties played an important role in the effort to redefine the nation as a community united by a continuous past and a common future.

Regional Cuisines in the Ancien Régime

To the Ancien Régime, France was a composite of distinct territories annexed at various times in the nation's past. People were generally aware of the distinctive features of the vast and often ill-defined natural expanses and historical provinces, cities, and towns that constituted the kingdom.

The rise of a centralized, absolutist regime had led, in Paris, to the emergence of a *grande cuisine* dedicated to the "glory of the king," and it was on this foundation that the reputation and prestige of French cooking rested. Elsewhere, however, in cities other than Paris as well as in the countryside, people's diets depended on their social status and the availability of local produce. These regional cuisines seldom made it into cookbooks, agronomic treatises, or travelers' accounts.

Well before the emergence of a French culinary personality, medieval recipe books reflecting the aristocracy's cosmopolitan tastes already mentioned such regional dishes as *tarte de Brie, brouet de Provence,* and *plat de navets comme en Beauce.* Many seventeenth- and eighteenth-century cookbooks attached regional epithets such as *à la provençale, à la bourguignonne, à la périgourdine,* and *à la flamande* to their recipes to indicate the use of ingredients from these regions. Since the sixteenth century, moreover, treatises on agronomy and food as well as manuals of practical skills had discussed foods peculiar to specific localities such as the cheeses of Auvergne and Brie, the capons and hens of Le Mans, the sweet tongues of Troyes, the chard of Lyons, the tub butter of Isigny, the barberries of Dijon, the apples of Normandy, and the candied olives, marzipan, and fruits of Provence, all of which already enjoyed a solid reputation. Finally, various works that took an interest in regional cooking mentioned the Gascons' fondness for millet, the Bretons' for oatmeal, the Cévenols' for chestnuts, the Limousins' for radishes, and the taste of southerners in general for garlic and onions. They also discussed special ways of cooking bream in Languedoc, squid in Saintonge, and ring dove in Gascony.

In the eighteenth century, improvements in bridges and roadways made it easier for Frenchmen and foreign visitors to learn about the various parts of the country, and travelers' reports continued to furnish information about the great variety of provincial customs. Among the many representations of provincialism, long dominated by sarcasms about old-fashioned regional ways, the image of the provincial as a person ignorant of Parisian refinements in culinary technique and gourmet taste was of particular importance. In François Marlin's account of his travels in the late eighteenth century, for example, he notes that while "a traveler should not in general keep a record of his meals and inns, such details are not always superfluous. . . . A cabaret anecdote . . . can give an accurate idea of the customs of a city or even a region."

Paradoxically, it was in this same period that philosophers and writers critical of the social and moral ills caused by rapid eighteenth-century urban growth began to represent rural, agricultural society in a new way. Although "the country bumpkin in Paris" remained a figure of mirth throughout the nineteenth century, new images of healthy rustics gained favor, and the frugal meals of solid country folk began to be noted with approval. Take, for example, one of the 157 accounts of travels in France that appeared during the decade following the Revolution— Saint-Amant's *Voyage sentimental et pittoresque dans les Pyrénées,* published in 1789. While traveling through a still-savage region whose people do not even speak French, the author observes the daily ritual of making soup at a peasant's cottage in Héas: "The bread, already prepared with a small lump of butter, sits in a big wooden bowl, boiling water is poured over it, and, presto, you have soup. To season it, the cook chews a clove of garlic and a raw onion and then spits into the bowl—the last word in culinary technique. The soup is served; it is excellent."

The Englishman Arthur Young, who during his travels in France discovered the refinements of a French cuisine "infinitely superior to our own," also explored local foods and culinary customs in various places along his route. In Strasbourg, for example, he ate *schnitz,* "a dish of bacon and fried pear which looks like something the devil might eat. Upon tasting it, however, I was surprised to find it passable." In *Les Landes de Bordeaux*, a work written by J.-S. Saint-Sauveur in 1791, we read: "The peasants of the Landes are not very civilized. The life they lead leaves them quite rustic and almost savage. . . . Their meals are frugal: they consist of a piece of *crucharde* soaked in a sauce made from bacon drippings."

Learning about the Diversity of the Landscape

In 1782, when he began writing about "progress in and details of" the art of cooking in France, Le Grand d'Aussy sought to demonstrate how culinary cultures are rooted in the soil and therefore able to resist change. To that end, he discussed at length observations made two centuries earlier by Jean-Bruyerin-Champier in *De Re Cibaria:* "As far as food is concerned, nearly all of his comments are still true today. And so they should be, since they are all based on what nature has seen fit to allow each of our provinces to produce."

The idea that the environment determines the peculiarities of each region dominated thinking about regional cuisines and cultures after the Revolution. Something had changed in the late eighteenth century, as local cultures absorbed the impact of new foods from the New World. Regional cuisines were not invented in reaction to this; they already existed, even if precise regional boundaries are hard to pinpoint. But people began to pay attention to regional specialties, to become aware of their existence. Jean-Louis Flandrin has made a fundamental methodological point about the history of representations—namely, that just because an innovation occurs at a given point in time, it does not follow that people inside or outside any given region are necessarily aware of that innovation. Only after the Revolution redefined the relation between the real and the imaginary and reshaped the representations and emotions that simultaneously established a bond and an antagonism between Paris and the provinces, the national and the local, the universal and the particular—only then did regional cuisines and specialties detach themselves from their geographic and social contexts and emerge as distinctive signs of locality; only then did they become perceptible indicators of the nation's diversity.

Paris discovered the gourmet delights of the provinces when the Frères Provençaux came to the capital from the Durance in 1786 and introduced such southern specialties as *brandade* and *bouillabaisse*. After the Revolution, however, the new nation felt a need to explore the way in which its resources were distributed within the boundaries of its new *départements*. The first culinary and alimentary geographies of France answered that need. In keeping with the goal of developing a system of national education capable of educating "friends, lovers, and spouses of the Republic," Alexandre Deleyre, an *encyclopédiste,* philosopher, and friend of Rousseau as well as a *député* representing the *département* of the Gironde at the National Convention, proposed what he called a "patriotic garden." Indeed, gardens and "theme parks" were all the rage at the end of the eighteenth century, and the point of Deleyre's proposed garden was to teach people about the geography of France—all of France, the "entire Republic, united and indivisible." His idea was to have schoolchildren walk across a map of France divided into *départements,* with each section of the map being a garden planted with vegetation typical of the region:

> Here, in the requisite number of squares, the *départements* of France would be identified and laid out. They would be set apart from one another by means of flowers, fruits, plants, and other products typical of, or found in profusion in, each *département*. In one square, for example, one might plant wheat; in another, millet. . . . In the squares for the Bouches-de-Rhône and the *départements* of the Var and Gard, one would see . . . olive trees or fig trees or pomegranate or orange, depending on the relative prevalence of one or another of these fruits. . . . The squares for the Calvados and Seine-Inférieure would be indicated by apple trees for cider; that of the Indre-et-Loire would contain a plum tree. Where unique products are lacking, or in gardens where the climate does not allow them to be grown, one would place a small column bearing an inscription marking a famous event or person suitable for distinguishing the particular *département* among the geographic squares. . . . One might choose memorable events or landscapes or buildings.[1]

In the patriotic garden, students thus learned about the nation by learning about local products and resources, where "local" was curiously enough defined in terms of *département* boundaries. These were taken to be as symbolic of the territory as a memorable event or a monument that a group might erect in honor of some individual or belief considered essential to the definition of its identity.

In a similar vein, Charles-Louis Cadet de Gassicourt's *Cours gastronomique,* published in 1808, set itself the objective of teaching readers about the origins of the food they ate and how various foods were used. One chapter, entitled "Let's Learn Something about Geography," was explicitly organized around the emerging concept of gastronomy. It took the same approach as the "patriotic garden" concept, dividing the country up in terms of the diversity of its resources. This "antiquarian" approach, which initially had been applied to other continents, was here applied to the *départements.* Cadet de Gassicourt's idea was to create a sort of museum of natural history and gastronomic curiosities. He offered, in the form of a "synoptic table," the first gastronomic geography of France, in which icons in the shape of bottles, chicken, fish, beehives, and terrines represented the chief food products for which each place was famous. The method drew comment, even before the book appeared, in the *Almanach des gourmands* for 1807: "Instead of the steeple of Amiens Cathedral, one sees a duck-liver pâté. At Nérac one sees a terrine of red partridge. In Toulouse another terrine of duck liver. Pigs' feet and head cheese in Troyes. A jar of mustard and barberry in Dijon." This graphic symbolism thus created a sort of star map of France in which each dot of light stood for a pâté or ham or terrine that shed its light on the land and instructed students about the fruits of the soil. Yet this was a period in which maps of France were rare. The average Frenchman seldom had access to one. The fact that popular images of France were shaped by compilations of regional culinary specialties was an indication of the status that would be accorded to such things in both the popular imagination and symbolic representations of national identity.

A Geographic and Mnemonic Bond

To study geography is also to connect with memory. After the Revolution, the French government undertook to catalog the country's natural and artistic wealth. A consular decree of Fructidor 14, Year IX, ordered the establishment of a series of provincial museums, thereby making local geography an object of study and a locus of memory in relation to which France defined its past. Because local culinary specialties exemplified the skills of a region's homemakers, artisans, and industrial workers, these regional foods became symbols of historical continuity and shared memory as well as tokens of community.

Although court cuisine remained dominant and even acquired additional luster from the talents of Talleyrand and Carême, the development of a provincialist culinary literature was the first important step toward the emergence of regional cuisines. These provincialist texts played down social, occupational, religious, and gender differences in order to embrace both the refinement of the wealthy provincial bourgeoisie and the rusticity of the peasantry within a single provincial culinary culture. Hence they expressed, first and foremost, a geographical solidarity, a geographic and mnemonic bond.

The first "regional" cookbooks were published in France at the turn of the nineteenth century. They were the work of both professional cooks and ordinary housewives. As time went by, the genre established itself and gained in popularity. The most successful bourgeois cookbook of the nineteenth century, *La Cuisinière de la campagne et de la ville ou la nouvelle cuisine économique* by L. E. Audot, was reprinted forty-one times between 1833 and 1900. In a sign of the times, the thirty-second edition, published in 1852, included both foreign recipes ("national dishes that we particularly liked and wished to see reproduced in our country") and recipes from Provence and Languedoc, because, "in addition to garlic and olive oil, which are very commonly used in the Midi, there are a number of specific methods and dishes not generally found elsewhere." Soon there was an outpouring of similar books, until nearly every region in France could boast of its own repertoire of recipes. Each region also had its culinary panegyric: *Le Cuisinier gascon* (1858) praised Gascony for its "excellent products, well suited in every way to the tastes, customs, and temperaments of the residents of our province." Savoy had *Le Cuisinier à la bonne franquette* by Mique Granchamp (1883); Burgundy, *Le Cuisinier bourguignon* by Alfred Contour (1891); and the Landes, *Le Cuisinier landais* (1893).

The second half of the century witnessed the appearance of more general works, providing not only recipes and lists of local specialties but also historical anecdotes concerning the dining customs of each region. Take, for example, Charles Gérard's *Ancienne Alsace à table* (1862), which inaugurated the genre, or Lucien Tendret's *La Table au pays de Brillat-Savarin* (1882), two "monuments" of regional publishing that remain in print to this day. The two works are similar: both were published by local publishers, intended for local readers, and organized around the local geography defined in historical rather than administrative terms. Both referred to provinces of the Ancien Régime and drew a parallel between political restoration and culinary traditions rooted in local history and geography. Both authors were typical regional dignitaries, local notables or scholars deeply attached to "the soul of the past" and determined to perpetuate a common heritage and identity.

From about 1900 to 1930 or so we witness a spate of Paris-published volumes celebrating the culinary riches of France in all its regional and social diversity. *L'Art du bien manger* (1901) by Richardin and Fulbert-Dumontheil, a "monument dedicated to French cuisine," was the first comprehensive survey of French culinary culture, purporting to include medieval recipes, "old" bourgeois recipes, strange recipes collected by various writers, artists, and amateurs, and local recipes communicated by "elderly housewives." Pampille's *Bons Plats de France* (1913) embodied the royalist, Catholic thinking of the Action Française movement as well as an emphasis on the primacy of rural over urban life, of the soil over city streets. In 1928 modernity capitalized on culinary memory by way of a radio contest sponsored by the firm of Corcellet, which invited female listeners to share their secret family recipes. A few years later Flammarion published *Les Plats régionaux de France*. Finally, Croze and Curnonsky's *Trésor gastronomique de la France* (1933) bestowed lasting legitimacy on a corpus of certified authentic regional dishes. In addition to regional cuisine, "the glory of our country . . . which epitomizes the tastes of each of our provinces," and peasant cooking, "which is improvised in the blink of an eye with whatever ingredients happen to be at hand," Curnonsky identified a third category, consisting of local dishes apt to become part of the national cuisine "because they are within reach of ordinary mortals," such as *confit* and *foie gras* from Périgord. Certain other local specialties, such as *garbure* and *crucharde* from the same region, he dismissed as unsuited to become "national" dishes because "it takes many generations to be able to digest them."

A National and Republican Culinary Model

Through historical commentary coupled with naturalistic, providentialist arguments adducing the natural diversity and richness of the soil and climate, the succulence and variety of local produce, and the cleverness and skill of the local populace, regional cuisines were given timeless roots in the local landscape. Regional cuisines are thus cultural constructs, rooted in the supposed eternity of the soil and in local memory. Allusions to the famous descriptions of French geography (*Tableau de la France*) by Jules Michelet (1833) and Paul Vidal de La Blache (1903), who stressed the influence of local factors on history, are more frequent than one might have thought. Of course, this rich literature only confirms the importance of the historical discipline in creating a national memory in the nineteenth century. But it also illustrates the role that local historians and learned societies took on after the creation of the Comité des Travaux Historiques in 1834. The learned societies served as "reservoirs of regional good will" and "megaphones" for trumpeting the history of the nation.[2]

In the last third of the nineteenth century, advances in industrial and agricultural technology, increased trade, improved communication and transportation, and the growing influence of urban lifestyles exacerbated the sense that rural communities were disintegrating and stimulated enormous interest in regional ethnology.[3] Perpetuating the romantic conception of the local as a conservatory of the sensibility of the past, a new system of representations emerged in which regional cuisines became the embodiment of local agricultural traditions and rural allegiances, family and religious customs, and nostalgic longing for a pre-industrial, pre-urban past. In 1882 Lucien Tendret was alarmed to discover that in Belley, where Brillat-Savarin had lived, "sound traditions and precious recipes are forgotten or lost." In 1901 André Theuriet of the Académie Française voiced his sorrow at the fact that for thirty years France had been losing its grip on "a joyful science, which we are in the process of forgetting," when as recently as the turn of the nineteenth century "every canton in France had its . . . special dish, its secret way of preparing some delectable morsel with devotion, tenderness, and love. . . . Strasbourg had its *pâtés de foie gras*, Metz its *mirabelles*, Nancy its blood sausage and macaroons." Protesting the triumph of chemistry, canning, and refrigeration, the chef Edouard Nignon deplored an age that no longer had any use for "the meditation and patience" that went into cooking in centuries past. "Down with chemistry! Down with speed!" he thundered in *Les Plaisirs de la table* (1926).

These reconstructed regional cuisines allowed modern urban society to resurrect its provincial roots by savoring dishes consecrated by memory. Peasants who went to Paris in search of employment frequently revived the atmosphere of the villages they left behind by choosing to live and associate with others from the same region. Often their social activities revolved around food. People liked to share regional specialties brought from home by the most recent arrival. For the provincial elite, whose fortunes in the capital prospered with the emergence of a republican "provincialism," food was one more way of maintaining a regional identity that was an important element in developing and maintaining networks of influence. Many joined circles or clubs for the purpose of perpetuating regional culinary traditions.

These "regionalist" gastronomic societies, founded by members of the provincial elite living in Paris, grew out of the encounter between a gastronomic sociability that first developed among the Parisian aristocracy; but later, as democratic culture took hold, they expanded to include the provincial bourgeoisie and a thriving regional culture movement whose goal was to preserve local dialects and customs.[4] When the Lyonnais of Paris met in 1872 to promote Lyonnaise cuisine, their number included such distinguished men as the prefect Lépine, Edouard Herriot, and Justin Godard. The Clafoutis, an eating club founded in 1884 that adopted as one of its rules never to include *clafoutis* on the menu, attracted many celebrated Limousins, including Jules Claretie. Other clubs included the Vin d'Anjou (1885), the Dîner Mensuel de l'Alsace à Table (1885), and the Bourgignons Salés (1890). La Prune held two annual dinners that shunned all regional specialties of the Lot-et-Garonne other than the *prunes confites* (candied plums) that were the "glory" of the region. Rounding out this brief list are the Betterave, which represented the Nord, and the Garbure, which represented Béarn.

Abetted by this regionalist discourse, gastronomic primacy shifted, at least symbolically, from Paris to the provinces, a shift further encouraged by the increased influence of small towns and agricultural areas under the Third Republic, which from the first sought to encourage prorepublican sentiment in a countryside that was still heavily Bonapartist. Although the new regime remained highly centralized politically and sought to integrate the nation by improving literacy, encouraging a modern outlook, and instilling nationalist consciousness, it also worked hard to establish local roots by espousing an official proregionalist policy that at times verged on outright favoritism toward agricultural interest groups. In this democratic and republican context, regional cuisines came to symbolize the diversity of local cultures and social classes within a nation united under the republican aegis. "Peasants and workers know how to eat, and in the country one meets farmers who are artists and barge men who are great chefs," observed Curnonsky.

The republic based many of its rituals on food. Seizing upon the centralizing model of the "government of the table," with the intention of both preserving a sense of locality and encouraging the new civic bond, the government staged banquets for local elected officials. These were both a sign of political equality and a commemoration of the republican nation. The banquets of 1889 and 1890 celebrated regional identities within a context of national cohesion. And the most spectacular of all the gourmet ceremonials connected with the construction of a new national memory was the gigantic banquet for nearly 21,000 mayors from across France, held at the Tuileries on September 22, 1900, in connection with the Exposition Universelle. For that occasion the menu was a judicious mixture of French—and by this point international—haute cuisine (*darnes de saumon glacées parisiennes, ballotines de faisans Saint-Hubert*) and local gems (*canetons de Rouen, poulardes de Bresse*). The republic chose to ignore archaic customs that constituted an obstacle to modernization, emphasizing instead only those cultural particularities that had the power to integrate the nation and relegating the rest to the category of picturesque popular traditions and regional folklore.

Tourism and Gastronomy

The new prominence of regional cuisines, which was linked to the change in their status and representations, also benefited from increased cultural consumption of local space during the Belle Époque, which saw an outpouring of regionalist novels and postcards featuring the provinces as a central theme. In this context, the rise of tourism that began at the end of the nineteenth century also led to increased exploitation of local resources.

As improvements and extensions to the rail network made travel for pleasure fashionable, series of tourist guides began to appear. Over time these codified the rules for taking in local sights. Culinary specialties joined other stereotypical representations of the local in the rhetoric of the guides, which featured local dishes, local sights, local landscapes, local architectural highlights, and local celebrities. Alongside descriptions of local geography and history, travel advice, maps, and itineraries, the *Guides Joanne,* which first appeared in 1840, devoted only a small amount of space to food, and even then only under the heading of "especially interesting industries and products." In Bourg, for example, we learn in the 1877 edition that there is a "fairly brisk trade in Bresse chickens." In Grenoble one can find "leather gloves," "Saint-Marcellin cheese," and "Chartreuse liqueurs." In the 1883 edition the tourist visiting Périgueux is advised to look for "flour, wine, brandy, livestock, game, fowl, truffles, and truffled pâtés known across Europe."

Thus with improvements in transportation and the growth of trade, what had once been a local resource now became primarily a source of industrial and commercial wealth. To see this change, one has only to compare Abel Hugo's *France pittoresque* (1835) with Ardouin-Dumazet's *Voyage en France* (1893–99). Whereas the former offers a picturesque account of various regions, the latter emphasizes agricultural and industrial traditions that promise to secure markets for the local economy. From the pages devoted to the city of Pithiviers, for example, we learn that there is "trade in honey and saffron from the Gâtinais" as well as "agricultural production in the form of *pâtés d'alouette* which have made Pithiviers famous as the source of one of the gastronomic glories of France."

In the 1920s the advent of the automobile encouraged tourists to explore the provinces for themselves. Regional cuisines now had an important role to play in the burgeoning "tourist economy." Michelin, which in 1901 inaugurated its *Guide Michelin pour les chauffeurs et les vélocipédistes,* was quick to grasp the implications of the technological revolution spearheaded by the automobile at a time when a general increase in the standard of living was leading to increased interest in leisure activities. The Michelin guides listed localities in a sort of dictionary, with brief indications of where to buy Michelin products and find service, along with local curiosities, itineraries, hotels, and restaurants. Thus the guides were intimately associated with a new way of discovering and consuming territory, which soon encouraged expansion of the hotel industry. But, here again, it was not until the 1920 edition that the first gourmet advice appeared: tourists were advised to sample the "hot pâtés, crayfish, and trout" in Belley and the "cassoulet" at Castelnaudary. In the same decade, the *Guides Bleus,* which replaced the Joanne series in 1910, began to draw the attention of their readers to the culinary specialties of the places featured. The *Guide Bleu Savoie* for 1922 inaugurated a "Dishes" section, distinct from the "Local Industries" section. In Annecy, for example, the guide recommended "potatoes au gratin, rissoles, trout, *omble-chevalier,* and wine" in the first category and "artistic pottery, chocolate, and cheese (reblochon and vacherin)" in the second. In the following year the *Guide Bleu Bords de Loire et Sud* included a section on "industries of interest to tourists, gastronomic specialties, and principal vintages." In the 1930s entire pages were devoted to the culinary specialties of various natural or historic regions.

How did culinary specialties come to be treated on a par with local celebrities, historical monuments, and the landscape as objects worthy of the tourist's attention? By this point, the literature on regional cooking was a flourishing genre. Nationalism was the order of the day, moreover, and this proved to be fertile ground for promoters of regional cuisines to exploit. Take the Club des Cent, for example. This was a club for sportsmen and gastronomes who, in addition, had to be well traveled, for members were required to have tallied at least 25,000 miles of touring by automobile. Since 1912 the club's membership had crisscrossed the provinces in search of fine dining, with the express purpose of maintaining the noble traditions of French cuisine in the face of competition from "international hotelkeepers, stateless by definition . . . who travel from country to country oblivious of the local spirit and who are capable of serving their clients in Bresse canned chicken from Chicago." Ultimately, it was in response to the needs of the tourist trade that the first gastronomic guides were published. These were based not on the *départements,* which tourists never accepted as part of their geography, but on France's historical provinces, to which they provided a gourmet's map symbolic of the enduring bond between tourism and gastronomy.

Marcel Rouff and Curnonsky inaugurated the genre in 1921. After an introductory survey that mingled modernity with tradition, they went on to publish a twenty-four-volume survey of France's gastronomic riches in *Le Tour de France gastronomique* (1921–28). Here the monuments, natural wonders, landscapes, and local celebrities are none other than truffles, *foie gras,* capons, and chickens. French history is everywhere present in these volumes by way of allusions not to royal entries or treaty signings but to the role, say, that gifts of pâté to *intendants* played during the Ancien Régime in Périgueux. Gastronomic high points became part of France's illustrious history, as the tour of France was firmly wedded to the national memory in gourmet cult and ritual. Between 1930 and 1950 guides dedicated to gastronomic tourism exhumed recipes from the depths of the provinces and assembled countless itineraries, routes, hikes, promenades, and tours that made aesthetic appreciation of local produce and cooking an essential part of the tourist experience.

Even as the era of the small farm was drawing to a close, regional cooking as a cultural phenomenon and economic resource was enlisting the support of various social and special-interest groups united by their desire to save a French identity ostensibly threatened by the globalization of commerce and trade. Regional movements sponsored celebrations in which local culinary specialties were served up against a backdrop of parades, colorful costumes, lectures in patois, and traditional folk songs and dances. They were slow, however, to cater to the tourist trade, which they initially suspected of perverting local cultures but ultimately accepted as a way of getting back in touch with tradition.

The theorist of regionalism, Jean-Charles Brun, wrote a brochure for the Touring Club de France entitled *Tourisme et Régionalisme* (1890), in which he tried to show how tourism could help to sustain and even develop distinctive regional characteristics. In 1913 a series of regional guides, *La France pittoresque et artistique,* surveyed local history, customs, traditions, folktales, legends, and literature. In these guides food was usually discussed in connection with local history and regionalist poetry, such as G. Spetz's paeans to the glory of Alsatian *choucroute* and Saint-Amant's to the glory of *tripes à la mode de Caen.* Recipes as such were generally avoided.

Finally, hotel and restaurant owners eager to attract new clients and stimulate the local economy worked hard to preserve and promote regional cuisines, family recipes, and local know-how. In this they had the support of the regional press, whose circulation was on the upswing. The history of this quest for "authenticity" has yet to be written. As Jean-Charles Brun observed, "A proper appreciation of their own self-interest has made excellent regionalists of ordinary hotel keepers keen to ensure that their own beautiful corner of France receives its share of the burgeoning tourist trade."

Thus the combined efforts of gastronomic associations, the regionalist movement, and professionals in the tourist and restaurant trade saw to it that local cuisines, reorganized and codified in such a way as to link specialty dishes to particular geographic sites—at times in a rather whimsical fashion—became the very embodiment of French genius in all its historical density and diversity. In 1923 it was regional cooking rather than French haute cuisine or the international cuisine of the great hotels that was consecrated as the "ninth art" at a triumphal Salon d'Automne, a show whose purpose was to encourage French art in all its forms.

On that occasion Austin de Croze insisted that "what is most attractive about French cooking is that it is quintessentially regional and yet, when taken together, constitutes a variegated yet homogeneous whole that cannot be improved upon: *French cuisine.*" More keenly attuned to the "nuances of the provincial soul," Jean-Charles Brun went even further: "Every province in France has its way of speaking, its unique sensibility, its literature, its art; it has its tricks and old recipes and gastronomic traditions. . . . You can't force people from the south to gorge themselves with butter or people from the north to use olive oil."

The nationalist fervor of the interwar years, which presaged the cultural program of Vichy, fostered a confusion of genres and epochs, and it was in that atmosphere that the myth of a renaissance of regional cuisines was created, a myth sustained by a number of energetic initiatives. There was the Association des Gastronomes Régionalistes, for example, founded in 1923, which organized dinners, celebrations, and colloquia all across France. *Grand Tourisme,* the travel agents' trade journal, surveyed eminent chefs and restaurant owners about the future of regional cuisine in 1932. And, finally, the Exposition Universelle of 1937 included a "gastronomic section" that sponsored a colloquium at the regional center.

The "awakening of the provinces" during the Belle Époque had made local culinary specialties symbols of a new model of national unity. Now the myth of a renaissance completed a process that began in the decade after the French Revolution, when local diversity was first reinterpreted as an expression of republican solidarity.

How unique was the French experience in this regard? In order to answer this question, we would have to learn more about the fortunes of regional cuisines in countries that had neither a centralized political regime nor a centralized cuisine. In Italy, a country with a wealth of regional cuisines but no unified culinary tradition, Vito Teti has explored the case of Calabria and has shown how the myth of a regional cuisine was created there in the late nineteenth century. This phenomenon both reflected the existence of a Calabrian cultural identity and signaled a heightened awareness of that identity. One is therefore tempted to speculate that, whereas "local dishes" based on locally available ingredients, family traditions, and market patterns are certainly found everywhere, what is interesting in Europe is the variety of ways in which such traditions were used to redefine local, regional, and national identities in the face of political, economic, and cultural change in the nineteenth century.

NOTES

1. A. Deleyre, *Idées sur l'Education nationale: Textes de la Convention nationale* (Paris: Imprimerie Nationale, June/July 1793), pp. 25–26. This proposed geographical garden seems

to have been the first of its kind. Similar proposals would follow, particularly under the Empire. It is worth noting that the ensuing process served as a pretext for satire and burlesque: in *L'École des gourmands* (1804) by Chazet, Lafortelle, and Francis, Gourmandin develops a method for teaching geography by associating cities and regions with their gastronomic specialties.

2. Pierre Nora, "L'Histoire de France de Lavisse," in *Les Lieux de mémoire,* ed. Nora, p. 318. Between 1862 and 1903 the number of learned societies increased from 204 to 915.

3. The Société des Traditions Populaires was founded in 1886; the Société d'Ethnologie Nationale et d'Art Populaire in 1885; the Muséon Arlaten, the first ethnographic museum, was created by Mistral, the originator of the Félibrige movement, in 1894; and the first regional ethnographic society, the Société Dauphinoise d'Ethnologie et d'Anthropologie, was founded in 1894.

4. The Félibrige, established in 1854, was the first regionalist organization. In 1888 the Union Régionaliste Breton was founded, followed in 1893 by the Escola Lemouzina and in 1900 by the Fédération Régionaliste Française, headed by Jean-Charles Brun.

BIBLIOGRAPHY

Agulhon, M. *Le cercle dans la France bourgeoise, 1810–1848. Cahiers des Annales,* no. 36. Paris: Armand Colin, 1977.

———. "Conscience nationale et conscience régionale." In *Histoire vagabonde,* 2:144–74. Paris, Gallimard, 1988.

———. "L'imaginaire des nations: Réflexions liminaires sur l'expérience française." In *L'imaginaire de la Nation (1792–1992),* ed. G. Dubois, pp. 13–18. Bordeaux: Presses Universitaires de Bordeaux, 1991.

Aron, J.-P. *Le mangeur du XIXᵉ siècle.* Paris: L'font, 1973. [*The Art of Eating in France: Manners and Menus in the Nineteenth Century.* Trans. Nina Rootes. New York: Harper & Row, 1975.]

Bernard, H. *La terre toujours réinventée: La France rurale et les peintres, 1920–1955, une histoire de l'imaginaire.* Lyons: Presses Universitaires de Lyon, 1990.

Berr, H. "Réflexions sur l'histoire provinciale." *Revue de synthèse,* 1900.

Bertho-Lavenir, C. "La géeographie symbolique des provinces: De la monarchie de Juillet à l'entre-deux-guerre." *Ethnologie française* 3 (1988): 276–82.

Boutier, J., A. Dewerpe, and D. Nordman. *Un tour de France royal: Le voyage de Charles IX (1564–1566).* Paris: Aubier, 1984.

Camporesi, P. *La terre et la lune: Alimentation, folklore et société.* Paris: Aubier, 1993.

Capatti, A. *Le Goût du nouveau: Origines de la modernité alimentaire.* Paris: Albin Michel, 1989.

Choay, F. *L'allégorie du patrimoine.* Paris: Le Seuil, 1992.

Corbin, A., ed. *L'avènement des loisirs, 1850–1960.* Paris: Aubier, 1995.

———. "Paris-Province." In *Les lieux de mémoire,* ed. Nora, III, 1:776–823.

Corbin, A., N. Gérôme, and D. Tartakowsy. *Les usages politiques des fêtes aux XIXᵉ et XXᵉ siècles.* Paris: Publications de la Sorbonne, 1994.

Croze, A. (de). *Le livret d'or de la section gastronomique régionaliste du Salon d'automne.* 1923; *Le Matin,* August 12 and October 4, 1912.

Csergo, J. "La constitution de la spécialité gastronomique comme objet patrimonial en France, fin XVIIIe–XXe siècle." In *Le patrimoine et la cité,* ed. D. Poulot. Grenoble: PUG, 1996.

———. "Livre de cuisine et conscience régionale: L'exemple de l'*Oberrheinisches Kochbuch* de 1811." In *Livres et recettes de cuisine en Europe, XIVe–XIXe siècle,* pp. 155–69. Cognac: Le Temps qu'il Fait, 1996.

———. "Nostalgies du terroir." *Mille et une bouches: Cuisines et identités culturelles, autrement, mutations/mangeurs* 154 (March 1995): 156–62.

Faure, Ch. *Le projet culturel de Vichy: Folklore et révolution nationale (1940–1944).* Lyons: Presses Universitaires de Lyon/CNRS, 1989.

Fèbvre, L. "Répartition géographique des fonds de cuisine en France." *Travaux du premier congrès international de folklore,* pp. 123–30. Paris: 1938.

Flandrin, J.-L. *Chronique de Platine: Pour une gastronomie historique.* Paris: Odile Jacob, 1992.

———. "Internationalisme, nationalisme et régionalisme dans la cuisine des XIVe et XVe siècles: Le témoignage des livres de cuisine." *Manger et boire au Moyen Âge: Actes du colloque de Nice, 15–17 octobre 1982,* 2:75–91. Paris: Belles Lettres, 1984.

———. "Problèmes, sources et méthodes d'une histoire des pratiques et des goûts régionaux avant le XIXe siècle." In *Alimentation et régions: Actes du colloque "Cuisines, régimes alimentaires, espaces régionaux," Nancy, 24–27 septembre 1987,* ed. J. Peltre and Cl. Thouvenot, pp. 347–61. Nancy: Presses Universitaires de Nancy, 1989.

Foncin, P. "Introduction à l'étude des régions et des pays de France." *Revue de synthèse,* 1900.

Furet, F., and M. Ozouf, eds. *Dictionnaire critique de la Révolution française.* Paris: Flammarion, 1988. [*A Critical Dictionary of the French Revolution.* Trans. Arthur Goldhammer. Cambridge: Belknap Press of Harvard University Press, 1989.]

Gasnier, T. "Le local: Une et divisible." In *Les lieux de mémoire,* ed. Nora, III, 2:463–525.

Hyman, Ph., and M. Hyman. "Les cuisines régionales à travers les livres de recettes." *Dix-Huitième Siècle* 15 (1983): 65–74.

"Identité culturelle et appartenance régionale." *Terrain: Carnets du patrimoine éthnologique* 5 (Oct. 1985).

Ihl, O. *La Fête républicaine.* Paris: Gallimard, 1996.

Ketcham-Wheaton, B. *L'Office et la Bouche: Histoire des mœurs de la table en France, 1300–1789.* Paris: Calmann-Lévy, 1984.

Knibiehler, Y. "Essai sur l'histoire de la cuisine provençale." In *National and Regional Style of Cookery,* pp. 184–90. London: Prospect Book, 1981.

Le Grand d'Aussy. *Histoire de la vie privée des François depuis l'origine de la nation jusqu'à nos jours.* Rev. ed. 3 vols. Paris: Simonet, 1815.

Lehmann, G. "Les femmes à la page et aux fourneaux: Le livre de cuisine en Angleterre aux XVIIe et XVIIIe siècles." In *Papilles,* 1:19–30 and 2:23–32. Cognac: Le Temps qu'il Fait, 1993.

Lorbac, Ch. (de). *Les Richesses gastronomiques de la France.* 2 vols. Paris: Hetzel, 1868.

Marlin, F. *Voyages d'un Français depuis 1775 jusqu'à 1807.* 4 vol. Paris: 1817.

M. ch. d'O. "Lettre du 15 août 1806." *Almanach des gourmands.* Vol. 5. Paris: Chez Maradan, 1807.

Nora, Pierre, ed. "L'Histoire de France de Lavisse." In *Les lieux de mémoire,* ed. Nora.

——. *Les lieux de mémoire.* Paris: Gallimard, 1986. [*Realms of Memory: Rethinking the French Past.* Trans. Arthur Goldhammer, ed. Lawrence O. Kritzman. New York: Columbia University Press, 1996–98.]

Nordman, D. "Les Guides Joanne." In *Les lieux de mémoire,* ed. Nora, II, 1:529–67.

Nordman, D., and J. Revel. "La formation de l'espace français." In *Histoire de la France.* Vol. 1, *L'espace français,* ed. A. Burguière and J. Revel. Paris: Le Seuil, 1989.

Ozouf-Marignier, M.-V. *La formation des départements: La représentation du territoire français à la fin du XVIIIᵉ siècle.* Recherches d'Histoire et de Sciences Sociales, no. 36. Paris: Éditions de l'École des Hautes Études en Sciences Sociales, 1989.

Perrot, J.-C. *L'âge d'or de la statistique régionale française (an IV-1804).* Paris: Société d'Études Robespierristes, 1977.

Pitte, J.-R., ed. *Gastronomie française: Histoire et géographie d'une passion.* Paris: Fayard, 1991.

——. *Les restaurants dans le monde et à travers les âges.* Grenoble: Glénat, 1990.

Pradei, A. (du). *Le Livre commode contenant les adresses de la ville de Paris et le Trésor des almanachs pour l'année bissextile 1692.* Geneva: Minkoff Reprint, 1973.

Rippert, A. *La carte postale, son histoire, sa fonction sociale.* Lyons: Presses Universitaires de Lyon, 1983.

Serres, O. (de). *Le Théâtre d'agriculture et Mesnage des champs (1600).* Grenoble: Dardelet, 1973.

Stouff, L. *Ravitaillement et alimentation en Provence aux XIVᵉ et XVᵉ siècles.* Civilisations et Sociétés, no. 20. Paris: Mouton, 1970.

Teti, V. "L'invention d'une cuisine régionale: Le cas de la cuisine calabraise." In *Alimentation et régions: Actes du colloque "Cuisines, régimes alimentaires, espaces régionaux," Nancy, 24–27 septembre 1987,* ed. J. Peltre and Cl. Thouvenot, pp. 411–21. Nancy: Presses Universitaires de Nancy, 1989.

Thiesse, A.-M. *Écrire la France: Le mouvement littéraire régionaliste de langue française entre la Belle Époque et la Libération.* Paris: Presses Universitaires de France, 1991.

Weber, E. J. *Peasants into Frenchmen: The Modernization of Rural France, 1870–1914.* Stanford: Stanford University Press, 1976.

CHAPTER 39

The PERILS of ABUNDANCE

Food, Health, and Morality in American History

Harvey A. Levenstein

The First Colonists: A Subsistence Economy

Europeans visiting the United States for the first time are often struck by the relatively large number of obese people one sees there, and they remark that Americans seem overfed. Although being revolted by girth is a fairly recent phenomenon, the idea of America as a land of food abundance is not. Throughout the nation's history, those who have praised or criticized its diet have agreed on that. Americans have proudly defined themselves as "People of Plenty," and this has primarily meant plenty of food. On the other hand, America has also been a home for countless schemes to limit partaking in this abundance—ranging from the zaniest of food fads to the most sober scientific theories.

Although the first settlers, in the early seventeenth century, suffered some difficult years, most of the inhabitants of Britain's American colonies rapidly established themselves as much better fed than their counterparts in the motherland. The ink was hardly dry on the French biologist Buffon's theory of how everything born in the New World was a stunted version of that of the Old when the colonists' abundant diet was helping to refute it. When the colonies rebelled against British rule in the 1770s, the American soldiers were, on average, much taller than both the British soldiers facing them and the French troops who came to their aid. Indeed, by the time of the American Revolution, white Americans had just about achieved their modern height—due mainly to the nutritional advantages of the land of abundance. Even their poorly treated black slaves were taller than European peasants and laborers. They were also much taller than the slaves of African descent in the Caribbean and South America. But the citizens of "the First New Nation" did not need comparative height data to prove that they were better fed than Europeans. The idea that their land provided them with enormous amounts of food was already enshrined in their folklore. It was natural, said the Philadelphia physician John Bell in 1793, that Americans, living amidst "superabundance," should be "great eaters."

For most Americans, abundance meant lots of meat—mainly pork and, to a lesser extent, beef—accompanied by breads made from corn (maize), rye, and, increasingly, wheat. Fruits and vegetables were plentiful in season (although in much of the country those seasons were not very long), and the immense stocks of fish and seafood along the coasts provided coastal communities with additional sources of protein. For much of the winter and spring most people in the middle and northern sections subsisted on a diet of preserved meat and bread, supplemented mainly by beans and root vegetables that they stored in cold cellars. Although they sometimes complained of this dietary monotony, they still took pains to impress foreigners with their abundant supplies of meat. In 1793 an impressed French traveler estimated that Americans ate seven to eight times as much meat as bread. The dearth of fresh vegetables was not regarded as much of a loss, for, like their British forbears, Americans were suspicious of fresh vegetables and preferred to cook them (and fruits, too) until they were almost mush. Indeed, despite the growing proportion of immigrants who did not originate in the British Isles, British traditions would prevail for almost the next two hundred years. An impressive number of new foods and tastes would be assimilated into the national diet, but mainly on British-American terms.

Modernization and Early Food Reforms

By the 1830s, impressive improvements in transportation—roads, canals, and steamboats—and agriculture were transforming the subsistence economy in which most of the country's farms operated into a cash one. A much wider variety of foodstuffs was now available for much longer periods of the year, particularly to the middle class of the towns and cities, which were swelling in the wake of this transformation. Perhaps, then, it was a feeling that they were being engulfed in agricultural plenty that made this new middle class so responsive to the first of what would be many attempts to regulate and restrict the national diet.

The food reform movement that arose in the 1830s and 1840s now seems quintessentially American, for it linked calls to avoid foods that science had deemed deleterious with strivings for moral purity. Its most famous advocate was the Protestant preacher William Sylvester Graham, whose scientific ideas were derived from the "vitalist" theories then circulating in France. He based his initial crusade—against alcohol—on the "vitalist" idea that the nervous system contained a force upon which all life depended. Alcohol, he said, overstimulated the nervous system and sapped this vital force, leaving the body prey to disease, debility, and death. He soon expanded the indictment to include other forms of nervous stimulation—particularly sexual activity and the consumption of meat and spices—adding a scientific dimension to traditional moral-religious prescriptions for sexual prudery and vegetarianism.

Graham's ideas also fit in well with the Romantic intellectual currents of the day, for he was suspicious of any food that had been altered from its natural condition. The cultivation of wheat, never too successful along the eastern seaboard, had boomed in the trans-Appalachian West, and Americans had been rapidly forsaking breads made of corn, rye, and whole wheat for white loaves made from bolted flour. This "denaturing" of wheat became one of Graham's main targets. Echoing the Protestant marriage ceremony, he thundered, "Let no man pull asunder what God has joined together." His followers set up the nation's first health food store to sell unbolted "Graham flour." (It was some decades later that commercially produced graham crackers appeared.)

This kind of appeal to science, nature, and God attracted many of the people swept up in other crusades of that great era of reform such as the antislavery, temperance, and women's suffrage movements. Prominent writers and philosophers such as Henry Thoreau tried vegetarianism and ate Graham flour. Fourierist phalansteries and other utopian communities adopted many of Graham's dietary ideas. The fiery preacher Charles Finney, who sparked the greatest Protestant revivalist crusade ever witnessed by the nation, was a Grahamite. Even Joseph Smith, polygamous founder of the Mormon Church, tried Grahamite vegetarianism.

Yet Smith and most of the other reformers eventually abandoned vegetarianism and returned to the pleasures of flesh-eating. The expansion of the railroad and cattle-raising into the West had encouraged hearty beef-eating, allowing the fulfillment of many an Anglo-Saxon dream. "We are essentially a hungry *beef-eating* people, who live by eating," a proud newspaper proclaimed in mid-century.

A Second Wave of Food Reforms

As the railroad networks expanded and domestic agriculture diversified, the tentacles of a tropical agricultural empire began to stretch out at home and then abroad. As a result, the plates of the wealthy, in particular, overflowed with an enormous bounty. Millions of immigrants from impoverished parts of Europe flowed in, providing a labor force for the railroads and other burgeoning industries. They also provided the servants to help prepare and serve the bountiful upper- and upper-middle-class meals. Often the upper-class versions of these meals, presided over by French chefs, were every bit as lavish as those of their Belle Époque counterparts in Paris.

By the 1890s, however, the seeds of a middle-class reaction against this kind of excess were finding fertile ground in the kinds of concerns that had given rise to food reform in the 1830s. Like the first wave of food reform, the turn-of-the-century one was grounded in new scientific ideas that were thought to advance both the health and the moral state of the entire nation. The first objective of the reformers was not the obvious one—the upper-class men who waddled about with enormous bellies, constantly complaining of dyspepsia, constipation, and other digestive ills. Nor, initially, was there much concern over the middle class and better-off farmers, who ate enormous quantities of heavy foods, particularly fried meats and baked pies. Rather, the food reformers first tried to change the diets of the working class, which was largely composed of immigrants who had come to America hoping to partake in the fabled riches of its tables.

The discovery that foods' energy could be measured in calories and that they were composed of proteins, carbohydrates, and fats, each of which seemed to have a unique physiological function, had revolutionized scientific thinking about food. A loose group of American nutritional scientists, social reformers, and home economists were struck by the apparent relevance of these new ideas—the so-called New Nutrition—to the horrific social problems created by industrialization and urbanization in America: ragged workers' families living in overcrowded, underheated, and unsanitary housing, drunkenness, child labor, and prostitution. They thought that if the working class could be taught that the proteins in beans, for example, were just as nutritious as those in beefsteak, they would be able to spend less on food and have more to spend on shelter, heating fuel, and clothing. Living standards would thus rise and they would turn a deaf ear to the radicals fostering anarchism, socialism, trade unionism, and other disruptive principles.

Unfortunately for the reformers, the working class was largely composed of immigrants, such as the millions from Italy's Mezzogiorno who had come to America hoping to eat beef, not beans. The reformers were generally ignored and derided by those they wished to help. (This was probably all to the good. Scientists, ignorant of the existence of vitamins, declared most fresh fruits and vegetables to be mainly water, so the New Nutritionists advised workers that they were wasteful extravagances. They were particularly frustrated by the apparent profligacy of Italo-Americans on this score.) However, by the early 1900s the New Nutritionists were beginning to have an impact on the middle class, who were again becoming responsive to calls for dietary change. This was due in part to the efforts of a number of other critics of the American diet, including a direct heir of Graham's ideas, Dr. John Harvey Kellogg, co-inventor (with his brother, William) of corn flakes and director of the famous "sanitorium" at Battle Creek, Michigan. This vegetarian health resort had been founded by Seventh-Day Adventists, a Protestant sect that had made many of Graham's food ideas part of its religious credo. The genial Kellogg, whose medical credentials were unimpressive and scientific ones nonexistent, had managed to turn the virtually moribund institution into a trendy health spa catering to a clientele of non-Adventists who were convinced that its cures reflected the cutting edge of nutritional science.

Many of Kellogg's ideas were simply Graham's dressed up in modern garb. At their heart lay the same warnings against eating those foods which overstimulated the nervous system—particularly meat, spices, alcohol—and succumbing to the temptations of masturbation. But he was also fixated on the terminus of the alimentary canal and was particularly enthusiastic about new theories concerning the dangers of "auto-intoxication," which blamed many illnesses on eating foods that encouraged bacteria to proliferate in the colon. By artfully blending new scientific theories such as this with older calls for moral uplift and an array of special vegetarian diets—high blood pressure, for example, was treated by putting patients on a diet of nothing but 9 to 13 pounds (4 to 6 kilos) of grapes per day—Kellogg managed to attract an impressive list of rich and famous people to the booming "San" as well as a lot of media attention.

One of the key people helping Kellogg straddle the gap between quackery and mainstream nutritional science was Horace Fletcher, a wealthy American businessman who had returned to an impressive nineteenth-century *palazzo* on Venice's Grand Canal. Like most faddists, Fletcher claimed to have discovered a miracle cure after indulgence in a rich diet had placed him at death's door. In his case, a drastic reduction in food intake and "thorough mastication" of his food had done the trick. Never one for half measures, Fletcher took his latter idea to an unheard-of extreme, advocating that each mouthful of food be chewed at least one hundred times. Prominent nutritional scientists, hoping that he might subsidize their research, pretended to subscribe to his theory that food was actually ingested by an unknown mechanism at the back of the mouth. However, they were able to take him more seriously in two regards. First, the fact that his feces were tiny and odorless did seem to demonstrate that "Fletcherizing" prevented "auto-intoxication." (Indeed, to make this point, he often sent them to leading scientists through the mail.) Ultimately more important, however, were his demonstrations that current estimates of human protein needs were much too high. People should eat only when hungry and then eat only enough to sate the hunger, he said.

The fifty-three-year-old Fletcher became famous for performing physical tasks beyond the capabilities of most twenty-one-year-old athletes on one-half to two-thirds of their protein intake. He advised the chief of staff of the U.S. Army on reducing the army ration and made prominent converts such as the novelist Henry James and his philosopher brother William. While most of them ultimately found "Fletcherizing" simply too tedious to maintain, his admonitions to eat less found increasing support among nutritional scientists and home economists, many of whom would shortly begin calling themselves dietitians. The downward revisions also found a receptive audience in the upper middle class, who were finding it impossible to imitate the culinary and entertaining styles of the class above them. The growing shortage of competent domestic servants made it particularly difficult to entertain in the sophisticated French manner. It was even difficult to fulfill expectations for family meals, which by the late nineteenth century had been invested with much of the somber moral significance of Protestant church services. The transient immigrant girls upon whom most middle-class women relied for help in the kitchen were of little use in preparing and serving these formal dinners. The women were therefore receptive to the reformers, who told them they should abjure the upper classes' fancy seasonings, exotic ingredients, complex preparations, groaning tables, and multicourse dinners. That these calls for restraining the pleasures of the flesh also struck a familiar Protestant chord did their prospects no harm.

These self-denying ideas received a big push during World War I, when the government organized a massive effort, led by Herbert Hoover, to persuade Americans to voluntarily cut back on consumption of certain foodstuffs—beef and wheat, in particular—so that they could be shipped to the U.S. and Allied troops in Europe. A major propaganda campaign was mounted to teach the New Nutritionists' rules of substitution and persuade Americans that eating less would not harm their health and might even improve it. Again, the working class remained generally unmoved by this information. They used fattened wartime paychecks to buy more beef. However, the campaign did have an impact on the middle class. Indeed, for many years thereafter they recalled how their diets had been "Hooverized."

"Vitamania," 1917–50

Even before Hoover had assumed direction of wartime food conservation in early 1917, the first vitamins had been discovered. Too little was known of them to have an impact then, but by the time he was elected to the presidency in 1928, the new nutritional paradigm revolving around vitamins—which its exponents called the Newer Nutrition—had come to the fore. Although it ultimately helped transform diets throughout the world, this new vitamin-centered way of thinking made itself felt particularly early in the United States. In part this was because the prewar and wartime food reformers had already primed middle- and upper-class Americans to accept the primacy of health concerns over gastronomic ones in making their food choices. Indeed, hardly anyone seemed to notice when the national law prohibiting the sale and consumption of alcoholic beverages from 1921 to 1933 virtually destroyed what remained of haute cuisine in America by forcing most fine restaurants, whose survival depended on profits from alcoholic beverages, out of business.

"Vitamania" was also fostered by industrial developments. By the mid-1920s, food production in the United States was being transformed into a series of highly organized industries dependent on large capital investments, mechanized production, sophisticated distribution networks, and—crucial from the point of view of dietary ideas—large expenditures for promotion and advertising. Vitamins, which are invisible, weightless, and tasteless, proved to be a food advertiser's dream. Citrus fruit growers, grape juice producers, flour millers, pickle producers—almost anyone could and did make extravagant claims. Fleischmann's Yeast Company, owned by Standard Brands (one of the two enormous new food conglomerates created by Wall Street–financed mergers in the 1920s), spent enormous amounts spreading the message that eating four of its slimy yeast cakes a day would provide enough vitamin B to "rid the body of poisonous wastes," raise energy levels, and cure indigestion, constipation, acne, pimples, "fallen stomach," and "underfed blood." The dairy industries were among the most successful at spreading vitamin consciousness. In the late 1920s, a process was invented to irradiate canned milk with Vitamin D. Its use was soon expanded to butter and fresh milk. The powerful milk producers' cooperatives and giant dairy companies, guarding the process from margarine producers, were then able to change the image of milk from that of a children's food into "the perfect food" for adults as well, one which contained virtually every nutrient necessary for good health. During World War I, coffee was the army's favorite beverage; during World War II, fresh milk was the G.I.'s overwhelming choice.

Vitamania had also helped revive Graham's idea that white flour was "denutrified." Critics charged that milling techniques introduced by large millers in the late nineteenth century, which made white flour much cheaper and even whiter than in Graham's time, were linked to national deficiencies in important vitamins. In 1940 and 1941, as America hastily rearmed in anticipation of being drawn into war, alarm spread over apparent deficiencies in vitamin B₁ (thiamine) in the national diet. In 1939 and 1940 physicians at the famed Mayo Clinic in Minnesota had put some teenagers on a diet very low in this vitamin and concluded that it made them surly and uncooperative. It was soon labeled "the morale vitamin," and warnings rang out that a nation whose staple was now white bread, from which most of this vitamin had been removed, would be weakened and vulnerable in the face of an enemy invasion. The government thus had millers restore the thiamine back into the flour and add two other nutrients, iron and riboflavin, for which deficiencies were thought to be widespread as well. The general public, however, seemed persuaded that taking vitamins would give them "pep" and energy, a notion mainly inspired by the fortuitous fact that *vita* means "life" and connotes vigor, verve, and vitality.

The organized medical profession was hardly enthusiastic about all of this, for they saw in vitamania a recurrence of the age-old threat that people would seek nonmedical help when stricken with illness. This danger to their monopoly on healing loomed particularly large in the late 1930s, by which time most of the vitamins had been synthesized and were being produced commercially, in the form of pills or tonics, and sold without prescriptions. Their recurring efforts to restrict vitamin sales were supported by many food producers. Unable to compete with the pharmaceutical giants selling vitamins in more convenient form, they dropped their vitamin-centered campaigns to focus on their products' other attributes, such as the "quick energy" that came from their sugar content. Most joined with the American Medical Association in promoting the doctrine that became the official government line until the 1970s: that the American food supply was unsurpassed in nutritional quality. The public was repeatedly assured that the vitamin supplements were unnecessary because they could obtain more than enough nutrients to ensure good health by simply eating a "balanced" diet.

The Era of the Baby-Boomers

Although a number of munitions manufacturers claimed that giving vitamin pills to workers raised their productivity, the entry of the United States into the war diverted attention away from vitamania and other health concerns. Food shortages and rationing became the national obsession, and for good reason: restricting how much of their favorite foods Americans could buy flew directly in the face of their perception of their country as the land of abundance. Although the ration was quite princely, even compared to the peacetime standards of other belligerents, Americans had difficulty accepting the idea that the shortages they faced were real. There were recurring rumors that supplies of food—particularly beef—were more than adequate but that foodstuffs were being wasted, destroyed, or otherwise kept off the market by an incompetent government, crooked middlemen, or various other conspiracies. The wartime resentment persisted into the postwar years, when the supply and price of beef became, at one stage, the most important issue in American domestic politics.

After 1948, when a semblance of order was restored to the markets and the feeling of being at the receiving end of the cornucopia returned, concerns over the healthfulness of the national diet remained in the background. The era of the baby boom, from 1946 to about 1963, was a time for family-building, when Americans set up millions of new households and were concerned primarily with managing them. In food, this meant that concerns of health or gastronomy took a back seat to "convenience," or what food processors like to call "built-in service." Producers and processors developed a host of new methods for growing, raising, preserving, precooking, and packaging foods. From 1949 to 1959, chemists alone came up with over four hundred new additives to help food survive the new processes. Any concerns over the effects of these methods on the nutritional quality of the foods were largely swept away by pride in American inventiveness. Government-sponsored exhibitions designed to impress foreigners with the achievements of American capitalism gave processed foods, kitchen appliances, and supermarket shopping center stage. In Moscow in 1959, Vice-President Richard Nixon waited until he was in the gleaming, fully equipped kitchen of one of those exhibits before engaging Chairman Nikita Khruschev in their famous debate over the relative merits of the two systems. When Khruschev visited the United States, he was taken through a supermarket.

Not everyone was impressed. A French woman, contemplating the monstrous turkey in the American display of a bountiful Thanksgiving dinner at the 1957 Dijon Food Fair, remarked with some disgust, "Who has an oven big enough to cook something like that?" Another wondered why the Americans had an exhibit at a gastronomic fair at all: everyone knew that everything they ate came from cans. Even in the United States it was sometimes said that "convenience" was taking a toll on taste. Yet gastronomical considerations had long since been relegated to the backseat when it came to food choices. Moreover, food tastes had virtually ceased to be an important marker of social distinction. Everyone seemed equally partial to beefsteak and potatoes, fried chicken, hamburgers grilled on the barbecue, and casseroles made with canned fish or meat, canned creamed soup, and topped with potato chips or crumbled crackers. Brightly colored Jell-O molds— canned fruits, vegetables, meats, or fish congealed in artificially colored and artificially flavored gelatin—graced the tables of all classes. There was hardly a dissenting voice as government, educators, the media, and the food industries regularly assured Americans that they were "The Best-Fed People on Earth." Indeed, after making his first visit to Europe in 1948, where he dined in Italy, France, and England, the nation's most prominent restaurant critic, Duncan Hines, assured Americans that their cuisine remained the world's finest. Only the English, whose roast beef he particularly admired, approached American standards.

A Time for Self-Criticism

This mood of self-satisfaction did not survive the late 1960s, when all aspects of American society were subjected to intense criticism. The public was suddenly made aware that millions of people were living in poverty. The fact that they had trouble paying for adequate diets seemed particularly scandalous in a nation producing an overabundance of farm products, storing mountains of surplus foods, and paying its farmers not to produce food. As in the depression of the 1930s, when socialists raised the cry that there were "bread lines knee deep in wheat," the charge that there was hunger in the land of abundance was a politically potent one. Programs to provide the poor with, first, the surpluses and then food stamps to purchase food had little trouble gaining public support.

But the issues that affected the middle classes the most had to do with their own health, not that of the poor. Indeed, even in the late 1950s the U.S. Congress responded to concerns that some food additives might be carcinogenic. Processors were allowed to continue using 704 of the chemicals then in use but were required to obtain government approval for any new ones by proving they did not cause cancer in mice. During the next decade, there was increasing alarm over the effects of the pesticides and chemical fertilizers that were now used extensively in farming and the antibiotics and other chemicals employed in meat production. Prewar concerns over the nutrient-depleting effects of processing arose again, stimulated in part by botched government attempts to stem another wave of vitamania by placing restrictions on vitamin pill sales. By the end of the decade, large corporations were being regularly denounced for being part of the "military-industrial complex" that had mired the nation in the Vietnam War. These critical eyes inevitably turned to the big businesses that now dominated practically every aspect of food production, processing, and marketing.

The best-known result of the new critical spirit was the vogue for "organic" and unprocessed "natural" foods. In a certain sense, this was a revival of the kind of mixture of health, morality, and romanticism that prevailed in the 1830s and 1840s. The drug-besotted hippies of the counterculture, with whom it was first associated, were hardly aware of or interested in past associations, but this kind of thinking also struck a sympathetic chord among the more conventional upper and middle classes. The health concerns were stoked by consumer activists such as Ralph Nader, an ascetic lawyer who turned his attention from the safety of automobiles to that of food. Young veterans of the "New Left," whose campaigns against racism and imperialism floundered in the early 1970s, redirected their moral critique of capitalism toward its effects on food and the environment. The giant corporations, it was alleged, used their immense advertising resources to brainwash Americans into eating their overprocessed, unhealthy, and environmentally hazardous products.

The food producers were thrown on the defensive, but not for long. Within months they were reformulating their products and emblazoning their packages with words such as "Natural," "Nature's Own," "Fresh," "Farm," and "Mountain Valley." Pet owners could even buy "natural" dog foods. Although the changes were often merely cosmetic and failed to satisfy most critics, they did help preserve sales. A much greater threat to producers' and processors' profits was posed by the disturbing turn that nutritional science seemed to be taking—away from the Newer Nutrition and toward what could be called the Negative Nutrition.

Negative Nutrition

After World War II, the government had embodied the lessons of the Newer Nutrition in charts portraying four different food groups—fruits and vegetables, dairy products, meat and fish, and grains—and telling Americans that each day they should eat some foods from each of these groups. Food producers supported this enthusiastically. Since every one of their products had a place in at least one of the groups, they could all be called essential for good nutrition. They helped make the "Basic Four" the core of nutrition education in the schools and the media.

The Negative Nutrition diverged markedly from this emphasis on eating enough nutrients. Instead, it warned against eating certain kinds of foods. A prime target, of course, was cholesterol, which, since the late 1950s, had been coming under increasing suspicion as a cause of heart disease and other deadly ailments. Sugar also became a favorite target. The white crystals were portrayed as an addictive drug, used by food processors to "hook" children on their products, and a leading cause of cancer, heart disease, diabetes, skin ailments, schizophrenia, hyperactivity, and assorted other physical and mental disorders. Clearly, the Negative Nutrition also echoed many Graham themes of the past—particularly when in the hands of moralists such as the sucrophobes, whose tales often echoed Protestant parables about those who have "fallen from grace." Graham and his followers would certainly have felt comfortable with the attacks on beef, the condemnations of the effects of industrialization on food, and the charges that greedy forces were foisting an unhealthy diet on the people. Nor would Fletcher, Kellogg, and their fellow advocates of restraint have felt alien in this atmosphere in which people such as the anthropologist Margaret Mead could blame "overnutrition" for the nation's ill health. Had they been aware of modern epidemiological evidence against it, they would almost certainly have supported that other important aspect of the Negative Nutrition—the attack on obesity. After all, their reduced estimates of protein requirements were important steps in what became a century-long buildup of claims that obesity caused a number of death-dealing ailments.

As in the previous eras, the food reformers were supported by important segments of the scientific community. Funding for health science research had been soaring since the late 1950s, and in the late 1960s increasing sums were allocated to studying the links between diet and health. Whereas the government, whose food research efforts were responsive mainly to agricultural interests, was slow to venture into the field, huge new nonprofit charities such as the American Heart Association and the American Cancer Society had no such compunctions. Not only did they subsidize research into the deleterious effects of various foods on particular ailments, they also took the lead in disseminating any adverse results. They began spending millions to warn the public of the supposedly terrible consequences of eating foods containing too much sodium, sugar, and animal fats as well as the perils of being overweight.

With such impressive backing, it is no wonder that the Negative Nutrition struck a responsive chord among the middle class and that within four years of being endorsed by the U.S. Senate in 1977 it became the core of national nutrition policy. In 1981 even the U.S. Department of Agriculture, which had fought a rearguard action against it on behalf of the powerful beef and dairy producers, endorsed its general goals. Of course, by then many of the processors who had initially been most threatened by the new paradigm had themselves adeptly picked up its banners. A wave of "low-fat," "low-calorie," "no-fat," "cholesterol-free," and "sodium-free" versions of their products now engulfed supermarkets. When the Reagan administration freed them in the early 1980s from previous restrictions on advertising health claims, the misleading labels and advertisements for their "heartwise" and "healthwise" products became the public's prime sources of information about the Negative Nutrition. Indeed, so great did the cacophony of half-truths and misinformation become that the succeeding Bush and Clinton administrations were forced to restrict it. However, new government guidelines, issued in the middle 1990s, seemed to provide additional scope for distortion. For example, the dairy and meat lobbies had managed to distort the government's advice that no more than 30 percent of calories be derived from fats to mean that this was the *lower*, rather than the *upper*, limit for fat intake.

The end result reflected many of the continuing paradoxes of American abundance. The middle and upper classes seemed swept up by lipophobia and took to dieting and exercising in an almost maniacal manner. Many of their daughters were overcome by eating disorders. Yet there is no indication of any decline in the average weight of Americans over the past twenty or thirty years. Indeed, quite the reverse seems to be the case. Although they have cut back on full-fat dairy products and their beloved beef, consumption of other fats, particularly in the form of crisp snacks (often eaten to banish the hunger pangs caused by dieting) seems to have more than counterbalanced this. The same goes for sugar, sodium, and other objects of Negative Nutrition scorn. To complicate matters further, there was a parallel, often contradictory, trend toward self-indulgence. The foreign travel boom of the 1960s and 1970s helped elevate gastronomic standards by developing a more adventurous and discerning clientele for diverse kinds of cooking. It also helped to once again make food tastes a sign of social distinction, just as they had been in the late nineteenth century. The narcissism of the middle-class "Me Generation" of the 1970s, which sought "self-fulfillment" in all things, including the pleasures of the flesh, provided a boost to this, as did the yuppie phenomenon of the 1980s, which defined people in terms of their consumption habits. Beneath it all, though, the Protestant strain of moralism persisted, along with its concomitant—guilt. In 1971 the magazine *Psychology Today* anticipated the next twenty-five years well when it noted that "food has replaced sex as an object of guilt." (Although Sylvester Graham would have preferred that food join sex in this matter, he would not have been displeased.)

But the targets of the guilt seemed to be constantly moving, multilayered ones. The Negative Nutrition paradigm had not really displaced the two previous ones—the New and Newer Nutritions; it had simply been superimposed on them. Americans were simultaneously trying to eat more of the foods that were supposed to cure illness, less of those deemed to cause it, more that promoted general good health, and less of practically everything that contributed to weight gain. To make matters worse, they were repeatedly fed new and often contradictory proclamations regarding what these were. Some observers began wondering how long this frantic search for ways to select from the abundance of available food choices could last. They suggested that the result might be a state of "gastro-anomie" in which people have lost confidence in all the experts and all the paradigms. But this seems unlikely in a culture that seems doomed to celebrate its food abundance while simultaneously avoiding enjoying it too much.

BIBLIOGRAPHY

Belasco, Warren. *Appetite for Change*. New York: Pantheon Books, 1989.

Carson, Gerald. *Corn Flake Crusade*. New York: Rinehart, 1957.

Conlin, Joseph. *Bacon, Beans, and Galantines: Food and Foodways on the Western Mining Frontier*. Reno: University of Nevada Press, 1984.

Cummings, Richard. *The American and His Food: A History of Food Habits in the United States*. Chicago: University of Chicago Press, 1940.

Green, Harvey. *Fit for America: Health, Fitness, Sport, and American Society*. New York: Pantheon Books, 1986.

Hooker, Richard. *Food and Drink in America: A History*. Indianapolis: Bobbs-Merrill, 1981.

Jones, Evan. *American Food: The Gastronomic Story*. New York: Random House, 1981.

Levenstein, Harvey. *Paradox of Plenty: A Social History of Eating in Modern America*. New York: Oxford University Press, 1992.

———. *Revolution at the Table: The Transformation of the American Diet*. New York: Oxford University Press, 1988.

Nissenbaum, Stephen. *Sex, Diet and Debility in Jacksonian America: Sylvester Graham and Health Reform*. Contributions in Medical History, no. 4. Westport, Conn.: Greenwood Press, 1980.

Root, Waverly, and Richard de Rochemont. *Eating in America: A History*. New York: Morrow, 1976.

Schwartz, Hillary. *Never Satisfied: A Cultural History of Diets, Fantasies, and Fat*. New York: Free Press, 1986.

Seid, Roberta. *Never Too Thin*. New York: Prentice Hall, 1989.

Shapiro, Laura. *Perfection Salad: Women and Cooking at the Turn of the Century*. New York: Farrar, Straus, and Giroux, 1986.

Whorton, James. *Crusaders for Fitness: The History of American Health Reformers*. Princeton, N.J.: Princeton University Press, 1982.

Williams, Susan. *Savory Suppers and Fashionable Feasts: Dining in Victorian America*. New York: Pantheon Books, 1985.

CHAPTER 40

The "MCDONALDIZATION" of CULTURE

Claude Fischler

In 1932 a writer living in New York conjured up an enthusiastic image of what the city would look like fifty years later in 1982: the population would have risen to 50 million, the Hudson and East Rivers would have been filled in, and traffic would move silently along elevated tracks attached to the sides of skyscrapers. Furthermore, the residents of the city "would live on concentrated food supplied in pill form."[1] The prospect of a purely functional form of eating seems to have alarmed no one at the time—at any rate, not the author and other avid proponents of scientific and technological progress. Despite (or perhaps because of) the Great Depression, people in those days displayed a deep-seated confidence in the promise of technology and the inevitable march of progress.

Fifty years later, many Europeans viewed with anxiety the prospect of a nutritional pill replacing the traditional meal, and many saw the industrialization of the food business as a step in that direction. In 1982 polls showed that for large numbers of people in France and elsewhere in the developed world, the food pill and everything that it implied was the ultimate symbol of Aldous Huxley's "brave new world." Here, for example, is the way one French journalist, writing in that year, described a housewife's shopping trip in the year 2000:

Nine o'clock in the morning, year 2000. Armed with a capacious shopping bag, Mme Lespinguette sets out to buy food on rue Lepic. Gone are the open-air stalls of another era. Now that fruits and vegetables stay fresh for weeks on end, they can be found only on supermarket shelves, wrapped in plastic. At the local butcher shop, Mme Lespinguette sizes up a nice roast. A sign stuck into the meat proclaims that it is "genuine beef." She emits a sigh. At today's prices, animal meat is a luxury that she can afford only for special Sunday dinners. Instead, she settles for a "100 percent pure vegetable steak" on a nearby shelf. Next, she heads for the new supermarket that has just opened on the boulevard de Clichy. In her cart she places a package of sliced egg, which she plans to use throughout the week for hors-d'oeuvres, a tube of instant omelettes, a package of pre-cut French fries, each precisely three inches long, and a couple of vacuum-packed fish, otherwise unidentified and supplied without heads or tails. To round out her purchases she picks up a couple of TV dinners, and with that our housewife of the year 2000 is ready to head home, where she can have both lunch and dinner ready in just a few minutes.[2]

At the time these lines were written, much of what the journalist portrayed as futuristic had already come to pass by 1982—the frozen fish fillets, the three-inch French fries, the textured soy protein added to chopped meat, the replacement of open-air stalls by supermarkets. The omelettes in tubes and the presliced hard-boiled eggs were unlikely to be in the shopping cart of the average shopper (then or now), but they were already being used in some restaurants. Nevertheless, the writer of the article missed most of the important changes in French eating patterns: specific products have changed, but the structure of the system remains. The distribution system has survived mostly intact. Despite the nostalgic allusion to open-air stalls, France, unlike the United States, still relies more on specialty shops than on supermarkets. What is most striking about this journalistic account is that the woman shopper is described as a housewife, which shows that the writer failed to take into account the massive entry of women into the workforce.[3] And our typical shopper is still described as carrying the traditional shopping bag of treated canvas or woven straw that Parisian housewives used to carry before the advent of supermarkets.

Why did this writer describe the present when she purported to be describing the future? Well, for one thing, forecasting, as one wag put it, is hard, especially when it comes to the future. That is why futurology usually involves extrapolating the major trends of the present moment. More important, however, is the fact that this pseudo-futuristic account obviously betrayed certain anxieties and fears on the part of the author and no doubt of her readers—a negative judgment about ongoing changes in the daily diet (and way of life) of the average person. Changes that were already visible in everyday life provoked and justified both anxiety about the future and nostalgia for the past.

From the Myth of the Pill to the Myth of the Invader

Our naive faith in technology and its promise of a better tomorrow has been shaken, to put it mildly, but our worries about the technological future are now couched in terms different from those used by the journalist in 1982. It is no longer the idea of taking our food in pill form that frightens us. Indeed, it is enlightening to discover that Marc Meneau, one of France's leading chefs, was commissioned to develop a range of high-quality freeze-dried foods for the use of French astronauts. Now, one might have thought that if purely functional food concentrates were right for anyone, it would have to be for space travelers. But in designing space food, the architects of the French space program felt that, on the contrary, the product should be as tasty as possible. Research showed that culinary pleasure was important for maintaining the morale of people forced to work in extreme conditions, in some ways more important than for people in more down-to-earth situations.

What replaced worries about food pills and other such futuristic notions was concern about two things: health and identity. The relative importance of these two concerns varied from country to country. In Great Britain, northern Europe, and especially the United States, the paramount concern—or fantasy, if you will—was health. In all the developed countries people can now expect to live longer than ever before. Life expectancy has almost doubled over the past century. Centenarians are no longer rare. Average height has increased significantly. Despite these signs of improved public health, there is widespread concern among medical professionals and the general public alike, and especially among the well-educated, precisely those who are most aware of the rules of hygiene and good nutrition and therefore least at risk, and much of that concern is focused on food. Cardiovascular maladies, especially heart disease, have been dubbed "diseases of civilization," as have many cancers. What is generally forgotten is that these maladies rarely strike people below a certain age; hence it is because we now live longer that we are at leisure to suffer from these afflictions of old age. In other words, getting old is bad for one's health—much worse, at any rate, than eating well.[4]

In France, Italy, Spain, and other traditionally Catholic countries, people also worry about their cultural identity, especially in light of what they perceive as threats to their culinary traditions. They are afraid that the importance of eating as a daily social act and form of pleasure and communication is being slowly eroded, chipped away, and dissolved by an inexorable process of "Americanization," symbolized not by the imaginary food pill but by the ubiquitous hamburger. (Very little attention of this sort attaches to the inoffensive pizza, which has nevertheless conquered the entire planet.) In other words, people today are afraid not of a "brave new world" but of losing their identity to "invaders." Europeans cast an anxious eye on the seemingly implacable "alimentary imperialism" of the Americans. The supposed "McDonaldization" of culture raises a question, however. Is it really the culmination of a historical process of rationalization, industrialization, and functionalization of eating? Or are we blinded by our own fantasies, projections, and "rationalizations" (in the psychoanalytic sense), which lead us to attach more importance to one aspect of the phenomenon while neglecting others, which we tend to underestimate or minimize?

Rampant industrialization, rationalization, and functionalization—there can be no doubt that all three dimensions are glaringly apparent in the changes that have transformed our relation to food since the nineteenth century. These changes have affected the entire food system—from production and distribution to consumption. Yet just because these things are glaringly apparent, we must be careful not to allow them to blind us to their complexity. If we are to grasp that complexity, we must first note certain paradoxical aspects of ongoing changes in the modern industrialized world. To be sure, today's food system is based on technology, industry, and functionality. But these are not its only dimensions, and in the absence of certain other conditions the system would not have developed as it has. Of the various other dimensions involved, the most important may at first sight seem paradoxical—it is pleasure. If we are to understand the processes now at work, we must first explore the close relationship between two seemingly antithetical aspects of the modern food system: functionality and pleasure.

From Henry Ford to McDonald's

In Europe the industrialization of food processing and the inception of a large-scale modern food distribution system are relatively recent developments, mostly dating from the 1960s. By contrast, industrial products such as Coca-Cola have been sold in the United States for more than a hundred years. In the 1880s and 1890s, companies such as Heinz, Nabisco, Kellogg, and Campbell already ranked among the largest American firms, and by the end of the nineteenth century "agro-business" dominated American industry. Paradoxically, the discovery of bacteria and the ensuing obsession with germs encouraged concentration in the dairy industry. By the early twentieth century, milk producers were obliged to pasteurize their milk, and only firms able to make the substantial investment required survived. A modern mass distribution system emerged in the United States in the 1930s.[5] By studying what happened in the United States—the first country to start down a path that others would later follow—we can better understand what has been going on in Europe over the past thirty years.

In most developed regions of the world, changes in eating habits have followed the same general pattern as in the United States. In western Europe, for example, the major change has been a shift toward more individualized, less structured patterns of eating. A similar change was already being noted in the United States in the 1960s.[6] Salient features of American eating patterns can be observed today to one degree or another in various European countries, especially in the cities. One important indicator of change is the increased processing to which food is subjected at every stage of the distribution channel, from farm to factory to the consumer's table.

During the second half of the twentieth century, agriculture became increasingly concentrated and intensive. Different regions specialized in different crops. The old practice whereby farmers grew a range of crops and sold much of what they produced locally gave way to single-crop farming over vast territories. Trade was globalized, and production for domestic consumption decreased. Industrial processing is more and more the norm.

The distribution system has also changed profoundly. In western Europe, supermarkets proliferated in the 1960s at about the same time as automobiles, television, and leisure time; living standards and levels of education also rose. The mass distribution revolution had consequences at least as important as those of the industrialization of agriculture and food production, on which it exerted a considerable influence. The market for food became a mass consumer market. Food became a high-tech product. Designed, packaged, marketed, and advertised with the help of the latest techniques, food was distributed through increasingly complex and finely tuned commercial channels, which relied on elaborate logistical systems. Many foods carried brand names, at least initially (distributors later began using their own brands), and considerable sums were invested in advertising.

Within the space of two or three decades, a substantial portion of collective culinary effort was redirected from the kitchen to the factory. The processed, "marketed" foods that one read about in ads thus embodied greater and greater amounts of added value. Value was added first of all at the stage of preparation as industry took over much of what had been domestic labor. Processed food figured as part of what B. Sylvander has called the "food-service industry."[7]

As more and more women in advanced western societies took jobs outside the home, time at home became increasingly precious, particularly since men did little more housework than in the past. In the 1960s supermarkets in western Europe began selling products designed to reduce the number of hours devoted to household chores. The advent of "light" foods, which integrated eating with dieting, offered yet another way to "add value" in processing. Industry had long since targeted the kitchen as a potential market, and now it targeted dieters as well.

Not all changes in what people ate came in response to consumer demand. Distribution played a decisive role as early as the 1960s. It was governed by a variety of imperatives—logistical, technological, and economic. Pressure from distributors led to the development of products that were easier to store, ship, display, and preserve on store shelves. Farmers selected products on the basis of appearance and shelf life. Everything from fruit to cheese was altered in important ways. Supermarkets encouraged the use of plastic packaging for such things as bottled mineral water and vegetable oil, also in the 1960s. Bottles made of PVC plastic quickly came into widespread use in France because they are lighter, easier to transport on pallets, and less fragile than glass; nor do they need to be returned after use. Only much later did people begin to realize the environmental implications of this change. Some shoppers in France began to complain that their favorite cheeses were now frequently pasteurized, that most apples were now of the tasteless Golden Delicious variety, that many fruits came to market before they were ripe, and that bread no longer tasted the way they liked. But the supermarkets sold food at excellent prices, thanks to substantial economies of scale.

Supermarkets also made certain innovations possible. Only they had the logistical and technical capacity to market new families of products, which soon found buyers. Examples in France include certain brands of yogurt and other "fresh dairy products" as well as mineral water in plastic bottles—both products of which the French happen to be the world's leading consumers.

After two or three decades of change due to the combined effects of industrial food processing and new channels of distribution, eating habits are today being subjected to new pressures. The average standard of living has continued to rise. Consumers' energy requirements have diminished. Competition for the attention of distributors and consumers has become increasingly fierce. Markets have become "segmented," to use the terminology favored by students of marketing, and value added now seems more crucial than economies of scale. Hence food processing has become even more intense. Value is added by using high-tech methods and improving quality.

To take a particularly striking case of market segmentation, consider whiskey. In the 1950s American mystery novels and detective films made scotch a favorite drink of European males, who saw it as a drink with sex appeal. The whiskey sold at that time was "blended." Since then the market has diversified. First came the "aged whiskies," the "twelve-year-old scotches." Lately, the fashion has been for "pure malt" and "single malt" (that is, whiskey that is not blended but comes from a single distillery). Along with this shift has come a notable increase in prices and profit margins.

Or consider another example: camembert from Normandy (although it is true that "camembert" from Denmark enjoys greater sales worldwide, a Frenchman may be forgiven for regarding the Norman variety as more authentic). As supermarkets began to claim a growing share of the market for cheese in the 1960s, many people predicted the demise of the old-fashioned camembert made with raw milk ladled into molds by skilled cheese makers who alone possessed the essential know-how. Indeed, many believed that all of the traditional French cheeses would soon be replaced by indistinguishable processed cheeses made with pasteurized milk. But what actually happened was that as the market segmented, and certain raw-milk camemberts were in fact improved through the use of modern, high-tech cheese-making equipment. The old-fashioned cheese makers were replaced by robots, and a camembert of quality—superior on average to the traditional cheese of yesteryear—proved to be a highly marketable and profitable commodity.[8]

Modernity at Home: Microwaves and Freezers

In recent years, large numbers of households have acquired microwave ovens and freezers. In France an organization known as the Centre de Recherche et d'Études sur les Conditions de Vie has monitored this phenomenon. In the spring of 1989, only 19.9 percent of those questioned stated that they had one or the other of these devices in their homes. By the spring of 1990, it was up to 24.9 percent. By the end of 1990, according to one estimate, nearly a third of French households were so equipped.[9] And in 1995 the same source put the figure at 50.31 percent.[10]

In France the acceptance of the microwave has gone hand in hand with the frank and unreserved acceptance of frozen foods, which 95 percent of French households now use at least once a year, according to industry studies. In the early 1970s the restaurant critics Gault and Millau searched through restaurant garbage bins and lambasted those establishments whose trash contained empty packages of frozen food. At that time frozen food was seen as utterly fraudulent, the ultimate abomination of the industrial wasteland. Since then, however, French consumers have come to see it as fresher than fresh, a superlative way of delivering fresh food to the table.[11] Other technologies have also created new markets—for prewashed salads, for example, or precut vegetables.

Apart from price, three factors contributed to the success of these new products: taste, healthfulness, and convenience. But taste comes first: the "organoleptic," or pleasure value, of food is paramount.

Of course taste and healthfulness are culturally relative terms. "Health" is understood differently in England than in France. Most people in England believe that cheese is high in saturated fats that threaten their arteries, whereas most people in France look upon cheese and other dairy products as rich in calcium and essential to a balanced diet. My own research has shown that the French have, on average, far less knowledge of nutritional matters than do Americans or Scandinavians. Yet epidemiological studies show that the French are less likely to suffer from obesity and that their rate of mortality from coronary disease is the lowest of all the industrialized countries with the exception of Japan.[12]

Convenience is also a crucial factor. This may account for a striking paradox: one finds that people in most of the developed countries, and especially France, ascribe significant nutritional virtues to vegetables, yet consumption of fresh vegetables continues to decrease. Consumption of vegetables in convenient boil-and-serve form is on the rise, however.

Eating Out

As the scale of the market for food was changing, so, too, was the restaurant business. Throughout history there has been an intimate connection between home and hearth: the kitchen was central to the very idea of home. But with the approach of the third millennium, eating is no longer so closely identified with domesticity.

The patterns of daily life have been profoundly altered by urbanization, industrialization, the entry of women into the workforce, the rise in standard of living and level of education, the ubiquity of the automobile, and expanded access to leisure activities, vacations, and travel. People eat more of their meals outside the home. Among the French, 82 percent say that they eat out at least occasionally, and the average person eats out five times per week.[13] Businesses, schools, and communities often operate cafeterias. Various types of self-service restaurants appeared in Europe in the 1950s. And in the 1960s the "chain restaurant" arrived from the United States by way of England, where the hamburger chain Wimpy's established a substantial presence before extending its reach to the continent.

Fast Food

Fast food, another American innovation, did not become a significant force in Europe until the late 1970s or early 1980s, however. Its rise to dominance in the United States began in the 1950s as the leading franchises established outlets on major highways, in urban centers, and in the new shopping malls that eventually became the commercial centers of the sprawling suburbs. In many malls space was reserved for "food courts," designated areas in which a variety of restaurants offered a selection of fast food, including pizza, hamburgers, tacos, Chinese food, Japanese food, Greek food, Middle Eastern food, and even the occasional croissant.

In Europe today, the term "fast food" does not evoke such a disparate assortment of cosmopolitan cuisines, however. It refers rather to the ubiquitous McDonald's-inspired trinity: hamburger, ketchup, and fries (or rather "French fries," an appellation that sounds rather strange to French ears). Fast food, which sallied forth from the United States to conquer the world, is the application of Taylorism, division of labor, and rationalization to the restaurant business. Where but in the United States, asks Harvey Levenstein in his history of eating in North America, would anyone have attempted, as Burger King did, to serve "a complete meal in fifteen seconds?"[14]

Visitors to the United States have long observed two peculiar features of the natives' behavior: on the one hand, Americans have powerful appetites; on the other hand, they are determined to eat as quickly as possible. This is especially true of businessmen in places like Chicago and New York. Since the turn of the twentieth century, self-service restaurants in both cities have catered to a white-collar clientele. Customers order lunch at a counter and then sit down to eat. The pace of the whole operation is so fast that these cafeterias are sometimes referred to as "smash-and-grab places."[15]

Writers such as journalist Paul de Rousiers in the late nineteenth century and novelist Paul Morand in the early twentieth century were already astonished by what they saw in businessmen's restaurants where meals were served and eaten in less than half an hour: "Lunch time. The streets fill once more. In New York nobody goes home in the middle of the day. They eat wherever they happen to be: at the office, while working, in clubs, and in cafeterias. . . . In blue-collar restaurants, thousands of people eat standing up, with their hats on, all in a line, like horses in a stable. The food is fresh and appetizing, though, and prices are lower than ours. While lines of men dig in to plates brimming with meatballs, others wait to take their place."[16]

Note what strikes the French observer's eye: the fact that people eat at the office, "while working," and that working men eat with "their hats on" and lined up "like horses in a stable" (in other words, in a manner lacking human warmth and conviviality). But the food is "fresh and appetizing."

Europeans are constantly surprised by the Americans' relationship to food. In the United States the dinner hour is not clearly set off from the rest of the day. It need not have a well-defined existence. People can work and eat at the same time. Indeed, they apparently can eat while doing almost anything. In Europe dinner is, or at any rate was, a ritual occasion assigned to a specific time and place and protected against chaos and intrusions. It was considered improper to phone during the dinner hour, much less to visit. It was (and, to a large extent, still is) unthinkable to eat in the street or while driving or in an elevator.

Iraqi spies in Washington might have been more effective had they paid closer attention to the eating habits of the U.S. military; they might then have been able to warn Saddam Hussein of the imminent bombing of Baghdad: on the morning of January 16, 1991, eight hours prior to the attack, Domino's delivered 55 pizzas to the White House (as opposed to the usual 5) and 101 pizzas to the Pentagon (as opposed to the usual 3).[17] In efficient America, the home of Yankee pragmatism, the purpose of eating is above all to aid in the reproduction of labor power with virtually no interruption of the productive process.

According to Levenstein, the success of the new fast food franchises in the 1960s was due in large part to the American obsession with hygiene. After Pasteur showed in the late nineteenth century that bacteria were the cause of certain infectious diseases, microbes became a paramount concern of restaurateurs and food packers. The first hamburger chains, which appeared in the 1920s, were called White Tower and White Castle. White dominated their decor. In fact, the owners of the White Castle chain, anxious to reassure customers concerned about the safety of chopped meat, announced that they had chosen "white for purity."[18]

Ray Kroc, the founder of McDonald's, is generally credited with being the inventor of fast food, but that honor really belongs to the McDonald brothers, Dick and Mac, who came up with the "concept." But it was Kroc who developed that concept and made it the global force that it is today. In 1937 the McDonald brothers opened their first drive-in restaurant near Pasadena, California. They hoped to profit from their fellow Californians' growing dependence on the automobile. Their specialty was not hamburgers, however, but hot dogs. After making a fortune in the 1940s with a much larger restaurant near San Bernardino, they ran into trouble when teenagers began hanging out in the parking lot and driving family business away. In 1948 the brothers totally redesigned their restaurant, focusing on hamburgers rather than hot dogs and aiming to deliver the fastest possible service at the lowest possible cost. They eliminated silverware and dishes and used cardboard and paper packaging in order to sell burgers for the ridiculously low price of fifteen cents.[19] Success came quickly: the restaurant ceased to be a teenage hangout and soon was filled with blue-collar families, for there was nowhere else that people of modest means could afford to take their children. Once again, cleanliness and hygiene were an important part of the equation: customers could see for themselves that the kitchen was spotless and that all the fixtures were made of gleaming stainless steel. From the first, children were the McDonald brothers' most devoted customers, and the children brought in the adults.

It was at this point that the two brothers fully embraced the logic of Taylorism, or, rather, of Henry Ford: they brought assembly-line production to the restaurant business. Using a small number of low-skill and therefore low-wage workers trained in standarized procedures on specially designed equipment, they were soon able to fill orders within seconds. Their success inspired imitators and led the McDonalds to think of franchising their formula.

Unfortunately, they were not very good at franchising. That is where Ray Kroc came in. Kroc, a kitchen equipment salesman who had supplied the McDonalds with mixers, purchased the right to sell and manage McDonald's franchises in 1954. To that end, he founded a company called McDonald's in Chicago. He brought to the task skills that the McDonalds themselves lacked and worked hard to ensure that franchisees would be successful. Among other things, he was ruthless about quality control and saw to it that all franchised restaurants met standards established by the McDonald brothers.

In the 1950s and 1960s other chains such as Kentucky Fried Chicken joined the fray, first in the United States and later abroad. At this stage some chains hit on the idea of capitalizing on "ethnic" themes.[20] As early as the 1950s, one of the McDonalds' neighbors in San Bernardino adapted their techniques to serving Mexican food such as tacos; this was the origin of the Taco Bell chain.

It was in the late 1950s that another vogue was launched, this time for pizza. By 1970 Americans were eating two billion pizzas annually, and Yankee know-how was applied to the problems of producing this Neapolitan specialty, which was still largely unknown in the north of Italy. On the West Coast the pizza market had been dominated since the early fifties by Greek-Americans. They developed a new technology for making pizza: instead of rolling and kneading the dough just before baking, it could be prepared in advance, stored in metal containers, refrigerated, and then popped into the oven directly from the freezer. The Wichita-based company Pizza Hut, today owned by Pepsico, perfected this technique, which transformed pizza into a true fast food.[21] Neapolitan pizza makers may have been upstaged, but, as a result, American-style pizza has triumphed the world over.

Hamburger and Pizza

After rising to a position of dominance in the United States, fast food entered an era of global expansion. Initial results were mixed, much like the reception of Coca-Cola after World War II. Europe, just then recovering from the devastation of the war, discovered Coke with a mixture of delight and ideological horror. Similarly, fast food at first ran into major political opposition. During the Vietnam era, for example, many Swedes vehemently attacked the Americans for trying to force healthy Swedish youth to eat "plastic food" alien to native traditions. Much later, when McDonald's tried to open a rather discreetly designed restaurant on the Piazza di Spagna in Rome, a thousand people demonstrated against it. They were determined to defend local culinary traditions against the barbarian American invaders. This was the inception of the "Slow Food" movement, which still exists to this day.

McDonald's initial misadventures in France are worth recounting. In the late 1970s a French entrepreneur by the name of Raymond Dayan obtained a McDonald's franchise on terms that were apparently quite generous. According to some sources, the U.S. firm considered itself fortunate just to gain a foothold in a country whose gastronomic traditions, culinary requirements, and reputation (to some extent exaggerated) for anti-Americanism seemed to stand in the way of its ambitious plans for expansion. Dayan opened the first McDonald's restaurant in a shopping mall on the outskirts of Paris. He soon opened a number of others, each more successful than the last. In 1982 McDonald's attempted to repurchase the franchise. According to the company, Dayan had violated contractual commitments pertaining to quality and hygiene. After a hard-fought legal battle, the company won its case in a Chicago court. Overnight, all the McDonald's restaurants in France changed their name to O'Kitch. The O'Kitch chain was later taken over by a European firm, Hamburger Quick. McDonald's then reverted to its original policy of steady expansion. Today it enjoys a powerful position in France and many other countries. Although French gastronomy remains what it has always been, that has not prevented the French from developing a taste for hamburgers.

In the ideological arena, however, the objections were as vociferous as ever. The criticisms that were leveled at hamburgers in general and at McDonald's in particular were not directed at other types of fast food. The reason was that, in the eyes of many Europeans, especially southern Europeans, McDonald's is the very embodiment of the American "imperalism" that they believe is threatening their culinary traditions, traditions to which they cling all the more tenaciously as global pressures impinge on all sides. To read the literature and interpret the polls, one would think that the hamburger was the devil incarnate. It is accused of seducing the young, of doing damage to health and well-being, and of posing a threat to national integrity and identity. To date, the pizza has been exempt from such criticisms.

Oddly enough, the market for pizza is today just as large as that for hamburger. Pizza is sold not just by fast food chains but by practically every company involved in the food distribution business. In France and other western European countries, pizza can be purchased in bakeries and groceries as well as from street vendors. It can be ordered for home delivery as well as in restaurants of every sort, from the neighborhood bistro to the food stands at ski resorts. Pizza is now sold everywhere from Paris to Cuba and Berlin to Calcutta,[22] yet no one worries that Italian imperialism poses a threat to national identity or nutritional well-being. One hears no outcry against pizza from either orthodox gastronomes or professional nutritionists (despite the high saturated fat content of the thick layers of cheese found on American-style pizza).[23]

Cooking by the Numbers

In the heart of old Europe, in the very fiefdoms of gastronomy, professional cooks have adapted to new techniques. Since the 1970s, both commercial and institutional restaurants have made increasing use of processed foods—first canned foods and then frozen and powdered products. The 1980s saw the introduction of ready-mixed sauces and sauce bases, fish flavorings, and similar cooking aids.

More recently, restaurants and others have begun to use vacuum-packed foods and vacuum cooking techniques, which permit the use of relatively low temperatures. Depending on the ingredients, vacuum-packed foods can be kept for five to twenty-one days. Here we see a perfect example of a more general trend, which is to shift the labor of cooking from the kitchen to an earlier stage in the distribution channel; rather than prepare a dish for the table, the cook orders it instead from a catalog of ready-made items that only have to be reheated, or else orders various ingredients (vegetables, meat or fish, sauce) that can be assembled and finished off to taste. Thus the cook increasingly tends to be a food distributor rather than a service supplier. Even the great chefs have experimented with vacuum cooking techniques, which enable them to achieve flavors that can only be obtained by cooking at low temperatures. For some years now, major French distributors have been offering a number of precooked vacuum-packed dishes, but purists claim that for health reasons most of these products are actually cooked at temperatures much higher than the 130 to 140 degrees Fahrenheit (55–60 degrees Centigrade) typical of true vacuum cooking. The process is thus closer to traditional canning, with deleterious effects on taste.

Although restaurants are increasingly likely to make use of these modern techniques, consumers are not yet ready to accept them. In a recent French television program, a reporter approached a table at which a number of diners were clearly enjoying a very rustic and traditional meal served on a red and white checked tablecloth. He asked one of the women at the table how she liked the food and received a very positive response. But when he revealed that the dinners were actually precooked vacuum-packed meals that had simply been reheated in boiling water, the woman's expression turned to shock and incredulity. Two restaurants that publicly acknowledged their use of vacuum cooking went bankrupt.

Nor do consumers seem ready to accept the use of irradiation techniques for improved food preservation, even though such techniques are already in widespread use in some countries. And they are even less prepared to embrace genetically altered foods, which in the United States have been revealingly dubbed "Frankenfoods" or "Frankenstein foods."

Global Homogenization?

The globalization of agriculture, food processing, and distribution has resulted in extensive culinary syncretism, quite similar to the cultural syncretism that Edgar Morin describes in *L'Esprit du temps*. Global agro-business does not purely and simply destroy local culinary particularities. It integrates as well as disintegrates, yielding a universal syncretic mosaic reflecting what Morin, speaking of mass culture, calls "a veritable analytic 'cracking,' which transforms natural raw materials into homogenized culture products suitable for mass consumption."[24] Thus, even as agro-business eliminates local differences and peculiarities, it adapts exotic regional specialties to the global marketplace and ships the resulting standardized products all over the world. Traditional cheeses, which nowadays are hard to find and expensive, have been replaced by pasteurized versions, but the new processed French cheeses are eaten not just in France but in Germany and the American Midwest. Nestlé has been surprised at the brisk sales of its frozen moussaka in France. Swiss muesli is now commonly found on breakfast tables in England and France. Global agro-business borrows from the traditional cuisines it helps to destroy in order to expand the worldwide market for its homogenized, standardized wares.

It is a mistake, however, to think that the industrialization of food processing, improvements in transportation, and the advent of mass distribution must inevitably lead to the elimination of distinctive local and regional dishes. In fact, modernity in some situations encourages the formation of local specificities. This assertion can be supported by another American example—a relatively recent culinary innovation that developed into a full-fledged local specialty as proud of its authenticity as cassoulet or bouillabaisse, even though it can only be described as a transcultural mishmash. The dish I am referring to is scarcely known outside of its native city. It is "Cincinnati chili," named for the Ohio city where it has been a popular menu item since the 1920s. A student of American folklore has provided a detailed account of the rise of this regional specialty.[25]

Cincinnati chili is made of hamburger and stew meat combined with a dozen or more herbs and spices, including cinnamon. The mixture is then simmered for three to four hours and served in a variety of ways. The basic version comes on a bed of spaghetti and is known as "chili spaghetti." Add a layer of grated cheese and you get what is called "three-way chili." Add chopped white onions on top of this and you have "four-way chili." And top the whole thing off with a layer of beans and you have "five-way chili." The rules for Cincinnati chili are as strict as those governing any traditional cuisine. The dish is served in sixty-five "chili parlors" owned by several fast food chains as well as in most Cincinnati restaurants. And residents of the city, who look upon the dish as a local specialty, also make it at home.

Cincinnati chili was invented by Tom Kiradjieff, a Bulgarian immigrant who was born in Macedonia. In the 1920s he sold "coney islands," or "chili dogs" (a variant of the hot dog), outside the Empress Theater, whose name became the name of the restaurant chain that Kiradjieff would later found. Instead of using his leftover meat to make Mexican chili con carne, a common practice in local restaurants at the time, Kiradjieff introduced several innovations. He made his chili with pure beef, served it with spaghetti, and, most significant of all, developed a "syncretic" sauce using a number of different spices, some borrowed from the recipe for a chili dog and others taken from the Balkan cooking he had known as a child. At first he mixed everything together, as in an Italian pasta dish. It was not until 1930 that he had the idea of creating a layered, unmixed version of the dish.

Like other fast food restaurants, several Cincinnati chili chains have sought to expand their market. So far as I am aware, however, they have not succeeded in attracting customers in other cities. The Cincinnati chili case is almost a laboratory specimen: one can use it to analyze the process whereby culinary folklore is created, spread, and possibly bastardized in the age of agro-business. In Europe a dish is not considered authentically traditional unless its roots can be traced back to rural civilization. Industrialization is seen as a destroyer of culinary traditions. Yet here in Cincinnati one has an example of the inception of a culinary tradition in a modern industrial city.

Rationalization, Regression, and Pleasure

Whenever one looks at fast food restaurants such as McDonald's, one question constantly arises: what accounts for their universal success? To this day, the Chicago firm seems never to have met with failure. A number of material, commercial, and financial factors have contributed to this unbroken record of success. The franchise system developed by Ray Kroc was based on a principle of mutual support: the company helped its franchisees to get rich, and in return the franchisees promised to abide by all its rules and to do nothing that might injure the reputation of the company. In the 1980s roughly a quarter of McDonald's franchisees in the United States were millionaires.

Still, additional problems stood in the way of exporting the successful McDonald's formula to other countries. There was, first of all, the problem of anti-Americanism. And there was another problem, one that McDonald's had learned how to cope with in the United States: while the chain owed much of its initial success to its popularity among young people, especially teenagers, it was far more profitable to target a family clientele.

In addition, there was the further difficulty, more complicated than is often realized, of adjusting McDonald's menu to other culinary cultures. At first sight the menu appears to be the same everywhere: hamburgers, cheeseburgers, chicken McNuggets, and so on. In fact, subtle variations exist from country to country. In France, for examples, the chain had to develop new sauces because its original ones were apparently too sweet. Elsewhere certain items are omitted from the menu. The choice of ingredients is not always the same. Meal schedules are a problem in some European countries. Take Disneyland Europe, for example (an operation in which McDonald's is not involved). Marketing studies in the United States estimated that 50 to 60 percent of visitors to the theme park near Paris would eat fast food during their visit. Whatever the validity of these studies, a European imponderable was left out of the equation: it appears that French, Italian, and other European tourists are not prepared to eat hamburgers at ten in the morning or five in the afternoon, as many Americans apparently are. At precisely 12:30 P.M., these Europeans tended to queue up outside the park's restaurants, abandoning all the other attractions. At other times, the restaurants remained empty. These movements interfered with standard crowd control measures. The park's designers had overestimated the flexibility of Europeans and the degree to which their eating habits had been "destructured."

No doubt the global success of McDonald's and other fast food chains is linked to certain culinary "universals." Fast food is not simply functional, and customers do not choose to eat fast food solely for reasons of convenience, price, and time.

In fact, the range of its tastes and textures amounts to a least common denominator of most people's preferences. The softness of the hamburgers and buns, the sweet sauce, and the sweet-and-sour ketchup reproduce the taste sensations of childhood, a kind of regression coupled with transgression. In the presence of their parents, who look on with fond approval, very young children are able to act independently: change in hand, they are free to march up to the counter and order their own burgers and Cokes. They can eat with their fingers, forgetting the table manners that are obligatory at home. Their little teeth can sink into the soft buns and chopped meat and the food that all the polls show they love best of all: salty, greasy French fries, crisp on the outside and tender on the inside.

Basic tastes, gratifying textures, transgressive freedoms, family consensus, convenience, price, hygiene, and standardization—no one anywhere has yet come up with a formula to compete with this, other than by imitation.[26]

NOTES

1. W. Parker Chase, *New York: Wonder City* (New York: New York Bound, 1983), originally published in 1932. Quoted in J. Gleick, *Genius: The Life and Science of Richard Feynman* (New York: Pantheon, 1992).

2. A. Oger, "Ils préparent nos menus de l'an 2000," *VSD,* no. 223, February 18, 1982, pp. 25–27.

3. In France, the most recent data from the Institut National de la Statistique et des Études Economiques show that only about three million women (15 percent) still stay home rather than work.

4. P. Skrabanek and J. McCormick, *Follies and Fallacies in Medicine* (Buffalo, N.Y.: Prometheus Books, 1990); C. Fischler, *L'Homnivore: Le goût, la cuisine et le corps* (Paris: Odile Jacob, 1990); Fischler, ed., *Manger magique* (Paris: Autrement, 1994).

5. H. *Levenstein, Revolution at the Table: The Transformation of the American Diet* (New York: Oxford University Press, 1998); and *Paradox of Plenty: A Social History of Eating in Modern America* (New York: Oxford University Press, 1993).

6. Fischler, *L'Homnivore.*

7. B. Sylvander, *L'Alimentation-service: Résultats des enquêtes* (Paris: Département d'Economie et de Sociologie Rurales de l'Institut National de la Recherche Agronomique, 1988).

8. See P. Boisard, *Le Camembert, mythe national* (Paris: Calmann-Lévy, 1992).

9. *Points de vente,* no. 393, 1990.

10. CREDOC, *Aspirations et modes de vie des Français,* ongoing survey.

11. This change came about largely because of the development of technology for freezing fish as it is caught. Between 1980 and 1988, consumption of frozen foods in Europe doubled. By 1988 it was on the order of 44 pounds per person per year in the most developed countries. In France, frozen-food consumption reportedly tripled between

1980 and 1994 (according to a 1994 report by the Association Nationale des Industries Agro-alimentaires). By contrast, sales of fresh vegetables and fish have been stagnant or on the decline. Already, for example, the French eat more frozen spinach than fresh spinach.

12. See, for example, M. Appelbaum, "La diète prudente est-elle bien raisonnable," in *Manger magique,* ed. Fischler, pp. 179–83.

13. P. Hébel and C. Renault, *La Restauration hors foyer en 1994,* 2 vols. (Paris: CREDOC, 1994).

14. Levenstein, *Revolution;* Levenstein, *Paradox.*

15. Levenstein, *Paradox,* p. 227.

16. Paul de Rousiers, *La Vie américaine* (Paris: Firmin Didot, 1892).

17. P. Tonello, "Undici miliardi di fette," *La Gola,* nos. 90–92, p. 26.

18. Levenstein, *Paradox,* p. 228.

19. J. F. Love, *McDonald's: Behind the Arches* (New York: Bantam Books, 1986).

20. For an interesting but controversial account of how big business captured the vogue for things ethnic, see W. Belasco, *Appetite for Change: How the Counterculture Took on the Food Industry, 1966–1988* (New York: Pantheon, 1989).

21. Levenstein, *Paradox,* p. 230.

22. In Cuba, according to newspaper reports, a state-run pizza shop is constantly forced to turn away customers.

23. The outbreak of "mad cow disease" in Europe has offered further encouragement to the consumption of pizza. Since March of 1996, hamburger consumption has suffered because of the suspicion surrounding all beef, especially industrially processed chopped meat.

24. E. Morin, *L'esprit du temps,* 2d ed., 2 vols. (Paris: Grasset, 1975), p. 85.

25. T. C. Lloyd, "The Cincinnati Chili Culinary Complex," *Western Folklore* 40, no. 1 (1980): 28–40.

26. Although there has been a recent onslaught in Paris of Italian *panini* revised and corrected to suit French taste. These are small breads filled with prosciutto, mozzarella, tomato, and olive oil and then heated in a two-sided grill that leaves marks on both sides of the sandwich. *Panini* will probably never outsell fast food, but they do open up a new market niche, offering a touch of the Mediterranean to city people obliged to eat on the run.

CONCLUSION
TODAY *and* TOMORROW

Jean-Louis Flandrin and Massimo Montanari

In the nineteenth century, militants of the Workingman's International used to chant about wiping the slate of history clean and starting over. To what extent has the capitalist economy of food succeeded in doing just that? What is left of the various "eating behaviors" that we have described in this book, behaviors that took centuries to develop? Do they still exist today? And if so, do they have a future?

Coca-Cola has long been drunk everywhere in countries whose cultures are as diverse as can be. Over the past thirty years, American fast food chains, led by Mc–Donald's, have come close to achieving a similar ubiquity. Nowadays, Europeans drink orange and grapefruit juice from cans, bottles, and cartons, thus obediently following the recommendations of modern nutritionists and celebrating the cult of the vitamin. Many of these fruit juices are also imported from America.

The power of American capitalism is not the only factor at work, however. There are even more pizzerias in Europe than there are fast food restaurants. In most of continental Europe, white bread has become the norm, even in countries where natural conditions make it difficult to grow wheat and where people of all classes once saw no shame in eating black bread. Everywhere the meat ration has increased, and class differences in meat consumption have decreased—even in Mediterranean countries where, until recently, a more vegetarian diet had been common.

Coffee drinking has also increased dramatically everywhere, even in Great Britain, where tea was traditional. It is increasingly common to drink beer, even in countries where the traditional drink was wine, cider, or mead. By the same token, wine has become more common in countries traditionally associated with beer, even as it has declined in countries noted for their production of grapes.

Some distinctive differences have even been stood on their heads: the Germans, who once consumed extraordinary quantities of meat, are now more likely to be vegetarians than the French. The same is true of the English. And the French, who for a long time shunned the grilled and roasted beef that their neighbors across the Channel loved, now seem more wedded to their daily beefsteak than are the English. But even these reversals are rooted in each nation's history, and in Europe traditional differences with respect to eating behavior have proved extremely persistent.

Although meat rations have been converging across the continent, they are still lower in southern Europe than in the north. Furthermore, each nation prefers certain meats over others: beef and mutton in England, pork in Germany, veal in Italy. As for fish—which, thanks to refrigerated trucks and railway cars, can be now be bought reasonably fresh in most parts of western Europe—the Swiss and Austrians still eat much less than do people in nonlandlocked countries.

Even though wine consumption has been rising in beer-drinking countries such as Germany, England, and Belgium, beer is still by far the most consumed fermented beverage. And even though wine consumption has declined in France and other wine-making nations, it is still much higher there than in the countries of the north.

Ireland, which was the first country to make the potato a dietary staple, is still the largest per capita consumer of potatoes. Next comes Germany, which also played a prominent role in the history of the tuber. And while the Germans now eat more wheat than rye, they still consume a far greater quantity of the latter than do the French. The same is true of the Poles. It is hard to decide, moreover, whether this difference between the behavior of the Germans and Poles on the one hand and the French and Italians on the other is due more to persistent differences in natural conditions or to durable habits and traditional tastes. Much the same thing can be said about buckwheat, which is virtually unknown in much of Europe but which still plays an important role in Brittany, where buckwheat pancakes are eaten, and in Poland, where it is used to make *kasza* (a sort of porridge of crushed buckwheat).

Furthermore, even when a food gains popularity across the continent, it is rarely the same in every country and may not be used in the same way everywhere. Take white bread, for example. Although more white bread than black bread is now eaten in all countries, it varies from place to place. The presliced, industrially baked white bread of England and the United States has little in common with French, Italian, or Spanish breads. This variety has a long history.

While most Europeans now drink orange and grapefruit juice, often with breakfast, as in the United States, the Americans and English drink vitamin-enriched juices, which many Europeans do not like and which are hard to find in some countries. And while Swiss chocolate has dominated the French market for some time, the Swiss chocolate sold in France is not the same as that sold in Switzerland. Even when the brand name is the same, the sugar content is adjusted to suit French taste. As for coffee, the beverage that goes by that name in the United States and northern Europe bears little resemblance to the coffee drunk in Italy or even in France. Nor is it drunk in the same way or in the same circumstances: the French, Italians, and Spanish generally do not take coffee along with their main meal, but Americans often do.

If Coca-Cola is virtually the same everywhere, its status varies. In France Coke is seldom drunk during dinner, at least by the older generation, whereas the practice is common in the United States regardless of age or sex. And if McDonald's is a cheap, popular place to eat in the United States, it is a deluxe restaurant in Moscow and Peking.

When it comes to cooking and serving techniques and table manners, the story is the same. Shorter cooking times and even uncooked foods have become popular in most European countries as the cult of the vitamin has captured new devotees. The new dietetics and the new aesthetics of physical beauty have forced cooks everywhere to limit the calorie and fat content of what they make: starches, flour-thickened sauces, sugar, butter, lard, and many other once popular ingredients are no longer in favor. Grilling is now in vogue for the same reason, and this has led to the development of new equipment for barbecuing and making fondues. Steaming in various kinds of baskets, couscous makers, and self-cookers has also become popular. Ready-to-eat foods and fast food restaurants are now common throughout Europe, so Europeans can now eat at any time of the day, as in the United States.

Although the French and English still sit at the table as they have always done—the French with their hands on the table, the English with their hands under the table—the French seem to have forgotten their traditional style of laying the *couvert* (setting) with a concave dish on the bottom and a convex one on top. Even in the most elegant restaurants (except for Troisgros), this custom seems to have gone by the boards. The hotel schools all teach restaurateurs to use the English-style setting. It has become common to serve dinner directly on the plate, simplifying both service and table manners. This custom seems to owe more to the traditions of India and Japan than to traditional western conviviality.

Nevertheless, it would be an exaggeration to say that cooking techniques, table service, and manners have been internationalized. The art of the sauce, which is all but unknown or misapplied in many European countries, continues to flourish in France and Belgium. The order in which dishes are served in France, though of relatively recent origin, is nevertheless strict. And it is just as strict, if not more so, in Italy, where pasta must be eaten as a first course, never as a side dish or garnish. The same countries are also strict about what may be drunk with dinner: wine, water, beer, or possibly cider may be served, but in principle neither soda nor fruit juice nor coffee nor tea is acceptable.

To be sure, sociologists and marketing experts have been somewhat too hasty to declare traditional dining patterns dead and buried. Even in big cities and among young people, regular meals are still the norm in France, Italy, and Spain. And if the distinction between a meal and a snack is less obvious in England, hours of dining are still just as rigid there as on the continent. In short, if anomic eating behavior is becoming more common in Europe, it is not yet as widespread as in America. Furthermore, it is not obvious that it will ever supplant traditional forms.

Indeed, the social function of dining is still important in Europe. Europeans do not eat simply to assuage a physical need but also to see relatives and friends with whom they like to share the pleasure of dining. In order to enjoy this convivial activity, they must keep to a common schedule and bring a certain ceremony to the occasion. In fact, eating rituals vary widely, not just according to country and social class but also according to the occasion and type of meal. No matter how simple, however—a snack shared between friends, say—there is a little more ceremony, a little more conversation, a little more social exchange than one finds around a bag of popcorn in the stands of an American stadium or on the living room couch in front of the television.

Clearly, then, the "standardization" of eating behaviors has not yet passed the point of no return. If consumption patterns are becoming increasingly similar, substantial differences remain. Appearances may be misleading, moreover, because common elements are interpreted in different ways in different countries. Local traditions, the result of a long and complex historical process, still exert a powerful influence.

Will this diversity survive? We think so, for the trend toward more homogeneous behavior tends to make many people react by developing a strong attachment to their own identity. Recent political events have demonstrated the truth of this assertion: wherever an attempt has been made to normalize and universalize identities, the reaction has been strong and sometimes violent. We see the same thing in connection with food and gastronomy—crucial elements in defining any historical identity, as we have tried to show throughout this book. Despite ambiguities and misunderstandings of all sorts, national cuisines have been "rediscovered" and local gastronomic traditions revived while at the same time the food-processing industry has tried to deny their importance. Regional cuisines are today a part of the national patrimony, and people are probably much more aware of them than in the past.

Indeed, in years past, every regional cuisine was inextricably intertwined with the local system of food production, at least as far the lower classes were concerned. Because of this necessary link, culinary traditions did not always engender a sense of pride at being a member of a certain community. In fact, tradition was often seen as a limitation or constraint, which people hoped one day to transcend. Peasants who worried about having enough to eat frequently relied on foods that could easily be stored for long periods. If this meant uniformity, that was a small price to pay for survival.

At the opposite end of the social scale, the elite contrived to enjoy an artificial cuisine assembled from every imaginable type of food; every vestige of local identity was erased, and this independence of circumstance became the principal mark of alimentary privilege. "Only the common man is content to eat whatever the land provides," Cassiodorus wrote on behalf of his sovereign, Theodoric, in sixth-century Gothic Italy. A thousand years later, Bartolomeo Stefani, the chef of the Gonzagos, wrote a treatise on cooking in which he explained that a nobleman should not have to worry about food being in season or about the natural limitations of the region in which he happened to live, because with a "substantial purse" and a "good charger" he could have whatever he wanted all year round.

In a sense, the food industry has today realized this ancient dream. Democratic as well as oblivious of regional differences, it has made it possible for everyone to eat whatever they like wherever they like, albeit at a price. The reaction, however, has been a frenetic, often chaotic quest to preserve local traditions. The food industry itself has been quick to seize on this novel trend—and we stress the word "novel"—by packaging and selling what used to be considered fit only for the poor as the very latest in elegant dining. Nowadays, local seasonal ingredients are highly sought after. This latest turn of events only seems paradoxical. In fact, it is the logical outcome of a transformation of the system of production that once appeared likely to have the opposite effect.

Thus to insist on regional differences and the preservation of cultural identity is not backward or reactionary. It is in fact the latest thing, an outcome possible only because of recent changes that have yet to be fully consolidated. A related point needs to be made as well, and it is worth making explicit even if it seems obvious: traditions are not really fixed once and for all at the moment of their inception. They are created, shaped, and defined over time as cultures interact, clash, and influence or absorb one another. This process has been quite evident in the pages of this book. Every culture is "contaminated" by other cultures; every "tradition" is a child of history, and history is never static. At the dawn of the Middle Ages, Roman eating habits were changed by contact with barbarian customs. Not only did Roman consumption patterns change but so did Roman taste. The same thing happened when Europeans discovered certain American plants and animals. But major cultural interactions of this sort are only part of the story. Every day people make new discoveries, encounter new foods, and have new experiences out of which they construct both individual and collective identities. Identity is both confirmed and reshaped by experience.

People speak, at times misleadingly, about a so-called Mediterranean pattern of eating, as if geographical circumstances alone were enough to dictate certain common choices and habits. But how many "Mediterranean diets" are there? And how many of those are "purely" Mediterranean? Think of what has gone into them: the American tomato, pasta (which came to Europe through exchanges with Arab traders), fruits and vegetables from Asia, and so on. Clearly, there is no such thing as a "pure" identity.

These considerations are especially important in this day and age, because food—and people—can travel more rapidly than ever before. What history teaches us is that change is inevitable and that there is no point in longing for the past—a past, bear in mind, that was often haunted by hunger.

Our generation, like those that went before, must learn how to manage the relationship between past and present, tradition and change. To do this in a reasonable, balanced way is a mark of intelligence. It also enables us to enrich our gastronomic heritage and explore that "proper sensuality" to which the humanist Platina devoted a famous book in the fifteenth century. It would please us, as it must have pleased him, to contribute to that end.

INDEX

Ale, 172, 278

Almanach de gourmands (Grimod de La Reynière), 364, 420, 476, 494, 504

Almond milk, 323

Almonds: in Arab cooking, 212, 215; in Carthage, 60; in classical Greece, 83; introduction into Europe, 222; in Jewish diet, 226, 227, 239; in Phoenicia, 56

Almosama, 228

Alphita, 81

Alziari, Dr., 425–26

Amadeus VIII of Savoy, 365

Amber, 212, 410

American Medical Association, 523

Amram Efratí ben Meru'am, 231

Anacreon, 103

Anchovies, 216

Ancienne Alsace à table (Gérard), 505

Ancien Régime, regional cooking during, 500–502

Andirons, 340

Androphagi, 157

Angoulême, Marguerite d', 359

Anima, 121, 122

Animal husbandry: in early Middle Ages, 169; in Etruria, 108–9; in Rome, 115; in Scythia, 157

Aniseed, 42

Anne of Austria, 386

Annona, 115, 127

Anonimo Veronese, 336

Antelopes, 120

Anthimus, 141, 150, 179

Antiphanes, 87

Aphrodisiacs: mandrake, 41; truffles, 218

Apicius, 132, 134

Appert, Nicolas, 463, 486, 494

Appetite: as expression of nationalism, 180, 431; role in food selection, 425

Apples: in Arab cooking, 212, 219; in Carthage, 59; in classical Greece, 83; in Jewish cooking, 225; in Phoenicia, 56; in Rome, 35; when to eat, 321

Apricots, 219, 321, 420

Arab cuisine. *See* Muslims

Archaeology, as source material on cooking, 296

Archilochus, 97

Ardouin-Dumazet, [name?], 509

Aristocracy. *See* Elites

Aristophanes, 84, 87, 154

Aristotle, 159–60

Aristoxenus, 102

Arouet, François-Marie (Voltaire), 387, 429–30

Arrian, 159

Art: classical Greek, 99; Etruscan, 110–11; Paleolithic, 26, 27; as source material on cooking, 296

L'Art de bien faire les glaces d'office (Emy), 399

L'Art de bien traiter (L. S. R.), 367, 407, 408, 419

L'Art du bien manger (Richardin and Fulbert-Dumontheil), 506

L'Art du cuisinier (Beauvilliers), 495

Artichokes: in Arab cooking, 216; Chinese, 361; in early modern period, 361, 363; in France, 404; Jerusalem, 358

The Art of Cookery (Glasse), 414, 417

Asparagus: in Arab cooking, 216; in Arab diet, 217; in early modern period, 361; in France, 404; in late Middle Ages, 265; preservation of, 487, 490; wild, in Rome, 121, 125

Aspic, 215

Assam, 391

Association des Gastronomes Régionalistes, 512

Assurbanipal, 36

Assurnasirpal II, 35, 57

Athenaeus, 106

Athens, 81, 86

Attica, 81

Audot, L. E., 505

Augustus, 115

Aurochs, 14, 26, 171

Australia, 393, 450

Australopithecus, 22, 23

Austria: fish consumption in modern, 449; potato consumption in, 445

Auvergne, 352

Avocadoes, 469

Chefs. *See names of individual chefs*

Cherries, 321, 420

Chervil, 316

Chesterfield, Lord, 367

Chestnuts: in Carthage, 60; in late Middle Ages, 270; pork and, 356; when to eat, 321

Chicken: in ancient Egypt, 42; in Arab cooking, 214, 215–16; in Carthage, 61; in Etruria, 109; in Great Chain of Being, 310; in Jewish cooking, 226; in late Middle Ages, 264, 265; modern consumption of, 449; in Rome, 120; sauces for, 323

Chickpeas: in Arab cooking, 215, 217; in classical Greece, 82; in early Middle Ages, 173; in Etruria, 108; in Greco-Roman period, 72, 135, 136; in Jewish cooking, 227, 231; in late Middle Ages, 265, 270

Chicory: as coffee substitute, 388–89, 453; in early Middle Ages, 173; in Rome, 135

Chidra, 85

Childbirth, Jewish celebratory foods for, 227–28

Children: at banquets, 94; butter consumption by English, 300; vegetable gardens and, 253, 265

Chiles, 358

Chili spaghetti, 544

Chinese artichokes, 361

Chocolate: Aztec preparation of, 385; introduction into Europe, 385–86; plantations for production of, 386; trade in, 360, 380

Cholesterol, food reform movement on, 526

Christianity: alcoholic beverages and, 201; Arab food habits and, 191–92; charity as public hospitality in, 288; forests and, 254; impact on Roman food culture, 117, 166; impact on sacrifice, 77; Jewish meat and, 190, 234–35; meat renunciation in, 183–84, 190; Muslim food taboos and, 191–92; sacred foods in, 166. *See also* Catholic Church; Fasting; Religious orders

Cicero, 134, 136

Cider, 272, 452

Cider vinegar, 318

Cincinnati chili, 544

Cinnamon: in Arab cooking, 212; in improvement of digestibility, 318; in Italian baroque cooking, 410; medicinal uses of, 316; in sauces, 323

Cinquanta cortesie overo creanze da tavola (Croce), 334

Circumcision feasts, 228

Cirio, Francesco, 487–88

Cistercians, 263

Citrus fruits: in ancient Egypt, 41; in Arab diet, 210, 215; in Byzantine Empire, 199; consumption in modern Europe, 550; diffusion of, 219; importation into modern Europe, 465; introduction into medieval Europe, 191; in late Middle Ages, 271, 298; nutrient content of, 465. *See also names of specific fruits*

City dwellers: Arab diet, 210; bread and countryside dwellers versus, 304; diets in Greco-Roman period, 76–77, 85–87, 120; diets in late Middle Ages, 249

Civility, concept of, 330

Civil War, in United States, 489

The Clafoutis (eating club), 508

Class, diet and differences in. *See* Status, social

Clausse, Jean-Claude, 1

Clibanus, 136

Clieu, Captain de, 388

Clinton administration, 527

The Clouds (Aristophanes), 84–85

Cloven hooves, 52. *See also* Taboos

Cloves: in Arab cooking, 212; medicinal uses of, 315–16, 316; in sauces, 323

Club des Cent, 510

Cluny, 260–63

Coca-Cola, 548, 550

Cocks, 82

Coconut oil, 458

Coconuts, 41

Cod, 314

Coena. See Cena

Coffea arabica. See Coffee

Coffee: introduction into Europe, 387–88; in modern Europe, 453–54, 549, 550; origins of cafés and, 387; preparation of, 386–87; production of, 388, 389; trade in, 360, 380, 388

Coffeehouses, 386, 390

Coffeemaker, Du Bellloy filter, 387

Cold versus hot foods, 316, 317, 318, 320, 321

COLE ACP, 470

Columbus, Christopher, 384

Columella, Lucius Junius Moderatus, 60, 130, 134

Colza, 82

Colza oil, 437, 457, 459

Comedic literature, as source on cooking, 296

Comité des Travaux Historiques, 507

Commerce. *See* Trade

Common Market, 460, 462, 463, 470

Compagnie du Niger Français, 461

Companagium: budget for, 303; definition of, 302

Compendium of the Effects of Different Foodstuffs (Simeon Seth), 202

Complantatio, 253

Conclusions sur le boire à la glace et à la neige (Alziari), 425–26

Condorcet, Marquis de, 387

Confitures, 395–96, 397, 409

La conserve alimentaire (Corthay), 495

Constantinople, 387

Consuetudines (Udalric), 260, 262

Contades, Marshall de, 1

Conti, Prince de, 475

Contour, Alfred, 505

Conuiuium (convivium), 124

Convenience foods, 524–25

Convivality: Cicero on, 136; dining and, 18–20, 370

Cookbooks: in Arab world, 210, 212, 218; cuts of meat specified in, 406; dessert, 397, 399; dietetics and, 322–24; English, 416; frozen food, 497; illustrations in, 399; innovations in, 396–400; organization of, 395, 396; origins of, 364–68; regional cooking in, 501, 505–6; Renaissance, 394–96; as sources on foods introduced into Europe, 222; as sources on medieval cooking, 296–97, 345; women

authors of, 366, 414, 416, 417. *See also* Literature, of food

Cookie makers, guilds for, 281

Cooking: acids in, 213–14, 215, 298, 408, 422; as art, 431; *la cuisine minceur,* 439; digestibility and, 317–19, 427; digestion as form of, 143, 316, 427–28; functions of, 76, 148; "good" taste in, 430; numbers of ingredients in early modern period, 380; numbers of ingredients in Roman, 134; regional, 380–81, 382 n.11, 440, 500–514, 543–44; versus rotten food, 121–23; seasoning and art of, 212–14, 298–99; social impact of, 25–26; source material about, 295–97, 361–62, 381; sun and, 119, 121; symbolism of, 29–30; techniques for meat, 17, 179, 215, 363–64, 406–7, 414–16, 422–23; techniques in early Middle Ages, 173–74; techniques in late Middle Ages, 259; techniques of modern, 550. *See also types of food preparation*

Cooking equipment, 233, 341–42; in ancient Egypt, 42, 43; in Arab world, 211–12, 215, 218; in classical Greece, 83; in early Middle Ages, 174; in Etruria, 110; in Jewish culture, 232–33, 235, 238; in late Middle Ages, 340–42, 346; in Rome, 135–36. *See also* Mortars and pestles; Ovens

Cooks: at court, 212; in Rome, 136; as specialists, 29, 86; women as, 212, 236. *See also names of individual chefs*

Coot, 314

Copper sulfate, 495

Copra, 458

Corcellet, 506

Coriander: in ancient Egypt, 42; in Arab cooking, 213, 217; in Jewish cooking, 239

Cormorants, 359, 404–5

Corn, introduction of, 355–56, 377, 443. *See also* Polenta

Correctives for Various Foods (Razes), 220–21

Cortés, Hernando de, 359, 360, 384, 385

Corthay, Auguste, 495, 496

Corvée, 264

Cottonseed oil, 460

Country dwellers: Arab diet, 210; bread and city dwellers versus, 304; in Greco-Roman period, 76–77, 84–85

Cours gastronomique (Cadet de Gassicourt), 504

Court: cooks at, 212; diets in Byzantine Empire, 201

Court-bouillon, 406

Courtesy, concept of, 330

Couscous, 210, 218–19

Cranes, 416; consumption decrease of, 359, 405; cooking for digestibility, 317–18

Cremonne, Baptiste Platine de, 400 n.2

Critias, 104

Croce, Giulio Cesare, 312, 334

Crop rotation, 254, 378

Croze, Austin de, 506, 512

Crusades, 315

Crustaceans: in Carthage, 61; in Etruria, 109; in Great Chain of Being, 309; in Greco-Roman period, 74; in Jewish culture, 48

Cuba, 392, 393, 547 n.22

Cubebe, 316

Cucumbers: in Arab diet, 217; preservation of, 487

Cuisine de santé (Le Cointe), 399

La cuisine minceur, 439

Le Cuisinier à la bonne franquette (Granchamp), 505

Le Cuisinier bourguignon (Contour), 505

Le Cuisinier français, 366, 407, 419

Le Cuisinier françois (La Varenne), 322, 396–97, 422

Le Cuisinier gascon, 2, 505

Le Cuisinier impérial (Viard), 494

Le cuisinier landes, 505

Le Cuisinier moderne (La Chapelle), 398

Le Cuisinier roïal et bourgeois (Massialot), 398

La Cuisinière bourgeoise (Menon), 399, 407, 408

La Cuisinière de la campagne et de la ville ou la nouvelle cusine économique (Audot), 505

Cumin: in ancient Egypt, 40, 42; in Arab cooking, 213; medicinal uses of, 316

Cupbearers, 34–35

Curcuma, 316

Curius Dentatus, 126

Curlew, 416

Curnonsky, 506, 508, 510

Cyceon, 82

Dairy products: in ancient Egypt, 41; ancient Hebrews and, 47, 50; in Arab cooking, 209, 211, 213; in Carthage, 61; in classical Greece, 82, 85; in early Middle Ages, 171–72; in Etruria, 109; fortification of, 522; in Jewish cooking, 227, 232, 239; modern consumption of, 450; in peasant diets, 450; in Phoenicia, 57; in Scythia, 157. *See also* Cheese; Milk

Dais, 114

Da quinquaginta curialitatibus ad mansam (de la Riva), 334

Dates: in Arab cooking, 212, 215; in Carthage, 60; in Jewish cooking, 225; in Muslim diet, 209; in Phoenicia, 56–57; in Rome, 129, 135; wine in ancient Egypt, 41

Datini, Francesco de Marco, 305

Dayan, Raymond, 541

The dead: Egyptian offerings to, 38; food of, 154. *See also* Funeral meals

De alimentorum facultatibus (Galen), 150

De antiqua medicina (Hippocrates), 148, 149

Decameron (Boccacio), 310

"Deceptive" dishes, 221

De civilitate morum querilium (Erasmus), 332

Deer: in classical Greece, 82; in early Middle Ages, 171; in Etruria, 109; in Mesolithic period, 14; in royal banquets, 35; symbolism of, 29, 31 n.15

Deforestation: effect of, 168–69, 254; meat-based diet effect on, 77–78; symbolism of, 167. *See also* Forests

De honesta voluptate et valetudine (Platina), 366–67, 395, 400 n.1

Dei, Benedetto, 304

Deleyre, Alexandre, 503–4

De l'honneste volupté (Platine), 400 n.2

Delicatessens, 282–83

Les Délices de la campagne (Bonnefons), 367

Della Casa, Giovanni, 332, 333, 335

Drinking societies, 368

Drunkenness, 372, 453

Du Bellloy filter coffeemaker, 387

Dubois, Urbain, 477

Duchesne, Joseph, 318, 319, 426–27

Ducks: in ancient Egypt, 42; in Arab cooking, 214; in classical Greece, 82; in early Middle Ages, 171; in Etruria, 109; in Great Chain of Being, 310

Dum, 41

Dumaine, Alexandre, 479

Dumas, Alexandre, 432

Dunkirk, 460

Dutch East Indies Company, 389

Dutertre, Father, 467

Dyer, Christopher, 303

Eagles: in English cooking, 416; in Great Chain of Being, 310

Earth, in Great Chain of Being hierarchy, 309–11

East Indies, 386, 388

Eating out, 537. *See also* Restaurants

Ecclesiastics. *See* Religious orders

L'École des gourmands (Chazet et al.), 513 n.1

Ecuador, 386

Eels: in ancient Egypt, 42; in Carthage, 61; in Rome, 130; salted, 314; sauces for, 323

The Effects of Good Government (Lorenzetti), 284

Eggplant: in Arab diet, 210, 217; introduction into Europe, 191, 221, 357; in Jewish cooking, 231, 238

Eggs: in ancient Egypt, 42; in Arab cooking, 213, 215, 216, 218; in Carthage, 61; in diets of monastics in late Middle Ages, 261; in diets of nobility in late Middle Ages, 259; in Etruria, 109; in Jewish cooking, 226, 227, 229, 238, 239; modern consumption of, 451; in monastic cooking, 184; in Rome, 125, 135; in royal banquets, 35

Egypt, ancient: alcoholic beverages in, 40, 41, 42; banquets in, 19, 38–39; condiments in, 42–43; cooking equipment in, 42, 43; cooking methods in, 43; dairy products in, 41; elite diet in, 13, 38–39; fish in, 42; food storage in, 43; funeral meals in, 38; legumes in, 40; meat in, 39, 41–42; number of daily meals in, 43; spices in, 42; tableware in, 43, 44; vegetables and fruits in, 39, 40–41; written recipes and, 16–17; yeast in, 39–40

Einhard, 179

Eiximenis, 336

Elderly: butter consumption by, 300; vegetable gardens and, 265; wine consumption by, 425. *See also* Age

Elegiac symposium, 103

Elias, Norbert, 332

Elites: Arab diet, 210; banquets and, 93, 123, 131; bread consumption decrease and, 361; cooking equipment of, 341; culinary regionalism of, 507; dietary studies of, 5; dietetics and, 142; diets in Byzantine Empire, 201–2; diets in late Middle Ages, 249; diets of ancient Egyptian, 13, 38–39; eating habits of modern, 552; French influence on European, 416; frugality and Roman, 137; game associated with, 29, 57; as gourmets, 367; lodging of, 473–74; mealtimes of European, 369–70; meat consumption by, 363; obligations of Roman, 130; pasta and, 283; plebeian dishes eaten by, 135; preserved foods and, 495; public hospitality and, 289; sauces and, 408; soft animal parts consumption by, 134–35, 405–6; starch consumption decrease and, 404; symposium and, 97–98; vegetables and, 421. *See also* Nobility

Ember days, 261

Emy, 399

Enclosure movement, 353

Endive, 173

England: attitude toward French cooking in, 416; banana consumption in, 467; beer consumption in modern, 452; books of secrets in, 366; bread consumption in, 303; butter consumption in, 300, 417; chocolate introduction into, 385–86; coffee introduction into, 388; cookbooks, 416; cooking tradition in America and, 517; diet

Food production systems. *See* Agriculture

Food quality, inspection for, 211

Food reform movements, 517–21, 522, 525–26

Food reserves, 26

Food riots, 249

Food safety, 286

Food science. *See* Dietetics

Food-service industry, 534–35

Food shortages: bread, 354–55; cooking fuel, 198; due to war, 523; grain, 352. *See also* Famines

Foreign aid, impact on local agriculture, 438

Forest famines, 175

Forests: as emergency food source in Middle Ages, 254; importance in Middle Ages, 178–79; peasant access in Middle Ages, 181, 248. *See also* Deforestation

Forks: history of, 332; use at table, 3, 368–69. *See also* Tableware

Forster and Smith, 459

Fourth Crusade, 196

Fowl. *See names of specific fowl*

Foxes: in classical Greece, 82; in Etruria, 109

France: alcoholic beverage consumption in modern, 452; aristocracy lodging in, 473–74; banana consumption in, 467; bread shortages in, 354–55; butter consumption in, 300–301; caloric intake in, 454–55; chocolate introduction into, 385–86; coffee consumption in, 453–54; cooking techniques in, 406–7, 422–23; dining rooms in, 368; egg consumption in modern, 451; export of cuisine of, 479; fast food in, 541; fat intake in modern, 461; fish consumption in, 372, 449; food industry in, 494–96; fruit consumption patterns in, 322, 362–63; hierarchical dining rituals in, 370; influence on European cooking, 366; landholding patterns in, 353; legume consumption in, 445; mealtimes in, 369; meat consumption in, 404–6, 414, 447, 448, 549; meat cooking technique changes in, 414–16; milk consumption in modern, 450; nutrition knowledge in, 537; oil consumption in modern, 451; origins of

restaurants in, 472; population growth in, 375; potato acceptance in, 444; potato consumption in, 357, 445; potato introduction into, 377; public inns in, 293; regional cooking in Ancien Régime, 500–502; salt consumption in, 412; shortening in, 462; specialty food shops, 531; spices in, 373, 408–9, 423; sugar consumption in, 392, 409, 446; table manners in eighteenth-century, 369; tariffs set by, 466; tea introduction into, 389–90, 391; tropical oils and, 459; vegetable consumption changes in, 404; wine consumption in modern, 451–52

La France pittoresque et artistique, 511

France pittoresque (Hugo), 509

Francolin, 214

Franks, 182. *See also* Barbarians

"Free people in arms," 181

Freezers, 536–37

French beans, 490

Frères Provençaux, 503

Friandise, 365

Friands, 431

Fricasses, 238

Fritters, 227

Frontal yoke, 253

Frozen foods, 497, 536–37, 546–47 n.11

Fruges, definition of, 117

Fruit: in ancient Egypt, 41; in Arab cooking, 210, 212, 215, 219; Bible on, 56; in Byzantine Empire, 195, 197–98, 199, 203; candied, 191; in Carthage, 59–60; in classical Greece, 83; in colonial America, 517; as desserts, 420, 424, 426; dietetics and, 321–22; in diets of nobility in late Middle Ages, 259; dried, in Jewish diet, 226, 231; in early modern period, 322, 362–63; Galen on, 321; in Great Chain of Being, 309; as hors d'oeuvres, 363, 364, 420; in Jewish cooking, 229, 231; juices, 454; in late Middle Ages, 271; in meal sequence, 321–22; measurements of, 37 n.8; mixed with meat in European cooking, 411; modern consumption of, 445–46; modern

Heat, in food preservation, 484–85, 486

Hebrews. *See* Jews

Hecataeus of Miletus, 58

Heddle, Charles, 458

Hedgehogs, 82

Height statistics, 351, 352, 516–17, 532

Heinz Company, 489, 533

Hemp oil, 458

Hempseed, 239

Herbs: in Arab cooking, 213; in early Middle
Ages, 173; in Greco-Roman period, 72; in
Rome, 118, 134. *See also* Spices; *names of
specific herbs*

Herodotus, 84, 156–58

Heron, 359, 405, 416

Herring, 314

Hesiod, 101

Hesychia. *See* Poetry

Heylin, Peter, 414

Hierophilos, 202

Hindus, food taboos of, 16

Hines, Duncan, 525

Hippocras (*hypocras*), 261, 283, 285

Hippocrates, 141; on age, 146; on balance in
health, 143; on cooking, 148–49; *Diet* of,
81–82; on foods, 144, 145; on gender, 147;
humors and, 75–76

Hispaniola, 388, 392

Hobsbawm, E. J., 448

Holidays, religious. *See names of specific
holidays*

Holland: chocolate introduction into, 385, 386;
coffee trade and, 388; fat intake in modern,
461; milk consumption in modern, 450;
potato consumption in, 445; potato
introduction into, 377; tropical oils trade in,
460

Homer, 58, 91, 96, 99, 154

Homo erectus, 25

Homo habilis, 22, 25

Honey: in ancient Egypt, 42; ancient Hebrews
and, 47, 51; in Arab cooking, 212, 215; in
Byzantine Empire, 199; in Carthage, 61; in
classical Greece, 82, 84; in Jewish cooking,
226; in Phoenicia, 57; preservation of, 42;
tastes of, 320

Honeycombs, 39, 135

Hoover, Herbert, 521

Horace, 133

Horse meat, 14, 26, 214

Hospitality: *cena* and, 125–26; desert, 209;
symbolism of, 33, 99. *See also* Banquets;
Public hospitality

Hot and dry foods, 316–17, 320, 422, 423. *See
also* Cold versus hot foods

Hoteliers, regional cuisine and, 511

Hot peppers, 358

Houten, Conrad Van, 386

Hugo, Abel, 509

Humbert II of Viennois, 295

Humors, four: in Byzantine Empire, 202; in
dietetics practice, 419–20; in Greco-Roman
period, 75–76, 143

Hungary, 358

Hunger, religious orders and, 183

Hunter-gatherers, 71–72, 258

Hunting: in Byzantine Empire, 202;
collaborative, 26–27; diversified, 24–26; in
early Middle Ages, 171; in Etrutria, 108–9; in
Greco-Roman period, 72, 73, 74; as image of
war, 178–79; in late Middle Ages, 265; in
Mesolithic period, 14, 15; in Neolithic
period, 29; nobility and, 178–79, 181;
opportunistic, 26; organized, 23, 26–27, 109;
in Paleolithic period, 14, 20, 26–27; in
Phoenicia, 57; prehistoric man and, 14, 23;
Roman breeding farms for, 120; versus
scavenger theory of prehistoric diet, 22–23,
24, 30n.9; as servile occupation, 121;
specialized, 26–27. *See also* Forests; Game;
Wild boar; Wild foods

Hylophagi, 158

Hymn to Demeter (Homer), 154

Hymn to Hermes (Homer), 154

Hypocras. See Hippocras.

Iambic symposium, 103

Ibycus, 103

restrictions on eating with *goyim,* 54, 190;
Rosh Hashanah, 225; Sabbath, 224–25;
seating arrangements at table, 330; spices in
cooking of, 239; Sukkoth, 226; tableware of,
233–34; taste characteristics of, 237; typical
daily diet of, 239; unleavened bread and, 227;
vegetables in cooking of, 225, 227, 229, 231,
238, 239; wedding celebrations of, 228–29;
wine in diet of, 226, 231; Yom Kippur,
225–26

John Cortasmenos, 203
John Kaloeidas, 203
John Lackland, King of England, 277
Joubert, Laurent, 425
Judah, 57
Jujubes, 41
Juniper berries, 42
Jurgens, Jan, 461
Jussieu, Antoine de, 388
Juvenal, 133

Kale, 173
Kano-Lagos rail line, 460
Kaplan, Steven, 354
Kausch, Joseph, 412
Keftiu oil, 43
Kellogg, John Harvey, 520
Kellogg Company, 533
Kentucky Fried Chicken, 540
Kiradjieff, Tom, 544
Kitchen accounts: in dietary studies, 5; as sources
of cooking information, 295–96, 361
Kitchens: in Arab world, 211–12; Jewish, 232–33,
236; in late Middle Ages, 259, 343; of
Muslims, 211–12; of nobility in late Middle
Ages, 259; of religious orders, 262, 263; of
Rome, 135–36; soup, 202; street, 471–72
Kneading basins, 235, 259
Knives: in ancient Egypt, 43; use at table, 3,
233
Kohler (chocolate factory), 386
Kohlrabi, 173
Komos, 101
Kondros, 85

Korsion, 40
Kosher. *See* Jews
Kosher, definition of, 54
Kraters, 71, 98
Kroc, Ray, 539, 540
Kulkas, 217

L. S. R., 367
Labat, Fr., 367–68, 415, 423
Labor: cooking and division of, 25–26; gender
and division of, 23, 212
Laboratores, 181
La Chapelle, Vincent, 398
Lamb, 35, 323. *See also* Mutton; Sheep
Lamprey: in Middle Ages, 171; sauces for, 323,
422
Lancellotti, Vittorio, 365
Les Landes de Bordeaux (Saint-Sauveur), 502
Landholding patterns: in Byzantine Empire, 195,
196; in classical Greece, 79–81; in early
Middle Ages, 167, 181; in early modern
period, 352–53; in Etruria, 108; in feudalism,
253, 254–57; in France, 353; in late Middle
Ages, 248, 257–58; of peasants, 195, 256,
352–53; of Roman Catholic Church, 183; in
Rome, 115, 117–18
Lando, Ortensio, 1
Languedoc, 351
Lard, 261, 273, 457
Lares, 118
La Reynière, Grimod de, 364
La Rochefoucauld, François de, 414, 416
Latium, 120, 269
Lauder, John, 417
Laurel, 265
Lauric acid, 458
Laurioux, Bruno, 315, 316
La Varenne, 396–97, 407
Leavening, sourdough as, 39–40
L'Écluse, Charles de, 357
Le Cointe, Jourdain, 399
Leeks: in Arab cooking, 213; in classical Greece,
82; in early Middle Ages, 173; in Greco-
Roman period, 72; in Jewish cooking, 225,

178–80; forests and, 254; hunting and, 178–79, 181; kitchens of, 259; landholding patterns of, 255–57, 353. *See also* Elites

Nomads: Aristotle on, 160; barbarians as, 71–72

Nomos gheorghikos (peasant law), 195

Noodles: in Arab diet, 215, 218; in Jewish diet, 230. *See also* Pasta

Norway, milk consumption in modern, 450

Nosoco, 461

Nostradamus, 366

Notarial records, as historical source material, 5

Nougat, 191, 225, 226, 239

Le Nouveau Cuisinier roïal et bourgeois (Massialot), 398, 399

Le Nouveau et Parfait Maître d'hôtel (Lune), 365

Nouveau Traité de cuisine (Menon), 398

La Nouvelle Instruction pour les confitures, les liqueuers et les fruits, 397, 398

Nuns. *See* Religious orders

Nutmeg, 212, 316

Nutrition. *See* Dietetics

Nuts. *See names of specific nuts*

Oats, 173; in early modern period, 377, 380; in Jewish cooking, 230; in late Middle Ages, 269

Odo, Abbot of Cluny, 181

Offal, 280

Oils: at ancient Egyptian banquets, 39; as condiment with beans in Rome, 134; cooking, in ancient Egypt, 43; cosmetic function of, 19; importation of tropical, 437, 457–63; at Mesopotamian banquets, 34; modern consumption of, 451; in Phoenicia, 56; salads and, 325; as symbol of civilization, 73. *See also* Fats; *names of specific oils*

O'Kitch, 541

Oleomargarine. *See* Margarine

Olive oil: in ancient Egypt, 43; in Arab cooking, 213; Catholic Church regulations and, 417; in classical Greece, 84, 86; in Jewish cooking, 237; in late Middle Ages, 271, 301; production in Syria and Palestine, 56

Olives: in Byzantine Empire, 195, 198; in Carthage, 59; in classical Greece, 80; in early

modern period, 363, 377; in Etruria, 108; in Jewish cooking, 229; in late Middle Ages, 271; in Rome, 125, 131; in royal banquets, 35

Onager, 214

Onions: in Arab cooking, 213; in Arab diet, 217; in classical Greece, 82; in early Middle Ages, 173; in Great Chain of Being, 309; in Greco-Roman period, 72; in Jewish cooking, 227, 238; in late Middle Ages, 265, 271; in Rome, 118

Opusculum de saporibus (Magninus of Milan), 316, 317, 318, 322, 323

Orache, 82

Oranges: in Arab cooking, 215; in early modern period, 361; extinction of varieties of, 437; modern importation into Europe of, 465. *See also* Bitter oranges

Organ meats, 280

Orgeat, 232

Oribasius, 141

Origo, Iris, 306

Orphics, 74

Ortelius, 384

Orvieto, 110, 111

Ostriches: eggs, in Carthage, 61; in Rome, 129

Other: definition of, 154–55; Greek concept of, 153, 155; pigs as symbol of, 191; Roman Catholic concept of, 192, 203; Roman concept of, 114

Otium, 124

Ouverture de cuisine (Casteau), 2

Ovens: in ancient Egypt, 43; in Arab world, 211, 215, 218; in Carthage, 59; communal, 340; indoor versus outdoor, 339; in Jewish culture, 235; in late Middle Ages, 259, 277; in Rome, 135

Oven tenders, 277

Ovid, 135

Oviedo, Fernández de, 384, 385

Oxen, 35, 170, 311

Oxtails, 406

Oysters: in classical Greece, 82; digestibility and, 319; in early modern period, 382 n.10; in Rome, 120, 122

P. Apuleius, 141

Packaging, for foods, 535. *See also* Storage of food

Padilla, 238

Pain à tout, 281

Pain de bouche, 281

Pain de mollet, 281

Pain de tout blé, 281

Pakistan, 469

Palaeologi, 198

Paleolithic period, 14, 20, 26–27

Palestine: citrus fruit production in, 465; olive oil production in, 56; wine trade in, 57, 58

Palm oil, 458, 460, 463

Pan cenceño, 231

Pandemain, 281

Papin, Dennis, 486

Paprika, 358

Papyrus Anastasi IV, 39

Papyrus rhizome, 40

Parboiling, 407, 415

Paré, Ambroise, 320

Parmentier, Antoine Augustin, 355, 357

Parsley: in Arab cooking, 218; medicinal uses of, 316

Parsnips: in early Middle Ages, 173; in early modern period, 361; in Rome, 118

Partridges: in Arab cooking, 214; in classical Greece, 82; in Etruria, 109; in late Middle Ages, 265, 323; social status and consumption of, 305, 311

Passion fruit, 469

Passover, 227, 238

Passover of the Huts, 226

Passum, 60

Pasta: development of trade in, 283; introduction into Europe, 191. *See also* Noodles

Pasteur, Louis, 484, 486

Pasteurization, 483–84, 486

Pastries: cookbooks on, 397; in late Middle Ages, 281, 341

Pastry makers, guilds for, 281–82

Pâté: makers of, 281, 473; origins of, 2; spices in preservation of, 314

Le Pastissier françois (Gaillard), 397

Patmos, 200

Peaches: proverbs against eating, 324; when to eat, 321, 420

Peacocks: in banquets, 359; consumption decline of, 405; in English cooking, 416; in Rome, 120

Peanut oil, 437, 459, 460, 461, 462

Peanuts, 358, 459

Pears: in Carthage, 59; with cheese, 325; in classical Greece, 83; proverbs against eating, 324; when to eat, 321, 322, 420

Peas: in classical Greece, 80, 84; flat, 265; green, 173; in late Middle Ages, 265, 270; preservation of, 487, 488, 490; yellow, 173

Peasants: ale and, 172; Arab diet, 210; bread in diets in late Middle Ages, 264; culinary regionalism of, 507; dairy products in diets of, 450; dietary studies of, 5; diets in Byzantine Empire, 198, 201; diets in classical Greece, 81, 84–85; diets in early Middle Ages, 169–72, 174; diets in early modern period, 381–82; diets in late Middle Ages, 248–49, 258, 263–66, 269, 270, 271, 272, 273; forest access of, 181, 248; function in Middle Ages, 181–82, 255; hospitality and, 291; hunger and, 183; idealization of, 501–2; Industrial Revolution effect on, 438; landholdings patterns of, 195, 256, 352–53; meat in diets of, 180, 273; nobles' diet versus, 178–80; taxation of, 255–56; tithes of, 170, 351–52; vegetable gardens of, 253, 265, 271; vegetables and, 181, 311–12, 420–21; wine in diets in late Middle Ages, 264

Pecudes, definition of, 117, 118

Peddlers, 279, 286

Pelicans, 42

Pellagra, 356, 443

Pelletier, 386

Penance: diets on days of, 265; Orthodox Church use of fasting as, 201; Roman Catholic Church use of fish as, 171

Pennyroyal: in classical Greece, 82, 85; medicinal uses of, 316

Carthage, 59–60; in classical Greece, 83; in Jewish cooking, 225; in Persephone myth, 154; in Phoenicia, 56; wine in ancient Egypt, 42

Pomelos, 465

Pompeion, 93

Pontac, Jean de, 473

Poo, Fernando, 386

The poor: Byzantine Empire banquets for, 201; dietary rules for, 142, 210; food for, in Rome, 128, 133, 134. *See also* Status

Popinae, 136

Poppy seed oil, 457, 459

Poppy seeds: in ancient Egypt, 42; in Arab cooking, 215; in classical Greece, 82

Population: agriculture impact on growth, 15, 350, 378–79; of barbarians, 375–76; distribution in Byzantine Empire, 195, 197; diversity of growth of, 374–76; England and Industrial Revolution growth of, 374–75, 378–79, 481; Middle Ages and growth of, 174–75, 252; migration patterns and, 442, 481; modes of growth of, 376–77; natural resources and growth of, 377–78; nineteenth century and growth of, 437–38; plague effect on, 236, 248, 350, 374–75, 376; potatoes and growth of, 379; source material for study of growth in, 375

Pork: in ancient Egypt, 41–42; in Carthage, 61; delicatessens in late Middle Ages and, 282–83; in France, 448; in Germany, 449; in Great Chain of Being, 311; in Greco-Roman period, 74, 77–78, 135; Hebrew taboos against eating, 47–48, 52–53; Muslim taboos against eating, 16, 191; as rural food in late Middle Ages, 249, 273; salted, 314, 364. *See also* Pigs

Porpoises: consumption decline of, 405; sauces for, 323

Porridge: in Arab cooking, 218; in early modern period, 380; invention of pottery and, 28; in late Middle Ages, 269; in Renaissance cookbooks, 396; in Rome, 132

Porta, Carlo, 331

Portugal: egg consumption in modern, 451; fish consumption in modern, 449; milk consumption in modern, 450; population growth in, 376; sugar consumption in, 299; sugar production and, 384

Posca, 131, 134, 198

Poseidonius of Apamea, 106, 107

Potatoes: adoption of, 357, 444; famine and, 378; introduction of, 355, 356–57, 377; macaque washing of, 18; modern consumption of, 445, 549; nutrient content of, 444; population growth and, 379; prejudices against, 356–57; as substitute for other foods, 382 n.11

Pots and pans. *See* Cooking equipment

Pottage, 29

Pottery, cooking and, 28

Potts, R., 24

Poultry. *See names of specific fowl*

Le Pourtraict de la santé (Du Chesne), 426–27

Prandium, 107, 124, 126

Prata, 118

Prehistoric man: diets of, 14, 21–22, 28; scavenger versus hunter theories of, 22–23, 24, 30n.9; seasonality in diet of, 22, 27. *See also* Hunting

Preservation, food: acidic liquids in, 213–14, 216; adulteration in, 495; basic ingredients for, 314; controlled fermentation in, 18, 486; decomposition control in, 485–86; definition of, 492; drying techniques, 211; of fruit, 59–60, 226, 231; of game, 487; heat in, 484–85, 486; ice in, 419, 425–26, 490, 496; industrialization of, 533–36; industrialization of bread, 483–84; industrialization of wine, 484–85; industry changes and refrigeration systems in, 483, 490–91; of legumes, 490; of meat, 17–18, 27, 41, 174, 198, 249, 382 n.10; of milk, 488, 489; origins of techniques of, 487, 488–90, 493–95, 533–34; research on, 496; salt in, 58, 211, 249, 412 (*See also* Salted foods); spices in, 313–15; sugar in, 486;

traditional methods of, 498; of vegetables, 412, 487, 488, 490, 497; wood role in, 342

Preserves, 395–96, 397, 409, 493

Prices, food: fruit shipments, 464; grain, 443, 482; oils, 463; in Rome, 115

Priests: food taboos and Hebrew, 47, 51; food taboos and Roman, 119; religious banquets and Mesopotamian, 36. *See also* Religious orders

Primates: as carnivores, 24; macaque potato washing, 18; omnivorous, 13

Primitive man. *See* Prehistoric man

Privacy, concept of, 333

Processed foods. *See* Preservation, food

Procope, 387, 472

Prohibition, 522

Projet de dixme royale (Vauban), 381

Prose Edda (Snorri Sturluson), 180

Protectionism, 462, 466, 467, 490

Protein sources: in early Middle Ages, 171; in late Middle Ages, 264

Protestantism, 526–27, 528. *See also* Christianity

Proverbs, dietetics and, 324, 325

La Prune (eating club), 508

Prunes, when to eat, 420

Prussia, 357

Psellus, 203

Psychology Today, 528

Ptisane, 82

Public hospitality: Catholic Church on, 289; charity as, 288; coerced sovereign, 288, 290; government regulation of, 288, 289, 291, 292; history of, 287–89; inns, 291–94; lower classes and, 289; in primitive cultures, 287; religious orders and, 289, 290; unconditional basic, 288, 290, 291. *See also* Hospitality; Inns; Taverns

Puerto Rico, 468

Pulmentarium, 131, 132–33, 174

Puls punica: eggs in, 61; recipe for, 58, 134–35

Pumpkins, 238

Punicum, 59

Purim, 226–27

Purslane, 82

Pythogoreans, 74

Quadrupeds. *See* Meat

Quail: in ancient Egypt, 42; in Arab cooking, 214

Quinces: in Arab cooking, 219; in classical Greece, 83; in Jewish cooking, 239; in Phoenicia, 56; when to eat, 321

Rabbits: in Arab cooking, 214; in Carthage, 61; in late Middle Ages, 265; sauces for, 323

Rabelais, François, 359

Racking, 485

Radishes: in Arab diet, 217; in early Middle Ages, 173; in Jewish cooking, 227; in Rome, 135

Raisins: in Arab cooking, 212, 215, 219; in Carthage, 60; medicinal uses of, 315–16; in Phoenicia, 57

Ramadan, 208

Randoin, Lucie, 378

Raoul of Houdenc, 296

Rape: in Greco-Roman period, 72; in Rome, 134

Rape oil, 459

Rare meat, 415

Raw versus cooked foods, 119

Ray, John, 414–15

Razes, 220–21

Razor fish, 109

Ready-to-eat foods, 550

Reagan administration, 527

Recipes: beef, 422–23; boar sauce, 134; broad beans, 134; first written, 16–17; how to read medieval, 297–98; in Jewish cooking, 237–39; in late Middle Ages, 297–98; meat sauces, 323; oysters, 319; pears in red wine, 322; in Persian cooking, 209; piquant sauce, 408–9; *puls,* 58, 134–35; sauce for fish, 239, 323; spices for sick persons and, 323–24, 424; *tharid,* 209; for Yom Kippur, 231

Red mullet, 61

Red pepper, 358

Reformation, 349, 372

Refrigeration systems: effect on food habits, 497–98; food preservation industry changes and, 483, 490–91; trade expansion due to, 464

Regimen conditum (Fagarola), 322–23

Regimen corpus (Aldobrandino of Siena), 316

Regimen sanitatis (Magninus of Milan), 318

Regional cooking, 380–81, 382 n.11, 440, 500–514, 543–44

Reindeer, 14, 26

Relatio de Legatione Constantinoplitana (Liutprand of Cremona), 203

Religious orders: chocolate and Mexican, 385; dietary restrictions on, 263; diets in Byzantine Empire, 200; diets in early Middle Ages, 174; diets in late Middle Ages, 260–63; fasting among, 183, 261; fish consumption by, 405; function in Middle Ages, 181; hunger and, 183; kitchens of, 262, 263; privacy concept and, 333; public hospitality and, 289, 290; renunciation of meat by, 183–84, 190; self-sufficiency of, 262; vegetables, 183, 184. *See also* Catholic Church; Christianity; *names of specific orders*

Religious rituals: bread and, 40, 240, 241; bread and Eucharist, 77; pigs in ancient Egyptian, 42; wine in, 57, 241. *See also* Banquets: religious; *names of specific holidays*

Renaissance period: courtly entertainment during, 329; printed texts of, 394–96

Residual analysis, 30 n.9

Resin, 199

Restaurants: Boulanger affair, 474–76; chain, 537, 539–40; definition of, 475; French Revolution impact on, 475–76; versus guilds, 474; Industrial Revolution effect on, 436–37; in nineteenth century, 476–77; origins of, 472–74; street kitchens, 471–72; tourism and, 477–78; in twentieth century, 478–80. *See also* McDonald's; Taverns

Rhizophagi, 158

Ribash, 231

Rice: in Arab diet, 210, 215, 218; consumption increase of, 444; introduction into Europe, 191, 221, 377

Riera, Jaume, 239

Ritz, César, 478

Roasting, 179; in Arab cooking, 215; larding prior to, 415

Rochefort, César de, 429

Rochefort, Jouvin de, 411, 412, 413

Rodinson, Maxime, 315

Roe, fish, 42

Roman Catholic Church. *See* Catholic Church

Rome: agriculture in, 72, 115, 117–18, 121, 129; bread in, 75, 125, 126, 131, 132, 303; *cena* in, 107, 114, 123–24; Christian impact on food culture of, 117, 166; classification of foods in, 121–23, 133; condiments in, 131, 134; conquest effects on food in, 129; cooked versus rotten food concept in, 121–23; cooking equipment in, 135–36; dairy products in, 133, 135; diet and conquest and, 161; dietetics in, 75–76; domestic versus wild meat, 119–20; fish in, 74, 120, 121, 122, 130, 133; food model of, 73, 77, 78, 129, 165–66; food symbolism of, 114–15, 116, 117, 125; food taboos in, 136–37; fruit in, 123, 125, 129, 131, 135; funeral meals in, 135; gardens in, 118–19; government regulation of food in, 129, 131, 132, 137; grains in, 72, 82, 85, 115, 119, 132; honor concept in, 114–15; hot versus cold meals in, 134–35; kitchens of, 135–36; legumes in, 72, 80, 82, 119, 133, 134, 135, 136; markets in, 115, 120, 121, 130; meal patterns of, 107, 124–25; mealtimes in, 124; meat in, 74, 77–78, 119, 120, 122, 133, 134 (*see also* Meat); "Other" concept in, 114; public hospitality in, 288–89; sacrificial animals in (*see* Sacrifices: of meat in Greco-Roman period); social status and food in, 128, 130, 134; sociology and study of food in, 137–38; spices and herbs in, 72, 118, 134, 135, 315; tableware in, 136; taxation in, 129, 130; vegetables in, 72, 118, 121, 125, 126, 127, 128, 133, 166; wine and, 71, 114, 125, 131, 134. *See also* Banquets

Roquette, medicinal uses of, 316
Ros, 264
Rösener, Werner, 270
Rose water, 212, 216
Rosh Hashanah, 225
Rotterdam, 460
Rouff, Marcel, 510
Rousiers, Paul de, 538
Rousseau, Jean-Jacques, 371
Roux, 407
Royalty, banquets of, 33–36
Rue, 202, 422
Rumination, 52
Rumpolt, 365
Rural areas. *See* Country dwellers
Rus, 121
Russia: importation of linseed oil from, 457;
    sugar consumption in, 392; tea introduction
    into, 391
Rye, 173, 377; in Jewish cooking, 230, 239; in
    late Middle Ages, 268; in modern period,
    443, 444

Sabbath, Jewish, 224–25
Saccaromycetes, 39–40
Sacchetti, Franco, 280
Sacchi, Bartolomeo, 366
Sacred land, 79–80
Sacrifices: in ancient Egypt, 41; of ancient
    Hebrews, 47, 51, 54, 230; blood, 90, 92, 113;
    Christian impact on, 77; game and, 74; Greek
    concept of, 153–54; human, 158; Jewish meat,
    240; of meat in Greco-Roman period, 74,
    82, 91, 113–14, 119, 121, 122, 123, 124–25;
    processed foods in, 51; study of
    Mediterranean society and, 137; in symposia,
    101
Safflower oil, 463
Saffron: in Arab cooking, 212, 213, 221; Fr. Labat
    on, 423; in Jewish cooking, 239; in Polish
    cooking, 413
Sage, 202; in late Middle Ages, 265; medicinal
    uses of, 316
Sailland, Maurice Edmond. *See* Curnonsky

Saints, Byzantine, 199
Saint-Sauveur, J.-S., 502
St. Anthony, 191
Salads: in Ireland, 411; in Jewish cooking, 238;
    proverbs against eating, 324–25; in Rome,
    118, 133
Salmon, 314
Salon d'Automne, 511
Salons de thé, 476
Salsify, 361
Salt: in ancient Egypt, 42; in Arab cooking, 213;
    in Byzantine Empire, 195; in Carthage, 61;
    European consumption of, 411–12; in fruit
    hors d'oeuvres, 363, 364; in Jewish cooking,
    239; medicinal uses of, 318; in Phoenicia,
    57–58; salads and, 325; symbolism of, 19, 33;
    taxation of, 411; *Le Viandier de Taillevent* on,
    323
Salted foods: alcoholic beverage consumption
    and, 413; in Arab world, 220; in early Middle
    Ages, 174; in early modern period, 364; fish,
    42, 314; in Great Chain of Being, 311; illness
    attributed to, 325; in late Middle Ages, 249,
    273, 285; meat, 122, 314, 325, 364; rarity of,
    314; in Rome, 136; taste for, 413; vegetables,
    412
Salumerias, 282–83
Salviat, François, 83
Santo Domingo, 388, 392
São Tomé, 386
Saqqara, 38
Sardines: in Arab cooking, 216; in Byzantine
    Empire, 202
Satires (Horace), 133
Sauces, 323; black pepper, 323; boar, 134; butter
    in, 407, 409; camel, 222; changes in making
    of, 407–8; dietetics and, 323; elites and, 408;
    fat- and sugar-based, 362, 407, 408; fish, 239,
    323; green, 408; *jance,* 323; in Jewish cooking,
    239; lamprey, 323, 422; meat, 323, 422;
    medicinal aspects of, 316; modern, 551;
    piquant, 408–9; in Poland, 411; spices in, 323;
    vinegar in, 323, 408
Sauerkraut, 412

179; dietetics and, 142, 182, 363; food and, in Rome, 128, 130, 134; food in late Middle Ages and, 260, 304, 305–6; meat and, 305, 306, 311; quality of person and, 182; of servants, 37 n.9, 307; source material on food and, 304–5; spices and, 314; vegetables and, 312

Steaming, of foods, 210, 550

Stearin industry, 458

Stefani, Bartolomeo, 552

Stews: in France, 406; in Jewish cooking, 225, 238; in late Middle Ages, 265; *pulmentarium* as, 132–33

Stimulants, 212. *See also* Chocolate; Coffee; Tea

Stoicism, 148

Storage of food: in ancient Egypt, 43; of grains, 211; in late Middle Ages, 343; in modern period, 443; wine, 343, 485

Storia Augusta, 78, 166

Storks, 359, 405

Stouff, Louis, 314

Strabo, 91

Strawberries: in Great Chain of Being, 309; when to eat, 420

Street kitchens, 471–72

Strontium/calcium ratios, 30 nn.1, 2

Sturgeon: in Byzantine Empire, 202; in Carthage, 61; salted, 314

Suchard chocolate factory, 386

Sudan, 460

Suet, 457

Suez Canal, 460

Sugar: in Arab cooking, 210, 212, 219; beet, 392, 437, 459; changes in use of, 424, 427; in colonial beverages, 360; consumption of, 299, 373, 384, 391–92, 409, 411, 446–47; in food preservation, 486; food reform movement on, 526; for ill people, 299, 324, 384, 423–24; introduction of cane, 191; in late Middle Ages, 282, 299; production of, 211, 360, 383–84, 392, 393, 437; sauces based on fats and, 362, 407, 408; in Spanish baroque cooking, 410–11; tastes of, 320. *See also* Desserts

Sugar beets. *See* Beet sugar

Suite des Dons de Comus (Marin), 398

Sukkoth, 226

Sumac berries, 213

Sumer, 19

Sunflower oil, 437

Supermarkets, 535

Swans, 359, 405, 416

Sweden: fish consumption in modern, 449; milk consumption in modern, 450

Sweet and sour tastes: in Arab cooking, 222, 223; in late Middle Ages, 299; in Rome, 135

Sweeteners, 215. *See also* Honey; Sugar

Sweetness and Power: The Place of Sugar in Modern History (Mintz), 391–92

Sweets. *See* Desserts

Switzerland: chocolate introduction into, 386; fish consumption in modern, 449; milk consumption in modern, 450; potato consumption in, 445

Sycamore trees, 41

Sylvander, B., 534

Symposia, 71, 92; ceremony in, 100–102; definition of, 97; elegiac versus iambic, 103; elites and, 97–98; as ethical experience, 98; food served at, 101; locations of, 100, 101; poetry associated with, 99, 102–4; purpose of, 99–100; religious symbolism of, 97–98, 101; sacrifices in, 101; symposiarch of, 101

Symposiarchs, of symposium, 101

Syria: banquets in, 19; olive oil production in, 56; wine trade in, 57

Syrups: in Arab cooking, 219; in late Middle Ages, 282

Tabernae. See Taverns

La Table au pays de Brillat-Savarin (Tendret), 505

Tablecloths, 333, 344

Table manners: in ancient Egypt, 43; in ancient times, 330; in Arab world, 220; body control and, 334–35; changes in, 3; in classical Greece, 92; courtesy concept and, 330; early normative accounts of, 330–31; in eighteenth-century France, 369; etiquette

Thuillier, Raymond, 479

Thyme: in Arab cooking, 213, 217; in classical Greece, 82; in late Middle Ages, 265

Tilapia, 42

Tithes: corn exempt from, 356; grain as, 351; peasant, 170, 351–52; pigs as, 170; potato exempt from, 444

Tobler chocolate factory, 386

Tomatoes: introduction of, 357; preservation of, 490, 497

Tomb of the Olives, 108

Tomb of the Reliefs, 110

Tongue: cooking for digestibility, 318; cooking techniques for, 406, 407

Le Tour de France gastronomique (Rouff and Curononsky), 510–11

Tourism: gastronomy and, 509–12, 528; guidebooks for, 509–12; restaurants and, 477–78

Tourisme et Régionalisme (Brun), 511

Tourist guides, 509–12

Toutain, Jean-Claude, 454–55

Trade: Arab world and, 219; in Byzantine Empire, 195, 196; changes due to Industrial Revolution, 437–38; in early modern period, 380; in fruit, 437, 465–68; government regulations of, 282–83; in late Middle Ages, 257–58; in pasta, 283; in Phoenicia, 58; protectionism, 462, 466, 467, 490; in Rome, 129; spices in, 359; technological advances and expansion of, 436–64; transportation in, 464, 482, 488; in tropical beverages, 360, 380, 388, 390; in tropical oils, 437, 457–63; urbanism and, 257–58; wine, 57, 58, 87; women and food processing and, 286. *See also* Guilds

Traité de l'usage des fruits des arbres pour se conserver en santé ou pour se guérir lorsqu'on est malade (Venette), 426

Traité des aliments (Lémery), 427

Traité des conserves alimentaires (Faucheaux), 495

Traité des livres rares, 431

Trajan, 160

Trammels, 340

Transportation: fast foods and, 539; regional cuisine and, 544; tourism effect on, 509; trade and advances in, 464, 482, 488

Travel writing, 501–2, 509, 510

Trésor gastronomique de la France (Croze and Curnonsky), 506

Tripe: in Jewish cooking, 238; in late Middle Ages, 280; in Rome, 133, 135

Les Trois Frères Provençaux, 475

Tropical oils, 437, 457–63

Trout, 171, 314

Truffles, 203; in Arab cooking, 218; in early modern period, 361, 363; preservation of, 488

Tujibi, 218

Tuna: in Arab cooking, 216; in Carthage, 61

Turkey (bird), 349, 359, 404

Turkey (country), 391, 450

Turkish coffee, 387

Turkish Delight, 220

Turks, 210

Turnips: in Arab cooking, 217; in classical Greece, 82, 87; in early Middle Ages, 173; in Greco-Roman period, 72; in *haricot de mouton,* 358; in late Middle Ages, 265; in Rome, 118, 133, 134, 135, 136; salted, 412; social status and consumption of, 312

Turtledoves: in classical Greece, 82; in late Middle Ages, 323

Tyre, 55, 57, 58

Udalric, 260, 262

Uncultivated lands. *See* Fallow land; Forests

Underwood, William, 488–89

Unilever, 461, 462

Union Régionaliste Breton, 513 n.4

United Africa Company, 461

United Brands Company, 467

United States: beef in, 518; cattle industry in, 489; colonial period subsistence diet, 516–17; egg consumption in modern, 451; fats in diet in, 528; food exports from, 489; food habits in, 534; food preservation industry origins in, 488–90, 533–34; food reform movements in, 517–21, 522, 525–26; hygiene obsession in,

539; mealtimes in, 539; milk consumption in modern, 450; pineapple imports of, 468; postwar abundance, 523–25; shortening in, 462; soldiers' rations in Civil War in, 489; sugar consumption in, 392; trade and transportation advances in, 464; vegetable oil exports of, 460; vitamins in, 521–23

U.S. Department of Agriculture, 527

U.S. Senate, 527

Urbanity, concept of, 330

Uterus, of pigs, 134

Vacuum-packed foods, 542

Variety meats, 280; gizzards, 135; tongue, 318, 406, 407; tripe, 133, 238, 280

Varro, Gaius Terentius, 107, 133, 137

Vautrin, Hubert, 371

Veal: in Arab cuisine, 221; in Great Chain of Being, 311; social status and consumption of, 306

Vegetable gardens: in ancient Egypt, 40; of peasants in feudal period, 253, 265, 271; in Phoenicia, 56; in Rome, 118

Vegetable oils. *See* Oils

Vegetables: in ancient Egypt, 39, 40–41; in Arab cooking, 213, 216–18; in Byzantine Empire, 197–98; in Carthage, 59; changes in French taste for, 404; in classical Greece, 82, 87; in colonial America, 517; in diet of nobility in late Middle Ages, 259; in early Middle Ages, 173; elites and, 421; in Great Chain of Being, 309, 311; in Jewish cooking (*see* Jews: vegetables in cooking of); modern consumption of, 445–46; peasants and, 181, 311–12, 420–21; in Phoenicia, 56; preservation of, 412, 487, 488, 490, 497; religious orders and, 183, 184; in Rome (*see* Rome: vegetables in). *See also names of specific vegetables*

Vegetaline, 462

Vegetarians: Adam and Eve as, 53; Grahamite, 518; in Greco-Roman period, 74; in modern Europe, 549; *prandium* meals and, 16; religious orders as, 184

Venette, Nicolas, 426

Venice, 196

Venison: salted, 314; sauces for, 323

Vetch: in classical Greece, 82, 84; in Greco-Roman period, 72; in late Middle Ages, 265

Le Viandier de Taillevent: on boiled meat, 422; competitors of, 394–95; development of, 297; on meat mixed with milk, 421; meats and, 322; on parboiling, 407; on salt, 323; sugar and recipes for illness in, 424

Viard, André, 494

Vidal de la Blanche, Paul, 506

Villard, François, 83

Vin-bois-charbon, 476

Vin d'Anjou, 508

Vinegar: in Arab cooking, 213–14, 215, 216, 217; in improvement of digestibility, 318; in sauces, 323, 408

Vineyards: in ancient Egypt, 41; in Arab world, 219; blight in, 484; in Byzantine Empire, 195; in classical Greece, 80; expansion in feudal period, 253. *See also* Grapes; Wine

Vitamin A, 239

Vitamin D, 522–23

Vitamins, 521–23

Vitellius, 114–15

Vladimir I, prince of Kiev, 189

Voltaire, 387, 429–30

Voyage en France (Ardouin-Dumazet), 509

Voyage sentimental et pittoresque dans les Pyrénées (Saint-Amant), 502

Waffle irons, 341

Wales, 300

Walnut oil, 271, 301

Walnuts: in Arab cooking, 212, 215, 219; in Carthage, 60; in Rome, 125, 135

Walpole, Horace, 414

Warblers, 415

War of the Roses, 375

War of the Spanish Succession, 376

Wars of Religion, 353

Water: drinking, 198, 202, 229, 232, 258; in Great Chain of Being hierarchy, 309–11; prehistoric boiling techniques for, 27; sources of, 211; wine mixed with, 172, 198, 199

Watercress: in classical Greece, 82; in late Middle Ages, 265; medicinal uses of, 316

Watermelons: in Arab diet, 219; introduction into Europe, 221

Weber, Theodore, 458

Wedum, Ulryk, 411

West Indies, 467

Whales, 57; blubber, 405; in Great Chain of Being, 310; salted, 314

Wheat: in ancient Egypt, 39; in Arab cooking, 210; in Byzantine Empire, 195, 196–97; corn as substitute, 356; cost of, 303; distribution as *annona*, 115, 127, 129; in early modern period, 380; as food of travelers, 126; in Greco-Roman period, 72, 82, 85, 115; importation of, 353–54, 437; in Jewish cooking, 230; in late Middle Ages, 268–70, 280–81; milling of, 86; modern market share of, 443–44; in Neolithic period, 28; in Phoenicia, 55; symbolism of, 127

Wheeled plow, 253

Whey, 215, 450

Whiskey, 535–36

White beans, 231

White Castle, 539

White Tower, 539

Whiting, 314

Widows, food choices of, 305

Wild birds, 310

Wild boar: Arab hunting of, 214; in classical Greece, 82; in early Middle Ages, 171; in Etruria, 109; in Mesolithic period, 14; recipes for, 134, 323; in Rome, 120, 134; salted, 314

Wild foods: as dietary supplements in Neolithic period, 28; in Roman period, 72, 121, 129. *See also* Game

Wild goats, 109

Wimpy's, 537

Wine: age of person and intake of, 425; in ancient Egypt, 41, 42; ancient trade in, 57; in Arab cooking, 213; at banquets, 35, 71, 94; barbarians and, 98; in Byzantine Empire, 195, 198, 202; in Carthage, 60–61; in classical

Greece, 71, 83, 86–87, 98–99; dietetics on iced, 419, 425; dietetic value of, 318; in early Middle Ages, 172; Galen on, 86; government regulations of, 231, 232; Greek terminology for, 83; *hypocras,* 261, 282, 285; industrialization of, 484–85; in Jewish diet, 226, 231; in late Middle Ages, 258, 265, 272, 343; in Mesopotamia, 35; modern consumption of, 451–54, 549; in monastic diets in late Middle Ages, 261; pasteurization of, 484–85; in peasant diets in late Middle Ages, 264; quality of, 272; racking of, 485; recipes with, 322; rituals associated with, 57, 241; in Rome, 71, 114, 125, 131, 134, 135; sales in taverns, 292, 473; salted food consumption and, 413; spices and, 261, 322; storage of, 343, 485; as symbol of civilization, 73; taboos and ancient Hebrew priests, 51; taboos and Muslims, 191; trade and, 57, 58, 87; water mixed with, 172, 198, 199

Women: at banquets (*see* Banquets: women at); as cookbook authors, 366; as cooks, 212, 236; dietetics for, 146; food processing and trade and, 286; industrial revolution effect on, 435–36, 437, 521, 531; table manners and, 335–36; vegetable gardens and, 253, 265; as workers, 546 n.3

Woodcocks, 265, 323

Workers: daily meals of agricultural, 382 n.12; food reform movement and, 519–20; Industrial Revolution effect on, 438; women as, 546 n.3

Xenia (Martial), 133

Yas-mah Addu, 37 n.3

Yeast: in ancient Egypt, 39–40; Jewish dietary laws and, 227

Yellow peas, 173

Yemen, 386, 388

Yogurt, 210

Young, Arthur, 367, 415, 417, 502

Yugoslavia, 451

Zimri-Lim, 37 n.3

EUROPEAN PERSPECTIVES

A Series in Social Thought and Cultural Criticism

Lawrence D. Kritzman, Editor